ROBERT A. HEINLEIN

IN DIALOGUE WITH HIS CENTURY

ALSO BY WILLIAM H. PATTERSON, JR.

Robert A. Heinlein in Dialogue with His Century:
Volume I, 1907–1948 Learning Curve

ROBERT A. HEINLEIN

IN DIALOGUE WITH HIS CENTURY

VOLUME 2

1948–1988
THE MAN WHO LEARNED BETTER

WILLIAM H. PATTERSON, JR. *1951*

TOR

A TOM DOHERTY ASSOCIATES BOOK · NEW YORK

ROBERT A. HEINLEIN IN DIALOGUE WITH HIS CENTURY:
VOLUME 2, 1948–1988 THE MAN WHO LEARNED BETTER

Copyright © 2014 by William H. Patterson, Jr.

A Tor Book
Published by Tom Doherty Associates, LLC
175 Fifth Avenue
New York, NY 10010

www.tor-forge.com

Tor® is a registered trademark of Tom Doherty Associates, LLC.

The Library of Congress Cataloging-in-Publication Data is available
upon request.

ISBN 978-0-7653-1961-6 (hardcover)
ISBN 978-1-4299-8796-7 (e-book)

Tor books may be purchased for educational, business, or promotional use.
For information on bulk purchases, please contact Macmillan Corporate and
Premium Sales Department at 1-800-221-7945, extension 5442, or write
specialmarkets@macmillan.com.

First Edition: June 2014

Printed in the United States of America

0 9 8 7 6 5 4 3 2 1

I haven't anything which could properly be termed a religion. My thoughts on religious subjects are matters of intellectual rather than emotional conviction. The nearest thing to a religious feeling I have, and, I believe, strong enough to justify calling it religious feeling, has to do with the United States of America. It is not a reasoned evaluation but an overpowering emotion. The land itself as well as the people, its culture in the broadest most vulgar sense, its history and its customs. I have no children and few close friends. I have no God. The only thing which always inspires in me a feeling of something much bigger and more important than myself, which calls up in me a yearning for self-sacrifice, is this country of ours. I know it is not logical—I presume that a mature man's attachments should be for a set of principles rather than for a particular group or a certain stretch of soil. But I don't feel that way. The green hills of New Jersey, the brown wastes of New Mexico, or the limestone bluffs of Missouri—the mere thought of them chokes me up. That is one reason why I travel so much—to see it and feel it. Every rolling word of the Constitution, and the bright, sharp, brave phrases of the Bill of Rights—they get me where I live. Our own music, whether it's Yankee Doodle, or the Missouri Waltz, or our own bugle calls—it gets me.

ROBERT A. HEINLEIN,
letter to John W. Campbell, Jr.
January 20, 1942

Contents

ROBERT A. HEINLEIN

IN DIALOGUE WITH HIS CENTURY

Learning Curve, the first volume of this biography, took Heinlein from his birth in 1907 through his naval career, destroyed by tuberculosis; a political career that ended in a personally disastrous political campaign; and a writing career that succeeded beyond anything he could imagine—only to be interrupted by the demands of engineering for World War II. After the war, his writing began to pick up again—but his fifteen-year marriage to Leslyn Mac-Donald Heinlein fell apart. After a year he was ready to remarry, a naval lieutenant he had met in Philadelphia during his war work.

It was a period of ups and downs—Heinlein's learning curve in the most literal sense. By 1948 he was coming to the crest of the curve, having learned better in many ways, with many more to come. But the core of his mind, formed as a radical liberal early in the twentieth century, held those values even as the world shifted around him. In particular, the leftward shift of American politics after World War II (among conservatives as well as liberals) put Heinlein in a widening gulf of values, increasingly at odds with both left and right. Heinlein engaged with his world, and his grappling was uncomfortable but necessary. Toward the end, as his personal fame grew, he became paradoxically almost invisible, and even his most approving readers reacted more to crude labels than to the actual content of his writing. More and more plainly he set out his message—"Again and again, what are the facts?"—and his readership grew into the millions, needing the affirmation of reason that includes the spiritual. The final products of his fertile imagination, dealing with taboos broken, men like gods, and a society, in Freud's terms, polymorphous perverse, are in no real sense the product of a "conservative" or "rightist" mentality.

By the time of his marriage to Virginia Gerstenfeld in 1948 (her first, his third), Robert Heinlein was halfway through his life, and he was essentially done with false starts. After the collapse of his marriage to Leslyn MacDonald, he had a long and painful creative dry spell, but he persevered and gradually discovered how to make his postwar "propaganda purposes" work, how to teach his fellow citizens (the current ones, as well as the teenagers who would move into responsible adulthood) how to live in, and how to take control of, their increasingly technology-dominated future. It was important work and satisfying, and for the new life he was building, at age forty, Virginia Heinlein was to become his perfect partner, in his writing business as well as in his life, steadily taking over the business aspects of his career so that he could concentrate on the art.

New markets continued to open up for Heinlein, and, so gradually he was never really aware of it, he became more than a successful popular writer in the mold of Erle Stanley Gardner or Rex Stout: He became a culture-figure, a public moralist, something like the role H. G. Wells had filled in the 1920s, and Mark Twain before him—but in a public much less open to moralizing, much more open to an irony that shells out important truths in the guise of fictions.

Although Heinlein died in 1988, his entire body of writing remains in print, selling even more widely than during his lifetime. Warren Buffett had not yet brought "value investing" back into currency at the time of Heinlein's death, but value investing is exactly what Heinlein engaged in for the last forty years of his life—investing in us (often as irony cast upon the waters, which comes back sevenfold!).

HALF DONE, WELL BEGUN

"I cried at the altar, and Ginny cried when we got outside and, all in all, it was quite kosher."[1]

October 21, 1948, was a beautiful, crisp fall day in Raton, New Mexico, just over the Colorado border. Snow gleamed on the distant mountaintops. Robert and Virginia Heinlein were finally married.

They had settled in Colorado Springs until the divorce from Leslyn was finalized, and they both struggled through the tumult of deciding on this new commitment, discovering that they both wanted this new life together.

Ginny, whose entire life had been spent in big cities, fell in love with that clean, mountain resort town,[2] and they began putting down roots. Their social life had been somewhat constrained by the need to keep a low profile—which is also why they went out of state for the wedding. Now, with the holidays coming on, in addition to working with a local radio station they joined a figure-skating club.[3] Ginny, a national ice-skating semifinalist, was asked to star as a featured performer in the Broadmoor resort hotel's Christmas-week Symphony on Ice program—an ice-dancing version of *The Nutcracker*.

Heinlein was sleeping well for the first time in years, his only health problem being a persistent sinusitis. Even his ex-wife Leslyn—now a long-distance problem—seemed to be straightening out after a very messy period of her life. Six months earlier, she had lost her job at Point Mugu—"compulsory resignation because of refusal to do work the way her boss wanted her to do it," their mutual friend Bill Corson wrote after talking with Buddy Scoles[4]—"complicated to unknown extent by liquor."[5] And then she disappeared. Not even their lawyer—Sam Kamens represented both Robert and Leslyn in the divorce action—had heard from her in more than a year. By September, Heinlein learned from friends, Leslyn had turned up in a sanatarium in Long Beach, "taking the cure." Her own letter to Robert had kindled hopes she would make a full recovery, since she had joined Alcoholics Anonymous.[6]

Reconnecting with friends after his period of self-imposed isolation, Heinlein wrote long letters telling them about the marriage to Ginny, glossing over the timing. He had strict personal rules about telling the truth, always, but sometimes telling the truth selectively helped your friends maintain your privacy—and other peoples' illusions, if necessary.

He had no illusions about getting back to work, especially now that he knew he could rely on Ginny as a helpmeet even with the writing, as Leslyn had been before the dark days (though in her own, different way). Heinlein was uncomfortably aware that the bank balance was dwindling away: Four months of unpaid labor on the screenplay for *Destination Moon* in the spring and summer of 1948 had put a severe crimp in their finances. He *would not* let Ginny go back to work. Heinlein's Navy pension and a small but steady trickle of reprint requests for his prewar stories almost covered current expenses. The script could potentially put them in the clear. George Pal was shopping the project around Hollywood (though without getting even a nibble of interest).

In the fall of 1948, Heinlein had three books in print: his second juvenile for Scribner, *Space Cadet,* came out in August—and the first, *Rocket Ship Galileo,* was still selling briskly. Fantasy Press issued the revised *Beyond This Horizon*. In five or six months they would have royalty payments that would cover next year's taxes and living expenses; he could feel reasonably confident that he wouldn't dip back into poverty, as they had in Fort Worth at Christmastime a year earlier. Gnome Press, another of the new, small specialty publishing houses, wanted to publish *Sixth Column* under the Heinlein name instead of the Anson MacDonald pseudonym it had borne when published in *Astounding Science-Fiction*. John Campbell, Heinlein thought, ought at least to have a coauthor credit, since it had been written from Campbell's (verbal) outline. He wrote to Campbell, and to Lurton Blassingame, asking what sort of fee and credit split would be appropriate. But Campbell did not want either money or credit.[7]

In the meantime, other speculative ventures were falling into his lap—two in one week recently: an offer to do continuity for a science-fiction newspaper comic strip[8] and a request from the A&S Lyons Hollywood agency to develop a science-fiction radio show, with him as the host.[9] Heinlein asked his cowriter of the *Destination Moon* script, Alford "Rip" van Ronkel, about the agency's reputation. It was a genuine offer, van Ronkel told him.[10] Heinlein was skeptical: He knew he had a good "radio voice"—better on radio than it sounded naturally—but felt he was not "celebrity" enough to carry such a show (though if they wanted to pay him—a thousand dollars a week was about right—he would put his objections aside).[11]

The regular writing was moving along: After thinking about it for a while, Heinlein had come up with a good idea for the scouting story that *Boys' Life* had been asking for. He originally intended "Nothing Ever Happens on the Moon" as a short story[12] about the first interplanetary Triple Eagle Scout, though it grew uncontrollably in the telling; by early November he had written twenty-five thousand words and struggled through multiple drafts with colored pencils, to cut it to nine thousand words. This produced a manuscript that looked, he said, like "modernist wallpaper."[13]

His professional life was flourishing, just as the demands of his personal life escalated: When Ginny was in Washington, D.C., during the war, she had been diagnosed with thyroid deficiency. In the fall of 1948 her medications were adjusted, and Robert was helping her keep to her medication schedule. "She takes a grain and a half a day and is repulsively energetic, unless she happens to forget to take her pills. I have posted a chart and award her gold stars for taking her pills."[14] Nobody else would recognize and validate that small-girl part of her personality—but Heinlein had quite a lot of small boy in his own makeup, which he rarely showed to anyone but her.

As she regained her full energy, Ginny took on the task of getting Robert's health in order. He had been sick the entire time she had known him, and when he was in Los Angeles working on the script for *Destination Moon,* his right leg began to bother him. Dr. King, the Los Angeles orthopedist he saw, had him doing stretching and strengthening exercises with orthopedic devices, to improve a postural imbalance he had picked up from fencing.[15] As their financial crisis eased, Ginny devoted more time and resources to the housekeeping and meal budget, stretching her talent and skills to make his meals sophisticated, flavorful, and sustaining. Robert had grown up on the heavy and undistinguished cooking of the Midwest: Vegetables that were not boiled to a limp mess and beefsteak rare and *à point*—not gray and overdone and tough—were new to him.[16]

But her program was derailed almost before it began. The doctor Heinlein was consulting about his sinusitis tested him for allergies. He tested positive for—well, nearly everything: "Seems I'm allergic to milk (ice cream, cheese, cream soups), corn (but not corn liquor), and lettuce. Why lettuce? Why not spinach? Ginny is beside herself trying to figure out how to feed me."[17] Heinlein took it in stride: "Me, I don't worry—anything is worthwhile to get the full use of my schnozzle again—and a little dieting will help my waist line. Ginny is such a swell cook that I have a strong disposition to over-eat."[18]

As they settled into their new life together, they began to take up their political interests, as well. They had moved to Colorado Springs too late in the year to register to vote: For the first time in Ginny's adult life, she would not be able to vote in a presidential election (Robert had filed an absentee ballot in California).[19] There was a good chance that President Truman might lose to Republican Tom Dewey (neither Dixiecrat Strom Thurmond nor Henry Wallace's Progressive Party stood any real chance in this election—but they both weakened Truman's support).

Robert had come to respect Truman's strength of character—particularly after his handling of the Democratic Party's racism at the nominating convention that summer:

> What I do like is the fact that Truman stood up to the southern "gentlemen" white racists and told them to go pee up a rope, and most especially the fact that the convention backed him up on it. If the convention had pussyfooted on civil rights I would have been strongly tempted to vote the vegetarian ticket. But it didn't . . . this was a time to stand up and be counted, and the count came out on the side of human decency, which made me happy and proud.[20]

Ginny was less enthusiastic about Truman.[21]

On election night, Robert stationed himself by the radio and stayed awake, tallying the overnight results as they came in. In the morning, he told her with great satisfaction that Truman had won—much in advance of the official count.

With the elections out of the way, Heinlein returned to the problem of his annual boys' book for Scribner. He had intended to build a story around undersea agriculture—a family of sea-farmers, since his editor, Alice Dalgliesh, wanted a prominent girl character this time. She had found his outline notes for *Ocean Rancher* "thrilling"[22]—but he needed to get in more suit-diving to finish off his background research. Ginny put her foot down: She had almost lost him last year.[23] *Ocean Rancher* was out.

Heinlein always had a hard time coming up with ideas for these boys' books. He had to invent something adventurous that boys would be interested in, without needing excessive background explanations. And it was always a problem to get the boys out from under the thumbs of their adult "protectors," because adventures were what they were being protected *from*.[24] Targeted at a general readership, these boys' books could not use the genre conventions of the science-fiction magazines—but he could use ordinary science.

His approach to the science-fiction juvenile was evolving. When he wrote *Rocket Ship Galileo* in 1946, the form of the juvenile was dominated by the Tom Swift/Motor Boys formula. *Space Cadet,* in 1948, was built around a group of teenagers, and so is still fairly close to the formula. His third book, however, would depart further.

His core idea came out of a story he remembered that Jack Williamson had cowritten with Miles J. Breuer in 1930, "The Birth of a New Republic"—"A very, very solid piece of work, one of my favorites, and miles ahead of the stuff . . . of the period."[25] A story began coming together in his mind, about a revolution on Mars against a distant Earth colonial authority. He wrote up a synopsis of the story as an outline-proposal and sent it to Alice Dalgliesh, by way of Lurton Blassingame.[26]

That November he wrote a story of a woman on a space station overcoming male chauvinism, "Delilah and the Space Rigger," aimed at *The Saturday Evening Post* (which found it too "technical"). Ginny suggested another story idea to work on while "Delilah" started on the rounds of other slicks:[27] In *Space Cadet* he had mentioned several iconic heroes-of-the-Space-Patrol. She suggested he write the story of Dahlquist, who stopped a military coup at the cost of his own life. During the first two weeks of December 1948, this turned into "The Long Watch"—a "downbeat" story, since the hero dies at the end, but it showed what had inspired those boys about the story: "The narrator is a hero in the mold that Heinlein perfected," Andre Norton later wrote of this story. "That is, he's an ordinary guy who must decide to do the extraordinary because of his belief in the American system of government."[28] Ginny cried when she typed it for submission—and every time she had to retype it.[29] Eventually, she said, her tears rusted out her typewriter.[30]

Heinlein had another writing chore he had been putting off since August: He wanted to do a really good story for John Campbell, as a major "thank-you" for his efforts to get Street & Smith to change its policy of buying and reserving "all rights."[31] Now they bought and reserved only serial and paperback rights, and this allowed Campbell to meet the conditions Heinlein set out two years earlier—rates respectable for pulp, if not as good as the slicks. All he needed was a good idea.

That, of course, is the hard part. Campbell suggested a dodge that would let them talk it over "in person": He had become interested in ham radio and threw himself into it with enthusiasm. There were a couple of hams in Colorado Springs, and Campbell arranged with one of them, Bill Talmaine, to make a connection on Friday, December 3, 1948.[32]

Astounding's November 1948 issue had come out the same week Heinlein remarried. In it, Campbell printed a "joke" letter from Richard Hoen—a "review" of the November 1949 issue, a year in the future. It was to be a glorious reunion of all the prewar greats, and Hoen had mentioned a new serial by Heinlein (as "R. A. MacH", referring to Heinlein's "Anson MacDonald" pen name), giving only the title "Gulf," and no other details (except that he implied it was not part of the Future History). It was a good joke, Heinlein told Campbell—and pointed out that he could top it: If Campbell would talk the other writers into doing stories with the titles Hoen had given, Heinlein could write something for the "Gulf" title and make Hoen's "prediction" come true.[33]

At that stage Heinlein did not have any specific idea for the story—he might be able to use some of the *Ocean Rancher* material, so the title could refer to the Gulf of Mexico, or—he kept turning the notion over in his mind but was getting nowhere.[34] He asked Ginny for a story conference. They scheduled a formal meeting, and he asked her to come with a few story ideas they could toss around.[35]

Ginny's help with the business side of the writing had already expanded well beyond that of a well-trained secretary. Much of her impact on him she could not really be aware of: Her "presence" was simply everywhere in his life, in big ways and little. The most casual remarks from her might spark a story idea, but she didn't even need to talk to inspire a story. One day, when she was putting away the wire recorder (since they were no longer using it for dictation) it *squawked,* and that gave Heinlein an idea for Willis, one of his Martian characters in *Red Planet*—that it would repeat sounds back at you, like a living wire recorder.[36] And the rest of his book's Martian biology built itself around that and integrated into the boy-hero's resistance to an attempted dictatorship on the Martian Colony. Ginny later commented, "Robert asked me to make notes when I had story ideas, and I always did. Sometimes they were simply notions for small things, other times they were bigger . . ."[37]

For this first story conference, Ginny's best idea was a variation on Kipling's Jungle Books stories—a human Mowgli raised, not by animals, but by aliens and then returned to Earth. It would be a satire, she explained. The boy would be like those goslings that imprinted on duck mothers, and the story built around his figuring out how to be a human being. Heinlein remembers the moment as linked to *Red Planet*, which he was researching and planning at that time:

Time after time ideas would beget more ideas, and I would have to lay the second generation regretfully away with the thought that the discarded notion was a little too involved and a bit too strong medicine for a boy's book. I collected quite a file of things about these Martians which had been left out of the book. One night, while discussing this Martian culture, I made some reference to Mowgli; Ginny speaks up and says, "There's your 'Gulf' story that you've been looking for."[38]

Heinlein wrote several sheets of notes by the time he ran out of steam for the night,[39] but the core of the book was already clear in his mind: he wrote the first and last chapter.[40]

But for the *Astounding* serial, this Martian Mowgli was *too* big an idea to be researched and written in the time he had. They continued discussing the "Gulf" story for the next several days. The Martians he had evolved for *Red Planet* were elder-brother types, and the boy they raise and use as a spy would probably turn out some sort of warped super-genius, like Odd John. "What makes a superman?" he asked Ginny, spontaneously. "They think better," she replied.[41] This was the germ of the spy/superman novella Heinlein later crafted for Campbell as "Gulf."

Heinlein put the superman idea aside, too, so he could finish some of the accumulation of work that was piling up.[42] He began revising and expanding *Sixth Column* for Gnome Press.[43] The revisions were ticklish:

> It was a hard story to write, as I tried to make this notion plausible to the reader—and also to remove the racism which was almost inherent to his story line.
>
> In revising the yarn for book publication (1947) I was lucky enough to find, in a respected British journal of science, some support for the notion that the subraces of h. sapiens might be told apart by spectral analysis of blood; I incorporated that idea in the book.[44]

In the middle of the *Sixth Column* revisions, Heinlein received another book offer: Shasta, a new publisher out of Chicago, had bought *Methuselah's Children* in the spring of 1948. Now the owner, Erle Korshak, wrote saying they wanted to make it a part of a *five*-book series that collected all of the Future History.[45]

This was a much better—and more realistic—offer than Crown had made him the previous year (for a heavily condensed, single-volume collection). Korshak wanted him to write all the stories whose titles he had put on his "Future History" chart but never written. Heinlein answered that he was interested, but he was also fully booked until February 1949:[46] Dalgliesh's approval of the

Red Planet outline came through, sometime in mid-December 1948, and Heinlein was ready to start writing the book after Christmas.

He found *Red Planet* a chore to write and spoke of it as "dull."[47] Dalgliesh had been very pleased with the outline discussion, but it didn't come alive for him. About a week before *Red Planet* would be finished, he took a day off and pitched Ginny's Martian Mowgli idea for "Gulf" to John Campbell in a long letter, so that he could have the benefit of Campbell's feedback before he had to start writing it. Now the "Gulf" had become interplanetary.

All the fundamental ideas of what would become *Stranger in a Strange Land* were there in this January 27, 1949, letter, including, explicitly, the Mars-Apollonian/Earth-Dionysian dichotomy, drawn from Ruth Benedict's 1934 study in *Patterns of Culture,* with flavors of two other classic superman stories, Olaf Stapledon's *Odd John* (1935) and Philip Wylie's *Gladiator* (1930), a book that is, for the most part, remembered today only as the direct inspiration for the Superman comic book character.

> The obvious tragic outcome is for him to retreat to Mars, just [as] a zoo animal, loosed, will slink back into his cage, unable to cope with the wild "natural" environment. Another solution is for him to become a messiah, either tragically unsuccessful, or dramatically successful. Or, on a less elevated plane, he could be the bridge across the gulf between Mars and Earth. . . .[48]

Meanwhile, back on Earth (or as close to Earth as Hollywood gets), van Ronkel wrote in January 1949 saying that a *Life* magazine article on rocketry had brightened up the climate for their *Destination Moon* spec script, and Louella Parsons had leaked the news that Pal was rounding up financing—somewhat prematurely, as the script was just being looked at. Pal had probably planted the leak himself, van Ronkel concluded, to create a "buzz" about the project. All the independent filmmakers were having trouble obtaining financing.[49]

Heinlein's second juvenile for Scribner, *Space Cadet,* had come out in August 1948, while he was still in Los Angeles, to generally good reception, but the reviews in the science-fiction fan press over the winter and into 1949 were not positive. In fact, for the past two years he had been getting very strange reactions from the science-fiction fans. Prominent fan Forrest Ackerman sent him a negative review by writer Robert Bloch that didn't seem to understand what was going on in the story at all. The fans—and in this case Bloch as well—seemed offended that he avoided the science-fiction genre conventions when trying to reach a general readership that didn't have robots and rockets and such at its fingertips. Exasperated, Heinlein wrote back to Ackerman:

> You know damn well that a story that *Astounding* will buy can not possibly be sold to the SEP—but through those stories I brought space travel to more people than has any other writer save H. G. Wells and Jules Verne—to more people than have all other *living* writers put together . . . So far as the general public is concerned I am the only space-travel writer, because I gave it to them in a form they could understand and made them believe in it. Would you criticize me for feeding pablum to a baby rather than rich, red beef steak?[50]

Nevertheless, Ackerman said, in fanzines and directly to Heinlein in correspondence, that the "slick" Heinlein set back the cause of space travel and only made him ill.[51]

Irritating—but just one of the many ways Ackerman was becoming a long-distance pain. The previous year, he had made a pest of himself over the Big Pond fund set up to bring the English editor of *New Worlds,* Ted Carnell, to the United States—as the "fan guest of honor" for the 1949 WorldCon in Cincinnati. As it happened, all of Heinlein's disposable income was going into care packages for the Carnells at the time, since England was still rationing food,[52] but Heinlein refused to explain himself to Ackerman. Now Ackerman was complaining that Heinlein wasn't giving him as much "access" as he wanted. Heinlein decided to make one more attempt to put the friendship back on a more reasonable basis:

> If you want to know me for *myself,* and not as a source of scoops, well and good. I like you and I regard you as an extremely idealistic sort of a guy, even though our evaluations don't match on various points. I don't like you simply as a source of nude pix, or a person from whom I can borrow s-f books, or as a bigshot fan; I like you for yourself—one of the sweetest guys I ever met (when you aren't off on a rampage). No doubt if we stay in contact you will sometimes get a scoop out of me, or an original manuscript, or a chance to see the inner workings of something. . . .
>
> . . . This letter has been painfully blunt, Forry, but, darn it!, you forced it on me. I prefer to stay on friendly terms with you; whether or not we do depends on whether or not you want to—as a friend, and not as Louella Parsons nor as a self-appointed critic.[53]

It was, by way of contrast, a pleasure to deal with someone as straightforward as L. Ron Hubbard, who wrote asking for a fifty-dollar loan so he could get to D.C. for a pension hearing. Twenty minutes after opening his letter, Robert was writing a response: Ginny volunteered to take the money out of her grocery budget and went downtown for a money order to be enclosed with the letter.

> You may attribute this on her [Ginny's] part to the fact that she put in four years in the outfit herself and lost her kid brother in the pig boats. She won't turn down a shipmate. As for me, it's partly because I remember you floating around out there in that salt water with your ribs caved in and partly because I have a feeling deep down that I could depend on you in a tight corner quicker than I could depend on some of my more "respectable" acquaintances . . . I think you are my kind of a son of a bitch and I don't think I would have to holler more than once.[54]

Hubbard's markets had never completely come back for him, while Heinlein's seemed to be expanding. Both Doubleday and Little, Brown had asked Heinlein for collections of his fantasy stories, and the discussions with Doubleday stretched over months, trying out various combinations of his short fiction. By April he reached an agreement with Doubleday on a four-book deal, beginning with *Waldo & Magic, Inc.* "It seems to me," he told his agent, "that [those two stories] go together about as well as mustard and watermelon, an opinion which was reinforced by trying to think of a title for the volume."[55] "Waldo" was a novella written in the opening months of World War II, built around Tesla's broadcast power and what the metaphysics of the new physics might mean. "Magic, Inc." was a prewar romp about commercial magic.

Back in Hollywood, van Ronkel had become very unhappy with his agent. Lou Schor had just lain down and gone to sleep on them, apparently expecting Pal to do all the rest of the work himself. Heinlein liked Schor personally, but it was hard to drum up support for someone who wouldn't cooperate. Reluctantly Heinlein gave van Ronkel an unlimited agency if he wanted to fire Schor.[56]

That was not all that was falling apart in Southern California: The hopeful expectations he had for Leslyn were dashed as reports came in. She was telling different stories to different people, and none of it was calming. "Heard from Sprague [de Camp] that she apparently has been working on the bottle to an extreme," Heinlein's Naval Academy friend Cal Laning, now in Washington, D.C., wrote Robert when she asked for a job recommendation.[57] Their mutual friend Bill Corson was even more depressing: "Oversimplifying things a trifle, I will express an opinion that she's nutty as a hoot owl . . ." he wrote, continuing sadly: "She aint the gal we used to know, Bob. There's been a vast change. It's a total stranger now, with only a physical resemblance to upset us."[58] Now she was demanding financial support from Robert, when he was close to broke.[59] She had run through the entire proceeds from the sale of the Lookout Mountain house in just two and a half years.[60]

Heinlein felt no need to help; even if he wanted to, nothing had ever helped Leslyn once she entered the bottle. So he went back to work. In January and February 1949 Heinlein began collecting notes for a mainstream novel set in the world of modern art, to be called *The Emperor's New Clothes*, something like Ayn Rand's 1943 book *The Fountainhead* (made into a movie in 1948).

But he couldn't afford to devote much time to speculative work.[61] The shorts he had written in November and December ("The Long Watch" and "Delilah and the Space Rigger") were bouncing from all the slicks.

In February 1949, Heinlein took up the Shasta proposal for a series of books of all the Future History stories. The series as a whole would be much stronger, he suggested, if he based each book around a typical personality of his era and wrote just the material—ten new stories altogether—that would finish the series off. Volume one would be about "Harriman and the escape from Earth to the Moon." Volume two would pick up with "Rhysling and the adventure of the entire solar system." Then a book about "the First Prophet and the triumph of rationalism over superstition," then "Lazarus Long and the triumph over death." The series would conclude with *The Endless Frontier*— his "Universe" and "Common Sense" stories about a lost spaceship, and a new novelette, "Da Capo," that would bring things back to Earth and the triumph of the human race over space and time.[62]

Heinlein knew what he wanted to write for the first novelette: the "prequel" to his 1940 story "Requiem," which had been about D. D. Harriman dying as he achieved his life's ambition to go to the Moon. The technical problem of the fusion of documentary with science fiction that he had worked into the *Destination Moon* script was outrageously experimental (for the time), and his "The Man Who Sold the Moon"—a story about the early days of space travel—continued to explore this new vein of science-fictional material. It wouldn't be science fiction at all, as the pulps understood the term—nary a space battle nor wondrous gadget in sight. It might be more suited to the general-fiction magazines—

—but Korshak wanted to premiere the story in *Outward Bound,* the first volume of the series, and that meant no magazine sale. Heinlein agreed to the restriction reluctantly: He could not afford to put any obstacle in the way of the advance for the book. His brother, Larry, had written asking for a loan of $100 for sixty days,[63] and Robert was embarrassed to have to tell Larry he didn't have it to give—unless one of the speculative ventures came through. "I hate like the deuce to have to put you off," he wrote Larry, "and it is almost as embarrassing to have to admit that I am myself strapped."[64]

There was one bright spot on his financial horizon: *Calling All Girls* magazine took his teenaged-girl ice-skating story "Poor Daddy," written in October 1947,[65] and paid $150 for the 2,700 word story[66]—about five and a half cents per word (compared to the new "highest-rate" Campbell had offered of two and a half cents per word).[67] The editor told him they could use more stories of the "Puddin'" type—and they didn't care that he was a man writing about a teenaged girl.[68]

Continuing to work as partners, Robert and Ginny had another story conference,[69] for the novella he needed to write for the first Shasta book of Future History stories—"The Man Who Sold the Moon."

As with *Rocket Ship Galileo* and *Destination Moon*, Heinlein could not, for storytelling reasons, reasonably expect to depict the long, slow buildup that a government-managed project would require, with hundreds of people involved.[70] As far back as 1947, when he proposed this story to *The Saturday Evening Post*, he had established its focus:

The background would be the same, at an earlier period, as my Luna-City stories; the story would be of D. D. Harriman, the first great entrepreneur of space travel. It would be concerned mainly with the financial and promotional aspects of the first Moon trip, rather than with the physical adventure. This is, I believe, a fairly novel approach to the space-travel story, and concerns what is, in fact, the real hitch in opening up the solar system—money, the huge initial investment and the wildcat nature of the risk.[71]

A personal fortune would only be a start on this project—it would have to become as much a glamour investment as a technical venture. The basic story was about a man obsessed with the Great Vision, finagling and flim-flamming the financing for a Moon rocket.

This prequel story to "Requiem" had to fit into a narrow time gap in his Future History chart. Robert and Ginny came up with many background bits to get the story to the correct length. "Robert would pace up and down the living room," Ginny later said, "and I would sit there and try to think of ideas that he could stick into this thing."[72] "We spent days discussing it. All sorts of things went into it—the Mississippi Bubble and things like that."[73] Heinlein started writing while Korshak prepared the contracts for the series.

At almost the same time, Scribner rejected *Red Planet*[74]—on just the points the editor had approved in the story outline.[75] Worse, Dalgliesh complained that this story was fairy-tale like and *wasn't technical enough*—after asking him to reduce the science from the level of his first two books for them. It was infuriating—particularly considering the struggle to make the thing work in the first place. Dalgliesh's idea of science fiction, Heinlein complained to Blassingame, was antiquated.

> Her definition . . . fails to include most of the field and includes only that portion of the field which has been heavily overworked and now contains only low-grade ore. . . .
>
> I gave Miss Dalgliesh a story which was strictly science fiction by all the accepted standards—but it did not fit into the narrow niche to which she has assigned the term, and it scared her. . . .
>
> Enough of beating that dead horse! It's a better piece of *science* fiction than the other two, but she'll never know it and it's useless to try to tell her.[76]

Dalgliesh had commissioned an evaluation reading by a professional librarian, Margaret C. Scoggins, who was enthusiastic about the book but noted potential problems with the boy's Martian pet, Willis, laying eggs in the protagonist's bed after "necking" with him ("She's got a dirty mind," Ginny remarked[77]), and a certain trigger-happiness among the boys.[78] The whole children's lit industry was under intense scrutiny at that time because of the public attention being given to gory and violent comic books. Young people bearing firearms absolutely had to come out; this was a point on which there could be no compromise. And even the suggestion of sex— the miscegenation that could be read into the egg-laying—was unacceptable to the librarians who had become the core of Dalgliesh's purchasers. "We value him as an author," Dalgliesh told Heinlein's agent, "but we have to sell books and we have to keep the reputation for integrity we've built up."[79] They weren't selling many books in bookstores, she told Blassingame, so the library sales were critical. This must have caused Heinlein's jaw to drop, as he was getting complaints from his family and from readers that they couldn't *find* the book in bookstores, the demand was so great.[80]

The day after the Scribner rejection, his spirits were bucked up when L. Ron Hubbard repaid the fifty-dollar loan—within two weeks and with an extra dollar for interest.[81] Heinlein returned the dollar, saying they didn't take interest from friends.

Having *Red Planet*—essentially a commissioned work—rejected after the outline was approved and the book written to outline infuriated Robert,[82] and he instructed his agent that he was going to insist on the advance, even if they had to sue Scribner to get it.[83] Blassingame agreed and brokered a compromise: Scribner agreed to accept the book based on its following the preapproved outline, but wanted some significant revisions. Though very doubtful about the practical nature of those revisions, Heinlein gave in:

> I capitulate, horse and foot. I'll bowdlerize the goddamn thing any way she said. But I hope you can keep needling her to be specific, however, and to follow up the plot changes when she demands the removal of a specific factor. I'm not just being difficult, Lurton; several of the things she objects to have strong plot significance . . .
>
> If she forces me to it, I'll take out what she objects to and then let her look at the cadaver remaining—then perhaps she will revise her opinion that it "—doesn't affect the main body of the story—" (direct quote).[84]

Some of the changes watered down the social philosophy of the book, in a way that was repugnant to him. "It appears that there is now a drive on to make the world safe for morons[,] and *Red Planet* got caught in the squeeze. Things that were okay in my last two books are now much too nasty for children. It's annoying."[85] He suggested bylining it by "Lyle Monroe"—or jointly by Robert Heinlein and Alice Dalgliesh—or "as revised by Alice Dalgliesh"[86]—proposals she rejected. Later, Blassingame told him that Scribner had panicked at the thought of diluting the Heinlein name recognition.[87] Dispiritedly he started marking up his manuscript to water down the book.[88] The contracts were finally signed on April 29, 1949. "I concede your remarks about the respect given to the Scribner imprint," Heinlein wrote to Blassingame,

> the respect in which she [Dalgliesh] is held, and the fact that she is narrowly limited by a heavily censorship-ridden market. I still don't think she is a good editor; she can't read an outline or a manuscript with constructive imagination.
>
> I expect this to be my last venture in this field; 'tain't worth the grief.[89]

For the time being, Heinlein had no choice: he had to do the work. Money was very tight going into April 1949. The revisions for *Red Planet* would take time, and "The Man Who Sold the Moon," which had been promised to *Astounding* as early as 1941, was tied up in the book publication and could not be sold to a magazine.

In the middle of the frustrating negotiations over the *Red Planet* revisions, Korshak wrote saying that Shasta couldn't possibly keep the terms of the contract they had offered for the Future History books; the royalty rates were too high to be a profitable venture.[90] Some of the terms, Robert felt he could live with—though it was no longer even a decent contract for him (he called it a "monstrosity" in a letter to Blassingame[91]). After weeks of back-and-forth, Heinlein decided to accept the bad terms, just to get on with the other writing he had stacked up.[92] "I have made great concessions; you have worn me out," he wrote to Korshak. "I want to sign your contract Monday morning 11 April or drop the whole matter. No more lengthy negotiations."[93] To his screenwriting collaborator, he complained:

> I've lost the last three weeks through the insanities of editors and publishers. On my latest novel [*Red Planet*] the editor thinks it's swell tomato juice but should be peed in to make it better. On a contract for five books with another house [Shasta] the publisher writes me *7000-word* letters explaining why he should have my other shirt and my one good testicle in the contract. All very time wasting.[94]

The contracts for the first two books in the Future History series were signed on April 19, 1949. Korshak irritated him by sending the $200 advance for the first book with the condescending message that the Heinleins could eat steak tonight on Shasta.[95] The advance Robert had just secured from Scribner was $500; he could have steak without Shasta.

Moreover, several of the stories in the first volume for Shasta needed revisions, minor and major. In particular, he wanted to bring the applied physics in "Blowups Happen" up to date, for which purpose he borrowed John Campbell's book manuscript for *Atomic Industries*.[96]

In April 1949 Heinlein needed to find a story manuscript[97] and spent half a day looking through his unlabeled boxes for it.[98] Through the middle of April,[99] Ginny organized his files for him: Each story, book, or article was assigned a work number on an index card, chronologically, like a composer's opus numbers. Heinlein went through the old manuscripts one by one with her, telling her from his recollections and from the notes on the storage envelopes which ones came before others or after, and Ginny made up a master opus list to reflect his recollections, putting the opus number on the files and organizing the files sequentially in the boxes, so the index cards would reference into the files without a long search through boxes and boxes. That brought him more or less up to date, with the *Destination Moon* script being #65. The Boy Scout story was #66; *Red Planet* #67, and so on. From that point forward, each time he started a project, he would put the next opus number on an index card and keep a running record on the card, instead of hiding the information away with the manuscripts.

The clock was running on his deadline for Campbell's "Gulf" story. Campbell had been fascinated with Ginny's Martian Mowgli idea—but Hoen had packed so many imaginary stories into his letter that Campbell couldn't possibly include them all, even if they were all shorts. He wasn't going to write a Don A. Stuart story for that issue, no matter what Hoen had "asked" for.[100]

Heinlein put the Mowgli story away and developed a suspense story (as opus #68) based on Ginny's comment about supermen thinking better than ordinaries. He started the story in mid-April but stalled for a month. Perhaps the "Gulf" story simply needed more thinking through than it had had to that point.

Royalty checks came in April, relieving any immediate crisis, so the Heinleins were able to take time off and enjoy the National Figure Skating Championships held that year in Colorado Springs.

The break probably gave him time to think about another important matter: The Department of the Navy had suspended his physicist friend Robert Cornog pending an investigation into his security clearance. After inviting the Heinleins to drop by Los Alamos on their way back from Philadelphia in 1945,[101] Cornog came out to Southern California and continued to be active in the movements to cope with the dangers of atomic weapons. The Los Alamos Scientists organization led to the Hollywood Writers' Mobilization asking Cornog to join in September 1945. That committee was later exposed as a Communist front organization. Cornog now asked Heinlein for an affidavit attesting to his character—and to his patriotism—when he contested the suspension.

That was a ticklish problem: Heinlein had belonged to some organizations in the thirties that were heavily infiltrated by United Front Communists. He carefully crafted a statement for the hearing coming up on May 26, 1949, that laid the groundwork for his own patriotism and leveraged Cornog's on that basis, giving the names of respected individuals who knew his opinion directly—John Anson Ford, who was still a Los Angeles County Supervisor; Susie and Robert Clifton; and John Kean, who had been his supervisor at the Naval Air Experimental Station in Philadelphia.

Cornog was, he argued, a prudent and close-mouthed individual—at the very most a "dupe," not even a fellow traveler. His involvement was excusable because "I can say from personal and bitter experience that it is very hard to spot immediately a clandestine communist."[102]

Identifying and getting Communists out of American political institutions, he conceded, was an important and increasingly urgent problem—but Cornog was certainly no Commie. The effort spent investigating him—and rocket expert Jack Parsons, a friend of Heinlein and Cornog both, who had recently been through the same mill—was better spent chasing down real traitors.[103]

Having defended his friend's integrity and dealt a blow against the Communists simultaneously, Heinlein learned that he would have to go back into the world he had left behind in Los Angeles: *Destination Moon* was going to be made into a movie. *Ad astra per Hollywood!*

Hooray for Hollywood!

The day before Heinlein sat down to write his Statement for Robert Cornog, which is dated May 17, 1949, he was able to tell Forrest Ackerman (in the same post in which Heinlein told his parents), that his movie script had sold and he would be coming to Hollywood as Technical Director for the film.

Heinlein's writing partner, Rip van Ronkel, had been making noises for months about an imminent sale of *Destination Moon.* RKO had passed on the project, but when the studio's president, N. Peter Rathvon, left to produce movies independently, he approached George Pal for a two-picture deal, including *Destination Moon* and a Christmas fantasy called *The Great Rupert,* on the theory that profits from a second picture could insure any losses *Destination Moon* might incur. By the beginning of April 1949, although no money had yet changed hands, Pal and van Ronkel were taking "notes" from the new producer. Rathvon didn't like the original ending, and Heinlein was skeptical about the prospects for finding a satisfactory "fix": "I find that when an unscientifically-trained buyer wants to rewrite science fiction, there is almost no way to satisfy him." But he gave van Ronkel several ideas for alternate endings ("I got a million of 'em, all equally stinky"[1]).

Heinlein remained pragmatically skeptical about the deal and would remain so until the check cleared the bank. "I'm a cash-at-the-bedside girl," he told van Ronkel, "which means that I won't actually *leave* Colorado Springs until I *see* some of it. I can't afford to."[2]

The Technical Director credit would entail a consultancy retainer for six to eight weeks' worth of work, in addition to the purchase of the screenplay and rights for *Rocket Ship Galileo,* the property from which it was derived. The motion picture and television rights were assigned to Pal as of May 9, 1949, and that made the deal official. That left only three weeks to make Pal's June 10 start date. "Pal must get on the dime now, or I'm out,"[3] Heinlein told van Ronkel.

Time pressure from minor staff doesn't usually mean anything in Hollywood: The producer sets the schedule, and everyone else either conforms or gets out. But in this case, Pal wanted Heinlein, who had already come up with dozens of innovative solutions to technical problems, with many more to work out. The assignment was likely to last only through July, but the Heinleins planned to stay until after Labor Day.[4]

Housing solved itself: On May 17, Willie Williams and Pat Morely, friends from their ice-skating circle in Hollywood, visited in Colorado Springs on their way to New York where they would stay until October. They offered their apartment, close to the Paramount studios at Sunset and Gower, where the set work would be done.[5]

Ginny started packing. They gave up 1313 Cheyenne Boulevard and put everything they weren't taking to Hollywood in long-term storage. Heinlein settled down to write the "Gulf" novelette, saying he had been "egg-bound for a month" on the project.[6] The superman—unaware he had introduced in the opening became part of an organization of other supermen, bent on guarding the rest of humanity from its own predators. He finished it at 5:30 in the morning of May 23. Three days to revise and retype left him a comfortable nine days before Campbell's deadline.[7]

The Heinleins made the travel to Hollywood a road trip, visiting friends in Los Alamos, then picking up some detailed photos of the surface of the Moon at Lowell Observatory in Flagstaff, Arizona, for Chesley Bonestell's use in painting the movie sets. Sightseeing at Boulder Dam on the border between Arizona and Nevada and a brief stop in Las Vegas for the slots rounded out the entertainment portion of the trip.

Heinlein plunged immediately into the production planning at the studio and was immediately overwhelmed. "Dateline is now Hollywood," he wrote on June 15, 1949, "and life is triple-geared. Some Monday I'm going to wake up and find that it's Thursday."[8] It was much easier to write about space than to film it, he found:[9] "This business of making a movie is a lot of fun," he told Lurton Blassingame, "but confusing. Sometimes I feel as if I were fighting a feather bed—so many people, so many details!"[10]

But the details did begin to come together. Chesley Bonestell (1888–1986) in particular was exactly on target. Heinlein said in a later speech that he had told Pal, early on: "if we could not get Chesley Bonestell, we should give up the project entirely."[11]

Heinlein originally chose to site the landing in Aristarchus Crater, but

Bonestell, seeing the site in his mind's trained eye, decided Aristarchus was wrong for the film: It was in the wrong hemisphere to get Earth in the background. He preferred Harpalus Crater in the Moon's northern hemisphere. Heinlein was awed by this implied feat of mental projective geometry.[12] Harpalus it was.

But Bonestell was not the only essential enhancement for the film. In his original ninety-eight-page treatment, written in the summer of 1948, Heinlein had suggested a cartoon to get the ballistics concepts across in an entertaining fashion. Pal talked his friend Walter Lantz (1899–1994), into introducing a real star into the film: Woody Woodpecker.[13]

After two weeks, the production team was rolling along, and Robert was able to spend more time with Ginny, who was somewhat at loose ends. Within a week, Pal told him the production would be delayed and his production team, once they got the current work out of the way, would be put to work on the second film Rathvon had ordered, *The Great Rupert*.[14]

That was a setback: Heinlein's consultancy fee didn't cover extra time in Los Angeles. He would have to do some fiction writing to bring in living expenses.

But in the month before the crew had to shift over to *Rupert, Destination Moon* moved rapidly into production. Set design had worked up a model of the principal sets, including a spectacular semicircular backdrop of six panels, each about six feet long and eighteen inches high, that Bonestell was painting for the interior of the crater. He was also doing an astonishing trompe l'oeil painting of the face of the Moon, more than six feet high—taller than he was, in fact: He had to use a ladder to paint the astonishing details on the upper limb of the Moon.

The demands on Heinlein's time eased off in July, and he and Ginny were able to take on a social life. They began to entertain, principally inviting Heinlein's old friend Bill Corson for dinner. They had the Bonestells over for dinner fairly frequently, and had lunch one day with one of Heinlein's personal heroes, mathematician, semanticist, and senior science-fiction writer Eric Temple Bell ("John Taine"), at the Cal Tech Atheneum Club. Taine's science fiction was being published in *hardcover*—in the 1920s!

Once they traveled south to Laguna Beach with another couple,[15] to visit with friends and fellow writers, Henry and Catherine (C. L. Moore) Kuttner. Over drinks Robert made some disparaging remarks about the tame-dog writer Rathvon kept in his office to write up his "stupendous" ideas for changing the *Destination Moon* script. "Hank blinked at me gnomishly and said 'I didn't know writers could live in captivity' and Catherine said, 'Oh, they'll sometimes live—but they won't breed . . .'" Ginny laughed so hard that she spilled her drink.[16]

On July 13, 1949, more writers arrived. The L. Sprague de Camps came visiting with their sons Rusty and Lyman. Fellow Navy man Cal Laning was to arrive the next day. Robert's brother Rex wanted to pay them a visit to see the set and also to work out what they were going to do for their parents' fiftieth wedding anniversary coming up in November—and Ron Hubbard wrote that he had been hired to oversee a Moom Pitcher[17] and would be joining them in Hollywood shortly. "We have had an endless stream of visiting firemen . . ." Heinlein wrote to Campbell. "[S]uch social matters plus the continuing matter of making a motion picture have kept me jumping and made it impossible, thus far, to get any real work done.[18]

They threw a cocktail party for the de Camps and introduced Sprague around to such Hollywood royalty as they had access to, including someone de Camp particularly wanted to meet, rocket scientist and occultist Jack Parsons.[19]

Cal Laning was a less high-maintenance guest, and one who turned out useful as well: On the day Robert took him to the studio to see the preparations, the team was stuck finding some excuse to get the characters out of the spaceship and onto the lunar surface, to make a plausible scene transition. Laning suggested radar failure, and voila.[20]

Ginny and Laning went to lunch together one day while Heinlein was showing Laning's two daughters around the *Destination Moon* set, and, knowing how close he and Robert were, she mentioned, casually, that they had lived together before marriage. Later, when she mentioned the conversation to Heinlein, "Robert was extremely annoyed with me that I had told Cal that we had lived together . . . and I never again mentioned the matter to anyone. I don't think Robert *ever* did."[21]

Amid the visits, he continued to be a working writer: On July 17, "The Long Watch" sold to *American Legion Magazine.* That did not, however, mean that things ran smoothly in Hollywood; some time in July, Pal conveyed another piece of unpleasant news: Rathvon had insisted Pal hire a screenwriter to punch up the script—make it more "commercial." It would take a complete rewrite. Pal tried to reassure Heinlein, saying that he had worked with James O'Hanlon in the past and Robert would find him a thoroughgoing professional. Robert did not find this reassuring at all: "Professional" of Hollywood writers often meant the writer would do what he was told and not make trouble, rather than fight for the right story. Heinlein listened with horror as Pal talked about turning *Destination Moon* into a musical comedy.[22]

Soon thereafter, O'Hanlon phoned Heinlein and asked for a story conference. He had six weeks to turn in his rewrite. Robert invited him over to the apartment. O'Hanlon started out asking about this "science-fiction business," which he seemed to think he could learn to work after half an hour's conversation. As he left, O'Hanlon told Robert, "You guys can write about gadgets, I will write about people."[23] Ginny Heinlein was present at the time. "It was a very unsatisfactory session," she later said, ". . . Robert was fit to be tied!"[24]

To give him a break from the tension, Ginny arranged for a weekend getaway in Ojai, revisiting Armelda's Farm, where they had stayed in 1947, and talked him into doing another book for Scribner, in spite of the row over *Red Planet*.[25]

Heinlein also had an order of sorts from *Boys' Life*: Irving Crump, the editor, had liked "Nothing Ever Happens on the Moon" so well that he asked for a serial. Heinlein had been collecting ideas for a 20,000-word novelette about a pioneer Scout on another planet, with the intriguing twist that he would actually have to create his own soil in order to farm it. Ginny suggested that, as his last boys' book was set on Mars, this should be the next step farther out—Jupiter.[26] He realized that he could make the novelette idea work also as a book, and that it was worthwhile to cultivate Scribner, even after the aggravating and drawn-out fight over social philosophy in *Red Planet*. ". . . [D]espite recent and current headaches, Scribner's has treated me well,"[27] he told his agent. He sent a proposal and outline for a four-part serial to Crump and received a positive reply before the end of July. He planned a 40,000-word draft which he would cut to 20,000 for Crump, then add 20,000 or more words to expand it to book-length for Scribner.[28]

He and Ginny both worked on the background for this one, calculating orbits and transit times for his new *Mayflower* and for an effect he intended to use—all the Jovian satellites lining up—and calculating the load for the artificial greenhouse effect that would support the terraforming project. Ginny worked on the ecology and agronomics aspects, including a unique one-page instruction of how to turn sterile rock into fertile soil. Into this story Heinlein worked a favorite theme: the human rationale for frontier-seeking, its background a grand recapitulation of the settlement of the New World four hundred years earlier. Without an expanding frontier, Malthus's depressing economic equations guaranteed resource wars. Serious realities—just the kind of thing his writer's sense told Heinlein that boys hungered for. "Kids want tough books, chewy books—not pap."[29]

Some of the material he had in mind was darker than usual. He asked Ginny's opinion about killing off one of his characters. Remembering *Little*

Women and the death of Beth, Ginny ruled it should probably pass.[30] "After all, death is part of life."[31] Heinlein was able to finish the book under the working title *Ganymede,*[32] in a month, on September 10, 1949. He set aside the cutting for later, since he now had other projects to get into shape. Bill Corson suggested a better title for this opus: "Farm in the Sky,"[33] and that gave Heinlein his book title: *Farmer in the Sky.*

Cosmopolitan approached him to do an article predicting what the future would be like in fifty years, and they were backing up the proposal with a small expense account. He also had to prepare the manuscript for *Waldo & Magic, Inc.* for Doubleday. With no access to his files, which were in storage in Colorado, he had to use tearsheets from old pulps.

He also wanted to write a glowing review of the new Willy Ley/Chesley Bonestell book, *The Conquest of Space.* Blassingame told him the magazines had already handed out assignments, except the pulp *Thrilling Wonder Stories,* which didn't pay for book reviews. It was against Robert's principles to write for-free-gratis, but he wanted to publicize Willy Ley's books, and the opportunity to push Chesley Bonestell at the same time was irresistible. Heinlein wrote about six hundred words for *Thrilling Wonder* and then wrote a more substantial thousand-word review pitched toward *The Saturday Review of Literature.*

Then James O'Hanlon turned in his rewrite of the *Destination Moon* script. It was a disaster.[34] O'Hanlon had, as expected, loaded it up with stale gags,[35] but he had also converted Cargraves, the driving force of the Moon landing project, into "a spoiled cry baby who blows his top and gives up at failure."[36] He had also enlarged the cast and sets in other ways, increasing the cost of the production, and added a beauty-contest-winning millionairess.[37] O'Hanlon had also come up with a new ending, about straightening the ship up for takeoff (which he was later to recycle into his *Conquest of Space* script for Pal[38]).

Even worse, this new script was subtly loaded up with Stalinist fellow-traveler propaganda: speech after irrelevant speech extolling man's glorious collective future in space, even including "the unselfish cooperation of big and little brother," a year after Orwell's *1984* had been published. The Comintern party line hadn't caught up to the obsolescence of one of its favorite terms. Heinlein restricted his written critique to just the dramatic mess the story had become, completely unsalvageable. To a friend in New York, he wrote:

> I am not yet sure just what sort of a picture we are going to get, i.e., whether it will be a picture of some stature and scientific plausibility or a wild sort

of Buck Rogers job. I am making the usual discovery that, in Hollywood, a writer sits well below the salt.[39]

If the film was going to turn into a travesty, there was no point in hanging around. His contract would be up on the last day of September, and as things stood, he was not inclined to renew. They might as well pack up and leave.

He turned down an invitation to the Children's Books and Art Fair in Coronado, California, for September 30, as they might no longer be in the area by then[40]—but did go to speak to a local group of about sixty children's librarians in the third week of September. He found to his surprise that he was not merely *a* guest speaker, but the *featured* speaker: "It developed that what they really wanted to hear about was space travel . . . . This turned out to be a purely 'Heinlein' meeting. It startled me a little."[41] He rose to the occasion. "You talked so easily and so to the point," the organizing librarian wrote, thanking him, "that it was a worthwhile occasion for all of us."[42]

That experience may have warmed him up a little, and it also gave him a direct impression of the potential audience of librarians—a parallax view to Miss Dalgliesh's sense of his market for these boys' books. It may also have helped him get a sense of proportion about the disaster that was developing at the studio—reminding him that he still had a career.

When a writer's magazine asked him for five hundred words on science fiction as "The Historical Novel of the Future," for their "Bookshop News" Department for February 1950,[43] he was able to provide the first of a series of short, thoughtful, and useful "beginners guides" to recognizing and buying science fiction. The same article was published in March 1950 in *Writer's Digest* under the title "Bet on the Future and Win!" Perhaps he found at that librarians' meeting a real hunger for quality science fiction—and science—that was reflected in the similar articles he was to do over the next several years.

HOLLYWOOD SHUFFLE

Pal had decided to use veteran actor-turned-director Irving Pichel to direct *Destination Moon* as well as *The Great Rupert*.[1] *Rupert* went into post-production, and Pichel phoned Heinlein to arrange for a sit-down talk.[2]

Pichel was a tall, lean, distinguished-looking person with a head of startling, prematurely white hair. He was also, Robert quickly discovered, keenly intelligent, with a wry and ironic sense of humor. The way Pichel talked about it—the elements he wanted to keep as well as those he wanted to get rid of—showed Heinlein that Pichel *understood* what *Destination Moon* was supposed to be about.[3] Directors almost always do the final version of a script, because the writers' script has the story but not the organization and plan for actually shooting the film. Pichel junked most of O'Hanlon's innovations and returned to the last Heinlein–van Ronkel script.

Heinlein felt he could trust this director not to turn the movie into a travesty. Pichel, he told his editors at Scribner, "is largely responsible for getting it back on track and away from a Buck Rogers musical comedy trend."[4] He sent a note to Ned Brown—Rip van Ronkel's Hollywood agent, who had agreed to represent Heinlein, too—saying he would accept a regular contract for technical direction. When his pre-production contract expired at the end of September, Heinlein told Lurton Blassingame:

> . . . I expect that a new one, until 1 December, will be signed if they will meet my terms. I think they will, as the production manager has suddenly discovered that I can save them money (as well as keeping the thing scientifically straight) at points where some of these other Hollywood characters were costing them money.[5]

This decision prompted Heinlein into sudden, high gear. Willie Williams and Pat Morely were coming back to Hollywood in October for a month and would need their apartment. Robert and Ginny found another place to live for the interim, a furnished apartment on Hollywood Boulevard[6]—hideously expensive by their standards, but he had a little "new money" coming in, so they did not have to touch their building/purchase/baby fund nest egg.

The *Cosmopolitan* prediction article went to contract, and Heinlein used the time while Pichel was rebuilding the script to start the research for the article, interviewing a wide range of sources, ranging from senior scientists like Fritz Zwicky at Aerojet in Pasadena, to his Aunt Anna, a longtime teacher of history.

Production work at the studio did pick up again. Through October and into November the lunar sets were going up in Hollywood, and the location Pichel had selected for exteriors in Apple Valley (in the Mojave Desert near Victorville, about sixty miles northeast of Los Angeles), was being prepared. The production carpenters built a house—at the ridiculous cost of $40,000 (at a time when tract housing usually sold for around $5,000)—to film Cargraves's domestic life.

The art director, Ernst Fegté, had done something bizarre with the lunar crater: It looked like a dried-up mud flat, which was absolutely impossible for the airless, waterless lunar surface. Robert was horrified.[7] Chesley Bonestell hated it. Everyone from the SF field he showed it to hated it. But this was one effect that stayed in. It was a perspectivizing trick, Pal explained to them: The painted backdrop for the set showed the crackles growing smaller in the "distance," to give the impression of vast spaces. They would help the effect along by shooting some medium-distance scenes with midgets in specially built space suit costumes.[8]

It was hard to argue with that logic, so Heinlein didn't. Technical direction was as much a matter of compromise as of creativity. The space suits were a case in point: His original design, based on what he remembered of the high-altitude pressure suit project L. Sprague de Camp had taken over from him during the war,[9] called for goldfish-bowl bubble helmets with 360-degree views. But glare from the overhead lighting would make those unfilmable with 1949 camera technology. They had compromised on a flat glass-plate front. The weightless scenes were even harder to work out and called for a complicated system of suspension wires painted the flat black of space. The whole set rotated on gymbals, but Robert figured out a dodge to make use of that very fact to conceal the suspension wires.

"Suggestions" continued to come down from the front office—Rathvon fiddling at long distance, demanding pointless, and sometimes just moronic changes. Once when the staff discussion was inclining toward something impossible for ballistic reasons, Heinlein remembered that Pichel's son was a rocket engineer and urged Pichel to phone him. Pichel did, and his son must have given him an earful about Heinlein's reputation for technical accuracy in his writing, for after that, Heinlein's word on technical points was final.[10]

But until the actual shooting began, work at the studio was at most a part-time occupation for Heinlein—distracting enough that he couldn't work up the concentration to cut his scouting novel set on Ganymede, *Farmer in the Sky,* from 60,000 words to 20,000 words,[11] but leaving him with too much free time on his hands to just stay idle. He took a quick trip to Berkeley for a visit with Robert Cornog and to consult with him about *Farmer in the Sky* and the *Cosmopolitan* article.[12] When he got back, he began accepting speaking engagements. An October 14, 1949, issue of *The Eagle,* the local John Adams High School newspaper, reported a radio interview with him and four ninth graders, for broadcast on the "Books . . . [sic] Bring Adventure" program in November.[13]

Heinlein also devoted some thought to the additional spec screenplays he wanted to do while out in Hollywood. He and van Ronkel had talked about doing another science-fiction script, but van Ronkel was off trying to get directing work, and Heinlein had the impression that van Ronkel was upset with him for staying with the film after Pal had turned down van Ronkel to direct it.[14] Ned Brown had suggested Heinlein do a script that made use of his ice-skating background—and he had also struck up a friendship with the PR man Rathvon had hired, Ben Babb (another Kansas Citian, though of a more recent vintage), and that was threatening to generate a comedy screenplay.

By the beginning of November, Willie Williams and Pat Morely left again for the winter, and the Heinleins were able to move back into their efficiency apartment near the Paramount studios.

Heinlein was able to pick up his correspondence again, writing a graceful note of congratulation to A. P. White ("Anthony Boucher") on the first issue of *The Magazine of Fantasy & Science Fiction,* which had come out in October. Blassingame sent a telegram saying that *Cosmopolitan* was cooling toward the prediction article and wanted to drop it. Heinlein was already irritated about the changeability of editors: He had put a considerable amount of background work into the article.[15] Blassingame sweet-talked the *Cosmopolitan* editors into keeping the assignment alive—but Heinlein told him, "[a]s for prophesies at the moment, I'm darned busy—please tell them that the immemorial rules of the fortune-tellers guild require that the palm be crossed with silver *before* the future is read. Check with any Gypsy."[16]

The studio had gone out of its way to be pleasant to the Hollywood press, which meant that Forrest Ackerman was at the studio frequently as production ramped up in October and November 1949.[17] Pal palmed him off on Hein-lein, and he often was asked to act as guide and host—not always a pleasant task. Ackerman seemed to be in an irritatingly lofty "science fiction c'est moi" frame of mind.

Ackerman had, without telling Heinlein, given away a Spanish language right for two of Heinlein's stories to a Mexican magazine he was agenting for, figuring it didn't matter, since Mexico didn't recognize U.S. copyright law—and the magazine didn't pay for content anyway. It was for "the good of science fiction," as defined by Forrest J. Ackerman—and therefore beyond objection. He handed Heinlein the August 1949 issue of *Los Cuentos Fantasticos* with "And He Built a Crooked House" translated as *"La Casa Descabellada."*[18] Heinlein objected. He later described the confrontation: "He simply looked puzzled at the notion that the *writer* might not choose to assist and encourage literary piracy even in a country where it was legal."[19]

Ackerman *would not* be called back to planet Earth, and against such a lack of comprehension, it was impossible to make any progress at all. "I let it go tell-ing him to knock it off!—where my stories were concerned, as I had already learned that it was useless to try to argue him out of his weird notions."[20] But it didn't "take." Ackerman continued shopping Heinlein's books to Hollywood studios without telling him. As Heinlein already had a working Hollywood agent, this could only cause trouble. Ackerman had also started telling the lo-cal fans "I don't think [Heinlein]'s very fond of fans" as an explanation of why he wasn't showing up at the LASFS meetings.[21] In fact, Heinlein's schedule had been completely booked for months in advance.

Principal photography was delayed until November 22, which was also Rex and Bam Heinlein's fiftieth wedding anniversary. The entire family was in town for the event, including spouses and children, most of them meeting Ginny for the first time. For this anniversary, there were so many guests that the children had rented a hall for a formal dinner.

At family gatherings, the Heinleins had the main table, and all the *aus-landers* from other families were relegated to side tables. Bam presided over one table as the Lyle contingent. At her golden wedding anniversary, the chil-dren took a solemn vote and decided she had done pretty well for the last fifty years and voted her an Honorary Heinlein and entitled to sit at the main table. But Bam insisted on keeping her place as a Lyle at the head of the in-law table. Bam was not very talkative—and Heinlein said of her that she "didn't let her fingers know what she was doing,"[22] but her natural reserve concealed a dry wit.[23] Ginny helped out with serving and entertained by playing the piano. Coming from a small and diminishing family, Ginny told Robert she liked the idea of being a member of a large family, for a change. "He looked at me as though I were crazy," she later said.[24] She especially cultivated brother Rex's wife Kathleen, and the two of them made opportunities for the brothers to visit each other,[25] as they had been estranged for nearly ten years.[26] When he was in Los Angeles a year earlier, Heinlein began planning for this occasion, and the brothers had agreed to "bury the hatchet."[27] Rex and the family had even visited Robert and Ginny in Hollywood at the end of July 1949, to see the preparations for the film. That meant a great deal to Robert.[28] Family is, after all—however irritating—family.

Heinlein was in Apple Valley nearly every day after the middle of November 1949. The production team had built a full-scale set of the rocket's tail section, and much of the shooting was done at night. The high desert gets very frosty at night. Pal remembered someone bringing in a thermos flask of grog to keep everyone going.[29] As filming started, Heinlein came down with a case of influenza, but he would not be diverted from overseeing things personally on the set. He was at the studio or the location every day, without fail, working through his sickness, though the sinusitis that came on with the flu would not go away. He took along with him the manuscript for *Farmer in the Sky,* working on the cutting in the intervals while sets were changed.

The front office kept sending down revisions. By now, Rathvon's wife was writing dialogue, too. On one occasion, a set of purple[30] revision pages came down. Each new revision to a page was mimeographed on a different color of paper. Purple indicated that these pages were on their seventh revision of the fourth script. Pichel called for everyone's attention. He read through the revision and then held it up for everyone to see. "This is what to do with those pages," he said, tearing them across. Pichel was a civilized, patient, and accommodating person, but contractually he had the director's final say over what went into the film.

In the meantime, the *important* part of filmmaking was getting under way. Ben Babb was in charge of the promotion and marketing budget (often called "A&P" for Advertising and Promotion)—$1.2 million, compared to the film's $600,000 production budget. Babb wanted to get "buzz" going. During the shooting, Heinlein sent Pal and Babb a requested list of the scientists he thought ought to be asked to observe the filmmaking process. Since he was already working on the preliminary stages of post-production—suggesting sound effects and having conferences with the film score composer, Leith Stevens—Heinlein was at the studio as much as at the set.

Everybody not directly involved in the shoot did local publicity work. It helped that Babb was an amusing and simpatico person, already developing into a good friend. Generally the effort paid off. "Colossal is a trite word in the industry, but it's the only adequate one to describe the job you all are doing on that picture," one of their contractors wrote, thanking Heinlein for his "personally conducted tour of the moon."[31]

Heinlein had three stories out in December—the second part of the "Gulf" serial in *Astounding*; his women-in-the-space-workforce story, "Delilah and the Space Rigger," in *Blue Book;* and "Rebellion on the Moon" (the new title they had given "The Long Watch") in *American Legion Magazine*. That one provided him some amusement later: One concerned reader wrote, anxious to know if the Russians could pick up atomic technology from the story. Alger Hiss's second trial was under way at the time (the first one, in the spring, had ended in a hung jury, but this one would convict him of espionage), and many Americans were anxious. The editor at *American Legion* wrote Heinlein this was a "very pretty compliment" to the verisimilitude with which he had invested the story.[32] Heinlein wrote directly to the anxious reader:

> I assure you that nothing in that story could possibly be of any military use to any enemy of the United States. I have had some ten years military service myself, and you may be sure that I would never under any circumstances offer anything for publication which could possibly give aid or comfort to our enemies. The facts about atomics, rocketry and so forth, given in that story, are well-known to everyone. There is nothing in it even slightly secret.[33]

Heinlein was more concerned about the copy editor's errors that had crept into the story—"libration" changed to "liberation" and "altitude" instead of "attitude" changed scenes into gibberish and invalidated the plot gimmick.

Being in the current issues of national magazines could only do him good—and Heinlein had a "prestige" item coming out at the end of December: *The Saturday Review of Literature* picked up his spec review of Bonestell and Ley's *Conquest of Space* and ran it in the December 24 issue under the title "Baedeker of the Solar System." That was the next step up from the slicks.

Even working on the film, Heinlein was able to maintain his writing career. Lurton Blassingame was whipping up foreign contracts for his older books: An Italian contract and a Dutch contract had come in in August for *Space Cadet*. Heinlein's return to Colorado Springs would be well funded—necessary, as he was thinking about buying a house there.[34] Heinlein also needed to get his sinusitis cleared up before driving into the mountains again, and both he and Ginny needed some extensive dental work. They planned to leave for Colorado just after Christmas.

But the shooting dragged on, from its scheduled two weeks to four weeks plus. Finally, the last shot was in the can shortly before Christmas. The local publicity work they had been doing was paying off: The buzz around Hollywood had reached a peak of excitement, and the wrap party, held on the "surface of the moon" (before the set was dismantled), achieved almost an A-list status. "Hollywood royalty turned out in droves," Virginia Heinlein remembered: "It was surprising that no one broke a leg or a neck: that set was hazardous for people in high heels, and there were plenty of those! . . . Not being especially a movie-goer, I didn't know most of them by sight."[35]

At the party, Robert and Ginny separated and mingled, each talking to different sets of people, as they normally did. When it was over, they were walking back to the car and Ginny asked if he had met Dorothy Lamour— *The Jungle Princess* and Hope & Crosby Road pictures girl in the sarong. Robert stopped dead in the street. "'Do you mean to tell me she was there, and you didn't invite me—get me over to meet her?' and I said, 'I'm afraid so.' And for two weeks he almost wouldn't speak to me."[36] After that, he decided he had *two* life's ambitions: to go to the Moon and to meet Dorothy Lamour.[37]

But it may simply have been that the dental work kept them from talking much with each other. Both were seeing the same dentist, and Robert finished cutting *Farmer in the Sky* for *Boys' Life* while Ginny was in the chair. He got it down from over three hundred pages to eighty-four a little after New Year's, and both manuscripts went off to Blassingame together.

A little before the New Year, Heinlein had the first inkling that the high level of publicity work Pal was doing on the film might have a down side: He got a note from L. Ron Hubbard saying that his film—*Rocket Ship X-M*— was going to use the publicity *Destination Moon* was stirring up.[38] There was nothing to be done about it: Pichel ignored it and went on patiently editing the film together. The subplot with all of Cargraves's home life wound up on the cutting room floor, which meant that O'Hanlon's net contribution to the script shrank again, to almost nothing.

Things were not going so swimmingly in the film's front office: *The Great Rupert* was released on January 8, 1950, and promptly flopped. Suddenly Rathvon was in a crisis of confidence. Pal was in no better position than Rathvon: He had put up his producer's share of the picture as collateral for the financing. His career as an independent producer, even more precarious than Rathvon's, could be over before he actually got it under way.

They had to make *Destination Moon* work.

Ben Babb was doing his part. His efforts to create buzz were very successful: Julius Schwartz, who had agented for Heinlein in 1939 and 1940, was
now an editor at DC Comics, and he shepherded a comic-book "preview" of
the movie into print (*Strange Adventures* no. 1). At *Astounding,* John Campbell wanted an article on the production. Dave Epstein from Pal's office suggested Campbell nominate a freelancer to do the writeup; he and Heinlein
and Bonestell would help freely with information.

Ginny coined a new verb that January, "to Korshak," as Erle Korshak began pestering them with last-minute details for Shasta's first volume of Heinlein's Future History stories, *The Man Who Sold the Moon.* Korshak's business
methods grated on their nerves: He had only two speeds—ignore everything,
then emergency full-rush must-be-done-yesterday.[39] Heinlein simply could not
accommodate that kind of irregularity in the middle of the rigidly organized
chaos of a film production. He had corresponded with L. Ron Hubbard over
the summer,[40] trying to get some perspective on what looked like gross irreg-
ularities in the royalty accounting Heinlein was receiving from Shasta, and he
told Hubbard they had gotten a triple-Korshaking that previous January
weekend: a frantic phone call followed by an after-midnight special delivery
of title pages to be signed for advance subscriber sales of the first edition—
and another special delivery before 5:00 A.M. the same day.[41]

Rogers Terrill, the editor at *Argosy,* had snapped up Heinlein's offer to do a
novelization of the *Destination Moon* story ". . . if we can beat the film,"[42] and
John Campbell had solemnly agreed with Ben Babb that Heinlein would be
the ideal person to write the article on the film for *Astounding.* Campbell
would need the manuscript by March to make a July issue—a difficult writing schedule if Heinlein were to leave Hollywood in February. And it would
be easier to coordinate with Pal's publicity department for photographs and
so forth if he did those two projects while he was still in Hollywood, but
Heinlein didn't see how he could make it work. He and Babb had been amusing themselves working out a comic satire of "the filmmaking experience" for
the Abbott and Costello comedy team. That would have to be turned into a
formal treatment[43] before it could be marketed. That could not be done before he got back to Colorado.

He would have to write the *Astounding* article in March.

RENT OR BUY OR BUILD?

At last the various writing jobs were done, and the Heinleins left Hollywood early in February 1950. They did little sightseeing this time and spent a few days in Albuquerque with Robert's sister Louise and his nieces and nephews. The oldest nephew, Bill Bacchus, was an Eagle Scout now—just the boy to try out some of the new story ideas he was cooking up for *Boys' Life*.

As they were preparing to leave Albuquerque for Colorado Springs, a phone call came from Rip van Ronkel, alerting Heinlein that Pal was going to give O'Hanlon a screen credit—and Robert might be left off the screenwriting credits entirely, except for the book.[1]

Robert was as angry as Ginny ever saw him.[2] He could not count on the Ripper to handle the situation: A clipping from the Dar Smith column in the Los Angeles *Daily News* revealed that van Ronkel was working on the screenplay for Pal's next venture, *When Worlds Collide*. Van Ronkel clearly considered his writing partnership with Heinlein at an end, and *sauve qui peut!*

They made for Colorado Springs, arriving February 12. Within three days they found a grim little house in the same neighborhood they had left in the spring of 1949.[3] Heinlein promptly collapsed with another case of influenza—a typical (for him) reaction to stress. And more poured on: *Cosmopolitan* rejected the predictions article, though they paid the $250 guaranty for expenses. That covered about half his out-of-pocket costs.

The Heinleins had another Korshaking when they arrived in Colorado Springs: They found Heinlein's author copies of *The Man Who Sold the Moon* waiting for them. The books were cheaply printed on a low grade of paper, "quarterbound" with a cloth spine and paper covers, a format Robert had specifically objected to—and the dust jacket said he had done postgraduate work in mathematics and physics at the University of Chicago. The deal with Shasta was turning out an unalloyed disaster.

But the film business would not wait. As soon as they got back to Colorado

Springs Heinlein objected—loudly—to the proposed writing credits van Ronkel had told him about. Pal's office offered a compromise: Heinlein and van Ronkel would take an "original story by" credit and share script credit with O'Hanlon. But Heinlein did not want O'Hanlon associated with his picture in any way. He took the position that O'Hanlon was hired to do work not found acceptable—either written out or dropped from the final edit—and that his payment for the work was all the remuneration he was entitled to. "I venture that not one line of dialogue can now be found in the edited version of the motion picture which appears as O'Hanlon wrote it."[4]

This is an astonishing argument for a Guild author to make; O'Hanlon's domestic soap opera material did wind up on the cutting room floor—but Pichel had shot it, and some of O'Hanlon's material *was* in the final edit of *Destination Moon*—particularly the irritating faux-Brooklyn comic-relief character that could be traced back to O'Hanlon's "trio of hepsters."

Perhaps it was the influenza talking, but perhaps also it was the first major indication that Heinlein was just not in sync with the Hollywood way of doing things. He imprudently insisted the matter be arbitrated by the Screen Writers Guild.

Before the SWG could act, though, another crisis erupted: Irving Pichel had earlier expressed himself satisfied with his director's credit, even though Pal went on to offer him an "adapted for the screen" credit. Now, though, Rathvon recut Pichel's final cut, editing out the context-setting speeches at the end—all the material "that make[s] the self-sacrifice more than Roverboy adventurism."[5] Disgusted, Pichel threatened to pull his own screen credit—a very loud and unmistakable message in the Hollywood community.

Within two days, both crises cleared: Rathvon restored enough to mollify Pichel, and the Screen Writers Guild gave their compromise recommendation: "Written for the Screen by Rip van Ronkel, Robert A. Heinlein, and James O'Hanlon, from a Novel by Robert A. Heinlein."

Even with influenza, Heinlein knew when to concede the field: He wired acceptance of the SWG compromise on February 27—the same day he signed the Scribner contract for *Farmer in the Sky*.

Alice Dalgliesh had been enthusiastic about *Farmer in the Sky*. She even suggested he could do publicity for a national children's radio show out of Chicago, *Carnival of Books,* hosted by Ruth Harshaw.[6] His professional writing was back on track, and he could move on to the next thing—in his case, house-building.

The Heinleins had considered buying an existing house before they left for Hollywood, but they decided instead to build and quickly found an appropriate site on Mesa Avenue near the edge of the Broadmoor resort property—a granite outcropping overlooking a canyon, with a view filled with giant pines and picturesque boulders.

Heinlein intended to design this house himself. Ginny had wanted a circular house, but this site could not accommodate a circular design.

The property had some other inconvenient features: The next-door neighbors' curving driveway encroached on the property—which didn't matter when the site was undeveloped but would make the Heinleins' access from the street difficult—and an open drainage ditch ran straight through the middle of the lot. Those features could be engineered away. "We planned the house to enjoy the more distant views, too," Heinlein later told a real estate agent. "The living room view window faces Cheyenne Mountain." He cleverly made use of the natural features of the site, enhanced with careful plantings, to make the house so private—screened from outsiders' views—that they could virtually live nude, if they wanted. Even Ginny's bathroom had a floor-to-ceiling picture window overlooking the arroyo.[7] Another bonus: The lot did not have a street number assigned—they could pick any number in the 1700s they wanted (the house on one side was numbered 1700, on the other 1800). They chose 1776.[8]

For years Heinlein had been accumulating ideas for single-family housing and had several plans and sketches in his files.[9] He settled down with his notes to get enough of a design on paper that he could turn it over to an architect as soon as they could find one. "[T]hat was a dream of his for a long time before we actually did it," Ginny Heinlein later commented:

> He had "built" dream houses on paper, and he was a very good designer for those. Before we did anything, he insisted that I read *Mr. Blandings Builds His Dream House.* We both did read it, in fact, and when it came to building, we did not make those mistakes, but we made others that that author had not thought of.[10]

Designing this house gave him a chance to put some of his labor-saving ideas into practice. The house would be hermetically sealed—the first of its kind in the Colorado Springs area. Everything that could be built in, was—no chairs or no standing lamps to collect debris and have to be swept under. Things that absolutely could not be built-in, like the dining room table, he put on casters. The rolling table could be moved easily onto the terrace for dining alfresco. He designed in a curtained gateway for the table, directly into the kitchen, so that Ginny could load even the most formal dinner in the kitchen and then roll it into the dining room.

He wanted as much automation as he could cram into the house, including a dish-washing machine (which he called a "robot dishwasher"): Ginny's kitchen would not only have a magnificent view, but it would take only a fraction of the maintenance effort a conventional kitchen required. He applied time and motion analysis, already in use in modern factories, to domestic architecture—and planned a separate garage that could be finished later for children.[11]

It frustrated him that he could not use any modern materials or methods—even though they were out in "the country."[12] Antiquated and featherbedding building codes forced him to work with methods and materials thousands of years old—literally: He wound up using Vitruvian bricklaying technique at one point, where he hadn't wanted masonry at all.[13]

Their Cheyenne Boulevard rental continued to be their headquarters until construction was finished, but it was run-down and infested with mice. They plugged up the mouseholes in the baseboards—after endowing the current residents with enough food to tide them over until they got out of the house. If they had a cat, it would not have been a problem, but Robert put his foot down: No cat until the new house was ready.

While waiting for the lot purchase to finalize, Heinlein threw himself into the last of the writing work he would be able to do for a while. Street & Smith suddenly withdrew its objections to paperback sales for some of the stories they had tied up, and Heinlein registered a number of reassignments of rights to his stories. Blassingame had been working on a paperback deal, and finally having the stories under Heinlein's direct control helped smooth the way.

On March 1, Rogers Terrill rejected the *Destination Moon* novelization—after assuring him that the story was virtually pre-sold. The novelization had the film's sober, matter-of-fact style—whereas Terrill wanted another "Green Hills of Earth." Blassingame told Heinlein he was handling it better than anyone had a right to expect—and *Collier's* might be interested in the novelization, if they could get it in print in time for the movie's premiere. The long lead-times the national magazines needed were closing the windows of opportunity. Heinlein had counted on the sale to keep them afloat a while longer, as they spent the script fee on building.[14]

He had one story ready to write; as soon as he turned the basic design over to the architect, he could sit down and write his second "girls'" story, "Mother and the Balanced Diet," about a teenage girl nick-named "Puddin'." By the time he finished it in early April, he retitled it "Cliff and the Calories (A New Puddin' Story)". The story was inspired by a stupendous meal they had experienced at the Christmas Tree Inn, in Arizona, on the way in to Hollywood. He asked permission of the owner, Mrs. Douglas—his "Mrs. Santa Claus"—to include her and the restaurant in the story.[15] Puddin's father, like Heinlein, has a wide spread of food allergies, but he found the meal worth every itch and sniffle.

Heinlein had several other urgent matters to deal with: Alice Dalgliesh had forwarded Clifford Geary's scratchboard illustrations for *Farmer in the Sky*. If he couldn't be illustrated by his first choice, Hubert Rogers, Heinlein thought Clifford Geary was turning out a very good substitute. "Ginny's first remark on seeing them was, 'gee, that man is clever!'—a sentiment which I echo."[16] Dalgliesh had also asked for some biographical information, and he hardly knew how to answer: "I've never done anything particularly interesting," he wrote her—quite seriously. He had a hard time imagining what kind of personal—as opposed to professional—data librarians might find interesting about him—that he could safely write about: military service *before* the war—not likely; socialist political activity, even less so. "I get tongue-tied and self-conscious over these personal details," he wrote, after sketching out the bare facts of his life. "I don't exactly see why the readers want to know such things about writers anyhow." He listed "talking" as one of his hobbies—"The last I do too much of."[17]

Meanwhile, Ben Babb had prepared a glorious tabloid-sized press book for *Destination Moon*.[18] Very impressive—but they were also talking about moving the premiere to August, to allow them more time to ramp up publicity. The two secret pre-screenings Babb had arranged in the sticks were uniformly positive: There were no negative comment cards at all, and 95 percent of the suburbanites attending the surprise showing said they would recommend it to their friends.[19] Word of mouth would work for them.

Heinlein had been corresponding since the previous summer with John Campbell and with L. Ron Hubbard about Hubbard's big psychology project and the book Hubbard was writing about it.[20] Campbell sent Heinlein a preprint of Hubbard's 16,000-word introductory paper, "Dianetics: The Evolution of a Science," which he would be running as a straight "science" article in *Astounding*. It was full of intriguing ideas, Heinlein thought, but he wanted to see the entire chain of Hubbard's reasoning before he commented on it. Hubbard's book, *Dianetics, the Modern Science of Mental Health*, was due out in mid-April; he would wait for the full exposition.[21]

By the time the article appeared in the May 1950 issue of *Astounding*, Hubbard and Sara Northrup Hubbard had a baby girl, Alexis Valerie Hubbard. The Heinleins sent a silver spoon as a birth-gift. Sara thanked them, saying it was better than being born with one.[22] Shortly thereafter, Hubbard's book on Dianetics came out. He sent them an advance copy, and Ginny read it first, since Heinlein was slaving over a hot drafting board. Ginny was, as Robert said, "firmly of the 'leave your mind alone' school of psychiatry,"[23] and it disturbed her. She made Robert promise he would not do anything public with it for five years. By that time, any furor it raised would have a chance to cool off.[24] Mystified, Robert agreed; he didn't have time to study it then, anyway—and he wouldn't do anything with it in any case until he felt he thoroughly understood it. "I tried lying down on the couch and asking myself questions," he wrote to SF colleague Robert Bloch, who was curious about the "ronetics" project, "but nobody answered. I guess I'll have to wait a few years."[25] John Campbell confidently—and somewhat chillingly—told him:

> I can tell you, Bob, that you're inevitably going to have to take up dianetics; it's inescapable for a man of your mental bent. For one thing, you won't be fully, consciously aware of the methods you are already using in writing until you have actually explored your own mind, to find what those techniques you use are.[26]

Heinlein responded frankly:

> I am interested in dianetics because you tell me that it is important and that I should be interested, but in my "case," if that is what we are to call it, I don't know what it is that we might be looking for . . . Maybe I need dianetics but I don't know why and I can't tell from the book what it is I am supposed to get out of it.[27]

Otherwise, trying to be an amateur architect as well as a professional writer was keeping him fully occupied. Irving Crump, the editor at *Boys' Life,* liked *Farmer in the Sky,* but not the title. After a little back-and-forth, he agreed to one of the alternative titles Heinlein suggested, "Satellite Scout." But Crump had trouble breaking "Satellite Scout" into installments and wanted yet another rewrite to put cliff-hanger endings into the second and third episodes of four altogether. Heinlein suggested instead dropping several thousand words of ecology and agronomy science exposition and collapsing the story into three episodes.[28] That satisfied Crump, who offered $250 each for three episodes, even though he had ordered and received a four-episode story—$750 for more than six weeks of work.[29]

Disgusted, Heinlein told Blassingame to accept that offer, since he needed the cash for house-building—but Crump was now up against his own deadlines: Blassingame should use this fact to leverage the purchase price back up to $1,000.[30] "I don't care whether he gets sore or not," Heinlein told his agent. "[T]his is my swan song with Crump; sales to him are not worth the trouble and worry. Don't get yourself in bad with him; blame it all on me."[31] But there would be more *Boys' Life* sales: Crump told Heinlein he wanted to see his next boys' book, too.

Blassingame was conducting discussions with New American Library, a major new paperback house that wanted to get into science fiction in a big way and were angling for Heinlein's whole body of work. They suggested they would be interested in seeing a follow-on to Donald Keyhoe's 1949 article in *True* magazine claiming that the UFOs people had been spotting obsessively for the last couple of years were alien spacecraft—an alien invasion story which the editors suggested two ways of developing. Doubleday, Blassingame suggested, would probably take a book based on either approach, as they liked "Gulf." Heinlein had already made notes for an alien invasion story. He combined his notes with the editors' suggestions and put it in the back of his mind to marinate.[32]

At the moment, Heinlein was trying to come up with a new boys' book: It always depended on finding some way to separate the boys from their parents or guardians so they could have adventures. "How about a story just the opposite of *Space Cadet*—" Heinlein wrote in his outline notes for *Between Planets*. "—a boy caught up in an interplanetary war? . . . . Don feels lost and left out; these other boys are getting ready for war; he is running away from it."[33] He worked up a complicated gimmick that involved dual citizenship and a spaceship in transit when a colonial revolt breaks out.[34]

There were other matters to deal with, so he put the boys' book on temporary hold until he got the Abbott and Costello treatment off to Ben Babb for final approval. If it was okay, Babb could walk it over to their Hollywood agent, Ned Brown. Then Heinlein turned again to the increasingly irritating Forrest J. Ackerman.

Ackerman had been nagging Heinlein for years to let him represent him as an agent instead of Blassingame, and it was becoming increasingly difficult to turn him down politely. Now Ackerman was trying to talk Howard Browne into buying serial rights for "The Man Who Sold the Moon" for *Amazing Stories* or for the new *Fantastic*. That story was tied up by contract with Shasta for another two years—which Heinlein would have told Ackerman if he had simply asked. Ackerman was trying to market a property whose availability status he did not know.

This was just exactly why Robert would not consent to have Ackerman represent him in any fashion. "I wouldn't let Ackerman negotiate on my behalf for a latch key to Hell," he told Blassingame. "I'd be afraid he would louse it up."[35] He wrote gently to Ackerman, thanking him for the tip, but telling him the story was tied up, and he couldn't authorize Ackerman to represent him without firing his existing agents.[36]

Bits of this and bits of that started to come together in Heinlein's mind about the alien invasion story idea the NAL editors had tossed his way—including a real incident, one he and Ginny had probably seen in a Movietone newsreel while they were in Hollywood, about boys in Iowa faking a flying saucer crash and charging tourists to see the fake. Heinlein's twist was that the fake was a *real* saucer landing *masquerading* as a faked crash, and the tourists were taken over by alien slugs that ran them like meat puppets . . .

He talked out the story to Ginny, and she didn't like it at all:[37] It was a shudder-pulp horror story, the way he told it—far beneath his present status as a writer for the prestige magazines. But Heinlein must have known the idea was ripe for the time. He had to raise more money for the house, so he took time out to write the book.

They found a local architect and a contractor for the house and began construction on May 1, 1950. Then, on May 7, Heinlein fired the architect (he never in his correspondence specified why, though at one point he refers to the architect as "incompetent"[38]), and took over all the preparatory drafting work himself.[39] Heinlein knew at least something about all the trades involved, and there were advantages to being able to oversee construction of one's own design. He began seeing a lot of the contractor, Albert L. Montgomery. Heinlein thought Montgomery was a blowhard and low-life—

I have seen him fly into a rage and get into a fist fight (at the age of 47!) because a plumber "answered him back." I have heard him naively boast of his crooked financial deals. He has never been known to pay any attention to traffic laws and he shoots deer out of season.[40]

—but he was available and his fee was "reasonable."

The plumber's charges in particular looked fishy; he could not possibly be laying as much pipe as he was billing them for—at least twice as many linear feet as the specs called for. But the contractor's instructions had the same inflated figures.[41] Montgomery was covering the plumber's peculations, and some of his own as well—he had built a casting floor for his own use, charging it to the cost of their foundation. Heinlein spent the entirety of one hot early summer day in the sun digging up the plumbing connections and measuring the actual piping installed.[42]

On May 19, Heinlein fired Montgomery, terminating his contract as of the end of that day. He wanted both the plumber and the contractor off the property. The plumber Heinlein was willing to see the backside of; when the final bill was presented, he would simply pay for what was actually installed, no matter what the guy claimed. But the contractor was another matter. Montgomery threatened to kill him. Heinlein began wearing a pistol on his hip everywhere he went, "Hopalong Cassidy style."

> Fantastic, isn't it? But *he* [Montgomery] keeps a gun, and he hates my guts—and he is, in my opinion, sufficiently emotionally unstable to use it. It's either be prepared to protect myself, or let him run me out of town. For a peaceable guy who pays his bills on time, I seem to get into the goddamdest messes.[43]

There were broader concerns in the background that spring. International tensions were escalating alarmingly, and there was a good chance the United States would be going to war again. Ginny's appointment as lieutenant in the Naval Reserve came through on April 25—the form commission typically referring to "he" and "him" throughout.

> Ginny came within a whisper of being recalled to active duty for the Korean War . . . [sic] but they still had no use for me. I planned to be a camp follower whereever they sent her . . . [sic] then when she was again released to inactive, I planned to join the Ladies' Auxiliary of the Colorado Springs American Legion Post. Petition, then make a stink over being turned down, that is.[44]

Ginny's father suddenly passed away in Brooklyn—not a bad way to go, so far as Heinlein was concerned, "still taking care of his patients on a Friday, then dropped dead on getting out bed the next day . . ."[45] Robert talked it out with Ginny, letting her give herself permission not to go back to Brooklyn and attend to the sad details herself.

Late in June 1950, the Korean War started. Laborers became scarce, and prices on materials began to skyrocket, increasing as much as 60 percent in one month. Heinlein laid in as much building material as he could afford—and that ate up the last of the *Destination Moon* money. Blassingame came to the rescue with another clutch of foreign book contracts—French this time, for Librairie Hachette.

Heinlein needed every new market Blassingame could come up with: Forrest Ackerman seemed determined to spoil the Hollywood market for him. About the time Ginny's father passed away, Ackerman wrote saying he had given "Universe," "Common Sense," and *Beyond This Horizon* to a producer he knew at Columbia Pictures, bypassing Ned Brown entirely.

Heinlein had to put a stop to this muddying of the already extremely murky waters in Hollywood. He wrote as strong and clear a cease-and-desist letter as he could manage while still remaining cordial:

> As you know, I have an agent in Hollywood, Ned Brown of Creative Artists Corporation, and an agent in New York, Lurton Blassingame. They completely cover the matter of representing me. You are not authorized to present my works to potential markets, and in my letter of 16 April 1950 I told you not to do so. Please withdraw any you may have presented *at once* and notify me. Please tell me what properties and what persons were involved. . . .
>
> For old friendship's sake I have tried to temper my refusals [but you] now put me in the position of being forced to class you as a special case to whom I will never pay a bonus under any circumstances. Kindly desist from any efforts on my behalf.[46]

Ackerman thought he was overreacting,[47] but Heinlein watched the negative ripples from Ackerman's interference continue to widen out: Kendall F. Crossen, whom Heinlein had not known was involved in the deal with Ackerman, got in a huff and told Columbia that Robert *would not* sell to them, now or in the future. Apparently Crossen was acting as a development consultant for various television and radio entities including NBC (and had been involved earlier in their purchase of "The Green Hills of Earth" for the radio adaptation that aired on June 19).[48] It took months of patient correspondence with Crossen to get him talked down off his high horse.

Heinlein could not stop the house-building once started; he had to get the grading done before the pumice-concrete foundation could be laid. His overtures to the Donelans—his next-door neighbors whose driveway encroached onto his lot—had been met with flat refusals to move the driveway. He told the Donelans that he had hoped to arrive at a resolution on a "fair and neighborly basis,"[49] but he had waited as long as he could.[50] The neighbor's son hired a lawyer to argue that they had a right to the easement by precedent and by right of adverse possession. But Heinlein knew hot air when it blew over him: He revved up his backhoe and graded the driveway out of existence,[51] then put up a strong fence on the property line—the last resort for manufacturing good neighbors out of common thieves—

—of which there were a sufficiency. Heinlein might have considered letting the matter of the contractor he had fired in May fade away without further action if Montgomery hadn't kept making threats:[52] Gradually Robert realized the only practical solution was legal. But Heinlein did not move fast enough, and the People of the State of Colorado got there first:

> The contractor I fired has finally been indicted for embezzlement and larceny as bailee [on August 2, 1950] . . . I should have had him indicted sooner; he found and fleeced another victim in the mean time—and man-aged to kill a man through negligence in the bargain . . . I don't want any trouble and won't have any unless he looks me up and forces trouble on me. But I intend to protect my wife, my property, and myself. So I'm carrying a gun and being damned careful to pull the shades at night.[53]

By a sudden stroke of luck, they had enough new cash in hand to get the framing of the house under way. "Your letter of 11 August arrived today," Heinlein wrote Blassingame,

> and caused us much jubilation . . . an advance check on the NAL contract twice the size we had expected, news that you had sold "Roads" for TV, and news of the Kellogg show for *Space Cadet*. Ginny and I are agreed that you are the original miracle man.[54]

On July 21, the advertising firm of Kenyon & Eckard picked up an option for their client, Rockhill Radio, on *Space Cadet,* to use as the basis for a television program (though the earliest scripts have a hero named "Chris Colby," struck out and "Tom Corbett" penciled over it). Best of all, the advance and weekly royalties were for a license to use "space cadet" in their show's title, *Tom Cor-bett, Space Cadet*. Heinlein didn't have to do any writing at all. He ceded also the rights for exploitation—free money for a right that didn't at that time have any value at all.

Heinlein didn't take the purchase of TV and radio rights seriously; there were (and still are) a hundred properties optioned for every one that gets made. But Kenyon & Eckard rapidly lined up Kellogg's, the cereal manufacturer, as a sponsor, and the show was ready to begin airing on October 2, 1950—fifteen minutes, three times a week. Robert and Ginny never got to see the show, as they had no television reception.[55] There was no television, Heinlein said, within a thousand miles of Colorado Springs.[56] The money spent well: Fifty dollars a week was very significant money in 1950 and covered their living expenses while they worked on the house. Heinlein asked for copies of the scripts.[57]

Heinlein was becoming a notable media figure in 1950 without stirring from his mountaintop in Colorado Springs. Ben Babb wrote with news about the national release of *Destination Moon* on August 15 (though it was showing in New York weeks earlier).[58]

There was an undercurrent of excitement building that couldn't entirely be accounted for by the $1.2 million publicity budget. Helen Gould, an influential film critic, summarized many developments happening at the same time in "Scientific Films Making a Comeback," in *The New York Times*. Harry Bates's "Farewell to the Master" had been picked up by Twentieth Century Fox to be filmed as *The Day the Earth Stood Still,* and Pal was working on *When Worlds Collide,* based on two Wylie-Balmer novels written in the 1930s.[59]

Heinlein was too wrapped up in building even to consider trips for the premieres. As he began putting up the walls late in June 1950, *Destination Moon* premiered on Broadway, and *Aviation Week* ran a very complimentary review early in July.[60] That seemed to set the tone for everything that followed. Virginia Fowler, his editor's assistant at Scribner, wrote excitedly about the hoo-raw in Times Square after a large ad appeared in *The New York Times* that featured his name prominently: "A three story shell of a rocket ship is wrapped around the corner of the movie house, and emits a hollow roaring sound, broken at intervals by an equally hollow voice which booms in a voice of doom—'Destination Moon'."[61]

Moreover, John Campbell told him, the theater's doorman was costumed in an orange space suit—in 90-degree heat![62]

The frame of the Mesa Avenue house was in place by mid-August, and the roof went up. City services were in—electricity and water. He rushed the installation of the exterior walls so that they could move into the structure on August 28, 1950.

The sales Heinlein had made in the spring began popping up to keep his name constantly before the public. The August issue of *Boys' Life* carried the first installment of "Satellite Scout" (the condensed version of *Farmer in the Sky*) and *Senior Prom* (the new name for *Calling All Girls*), a magazine for teenaged girls, ran his new "Puddin'" story, "Cliff and the Calories." Also in August, Shasta released *The Man Who Sold the Moon,* and Scribner brought out *Farmer in the Sky. Short Stories* magazine ran the *Destination Moon* novelette in its September issue, capitalizing on the movie's first-run success. He was in boys' and girls' markets, books, pulps, and film, all at the same time. His postwar plan to break out of the pulp market was a complete success.

ALIEN INVASIONS

Robert and Ginny Heinlein spent Labor Day (September 2, 1950) floating 12" × 12" glass bricks on oakum to close the clerestory windows between roof and exterior wall, which would make the house weatherproof. "I am still much badgered by bills, mechanics, unavoidable chores and such," he wrote to Blassingame, "but I have a place to write and should now be able to resume writing without delay and be able to continue at it fairly steadily."[1]

He had two books ready to write any time he could get away from building—but first he had to cut a cat door for the marmalade kitten Ginny had acquired (and named Pixie) just a couple of days after they moved in.[2] She had conspired in her stealth cat-acquisition project with G. Harry Stine, a young fan in Colorado Springs. Stine was a hi-fi enthusiast, and Robert set him planning a state-of-the-art stereo system for the house, with concealed speakers and volume controls in every room.[3] Stine was also a beginning writer, and Campbell had urged Heinlein to help him out with his writing. "I think quite well of Harry," Heinlein wrote, "and think that he will make a good writer in time. He is intelligent, willing, and his shortcomings are the limitations of his years. I am giving him such help as I can."[4] (Ginny recalled that Stine ignored everything Heinlein tried to tell him—and sold his first story to Campbell later in 1950.)[5]

Designing and building your own home lets you customize it to your lifestyle. His and her bathrooms were built into the plan.

Ginny's bath is not just a place with plumbing. Her sybaritic attitude toward baths matches that of the decadent days of the Roman Empire; her bath is her favorite living room and I designed it most carefully to her tastes . . . . I heated the tub itself, Japanese style, and brought a big picture window right down to the edge of the tub . . .

Ginny fills this tub to her chin (it is big enough for four people—six if they are well acquainted), surrounds herself with cigarettes, ash trays, drink, chewing gum, mail, book and book rack, magazines, puts on a stack of records or turns on FM (I piped sound in, with local controls), switches off the telephone—and stays there, happy as a frog, hours at a stretch, surrounded by cats.[6]

It was around the matter of Ginny's baths that the Heinleins developed their own private form of telepathy: Ginny would settle into the water and train her mind on Robert to bring the cigarettes she had forgotten, and presently he would turn up with cigarettes and ashtray, almost without fail.[7]

His own bathroom was more austere, by comparison, and the pictures varied from time to time, from an aquatint of the Taj Mahal, to a waterproofed lithograph titled *Medusa*.

The place turned out not quite so inaccessible as Heinlein had planned: On one occasion, a fan from out of town—Curtis Casewit—decided to look around the house before knocking on the door and peeked into Ginny's bathroom, startling her out of the tub with a shriek that brought Robert running in alarm.[9]

The telephone was the only flaw in an otherwise comfortable life. They had been given a four-party line—a technological affliction fortunately no longer common. A single telephone line is run to four (or more) different houses, so that any incoming call would ring in all the houses—a different ring tone for each party. You could not use the telephone when anyone else was on it—and more gossipy neighbors made a nosy habit of picking up the phone to listen in on other families' conversations.

One evening, someone was calling every twenty minutes or so, trying to reach a neighbor who wasn't home, for hours. Ginny could not get to sleep. Presently, Robert took the telephone and lay down on the bed next to her and began, calmly and methodically, going up the chain of command from operator to supervisor to department head, asking for a better grade of service—and being turned down, and going up the next step in the chain.

Somehow he was put in touch with the regional vice president for Mountain States Telephone, who was vacationing at Sun Valley. The man was outraged that anyone should call him at this ungodly hour—and Robert pleasantly agreed with him. That, he explained, was exactly the problem: Somebody else's caller was keeping his wife awake. By the time he was finished, the man agreed to upgrade their service—a private line to be installed the next day.[10]

While they were smoothing out the bumps in their new life, the Heinleins also got to know some of their neighbors. Ginny had particularly taken to the nearest, Doc and Lucky Herzberger. Lucky was a lively blonde who rode show horses and kidded Ginny about her effete Central Park riding background. They received impromptu dinner invitations from the Herzbergers, and they learned to "dress for dinner" automatically, since they never knew what they would find—a cozy dinner *en famille* (Lucky's signature hot dog dinner) or a carefully orchestrated "society" dinner for thirty.

Heinlein grumbled about the dinner dress at first. His formal wear was all heavy serge fabric with the severe Navy cut. Ginny took him to a good tailor and got him outfitted with lighter, tropical-weight evening wear. After that he delighted in dressing for dinner whenever possible.[11]

Heinlein's start on *The Puppet Masters* was delayed by a very strange crisis: He got a letter from Sam Kamens, his lawyer-friend in Los Angeles, dated September 18, 1950, saying that Cats Sang (Mrs. Henry Sang)—his friend from Philadelphia during World War II—was trying to reach Leslyn's cousin, Marian Beard. Over the summer, starting on July Fourth, Leslyn was in the hospital following a series of strokes.[12] The most recent one had put her in a very bad way, and Cats was trying to locate Leslyn's only surviving relative. The doctors gave Leslyn only a week to live and Cats was trying to assure that the body would not be shipped to Heinlein in Colorado Springs. That mystified him:

> I can see from Cats' note that she felt that she was acting in my best interests. I appreciate the good thoughts. However I did not see it that way from what information was available to me . . . She [Leslyn] married Mocabee in November 1949—why in the world would anyone ship Mrs. Mocabee's body to *me*? And who would do so? Mr. Mocabee?[13]

Further complicating matters, Cats had contacted Heinlein's mother before reaching Sam Kamens, so the non-event continued to reverberate through his family and acquaintances in Southern California.[14]

On October 1, 1950, Heinlein was finally able to settle into the writing of his flying saucer book, *The Puppet Masters*. It went very rapidly—100,000 words of draft in about five weeks. It was turning out a very timely book.

During World War II, pilots had reported seeing unidentifiable "foo fighters" in the sky. For the last year or so, since 1947, flying saucers and strange blue lights in the sky had attained almost the status of a craze, particularly in the late-summer "silly season."[15] The media were making their own kind of "alien invasion" story: Alger Hiss's first trial in July of 1949 (which had ended, in a hung jury, on Heinlein's forty-second birthday), was the start of a period when Congress, the FBI, and the newspapers, too, were doing their best to whip up hysteria about "Communist infiltrators." Hiss, just convicted of spying for Stalin, had been a very high official in the State Department (he was with Roosevelt at the Yalta Conference five years earlier). There were, in fact, Communist spies working at the highest levels of the U.S. government. This was a genuine—and a very serious—problem, which needed to be dealt with forthrightly, and so far as Heinlein was concerned, the hysteria was only getting in the way of the real job:

> Spies have had access to top secret information, and loyal men are being prevented from working where they can do the most good through 'guilt by association' and other methods having roughly the scientific accuracy of witch smelling. It's ridiculous![16]

The arrest of Julius and Ethel Rosenberg in August that year (very minor cogs in the Soviet espionage network) showed very plainly that even unsuspected neighbors might be aliens in disguise, working to enslave you.[17]

Even some of his old liberal friends had drifted away from the Jeffersonian eternal-vigilance-is-the-price-of-liberty that was the core of Heinlein's values.[18] Perhaps the drift had been there all along, and it took a touchstone issue like this Hiss-Rosenberg thing to cast the erosion into sharp relief.[19]

It was not just some drift in some of his friends: He could see evidence everywhere he looked. Since the war, there were too many bleeding hearts— some of them in very unexpected places. Earlier in the year he had let John Arwine have it with both barrels, over trying to salvage a Communist:

> I can't go along with your thesis that your friend is a brand to be snatched from the burning. Dammit, John, anybody who hasn't got the horse sense to see the stupidity, the asininity and the contradictions of Communism by April 1950, is not a brand to be snatched from the burning no matter what other talents he may possess. He's too damn stupid, quit wasting your time. Don't take that as advice, but simply as emotional blow-off.[20]

With *The Puppet Masters,* Heinlein was "in tune with the Zeitgeist." It was worth the effort to create his "thinly-disguised allegory, a diatribe against totalitarianism in all its forms."[21]

He couldn't do anything about the state of the culture. What he *could* do was to keep putting solid American liberal values before his readers, children and adults—"love of personal freedom and an almost religious respect for the dignity of the individual."[22]

Horace Gold, who was editing a new SF magazine, *Galaxy,* had sent him the first two issues to entice him into letting *Galaxy* have "Pandora's Box," the predictions article *Cosmopolitan* had commissioned, then abandoned. At first, Heinlein tried to talk Gold out of it: That one had been written for an audience of clubwomen and would look hopelessly naïve in a science-fiction magazine. It would be an embarrassment.[23]

But Gold knew what he wanted and thought Heinlein was high-hatting him—sneering at *Galaxy.* He had "heard" from unidentified sources that Heinlein would not sell except to the slicks anymore.[24] No, Blassingame—then Heinlein himself—assured Gold, just the opposite: He wanted his debut in *Galaxy* to show him at top of form.[25]

Gold was firm: The field was changing in ways Heinlein might not see; and a predictions article written for a general audience was exactly right for *Galaxy* in 1950.[26]

It was a mystery to Heinlein, but "the customer is always right." "Pandora's Box" went to Gold "as is."

By the time Heinlein was ready to send out his most "adult" novel, *The Puppet Masters* (December 2, 1950), he was wrestling with an interesting request from the editor of *Child Life,* a magazine for very small children, to write stories that could take his audience down to the six-year-old level. The technical restrictions were even more difficult than those for the juveniles—800-word stories using a vocabulary of about 250 words. The payment for each individual story was small—only $30—but the secondary and reprint markets for these things could make up for the low initial sale. He worked out a possible plot for a serial and agreed to think about it.

In the meantime, he had to get all the writing done that he could, before Ginny was called up for the Korean War and he would need to take off to be her camp-follower. He shut his ears to the war news and pushed out another "Puddin'" short story for *Senior Prom*, "The Bulletin Board."[27]

The same considerations were driving the house-building: He had to write the next boys' book for Scribner in order to get enough money to hire the necessary trades—and of course that meant he was tied to the typewriter and could not build. "If I ever try to build a house again," he told Blassingame, "I hope they lock me up first."[28]

It initially looked as if he had succeeded too well at *The Puppet Masters*: It was too creepy. *The Post* passed on it, as did *Collier's,* which had just bought its own alien invasion story, the science-fiction horror classic *The Day of the Triffids* by "John Wyndham".

The readers for Doubleday downchecked *The Puppet Masters* as "squeamish" and said that "no woman would read it,"[29] but Walter Bradbury, the editor at Doubleday, overruled them: It was hitting its target audience, if maybe a little rough. Bradbury asked for a little cutting, from 90,000 words to 75,000 words, and a little softening of the sexual titillation and the horror elements.[30]

In January 1951, Heinlein received a dozen scripts from the *Tom Corbett* show that had been airing since October and found they did not carry a credit for the book.[31] He still had the option of trying to get a card on the show, but what he saw appalled him:[32]

> The show is so moronic, the motivations and implied ethical standards so false that I can conceive of no circumstances under which I would want my name mentioned in connection with this show. I am satisfied to take my thirty pieces of silver and remain anonymous.[33]

When it came time to assemble the manuscripts and tearsheets for his second Future History collection for Shasta, *The Green Hills of Earth and Other Stories,* the line editor for this project, Ted Dikty, asked for some minor revisions for continuity—and some major revisions to bring " 'We Also Walk Dogs' " into the Future History (Korshak had simply listed it in the original contract).

Heinlein put his foot down: He was at the end of his rope with Korshak. Among other things, he *could not* get Korshak to answer routine business correspondence, and Korshak had recently added insult to injury: When Heinlein found out that Korshak had granted a Braille right instead of forwarding the request to him, as any normal publisher would have done, he became coldly furious.[34] "This incident," he wrote to Ditky, "typifies why it is so distasteful to do business with you people: you do not even have the grace to permit an author to perform his own acts of charity."[35]

If he could manage it, Heinlein wanted out of the contract with Shasta. But he sent the manuscripts on January 15. He had elected, he told his agent, to try to achieve a more professional, arm's-length relationship, rather than force an arbitration on the contract at this time.[36]

Shasta was not his only problem. He had expected royalties to start coming in from *Destination Moon* before Christmas, but no word came from Rathvon. Heinlein didn't have any hard numbers to go on yet, but a rough calculation based on number of theaters times showings per day times average ticket price suggested the film must have broken even by now.

At the six-month mark, the initial release showed no signs of fading: Their

$1.8 million baby was making a strong showing. Heinlein got a notification from George Pal Productions that they were up for an Oscar: The art director, Ernst Fegté, had submitted three scenes to the SFX (Special Effects) Committee of the Academy of Motion Picture Arts and Sciences—"Take Off," "Rescue," and "Landing on the Moon."

The prestige was tremendous—and exactly how many square feet of drywall would the honor get up?

Everybody involved with *The Puppet Masters* was acting somewhat "cracked." Blassingame had submitted the book to *Galaxy*, since Gold's rates were competitive. And Gold wanted it—and he didn't want it—or something a little like it, perhaps. Heinlein could cope with the request to cut the story—sixty thousand words was about right for a pulp serial—and he knew he would have to cut some of the titillation for magazines, but Blassingame agreed the revisions Gold wanted were excessive. "In fact," Heinlein wrote Blassingame,

> . . . they amount to an order for an entirely new book, one bearing a vague relationship to the one in existence but requiring complete rewriting with new incidents, new complication, a vastly different plot and a different solution.[37]

Some of Gold's criticisms might be addressed by the editing Walter Bradbury wanted done for Doubleday—tone down the horror and tone down the "prurience" (though the book scarcely ever rose above the level of titillation). Heinlein asked for some more specific guidance: What exactly was Doubleday looking for? Bradbury startled (and dismayed) him when he said, "You've got to remember your juvenile audience, and you've got to recall you're writing for them."[38] This particular book *could not possibly* be reoriented to a juvenile audience: It was a horror story for adults, from the ground up. "I have caught myself neatly in a trap," he told Ginny, "one of my own devising, by writing for juveniles and trying to write for adults at the same time and under the same name."[39]

And then Leslyn surfaced again, with no sign of her supposed brush with death—though whether in some sense "recovered" was an open question.

Leslyn had written to them, direct to Mesa Avenue, late in 1950—"all sweetness and light to us"[40]—but it became clear that letters she sent to his friends and business associates were another matter: Doña Smith (the former Doña Campbell) mentioned receiving one and, at Heinlein's request, sent it on to him in February 1951[41]—a classic poison-pen letter in the venomous mode of Leslyn's dead mother. Heinlein read it with amazement, mounting to alarm, changing to disgust. Disgust gave way to sorrow and then to an abyss of pity: His Leslyn, his Piglet, was finally and completely gone, the once-beloved body possessed by the untidy ghost of her mother.

> I had hoped that time would eventually make me of little importance in her mind but apparently her hatred of me is even stronger than ever. . . .[42]
>
> I married a sweet and intelligent girl back in 1932, twenty years ago. The first five years were happy on the whole, though I should have spotted the storm warnings. The second five years were kept pleasant in part only by difficult adjustments—and by the fact that we were too poor to give her much leeway—or much liquor. The third five years are better left undescribed. I learned to smile no matter what happened. After the war I tried very hard and with expense no object to get at the root of the trouble. I failed and became desperate and did many foolish things and estranged many of my friends. But once I was away from her I got well in a hurry, almost at once. I have often wondered to what extent my own acts or omissions contributed to her illness. "Not much" is my honest belief; I think it was latent in her, from her mother; I think it simply took a number of years for it to develop.[43]

Everyone was getting Leslyn's poison-pen letters—friends and former friends, editors and publishers, even Lurton Blassingame. Heinlein had been through this cycle before, too many times, and knew there was no point even in entertaining hope: His best strategy was to make no reply at all.

> Through experience with her and very similar experiences with her mother I have found that the only defense, poor as it is, is silence, complete silence, and a refusal to offer defense or explanation even when she manages to convince some third party . . . This last letter doesn't look to me as if it could fool anybody—and yet I would venture a guess that she could be quite convincing in her more lucid moments.[44]

Nor was Leslyn the only source of confusion that spring. Not quite a year after L. Ron Hubbard's book was published, Dianetics seemed to be generating a lot of attention in the world at large—but it also seemed to be imploding. Heinlein mildly characterized the troubles he was hearing about as "growing pains" in a letter to John Campbell on February 26, 1951, and Campbell reported back that the California organization had come under attack by Communists—focused on Sara Northrup Hubbard.[45] It was hard to tell what was actually going on: The gossip Heinlein received from friends on both coasts was confusing. Heinlein was too busy to delve deeply into the issue in any case; spring was coming on, and he would soon be able to hire trades and get the interior of the house finished—always assuming the Army didn't get all the skilled construction workers. The invasion of South Korea was almost a year old now, and yet, there was still no sign of a definite commitment on President Truman's part or Congress's—and thus still no telling when Ginny might be called up. As he got the major manuscripts done, Heinlein dealt with business matters that had accumulated, so he could go back to house-building.

Alice Dalgliesh was happy with *Between Planets*—mostly (though a little dubious about the ambiguous boy-meets-girl subplot that Heinlein had put in because he was actually getting more fan mail about these books from girls than from boys).[46]

Doubleday asked him to edit a science-fiction anthology for their line (science-fiction anthologies were selling better than novels at the time).[47] Heinlein initially turned them down flat, but Blassingame persuaded him that the continuing exposure would be good for keeping up name recognition. Doubleday offered to have Fred and Judith (Merril) Pohl run down the rights, with Walter Bradbury overseeing the project. Reluctantly, Heinlein agreed, and that started a months-long cycle of reading and passing tearsheets back and forth with his other three editors and discussing the contents. By August 1951 the project was under way, and Heinlein's main contact, Truman Talley, reported "The team play between Fred and Judy, Brad, and ourselves is going along without a hitch."[48]

The previous summer, a deal had been negotiated with New American Library to take all of his books to paperback under the Signet imprint (*Sixth Column* to be retitled *The Day After Tomorrow,* since the pre–World War II reference in the title was no longer topical). Blassingame included the Shasta books with the deal, but with the advances and royalties paid directly to Heinlein. Heinlein then forwarded to Shasta their contractual share of the advances. It was a pain to do things in reverse—the author pay the publisher instead of the other way around—but he was already doing this with secondary rights for the stories they had under contract. It was the only practical way he could work out to reduce the free-for-all grabbing of his rights. "Shasta is entitled under contract to a percentage split in this matter; there Shasta's interest ends, and I intend to keep it that way."[49]

However, Heinlein did not yet understand that Shasta could not be reined in: Korshak was already selling secondary rights without telling him *or paying for them,* and he had just sold an anthology right to SF editor Don Wollheim for "Life-Line."[50]

This was not a problem unique to Shasta, though Korshak was by far the worst offender of whom Heinlein had experience—an unacceptable degree of casualness about other peoples' property rights seemed endemic among the fan press publishers: Fantasy Press's agent, Abe Klein, had negotiated a reprint sale of *Beyond This Horizon* to Grosset & Dunlap, with an introduction by Groff Conklin, without even telling Heinlein about it. Heinlein did not like either side of this deal. In the first place, Fantasy Press did not have the contractual right to make a secondary sale of the book;[51] in the second place, he thought Grosset & Dunlap's "SF Classic" line of books flimsy and unattractive.[52]

And in the third place, he had avoided being associated with Groff Conklin since the Crown anthology. Immediately after the war, Conklin was just a little too willing to tolerate and even justify Stalin for Heinlein's taste.[53] When Conklin wanted another story for a new anthology—"Columbus Was a Dope"—they had a little frank conversation on the subject and cleared the air. It appeared that Conklin had modified his uncritical political positions, and Heinlein felt he could now work with Conklin. "I may be mistaken," he wrote to his agent, "but I propose to give him the benefit of the doubt. Just the same, these soft heads have put this country in danger much more than the outright Russian agents."[54]

A smart man learns from experience; a wise man learns from the experience of others. As of 1951, Heinlein learned he was still only "smart" when it came to management of his business affairs. *Tom Corbett* had already spun off comic books and a newspaper strip as of April 1951, and the merchandising rights to the "Space Cadet" name he had essentially given away began coining money for the show's producers as their space suits and ray guns became what *Newsweek* magazine called "a national craze."[55] Over the summer, Blassingame reported: "I also heard that the space suit[s] are selling madly; the police had to be invoked to save a Los Angeles store the day they went on sale there and the kids were lined up for blocks." He concluded ruefully: "Too bad we didn't hold on to these rights or demand a lot more cash for them."[56]

Heinlein had already shrugged it off philosophically:

As to the commercial rights, money is a relative thing. I can remember once being terribly hard up for fifty cents—stranded, broke, and hungry. I remember another occasion when I hocked my (sacred!) Annapolis class ring for seven dollars. At the time the money they paid me for the commercial rights was ransom money which got me out of a most unpleasant hole. I don't regret it for myself but it may not have been fair to you in the long run.[57]

Blassingame kept delivering royalties and advances, and construction on the house moved along. At one point in May 1950, though, H. L. Gold was weeks late with his payment for the *Puppet Masters* serial, and the finances became "iffy." A few weeks later, the squeeze had become critical:

H.L. Gold's delay in paying off on *Puppet Masters* is becoming quite embarrassing—if he does not get the money to me by this coming Friday the 25th, I'll probably have to let my mechanics go (and God knows when I'll be able to get them back!). This housebuilding game is wonderful—just like pouring money into the sea.[58]

Blassingame wired them $500 out of the blue, which Heinlein later concluded had been a loan, or advance, out of pocket. It was a good risk, though: Three days later, the prestige general-fiction magazine *Blue Book* took the serial rights for *Between Planets,* which they would retitle "Planets in Combat" when it came out in September and October.

In May 1951, John Campbell resigned from the Dianetics organizations. His "explanations" were hard to follow: When the subject came up in letters, it sounded as though he was accusing Hubbard of ideological impurity or counter-revolutionary tendencies or something.[59] Isaac Asimov undoubtedly put his finger on an important factor in the split, in a witticism widely quoted at the time and repeated often since: "I knew Campbell, and I knew Hubbard, and no movement can have two Messiahs."[60]

The science-fiction field was expanding explosively in 1951—radio, television, comic books—and Heinlein was contacted by a woman who wanted to adapt *Red Planet* as a stage play for the Tenth National Play Competition sponsored by Seattle Junior Programs, Inc. It was not a medium he had much interest in himself, but he wished Minta Meier good luck with the contest as he granted and then next year renewed rights for her one-hour-and-forty-minute adaptation.[61]

In the meantime, Shasta had been too quiet. Korshak had again refused to let Heinlein see corrected proofs, and on June 26, 1951 (just a week after Heinlein had sold a radio right for "Green Hills" for the *Dimension X* program), a delivery man showed up on the Heinleins' doorstep with eleven cartons of advance-order copies of *The Green Hills of Earth and Other Stories* for him to autograph—shipping charges COD. Heinlein refused delivery: He was not contractually obligated to pay Shasta's shipping charges.[62] A month later, the cartons came back, shipping prepaid this time, both ways. He looked the books over before starting to sign them and found Shasta had changed the order of the stories and had not made some of the proofreading corrections. Even more embarrassing, they had dumped the introduction L. Sprague de Camp had written and substituted a new one written by Mark Reinsberg. That angered him more than any wrong done directly to him. Reinsberg was a friend, too,[63] so there was nothing wrong about that—but it was a slap in de Camp's face. Heinlein wrote to de Camp:

> Sprague, I see that Korshak (a man always full of little surprises) has substituted an introduction by an ex-fan named Mark Reinsberg in *The Green Hills of Earth* for the wonderful introduction you wrote. Can you tell me what happened? Korshak never tells me anything; he just goes ahead and does things—the *fait accompli* is his Standard Operating Procedure and he rarely answers my letters. . . .
>
> His infinite variety in thinking up new ways to be an unbearable jerk continues to amaze me. They range from "selling" rights of mine not controlled by Shasta to long-distance phone calls in the middle of the night. His latest stunt is to refuse to honor author's corrections over proof. Grrr![64]

Blassingame just wanted to clean up the immediate mess: He suggested that Heinlein sign the books, send them back to Shasta, and start an arbitration when he was next in New York. Business was booming, and that's where Heinlein's time and attention should be going:[65] *The Post* wanted another Heinlein story; the Doubleday anthology was shaping up after a time-consuming but rewarding round of reading and correspondence about its contents; and foreign rights and anthology reprint requests were coming in steadily. Martin Greenberg had recently requested "Columbus Was a Dope," too, for a Gnome Press anthology—the same story Groff Conklin had wanted. Heinlein was a little mystified at the demand for that story: "The story was slanted for the general magazines and intended for the public rather than the regular readers of science fiction . . . it will seem like pretty thin beer to the jaded appetites of the s-f afficianados [sic]."[66] If all Greenberg wanted was the drawing power of Heinlein's name on his contents list, Heinlein was not inclined to cooperate: He told Blassingame to offer it under the "Lyle Monroe" name. If it somehow turned out Greenberg wanted the *story,* Blassingame could give him the

Heinlein name gratis: "I'm often wrong; if he believes in the story . . . I'll back him with my own name."[67] Heinlein *was* wrong—or at least Greenberg so convinced him: "Columbus Was a Dope" appeared in the Gnome Press anthology *Travelers in Space* later that year. The many mansions of science fiction had added several new tracts of public housing since the war, and Heinlein's fluff-for-John-Q.-Public was not merely accepted, but had become part of the way science fiction presented itself to the public.

Now that the house was done, they had had their first house guests (a very unsuccessful visit from Bill and Lucy Corson early in August 1951[68]). The house-building had drawn local attention. The *Colorado Springs Gazette-Telegraph* sent a stringer, Dorothy Shanahan, to get an extensive interview with both of them, and ran an article that went on for pages, heavily illustrated with photographs, mostly of Ginny and her proud possession of a "push-button" home. The built-ins and amenities were sources of gushing wonder, as was the sound system G. Harry Stine had helped build into every room in the house, with independent controls in each room. Shanahan seemed particularly fascinated by Ginny's dining table on wheels.[69]

The article appeared on September 30, 1951, as they were ramping up for their first real opportunity to entertain in their new home: They hosted a wedding reception of G. Harry Stine and Barbara Kauth, his college sweetheart, before the newlyweds had to take off for New Mexico and Hank's brand-new job as a rocket engineer at White Sands.[70]

It might have been the newspaper article that brought the Heinlein house to the attention of *Popular Mechanics*. In November 1951 *PM* sent their Western editor (and photographer) Tom Stimson (who had written their very flattering coverage of *Destination Moon* in 1950), to do a similar piece. Stimson's article appeared in the June 1952 issue of *Popular Mechanics*.

The Stimson interview had been a welcomed break from the Martian Mowgli story, which had gone sour on Robert after he got an introduction on paper.[71] He put it aside and cranked out an idea that had been tickling in the back of his mind since Robert Cornog had loaned him a copy of *Cycles* in 1949—a book on cycles of all kinds—sunspots, cicadas, economic cycles, women's hemlines, and so forth.[72] A number of unrelated cycles were scheduled to peak—or trough—simultaneously in 1952.[73] "The Year of the Jackpot" would be topical, if a little depressing, since he imagined a rather permanent bottoming-out of all humanity's cycles while everyone around his protagonist goes nuts.

It seemed like a timely idea,[74] but the story bounced around a few times until Blassingame offered it to *Galaxy* in October 1951. Gold wanted it—but he asked for so many and so substantial revisions that it would have essentially required Heinlein to write a new story (the happy ending Gold wanted was particularly problematical). Heinlein told him "no" on the revisions, adding privately to Blassingame: "Gold is such a fusser and tinkerer that I believe that sales to him are worth while only on a take-it-or-leave-it-basis—and I think he will buy on that basis."[75] And if not . . . Street & Smith had just changed its policy to buy only serial rights. Campbell was an editor he knew he could work with.

By October 1951, the first two installments of *The Puppet Masters* were out. Heinlein was appalled at how much editorial fiddling Gold had done with it—he had gone through the manuscript like a steamroller: "Gold turns out to be a copy messer-upper; there is hardly a paragraph which he has not 'improved'—and I am fit to be tied."[76] Heinlein was particularly agitated about the wholesale destruction of his carefully built-up prosodic effects. He didn't have high style going for him, he wrote to Gold; all he had to give the consumer was his "voice," his effects, "as calculated as a whore's sighs—and it is my whole stock in trade."

> A word misused on p. 10 and again on 73 does not have its intended effect until it is again used on p. 213—and then damn it! somebody comes along with a blue pencil and takes it out as unnecessary on 10! It was unnecessary on 10, but it wasn't 10 I was shooting at; it was 213 . . . . I am aiming at certain built-up emotional effects and I don't want the style to be noticed as such.[77]

Gold acknowledged that his editing was obtrusive here. Perhaps he was distracted by *Galaxy*'s change of ownership over the summer—in any case it wouldn't happen again. He restored the language for the third installment—thereby, of course, compounding the mess.[78]

Now that the foreword to the Doubleday anthology (*Tomorrow, the Stars*)[79] was turned in and "Year of the Jackpot" was sold, Heinlein had a little time. Ben Babb had come up with an angle that might rescue their Abbott and Costello treatment, reslanting it to the new comedy team of Dean Martin and Jerry Lewis. It wouldn't require any substantial commitment of time; Heinlein took a few days off and went to Denver to record a radio program at the KOA radio station for the kids' book review show Dalgliesh had recommended to him, *Carnival of Books*.[80] Its host, Miss Ruth Harshaw, had arranged for four boys to talk about his latest juvenile. The boys made a fine panel, and the experience was undoubtedly enhanced when Miss Harshaw said her favorite was *Red Planet*.[81] Thereafter he made opportunities to appear on *Carnival of Books* whenever he could manage it.

A TV adaptation of "Ordeal in Space" (Heinlein's Future History story about an agoraphobe who cures himself by rescuing a kitten on a ledge) aired on CBS's *Out There* program on November 4, 1951.[82] The adaptation was made by "Edward Waldo," which might have been a pseudonym of Theodore "Ted" Sturgeon, whose family name (and his birth name) was Waldo. Rod Steiger appeared in this episode. Over the summer of 1951, just before the *Green Hills of Earth* books arrived on Heinlein's doorstep, Sturgeon was involved in setting up a "writers cooperative," Tomorrow Is Yours, Inc., to provide content for a television series under development.[83] The producer wanted the best of science fiction, and Heinlein was one of the first fourteen writer-members Sturgeon asked to participate. Heinlein looked over Sturgeon's prospectus and noticed some flaws in the setup. He did not think the contract was salvageable and wrote a detailed analysis—and then a shorter, "fluff" letter to let Sturgeon down easy that he wasn't going to be participating. He gave both letters to his agent and let him make the decision which to send.[84] Blassingame opted to send the longer letter, on the theory that Sturgeon could get some practical use out of the analysis.[85]

Heinlein was writing a new story, about using psychics—telepaths, clairvoyants, telekinetics—as weapons of war, but it got away from him. He finally wrestled "Nightmare Race" to a close at 14,000 words and struggled to cut it to a more saleable length.[86] In a month he went from 56 pages to 34, to 31 and finally to 28 pages, changing the title to "Project Nightmare"—and the first editor who saw it (Knox Burger at *Collier's*) said it was frantic and read as if it had been cut too much.[87] (Also, the war scare with the Soviet Union was passé.) None of the slicks, then none of the reputable magazines would take it. In 1951 Heinlein was still laboring under the impression that science-fiction magazines would not be interested in material written for a general audience.[88] The story was never offered to Campbell, for example—who in any case did not develop an interest in psionics until years later. Howard Browne purchased it for *Fantastic,* the new sister magazine for *Amazing,* but *Fantastic* ceased publication and it wound up at *Amazing,* where it was published in the April–May 1953 combined issue.[89]

Ginny noted thoughtfully that he had spent more time on those two stories—"The Year of the Jackpot" and "Project Nightmare"—than he had on any of his books and earned only a fraction as much.[90] Heinlein realized she was right and took the conclusion as his own:

. . . purely from the standpoint of economics a novel with a slow, steady sale is more rewarding in the long run than a large number of short stories later gathered as a book. On the other hand, literary reputation is more enhanced by short stories widely anthologized. But the collection [Opus] #87 [*Green Hills of Earth*] cumulatively represents more than two years of hard work while this one novel [*Between Planets*] represents less than 2 months work. I have concluded that I need novels to eat on and shorts for display purposes.[91]

For nearly a year they had been "eating on" the royalties from *Tom Corbett, Space Cadet*. That November, the Kellogg's company held an executive conference at the nearby Broadmoor resort:

. . . Kenyon & Eckhardt, the adv agency which has *Space Cadet* from Rockhill Radio, is presenting a supercolossal (!) spread of the TV show, etc., to them. I am helping out with exhibits and some sort of a talk. An odd sort of a clambake but I will do my best to be helpful.[92]

It would also be a chance to see special screenings of some *Tom Corbett* episodes on kinescope. He saw nothing that caused him to change his position.

Neither did the news about L. Ron Hubbard. The rumor mill was starting up again: Heinlein heard, for example, that Hubbard was paralyzed and hiding out somewhere in the Midwest. "I doubt very much the rumor about Ron being paralyzed," he wrote to Robert Cornog. "I have heard from him a few times. He is living in Wichita and—by his statement—is doing some flying."[93] In fact, their mutual friend John Arwine had had a long, rambling phone call from Hubbard recently.[94]

And while the initial organization was imploding, Dianetics "auditing" was taking over science-fiction fandom, as a parlor game played like one of the old "Freuding" parties of the 1920s.[95]

Heinlein had no time to investigate or play parlor games with his head: By November 1951 it was time to start his annual boys' book for Scribner, and he didn't have even the glimmering of an idea. Heinlein asked Ginny what he should write about.

"Why don't you write about a pair of mischievous twins," she suggested, "always getting into trouble"[96] (Ginny had always been fascinated by twins). Robert S. Richardson had written recently, wanting to see more of a minor character in *Red Planet*—the boy student-businessman at the school. Heinlein combined the two ideas and split the *Red Planet* boy into twins. He started on the story that would become *The Rolling Stones*, giving it a light, realistic treatment like a *Post* story—or a series of *Post* stories—following a middle-class (well, *upper*-middle-class) family on their grand tour of the Solar System.

Since he worked until very late at night, and Ginny got up very early, Heinlein had developed the habit of leaving the pages he had just finished on the kitchen counter for her before going to bed. Once Ginny had her OJ starter, she read the new pages, and later, Heinlein would collect any notes she had made for him.

Ginny was finally beginning to be comfortable in what she saw as her role in Robert's process. She could give him a place to start, and that was what he mainly needed. Heinlein was more emphatic: He told her she had given him his "finish" as a professional writer, her marginal notes on his draft always carefully pinpointing stylistic or grammatical awkwardnesses, or lack of clarity in his expression.[97] Heinlein formed a habit of asking her before each writing session what he ought to write about next—and almost always she would be able to come up with an idea he could use.

The book was turning into a comedy—not the kind of thing he felt most comfortable with—so he had to work hard on his family of seven intelligent, engaging people.[98] His characters and situations came from many different sources: Having the boys sell bicycles in space was his own idea,[99] as was the alien species of affectionate pets—flat cats, based on Ellis Butler Parker's comic short story "Pigs Is Pigs."[100]

> Ginny dreamed up the red-headed twins; I provided the other characters; we both provided incident. I did not need to draw on the Gilbreths; I am one of seven children. Dr. Stone combined my mother and her father, an M.D. As to the baby who plays chess well at four, that's myself in that aspect—my Grandfather, Dr. Lyle, was my playmate at that age; I played a better game of chess then than I do now. Children's minds are just as competent as adults for abstract reasoning and they have less to distract them—the world has not yet crowded in.
>
>   Hazel combined my Aunt Bam, an old heller who died at 99 and was forever traveling, and my Aunt Anna, a professor of history, who is still living at 78, having retired at 76. She's tough and she's brilliant and she has a whim of iron."[101]

Roger Stone, paterfamilias, sounds like Heinlein again, in his "Daddy" persona from the Puddin' stories, who played straight man for everyone else.

He finished the draft of *The Rolling Stones* a couple of days before Christmas and found that his usual "tightening-up" edit—striking unnecessary phrases, surplus adjectives, and so forth—was almost not needed this time. The draft manuscript was so clean that, except for a few pages, it would not even have to be retyped.

There were several minor matters that needed attention before the end of the year. The payout from *Destination Moon* was nearly two months overdue. Unless one of the story sales came through, he would not have enough cash to pay his taxes. He might have to mortgage the house—a very unpleasant prospect, since it was essentially borrowing to pay current expenses. But he considered it because he was "anxious to get off the hook as soon as may be; I don't like to owe money—it makes me feel mildly dishonest."[102]

And there was another thing: Over the last few months, he had developed twinges and pains in his gut and his bottom. His health was otherwise good, but he feared this might be cancer. Exploratory surgery was scheduled at a cancer clinic early in January. He sent the *Rolling Stones* manuscript to Blassingame on December 31, 1951, and went into the hospital on New Year's Day 1952. His surgery was the next day.

REALITY BITES

Publishers normally forward mail they receive for an author, to protect privacy: Instead, Shasta gave out Heinlein's home address to a fan. This was not the kind of thing he wanted to have to deal with while weak from surgery (not cancer, thankfully, but a late complication from the botched hemorrhoid-correction surgery he had in Philadelphia during the war).

But news on other fronts was good: Fred Pohl wrote, wanting a "light story"—"Beyond Doubt"—to counterbalance a "fairly ponderous" anthology he was assembling, *Beyond the End of Time* (Perma books, 1952).[1] Heinlein contacted Elma Wentz, his coauthor: Pohl could use Heinlein's own name, but Elma Wentz (now LeCron) used "Miller" as her pseudonym.

Galaxy rejected *The Rolling Stones* for serial publication; Campbell rejected it, saying he expected more "philosophical" material from Heinlein. Alice Dalgliesh's reaction, however, was enthusiastic:

> You are a wonder! All morning I've been hanging breathless on the pages of *Rolling Stones* and laughing out loud as I read, too. When I came to where Dr. Stone is transferred from one ship to another I practically collapsed. And the flat cats! How do you do it[?][2]

That was encouraging: If the Scribner contract and advance came through early enough, he might be able to keep the IRS wolf away from the door. He could only sit up to work for about an hour a day—and he was fuzzy all the time with the drugs they were giving him.[3] Nevertheless, he sold a TV option for "Let There Be Light" to Teo Savory Productions a week into 1952 and entered negotiations with Ely Landau, Inc., for an original screenplay based on *Between Planets,* to be the pilot M.O.W.[4] for a series. Landau probably thought Heinlein was naïve: He offered him "hack's rates" for the original work they wanted, Heinlein told Blassingame.[5]

The *Destination Moon* payouts continued to be late. Blassingame contacted United Artists, the picture's distributor, directly. They acknowledged the existence of "deferments" still to be paid to van Ronkel and Heinlein, plus Chesley Bonestell and Pal himself, but claimed that there were huge amounts to be paid preferentially to someone called "Motion Picture Capital Corporation" before any payments would be made on the deferments. They would not say how much the picture had taken in, or how much they were holding undisbursed.

Gradually Blassingame got the full picture: Heinlein and van Ronkel had made their deal with Pal for 10 percent of the producer's net, and Pal had pledged the entire producer's share to cover the financing. When *The Great Rupert* bombed, it took down the *Destination Moon* profits: Everything went to Rathvon, to pay back *Rupert*'s losses. Lou Schor, their agent on the deal, wrote that he didn't think they would ever see any money out of Pal and Rathvon unless they sued. It was questionable under current law whether Pal had the right to dispose of the part of the producer's share he had already pledged to Heinlein and van Ronkel, and that was the question that might be brought before a court—a prospect of which Heinlein said "I view coldly, having never gotten anything but headaches and lawyer's bills out of law suits."[6] The most they might be able to achieve would be to drive Pal into bankruptcy. Reluctantly, Heinlein wrote Blassingame that he could not see making a trip to New York if United Artists was not going to pay out—which meant he would not be able to proceed against Shasta.[7]

Even if he got none of the film's profits, he had gotten his house-building started on the script proceeds, and he had achieved enough, very minor, celebrity out of the deal to be an annoyance.

Leslyn was writing another spate of poison-pen letters this year. This new series of letters was so over-the-top nuts that anyone who looked at them would conclude she was insane: "The accusations and insinuations about me in the letters . . . are somewhat less lurid than those she has sent to other friends of mine," he told Lurton Blassingame, who had already received two such poison-pen letters by February of 1952.

Ginny and I are accused of having attempted to murder her, I am accused of exploits that would have kept Casanova busy several life times, I am held responsible (with a threatened suit for $14,500) for her "loss of earning power" from '48 to date, I am alleged to have obtained "radiating atomic material" from "two little German prisoners of war" which I then am alleged to have used in several different foul and dastardly fashions, all mutually contradictory . . . .

The only thing that really worries me—and this scares the hell out of me—is that someday she might get out of bed, hop a bus, and show up here.[8]

He consulted a lawyer and was advised his best course was "to sweat it out and ignore it."[9]

Otherwise, Heinlein's slight degree of fame outside the book field kept other offers coming in. The station manager for KVOR Radio in Denver wrote asking him to be on Edward R. Murrow's "This I Believe" radio program. Murrow had become a popular and recognizable radio newsman during World War II, and Heinlein knew of his reputation as a patriot. This was a nationally syndicated show, with slots assigned to CBS's regional affiliates. Heinlein was one of Denver's nominees.[10]

"I'm flattered," he told Irving Pichel the following day, "but am thinking of turning it down; I don't relish getting on a national hook-up and doing an emotional strip-tease. Furthermore such things take me away from my regular work by distracting my mind, sometimes for days, from story."[11] Blassingame talked him into it, though: It would be good exposure. Heinlein would have until May to figure out what he wanted to say—in three and a half minutes, tops.

He had better keep a grip on his credo: Erle Korshak had dropped by Blassingame's office early in February (while Blassingame was out with influenza), to inform him that Shasta had retained the Authors Guild's lawyer to sue Heinlein, if need be, to get him cooperating again. Actually, Blassingame said, they were fishing for a buy-out offer for Heinlein's contract. Adding insult to injury, Blassingame discovered that Shasta had sold the Australian rights of "Life-Line" for just $10![12] As much scam and scandal as Blassingame had seen in his long career as an agent, this was beyond even his experience.[13]

In February 1952, Charles Scribner died following a heart attack, and Dalgliesh wrote saying that young Charles Scribner would take over the management of the firm. She asked Heinlein to change the name of a slightly unsavory character in *The Rolling Stones* (his current book), "Old Charlie." Exasperated, he refused the change, telling Blassingame it illustrated "how far afield she has gone to find trouble" and added "How silly can one get?"[14]

With the major manuscripts out of the way and his health on the mend, Robert could relax and enjoy life once again—and there was a great deal to enjoy in their "scissorbill town," as Heinlein sometimes referred to Colorado Springs.[15] The weather turned warm and mild in February, and the Heinleins installed a tightwire in the backyard, eighteen inches off the ground, and practiced wire-walking. Ginny could make it all the way across; Robert usually fell off two-thirds of the way.[16] They talked about politics in a desultory way with friends and acquaintances.[17] This was an election year, and none of the candidates looked very promising. Eisenhower might be the best of the lot—Heinlein had become quite disillusioned with the Truman administration.[18] He was rooting, instead, for the "Double Deal Party."[19]

As "Year of the Jackpot" appeared in *Galaxy* in March 1952, Heinlein took up the manuscript of *The Rolling Stones* to cut it for *Boys' Life*, the only real serial market he could see for it. His concentration was broken almost immediately: Miss Dalgliesh wrote with some "questions"—unpleasantly Freudian—about the "repulsive love habits" of the flat cats. This was more of the amateur psychoanalysis of the *Red Planet* days. Heinlein immediately and flatly rejected the Freudian interpretation and demonstrated his point by giving a lengthy Freudian reading of one of Miss Dalgliesh's own juveniles. He was still fuming the next day: "Her letter was rather horrid and I was quite offended . . . . enough is enough and I do not intend to tolerate any more of this sort of thing . . . . Amateur psychoanalysis makes me sick!"[20]

Miss Dalgliesh wrote back, explaining that she was not herself a Freudian, as he had assumed—"but am aware that the world at the present time is full of pseudo-psychologists who pick up all kinds of things in books for young people . . . I don't argue—but I simply try to head them off. Of course I don't think you write 'dirty books.' Neither do I."[21]

That settled his mind somewhat:

It is an enormous relief to find discover [sic] that you are not one of the "enemy," but an ally. But I had to get angry enough to cease being diplomatic to find that out. Under any ordinary circumstances I will not argue Freud with a Freudian, astrology with a believer in astrology, ghosts with a spiritualist, theology with a priest or minister, economics with a Marxist. It does no good. . . .

. . . Look, as long as we are on the same team, rather than fighting each other, you won't find me difficult about changes. Any more you want to make?[22]

He was able to send Blassingame the cut magazine version of *The Rolling Stones*, retitled "The Unheavenly Twins," on March 17 and move on. Crump bought it on April 10, retitling it "Tramp Space Ship."

Life *chez* Heinlein came to a standstill in April 1952: The National Figure Skating Championships took place in Colorado Springs, and Ginny was on the hosting committee—chief accountant supervising the relays of clerks necessary to compute the judges' tallies. Robert was on the trophy committee, which meant his part was over before the event began, and he could indulge in spectating. He valued the skating they did, not the least because it threw him "into social contact with dozens of children from two years to twenty several times a week."[23]

Once the Championships were out of the way, they could both relax a little. Ruth Harshaw's *Carnival of Books* program on *Red Planet* aired on April 12, 1952 (with a tag publicizing *Between Planets,* which was just out). Shortly thereafter, the renowned poet John Ciardi wrote Heinlein in his capacity as editor for the Twayne publishing house, asking for an introduction to a collection of L. Sprague de Camp's stories, *The Glory That Was.* Heinlein still felt he owed de Camp something because Shasta had dumped de Camp's introduction for *The Green Hills of Earth.* He wrote back that he would be honored to write this preface.[24] Ciardi took the opportunity to ask for "any book-length Heinlein ms."[25]

On April 22, Heinlein took Ginny ice-skating and suggested they drop by Lucky's house on the way home. The door was flung open and everyone Ginny knew in Colorado Springs shouted "surprise." Robert had put together an "over the hill"–themed surprise party for her thirty-fifth birthday.

Also and more seriously over-the-hill, Heinlein's 1939 car, *Skylark IV,* "now threatens to quit every time we take it out of the garage"[26] and would never stand up to a long road trip. They started looking at cars, both new and used.[27] April was royalty statement month (though also tax month!), and the influx of cash gave them a little leeway—until nearly all the gadgetry in the house went on the fritz at the same time, including the plumbing, which he discovered had been creatively "revised" from his original design and had to be dug up and reinstalled correctly.[28]

In the middle of the work on the house, they found a used 1949 Cadillac, a thing of beauty. "It is a well-nigh perfect piece of machinery," Heinlein wrote of the car, within the limits of the art of the time—solidly built as only mid-century Caddys were.[29] And they were able to purchase *Sweet Chariot* for cash in hand, without taking out a bank loan: Without warning, Pathé—not United Artists—paid Heinlein 95.23 percent of the "deferments" on the *Destination Moon* project, $4,285.30 (of which Blassingame's commission was 10 percent).[30] The deferments, being production expenses, were paid out before profits. If Pal got any, he would then pay Heinlein and van Ronkel their 10 percent of his share.

Heinlein pulled out the abandoned manuscript for the Man from Mars book, but it did not come together for him this time, either, so he put it aside again and wrote the script for the "This I Believe" radio program. He decided to avoid religion entirely and talk about his opinions—philosophy—about what being an American meant to him.[31] "My religious beliefs are private to me," he began,

> . . . and I suppose that yours may be to you. I am going to talk about more homely matters, matters so simple and obvious that it has almost gone out of fashion to talk about them—trite things, as trite as approving of good roads and good weather, or declaring for the American home and the American flag.
> I believe in my neighbors.[32]

The Edward R. Murrow staff were delighted with it—"The simple, direct and personal treatment of your creed is the kind of statement we always hope to get," the producer's assistant wrote back to him.[33] They instructed him to arrange with KVOR in Denver to make a disk of him reading it for later broadcast.

In June, the *Popular Mechanics* article on the house appeared, and Arthur C. Clarke announced his arrival in New York on a promotion tour. Heinlein had been corresponding with Clarke since January 1947 through the British Interplanetary Society, of which Clarke was an officer (Clarke had also begun selling science fiction to *Astounding* in 1946). When Clarke's new book, *The Exploration of Space,* sold to the book-of-the-month club, Heinlein arranged for G. Harry Stine to give Clarke a tour of the White Sands missile proving ground while Clarke was in New Mexico on his way to Los Angeles. He invited Clarke to stay with them in Colorado Springs on the way back.

While Clarke was with the Stines—and Clyde Tombaugh—early in June, and then on to Los Angeles, Heinlein tried again to work on *The Man from Mars,* but put it aside again. Clarke arrived in Colorado Springs on schedule, on June 25, for an extended visit.

Ginny had thought, since food rationing was still so tight in Britain, that Clarke would appreciate some delicacies, but found that Clarke was not much interested in food.[34] He and Robert talked incessantly, even as they went sightseeing, climbing Pike's Peak on its funicular railway (Ginny stayed behind, as she had trouble breathing at that height),[35] and, on another occasion, being lowered in a bucket into a Colorado gold mine. Clarke recalled the trip for his authorized biography:

"We spoke about everything under the sun," recalls Clarke, "but especially the film *Destination Moon* . . . We both felt very strongly about the production . . . Bob and I were both crazy about it" . . . It was, according to Clarke, a "wonderful visit," that transformed a growing friendship into a close one.

Clarke remembers Heinlein as "very protean. Heinlein was everything—like Walt Whitman."[36]

Shortly after Clarke left to continue his book tour, Heinlein heard from Bill Corson that their rocketry friend Jack Parsons had died in an explosion on June 17, 1952. L. Sprague de Camp forwarded a newspaper clipping that assumed it was murder:

> . . . somebody set off a bomb underneath him apparently, though the article was almost entirely devoted to his "weird sex cult" as they express it and gave no details about the actual demise, e.g., where it took place. Parsons' mother committed suicide a few hours after Jack's death. No mention of any widow, though when I got a letter from Jack a few months ago he said something about being back with "the witch" whoever that may have been. Thought you'd like to know.[37]

Ave atque vale.

Describing the summer's accumulation of interruptions, Heinlein wrote to Blassingame,

> Yes, I am still having trouble with that novel [*Stranger*]. Trouble is all I am having—trouble with the story itself and trouble with my surroundings. I have lost almost a month to houseguests, Arthur C. Clarke followed by the [George and Doña] Smiths—and now we are about to spend a week in Yellowstone and Sun Valley, leaving tomorrow. I could cancel this trip but there are reasons why it is desirable not to cancel it. Furthermore I hope that a few days away from that constantly ringing phone will help me to straighten out this novel in my mind. (Sometimes I think that everyone in the country passes through Colorado Springs in the summer!)[38]

Heinlein planned out a circle-tour itinerary that would take him and Ginny to a number of the National Parks in the region, and they packed up for an extended trip, leaving on July 17 for Jackson Hole and on in a few days to Grand Teton National Park, and to Yellowstone for the bears and the geysers. Then on to Sun Valley for outdoor ice-skating—in July!—and Salt Lake City for the "Days of '47" festivities commemorating the founding of the city, and on to Zion National Park.

From Zion, they went south to the North Rim of the Grand Canyon. Overlooking the canyon, they turned on *Sweet Chariot*'s radio and listened to the Republican National Convention nominate Dwight D. Eisenhower for president. They stayed for a few days in a log cabin and took a mule ride down the Bright Angel Trail to the bottom of the Canyon.

They then turned east again, stopping by Bryce Canyon. They motored on to Aspen, and then home to Colorado Springs—"to find a bushel of mail and a constantly ringing phone. I don't know why we ever came back."[39] This trip had been a much-needed tonic for the stress of the last couple of years—and Ginny gave every early sign of having "caught" on this trip and might be pregnant. It was too early to ask the rabbit.[40]

Blassingame expressed interest in paying them a visit that coming winter— a hunting trip possibly, since they had elk there in Colorado. Blassingame had developed into a very good long-distance friend, though they had met only briefly on a trip to New York in 1948.

Also among the piles of accumulated correspondence were two irritating and presumptuous letters from Forry Ackerman, peeved that Heinlein refused to join the Science Fiction Writers of America[41] (an organization Heinlein had never heard of until this mention), chiding him for—wholly imaginary—incidents of spite toward fans, toward himself, and toward Ray Bradbury, and for costing him—and himself!—a cash customer by the "rude" way he had treated a fan Ackerman had sent for an unannounced and unwelcomed visit. "Antagonism breeds antagonism," Ackerman wrote sententiously,

and old tales about Heinlein are dragged out for counteraction . . . but I can only gulp and go inarticulate at the mystery of Heinlein the man, Heinlein the mystery, Heinlein the enigma, Heinlein the fan-hater, Heinlein the recluse . . . .

Are you a happy man, Bob Heinlein? You are in no way beholden to me to answer that question. But the recent conjecture that has reached my ears is that you aren't, couldn't be with all the venom you pour forth and irritation that radiates from you.[42]

Heinlein wrote back, summing up his dissatisfaction with Ackerman's criticisms, and his curious version of "friendship."

This "Heinlein the recluse" talk is rather silly. It is high time you stopped it
. . . . It is none of your dam[ned] business whether I go to such things or
not. You have been going on tediously for years on the subject and it is time
you shut up. . . .[43]

Patiently he covered each of Ackerman's points in detail—and he told Ackerman bluntly it was a case of rank impertinence for Ackerman to set himself
up as judge of Robert's and Ginny's social correctness.

Heinlein was beginning to realize it was not so much he had a "problem"
with fans as that he had problems with one, very specific fan:

Ever since the war my relations with you have been one long series of demands, alternated with criticisms and sarcasm. I repeat, I will not buy your
friendship. If it is true friendship, freely given, I will be most happy to have
it. But I shall make no further effort to live my life to fit your ideal concept
of what I ought to be (a tail on Forry's kite, apparently!) and I shall put up
with no more of your diatribes . . .[44]

At this point, nothing but an apology from Ackerman would do. And there
the matter stood.

One day in mid-August, a man named Jack Seaman telephoned saying
he was in Denver and wanted to come down to Colorado Springs for a visit
about a television series he was putting together. Robert listened politely
as Seaman explained that Forry Ackerman had put him in touch with Ned
Brown at MCA[45]—and, indeed, in the mail shortly afterward was a letter
from a Malcolm Stuart at MCA about Seaman: He was a former stuntman,
now turning producer, and he had a half-hour science-fiction anthology series
already financed, to be called *The World Beyond*. Seaman wanted to buy as
many as thirteen new stories from Heinlein—plus TV rights to stories Heinlein had already written.[46]

Seaman turned out to be an engaging fellow, reasonably knowledgeable
about science fiction, with workable story ideas of his own and enough story
sense to know what was doable—and his project was not speculative: It was
already funded.[47] Seaman had in mind a collaboration, developing the thirteen original stories together (at $400 per story, split two ways), and then the
producing company, Clarinda Pictures, would have an option for them to
write screenplays from the developed stories (at $500 each, again, split two
ways).[48] If Clarinda purchased any of Heinlein's older stories, Robert would
get the story payment, but they would split the script collaboration. Seaman's

proposal was "adequate without being financially exciting," Heinlein remarked:[49]
He would not net as much as the same effort put into a new book for Scribner.
But he agreed. Seaman could come back in two weeks to work on the first
thirteen stories.

Seaman went back to Hollywood to work out the contract, and Heinlein
concentrated on clearing his desk. The article for the School Library Association of California was a chore: "This sort of writing I find difficult, as I am
not a literary critic and it makes me rather self-conscious to write about my
writing. Telling stories is easier."[50] Dalgliesh liked "Ray Guns and Rocket
Ships" so well that she asked if she could submit it to *Library Journal* on his
behalf (although they cut nearly eighteen hundred words out of the version
they eventually published).[51]

Before the winter visitors started arriving, Heinlein had time to write the
short story he had promised *American Legion Magazine,* but he didn't have an
idea, so he turned to Ginny, his personal font of all ideas. She remembered
when she was a child—in 1925—reading newspaper stories about a dogsled
race to Nome, Alaska, rushing medical supplies to relieve a plague. Ham radio operators all over Alaska had followed the incident and relayed the reports
nationally.[52] Robert rethought the incident in science-fictional terms and
centered the story around the crushing acceleration a relief pilot would have
to endure for days at a time on an interplanetary serum run. It would disable
him for life. He completed "Sky Lift" on September 4, 1952.

The deal with Seaman and Clarinda Pictures turned out more complicated than he and Seaman had discussed, and the contract negotiations
dragged out. The head of the company, Sam Norton, wanted to decrease the
option and writing money. The deal had started out marginal for Heinlein in
the first place, and that reduction would drive it into the category of not-
worth-wasting-time-on.[53] But Seaman continued negotiating with Norton as
the month Robert set aside for the project dwindled away.

Robert and Ginny decided to take up an invitation from G. Harry Stine to
go to White Sands for the public launching of the last of the V-2 rockets. The
American Army had captured parts for about a hundred V-2s in the Harz
Mountain manufactories, and there was now only one left—a "hangar queen"
that was never supposed to have flown. The Heinleins flew to Las Cruces,
New Mexico, the day before the launch and rented a car. They had been able
to get a reservation at the El Amador, a converted coach house so old that the
wooden floors had waves worn into them where so many had walked. Heinlein spoke before the Rocket Society there, and they had an early dinner with
Jack Williamson.

After an additional day's delay (someone had forgotten to order the liquid oxygen part of the fuel) they found themselves with Jack Williamson, Harry Stine, and Clyde Tombaugh close to an otherwise unidentified site named "Station Easy."[54] The rocket lifted breath-stoppingly slowly, majestically, and picked up speed, gaining altitude until it was directly overhead and seemed to—hesitate. Ginny, whose eyesight was still very sharp, said "there is something wrong with that rocket,"[55] but the men assured her she was imagining things. Ten miles up, it seemed to be shooting off its carbon vanes—

And the sky was suddenly full of debris, and the V-2 seemed to be falling back on them. There was no place to run: The falling debris was everywhere.

The rocket crashed half a mile away, taking out a telephone pole near the Navy blockhouse, and the fuel, ten tons of liquid oxygen and hydrogen peroxide, exploded. "And there was the most beautiful—well, it looked like a nuclear explosion at first," Ginny Heinlein recalled. "Great big flame . . . silvery . . . around the edges."[56] Stine later speculated that the hydrogen peroxide sitting overnight in the tanks, waiting on the forgotten LOX, might have corroded the tanks.[57]

The delays with the Seaman project continued, and Heinlein continued to work on other things: He wrote a short review of a new space book, *Across the Space Frontier* by Cornelius Ryan, titled "The Ever-Widening Horizons," for the *Colorado Springs Sunday Free Press,* that appeared on September 28. On September 30, the people at Rockhill Radio informed Blassingame that Kellogg's was dropping *Tom Corbett, Space Cadet,* and the weekly checks would therefore stop.[58] Rockhill would continue to look for a new sponsor. The royalties would be missed, but his print publication was going strong—*Boys' Life* began "Tramp Space Ship," his three-part adaptation of *The Rolling Stones,* in October.

Seaman worked out a deal satisfactory to all concerned: His company, Clarinda Pictures, set up a new company for the series, Planet Pictures, and all the contracts were drawn and executed by September 23, 1952. Seaman was finally ready to work on the scripts in October. Rather optimistically, Heinlein thought, Seaman wanted to push out the first thirteen or fourteen scripts in one week, with the pilot turned into a M.O.W.[59] They would break for an overnight visit from Robert's brother Rex, followed immediately by Blassingame's visit, then resume work around the twenty-first of October. "For a guy who prefers to be a bum I sure get myself tied up. But I'll bet I'm the first writer to get an elk-hunting trip specifically written into a Hollywood contract (Ginny takes a dim view of all of this.)" [60] They also got a pregnancy exception written into the penalty clause.

Seaman duly arrived early in the morning of October 5, and they started to work on the lineup. He came with a list of story ideas they had worked out together. For some of them—a few—there were story development notes. They had decided on a framing situation for *The World Beyond*. Heinlein wrote a short, three-page hook, which he called a "patterned opening." Each episode would begin in a futuristic schoolhouse, with a lecturer who would tell his class the story we would see this week, as an incident out of their history. As he lectured, the teleplay story would start.

But Seaman never actually did work out the contractual deals for the original stories (Ginny said that Robert called Seaman a "walking writer," who talked out his ideas pacing,[61] and then Robert did the actual writing). Heinlein worked up his idea for the pilot—tentatively titled "Ring Around the Moon"—into a M.O.W. script, about a woman-and-man team of pilots marooned on the Moon and marrying to preserve the proprieties—an idea that seemed much more "reasonable" in 1952. Seaman gradually, one by one, replaced the original stories with workups of Heinlein's older stories, until the final lineup was:

> Pilot—"Ring Around the Moon"
> 1. " 'It's Great to be Back' "
> 2. "Space Jockey"
> 3. "The Black Pits of Luna"
> 4. "The Long Watch"
> 5. "Ordeal in Space"
> 6. "Delilah and the Space Rigger"
> 7. "Project Nightmare"
> 8. "Life-Line"
> 9. "Requiem"
> 10. " 'And He Built a Crooked House' "
> 11. " 'We Also Walk Dogs' "
> 12. "Misfit"
> 13. "Home, Sweet Home"

Of the thirteen episodes that fulfilled the original contract, "Home Sweet Home" was the only Seaman-Heinlein collaboration as to story, and it existed only as seven pages of a more-or-less-completely-developed story idea. In any case, all the scripts were to bear the name of the writing partnership—Robert A. Heinlein and Jack Seaman—no matter who did what part of the actual work. "Home, Sweet Home" and another original story, "The Tourist," were removed from the lineup as too expensive to produce.[62]

This arrangement worked out well for Heinlein in a financial sense, since he didn't have to split the story fee, but it contributed to a growing frustration with Seaman's working methods. He was pleasant to work with, but he seemed to have no concept of time or deadlines, his own or Heinlein's, and the delays pushed Heinlein's other writing commitments farther and farther behind schedule.[63] Of the month Seaman had committed to be there—the second month Robert had set aside to work on *The World Beyond*—his working days totalled only eleven, and the scripts he started were never done properly before he turned them over to Robert to finish.[64] Heinlein finished the pilot script and turned it over to Planet Pictures to fulfill the secondary contract. Rex came and left, and then Blassingame arrived.

Ginny had been able to obtain a hunting license for Blassingame, and Heinlein found them a "native guide," Floyd Woodings. Together they packed by horse into the mountains near Gunnison, Colorado, so far that they outdistanced all other hunters, to the 10,500-foot level near the Continental Divide— "magnificent, rugged country, flaming with autumn colors."[65]

Above the timberline it was already winter. They had a very rough camp, sleeping on the frozen ground. One memorable morning, Heinlein finished making the coffee, poured himself a cup, turned away to pick up his plate, and turned back to find a rime of ice on top of the coffee.[66]

Blassingame did get his elk—a magnificent, 1,200-pound specimen of Royal Elk, with a rack of 12 points on a span of 42 inches. They skinned and butchered it on the ground and packed it out, meat and trophy, using all four horses—which meant Heinlein hiked out leading two of the horses, fording icy mountain streams on foot. Heinlein assured Blassingame that despite the discomforts, "Nevertheless I had one hell of a time and would not have missed it for worlds."[67] Blassingame looked at it as "one of the high moments of my life."[68]

The full writing schedule for *The World Beyond* resumed immediately. Seaman was due back in November, and again on December 5, and theoretically they would have the first thirteen scripts finished by December 22.

The first broadcast of Heinlein's "This I Believe" piece took place on CBS radio on December 1, 1952. Willy Ley and Jack Seaman both arrived on December 5 (Ley had been attached as a technical advisor to the production of *The World Beyond*).[69]

Ginny was already Christmas shopping and mailing off packages. By now it was clear that her pregnancy alert after they came back from the National Parks trip was a false alarm. More consultations with doctors, and they did find

> . . . a minor malfunction that might have been corrected with estimated 25% success through prosthesia involving a laparotomy for her . . . [sic] I did not like those odds for her as she was then 36 when we pinned it down— and I was too old for a legal adoption—so we accepted the situation.[70]

As soon as he got the *World Beyond* work out of the way, Heinlein had to start on his next boys' book for Scribner. Dalgliesh cautioned him to not be too definite about the boy's age in this next one: They had lost a portion of their usual army base sales for *The Rolling Stones* because the twins were sixteen, rather than eighteen.[71]

The actual filming of the *World Beyond* pilot M.O.W. was to commence by the end of December, at the Hal Roach studios in Hollywood.[72] Seaman was short of cash, and Heinlein made him a personal loan of one thousand dollars, to be paid back out of the proceeds of their collaboration.[73]

On December 20, Seaman informed him by phone that the producer agreed that the contract had been fulfilled. Utterly predictably, they had changed the title for the pilot to *Project Moonbase* and decided to cut it loose from the television series. They had Heinlein write a voice-over introduction and enough new material to bring it up to 63 minutes.[74] He sent the last TV script on Christmas Eve—and started immediately on the Scribner book, without a story to tell.

He idled while waiting for inspiration, fiddling around with the relatively undemanding make-work of correspondence. Sprague de Camp, who was gathering materials for his *Science Fiction Handbook*, had asked about *Destination Moon,* but he also raised a question about one of Heinlein's five rules for writing, articulated in his 1947 article, "On the Writing of Speculative Fiction," which were becoming somewhat famous in the science-fiction community— advice to the beginning writer:

1. You must write.
2. You must *finish* what you start.
3. You must refrain from rewriting except to editorial order.
4. You must put it on the market.
5. You must keep it on the market until sold.

The rule about not rewriting, de Camp thought, needed some clarification. His own practice, Heinlein explained, was to combine the functions, cleaning up the manuscript by cutting surplusage, adding:

> I do a certain amount of true rewriting these days (other than rewriting to editorial order, which is always admissible)—but I still do damned little and I would never advise a beginner to rewrite. He can learn more by starting a brand-new story and doing his best on it.[75]

There was a lot of promiscuous kissing at the New Year's Eve party that year, and Heinlein caught a case of flu—his first real illness in four years.[76] But he also got an idea for his next Scribner book.

OUT AND ABOUT

Some months back, Stan Mullen, a local Colorado Springs science-fiction colleague, had shared a historical curiosity over dinner, when the conversation turned to what Heinlein would write about for his next boys' book for Scribner:[1] a China clipper had set sail from its home port, Boston, in the nineteenth century and come back, years later, with a former cabin boy commanding the ship as its captain.[2] A story grew around the idea in January 1953[3]—imagining a future for space technology in which starships could be as out of touch as were nineteenth-century whaling ships. Heinlein decided the boy had lied to get into space in the first place—and the ending would necessarily be the decision to take his punishment and live with the consequences as an adult.

There were problems to be cleared, though, before he could begin writing *Starman Jones*. Shasta was already trying to sell paperback rights for the third Future History book, even though Heinlein had so far refused to sign the contract for it. Even Blassingame's patience had run out; he found out Shasta's own attorneys were disgusted with them, since Korshak was ignoring their recommendations. Also, it developed, the Grosset & Dunlap contract Fantasy Press had placed for *Beyond This Horizon* was throwing a monkey wrench into the negotiations with NAL for paperback rights.

But not everything was in turmoil: Rockhill Radio found a partial sponsor for the *Tom Corbett* TV show and might be able to go back into production. Even with Jack and Blanche Williamson in for an overnight visit—welcomed houseguests—Heinlein was able to write an introduction for editor Sam Mines who was assembling an anthology for his magazine, *The Best from Startling Stories*. Mines could use any boost Heinlein's name might be able to give: SF was booming in 1953, with more than forty new magazine titles on the newsstands—stiff competition. Later in the year, A. P. White ("Anthony Boucher") and Mick McComas gave Mines's anthology a good review in the *Magazine of Fantasy & Science Fiction*—and promptly asked for a Heinlein piece they could use for their own annual anthology. Heinlein felt he had to decline: It would stir up animosity with both John Campbell and H. L. Gold:

> For strictly personal reasons (not business) I will never let either one of them know that I think your book [*F&SF*] outclasses theirs. For me, it would be too much like telling a fond parent that his child is homely and stupid—or that the child next door is prettier and brighter . . . . Which makes me look like a heel [but] I wish to avoid even the suggestion of choosing between friends—
>
> (If your magazine actually were a stinker and you were both financially insecure in consequence, I could easily be persuaded. I would prevaricate or lie for a friend gladly . . . .)[4]

Heinlein was able to start *Starman Jones* on February 2, 1953, and finish up on February 28, averaging twenty-three hundred words a day and working without an outline, even through distractions: Mick and Annette McComas visited in Colorado Springs for a day in the middle of the month.[5] And John Campbell was writing distracting letters about his break with Hubbard's Dianetics project, saying Hubbard was a "first rate mystic" but an "erratic investigator."[6]

On the day Heinlein wrote "The End" on his draft manuscript, principal photography of *Project Moonbase* wrapped at the RKO studios in Los Angeles.

With the boys' book finished and the TV series out of the way, Heinlein set arbitration with Shasta in motion, dealt with a proposal from Gnome Press for another collection of novellas (that ultimately never went anywhere), and scheduled another hospital stay for the middle of March, for the last of the series of reconstructive plastic surgeries that would take care of the botched wartime hemorrhoid operation.

But things kept coming up all month, and he kept putting off the surgery. Rip van Ronkel wrote saying he had hired a lawyer to sue Pal for collection, and that set off a round of investigation as to whether he should join the suit. Rex was promoted to full colonel. The student newspaper from Heinlein's old high school, Central High in Kansas City, contacted him for a long-distance interview . . . there was simply no way he could take time out to recuperate from surgery now. It had to wait until the first week in April.

Leslyn somehow heard about his planned operation and incorporated it into another round of poison-pen letters that went out to as many of Heinlein's colleagues and friends as she could reach in 1952 and 1953. Heinlein asked friends to send him any such letters they received from Leslyn and began collecting a file of them, in case he should have to defend the lawsuit she threatened.[7]

John Campbell wrote psychologizing his hospital stay as a workaholic in need of a vacation. "Slow down a bit, don't have so much pleasure on pure effort, and you'll have less flu, and fewer visits to the hospital. The net result will be greater total effort-output." [8]

Robert was a little exasperated:—H. L. Gold had made similar comments, psychoanalyzing his "bottomry" and enough was too much. He wrote firmly to Campbell:

> Now about your long-distance diagnosis of my "troubles"—in the first place I practically don't have any, being solvent, happy, and in excellent health. I've merely been busy from having my time wasted by a Hollywood producer who has no sense of clock or calendar . . . This was further complicated by flu—but it was the first time I had been ill in four years. . . .
>
> Still I do intend to slow down and relax. I have spent five years scratching to make up for having been cleaned out financially. I have now recovered the lost ground and then some; I can do pretty much as I please.[9]

By late March, Alice Dalgliesh had reviewed *Starman Jones* and told Blassingame she wanted some changes. Her complaint was that the Montgomery character, who nearly beat the boy the first time he met him, was too pulpvillainish. She thought it would be more believable if the conflict built up over a period of weeks or months. The last chapter she also thought a little rushed.[10]

Heinlein was not convinced that the changes Miss Dalgliesh wanted were either necessary or desirable. In a letter to Blassingame,[11] he explained that trying to accommodate a slow buildup of a bad home situation might have been right for *Huckleberry Finn,* but these juveniles had a much smaller scale. That kind of slowdown would destroy the balance and pacing of the first half of the book (and add probably fifteen or twenty thousand words to it—too large for a juvenile publisher at the time). In the second place, the portrait of Montgomery was the only one in the book "drawn from life": It was a portrait of the contractor who had threatened Heinlein's life while he was building the house, three years earlier—a mean one, at the very least, and a true-to-life Ozark type.

In any case, the end of the story was in the next-to-last chapter.

> The real issue is the one in which a man must decide whether or not he is morally justified in lying to get around a basically unfair situation. I kicked

that one around quite a bit both with Dr. Hendrix and with Mr. Walther. In my opinion it is almost unanswerable . . . . Was Max morally justified in lying his way into the space merchant service? I don't know, I really don't know—but my sympathies were with Max.

I don't much like handing kids ready-made answers in any case.[12]

The day before he went into the hospital in April, Robert's brother Larry proposed the men in the family club together and give their parents a "circle tour" of the United States, to visit everyone in their now widely-dispersed family. Since Robert was in the hospital, Larry, Ivar, and Clare would underwrite the trip: Robert and Ginny could pitch in when he had recovered enough to be able to contribute.

The last time Heinlein was in the hospital, he had frightened the staff by getting up immediately after the surgery, before the anesthesia had completely worn off, and locking himself in a bathroom. He was better behaved this time: "I distinguished myself by kissing the operating nurse—twice!"[13]

While he was recovering, Carey McWilliams, the editor of *The Nation*, wrote asking for a list of his six favorite recent SF novels. He sent his reply on a postcard, and it was published, along with similar replies from Anthony Boucher, Kurt Vonnegut, and H. L. Gold, as a sidebar to an article about Ray Bradbury:

> *The Demolished Man* (Alfred Bester)
> *Player Piano* (Kurt Vonnegut)
> *What Mad Universe* (Fredric Brown)
> *Pebble in the Sky* (Isaac Asimov)
> *Rogue Queen* (L. Sprague de Camp)
> *1984* (George Orwell)

Dalgliesh informed him Scribner had ordered a special second printing of *The Rolling Stones* to handle the demand. Since they seemed to be selling everything they printed, that worked to Heinlein's advantage. His short stories were not faring so well. "Project Nightmare" had been rejected by every prestige magazine and finally went, at "firesale rates" to bottom-of-the-barrel *Amazing Stories* where it appeared in the April 1953 issue, *Amazing*'s twenty-seventh-anniversary issue.[14]

On May 1, as the arbitration action against Shasta began to ramp up, Erle Korshak visited Lurton Blassingame in his office in New York and apologized for the trouble, pledging better behavior in future. Blassingame professionally was inclined to go along for the sake of peace and uninterrupted author royalties—but he noted dryly in his report to Heinlein that Korshak showed signs of reverting to type even before the conversation was over.[15]

While Heinlein was still recuperating from his surgery—and coming up with a new story—they got word from Rockhill Radio that a second partial sponsor had been found for the *Tom Corbett* TV show: The International Shoe Company of St. Louis was willing to pick up every other Saturday.

Robert and Ginny got a call from a local doctor they didn't know, Dr. Howes. He invited them to come visit his home that night while A. E. van Vogt was in Colorado Springs coming down from a big Dianetics conference in Denver. Dianetics "auditing" was still enjoying status as a craze among SF fans, and van Vogt had been one of Ron Hubbard's early "converts," rising to prominence in the Los Angeles organization. They found a surprising number of the old Korzybski/General Semantics crowd there, but also another friend and colleague, Robert Moore Williams, who Robert thought had a touch of genius as a science-fiction and fantasy writer: "I think you are one of the dozen sensitive and imaginative artists in the field," he had written to Williams years earlier.[16]

Dr. Howes turned out to have an Sc.D in physics, rather than an M.D. There were no science-fiction fans at the gathering, but a number of people Ginny later characterized as "very odd."[17] The setup looked like a doctor's (medical doctor's) waiting room. People disappeared for a while into the back rooms, and then reappeared after being audited by Dr. Howes. When van Vogt finally appeared, he spoke briefly with Robert and Ginny and told them that Dr. Howes was the only Dianetics "Clear" in the world.

Van Vogt himself Heinlein found rather less "nervy" than he was before the war, more self-assured[18]—much the same results John Campbell had reported of Ron Hubbard—as a result of his exposure to Dianetics.

> He is peddling Ron's newest twist, "Scientology" (sic!) but tends to disparage Ron himself—which same seems to be true of the whole group, i.e., Ron is a jerk, Ron is a nut—but nevertheless he is the prophet of the One True Faith.
>
> Me, I smiled, I did not argue, I asked questions—I listened to horse manure with a straight face.[19]

Robert Moore Williams went home with the Heinleins for more shop talk. He had been through the Dianetics mill himself a couple of years before, and thought it based on hypnotism—"powerful and exceeding dangerous."[20] Robert had kept his promise to Ginny not to take up Dianetics for five years. "I never have been exactly sold on Dianetics," he told Campbell—

—not that I was "agin" it; I just tried to keep an open mind until I had enough data, data which was impossible to gather here. Ron's book certainly was not adequate basis for judgment. I think you probably realize now that Ron's book was so poorly written from a standpoint of scientific method as to be (although interesting) impossible to evaluate. But I was very pleased to see the orthodox psychiatrists and most especially the psychoanalysts given the hot foot. Whether or not Ron was right, the orthodox practitioners are most certainly wrong . . .[21]

Such events as he had just attended offered very little attraction for him.

And in any case, he had other matters to attend to. He pulled the old manuscript for *The Man from Mars* out of his files for another attempt to write through his block, after he replied to Rip van Ronkel that he would join in a suit against George Pal. He was shocked and distressed by van Ronkel's news that their agent, Lou Schor, had obtained—and later sold—a 10 percent interest in the action on *Destination Moon,* points gross: Schor could not possibly have bought the interest in the production—he was hard up at the time and borrowing money himself. Nor could he have earned that in any legitimate way; it was clearly a conflict of interest and unethical conduct for an agent.[22]

But there was little that could be done about it—and as Irving Pichel pointed out, it was Rathvon who had the money—and Rathvon, in a perfectly legal arrangement with Pal, *had no duty to them.* Moreover, what Pal had done was something approaching "standard practice" in the industry. Hard on them, but there was nothing for them to enforce—and the amount in controversy might not be enough to justify the expenses of a lawsuit. Pichel felt sure they would see something from Pal eventually, even without suing.

Pichel was gradually being "frozen out" of the Hollywood filmmaking community, for his liberal activities in the 1930s, before he began directing. Fortunately, he had been offered a professorship at UCLA in the wake of his successful biopic, *Martin Luther,* for a German production company. Pichel was a casualty of the Hollywood blacklists—a clear warning to Robert, who had "then-liberal-now-subversive" politics in his own past.

Nor was the arbitration with Shasta going well. Doubleday would pick up the contract for the third Future History book, Blassingame told him, only if Shasta could be gotten entirely out of the picture. Blassingame had retained a new lawyer, and Heinlein was shocked that the lawyer thought their case "iffy" on the merits and that they ought to settle.

Heinlein instructed Blassingame to drop the negotiations with Doubleday while he figured out what to do about Shasta. He had originally wanted just to rescind the contract and walk away. His own lawyer in Colorado Springs thought he would probably be able to make that stick. But it was becoming clear that the simplest way to unblock the secondary (paperback) sales was to give in.

On June 17 he executed the contract with Shasta for the third Future History book, about a Second American Revolution against the American theocracy Mark Twain had predicted,[23] the human race then picking up where it had left off in its journey out to the stars. Korshak came to Colorado Springs for a personal visit, and they all went out to dinner at a hotel—Ginny not wanting Korshak in their home.[24] Korshak convinced Heinlein that he was capable of turning a new leaf—which Heinlein was willing to believe, since it only worked in Korshak's best interests. And the new contract had termination provisions he considered adequate.

The new Shasta book gave an excuse to put *The Man from Mars* away; the writing was not going well: Fifteen thousand words into his manuscript, "I am as confused as the characters," he told Irving Pichel. "But that is a standard complaint at this stage. Perhaps I can work it out."[25] His local friend and SF writer–colleague Stan Mullen gave him a "pep talk" about the project, so he went back to work on it for a short time,[26] even though something about it was evidently not quite right, and he ground to a halt again.

He went to work on the Shasta book revisions.

"Coventry" didn't need any substantial revisions; nor did "Misfit." But the cornerstone of the book, "If This Goes On—," was too dated, too pulpish to fit with the others. Heinlein added a subplot about John Lyle's discovery of the founding documents of the first American Revolution, got rid of his pulp heroine, introduced a more "realistic" sex interest for Lyle, and in general added more than twenty thousand words, bringing it up to fifty-five thousand words. He also allowed his revolutionaries an effective doubt about the idea of brainwashing the electorate, even though their motives were pure. Now he evidently felt it belonged in the same universe as "The Man Who Sold the Moon."

Shasta wasn't thrilled with his suggested title for the book, *A Hymn Before Battle,* and neither was NAL. Heinlein suggested other titles—*Revolt in Paradise* or *Revolt in 3000 A.D.*—and they didn't fly, either. Somehow, between the two of them, Ted Dikty, the editor for Shasta, settled with Truman Talley at NAL on *Revolt in 2100*—a title Robert could not understand at all, since there was nothing in the book that took place in 2100 A.D.

The summer resort rush was in full swing in July, making writing difficult, between the houseguests and visitors. Heinlein had three sets of houseguests expected within a three-week period—the McComases, his old high school principal, Otto DuBach (who was spending his retirement traveling around visiting people he had known earlier), and his parents on their circle tour of family. They were coming in later than scheduled, since they had doubled back for a second visit with Rex in D.C., where he was teaching electronics at West Point.

Their new schedule was particularly inconvenient as Heinlein also had a deadline of July 31 to revise some stories for a new collection for Fantasy Press, *Assignment in Eternity.*

Heinlein gave a large garden party for his Colorado Springs friends and acquaintances (including visitors Mick and Annette McComas)[27] on the Fourth of July that year, and he wired the garden for sound and laid in a fully-stocked bar for the occasion, with champagne and brandy and lemons for Ginny's favorite cocktail, the French 75.

Robert's father and mother arrived in the middle of July, and Mr. Dubach joined them on the 27th. They also invited T. O. Johnston, another Centralian who was working as publicity director at the nearby Broadmoor resort-hotel, and a photo duly commemorating the reunion appeared in the *Colorado Springs Gazette-Telegraph* on July 30. Ginny was not in this photograph: She was suffering from an attack of poison ivy at the time. On a side trip to Seven Falls, Robert was recognized—a local celebrity!—by the boy parking his car. He was secretly pleased that this happened in front of his parents;[28] he always felt his father regarded his writing career as not quite something a gentleman would do: Rex and Larry were the "good sons." He was the black sheep.[29]

Heinlein's father's disposition had not improved by being nearly catatonic for more than fifteen years.[30] He and Bam bickered continuously—very unpleasant in the confines of the small house. In particular, Rex wanted Bam to see about getting an old-age pension from the government. Of course, she was not eligible for it: She had never been employed by anyone who might give a pension—or Social Security for that matter.

> But Dad nagged her about it so continuously and painfully while they were here that Ginny and I decided to take action at once. We are now sending them (and have been since the month of July) $40 a month, made out to Mother and somewhat jokingly referred to as "Mother's Old Age Pension." . . .[31]

The others could chip in if they wished; Robert and Ginny didn't want to cut anyone out.

Robert's parents finally left on the first or second of August, and he and Ginny breathed a sigh of relief as they passed them on to Louise in Albuquerque. His father's bread-and-butter note dated August 5 was rather salty.[32]

Over the summer, Seaman had found a distributor for the film made from the TV show pilot Heinlein had written, *Project Moonbase,* and the movie was released by the Lippert organization in August 1953,[33] to unfavorable reviews. The *Hollywood Reporter* covered it on August 28, 1953:

> *Project Moonbase* makes a pitch for the juvenile science-fiction market, but its complete ineptitude will make it an object for derision even from the Saturday matinee kid audience. A depressing combination of inane story, atrocious acting and amateurish direction, this Lippert release will have trouble getting bookings in the most product-starved situations.[34]

Bad news from Hollywood (even if not entirely unexpected) was met by good news oveseas—and at home. Blassingame's effective work lining up foreign editions of the juveniles was no longer being siphoned off by building. They had briefly considered using their hard-won expertise to build another home to rent out, but joining the landlord class did not appeal.[35] Heinlein has said that he conceived the idea of a trip around the world and convinced Ginny, around the middle of June, by being stubborn—but not too stubborn. "I am going around the world. You are going with me because I need to keep you in sight where I can watch you and keep you out of trouble."[36] Within a few days of his parents' leaving, Heinlein had told Blassingame about the trip; by August 19, Ginny wrote for both of them to the Department of the Navy seeking permission to travel internationally.

After that it was passports, visas, inoculations that sometimes left him queasy and almost always incapacitated Ginny for a day or more, and wardrobe and luggage. Robert was dismayed by Ginny's idea of the proper amount of luggage for a six-month trip: "I notice that she is planning to wear a different evening dress every night however, and she has bought me a white tuxedo. I think she has herself mixed up with the Duchess of Windsor—probably progressive delusions. I'll lead her home on a leash."[37] Also significant was the ever-problematical matter of travel arrangements. Most of the initial struggle fell to Ginny—only natural and entirely appropriate, since it was two of her crotchets that were making it so complicated:

> . . . Ginny is opposed to flying, an attitude she picked up from too many years testing airplane materials, and she did not want to go too close to the Iron Curtain. That last is regrettable, as my next older brother [Rex] is in Zurich and my eldest brother [Larry] is in Heidelberg. But I hope to see them next year, maybe, and catch a little European culture out of bottles.[38]

Heinlein probably intended from the first to get a travel book out of the experience (not just general background that might go into anything). He helped with the arrangements between writing sessions, but a multitude of obstacles came up: American President Lines cheerfully returned their deposit, telling them their world tours were fully booked up two years in advance. Their travel agent, Mrs. Feyock, showed them how to book each leg of their trip independently—which gave them a lot of freedom to stop and explore, not bound by the schedule of a package tour. It was a project only possible because travel agents at that time were paid on a commission basis by the hotels and transport agencies they booked.

But the problem they could *not* overcome, singly or working together, was transportation for the last leg of their trip: There simply *was* no available transportation of any sort from New Zealand to anywhere on the North American continent. Robert and Ginny decided to keep their stay in New Zealand open-ended while they worked out arrangements on the spot. As late as October 24, when Robert gave Blassingame their schedule, he noted they had no fixed schedule after arriving in Singapore on January 29, 1954.

Heinlein mounted a full-scale attack on his piled-up backlog of work to make the trip financially possible. The major task was his annual boys' book for Scribner, which had to be finished by the time they were scheduled to leave. He had a "Swiftian fantasy" in mind this time—an animal story with a science-fiction twist, in which nothing is as it seems. Casting it as a thinly disguised science–fantasy would let him play "fast and loose with scientific orthodoxy."[39] An overgrown alien pet turns a village upside down and then embroils the entire Terran Federation in a conflict that could turn into interstellar war.

He started writing *The Star Lummox* on August 26 and promptly ran into a snag: It was too static, with not enough action or conflict. Ginny came up with a fresh way of starting the story, jumping directly into action *and* conflict, and that unblocked his progress. He was able, even with interruptions, to finish the entire seventy-five-thousand-word book by September 26 and invite his local lawyer over to dinner to check on the authenticity of the courtroom scene.

The Star Lummox started out a romp, but turned out to be his last visualization of the peaceful world-state ideal of his socialist youth. By 1953, America itself was becoming an empire, and not without growing pains. Pundits in the current-events magazines solemnly discussed the transformation of the American democracy on the world stage, and some of this very adult agonizing over the fate of democracy Heinlein poured into his Swiftian animal story.

When the manuscript for *The Star Lummox* was professionally typed, he turned it over to Blassingame, along with an itinerary and full Power of Attorney to use for any business decisions necessary while they were out of the country. He also forwarded copies of their wills and had the instruction added to contact Blassingame in case of emergency. Lucky Herzberger's parents, Dr. and Mrs. Knowles, had volunteered to house-sit and take care of Pixie, so he wouldn't have to be kenneled.

One last item was included in his instructions to Blassingame:

You may possibly hear from a Dr. Phineas Bernstein of this city, telling you that he expects to have an "article" ready for delivery about such-and-such a date—in which case get in touch with us by fastest means. We have instituted proceedings to adopt a child; the "article" will be a baby.[40]

The Heinleins shipped half their luggage ahead to their port of embarcation, New Orleans, but at the last minute they received a wire saying that the *Gulf Shipper* would be delayed an additional three days, so they canceled their airline reservations and booked a Pullman car instead, for a leisurely two-day train trip by way of Fort Worth. Even though the railway station was cold the evening of November 12, a crowd of friends came to see them off—including most of the staff of the travel agency (a world trip was an exciting project for them), and they received parting gifts of candy and Ginny's favorite green cymbidium orchids. They arrived in New Orleans on Sunday morning, and "We began to dig our graves with our teeth, wide and deep, a process likely to continue for 40,000 miles."[41]

Two days of genteel carousing in New Orleans nightclubs capped off their five months' of exhausting work. When they boarded the *Gulf Shipper* on the morning of November 17, 1953, and she warped away from the dock around ten o'clock in the morning, they were ready to collapse. Heinlein mustered the energy to follow from the deck the afternoon's cautious progress out of the ever-changing Mississippi Delta under the direction of a special pilot whose sole duty it was to get the freighter out into the Gulf of Mexico—a process like something out of Mark Twain's *Life on the Mississippi*.

Then they went to bed.

WORLD TRAVELERS

"I recall quite well," Ginny later remarked, "that the first long sea voyage we made together it took Robert five days to get the gumption to load a camera!"[1] The *Gulf Shipper* was a passenger-freighter, with excellent, though not luxurious, accommodations. The Heinleins began making shipboard friends, and Robert took the opportunity to show off Ginny's talent and good nature, offering her barbering skills to the entire crew—all forty-seven of them. It took her all of one day, but netted them a fifth of Scotch whisky.

The ship made for the Atlantic side of the Panama Canal, an approach familiar to Robert through many transits while in the Navy, but not to Ginny. Seeing the operation of the locks, raising the whole ship eighty-five feet in a concrete box, to float out into Gatun Lake, was as fascinating and awe-inspiring for her as it still was for him, and the reverse process, lowering in the Miraflores Locks to the Pacific, was just as impressive.

Their first real port of call was Buenaventura, Colombia. It rained almost continuously while they were in port—Buenaventura gets 350 inches of rainfall each year. Nothing dried out—ever. Heinlein developed a bad case of athlete's foot overnight, and his portable typewriter froze up, rusted to immobility.[2]

By the time they got to Callao, the seaport of Lima, Peru, they were out of the tropical summer and into more temperate climates. A routine delay gave them an extra day for sightseeing in Lima, and they had a chance to see Pizarro's mummy, parks, and the slums by which Heinlein gauged the "real" standard of living of the countries they were visiting. They chatted amiably with anyone they were thrown together with, and Heinlein found his own assumptions and world view challenged by the understandings and assumptions that made South American politics work.[3]

The news from the United States was filled with the doings of Senator Joseph McCarthy. Of his general attitude toward McCarthy, Heinlein later explained,

"Let me take time to make it clear that I regard McCarthy as a revolting son of a bitch, with no regard for truth, justice, nor civil rights—also that I think his purposes were demagogic and personally ambitious, not patriotic. All clear?"[4] The local news was a sharp and strange contrast. His attitudes toward the McCarthy hearings, he said, were shaped by what he saw there:

I read most about them while in Lima, Peru—and at the same time passed back and forth in front of the Colombian Embassy where Haya de la Torre had taken sanctuary. Here was this poor devil, on the short end of a South American political difference, hiding in one room for years on end, because the alternative was to come out and face a firing squad. I could not help comparing him to Fifth Amendment "martyrs" [in the U.S.]. I concluded that the whole McCarthy incident was a shining example of just how strong our Bill of Rights can be . . . .

I think that the most regrettable thing about the whole McCarthy tea-pot tempest is the way hordes of usually sensible people let themselves be panicked. "Run, run, the sky is falling!" If we can't stand up to a pipsqueak threat like McCarthy, what would we do in the face of a real menace? Pre-posterous! All out of proportion to the irritation. Have we lost our wits, to let such a bogeyman frighten us?[5]

Dismayingly, he found almost zero comprehension of what the American ideal of political freedom might mean in practice. Even when otherwise sophis-ticated people believed what they heard of American political life (not univer-sally the case), they reinterpreted the reportage to fit their own customs and conditions. "McCarthyism"—which, he observed, "they conceive to be a policy of take-him-away-and-lock-him-up-I-don't-like-his-politics"—was ramping up, and there was a disturbingly widespread assumption that the McCarthy "reign of terror," an expression understood in the United States as metaphorical (though serious), had the scale and violence of the French Revolution:

. . . the political institutions of another country are hard to understand. Outside the United States very few people comprehend the nature of a con-gressional investigation and it is almost impossible to explain it to them. They have it mixed up with the Inquisition, with Senator McCarthy having all the functions and powers of Torquemada. The idea that a private citizen can answer or refuse to answer a series of questions put to him by a senator [as to treasonable activities] . . . and then get up and walk out a free man—is so foreign to most other people that they simply cannot believe it.[6]

It was a theme he encountered over and over again throughout this trip—and the others he made in later years. It seemed to him that virtually *nobody* got the essential lesson here: Nobody was killed in the United States; nobody was even jailed except by due process of law; the worst that happened was that some people had reputations blackened, possibly deservedly if they had in fact been engaged in treasonous activities. The system worked exactly the way it was supposed to—protecting the rights of individuals. Heinlein was resilient, but it did take some of the shine off his long-standing one-world sentiments. How could people unite in mutual self-interest if they couldn't even comprehend that politics might not be pursued by Latin *vendetta*?[7]

> . . . in the wider sense we have made the greatest cultural contribution of any society to date, by demonstrating that 160,000,000 people can live together in peace *and* freedom. Nothing else in all history even approaches this cultural accomplishment, and sneers at *our* "culture" are both laughable and outrageously presumptuous when emanating from a continent that habitually wallows in its own blood. I'll take Coca-Cola, thank you; it may be vulgar, no doubt it is simply impossibly American, it may lack the bouquet of a Continental wine—but it is not flavored with ancient fratricidal insanities.[8]

From Lima the *Gulf Shipper* made for the Chilean port of Arica. Heinlein occupied his time brushing up his navigation skills and shooting the sun each day with the ship's navigator.[9]

Their time aboard the *Gulf Shipper* came to an end early in December—midsummer—in Valparaiso, Chile. They gave a farewell dinner party the night before they left the ship, exchanging addresses with newfound friends. The line's local agent shepherded them through customs and onto a train bound for Santiago, where they would spend a week or more at the luxurious Hotel Carrera.

There, Robert drafted a brief portrait, about eight thousand words, of the bemused and somewhat surreal mental state they were enjoying, "Ms. Found in a Pisco Bottle *or* Around the World Backwards and Upside Down"—the introduction of which would become the opening paragraphs of chapter 2 of his travel book *Tramp Royale*.[10] They enjoyed Chile enormously but had a deadline to meet in Buenos Aires, Argentina. They flew across the continent on December 12, 1953, to catch the ship for the next leg of their trip and get back on the schedule laid out in their itinerary. Both of them were apprehensive about going into Argentina, the last fascist state left over from World War II.

This trip was three hours across the continent (though they did get to see the enormous Christ of the Andes statue from the air) and three hours getting through customs. Ginny had scheduled them for only four days in Buenos Aires—the original Big Apple—on the theory that that was the absolute maximum length of time she could possibly keep her mouth shut (Robert thought she was unduly optimistic).[11] Then *Ruys* delayed in sailing, and they had more time. They were, therefore, relieved and pleasantly surprised to find that they *liked* Juan Perón's Buenos Aires: It was relaxed and above all *civilized*. Perón's presence was felt everywhere, true—but the general run of opinion seemed supportive, popular attitude mirroring in an apparently genuine way the *Perón cumple* posters seen around town: "Perón keeps his promises"; "Perón performs." Santa Evita had been dead for only a year and a half, and her memory was everywhere, too. Unlike her husband, though, Eva Perón seemed to be almost universally despised—by the middle classes.

The major hazard to the tourists, Robert remarked, was the alligators—the empty ones sold as bags and shoes.[12] But they found some of Robert's books on sale, and once when they were out trying to find American cigarettes on the black market (Heinlein's attitude toward a wartime black market was one thing—but to black markets created by busybody regulations he had a strictly pragmatic attitude), Heinlein incautiously admitted to the man giving them directions that he was a writer. Word spread quickly, and he was besieged by reporters. He agreed to a radio interview on Friday, December 18, 1953, for the *Servicio Internacional*—the International Broadcasting System of Argentina[13]— that went surprisingly well despite some cultural differences that made him uncomfortable.[14] One part of the interview he feared might give him trouble: He was expected to say "something really nice about Papá."[15] He was able, however, to approve at least one sentiment seen around town on banners prominently displayed: "In the new Argentina, the only privileged ones are the children."

After eleven days they boarded M.V. *Ruys* for the next leg of their voyage, to Brazil by way of a two-day stopover in Montevideo, Uruguay, where a chance meeting in a sidewalk café, five minutes socializing with a spaniel and its human family, led to a warm personal relationship with a young Uruguayan diplomat, Mauricio Nayberg, and to introductions around the world, particularly in Singapore, that would open unexpected doors.

They had only three days in Brazil, so started inland by bus the first day from booming, industrial Santos to São Paulo, and then overnight, two days before Christmas, up the coast to Rio de Janeiro.[16] They had only one day in Rio, a native guide who spoke almost no English, and a day of overpowering heat and humidity—but they drove up Corcovado mountain to see at first hand the monumental Christ the Redeemer statue overlooking the steep hills over Rio—and, what the Heinleins may not have realized they were overlooking, Rio's *favelas,* some of the worst slums in the world, so legendary in their poverty, violence, and crime that they are still being used as the setting for many "shooter" video games.

Ruys headed for Cape Town, South Africa, next, and the weather was rough. There was a fire extinguisher low outside their stateroom door that would catch them whenever the ship lurched. Ginny, who always bruised easily, got a vivid collection of bruises from hip to knee. One day she startled some of the South Africans returning home, who were lounging by the ship's swimming pool. "What happened to you?" they asked, concerned. The devil got into Ginny at that moment: "My husband beats me," she told them. They were indignant on her behalf—never stopping to ask themselves why a wife-beater would localize his abuse to her upper legs. Ginny let them go on, amused. But it got around the ship that Robert was a wife-beater. One of them even wrote him a stern letter about it. It was the kind of thing it was hard to take seriously—but also hard to shrug off. Fortunately, they would leave it behind them when the ship got to South Africa.[17]

The captain decided to risk an unscheduled stopover at the most isolated inhabited spot on Earth, the island of Tristan da Cunha—an opportunity like catnip to Robert in both his "official" capacities as loafing tourist and working writer. A British possession midway between South America, Antarctica, and Africa, Tristan da Cunha rarely had ships more often than once every three to seven years. *Ruys* arrived on January 2, 1954, and Heinlein posted a handwritten letter on ship's stationery to Ron Hubbard—also an avid world traveler (and member of the Explorer's Club)—for the curiosity value of the postmark.

The Tristans were friendly and hospitable, but lack of cultural context made it nearly impossible to converse with them—a stark contrast with the way they had managed to chat with strangers with whom they had no language in common over all of South America. They were able to conduct commerce, however: Crew members bought some penguins from the islanders. But the Tristans did not have disease resistances the others all shared: A cold was going around the ship—a very minor thing that didn't even disturb the ship's surgeon's routine. But the islanders caught it from them, and four of them died in the ten days after *Ruys* left.[18]

Two days later, the ship grounded at the Cape of Good Hope.

South Africa under apartheid was a problem for Heinlein, his aggressive anti-racist impulses at continuous war with his deliberate policy of openness to *autres moeurs,* of trying to understand the different folkways, how they came to be and what functions they served in a living society. But South Africa was an intensification of his dilemma at home. The Union of South Africa is the *other* USA, and his dilemma is set out on the first page of the South Africa chapter of *Tramp Royale*: It was, like Robert's USA, a stunning, gloriously beautiful country—"a paradise where you expect to wake up some morning with your throat cut."[19]

They had ten days to get overland from Cape Town to Durban to join their next ship. One of their shipboard friends on *Ruys,* Sam (not otherwise identified), invited them along on a road trip overland from Cape Town to Johannesburg, through the Karoo Desert, where they encountered African cattle (rangier than their American counterparts), exotic birds, and springboks, the national emblem of South Africa, a kind of gazelle that has no American counterpart, through the Orange Free State and into the Transvaal (literally, across the Vaal River).

Johannesburg was where their host's trip ended,[20] and the Heinleins rented a taxi for a day to tour Kruger Park. No zebras, unfortunately, and no rhino, but an abundance of birds, impalas and other African gazelles, and even buffalo. And many lions—out of season and therefore unexpected—blended into the landscape and looking like termite hills, like abysses looking back at you.[21] Robert was shaking with excitement. This was the Africa he had come for.[22]

They almost did not get back. Their train was fully booked, and they had to stay overnight in Nelspruit and hire the taxi to drive them back to Johannesburg the next day—expensive, but it did give them a chance to inspect the Voortrekker Monument outside of Pretoria, a brother-under-the-bronze of the Mormon migration monument in Salt Lake City.[23]

From Jo'burg, they flew to Durban in a DC6B workhorse. *Ruys* was delayed an extra day, which gave them a chance to make a hundred-mile day trip into Zululand and visit the atelier of Ntuli, then a world-famous African sculptor. They bought a bust of a Zulu Matron, "strong and proud," for a ridiculously small fee. "And I met Ntuli himself—" Heinlein wrote later to a friend:

[I]t turns out that we are twin brothers, save that he is younger than I am and (of course) several shades darker as he is a Zulu. But our skulls have the same bony structure and the close resemblance is unmistakable—I got Ginny to preserve the fact in Kodachrome, the two of us."[24]

They returned to Durban with enough time left over to try to book the leg from Singapore, where they would leave *Ruys,* through to Australia by way of Indonesia—perhaps by way of Bali. Heinlein wanted to see for himself the bare-breast fashion in sarongs that was even then being suppressed by the new Indonesian government.[25] But Bali was not possible this trip.

They left *Ruys* in Singapore early on the morning of January 29. Ginny's sense of humor was not always appropriate for the perilous world outside America. To the routine inquiry "Anything to declare?" when they were going through Singapore customs, Ginny replied tartly, "Two pounds of heroin." Robert went cold, and the customs inspector's eyes bugged out. Though Ginny remembered only that he said "Oh, you Americans!" and stamped them through,[26] Robert remembered it differently: ". . . he decided to treat it as a joke, laughed hollowly, said, 'Yes, yes, no doubt,' and refrained from searching us. But I did not draw a breath until we were outside and in a taxi."[27] He never did succeed in impressing on Ginny how very much real trouble they had narrowly escaped.

Singapore was "a three-ring circus and a year-long Mardi-Gras,"[28] with a million people packed into a space that could not possibly hold more than fifty thousand. Predominantly Chinese in population, "properly speaking, the whole city is a slum, so tightly stacked they are one on another. But it is so alive, so cheerful, so bursting with energy that the slumlike quality of it is not depressing."[29]

They settled in for a week or more at Raffles, a hotel chosen for its associations in romantic fiction. They wound up with Nelson Rockefeller's suite and enjoyed "Oriental splendor" that they almost could not have imagined—including the services of a sixty-year-old "houseboy," Foo, who lavished attention on them. In the hotel's gift shop Heinlein found a *Tom Corbett* comic book, which he purchased for his working files back home in Colorado Springs.[30]

Their pick-up acquaintance with Mauricio Nayberg in Montevideo had resulted in an introduction to one of his father's business connections, a Mr. Ho Chuy Moo. Mr. and Mrs. Ho lavished hospitality on the Heinleins, even more startling and abundant than the Naybergs'—superlative Cantonese food (plus instruction in the use of chopsticks), introductions to tailors, amusement parks, a day trip to the Sultanate of Johore, and the Tiger Balm Garden/Har Paw Villa (an extravagant oriental garden and collection of exotica built by the heir of the Tiger Balm fortune) that stretched even the imaginative/descriptive faculties of this science-fiction writer.

The Heinleins were finally able to book passage to Brisbane, on the northwest coast of Australia, by way of Indonesia on a China coast vessel, *Tjibadak*—the last cabin left. Their preferred route from the west coast of Australia, possibly Derby or Darwin in the north, or even Perth in the far south, then by rail to Sydney on the east coast, was not possible. Australia and New Zealand were open-ended for them now, since they had not yet been able to find transport back to the United States.

With Mr. Ho's assistance, they were even able to obtain an Indonesian visa—not for Bali, but for Jakarta, where they would have a three-day layover. They sailed from Singapore on about February 10.

On the night before they left, they decided to give a thank-you dinner for the Hos at Raffles. While they were dressing for dinner, it suddenly occurred to Heinlein that Raffles might have the same "non-European" prejudice they had run across everywhere from Africa to Asia. The telling of this incident in *Tramp Royale* (at pp. 225–6) is more genteel than the somewhat more blood-thirsty version Robert saved for friends: "Say, hon," Robert remarked to Ginny,

"I don't recall having seen any orientals in the dining room—is this joint still 'pukka-sahib' and all that crap? We don't want to embarrass Mr. and Mrs. Ho."

Ginny went right on dressing. "Don't give it a thought."

"Huh?"

"If they try to keep our guests out of the dining room, we then go straight to the front desk and check out—and once our luggage is outside, we set fire to the place."

She's a practical woman. Get the luggage out first—

. . . . So I suppose I will never be a real literary-type author, because I can't learn to be a detached and analytical observer; I get involved, I take sides.

And so does Ginny. But she need never worry about my getting annoyed with her over this, because her instincts in such matters always suit me. She is what I feel to be a good person in the word's simplest and plainest meaning. Which includes lashing out with her claws on some occasions when others may consider it improper—I don't give a damn whether Ginny is "proper" or not; I like her. I like her values.[31]

But Raffles was civilized: They were not put to the necessity of rescuing their luggage.

Tjibadak is not mentioned by name in *Tramp Royale*, because it was a filthy and appalling tub—an unpleasantly fitting introduction, as it turned out, to

Sukarno's Indonesia. "[W]e could have quit this ship only at Djakarta [as it was then spelled]—which we would have done had Djakarta been an improvement, which it is not."[32]

Heinlein does not mention the fact in *Tramp Royale,* but the "body search" to which he was subjected at Indonesian customs (while Ginny was waved through), was conducted at bayonet-point[33]—which could only have reinforced the advice given them in Singapore not to argue with an Indonesian policeman or soldier, as they would have no hesitation executing you on the spot if angered.[34]

Jakarta itself Heinlein characterized in 1954 as a city the size of Chicago, but without plumbing of any sort, except for a foul canal running through the city, which was used for *all* water purposes. They did locate a friend of a friend at the city's one modern hotel, Hotel del Indes—Lothar Wolf, the producer of Irving Pichel's *Martin Luther,* who was there to help build up an Indonesian film industry.[35] They stayed aboard ship that night and watched the festivities for Chinese New Year celebrated by the largely Chinese crew. On the second day, they were scheduled to visit the botanical gardens in Bogor, sixty kilometers south of Jakarta. Ginny defied currency restrictions and smuggled cashier's checks off the ship, to buy batiks and sarongs. Cashier's checks they found not as desirable as cash—they can be traced.

The passage to Brisbane—the first place they could realistically get off *Tjibadak*—took an additional two weeks around Australia's northeastern "corner." They were in rough weather, having clipped the edge of a cyclone that was wreaking havoc at Queensland. By that time, most of the remaining passengers were Australian sheep men and their families, returning home, whom the Heinleins found almost uniformly rough but sociable—"easy as an old shoe."[36]

They arrived in Brisbane on about February 15. Brisbane's "feel" reminded Robert overpoweringly of "home"—the American Midwest, circa 1920–30. "I liked Australia and wanted it to like me."[37] They had only a few hours in Brisbane and elected to see teddy-bear koalas at a private zoo just outside town. Koalas are cuddly creatures—"left to themselves they cuddle with each other."[38] Ginny was given Little Mo to cuddle and had her picture taken. Little Mo was then returned to her cage, stopping to nibble at the concrete curbstone. Robert and Ginny were delighted with them: Their "unique genius for being pets"[39] makes them Earth's natural flat cats. The other Australian fauna they saw delighted them as "determined to be as exotic as possible . . . they are *all* on the lunatic fringe of the animal kingdom."[40]

Later that day they made their way the few hundred miles down the coast by a commuter vessel.

The Heinleins had originally planned to spend a month or more in Sydney, but the combined delays had reduced their time to only nine days before their March 1 sailing date for New Zealand. In addition to the normal planned tourism—the Sydney Zoo they found one of the most interesting on the entire trip—there was business to be attended to in Australia.

Australian laws prohibited American publications—which Heinlein referred to as a "sinful embargo on American Books"[41] (with the result that the bookstores and newsstands were filled with "some of the most amazing trash to be found anywhere"[42]). An Australian publisher had produced a pirate edition of "Life-Line"—a 7,200 word story—in paperback format. Shasta had sold the rights (for a mere ten dollars) and never even reported it, but just pocketed the money.[43]

Blassingame had found a solicitor for them, J. A. Campbell, Esq., to pursue the matter of literary piracy. Mr. Campbell was retained to see what recourse they might have on the Australian end. Not much, it turned out, but he had also agreed to act as their local business agent, which would be useful since Blassingame had been selling Australian rights for the Future History books for the last couple of years.

Their solicitor had a largish amount of mail for them. Blassingame had forwarded some business mail, as expected—Scribner wanted a retitle for *The Star Lummox* as there was another book on the stands currently with "Lummox" in the title. But the rest was fan mail. Their Colorado Springs house-sitters, Doc and Mimi Knowles, had apparently forgotten that they had asked that the fan mail *not* be forwarded. Wearily Robert and Ginny set out to answer the fan mail by handwritten postcard, since they didn't have access to typewriters.[44] Regrettably, they had plenty of time for the chore, as Australia's bizarre income tax requirements kept them tied to Sydney and haunting government offices nearly every day, and there was literally *nothing* to do on weekends in Sydney: *Nothing* was open for business![45]

Some of the fan mail was from schoolchildren on class assignments. In recent years, elementary school teachers all over the country had taken up the inconsiderate practice of having entire classes write to authors, often bombarding them with questionnaires for class projects. How a writer was supposed to get any writing done was a mystery best left unexplored.[46]

Somehow, word got out that he was visiting Australia, and Heinlein was lionized by Sydney science-fiction fandom, prevailed upon to give a "very interesting talk" to the Futurian Society of Sydney in the Club Room on Thursday, February 25, 1954.[47] He offered copies of all his books to the club library.

It was New Zealand that turned out to be the great disappointment of this

trip. Heinlein had been fascinated by the country for decades and was looking forward to encountering its legendary grandeur for himself. The statistics
and articles he had been reading for twenty years made it sound like the kind
of working, progressive socialism he had labored toward for decades. Their
union policies alone sounded like a worker's paradise.

Monowai cast off just two days after the then still-secret Castle Bravo
H-bomb was detonated at Bikini Atoll. They docked in Auckland on March
5 after an uneventful passage of four days. Their stateroom had been uncomfortably cramped, but at least the ship was clean. Not as much as could be
said for the hotel in Auckland—and the food they were given all during their
stay in New Zealand.

They arranged a tour of the countryside as fast as possible, running into a
snarl of red tape and incredible union featherbedding that gave his professional Democrat's conscience twinges. They endured several days in Auckland, over a weekend buttoned up tighter than even Sydney—"Australian
closing hours are inconvenient, but New Zealand closing hours are more in the
nature of paralysis"[48]—before they were able to book a tour of North Island—a
beautiful place. Waitomo, their first stop, did a great deal to take the taste of
Auckland out of their mouths. The Glowworm Grotto fascinated them.

Otherwise, the trip itself was moderately grim. In the thermal geyser
country of Wairakei and Rotorua, a guide, displaying all the characteristics
of petty bureaucrats everywhere, disparaged Yellowstone's geyser field, and
Robert had enough. For a moment he lost his temper and sense of discre-
tion enough to point out the facts and drew down the guide's righteously
arrogant—and factually wrong—wrath.[49]

Of New Zealand in 1954, he said it was a place, "where no one goes
hungry, but where life is dreary and comfortless beyond belief, save for the
pleasures of good climate and magnificent countryside."[50] Worst of all, it was
grim *because of* the very features that had made him most hopeful for it—the
British pattern of socialism, the overpowering, oppressive, death grip of the
unions stifled all spirit of progress, all incentive to better the thousands of
petty, daily inconveniences this often truculent, beaten-down people burdened
themselves with as much as their visitors.[51] "New Zealand is a fake utopia,"
Heinlein concluded, "a semi-socialism which does *not* work and which does
not have anything like the degree of civil liberty we have. In my opinion, it
stinks."[52]

They left New Zealand on a DC6 sleeper to Hawaii (by way of a dinner
stopover in the Fiji Islands). In the eleven days they were in New Zealand,
Ginny lost eleven pounds—and it was probably here, also, that she contracted

both scurvy and pellagra. In the future, they carried vitamin tablets with them while traveling.

They were met at Honolulu customs by Bob and Violet Markham, shipboard companions from *Gulf Shipper*. The Markhams took them home out beyond Diamond Head and pampered them while they recovered from the assorted shocks of New Zealand (and of air travel, for Ginny).

Hawaii is nominally "home," though they had several thousand miles yet to go. But it was an ideal place to recover from repeated culture shock. They continued as tourists, visiting pineapple fields and staying overnight at the hotel overlooking the Kilauea volcano, where Ginny enrolled herself in the cult of Pele, Hawaiian volcano-goddess. She gained back the weight she had lost, and Robert put on some extra weight, too: He was getting to be, if not quite "stout," then "well fed."

They found in Hawaii more mail from Blassingame: Miss Dalgliesh was disturbed by the girl-who-divorced-her-parents in *The Star Beast* (the new title for the *Star Lummox* book). Children "divorcing" their parents was a part—unpublicized—of our own legal system, not one of Heinlein's fictional inventions. In any case, he didn't need to do anything about it—Blassingame had arranged a compromise: Miss Dalgliesh would edit to minimize the impact.

It was probably on this trip that the Heinleins made their one visit to the Pearl Harbor Memorial. Cal Laning had been at Pearl the morning of the attack in 1941, but it was other friends and colleagues and shipmates Robert wanted to remember:

> I have returned to Oahu many times, but I have been out to see USS *Arizona* just once, did not go aboard, did not stay long, and do not intend to go back a second time. Somewhere, down inside her, are more than a thousand bodies; one of them is my former Commodore, Captain van Valkenberg, commanding. Another is Tommy McClelland; we were cadet captains together in high school, corporals together in the 110th Combat Engineers. I don't wish to stand over their bodies or any of the others. "They shall not grow old as we that are left grow old, age shall not weary them nor the years condemn; At the going down of the sun and in the morning, we will remember them . . ."[53]

Standing over the skeletons of his comrades, picked clean by the crabs and the fishes of the sea, must have been an emotional capstone for the trip.

Many things had changed for him and in him, many opinions overthrown. The great socialist ideals of his youth were wonderful dreams, but if his encounters on this trip meant anything at all, it was that the materials did not exist in the world to make them into reality, and even the attempt to put them into practice could do more harm than good.[54] No world federation had a chance to be an instrument for liberation. The voice he had raised for such things he would still.

It was a short sleeper flight from Honolulu, orchid leis around their necks, to San Francisco on March 28, 1954. Robert had caught a cold and spent much of their three-day stay at the Hotel California resting, while Ginny shopped on Union Square. In the evenings they visited with friends and colleagues.

A. P. White now lived in Berkeley, and they were able to spend an entire evening with him—though Robert was not able to get any resolution on those mysterious remarks about differences of political opinion White had been making in correspondence for the last several years. Heinlein began to suspect it was not *he* who was turning away from traditional liberalism: White was evolving into something incompatible with liberalism as Heinlein understood it: he was becoming a leftist. Nor was he the only person making that evolution. As Lester del Rey later put it, the country was drifting to the left, "leaving those with mature ideas about what should be our political stances appearing to move rightward."[55]

There was a gulf opening up in American politics, and Heinlein found himself on the far side of the divide: "leftism" was not "liberalism," and he was *and would remain* a liberal.[56]

On March 30, they flew to Denver and just missed the day's last shuttle flight to Colorado Springs. They were stuck just twenty-five minutes by air from home. The next day, they boarded the shuttle. Ten minutes into the flight, literally within sight of Cheyenne Mountain, the cabin began to fill with smoke "so thick that you could not see your hand in front of your face."[57] It wasn't anything dangerous—excess oil smoldering in the cabin's heating and air-conditioning system—but the pilot banked into a U-turn and headed back to Denver.

The second try was uneventful. They deplaned at Peet Field, met by friends and neighbors. Thirty minutes later, Pixie was greeting them, stropping their ankles, and they were home.

SOME BEGINNINGS OF SOME ENDS

Ginny urged Robert to start on the travel book he had been making notes for right away, while all the memories were still fresh, but their time was relatively short: Heinlein's twenty-fifth Annapolis class reunion was late in May, and they planned to make it an extended trip east this time, spending several days in New York. The five or six weeks he had before the trip wouldn't be enough time to organize and write the book—and there was a huge pile of mail to deal with.

In the backlog of correspondence Heinlein found the editing Dalgliesh had done on *The Star Beast,* cutting to minimize Betty Sorenson's "divorce" from her parents, with a note, saying: ". . . it is hard enough to sell books these days without having them kept off lists by something that foolish people take too seriously. I think as I fixed it the omission doesn't hurt the book at all, but as I told you, it is up to you[.]"[1]

Heinlein wrote that he didn't see what the fuss was about: There were many more unorthodox ideas in that book, and he didn't much care for this kind of censorship. But since Blassingame had allowed it, he would let the editing stand. *The Magazine of Fantasy & Science Fiction* had the first of three installments of the book in print this month, under his original title of *The Star Lummox.*

Heinlein went into downtown Colorado Springs to find a newsstand that still had a copy of the current (April 2, 1954) *U.S. News & World Report:*[2] They were publishing a complete book, *The Final Secret of Pearl Harbor,* by Admiral Robert A. Theobald, with corroborative forwards by Admiral Kimmel, who commanded Pearl Harbor on December 7, 1941, and Admiral William H. Halsey, wartime commander of the Third Fleet.[3]

Admiral Theobald "puts the responsibility for Pearl Harbor on one man: President Franklin D. Roosevelt."[4] Theobald argued that Roosevelt arranged for the Japanese to be pressured into declaring war on the United States and concealed (or engineered the concealment of) relevant diplomatic dispatches in order to make the incident happen.

Although Heinlein knew that Admiral Kimmel was derelict in not having the Fleet at sea during an international crisis, he felt compelled to believe the truth of Admiral Theobald's position. It was widely known that Roosevelt wanted the United States to intervene on Britain's behalf; he wanted to get the United States into the war in Europe. The book[5] clearly implied Roosevelt had manipulated the country into World War II—and was, therefore, personally responsible for the carnage at Pearl, and for all the hundreds of thousands of American casualties in the war.

After thirteen years, Pearl Harbor was still a hot-button issue in American politics. Roosevelt had been near-deified in popular opinion since his death; his policies—or what his surviving followers *thought* were his policies—had been elevated into cornerstones of Democratic Party platforms, and even the new Republican administration of Dwight D. Eisenhower had to deal with Roosevelt's legacy through Truman. Some aspects of "Pearl Harbor Revisionism" are now considered historical orthodoxy, as individual pieces of information can be fit into the overall picture. It is no longer thought, for example, that the attack was purely motivated by evil intent on the part of the Japanese high command, though the situation was much more complex than even Theobald knew about in 1954: It was not yet clear, for example, that Japan was being oil-starved by its Axis allies. Other revisionist elements remain controversial, and some are simply lumped together by historians as "conspiracy theory."

The *Final Secret of Pearl Harbor* painfully shook Heinlein loose from his personal attachment to the memory of his Roosevelt. "Robert felt that the Navy had been betrayed," Ginny said later, "and he felt for his classmates who had been killed in that attack."[6]

But this revisionism was working alchemical changes in Robert, more and different than the general public understanding of Roosevelt's personal complicity.[7] Heinlein had just had a shock to his world picture. This trip had shown him graphically how little the world was ready for his radical-liberal One World enthusiasms. Perhaps he might have recovered from that destabilizing confrontation with uncomfortable realities, but the careful nonconfrontation with A. P. White in San Francisco added a harmonic to this discord.

The Theobald Report offered a harsh and unwelcomed glare of more light. Superficially, perhaps, it exposed Roosevelt as a skilled politician—and it does not hurt to have an appreciation of what is real versus the god-king myth—but it made Heinlein reconsider also, what he, himself had wrought.

For one thing, it threw into sudden, high relief the differences between the New Deal and Upton Sinclair's EPIC that had been nearly invisible to Heinlein at the time—differences of tactics rather than of basic philosophy.[8] At the time, they both "felt" like they were building Wells's managerial socialism—hesitantly, experimentally, sometimes using very unlikely materials in unlikely ways (for example, Wells's odd early [1907] enthusiasm for professional realtors). By 1954 Heinlein was no longer quite so sure. It was not that he now had a problem with socialism per se—

> Socialism can be good or bad, depending on how it is run. Our national parks are an example of a socialist enterprise which is beautifully run . . . . Here in the USA, where we have much more socialism than most people appear to believe, we are good at it in some spots, fair in others, lousy in some. In general I have come to believe that we here are usually better off with private ownership government policed than we are when the government actually owns the deal and a bored clerk looks at you and sneers when you complain. But I don't hold it as an article of faith, either way—people ought to be able to organize their affairs to suit their convenience, either individually or collectively. They ought to be free to do either one. They ought to be free.[9]

Perhaps there had been embedded in Roosevelt's New Deal the seeds of this current leftism that was softening the brains of otherwise bright and well-intentioned people, who seemed not to realize that they had conceded important intellectual and moral ground to that stunted and malign child of socialism, as Wells had called Lenin's and Stalin's Communism. America's leftism now had no room for that strain of American progressive optimism and benevolent patriotism that married love of country to love of the great ideals of the Founders, that went back to the last century, through Emerson and back even to that old Puritan thunderer Jonathan Edwards.

Heinlein resigned from the Democratic Party in 1954 and for ten years remained unaffiliated, voting a split ticket.[10] Doubtless he wanted to be free of that now-tainted legacy—but he may also have foreseen that he would be forced increasingly into conflict with his party as leftism continued to overwhelm and then displace liberalism. "So everyone is out of step but Willie. This may be the March of History. I think it may be. I strongly suspect that the process is irreversible and that I am utterly out of step with the times."[11]

With these ideas starting to percolate through his mind, he traveled to

Annapolis for his class's silver (twenty-fifth) reunion, a journey back in time for him: During the reunion on May 22 and 23, 1954, he and Ginny stayed at Carvel Hall, the old Paca Mansion across from the campus, where Robert had stayed the night before he took his Midshipman's Oath in 1925. They moved on to Philadelphia on the 24th, to see the de Camps, and Sprague introduced him to a young friend and budding writer then in med school, Alan E. Nourse, who was also the president of the Philadelphia SF Society.[12]

The next day they went on to New York, where they had dinner with Isaac Asimov and the Blassingames on May 25.[13] Isaac Asimov remembered that dinner: Heinlein was trying to talk him into listing with Blassingame, but he was put off when Blassingame's wife, Peggy, sampled his Shrimp Fra Diavolo. Asimov was extremely territorial about his food.[14]

Ginny was suffering from a slight bladder infection and took an early flight back to Colorado. Robert stayed behind, bunking with John Arwine, in order to have a long, face-to-face talk with John Campbell.[15]

Campbell had been writing for some time about his own, independent psychological researches now that he had left the Dianetics movement. He and his new wife, Peg, used each other as subjects—but it was hard for Heinlein to grasp exactly what it was they were doing from Campbell's "frustratingly inconclusive"[16] letters. He had a deep suspicion, he had told Campbell, of figures of speech used as if they were rational arguments[17]—to which Campbell was particularly prone, because of his analogical style of argument.

Campbell had arranged to have the house in Westfield, New Jersey, to himself one evening and invited Robert. He had an overriding agenda in mind and didn't allow small talk to get in the way: Without even asking about Heinlein's trip around the world just concluded, he took Heinlein to his basement workshop for hours of increasingly mystifying and increasingly frustrating—and then downright insulting—lecture.[18]

It had started out cordially enough: Campbell had come up with "a new concept of distance" that seemed somehow to be pivotal to his psychological researches. As Campbell went on lecturing, though, it got foggier and foggier. Heinlein tried to understand it from the ground up: What were the *data* on which Campbell built his superstructure of philosophical ideas?

But the data—even the actual description of the new concept of distance— was "confidential." Heinlein could get nothing out of Campbell about methods, or data, or even tentative conclusions. Campbell repeatedly told him he didn't understand—true enough—and that he lacked the patience—and the math (Heinlein was a better mathematician than Campbell)—for this kind of painstaking work in any case. Campbell was going to develop a radio that was not subject to the inverse-square law. "Good trick," Heinlein remarked dryly. "John demands applause now for results he is going to produce tomorrow."[19]

At last, Heinlein's Semantic Pause gave out: "I finally told him that until he disclosed his data and explained what he was doing nobody was obligated to take his work seriously."[20]

He never did find out what Campbell supposedly wanted to communicate to him. The meeting broke up after four exhausting hours with Campbell telling Heinlein that he lacked the "serious social purpose" that Campbell had—which caused Heinlein to think unkind thoughts:

> After four hours of bullyragging I felt insulted—not only my intelligence insulted by prime damfoolishness, but personally and emotionally insulted by being told repeatedly that I did not understand simple statements—and then told I was a slacker because I did not drop everything and follow him!
>
> (Goddam[n] it, I was working my heart out and ruining my health during the war while he was publishing *Astounding*—doing what I could when they would not accept me for combat. I don't need JWC to tell me my duty. As for space flight, who is actually sweating to achieve it? You [Stine] and the boys with you, eating sand and wind at 130 degrees in the Jornado basin? Or John Campbell sitting on his fat buttocks back in Jersey and laying down the law from his easy chair?)
>
> Hell and Maria, John has never seen a big rocket. He (so help me!) had never even been up in an airplane until the Navy gave him a free ride down to Washington the week the war ended . . . .[21]

But that was not the worst of it: Campbell went on that he lacked serious social purpose *because he did not have children*. At that, it was past time to shut up, but he went inexorably on:

> . . . if only I had his feel of social responsibility to the next generation I would join up under his leadership and solve these problems (what problems I still don't know!) in time to stop the Russian H-bombs . . . . Me, I'm just a butterfly with no progeny; I can't be expected to have any social responsibility, natch![22]

Heinlein got out of there. "I did not take offense; I don't think he knew he was being insulting. I remain fond of John, but some of his bullyragging is hard to take."[23]

He did not tell Ginny about this incident: Ginny would have been offended by that no-kids-equals-no-social-consciousness crack—but she knew something he did not. In their last round of fertility testing,[24] the doctor had let her see the slides of Robert's sperm sample: There were no wigglers living in it at all. "I never told him that," Ginny later remarked. "He would have been devastated. I just let him think that it was that 'mutual infertility.'"[25]

This generation of Heinlein's family all had low fertility. Neither Rex nor Clare had natural children, either, while Larry had a son by his first marriage (Lawrence Lewis Heinlein) and three girls by his second. Perhaps in Robert's case it was due to childhood malnutrition. Or perhaps the measles he had had in 1914 caused the infertility—or the succession of genito-urinary tract infections during his Navy years.

Heinlein would probably never have said anything about the incident with Campbell to anyone, but Campbell made the disagreement rather "public" by writing a seven-page letter to G. Harry Stine at White Sands, complaining about Heinlein's close-mindedness. Stine wrote to Heinlein, expressing his confusion: Campbell's intuitive, Fourth-of-July sparkler was very different from Heinlein's careful building of foundations from which inferences could be made—but belittling Heinlein was out of bounds.[26]

Heinlein was outraged that Campbell should expose their disagreement to any third party—but at the same time it gave him someone he could talk to. He was grateful, he told Stine, for the reality check.

> Your remarks about John did my heart good, as I have been much disturbed to know that he would write a long letter to another person about the argument we had and have been doing some soul-searching to try to decide whether or not I had been out of line in what I said to him.
>
> As an admittedly biased judge, I am forced to say that I do not think I was out of line. On the contrary I think I was very slow to speak and long suffering . . . .[27]

The travel book was nearly done in draft. He sent out the first half of the book to Blassingame, to begin showing around. Walter Bradbury at Doubleday passed on *Tramp Royale*—he was charmed by it, he told Blassingame, but travel books were a tough market to crack, and this book didn't fall into any of the usual categories.[28]

That must have been irritating, of course, but Blassingame continued to shop the book around while Heinlein finished writing it—between squiring drop-in visitors around Colorado Springs. He also wanted to do an "adult" book before starting on his annual boys' book.[29] He was growing tired of the petty censorship in the juvenile market, but Blassingame convinced him Dalgliesh was "just doing her job," and so Heinlein planned to write another again this holiday season. Once the travel book had made its first rounds, Heinlein asked Blassigname to send back the half-manuscript for *Tramp Royale,* so that he could finish the book and get it out of his system.[30]

He had been trying out a couple of gimmicks to lighten the sheer physical work of production. He was sold, now, on electric typewriters, for their light, instantaneous touch, though the clatter of the keys against the platten was enough to raise complaints from Ginny two or three rooms away. But he could work longer hours if he didn't get tired punching the keys, and it was his style to work steadily from "can" to "can't." He found an ideal solution: On July 29, 1954, he purchased an Underwood Model 12 "Silent" typewriter that had been built for a funeral home, with a silencer—a case built around the works, enclosing everything but the keyboard. Ginny called it a "baby's coffin."[31] It cost as much as the advance for an entire book.[32]

That summer of 1954, Heinlein's brother Rex came through Colorado Springs with his wife and family. A year before, Rex had retired from teaching at West Point (at age forty-eight), and he had taken the entire family to Switzerland for a year so his daughters could attend a Swiss finishing school.[33] On their way to the West Coast (eventually winding up in Palo Alto, California), they stayed with Robert and Ginny, overcrowding the Mesa Avenue house, which was rather too small for that many people. Robert and Ginny gave up their bedroom and slept in Robert's study, while the girls slept on the built-in couches in the living room, or in Ginny's office—but they gave everyone a good time. Karen sent them a bread-and-butter note two months later:

> Every minute we were there was so much fun. Lynnie and I had always hoped for the chance to ride a horse for the first time and you made that possible for us. And skating in the middle of summer was a treat for us especially since we did very little in Switzerland . . . . You really kept us busy doing wonderful things while we were staying with you in your lovely home.[34]

The rest of the Heinlein family was again in a state of agitation during that summer: Father Rex had lapsed back into that state of depression the doctors had been calling Involutional Melancholia and was back in the hospital.

John Campbell seemed to be getting over his snit in the fall: He sent them some LPs of Tom Lehrer songs that were funnier even than *Pogo.*

We have played them repeatedly and we are forever grabbing people, telling them to sit down and listen carefully—then we watch their expressions with glee. Ginny and I sing the "love" songs to each other in saccharine tones, assuring each other that in twenty years or so we'll wish the other one dead.[35]

On the same day Heinlein wrote to Campbell, a librarian-reviewer with the unlikely name of Learned Bulman wrote to Alice Dalgliesh saying the child-divorce in *The Star Beast* was objectionable and ruined the book, and he would have to say just that in his review for *Library Journal*. Could that not be edited out of the second edition? Dalgliesh ducked the issue, saying Heinlein felt strongly about leaving it in. She forwarded the letters to Heinlein, with a handwritten P.S.: "Perhaps this gives you some idea of what an editor is up against!!"[36]

Heinlein answered Bulman mildly, pointing out that the child-divorce was legitimate, straightforward extrapolation from current social trends—and that *any* change of customs will always displease some.

> Mr. Bulman wrote to me that he did not object to the idea of "divorce" for unfortunate children in itself, but that one of the characters was "flippant." This epitomizes the nature of the objections; these watchful guardians of youthful morals do not want live characters, they want plaster saints who never do anything naughty and who are always respectful toward all the shibboleths and taboos of our present-day, Heaven-ordained tribal customs.
>
> I could write such books, of course—but the kids would not read them.[37]

With Dalgliesh, however, Heinlein was less gentle.

> I am sure that you feel that you defended me in your letter to Mr. Bulman and I am sorry indeed not to agree. You told him that you discussed the "divorce" matter with me when the manuscript came in and that I was very firm about leaving it in. You specify that you yourself hold no brief for the idea. Then, having made it empathetically clear [possibly Heinlein means "emphatically"] that you have no liking for the notion and that you tried to talk me out of it, you do discuss it in general terms and suggest that it won't hurt young people to think about odd ideas.
>
> If you will think back you will recall that I was out of the country when the manuscript came in and that you got permission from Mr. Blassingame to revise the "divorce" matter to suit yourself—which you did . . . The version

Mr. Bulman saw was precisely as you had revised it. If you will think back still further you will recall that I have always, without exception, approved any change you asked for when the reason was to avoid trouble with librarians or teachers—no matter how little I liked the changes.

You can imagine how surprised I was to find you telling Mr. Bulman that I overruled you on this . . . Over the years, out of eight books, this is to the best of my knowledge, the *first* time that any librarian, teacher, or parent has ever objected to anything in any of my boys books. Now, when the first attack does come along, I trust that you will understand the shock with which I find my editor promptly assuring the attacker that she knew I was guilty all along but could not talk me out of it. . . .

Even if it had been true, I am surprised . . . that you would disavow my work to an outsider. I am wondering how Scribner's handled the complaints about *From Here to Eternity*? Did the firm stick up for Mr. Jones?. . . . [38]

(I agree with you heartily; the lot of an editor is not a happy one.)[39]

Dalgliesh wrote back, complimenting him on his mild-answer-turneth-away-wrath—but noted he was taking this too seriously.[40]

This was not a reply calculated to settle Heinlein's temper. In a scorching letter—possibly never sent, as it survives only in draft—he demanded to know, if *she* didn't take her line seriously, how could she expect Bulman to? And if nobody takes him seriously, why should we? "I no longer take Bulman seriously because I no longer give a hoot about selling (or writing) juveniles under such circumstances. But I take your handling of this most seriously."[41]

Up until this incident it would never have occurred to me to question it. I had thought being with Scribner's was almost like being in a family, with the writers proud of the publishing house (*I* certainly was!) and the house proud of its writers. I had assumed without thinking about it that in event of attack from the outside we would stand shoulder to shoulder beyond any question . . . . your very last statement to me assumes that I should understand that, in disavowing me, you were simply doing what was inevitably necessary under the circumstances.

I don't agree.

I would not agree even if the facts had been as you alleged. I had thought that we were all one team so far as outsiders were concerned; I had never dreamed that locker-room differences of opinion could be carried out on the field and offered gratis as an advantage to someone who opposed us.

I am as humiliated and mortified and astonished as you would be if you were to find me undercutting Scribner's position.[42]

This nonsense over the juveniles, he told Blassingame, was becoming so vexatious, so repeatedly irksome, that he wondered if he should give them up entirely and concentrate on "adult" novels instead. Blassingame wrote back with the calm, measured, practical advice Heinlein so valued: Dalgliesh was doing her job—which was selling his books to librarians and teachers. Go on to your adult books now, he urged, and revisit the question of the juveniles if the book actually took a hit in sales because of Bulman's negative review.

The "adult" novel didn't get written that year, though. Ginny had remarked one day about the "class honeymoons" that seemed to pass through Colorado Springs in waves that year: Graduating classes in high schools organized group trips to the Broadmoor or to places like Garden of the Gods, cluttering up the tourist sites when they wanted to take friends and family out.

And that was a germ for his next juvenile: The class honeymoon became an interstellar survival exercise for a high-school class—an idea much more radical in 1954 than it is now (parasitic exploitation of other peoples' ideas in, especially, the film industry makes it sometimes difficult to remember how fresh and arresting these ideas were when they first appeared). The young people are marooned on an alien and unexplored planet by an astronomical accident and must band together to survive and keep civilization alive. Heinlein began writing *Schoolhouse in the Sky* on November 11, 1954, finishing the 76,000-word draft on December 10, ahead of his usual work schedule, with ample time over the holidays to trim it and have it professionally retyped. He solicited Blassingame's advice on the hunting sequences.

This time, Dalgliesh's only major request was for a change of title—titles with "Schoolhouse," she explained, didn't do very well with teenagers. He suggested *Tunnel in the Sky* instead—one of the "working" titles he had used occasionally in correspondence with Blassingame. That was satisfactory. But, she warned him, the racial mix of the class[43] and the implication of miscegenation at one point, where a Zulu-descended girl was contemplating marriage with his protagonist, would cost them sales in the Deep South—and the reference to an "Australasian," implying that in the future British Australia would be overrun by Asians—would dampen sales in Canada (and possibly other Commonwealth countries)—though "I'm with you, of course."[44]

This prospect bothered him not at all, though he acceded to her other suggestions—and some new ones Blassingame had made. It was possible

Dalgliesh might reject the book. He wrote to Fowler, Dalgliesh's former assistant who was now at Holt:

> . . . I have written one more boys' book which will be submitted later this month [January 1955] to Scribners. If Miss Dalgliesh turns it down—which is a distinct possibility—then it will be available to the trade early in February.
>
> But will I in fact have any more freedom with one editor than I have with another? They all have to sell to the same librarians, please the same teachers. It may well be that I should quit the juveniles entirely, even though they have proved quite satisfactory financially and not unrewarding professionally . . . .
>
> If I find I cannot buck this asinine censorship, I am simply going to get out of the field—but that is not important. What does strike me as woefully important is this attempt to cope with serious and tragic matters by quack methods, as futile as a poultice on a cancer . . . .[45]

He had built into this book—and not for the first time—a factor he thought would be completely unacceptable to Dalgliesh or to any other mainstream publisher: His protagonist, Rod Walker, was a Negro. He had not said so, not in so many words (he was not suicidal, after all, considering the public furor a few years earlier over Sinclair Lewis's race-relation novel *Kingsblood Royal*[46]), but there were details that made it clear, to anyone who cared to think about it. He kept it to himself as the book wound through the publication process in 1955.

By sheer coincidence, another book dealing with a similar situation had just come on the market, having been rejected by a succession of twenty-one publishers. William Golding's *Lord of the Flies* just skirts science fiction, with backstory elements that could be read as future war. Golding's book takes a very different approach to the problem of an accidentally isolated group of young people—a speculative-realistic novel set in a timeless context that holds civilization is a thin veneer, to be discarded. Heinlein takes the contrary view that civilization is humanity's proudest invention, something we will take with us, to the stars.

Both books are still in print, more than fifty years later.

VINTAGE SEASON

By 1955, much of the Heinleins' socializing revolved around dancing: Ginny's ice-dancing, of course (and Robert had achieved enough skill, at last, to keep up with her on many of the figures). Gradually, they had added several kinds of off-ice dancing as well—round dance, cotillion, and Viennese waltzing. That winter (1954–55), they added square dancing in Pappy Shaw's "Calico and Boots" club, often inviting the entire club home for an impromptu party.

Heinlein once again picked up the manuscript of *The Martian Named Smith* (after stalling on the book in 1952). By February 1955 he was 36,000 words into it,[1] but it just *would not* come together for him. In a letter to Theodore Sturgeon, he complained: "I am at present stuck on 148[2] of the best set-up for a novel I ever had in my life and I *cannot* get the Goddam thing to jell!"[3] Frustrated (in his letter to his agent, he said the novel "aborted" at about 54,000 words),[4] he set it aside to deal with Shasta's request for revisions to *Methuselah's Children,* which had now been hanging fire for eight years.

Methuselah's Children would be the fourth of their five projected books in the Future History series. Shasta also wanted him to write another long novella, "Da Capo," for the last book, under the same restrictive terms as he had done "The Man Who Sold the Moon" five years before. Heinlein had lost so much secondary income on that deal that he couldn't work up any enthusiasm for a writing project that was too "da capo" for his own commercial interest. "Of course I may never write 'Da Capo' anyhow," he told his agent, "since I am tired of this series [the Future History]—but I certainly am not going to contract to write it and agree to throw away the major return on it."[5]

A very *odd* request came in from Theodore Sturgeon. Sturgeon was badly blocked and out of cash. He needed help—anything that might kick-start the writing process. Heinlein was flattered by the request—"To have the incomparable and always scintillating Sturgeon ask for ideas is like having the Pacific Ocean ask one to pee in it."[6] He spun off a couple of dozen "Sturgeonish" ideas that might sell quickly to Campbell, ranging from "tag lines" that might start a story rolling—

- "June 28—the new bull calf looks better all the time. Met a leprechaun today. Nice little guy. I'm going to have to drain the south forty . . ."
- "This guys sells soaps and cosmetics, door to door like the Fuller Brush man. She tries their beauty soap; she becomes beautiful. So she tries their vanishing cream . . ."
- "A little cat ghost, padding patiently around in limbo, trying to find that familiar, friendly lap . . ."

—to fully developed ideas that only needed writing out.[7] At Ginny's suggestion, he also enclosed a substantial check that would help with immediate expenses.

Ginny filled in the hours when Robert was at the typewriter by auditing courses at nearby Colorado College—harmony and music theory in 1955—and precinct work with the League of Women Voters. She also started working with the local little theater group, acting as wardrobe mistress for their production of Arthur Miller's *The Crucible* and then for *The Tea House of the August Moon.*

Ginny's actors and behind-the-scenes staff from the little theater were a mix of raw amateurs and seasoned semi-professionals, and Robert was usually ready to quit work for the day when Ginny brought them home with her in February of 1955. He must have listened thoughtfully as the new-to-him shop talk circled around. At some point it must have occurred to him that a theatrical background might give his next book just the novelty twist he needed. He asked leading questions—about makeup and other details he might use—and soaked up the theatrical lore that flew around the room without any prompting from him.[8] The book that came out of all this, *Double Star,* turned on an actor hired to impersonate—double for—a politician who has been kidnapped to precipitate an interplanetary crisis—and matures into a thoughtful adult by this experience.

Double Star is one of Heinlein's most charming entertainments, one of several masterworks of his 1950s, written ingratiatingly with what he called "the heroic hijinks with which the story is decorated, such as kidnapings and attempted assassinations," lifted from English, Roman, and Chinese history[9] (but mostly based on the long literary tradition of doubles, from *The Man in the Iron Mask* to *The Prince and the Pauper*). Heinlein had reached in his writing for young people a pinnacle of skill in seducing and pleasing his readers, gently teaching without seeking to challenge. Although *Double Star* was nominally written for adults, it fits comfortably with the juvenile novels he was writing at this period. Speaking of *Double Star,* Heinlein later defined his "pedagogical" intent:

> I think that a person with enough empathy to recognize and respect a horse as part of the Living Tree with a personality and feelings of his own is more likely thereby not to join in a lynch mob.
>
> I may be entirely mistaken in this; I have no scientific proof. But it is a theme which has run consistently through all my stories . . . the theme that the human race is not alone in this universe and it had better get over its xenophobia . . . the notion that human beings should seek to find friends among other types of beings and not automatically assume that they are enemies.[10]

The book was finished by March 23 and edited for the typist three days later— less than a month before they were scheduled to leave for a trip to Europe.

Travel permissions with the Naval Reserve were becoming more and more cumbersome for Ginny. She asked for and obtained an Honorable Discharge on April 21, 1955, the day before her thirty-ninth birthday.

Ten days later, the Heinleins left Colorado Springs for New Orleans to board the *Tillie Lykes* for stops in Savannah, Georgia; to the Azores; to Genoa; Naples; Rijaka, Yugoslavia; Venice; Athens; Istanbul; Alexandria—and on to Heidelberg where they would camp out with brother Larry and family, making side trips ad lib for four or five months. One of those side trips they initially planned would be to Sweden—"One purpose of this trip to Europe was to look into the possibility to adopting a Swedish child—but for various reasons we have decided against that, so now the trip is just for pleasure and education."[11] Heinlein was now too old to adopt under Colorado law—he would turn forty-eight while they were gone—and in any case, the state of the world was just too uncertain.[12]

In early June 1955, they were in Yugoslavia, where they made friends with their guide, Mary Dinaka—a WWII resistance fighter. While there Heinlein saw something that affected him profoundly—at least as deeply as the Pearl Harbor exposé: He witnessed a ceremony at which American tanks were handed over to Tito's Communist Yugoslavia. Marshal Josip Broz Tito (1892–1980) had broken with Stalin in 1948, but he was still a Communist and a violently anti-democratic dictator. The idea—postwar policy for decades—of arming one set of dictators against another set stuck in Heinlein's craw.

> . . . [T]hose two things, the truth about Pearl Harbor and seeing with my own eyes American arms being given to a communist dictator, were things that said to me: "Brother, you aren't just in the wrong pew, you're in the wrong church . . ."[13]

From Yugoslavia to Venice to Athens, arriving at the Piraeus (the port of Athens) at night during a full moon. They took advantage of the ideal circumstances for viewing the Acropolis, its damage softened by moonlight.

They had planned to fly from Alexandria to Heidelberg, but instead left the *Tillie Lykes* at Istanbul: The Chief attacked the radio operator in the Captain's mess one day—unprovoked so far as anyone knew—and tried to kill him. Instead of convening a court of inquiry, the Captain elected to hush it up—despite a doctor's warning that the man was mentally unbalanced. There was a second attack, this time *in the Captain's presence,* and he still did nothing. This ship, Heinlein concluded, was too dangerous to risk: He and Ginny cashed in their tickets and flew directly to Germany.[14]

Heinlein's brother Lawrence was stationed in Heidelberg with the U.S. Army of Occupation. Robert looked around once they got out of the airport and exclaimed that they were speaking English—but they weren't: Ginny heard only Hochdeutsch, a little *schlamperei.* The accents and speech rhythms of Bavarian German must have triggered long-disused mental circuitry in Robert, left over from the neighbor woman—Mrs. Oehlschlager—who had "borrowed" five-year-old Bobby and spoken German to him as she made gingerbread cookies.[15]

From Heidelberg they could make "loop trips" in any direction, coming back to Heidelberg as a base. The French Riviera caused Heinlein's eyes permanently to bug out, he said, because of the new bikini fashion in swimwear.[16] Ginny went shopping for one, and consequently had the first bikini to reach the United States (that she knew of).[17]

One side trip was just for Ginny's benefit: the Bayreuth Festival. She loved Wagner's music, and being in Germany during the Festival was an opportunity not to be missed. The Festival was held annually to play the entire Ring cycle in the theater Richard Wagner had designed and built for his own *Singspiele.* Almost seventy years after Wagner's death, the Festival was then still being managed by his grandchildren. Wieland Wagner gave it a modernistic production with dramatic lighting on a bare stage. Robert tagged along for the exhausting experience (some of those operas are eight hours long!). His reaction was about what Mark Twain's had been.[18]

Their itinerary took them from Heidelberg to Paris near the end of August, and then to London for a short—too short[19]—visit with the Carnells. Then a swing around Ireland, Wales, and Scotland. The English leg of the trip they found oddly disappointing, dirty and inconvenient—"the goddamdest aggregation of stopped-up toilets, dirty trains, dirty beds, dirty places, and fouled up schedules."[20] It was New Zealand all over again, they concluded when they found that union rules prevented their London hotel's floor maid from changing a burned-out light bulb in their bedside lamp. Ginny wasn't even permitted to change the bulb herself: An electrician had to be called.[21]

After a too-short visit in Scotland, they flew to New York from Glasgow on September 12 and 13, 1955, and spent a week in Lurton Blassingame's care, then back to Colorado Springs.[22]

Once they got settled in and caught up with mail and ledger entries, there was a party. Ginny brought out her bikini. The men's reaction was gratifying enough, but it was the women's reactions that were startling. They all oohed and ahed over it, and wanted to try it on. They might do so, Robert ruled—if he could photograph it on them. Giggling, they all agreed, and each one changed into Ginny's one bikini and came out to model it for the party—big ones, small ones, short ones, tall ones, all in Ginny's bikini. It was a wonder of persuasion on Robert's part, and he captured it in slides (which are preserved in the Heinlein Archive).

It was time for him to start thinking about his next boys' book—if he was going to do another one. Ginny suggested another book about twins, a particular fascination of hers (she had always wanted to be a twin[23])—and he started thinking along those lines. Twins suggested Einstein's Twin Paradox: What if you had a pair of twins and sent one off on a spaceship traveling at a significant fraction of the speed of light. The Lorentz-Fitzgerald contraction suggested that, from the perspective of the boy left behind on Earth, his twin on the ship would stay young while he aged. Heinlein started jotting notes of an outline for a story he called "The Star Clock"—or possibly "Dr. Einstein's Clock" or some variation thereof—on November 5, recycling some of his thinking about long-lived families for people who lived out-of-phase with their culture.[24]

The Shasta deal was finally breaking his way: They had not made payments on their contracts in more than a year, and the contracts voided automatically after a thirty-day arrearage. Since they had sold properties they did not own (and kept the proceeds from the sales), even Blassingame-the-peacekeeper was willing to call it quits. On November 3, 1955, Blassingame wrote to Oscar Friend, Shasta's agent in New York, canceling the contracts and making an attempt to rein in the piracy.[25] Heinlein said he was not angry, but he was sorry it should end like this—and Blassingame should bend every effort to get the manuscript for *Methuselah's Children* back.[26] Doubleday had said they would publish it if Shasta were out of the picture.

Double Star was *very* well received, running to almost universal acclaim in *Astounding* in February, March, and April 1956. It was, in fact, so well liked that it was given the Science Fiction Achievement Award as the Best SF Novel of 1956 at the World Science Fiction Convention held the next year in New York.[27] These awards, nicknamed Hugos for the founder of the first science-fiction magazine, Hugo Gernsback, had been given out for only the last few years—the first time in 1953 and then commencing uninterrupted from 1955. They were miniature rocket ships, just over a foot tall, with short, stabilizing fins—just like his original design for the ship in *Destination Moon*!—executed by hand in chrome steel.

Howard Browne had recently changed the format of *Amazing Stories* from pulp to digest-sized magazine[28] and made a proposal: He wanted a "predic-tion" article from Heinlein for the magazine's thirtieth-anniversary issue in April 1956 and offered the astonishing amount of one hundred dollars—an offer Heinlein could not very well refuse. He put it on his work agenda for January, and in November 1955 started to write *Time for the Stars,* about tele-pathic twins recruited to provide communications for exploring starships.

Toward the end of 1955 Heinlein received an advance copy of a book that Morey Bernstein had been researching nearby in Colorado for the last couple of years, *The Search for Bridey Murphy.* Its past-life regression stuff looked interesting—another datum to be filed with J. B. Rhine's books on telepathy, clairvoyance, and other "psychic" phenomena. It was not precisely that he "believed" Bernstein's conclusions in *Bridey Murphy*—but they were compat-ible with his own experience, superficially plausible, and the *kind* of thing that appealed to his sensibilities as a writer. He decided to include something from it in his "prediction" article for *Amazing.*[29]

By the end of January he was generating a new "adult" book. He had an engineer/inventor on a bender because his wife dumped him to marry a rich man. But the elements weren't coming together quite right, and he kept turn-ing them over in his mind, changing a bit here and a bit there and seeing how the fit-together improved.[30] One late January morning at breakfast, Ginny crossed his field of vision, being led-between-the-legs by their cat, Pixie. Bemused, he watched her open a people door for him and wait while Pixie sniffed disdainfully and turned away from the snow, complaining vocally at Ginny's mismanagement of the weather. There were seven people doors leading out, and the same little playlet was reenacted at each door. When Pixie had rejected the last door and stalked away, indignant, Ginny shrugged. "I guess he's looking for the door into summer."

Suddenly, all the jumble of story elements he had been fiddling with fell into place in his head—a completely different configuration, and one that felt perfectly *right*. "Don't say another word," he said. He got up and almost ran to his office, eager to start getting the story down on paper. Thirteen days later, *The Door into Summer* was finished—the shortest length of time he had *ever* taken to write a full (if short) novel—and nearly perfect as it came off his typewriter.[31] Pixie was the missing element; Robert's familial affection for "the old warrior" gave the book its emotive core and tied all the incidents together in another ingratiating, seducing book.

Once the finishing work was done, the Heinleins took an eight-day driving vacation in New Mexico seeing friends in March, making the rounds from Albuquerque to Las Cruces and to Portales, where Jack Williamson lived.[32]

The Door into Summer did not have instant success: John Campbell rejected it through Blassingame, but A. P. White ("Anthony Boucher") picked it up for *The Magazine of Fantasy & Science Fiction*. Blassingame sold the book rights to Doubleday, and that was the last of Heinlein's four-book option contract with them.

Pixie, though, did not live to see "his" book published. He had already contracted uremia, and soon the pain would become unbearable. Months later, in the dead of winter, their neighbor Art Herzberger, a practicing veterinarian, came over and put Blassingame Pixilated Arroyo—The Only Cat—to sleep.[33] Robert used a new shirt for Pixie's winding sheet, and they planted a memorial tree over his gravesite, so that the local coyotes would not dig up the grave. Ginny retired the name. He had been Pixie Three: There would never be another Pixie.[34] Heinlein scheduled some mindless physical labor for himself and installed an irrigation system to prevent having to carry bathwater again, to save Ginny's vegetable garden during droughts.

In February 1956, Heinlein received a check from George Pal Productions: $748.83, and that was his entire proceeds from *Destination Moon*. The production company had gone inactive. That portion of his life was over.

He had several "releases" of a sort that year: In February his mother wrote saying that she no longer needed the "pension" he and the boys were giving her, since Rex's pension from International Harvester had increased. Dad's health was improving, too, and there was a possibility he might make a full recovery.

The experience of writing *The Door into Summer* almost in one straight-through burst ushered in a very productive period for Heinlein. In June 1956, he wrote a Future History story, aimed at *The Saturday Evening Post.* "Jeff and the Menace From Earth" had come off the typewriter at 14,000 words—much too long for *The Post,* so he cut it in five successive drafts to 6,000 words. But *The Post* wasn't in the market, and Blassingame sold it to A. P. White ("Anthony Boucher") for *The Magazine of Fantasy & Science Fiction.*

Heinlein cautioned White that the story might have been cut too much.[35] White asked to see the longer version, which he found so much better that he repurchased the story at novelette length—another reason *F&SF* had turned into the premier SF magazine of the 1950s.

Summer 1956 was, again, a rush of visitors. Lawrence and Kathleen stopped by on their way back from Germany to Kansas City, and Rex Ivar's daughter Lynnie arrived, too, taking them up on Ginny's invitation two years ago to spend the months of July and a week of August with them and continue her lessons in equitation begun with Lucky Herzberger. Lurton Blassingame visited again, and Ginny arranged for him to be able to hunt on a resident's permit.

Leslyn started another round of poison-pen letters. Her letters had become more rambling and more vile over the years.[36] A. P. White made a passing reference to St. Dymphna when he mentioned one of her letters to Heinlein. Heinlein had to look up the reference: St. Dymphna was the patron saint of the mentally afflicted. There was nothing he could do about it, so he tried to put it out of his mind and get on with his own work: "Like her mother, as long as she is alive she is a potential for mischief . . . So, while I shall rest easy and do nothing, I shall not feel entirely easy as long as she remains a potential source of animosity."[37]

Boys' Life still wanted a serial, so he started an interplanetary scout-and-his-dog story early in September. *Boys' Life* picked up "A Tenderfoot on Venus" but wanted it cut to less than 15,000 words for publication in the June and July 1958 issues as "A Tenderfoot in Space."

And then it was time for the annual chore of ginning up another boys' book for Scribner. He was very tired of these, he had told Blassingame on this last hunting trip, and was thinking about getting out of science fiction altogether. Blassingame suggested he stray not too far from his proven strengths—perhaps a modern, contemporary-scene novel about scientists working to make space travel possible.[38] Heinlein routinely followed technical developments in general literature, as well as in the specialized field of science fiction, and recently he had been trying out new techniques that would perhaps not be suitable for science fiction:

> . . . I have been fiddling with experimental methods of storytelling (none of which you have seen) and I am beginning to think that I may be developing a new method which might turn out to be important. It is a multiple first-person technique, but not the one used by John Masters in *Bowhani* [sic: Bhowani] *Junction* [1954, filmed 1956]. Mine calls for using camera cuts and shifts as rapid as those in the movies; the idea is to give the speed of movies, the sense of immediacy of the legitimate stage, and the empathy obtained by stream of consciousness—a nice trick if I can bring it off! The greatest hitch seems to lie in the problem of shifting viewpoints, both without confusing the reader and without losing empathy through cumbersome devices. But I think I am learning how to do it.
>
> I don't want to use this technique on commercial copy until I am sure I can force the reader to go along with a novel technique . . . if I do have here a usable new technique I want to polish it to the point where it can stand up in the open market in competition with the usual wares whose values are established and recognized.
>
> Ginny suggests that I not use it in science fiction in any case, but save it for a lit'rary novel. She has a point, I think, as it would not be seriously reviewed in an S-F novel. We'll see.[39]

The international news turned shocking on October 23, 1956, when Soviet troops occupying Hungary fired into a crowd of demonstrators in Budapest—labor union members agitating for relaxation of the strings on the puppet Nagy government. Labor unions have traditionally been greater enemies of Communists than of capitalists.

At first, the occupying troops—mostly Ukranians who had firsthand experience of Soviet massacres—refused the order to fire on the crowd, and Hungarian independence was declared. The revolution lasted ten days: On November 4, 1956, the Soviet Union rushed in two thousand tanks and two hundred thousand troops to depose the Nagy government. And then the slaughter began: Thirty-five thousand Hungarians were killed by the Soviet troops; thousands more fled the country.

The memory of Soviet Premier Nikita Khrushchev as "the Butcher of

Budapest" made an indelible impression on Heinlein. He had been watching the presidential election campaign with a degree of horror and disgust this year, as the Democratic Party imploded. He wrote to his brother Clare:

> I have witnessed the intellectual bankruptcy of the present Democratic Party and my stomach is still doing slow rolls and wing-overs. The only man I wanted to vote for was Stuart Symington and they never put his name in the hat . . . I am impressed by Mr. [Adlai] Stevenson—I think he has raised sheer stupidity to a high art, to a level of genius not achieved since the late and unlamented Immanuel Kant.[40]

He was not a Republican, but he voted for Eisenhower—probably the least harmful choice that year.[41]

After the election, he started writing *The Chain and the Stars*. Over the years, starting with *The Rolling Stones* in 1952, Alice Dalgliesh had given him contradictory advice about the age of his protagonists. "Miss Dalgliesh was always complaining," Ginny Heinlein recalled, "and Robert got very upset about it. She complained once that the hero was too young and lost the sales to the services; another time, the hero was too old and lost the Boy Scout types—things like that."[42] To Blassingame, Heinlein wrote:

> I can make my central character *any age she wants* at the opening of the story. But it can only be one age. If she will tell me what age she thinks is best for the market, I can tailor the central character of my next book to fit. But I can't make him simultaneously of draft age and of junior high school age. Nor can I keep him from growing up as the story progresses without limiting myself to a simple action story spanning not more than a few weeks. This is difficult to do in space-travel stories—but I can do it if she wants it.[43]

For the new boys' book Heinlein decided to abandon his usual formula and just write an adult novel, leaving out a love interest, and have the protagonist range from preteen to twenty or so. It is not clear when Heinlein began making his outline notes, but they show his book starting with the nursery rhyme quotation "Rich man, poor man, beggar man, thief," and evoking the atmosphere and exotic setting of *The Arabian Nights* and *The Prince and the Pauper*. "Our hero is a beggar-thief in a big city, an orphan brought up by Uncle Jules (no relation) who is his (Oliver Twist's mentor Fagin—maybe)." Another set of notes[44] explores the basic setting of the interstellar trading vessel run by an extended family. Initially his "Dave Devro" is captured by "the space guards, the family broken up, and Dave forced into a school (state) for boys his age. The rest of the book could be concerned with his efforts to break loose, to get his family together, to go out into space again."

But, as had happened before, when Heinlein started writing, the combined story underwent a transformation—this time into a passionate anti-slavery book inspired, perhaps, by the recent Hungarian revolution. His Thorby is bought as a slave boy of ten or eleven, freed, and searches for the meaning of his life in his extended families of trading ship *Sisu* and of the Hegemonic Guard space navy—and then the birth family he had lost long ago. At each stage Thorby learns to value and protect wider social values, from family to the whole of his civilization. But even restored to his planet and place of birth, he cannot rest until he brings all his resources to bear in the fight against slavery—the passion of his first adoptive father, the beggar who had bought a scared slave boy and raised him as a son. *Citizen of the Galaxy* is Heinlein's most wrenching exploration of the young adult's individuation crisis, and Thorby's relationship to his family values—multiply layered—is a finely nuanced statement of what it means to become an adult and a true citizen.[45]

The book was written over a three-week period from November 12 to December 8, 1956, with four alternative titles, but when he had the manuscript professionally retyped for submission, he gave it a new name: *Citizen of the Galaxy*.

Early in January 1957, Heinlein received a glowing review of *Time for the Stars* by Hermann Deutsch, one of the editors of the *New Orleans Item*. In correspondence, Heinlein and Deutsch discovered they had mutual acquaintances (including the Bill Deutsch Heinlein had met at Denvention in 1941 and since lost track of). Deutsch invited Robert and Ginny to stay with them when next they were in New Orleans.

That fall and winter of 1956 Ginny had been suffering from a case of amebic dysentery—contracted, she said, from wild watercress served at a garden party by a local chef who really ought to have known better.[46] The doctors found a Giardia colonization as well (a different brand of parasite). Possibly she had had it for years, since their visit to Java in 1954, and the watercress incident had just brought it out. Possibly it was contracted from the "filthy water" supply in Colorado Springs (about which the new Air Force Academy was already complaining to the city).[47] On top of the dysentery, her chronic bursitis, left over from her basic training in 1943, flared up. This time the pain was incapacitating, despite treatment with Novocaine, codeine, cortisone, heat, and massage. A hot, dry climate might help, so Robert decided to take her to the desert after he fulfilled a commitment to give a lecture in Chicago.[48]

Mark Reinsberg, the Chicago fan who had gotten him involved with Shasta in 1948, was now teaching a night-school class in writing at the University of Chicago. He asked Heinlein to be part of a lecture series he was organizing for his writing class—not something Heinlein would ordinarily do (and the honorarium of $50 would not even cover expenses)[49]—but he agreed this time, and this lecture, to be delivered at the beginning of February 1957, was on his mind all that winter. The last time he had written such a thing was ten years earlier, the 1947 essay written just after the breakup with Leslyn, which had been published as "On the Writing of Speculative Fiction." At that time, there was not one word of formal SF criticism in print—though both Gernsback and Campbell had talked here and there about the theory of science fiction in their magazine editorials over a period of more than twenty years, and important scholarly groundwork, such as bibliographies, appeared earlier, notably in A. Langley Searles's fanzine *Fantasy Commentator*.[50] But it is J. O. Bailey's *Pilgrims Through Time and Space,* published in 1947, which is regarded as the start of science-fiction criticism.[51]

During the 1950s, there had been a blossoming of thinking about science-fiction theory and criticism, mostly mediated by fanzines or the SF magazines themselves (there being no professional or academic journals willing to print essays on science fiction), and the beginnings of the development of critical standards for science fiction. Heinlein followed the entire development from J. O. Bailey's *Pilgrims through Space and Time* and E. F. Bleiler's *Checklist of Fantastic Literature* (1948)[52] through de Camp's *Science Fiction Handbook* (1952) and the latest (and most influential), Damon Knight's *In Search of Wonder* (1956). What Heinlein had been doing for some time was not genre science fiction by the strict standards of early pulp—which is why Heinlein had originally begun to use the term "speculative fiction": His focus from the start was in general literature rather than in genre science fiction. The hurdle he had been helping his librarians over was the idea that SF, being pulp in its origins, was *escape literature*. In a letter to a librarian concerned to develop purchasing standards for science fiction two years earlier, Heinlein wrote:

This genre is *not* a sub-genre of adventure fiction (even though many of the tales in it are adventurous) . . . This field is concerned with new ideas, new possibilities, new ways of looking at things . . . which is precisely why it is so attractive to young people and so little read by older people, i.e., read only by those who have kept their minds young. Now if a story does not take the cultural framework we live in, stretch it, twist it, turn it upside down and examine it for leaks, rearrange the parts and see how they would relate in a new arrangement—in short, explore possibilities and play games with ideas—it is not really a story of this genre at all but merely a western translated into the wider open spaces of the stars.[53]

At its best, science fiction tried to get its readers to *engage* reality at the highest levels. "Imaginary-but-possible" meant that science fiction was a branch of *realistic* literature, also distinguished from contemporary-scene fiction that had wandered (too far in his opinion) in the James M. Cain direction of Zola-esque realism: "[S]peculative fiction is much more realistic than is most historical and contemporary scene fiction and is superior to them both."[54] He wrote the bulk of the lecture, titled "Does Science Fiction Have Any Virtue?" on February 5, 1957, and two days later flew to Chicago. He had a quick meeting with Erle Korshak, who promised to turn over a new leaf—and who knows, perhaps the horse will fly?

The morning of the lecture, February 8, Heinlein gave a radio interview for WFMT, with interviewer Bob Luefley. In the afternoon, after a lunch with Miss Harshaw at the Arts Club, he taped *Carnival of Books* at the WMAQ radio studios. *Time for the Stars* was getting him a lot of good press: Even Learned Bulman liked it in his *Library Journal* review.[55]

The lecture that evening went very well, with a question-and-answer period following, in which Heinlein had an opportunity to discuss the making of *The Puppet Masters*.[56] After the taping, a local fan (and another friend of Mark Reinsberg's), Earl Kemp, arranged for a pub crawl of the local strip clubs. On Saturday, Heinlein met with the University of Chicago Science Fiction Club and was given a reception with local professional colleagues at Mark Reinsberg's house. Fritz Leiber, who was living in Chicago at that time, memorialized the occasion with a clever sonnet, working a number of Heinlein's titles into the rhyme scheme:

For Bob Heinlein

> Bob, here's to say we're deeply in your debt
> For letting us raise ship with Starman Jones
> And share the training of Space Cadet;
> For introductions to The Rolling Stones;
> For Farmer in the Sky and "Goldfish Bowl,"
> "If This Goes On—" (Thank God, it has so far!)
> Red Planet, "Waldo," "They," "The Roads Must Roll,"

Methuselah's Children, *"Life-Line,"* Double Star.
Thanks, Bob, again, for all these fancy trips,
For "Misfit," "Universe" and "Common Sense,"
For "Blowups Happen," "The Long Watch," ("Eclipse");
They're luxury cruises, sparing no expense;
There aint a finer (this I testify)
Door into Summer, Tunnel in the Sky.

Fritz Leiber
2-8-57

Heinlein flew back to Colorado Springs the next day, then went for a desert rest-up with Ginny.

Their base of operation for the next three weeks was the Arrowhead Motel in Nogales, Arizona—baking warm even in February. Robert set up his portable typewriter in peace and caught up on correspondence while Ginny recovered from her bout of bursitis. They visited with Heinlein's science-fiction colleagues Fredric Brown and Stuart and Mildred Clingerman and made their leisurely way back home early in March by way of the Stines in Las Cruces, New Mexico.

They arrived back in Colorado Springs on March 13, just in time to be snowed in and housebound. Ginny's bursitis was better, but she was very wobbly on her feet, and so dizzy when she got out of bed that she could hardly stand or walk. Her doctors diagnosed a bizarre late-onset menthol allergy and Shigella bacillary dysentery on top of the Giardia—somewhat alarming, since Shigella had an 18 percent mortality rate. She had probably had a subacute infestation for some time. Robert probably had it, too, since he was feeling draggy and "full of vague aches," which he had attributed to advancing old age.[57] He took the cure with Ginny.

But he was able to work. Being with Ruth Harshaw and her bright, earnest teenaged co-interviewers must have given him a lift, restoring his enthusiasm for the juvenile series: "my stuff for kids is the most important work that I do . . . I hope to keep it up a long time."[58] He seemed to be contributing in a minor way to relieving the crisis in technical education: Kids need to know what tools they need. "I feel a degree of obligation to the kids," he told an educator who wrote him in enthusiasm for *Tunnel in the Sky.* "Therefore, no matter how much cops & robbers I put into such a story, I always get in a plug for technical training in general and for study of mathematics in particular."[59]

At the beginning of March 1957, a group of science-fiction writers launched a mimeographed professionals' discussion magazine, *SF Forum.* Heinlein would

never be comfortable with the sniping and backbiting contained in this kind
of fanzine-for-professionals, but other writers did not have his reticence about
slamming their colleagues in print—and Heinlein was the biggest target
around. James Blish used *The Door into Summer* to kick off an amateur psychoanalysis of Heinlein as seen through the lens of his many first-person
narratives—impertinent, infuriating, and imprudent.[60] "Any writer learns to
expect unfavorable reviews," Heinlein wrote directly to Lester del Rey, the
editor of *SF Forum*:

> he must accept them, along with bad weather, flat tires, and other such.
> Any professional writer is aware that his published work is open to public
> literary criticism within the limits of the "Fair Comment" rule.
>
> But it seems to me that this article is only secondarily a review, not liter-
> ary criticism at all in most of its details, and is primarily a vehicle for *per-
> sonal* criticism, improper where true and much worse than improper where
> false . . . .
>
> The prudent thing to do was probably to keep quiet and try to forget it.
>
> But I found that I was not forgetting it, that it was on my mind, interfer-
> ing with work, preventing sleep. I felt as if I had been invited to tea, then
> sandbagged as I walked in the door.[61]

Blish's notions about what a critic could infer directly about the psychology of
a writer—of Heinlein, at any rate—were wrong: The "unconscious" effects
Blish was trying to analyze were storytelling devices; Blish did not seem to be
able to tell artifice from accident.

> None of these things is done "by instinct." I sweat like hell to make it a
> rousing good story while getting in the preaching I want to preach. . . . I
> suggest that to the extent that they are used unconsciously, unwittingly
> "instinctively," they are sloppy craftsmanship and likely to be bad art.[62]

There were four "themes" he did use over and over—deliberately and not "by
instinct":

> One is the notion that knowledge is worth acquiring, all knowledge, and
> that a solid grounding in mathematics provides one with the essential lan-
> guage of many of the most important forms of knowledge. The third theme
> is that, while it is desirable to live peaceably, there are things worth fighting
> for and values worth dying for—and that it is far better for a man to die

than to live under circumstances that call for such sacrifice. The fourth
theme is that individual human freedoms are of basic value, without which
mankind is less than human.[63]

After weighing the worthwhileness of raising a fight over this issue, he concluded not this time—but:

> . . . a more temperate tone would, I think, bring higher respect, as well as
> being kinder. Horace, Tony, Larry, John, Bob, etc.,[64] are all doing the best
> they can; give them credit for honest effort.
>
> The above remarks apply even more strongly to the writers. I myself am
> one of the lucky ones who never has any trouble in selling; science fiction
> has paid me so well that my only financial problems in years has been [sic]
> where and how to spend it all—so all of you are invited to lambast my sto-
> ries to your heart's content, so long as you stick to the rule of "Fair Com-
> ment" and leave my private life and personality out of it. I won't care very
> deeply what you say; the literary criticisms I am interested in come from
> my agent, my editors, from librarians, and from the mail of unorganized
> fans—the general reading public. But my relatively well-armored state is
> not enjoyed by many writers; I know, from the dozens of aspirant and
> beginning-to-sell writers I have worked with that the relatively insecure
> writer is just a mass of raw nerve ends. Unfavorable criticism, to be of any
> use to him at all, *must* be couched in thoughtful language, temperate tones,
> and so phrased that he can use it to do better next time. If he is simply
> lashed, ridiculed, held up to scorn, it does him no good at all—on the con-
> trary it is likely to make it impossible for him to write for days on end.
>
> I suggest that it never helps anyone to tell a mother that her baby is
> ugly.[65]

John Campbell took *Citizen of the Galaxy* for serialization in *Astounding* in
a long letter concerned with the sociology of chattel slavery, concluding:

> You know, Bob, I'm tempted to retitle that story of yours "The Slave." Thorby
> was a slave every paragraph of the way—including the last. Margaret pointed
> out his slavery in the Free Traders; Wing Marshall Smith pointed out his
> slavery in the end.[66]

It took several exchanges of correspondence, and a small modification to
the text, to get Campbell off the focus on slavery and onto citizenship.

Puh*lease* don't change the name of "Citizen." I admit that there is a modicum of "There is no freedom" in the yarn; but that is not my theme—my basic theme is that all creatures everywhere are constrained by their circumstances but that a mature creature (that is to say, a "citizen") faces up to the constraints in a mature fashion, not evading, not ducking, not taking the easy way. This certainly does not make him a slave even though it may require of him a self-discipline more stringent than the externally-imposed discipline of a slave . . . .

But the most important point is that the trade book will use that title and I don't want a single customer to buy the trade book under a misapprehension. If you must change the title, talk it over with Scribner's and settle between you on a mutually agreed title—but only one title. Call it "Uncle Tom's Cabin in the Sky" if you both agree on it. I just want to play fair with the cash customers.[67]

Campbell asked him to add the phrase "citizen of the galaxy" into the text at some point, to clarify his aims,[68] and Heinlein made the requested change.[69]

But the Scribner edit of this book was going off the rails, as well: Dalgliesh had made some minor cuts—a reference to Grandmother *Sisu* being shocked at pinup pictures; Baslim's dismissal of the state religion of Jubbalpore—and in her accompanying letter she wanted to cut, too, the reference to "girlie magazines" used as trade goods.[70] There was a certain amount of . . . *sensitivity* . . . on this subject at this time, particularly in New York state, due to the recent furor over violent and gory comic books.

This was trivial, by comparison to the *Red Planet* fight. He started a letter giving permission for the changes, though he could not *approve* of them. He did not see the *point* of these changes. Was a reference to grandmothers not always seeing eye to eye with their junior bachelors and their chosen entertainments really all that offensive? And as for the Jubbalpore religion—

This state religion is a vicious thing, upholding slavery, permitting gladiatorial combat, setting up the emperor as a god or demi-god with divine attributes . . . so what should I do? Show the old man teaching the kid to respect this religion?[71]

Argue he might; ask for rational explanations he might; but he knew it was ultimately futile. Dalgliesh was watching out for his interests as a commercial writer: *Any* appearance of questioning religion (*any* religion, even his made-up one) would draw down hellfire from librarians and teachers and parents.

By the time he finished with the letter, he wanted to revoke the sale and get the manuscript back from Scribner—but they had already set it in type, incurring production expenses.

Ginny was appalled when he showed her the letter and made him rewrite it.[72] He struggled with several drafts of a more diplomatic version. One pencil draft begins "[m]ake any changes you wish" and continues "I have never been in sympathy with this policy of catering to the smugly self-righteous prejudices of the ignorant and the half-educated in an attempt to sell more books . . ."[73] (Diplomacy was, apparently, a moving target.) Finally he produced a sixth draft, a blunt, one-page letter, which he forwarded to Blassingame for comment and so that Blassingame would know how seriously this conflict was affecting him. "This whole matter has been growing in my mind for years and yet it is so vexatiously difficult that I can't see any good answer."[74] In a later letter to Blassingame, he talked more about the upset the conflict had engendered in him:

> I know I have not made clear why two changes, admittedly easy and unimportant, threw me into spin and lost me ten days' working time, cum much anguish. I don't know that I *can* explain it, but it is true. Part of the reason lies in that Chicago lecture of mine you recently read; I necessarily write science fiction by one theory, the theory of extrapolation and change—but once it reaches the editor (in this case) it is tested by an older theory, the notion that this our culture is essentially perfect and I *must not* tinker with any part of it which is dear to any possible critic who may see the story. These things have now added up to the point where I feel unable to continue. I *may* write another. I don't know yet. I can't until some of the depression wears off. But I don't know how to tell her that I probably won't deliver the story she is expecting—I've tried six or eight times, wasted many days, and all the ways I can express it either sound rude or inadequate. I know this sounds silly but it is true . . . .[75]

It was probably a good thing Ginny was feeling well enough to intercept his rants. Her health was improving, though slowly. She sometimes felt up to gardening—and they were able to go out sometimes, for dinner. The doctors had found another intestinal infestation and a cyst on her scalp that would have to be removed surgically in June. The cyst might be contributing to her debilitating facial neuralgia, and that would relieve some of the pain—but her balance might be gone permanently: She might never be able to skate again.

Heinlein's own health had improved: He had a physical on his fiftieth birthday, and his heart was in good shape. Nor was his professional life *all* frustration: Martin Greenberg at Gnome Press offered him a contract for *Methuselah's Children*. Now that Shasta was going out of business, Gnome was one of only two specialty presses left in the science-fiction field. Greenberg wanted one or two collections of Heinlein's short stories.

The Magazine of Fantasy & Science Fiction brought out "The Menace from Earth" in its August issue, and a new magazine, *Saturn,* bought "The Man Who Traveled in Elephants" in October—a sentimental favorite he had written nine years before and had never been able to sell. The seller's market for science fiction was helping to reduce his backfile.

As to the juveniles—"I feel I have reached an impasse in this branch of fiction," he had told Blassingame in May.[76] But in one of his discarded draft letters to Alice Dalgliesh the next day, he told her,

> You can edit me because you're better at it than I am; other editors I won't allow to change anything because they're not. In short I want to go on writing boy's books and I want to write them for you.
>
> But unless I can get this worked out I probably won't be writing them for anybody.[77]

The problem was not resolved, but timing was forcing his hand: If Heinlein was going to do another boys' book in 1957, he would have to start it soon: He planned to be traveling over the holidays—the Far East and India this time (he was finally going to achieve a life's ambition and see the Taj Mahal in person—by moonlight if he could manage it).

He began turning over material in his mind. On the evidence of what wound up in the book, he found his story material in what was topical. "Juvenile delinquency" was in the news and editorial pages, but that was not the kind of book Heinlein had been writing. On the personal front, his neighbor, Lucky Herzberger, was still thanking them profusely for "teaching" their daughter, Barbara, how to read over one weekend visit while Lucky and Art were out of town—but that was absurd: Ginny had simply handed her a book one day, and Barbara began reading on her own.[78] What that might say about local schools really didn't bear thinking about, but Heinlein was more or less forced to think about it when he went to a large newsstand downtown looking for a copy of *Scientific American*. He could not find one copy—the stand had sold the three it took—but he counted *twenty* astrology magazines.[79]

Heinlein framed all his concerns about intellectually-soggy American youth in a story about a space-struck boy accidentally prepared to take advantage of the slings and arrows fate threw at him amid the game shows and jingle contests that made up American television in the 1950s—and let the boy stand up as a proud representative of humanity in a kangaroo court of aliens. He titled his book *Have Space Suit—Will Travel.*[80] The title had plot significance, of course—in fact, that *was* the plot for the first several chapters.

Heinlein did his usual careful research and preparation—sizes of various galaxies, surface temperatures on planets, calculating travel times to Pluto and beyond. At one point, he needed to know the volume of air an empty space suit would contain, and did the calculations. But the answer didn't seem right to him, so he took his worksheets to Ginny. She did a completely independent calculation that came closer to what he thought it should be. It didn't seem to be the arithmetic that was at fault: Comparing their worksheets, they traced the difference to a single critical figure. He had used the figure in *Marks' Standard Handbook for Mechanical Engineers,* the handbook he had learned engineering with at the Naval Academy and had used ever since. Ginny had taken hers from the *Chemical & Rubber Company Handbook,* the chemist's traditional sourcebook. The CRC clearly had the right figure: Robert penciled the correction into his *Marks'* and wrote them a letter (and found the figure corrected in the next edition).[81] After that he would not rely on a single source for critical figures.

Ginny also helped out by composing a musical "speech" for the Mother Thing, a music-speaking "beat cop," with Robert looking over her shoulder and with a veto: He didn't want it to sound like anything human. Together they got the effect he was after. The whole book was a pleasure for both of them—". . . pure fun all the way through."[82]

Heinlein finished *Have Space Suit—Will Travel* on August 30, 1957, just as the first installment of *Citizen of the Galaxy* began to run in *Astounding.* While he was tightening up the manuscript, his Hollywood agent, Ned Brown, forwarded an offer for him to script Herman Wouk's *The Lomokome Papers* (1947), a science-fiction satire of the Cold War, about a naval lieutenant's trip to a hollow moon. But he was able to turn it down with a clear conscience: He had already paid a nonrefundable deposit for their sailing date in November. At least this proved there was some activity in Ned Brown's office. He put off the question of switching agents in Hollywood for another time.[83]

GOING OFF A BIT

On October 4, 1957, the Russians launched an earth-orbiting satellite, Sputnik 1, a twenty-two-inch metal sphere with four whip antennas, broadcasting a continuous *beep-beep-beep* as it sped across the sky completing an orbit in ninety-six minutes. "I am very shook up," Robert told Buddy Scoles, ". . . on the basis of payload and performance . . . it appeared that they [the Russians] had solved the problem of precision positioning and that it must be assumed that we were sitting ducks . . ."[1] The Eisenhower administration, he went on to say, had dropped the ball—badly: ". . . everybody from the President on down was caught flat-footed by a degree of Russian engineering achievement we had not suspected they were capable of."[2]

After the initial postwar flush of enthusiasm for guided missiles, funding in the United States for basic research had been cut back, and progress had reached a virtual standstill. The promise of space travel, that had been piggybacked on missile development, was deferred and deferred—and now the Russians had seized their opportunity. When Robert's phone rang that morning, it was the local newspaper wanting him to tell them what Sputnik really meant.

> I told the press that if the Russians could put that payload in that orbit then it seemed extremely likely that they could hit us anywhere they wanted to with warheads—and any time, depending on whether they had the hardware on the shelf or had to stop to build it.[3]

Heinlein spent the next month, while Sputnik beeped overhead for twenty-three days, trying to round up a new job for G. Harry Stine, who had been summarily fired by Martin Company (predecessor to today's Lockheed-Martin) for saying much the same thing to United Press when asked, just an hour after Heinlein spoke with the local press in Colorado Springs. Heinlein also dedicated the book he was working on—*Have Space Suit—Will Travel*—to Hank and Barbie Stine.

Shortly after Sputnik went silent, the Russians did it again, launching Sputnik 2 into Earth orbit, with a dog as "passenger." "Sputnik" means "traveling companion." The papers dubbed this one "Muttnik," but no one was laughing. Robert sent A. P. White a characteristic bit of doggerel on the subject that showed how he was leaning, "with apologies to Robert Herrick":

> *Gather ye rosebuds while ye may*
> *Old Sputnik's still a-flying.*
> *For while we still are here today,*
> *Tomorrow we'll be dying.*[4]

The Heinleins left Colorado Springs a little early to have a few days with Robert's brother in Palo Alto and a few days more at the Mark Hopkins in San Francisco, where he could hook up with Robert Cornog and A. P. White. White had lined up a number of his Bay Area colleagues to meet, including Poul Anderson, and a relative newcomer, Philip K. Dick.

They sailed on the S.S. *President Monroe* at noon on November 26, and were surprised to find a telegram waiting for them on the ship—from Margaret Sanger. "Delighted to learn from Lloyd Morain [a friend of Ginny's] you arriving Honolulu. Please phone me Reef Hotel[.] Many mutual interests to discuss."[5] That was more like a summons for a command performance from one of the true royals of the century. Margaret Sanger, just a couple of months younger than Heinlein's mother, was one of the pivotal figures in the birth control and planned parenthood movements; had smuggled diaphragms into the country in bottles of brandy when it could still mean a jail term; was the scandalous lover of both H. G. Wells and Havelock Ellis. Her *What Every Girl Should Know* and *What Every Mother Should Know,* distributed as Haldeman-Julius Little Blue Books, were virtually the only reliable sex information widely available when Heinlein was growing up. Her good-socialist opinions about eugenics and population control had deeply influenced his—particularly her opinion that war was driven by excess population.

They met Sanger for lunch in Waikiki. Her energy at age seventy-seven was astonishing: She was planning to open family planning clinics in India that year, and in Italy—right in the Pope's teeth.[6] She also must have had the constitution of an ox: She had brandy after brandy all afternoon. Ginny stopped drinking relatively early (she didn't much care for brandy), but Heinlein got spliffed matching her drink for drink.[7] "It was a little like meeting Santa

Claus or some other semi-mythical creature," Heinlein told Alice Dalgliesh, who also knew Sanger.[8]

Dalgliesh's initial reaction to *Have Space Suit—Will Travel* was very enthusiastic (though she bizarrely thought it must be a "spoof" of some kind), but by now she was moving on to pettifogging details. One request for an edit he had to think about—over a *very* rough Pacific crossing: *three* typhoons and into the eye of Tropical Storm Nina to succor a Greek freighter in distress. Coming out was even rougher: The ship rolled over 43 degrees. Thanks to Bonamine, the new motion-sickness drug, he weathered the crisis without an attack of seasickness (never a problem for Ginny).

Dalgliesh wanted him to soften the scene where Kip stamps on a Wormface skull. Ultimately he decided *not* to make the revision, explaining

> The United States is today in the greatest peril in its history and I do not think we have better than an even chance of living, as a nation, through the next five years—and I am convinced that our present terrible peril has been brought on in large measure by weak-stomached ladies of both sexes, tender-minded creatures who fear fighting more than they fear slavery. This boy is fighting bare-handed against a truly evil creature, not only for his own life but for the life of a small female of his own species. He fights in terror and in great physical repugnance—but he fights, he is heroic.
>
> I don't want to reduce that scene to cardboard. It is honest the way it is. Alice, the time is very short, we may have lost already, and I don't ever want to pull my punches again.[9]

They arrived in Yokohama days late and decided to stay in Japan and fly to join the ship later, in Hong Kong. General Smith, a longtime friend and the commander of the U.S. Forces in Japan, put a car and driver at their disposal while they were there. The special treatment they received might also have been a compliment to Robert's brother, Larry, who had been one of the first Americans in Japan at the end of World War II. While they were there, General Smith invited them as the only civilian guests at an elaborate military staff dinner party—a true Lucullan feast, with pheasants roasted whole and put back into their feathers, and a *piéce monté* ice-cream dessert in the shape of Mt. Fuji, which the waiters flamed and put in eruption.

It was almost a shame to fly to Hong Kong, which was crowded with refugees fleeing Indonesia.[10] While in a Hong Kong night club, Robert and Ginny essayed a tango—a dance he particularly loved—and were congratulated by a ship's officer—the chief mate—of a British freighter in port. Robert stood him a drink, and one thing led to another. He brought his captain over, and on being assured that Ginny was broad-minded, the captain brought over their "dates," a couple of working girls, and they had a party. They had no language in common, but somehow managed to piece together the girls' story—swimming across the Kowloon Strait to get out of Communist China. When the officers found out who Robert was, they treated him and Ginny to champagne, which flattered his ego: Nobody on the *President Monroe* read science fiction, so he had "passed" without being recognized.[11]

The next morning he visited the freighter at their request, for tea and to autograph their first (British) editions of his books in their ship's library.

They arrived in Singapore late on Christmas (after Heinlein played Santa Claus in traditional red, fur-lined suit for the children on board the S.S. *President Monroe*). "The Santa Claus suit I'm to wear," he had told Lurton Blassingame a few days earlier, "encloses me completely—mask, beard, stocking cap, and heavy suit—in this weather. I have Santaclaustrophobia."[12] But Ginny said, "He did it beautifully."[13]

They were astonished the next day when the doorman at Raffles greeted them by name, as if the three years since they had been there last never were (unfortunately, they did not get the incomparable Foo as their floor boy this time).

They had a blissful five days in Singapore. They were immediately invited by the ever-generous Hos to their twenty-fifth wedding anniversary. Bearing as their hostess gift a basketful of orchids which Heinlein said "looked like something fit for a gangster's funeral," they arrived at a large, formal Chinese banquet. "The room held its breath when we sat down, to see whether we could handle chopsticks. We both picked them up and used them like old hands, so there was a sigh of relief around the room—we weren't barbarians after all."[14]

Next was a flight to Bangkok. They wanted to go on to Angkor Wat, but the flights were all oversold, so they extended their stay in Thailand. The water at their hotel was so bad—directly out of the klongs without any kind of filtration at all—that they bought bottled water and bathed together in that, soaping themselves with one bottle and rinse-showering with the next several. On New Year's Eve, the *President Monroe* sailed up the west coast of the Malay peninsula to Penang and then made a leisurely way to Bombay. From there, they were to fly to Delhi and proceed by hired car to Agra.

They saw hundreds of people—possibly thousands—sleeping on the streets in Bombay. We have become inured—somewhat—to the homeless, but in 1958, this was shocking and disgusting to an American's sensibilities.[15]

Even the Taj was a letdown for them: The famous reflecting pool was filled with green slime, and the Arabic inscriptions inlaid into the marble were unexpected and unsettling.[16]

The next leg of the trip—to Karachi, through the Suez Canal and up to Naples by way of Port Said and Alexandria—did not leave much of an impression by comparison to India. They left the ship in Naples because Robert had arranged to meet Cal Laning there while the *President Monroe* went on to Marseilles. They did make some planned side trips: Robert particularly loved Florence. They arrived just at sundown, and it was dark by the time they checked in. Robert was reluctant to tackle a new city at night, but Ginny dragged him into the narrow streets, and they were soon lost—

—and turned a corner into a square and I was staring right straight at the Cellini's Perseus and not so much as a velvet rope to keep me from walking right up to it and touching it—which I did, feeling breathless!

And right next to it the Rape of the Sabines. Not copies—the real thing.

Ginny soon had a crowd of the locals around them giving directions in a macaronic mix of Latin and French cognates, since none of them spoke English.

No matter, we got a personally guided tour and ate dinner with them all . . . and by the time the evening was over she was talking a bastard, uninflected Italiano but with excellent accent. This is why I will go anywhere without a guide; I'm married to one.[17]

In Vienna they danced to "The Beautiful Blue Danube" waltz where it was invented, so gracefully that the local dancers cleared the floor to watch them.[18]

Ginny succumbed to a bladder infection—not incapacitating, but not very comfortable, even with morphine and Demerol. They were more than ready to rejoin the ship in Genoa on February 4 for passage back to New York, where they stayed with the Blassingames and saw *My Fair Lady*. Dalgliesh asked Ginny to come along to a story conference. *Have Space Suit* was already in production, but Dalgliesh was still trying to get Robert to soften it: She objected to the very last scene, where Kip throws a malted milk into the face of a jerk who had been heckling him. She must have thought Ginny would support her objection, but Ginny told her bluntly she didn't see anything wrong with it: It was a good ending for the book—it certainly showed the boy's character change in the most graphic possible way.[19]

The book stayed "as is."

Ginny's bladder infection wasn't getting any better. Robert had business to attend to—instituting the suit against Shasta—but he put her on a DC7 bound for Colorado Springs. "Crashed in Kansas," she wired him from the Biltmore on February 28, "came in by dog sled love. Ginny."

Blassingame had received an inquiry for *The Puppet Masters* from a Hollywood lawyer—but he wanted rights for a one-hour television show of the book, which both Heinlein and Blassingame doubted could reasonably be made. Blassingame turned this offer down by setting the option price too high for television, but about right for a film option: $7,500.

Heinlein also made a "promotional" stop at a fan meeting of the Eastern Science Fiction Association in Newark, New Jersey, in February 1958, where he had a chance to meet with Sprague de Camp, Willy Ley, and Cyril Kornbluth. Kornbluth took the opportunity to stir up bad blood: When he congratulated Robert on winning a Hugo Award for *Double Star,* Heinlein did not know anything about it—did not even know it had been nominated.[20] Kornbluth said, "What? You mean Ackerman didn't give it to you?!?"[21] This was just mischief-making on Kornbluth's part, as it appears that *no one* had accepted the award for him and it simply took more than six months for the statuette to get to Heinlein. But it added fuel to Heinlein's resentment of Ackerman that would never be set straight in his lifetime.

From New York Heinlein took a train to Washington, D.C.,[22] and then flew to Chicago for a conference with a lawyer about the suit against Shasta— the only option he could see to get them to stop selling rights out from under him they didn't own. The attorney—who also represented the *Chicago Tribune* and therefore had some expertise on publishing issues—was doubtful about the clear-cutness of some of the contract issues, and that took some of the wind out of Heinlein's sails. "So I am resigned to continuing this guerilla warfare indefinitely, without going to law, unless some change occurs which strengthens my position."[23]

The visit was capped off with a case of the end-of-winter cold going around Chicago. He was glad to fly back to Colorado Springs early in March 1958, and he recuperated while Ginny recuperated also from a case of flu. Damon Knight wrote that Cyril Kornbluth had suddenly dropped dead, after shoveling snow out of his driveway, on March 21, 1958. Knight was soliciting contributions for Kornbluth's widow, who was virtually penniless. Robert made out a check automatically—then stopped Ginny from sending it. He was essentially a stranger to Kornbluth's family, and he had no idea whether they would be willing to accept charity from a stranger. He contacted the artist Ed Emshwiller, who was in a better position to know the Kornbluths and their situation, and sent the check to him instead, to forward it if it seemed appropriate. A note of condolences went to Mary Kornbluth directly. A year later, Emshwiller wrote saying that he had given her the check.[24]

Around the end of March 1958, Heinlein took out the *Man from Mars* manuscript that had crashed on at least three previous occasions. The manuscript was about 54,000 words long, and he had gotten his characters out of the clutches of the government, but the story had just stopped moving for him the last time he had worked on it, in 1955. At the time, he told Blassingame, "Ginny says that it cannot be salvaged, and I necessarily use her as a touchstone. Still worse, I suspect that she is right; I was never truly happy with it, despite a strong and novel theme."[25] He gave the manuscript a new title, *The Heretic,* prepared to write through his block with the story.[26]

On the morning of April 5, 1958, Ginny broke a house rule and woke him early. He normally worked late into the night when everything was quiet enough to develop perfect concentration, which meant he often did not rise until noon or later. This morning Ginny was grim, but wouldn't say what was wrong. He had never been a morning person and wasn't good for anything until his second cup of coffee anyway.[27] He bathed and dressed and sat down at the table Ginny had rolled out laden with his morning bacon and eggs. She put down before him the local newspaper, the *Colorado Springs Gazette-Telegraph,* turned to a full-page ad, and waited for him to finish reading.

A "Committee for a SANE Nuclear Policy" wanted to wallpaper the White House with petitions for a unilateral halt to American nuclear testing. He started a slow burn as he finished the ad. That day, he described his reaction to Lurton Blassingame.

> Ginny and I read it and felt sick. I've hardly stopped shaking all day. In beautifully persuasive language this committee proposes that we simply surrender to the sort of "disarmament" that the Kremlin has proposed ever since the end of World War II. It reminds me of the Oxford Oath and the "You Can Do Business With Hitler" and the Munich "Peace in Our Time" sell-out of the 'thirties. Can't those bloody fools see that there is no point in rely[ing] on the "honor" of the Butcher of Budapest? Don't they know that lambs don't sign vegetarian treaties with lions? Can't they figure out that if

warfare is limited to old-fashioned "humane" weapons then 170,000,000 are certain to lose against a combine of over a billion?

Apparently not.[28]

At the very least, these proposals would concede the entire ground for negotiations to the Soviets and cripple the United States' negotiating position—to say nothing of the misery and despair the whole human race would be plunged into if Stalin's successors were not prevented from reenacting Budapest in hundreds of cities all over the world.

"And what are we going to do about it?" Ginny demanded.[29]

There was only one thing you could do: it was time to ante up—your lives, your fortunes, your sacred honor, one per customer. He went into his study[30] and worked up the text of a short call to arms—a full-page ad of their own for the *Gazette-Telegraph*:

WHO ARE THE HEIRS OF PATRICK HENRY?
STAND UP AND BE COUNTED!

Is life so dear, or peace so sweet, as to be purchased at the price of chains and slavery? Forbid it, Almighty God! I know not what course others may take, but as for me, give me liberty, or give me death!

—Patrick Henry[31]

In about 2,200 words, Heinlein laid out the meaning of the SANE ad in its historical context, showing how the ad reflected the Stalinist line.

> This follows the pattern of a much-used and highly-refined Communist tactic: plan ahead to soften up the free world on some major point, package the propaganda to appeal to Americans with warm hearts and soft heads, time the release carefully, then let the suckers carry the ball while the known Communists stay under cover . . . .
>
> These proposals are not a road to world peace, they are abject surrender to tyranny. If we fall for them, then in weeks or months or a few years at most, Old Glory will be hauled down for the last time and the whole planet will be ruled by the Butchers of Budapest.

There is no solution, Heinlein said, except the hard one of supporting the liberal values America stands for in world history—freedom as against tyranny, a choice offered again to each generation: It would mean decades of weary, unremitting work, and higher taxes, but "The risks . . . can be reduced only by making the free world so strong that the evil pragmatists of Communism cannot afford to murder us." He continued, urging anyone not in Colorado Springs to start a local chapter of a "Patrick Henry League":

> You are a free citizen, you need no permission, nor any charter from us. Run an ad—quote or copy this one if you like. Dig down in the sock to pay for it, or pass the hat, or both—but sound the call in your own home town, mail copies of your ad out of town, and get some more letters started toward Washington.
>
> And let us hear from you!

And it concluded with a form letter addressed to the president.

Even in a local paper a full page is expensive. But money was not the only cost of this act: "You do realize," Ginny said to Robert, "if we run this ad we're going to lose half our friends in town?"[32]

They went to the newspaper office in downtown Colorado Springs. The advertising manager hesitated when she saw the piece and sent them to talk to the editor, Robert LeFevre, who read through the copy line by line, nodding pleased agreement until he got to the last lines, the part about gladly paying higher taxes, and his smile evaporated instantly. That sentence—not so very different from President John F. Kennedy's "pay any price, bear any burden" speech just a few years later—marks Heinlein's political stance in 1958 as solidly, centrist American liberal, in the progressive tradition. Robert LeFevre, who was later to become a well-known libertarian pacifist, would not print "Who Are the Heirs of Patrick Henry" as editorial content (few libertarians will go along with higher taxes under any circumstances—a view conservatives of many stripes share with them). They went back to the display advertising office, where they scheduled three insertions, on April 12 and 13 and again on April 18.

As the ad was set into type, Robert and Ginny had several proofs pulled and sent them out to their closest friends and acquaintances, asking for donations of two dollars to defray the expenses of the ad there and in the Colorado College newspaper. H. L. Gold wrote back, remarking about the ad's tone. Heinlein explained:

> You say you envy our "certainty"—but we have no such certainty. What we do have is resoluteness. Certainty is impossible to a logical man—but a

logical man must behave in a crisis as if his calculated risk were indeed a certainty . . . [33]

What they had, instead of certainty, was *style*.

They rented one of the new, first-generation commercial photocopiers from 3M—a two-paper process in pink and white that faded after a few years— and set up a campaign office in their living room. They mailed out copies of the ad to almost their entire personal and professional address lists (Heinlein would not send them out to any military personnel on active duty). Money they would accept, of course, but what they were looking for was people who would set up core campaigns in their own locales. As in all grassroots campaigns, *local* organizers are pearls beyond price—

And that is just what this Patrick Henry Campaign was—grassroots politics on a national level. Robert and Leslyn had worked many such projects, in Los Angeles, and for the California State Democratic party, always on a local level. This was the first time he and Ginny had worked on a political project together. Robert and Ginny Heinlein worked together as smoothly and as concentratedly as Robert and Leslyn Heinlein had.

They worked sixteen- and seventeen-hour days for six weeks, handling a very taxing volume of mail, appearing on local television, and giving talks at meetings. Expenses mounted.

The earliest returns were very encouraging. Lurton Blassingame not only signed the letter and made a useful cash contribution, he showed it to the editors of *American Legion Magazine* and reported that they might want to give it national exposure in a month or two.[34] That could help a great deal.

The only stiffly unfavorable replies they received, as expected, were from the local group that had sponsored the SANE ad, plus two others—a man who wrote that he was all in favor of freedom but didn't think he cared to die for it, and a woman who wrote that she "agreed with us in every particular but was unwilling to pay higher taxes for any reason whatsoever."[35]

After an initial burst of approving response, incoming mail slowed to a steady dozen per day. Nevertheless, they could not be even cautiously optimistic: The rest was silence—and expensive silence at that. Some, like Alice Dalgliesh and John Campbell, wrote back agreeing with his positions but refusing to sign the letter. Most simply ignored it. In addition to newspaper ads and (mostly local) speeches, they (Ginny did the donkey work) mailed out several hundred individual appeals to a list that included rocket and missile engineers and a sampling of Naval Academy alumni now in civilian life, many of them Robert's classmates.

It was perhaps not entirely surprising that they heard almost nothing from the rocket men: They were under such tight security and such oppressive scrutiny that they were effectively locked down and could not speak freely. But the response from his classmates was disillusioning: Only 8 percent responded at all.

They would have given it up after a few weeks except for two letters.[36] One came from the outgoing chairman of the new Atomic Energy Commission, Admiral Strauss. The other was from Dr. Edward Teller, the inventor of the H-bomb.

> Each of them told us that they knew of no one else anywhere in the country who was trying to organize support for their policies. Strauss wished us good luck in the tired manner of a man who has tried hard and knows that he is whipped; Dr. Teller's letter was such that you could almost hear a sob in his voice: "Yours is the first one. Yours is the only one. I hope that you will not remain the only one!"[37]

There were some other encouraging developments: A group in San Francisco got a modified version of the ad printed in a local paper; General Gruenther wrote, "The United States owes a vote of thanks to Robert and Virginia Heinlein."[38]

Heinlein took every opportunity to speak to groups outside Colorado Springs, as local resources were running dry. An overnight visit with Hermann Deutsch in New Orleans resulted in a very encouraging column publicizing the cause.[39] A cold caught in Florida turned into chronic bronchitis and laryngitis, yet he *could not* put off these requests until he should heal up: He developed a routine of chewing one Aspergum twenty minutes before he was scheduled to speak, and another while he was being introduced carried him through the speeches—but he could not shake the sore throat, and it did not get any better. "[T]he next morning," he told his brother Rex, "I'm in as bad shape as ever."[40]

Time magazine put a letter out in all their foreign editions—but not the domestic edition. One of the editors of *The Saturday Evening Post* responded favorably, and Heinlein considered reworking his writing output to concentrate on *The Post* again and shuffle his book contracts around so that he was placed only with publishers he could rely on.[41] He knew he would lose money that way—"but at least I would have the satisfaction of doing business with patriots."[42] Jinny Fowler at Holt had ignored the letter, too:

> . . . if she had signed I would have moved my juvenile books over to her list; I am staying with Miss Dalgliesh (if I ever write another one) simply

because I do not know of a juveniles editor in the trade who is firm on this point—if you know of one, let's grab our hats and go![43]

But by June it was clear that the struggle was not catching on. The Cold War dynamics played themselves out on the small scale, confirming his realistic estimate of their chances written at the start of the project: "[T]he efforts of two people seem too futile in attempting counter-propaganda to 176,000,000 people who have already been reached by the original propaganda on a thoroughly organized and highly expensive scale." [44]

That coordinated propaganda was working: Late in May, Robert took time off while Ginny kept the campaign going in Colorado Springs to go to Denver for an Air Force–organized Symposium on Manned Flight in Space. "I know now why the Russians beat us into space," he wrote a furious note to himself. "A panel of learned defeatists—thank God they didn't advise the Wright Brothers." [45]

The prospect looked bleak. Given that the Soviet Union under Nikita Khrushchev was playing an "A" game—and Eisenhower's United States was not—the most likely prospect, Heinlein concluded, was not nuclear war, but a prolonged surrender, with America's nuclear weapons placed under United Nations control, which effectively meant Soviet control. They were left with prospects Heinlein had articulated very early in the campaign:

> I don't really expect World War III. I think we are going to go under through capitulations, the way Czechoslovakia did. I think we will suspend nuclear weapons testing, in response to "World Opinion," after this present series this summer—and I don't think we will ever set off another nuclear explosion. Then, after some years of apparent peace and good will, when we have effectively disarmed, something will happen (be caused) which will really annoy us. When we object, we will be handed an ultimatum—and it will turn out that we no longer have the potential to win. And we will surrender.
>
> I've skipped a lot of stages in the above—but that is the route we have been following. I see no strong prospect that we will change.[46]

The Heinleins were not the only ones who thought this way: The phony "missile gap" issue swept the Republicans out of the White House in the 1960 elections, and a few years later President John F. Kennedy did draw a line in the sand—a cordon around Cuba—when the Soviets installed nuclear missiles ninety miles from Florida. That was forthright action for the highest good, both for the United States and the entire world—stakes worth the risk, and prideful enough to suffer, if not to forgive, the Bay of Pigs bungling. But the horrifying foreign policy continued, and it is America's continuing support of dictators around the world that sowed the desert whirlwind we reap in the Middle East of the twenty-first century.

As Ginny had predicted, the Heinleins did lose the better part of their friends, not only in Colorado Springs but among Robert's colleagues in science fiction. Some—Mick McComas and A. P. White—simply dropped him. Others, ditherers such as H. L. Gold and John Campbell, and the pacifists, Robert Bloch and local Colorado Springs artist Lew Tilley, he dropped.[47]

They quietly let the campaign lapse, and it ran down of exhaustion. When they zeroed out the accounts, they found their six weeks of effort had put five hundred signatures on President Eisenhower's desk—at a net cost to them out of pocket (that is, after donations were deducted from expenses) of $1,000. Two 1958 dollars per signature was poor economics in the first place—and even poorer politics when it was producing apparently no results at all: President Eisenhower announced a unilateral cessation of American nuclear testing.

"If you can think of anything more that we can do, along different and more effective lines, please tell us," Robert wrote Blassingame. "We are anxious to start working again—but we don't relish running in circles."[48]

"[A]s an old ward-heeler," he wrote Hermann Deutsch, "I can see the bleak fact that my methods did not work, especially as the movement did not effectively take root elsewhere."[49]

WAITING OUT THE END

As the Patrick Henry campaign wound down in June 1958, Ginny became ill: She was testing positive for dysentery again—several organisms. Robert recovered from his bronchitis and was only a little "nervy" from exhaustion—which meant a return of his recurrent insomnia. They tried to rest, not going out, not entertaining anyone. Morale was not good.[1] Robert had done virtually no writing for more than a month, and the correspondence and business details piled up. Korshak made an absurd offer to let him purchase Shasta's stock and the printing plates for the three Future History books for $4,000, just about what one of the books had earned in royalties. Heinlein wanted to be shut of Shasta, but not that badly.[2] Korshak was still selling secondary rights he didn't own, despite serious efforts by Blassingame to call a halt to his villainous business practices. In mid-June 1958, Heinlein bluntly told Korshak and his remaining business partner in Shasta, T. E. Dikty,[3] that he held off legal proceedings only because he did not want to appear harsh—"But my forbearance has been ill paid; there have been many annoyances in the mean time": illegal sales continuing even after they had been caught and warned off, a "contra-accounting" scheme that resulted in Robert's royalties being diverted—

> And now, to top off all these, I learn (as usual, by accident, through subscribing to a British magazine [probably Ted Carnell's *New Worlds*]) that the SFBC of England is offering as its July/August 1958 selection something called a "Robert Heinlein Omnibus" published by Sidgwick & Jackson and offered at the preposterous price of 5s. 6d or $.75! I don't know what it contains; you haven't told me about it[.][4]

Shasta was keeping all the monies they got by selling rights they didn't even own.

International news continued depressing. Sputnik 3 went up, and the press was silent about it. Heinlein fretted about the implications of this news blackout: ". . . when Russia put up Sputnik #3, the giant one, I followed the papers and the news very closely because I wished to see it." He had even gone downtown to look at the wire services feeds directly, but found no coverage at all.

> . . . did the word go out quietly from the White House (Adams, maybe[5]) to play it down, pay little attention to it, sweep it under the rug . . . don't get the peepul stirred up . . . I find it downright chilling that that thing should be going by overhead, with all that it implies about the future, and no real news about it in the papers.[6]

There was too much that was not being talked about, that ought to be shouted from the rooftops: Russian submarines were spotted in offshore international waters almost daily, and nothing was being done about them, nothing at all.[7] Earlier Heinlein had expressed his opinion of the administration's response succinctly, to Alice Dalgliesh: "I can't figure out whether Mr. Eisenhower is senile or simply stupid and irresolute."[8]

Heinlein was also disturbed, he told Hermann Deutsch, by the silence on the issue of the unknown number of American prisoners being held by China.

> I've heard figures running from four to over three thousand. There are some nasty rumors going around that a great many of our soldiers officially listed as "missing in action" in Korea are actually prisoners in China . . . and that the administration would rather not hear any more about it because they do not intend to do anything about it.[9]

When Captain Eugene R. Guild (U.S. Army, Retired) formed a lobbying organization to keep the Korean War POWs alive as a public issue, Robert and Ginny contributed generously to Fighting Homefolks of Fighting Men and repeated their gifts year after year.

On July 11, 1958, Heinlein sat down at the typewriter and banged out in one long session a 4,500-word story aimed at *Playboy*. He had been fascinated by the "circle in time" gimmick for a long time, and he apparently had the odd but original idea to combine it with some topical material—that 1947 nonsense song "I'm My Own Grandpa"[10] (that was, in fact, one of the titles he considered for the story), and possibly also the gender-reassignment surgery Christine Jorgensen had made world headlines with in 1952.

Heinlein started out with a natural hermaphrodite, a rare but legitimate medical condition in which a child is born with both sets of sex organs, and gender assignment is largely a matter of choice on the parents' part anyway. Heinlein has his hermaphrodite raised as a girl and impregnated by a time-traveling male version of herself, later on in her/his personal timeline—giving birth to himself (only one set of genes to draw on), and since the male would have to be able to travel back in time, he could put himself into a foundling hospital, too. The time paradox was expressed in a single character, and it was a neat reversal on the old "you can't kill your own grandfather" time paradox. The him/her personal timeline is an Ouroboros snake, swallowing itself perpetually. He initially titled it "The World Snake," but changed it as he spent the next two days cutting and revising it, to something his character said in one of the last, pathetic lines of the story: "All You Zombies" (Zombies were big that year). *Playboy* promptly rejected it, the editor saying the implied sex made him queasy.[11] It circulated for a while to the stag magazines, but without any takers. In November, editor Robert Mills picked it up for *F&SF* (A. P. White—"Anthony Boucher"—had retired earlier that year).

Gnome Press had brought out a very disappointing-looking hardcover issue of *Methuselah's Children*. Heinlein was very unsatisfied and told Greenberg so in very clear terms: "[T]he book looks and feels, in all respects, like a cheap reprint of a trade edition. In effect, that is just what it was—because you went almost immediately into your cheap book-club promotion on this book."[12]

The last installment of *Have Space Suit—Will Travel* appeared in *F&SF* in October. Heinlein must have been generating a new book idea while recuperating from his amebic and bacterial infections, for he outlined and on October 14, 1958, began to write *Podkayne Fries: Her Life and Times*, with a female teenaged protagonist, and written in the first person—"unheard of in the genre."[13] Even aside from the aftereffects of dysentery, though, he found it unusually difficult: "Right at the moment I am having a hell of a time trying to start a novel. I find myself more and more out of sympathy with the spirit of the times, which makes it hard for me to write popular fiction."[14]

Ginny had started to study the Russian language in an extension course offered by the local high school (with teachers from the University of Colorado).[15] The students were mostly military men from one or another of the local military bases—twenty-one to start with.[16] She worked hard at it, and strained her eyesight: Some of the letters in the Cyrillic alphabet have small tails distinguishing them from letters without the tails. Ginny had to get glasses to see the tails.

At some point Heinlein must have proposed to Ginny that they make their next trip inside the Soviet Union, to see Communism at firsthand, and from the inside. The USSR had an international travel agency, InTourist, which would allow them to book the trip.

Ginny cannot have been enthusiastic about this proposal, having no desire to be behind the Iron Curtain—but they had been in the buffer states on their most recent trip and nothing untoward had happened. Perhaps it was her Russian classes that tipped the balance in favor of going.

Early in November, Blassingame received a "heads-up" letter from Doubleday: A Robert Kent in Los Angeles had written to Heinlein's publisher about a new cheapie film that had just come out from American International Pictures, *The Brain Eaters,* that seemed like a plagiarism of *The Puppet Masters.*

There was perennial interest in that property in Hollywood—Blassingame had recently received a couple of nibbles for options at $2,500 and $3,500, respectively, offers so low that they could be ignored. Ned Brown, on the other hand, was fielding a more serious offer: One of his clients, actor-turned-producer John Payne, had made a similar lowball offer to purchase the property, and Blassingame had set a $15,000 total value on it: $5,000 on signing, $5,000 when it went into production, and $5,000 on release.[17] Payne was hesitating, but his hand was inching toward his checkbook.[18] If this *Brain Eaters* was a real piracy, it might render the property valueless. Heinlein should see the picture and let Blassingame know what he thought—but it was not due to hit the Colorado Springs area until the end of December 1958.

Heinlein took *Podkayne Fries* off his agenda: A hundred pages into the manuscript, it just was not coming together for him. He must have been mulling over the intertangled notions of freedom and responsibility, duty and moral self-discipline and citizenship—subjects possibly suggested by the depressing reception of the Patrick Henry campaign, but also by his brother Larry's promotion to the rank of brigadier general of the Army Reserves:[19] Larry "did it the hard way . . . he took the long route, all the way from private to general officer."[20] Another story came to him: *Starship Troopers.* Later, Robert recognized the origin of the story in something his father had said when he was just five years old: "I just remembered where I got the basic thesis of S. Troopers. From my father—his conviction (1912) that only those who fought for their country were worthy to rule it."[21]

In 1912 the country was in the middle of the militarism associated with the Progressive movement—a time and place in the culture that persisted all through Heinlein's own upbringing, and of which the Civilian Military Training Corps Heinlein attended while he was in high school was a part. It was undoubtedly that connection that suggested a young man undergoing military training (and that, in turn, may have suggested Kipling's "The 'Eathen" [1896] as its basic story arc,[22] which he may also have melded with a wartime novel by H. G. Wells, *Mr. Britling Sees It Through* (1916): "Conscript soldiers are the ruin of war" [327]).

If the militarism of the Progressive Era was the starting point, the idea certainly underwent a great deal of reprocessing before the typewriter went clicking. Perhaps this aspect of *Starship Troopers* derives from another book that had influenced him highly in the past, Edward Bellamy's *Looking Backward* (the book of which *For Us, the Living* was a modernized retelling). Although Bellamy's "industrial army" is officered by a strict meritocratic review, there is one great exception to this schema: The head, or general, of each guild is chosen by vote of the *veterans* of the guild.[23] Certainly Bellamy interchanged military and civilian descriptions of the structure of the industrial army, and Heinlein's story also mixes freely the civilian and the military in the makeup of his world. He made his far-future military 100 percent voluntary, to discourage the chaff, and turned it into a kind of Darwinian evolutionary filter.

> I do not know that this system would result in a better government—nor do I know of any way to insure "knowledgeable" and "intelligent" voting. But I venture to guess that this fictional system would not produce results any worse than those of our present system. Not that I think it is even remotely likely that we would ever adopt such a system—[24]

Moreover, from the evidence that this was the story Heinlein did write and did complete, it must have had that ring of "relevance," of engagement, he had been missing with the Podkayne story. He later explained some of his thinking in generating the story to colleague Theodore Sturgeon:

> . . . I'll state explicitly the theme of *Starship Troopers*: it is an inquiry into why men fight, investigated as a moral problem . . . . being a novelist, I tried to analyze it as a novelist. Why do men fight? What is the nature of force and violence, can it be morally used, and, if so, under what circumstances? . . . .
>   What I tried to do . . . was to find, by observation, a fundamental basis for human behavior—and I decided that the *only* basis which did not call

for unproved assumptions was the question of survival vs. non-survival in the widest possible sense—i.e., I defined "moral" behavior as being survival behavior . . . [sic] for the individual, for the family, the tribe, the nation, the race.

Now this thesis may or may not be true, but it is the theme of the book, explicitly stated over and over again—and every part, every incident, in the story merely explores some corollary or consequence of the basic theorem. Is conscription permissible morally? No, because *moral* decisions cannot be determined by law, by committee, by group—to fight or not to fight is a personal, moral decision . . . .

Everything in the book turns on this single theorem . . . [25]

He framed his ideas slightly differently for Alice Dalgliesh:

Let me state the theme of my story: the central theme of the story is John XV 13: "Greater love hath no man than this, that a man lay down his life for his friends." The story starts with a boy, a child, a spoiled son of the extreme right, one who is utterly incapable of conceiving this ideal. The story ends when he is perhaps only two or three years older, but fully matured, a lined and tempered adult wholly dedicated to that simple, selfless proposition.[26]

The story came together along the same basic lines as *Space Cadet*: a high school graduate going into the army and coming of age as he comes to understand the emotional and moral meaning of the theme—why people would fight and die to protect their homes. Presumably to clarify the individualist nature of the moral theme, Heinlein made the antagonists soulless hive-creatures, representing the forces of totalitarian collectivism that were threatening to overwhelm the free world. Later he said:

Starship Troopers describes a libertarian, democratic, almost idyllic utopia—but under wartime conditions and told through the eyes of a young, inexperienced man who has to form his own philosophy under those conditions.[27]

And the philosophy of life his high-school-aged hero develops in the crucible of war is embodied in lines one of the characters quotes to Johnny Rico, from the fourth stanza of "The Star Spangled Banner":[28] "Oh! thus be it ever, when free men shall stand/Between their loved home and the war's desolation!"

Space Cadet had been about the military in peacetime and played itself out in the sanitized "social service" aspect of the military—as had much of Heinlein's own service. But this book was set in the military in time of war, and required a more realistic picture of what the military means.

He started writing *Shoulder the Sky* (the title a reference to Atlas holding up the sky)[29] on November 8, 1958. He used all the skill he had at his command to make the violence of the combat in the opening chapter nauseatingly real, but his protagonist likable and "identifiable." This forced his young readers to entertain two mutually contradictory self-pictures in their minds—a "nice" guy who wreaked incredible violence in the best of causes—the strongest possible argument against namby-pamby pacifism he could mount.

Some people were not going to want to hear these things. Alice Dalgliesh was not going to want to hear these things.[30] But these were things that needed to be said in the intellectual and moral climate of 1958:

Why have I written a book which I judge ahead of its time is likely to displease quite a few people?

I could answer that almost everything I have ever written does not please most people and that answer would be true. But not sufficient.

I wrote this book because it is in tune with the times, although not with popular beliefs. It has something important to say about war, about juvenile delinquency, about the civic responsibility of the citizen, about education, about a young man's proper role—his *duty*—in his social group. What I am saying to my young reader is: "Look, son, this is not an easy world; this is a grim and dangerous world—and it is quite likely to kill you. But you have a free choice: you can go to your death fat, dumb, and happy and never understanding what is happening to you right up to the time the bombs fall . . . [sic] or you can grow up, face up to your harsh responsibilities, look death in the face and defy it, and thereby enjoy the austere but very real and deeply satisfying rewards of being a man. But the choice is yours, and neither your mother, nor your teacher, nor the state can in any wise release you of it."

I could have written this as an essay—and no teen-ager would ever bother to read it. Instead I cast it into the form of an adventure story in the belief that many would read it, and some would understand it and profit by it . . . .

As such, the story is timeless; I dolled it up with futuristic gadgets and strange planets simply to flavor it for the kids. And, as such, it is most timely—for this is exactly what our boys in high school face . . . . What has happened to our boys in a single generation? I am not sure—but the results terrify me.[31]

In the writing, the title had changed from *Shoulder the Sky* to the more descriptive and catchy *Sky Soldier* and then to *Starside Soldier*. He finished the 60,000-word draft at 5:20 A.M. on November 22 and left it on the kitchen counter for Ginny to first-read. When he woke up, he found a note from her: "Darling—I read the end—you will be pleased to know I cried—maybe others won't; but I did. I'm at Lucky's. Call me. All my love, T."[32] That ending was a good stroke—his protagonist's life choices validated by his father, creating a wholeness to the boy's life. He was about to make another combat drop—and the implication was that neither Johnny Rico nor his father would survive it, though Heinlein had not written that in explicitly.

What he had been explicit about, however, was that the boy was a Filipino. He had sprinkled the early part of the book with a lot of Spanish names, but mentioned close to the end that Tagalog was the boy's milk-language. Perhaps because his editor had not noticed when he put in a Negro hero (in *Tunnel in the Sky*, 1955), Heinlein felt the need to be more explicit about this Asian hero (the first in science fiction).[33]

He spent a couple of weeks cutting and polishing the manuscript and sent it to a professional typist early in December—which gave him a little time free to deal with the possible filmed plagiarism of *The Puppet Masters*.

Over the 1958–59 holidays, almost two months into its national release, *The Brain Eaters* reached Colorado Springs, and Heinlein saw it on January 2, 1959. There really couldn't be any doubt about it: "I counted too many identities of 'gimmicks' as well as the basic plot to be in any doubt in my mind about it."[34] Even worse, the production was very low quality, and they had ripped the guts out of the book, turning it into a hack weird-menace shudder-pulp story. "[T]he whole thing was done in such atrocious bad taste and with such wild illogic that the useless use of sex hardly stood out."[35]

On top of the continuing runaround he was getting from Jack Seaman's successors over the profits (if any) from *Project Moonbase*, Blassingame was now telling him *The Brain Eaters* would kill the option-purchase deal they had been negotiating for *The Puppet Masters*. He would have to sue American International—just as soon as Blassingame could find the right lawyer to handle it.

Heinlein sent the clean retype of what was now titled *Starship Soldier* to Blassingame and, simultaneously, to Scribner, on January 10 and braced himself. He had done this one, he told Blassingame, as he had done *Citizen of the*

Galaxy two years ago—written what was essentially an adult novel, but one his kids should find interesting.[36] Blassingame liked it—it gave him a bang, he said, though it also sagged in places, bogging down in the middle with the lecturing.[37]

The reaction from Dalgliesh, however, was a flat rejection. This was not adventure, she said, it was social commentary and the boys wouldn't want it at all.[38] He should put it away for a year, she told him: Perhaps he would feel differently about it after he had cooled down. She also enclosed a lengthy personal letter of rebuttal: "Having bounced the book," Heinlein told Blassingame, "she now seems to want to continue the argument: she sent me a quite unnecessary (and snide!) letter, raising points better not raised over a manuscript she has returned. But I'm damned if I'll fight with her."[39]

Dalgliesh had made one useful suggestion, though: He could try marketing it as an adult serial[40] . . . but Doubleday passed it up as *too* juvenile (though admirably loaded with technique),[41] and a week later John Campbell passed it up for *Astounding*. Again it was too juvenile.

So it was too "adult" for the juvenile house and too "juvenile" for the adult publishers.

That February, Heinlein made a loan to Ben Babb's wife Betty Jane (Ben had been sick for a long time already, and they were in desperate straits). The "loan" (Robert and Ginny knew quite well it was a gift) was inconsiderable, and they were glad to be able to help. She had done the right thing in coming to him, Heinlein assured Betty Jane Babb—but he also cautioned her about keeping this kind of secret from her husband. It was the kind of thing that could be soul-destroying:

> A lot of wives . . . think they are being "faithful" as long as they don't take a roll in the hay with some other male, no matter what they do to kill the spirit of the man they promised to cherish. They never get it through their silly heads that a mere roll in the hay could be no more important than a bad case of hangnails—certainly no worse than a bad cold—if they paid attention to the essence of the contract, "to love and cherish" come what may—buck him up and keep him going, *somehow,* against an unfriendly world.
>
> That is what marriage is all about—sex is at most a minor aspect of it: a partnership between two people, in which each places the other's welfare as the paramount value in a shifting and uncertain world . . . There have been more than a few honest and loyal wives who have hit the streets to support sick husbands—and let us now have a moment of silence in honor of their gallant souls.[42]

Immediately after receiving Dalgliesh's rejection of *Starship Soldier,* Heinlein had tried to reply and found himself in the same round of write-and-tear-up-drafts that had made him jittery and insomniac after *Citizen of the Galaxy.* He had finally reached a draft of a letter he—and Ginny—could live with, explaining the points of his own experience and thinking that had gone into the book—and showing how *Starship Soldier* fit into the juvenile series he had been doing for the last twelve years. Something in that long letter[43] apparently reached Dalgliesh in some fashion: She asked Blassingame to return the manuscript so she could reconsider it.

In the meantime, Heinlein tried a "backchannel" letter to an acquaintance in the Scribner editorial board (identified in the correspondence only as "George" and "McM") asking for an opinion as to why it had been rejected so summarily and suggested that he might be able to use the input to salvage the book for Scribner.[44] A week later he heard back from George saying that he believed rejecting the book was the appropriate thing for Scribner to do: The story was weak, the didactic approach was weak, and it would not do his reputation any good. Couple those considerations to the objections certain to be raised by librarians—"and I don't think it's appropriate."[45]

Blassingame put it on the open market, and *Fantasy & Science Fiction* picked up the serial rights, requesting a condensation of the book to 20,000 words. The editor, Bob Mills, was jittery about it. Alfred Bester had talked Mills into letting him read the manuscript and wrote Heinlein a long letter first complimenting him on a crisply told story, but voicing his concern and Mills's about the direction it was taking: He warned Robert not to fall into the jingoism trap Kipling had got himself into that "makes his name odious today as a thinker (but *never* as a writer)" and suggested a rebuttal story or two.[46]

To Bester, Robert made a temperate reply: He and Mills certainly were free to say whatever they wished in print, "But I may not like what you have to say and I certainly will not answer it." He abhorred personal arguments and had never—and would never—write anything for publication, or say anything in public "knocking my colleagues or their works."[47]

But if they were that jittery over it, they shouldn't even be considering it: Heinlein told Blassingame to withdraw the book from *F&SF* and get the manuscript back.

I don't know whether he [Mills] got cold feet on his own, and then called in Alfie Bester and suggested that Alfie write a rebuttal, or whether it was the other way around—cold feet contracted from Alfie after he let Alfie read it. It doesn't really matter which was cause and which was effect; the end result was that he asked Alfie to write a rebuttal to my story and asked me if I would mind if he introduced my story with a statement that he, the editor, totally disagreed with it.

Well, I do mind, on both points. It is all right for the umpire to wear a plain blue suit, but when he puts on the other team's uniform and tells the cash customers that he is agin me from scratch, that is another matter entirely—and when I find that the umpire is coaching the opposition against me, then I *know* I'm in the wrong ball park.[48]

Shortly after Miss Dalgliesh had bounced *Starship Soldier* the first time, Heinlein had received an inquiry from a Hollywood-based television producer, Tom Swicegood, who was the president of Pine-Key Productions. He and his partner, Jim Doherty, were working on a half-hour SF series for fall 1959, *Crater Base One,* and wanted one or more Heinlein stories for the series.[49] Things run in cycles, especially in television, and this season another production company, Ziv-TV, had another half-hour space show in collaboration with Ivan Tors, *Men Into Space*—about the colonization and settlement of the Moon[50] (with newcomer Angie Dickinson in the pilot, which aired in September 1959).

Heinlein was cautiously interested: He had been badly burned twice by Hollywood. But the series "bible" he found encouraging.[51] In the Producer's Notes section of the bible he found among the instructions to writers:

CRATER BASE ONE is a new kind of television format. It is not a detective story in a moon setting. Nor is it a hide-and-seek cowboy story which is doctored up by placing the hero inside a space suit and sending him off to "get the bad guys." Rather, CRATER BASE ONE is the story of intelligent pioneers in a very hostile world, living only in the minds of men with *imagination.*

We need adult stories, the key to which is *characterization.* A believable, interesting character is far and away the best approach to what we want. Two-dimensional characters are for kid shows.

Any comparison between CRATER BASE ONE and shows like FLASH GORDON, CAPTAIN VIDEO, etc., is absolutely not desired . . . [sic] Our stories, sets, costumes, and other details are to be handled with realistic honesty throughout.[52]

The background was thoughtfully worked out, Heinlein thought—tangled international jurisdictions over the Moon base seemed to be the key issue in the series[53]—but he found the pilot script frankly incompetent: Not only was it dull, lacking in dramatic values, but it didn't make any coherent use of the series premises. It was hard to believe that it had come from the same shop as the bible.[54]

Swicegood's initial proposal to Heinlein was for an outline of a story from him, five to ten pages—for which he was to be paid a flat fee plus residuals.[55] Unfortunately, the sample contracts Swicegood sent him would require him to join the Screen Writers Guild. The Authors Guild used to have reciprocity with the SWG, but Heinlein didn't know if that was still the case—and he thought it absurd to have to join a union just to work on the series. And in any case he didn't like the "closed shop" aspect of the thing.

> Writing is not bricklaying and I am of the opinion that my grocer should be as free to write anything he wants to write and to sell it in any market as I am—even though I am a dues-paid-up member of my guild and he is not, i.e., I don't own the writing trade and I don't think anyone, or any group, should be allowed to own it, or any part of it, or to require anyone to pay a fee nor to submit to a set of rules in order to compete with me or my colleagues in the market. Writing, like speech, is a basic freedom . . . [sic] and not merely my way of making a living.[56]

Swicegood suggested they pay him for one story, and he could see how it worked out: He would in any case have been paid for the work.[57] Heinlein forwarded the contract to Lurton Blassingame (his relationship with Ned Brown he thought was coming to an end) for review. He decided instead to do the work "on spec" and suggested a dozen technically trained SF writers who could be approached for a series like this.[58]

Heinlein never did produce an outline (a conventional stage of television series writing). Probably the process of thinking in visual screens so the story could be translated into a script—so that he could then write a narrative story—was too cumbersome, and he was preoccupied in March 1959 with assembling a collection for Gnome Press of miscellaneous, more-or-less science-fiction stories he had written since taking up writing again after the war, *The Menace from Earth*.[59] But on April 11, 1959, before going off to Las Vegas for the World Congress of Flight,[60] he mailed a twenty-eight-page script to Swicegood that reused one of his own titles, "Nothing Ever Happens On the Moon." This original story had nothing in common with the Boy Scout novelette he had written ten years earlier; instead, it had a funding committee VIP trapped on the Moon during a destructive quake, a scenario that would give plenty of room for exposition of the complicated situation in the *Crater Base One* bible.[61]

After the Las Vegas trip, Blassingame found a suitable lawyer to institute Heinlein's plagiarism suit against the producers of *The Brain Eaters*: Harold A. Fendler, Esq., of the Fendler & Lerner Beverly Hills law firm, wrote to Blassingame on April 24, 1959, that they had seen *The Brain Eaters* in the company of Ned Brown, still Heinlein's Hollywood agent. "We were all of the unanimous opinion that a copyright infringement exists and that suit should be filed," Fendler told Blassingame.[62]

While waiting for the Pine-Key notes on his draft script, Heinlein did some professional writing for Ginny: Their one year of Russian class was coming to an end. But one year of Russian language study is not enough to become proficient. Russian is very difficult to learn as a second language, with verbs that change roots in the middle of conjugations, and—never mind the jawbreaking consonant clusters!—sounds that don't exist in English. Ginny asked Robert to write up a petition to the University to provide an extra year of instruction. It was successful. She also hired a tutor—an elderly (female) White Russian refugee—and continued with additional lessons daily.

When the tutor found out who Robert was, she told him she was sure she had read "The Man Who Sold the Moon" in Russian.[63] The Soviet Union did not subscribe to any international copyright convention and it might well be that they pirated his stuff ad lib. He would have to look into that when he got to Moscow. The Russians had a reputation of paying up when caught with their hand in the till—so long as it was paid and used locally.[64]

In June, Heinlein assembled another short-story collection for Gnome, of more-or-less fantasy stories, *The Unpleasant Profession of Jonathan Hoag*.[65] Both *Menace from Earth* and *Unpleasant Profession* were better printed and bound, and both sold promptly to paperback houses, which was getting to be where the money was, though with some unusual contract provisions: *Menace* was brought out in several different versions, with differing numbers of the stories in the various paperback issues, and *Unpleasant Profession* became part of a series of "number times something" paperback titles Gold Medal was bringing out. His became *6xH* for "Six times Heinlein." And with "The Menace from Earth" and "All You Zombies—" in print he was more or less up to date, ("Zombies" had just been published in *F&SF,* in April 1959) all his stories collected between boards, except for three very early stories that he hadn't been able to do anything with over the years. The SF market was in the worst slump since the war.

In mid-June, Heinlein made a trip to Kansas City for a niece's wedding and took the opportunity to visit the family homesteads and stomping grounds. The house on Cleveland his family had lived in before 1920 was vacant and about to be torn down. The other sites—churches and schools—were a little older, a little more worn, but still going. Someone had torn out the maple tree they had planted at the house on 36th Street. And of course he saw Swope Park. He even chartered an airplane (for the munificent sum of $24.00) and flew to see his grandfather's house in Butler.

Swope Park must have brought back memories—perhaps of playing Tarzan in the nude there, at age five, and that may have led to recalling his adult fling, now nearly thirty years ago, with naturism. In June he began contacting some of the nudist/dude ranches around the country. He got back in touch with the Garrisons, who had founded an unlanded nudist association in Denver that Robert and his then-wife Leslyn had joined when he was hospitalized at Fitzsimmons in 1933 and 1934. Heinlein had put them into *The Door into Summer*. The Garrisons remembered him, of course, but had sold the Colorado Sunshine Club to the members the year before. It was called Mountain Air Ranch now.

Robert and Ginny made a reservation at the Lazy Bears Dude Ranch in Kemmling, Colorado, for two weeks in the middle of July and bought association memberships. They added subscription memberships to the national nudist organization, the American Sunbathing Association.

Things had loosened up a bit in the last twenty-five years, but it was still in 1959 necessary to be discreet. These resorts did not want to get a reputation as catering to roues and libertines and so discouraged singletons of either sex—but particularly men without their wives. Ginny knew Robert would be looking up these places whenever he traveled, and she was studying hard at Russian and couldn't always get away. She wrote a handwritten blanket permission Robert could show the owners of these colonies and ranches, if she wasn't with him:

I am aware of and fully approve of my husband's nudist activities.

Virginia Heinlein[66]

Ginny accompanied him for the first weekend of their nude dude ranch mini-vacation. Robert rode and swam, lifted weights and bounced on a trampoline "in a gingerly middle-aged fashion" and even helped out with the ranch chores, digging postholes and so forth. He got a fine overall tan—and a "fancy collection of saddle sores"—and enjoyed himself immensely.[67]

Ginny never really became comfortable in skin with strangers (around the house was another matter).[68] Nor did she find the experience particularly congenial: "I did not like such places, or the people I met there," she later said succinctly.[69] One weekend was enough for her. When she took her planned break for her Russian language class, she stayed in Colorado Springs and used the vacation from the vacation to study a little harder, to be prepared for their trip to the Soviet Union, less than a year away.

Swicegood and Doherty had been congratulating themselves on their good fortune in getting a story from Heinlein for *Crater Base One*. He was far ahead of them, Swicegood told him.[70] But Heinlein's script presented technical problems Swicegood had probably wanted to avoid. The story was quite good—but the way it was told was just too different from what the audience (and more importantly, what the *sponsors*) would expect to see:

> It makes excellent *reading,* like just about all of your published material and letters, but . . . for half-hour (or any length) *dramatic* show, it would be sudden death! As you had it there were so many requirements for a television show that were entirely disregarded[71] that the average editor would throw up his hands in despair, never even considering the slim possibility of scissors and paste . . . . However, I've gotten some damn good stories by offering my inept suggestions and having the authors come back at me with, "To hell with that foolishness! But—instead, suppose such and such," etc. Sometimes it works.[72]

Not this time. Swicegood reworked the story and retitled it "Moonquake" for the second version of the script,[73] cutting out most—but not enough—of the dialogue establishing the base's conflict with the funding agency Earthside, and he discarded the original work-together-and-learn-better ending in favor of some foolery with a spaceship toppled in the quake (why this particular gimmick was so attractive to TV and film people was a mystery). The revised story was now inconsistent in terms of the characters' motivations—there was, for example, no reason for his VIP to be there at all—and the ending had nothing logically to do with the setup. It was, Heinlein told Swicegood and Doherty, part horse and part cow, a chimera too mismatched to live. It would be better to junk the resulting mess and start over.[74]

Probably this was looking like more work than the project could justify. On the last day of July, Swicegood wrote his regrets:

> I haven't wanted to write this letter, but there doesn't seem to be any way out of it. Your comments about putting the horse and the cow together are

entirely correct—which unhappily leaves us little alternative other than to take your own advice and "DON'T!"[75]

Swicegood himself was already on to the next thing, an anthology series of true sea stories. Ultimately, *Crater Base One* was never produced.[76] Apparently, Heinlein was never paid for his work, either.

Alice Dalgliesh's "reconsideration" of *Starship Soldier* had no different results, but it hardly mattered. G. P. Putnam's Sons wanted the book very badly. One of Putnam's senior editors, Peter Israel, told the owner and managing editor of Putnam's, Walter Minton, that a Heinlein juvenile had come on the market. Minton told him to grab it, sight unseen.[77] Heinlein's reputation in the children's lit publishing industry was solid—though apparently, he was a profit without honor in his former home at Scribner: Miss Dalgliesh had told him once that his books had kept her department in the black for years—yet Charles Scribner himself had been involved in the rejection of this book and had voted to dump him—a discourtesy Heinlein felt deeply (and said so repeatedly).[78]

Peter Israel ducked the issue of whether it was a juvenile or an adult novel: He simply presented it as a "new book by Robert Heinlein" at a sales conference, saying, "Let's let the readers decide who likes it."[79] They would bring it out by the Putnam's Children's Department, but design and promote it on their adult list.

They would publish it as-is, William McMorris, Heinlein's line editor, told him,[80] but they went over the manuscript practically line by line, rebalancing the text and working through alternative titles until they settled on *Starship Troopers*.[81] McMorris's suggestions for revisions were cogent, improving the story by adding, for example, another combat scene, and sending his hero down into one of the bugs' tunnels.[82] Heinlein added an entirely new section of 30,000 words before his final scene, with Johnny Rico in Officer Candidate School, bringing the total word count up to 90,000.

During the revision process for *Starship Soldier,* John Payne was talking about having Heinlein come out to Hollywood to script *The Puppet Masters* for a full production—*and* he accepted the price Heinlein had set for his services (based on a calculation of his earning power at home in Colorado Springs similar to that he had done in 1949).

And then Payne saw *The Brain Eaters.*

"It's a crying shame that some character could take the elements from *The Puppet Masters* and demolish the concept," he wrote Heinlein.[83] His bankers and loan sources refused to back any production with such a spoiler already out in public.[84] Payne abandoned the project.

It wasn't a total loss: Heinlein's attorneys could now prove definite damages to Heinlein's commercial property as a result of the *Brain Eaters* infringement.[85] Payne offered to testify on their behalf[86]—but how much money they could pry out of American International was anybody's guess.

Heinlein was invited to speak at an Air Force Association conference in Tampa in September 1959, which gave him an opportunity first to stay at The Floritans nudist resort in Tampa, and then go on to Cape Canaveral to see a static test of an Atlas launch vehicle. He came back to Colorado Springs by way of a business-pleasure stop in New Orleans to visit with the *Item* editors and Hermann Deutsch. Deutsch had introduced him to another science-fiction colleague whose fresh and original approach Robert particularly liked, Dan Galouye.[87] "Most sci-fic has become formula-ridden and standardized. We need more new blood and new ideas, such as Dan provides."[88]

Ginny had other matters on her mind. Robert had been handed a flyer on one of his recent travels—a Seattle-area character wanted to found an anti-Communist society named after an American soldier killed by the Communist Chinese. Ginny was immediately interested—so interested that she wanted to attend this organizing seminar at the Olympic Hotel on September 25, 1959. The organizer's name was Robert Welch, and his project was the John Birch Society. His message fit right in with their recent charitable interest with Eugene Guilds and the Korean War MIAs, and Welch's magazine, *American Opinion,* had some thoughtful material to offer. An observer named "Clise" who took extensive notes of the meeting described Heinlein as "an independent writer of philosophical fiction" whose "prime interest" was winning the release of American prisoners held in the Soviet Union.[89]

Single-issue politics often makes *very* strange bedfellows. As disconnected as Robert felt from his own party, anything was possible—any kind of ad hoc coalition of interests. The Heinleins also found Welch personally sociable—a pleasant drinking companion in the hotel bar.[90] They would not offer to found chapters in their locale, but they did purchase several gift subscriptions to the magazine, and they contributed money to Welch's anti-Communist effort (and later found he had enrolled them as members, which was not what they had in mind at all. They asked to be taken off his lists.).[91]

After a side trip to Camp Forestia, the Fraternity Snoqualmie nudist resort[92] (Ginny not participating), they flew back from Seattle to Colorado Springs. Heinlein was in some discomfort, as he had an ulcerated molar. They were immediately snowed in—in September!—with forty inches of very wet snow, a four-day wait to get to the dentist, and many days afterward doped up and unable to work.

When he was finally able to concentrate, he fiddled around with a number of ideas. The steady stream of domestic anthology rights, and the foreign sales, individually smaller—a *lot* smaller—than his domestic sales, added up to a substantial income when combined with his domestic book contracts. In the last eighteen months Blassingame had placed a British contract for *Revolt in 2100*, Danish contracts for *The Puppet Masters*, *Space Cadet*, and "The Green Hills of Earth"; Finnish rights to "Ordeal in Space," a Dutch right to "The Long Watch," Italian rights for *Red Planet* and *Revolt in 2100* again, and a Japanese contract for "They." He was also negotiating a Japanese contract for *Methuselah's Children* and a Portuguese sale of *The Green Hills of Earth and Other Stories*. Blassingame disclaimed any responsibility for that success: "Your foreign sales are 'fabulous' because of your stories—and subject matter," he told Robert.[93]

Other friends and family were not doing so well. When Heinlein visited Kansas City, he had been brought back in contact with family members still living there, including "Bud" Heinlein, his brother Larry's oldest boy with his first wife, Alice.[94] Bud called Heinlein, late in October,[95] wanting him to drop everything and come to Kansas City because he and his wife Donna were in desperate straits.

The problem seemed less the money than a complete unwillingness to come to grips with the situation. Heinlein made them a cash loan to take care of immediate expenses, "secured" by their furniture (actually a way of taking the storage problem off their hands, since they wanted to give up their jobs and move, to make a fresh start).[96] When he got back to Colorado Springs, Heinlein supplemented the original loan with another and wrote a long and detailed letter of advice about how to reverse their downward financial spiral, advising them to pull back to the bedrock of their marriage partnership—the way he and Ginny had to economize the winter of 1947–48 while they were in Fort Worth[97]—and build from there.[98] Bud's response was to use his credit to get deeper in debt. Bud's next letter was resentful and frankly offensive, threatening to punch Robert for making Donna unhappy to read his October 29 reply.[99] And then, just a few days later, an abject apology.[100] It was hard to believe these letters came from the same individual.[101]

Bud would flip from rage to despondency overnight. Robert recognized this was something that money would not solve, and it was the same kind of emotional black hole his relationship with Leslyn had become at the end. He gave Bud's mother Alice a release of their furniture[102] and wrote a firm and clear letter to Bud, detailing what course of action he needed to take, concluding:

One last word: Bud, I would not be going to this much agonizing trouble if I were not very fond of you and deeply concerned with the welfare of your entire family. I hope that you will take this letter calmly and be guided by it. But if you blow your stack instead, I can't stop you. The most I can do is to try to help you in helping yourself. I can't live your life for you.[103]

Probably Bud's emotional situation was made worse by the agony the whole family was going through at the same time. Robert's father had seemed to get better early in the year, gaining a little weight. But just weeks before his sixtieth wedding anniversary in November, Rex's health was obviously declining, and he had only days to live. Bam wanted him buried in Kansas City, next to Rose Betty's grave—and with military honors. Rex Ivar Heinlein's service in the Spanish-American War had been the defining moment of his life, in his own mind. As the oldest son, Larry began making those arrangements.

Rex passed quietly on November 13. Robert flew to Kansas City immediately to finalize the funeral arrangements while Bam accompanied the coffin by train (a requirement of the railway). He signed for the entire funeral and burial arrangements as a package.

The service at the grave was short—the Methodist ritual. (I intended to say earlier that we used the 23rd Psalm and "In my Father's House are many mansions—" at the chapel.) This was followed by the military part . . . [sic] and it was over.

I was particularly glad that Mother decided to use the military ceremony. I did not urge her to; none of us did so—she decided it herself. But we all know how proud Dad was (and rightly so) of his service to his country. It made me happy and proud—even though I was blinded by tears—that he had it.

The honor guard and bugler were supplied by my [Robert's] old outfit, the 110th Engineers, doing their own proud. The riflemen were all master sergeants.[104]

Then the Bugler played taps:

Day is done
Gone the sun—
   From the hill
   From the lake
   From the sky . . . [sic]
Rest in peace

Sol . . . [sic] dier Brave
God is nigh.

I couldn't take it, of course—I can't take hearing it even when it is not someone I love. It was all I could manage to remain at attention and not let my sobs be audible. But, hurt as it did, I am glad Mother decided to use it—for I know that it was done precisely as Dad wanted it . . . [sic] The full honors that are meet and proper for a man who loved his country and had served it proudly and honorably.[105]

Rex Ivar Heinlein's long and sad struggle was over at last, and he was laid to a rest he could never achieve in life. It was appropriate he should be beside Rose Betty, for her accidental death thirty-three years earlier[106] was as defining for his life as his military service had been.

Robert would never know if his father realized how much his example of strength had meant. He knew he had never been the son his father had wanted him to be; his brother Rex had won finally and for-ever on that count.[107]

"May the Lord make His face to shine upon thee and give thee peace."[108]

"My Own Stuff, My Own Way"

Virginia Kirkus operated a book review service widely used by libraries and some bookstores as a purchasing guide. The short, pithy, often negative reviews were looked on by publishers as a significant pass/no-pass gateway to library sales. On October 1, 1959, Kirkus reviewed *Starship Troopers* generally positively, as a "weirdly credible adventure revolving around moral philosophy and entomology," though "somewhat pretentious in style and proposed scope, often slightly confusing to the non-aficionado."[1] On October 5, Kirkus took the unprecedented step of publishing a second review, *reversing* the first one:

> A report on this title appeared in the last issue, but additional material has reached us which necessitates a completely revised viewpoint and a new report. Heinlein is generally regarded as one of the most dependable of the SF fraternity, and this is a weirdly credible adventure revolving around a youth in his late teens, a citizen of Terra, who enlists as an interstellar soldier. His journeys not only include fantastic journeys through space, combats with insect enemies, and so forth, but they extend to the battle front of the mind, and it is on this level that the book must be more closely analyzed. Quite evidently Heinlein is projecting his own justification of the moral validity of war, of a proper military order dictated by reason, of a moral philosophy which advocates capital punishment, military violence dictated by "older and wiser heads," and a virtual reign of terror by force, but he attacks concepts and historic figures with vitriolic hysteria. Any realization of this as presenting characters engaged in philosophic discussion—which Heinlein would perhaps suggest—is far from the truth. It reads rather as dogmatic airing of very personal attitudes—a somewhat menacing sort of "brain-washing" for the uninitiated and acceptant readers.[2]

Peter Israel, Heinlein's editor at Putnam's, was surprised and disturbed, but Robert shrugged it off: It was certainly odd, but,

> the tone of the second review was about what I expect this book will get from quite a high percentage of reviewers with pacifist-socialist-internationalist leanings . . . [sic] who are very numerous, as you know. I simply hope that they do not smother it in silence—their usual technique.[3]

He sent out twenty-one copies inscribed to friends and family.[4] "Ordinarily I do not give away my own books," he told William McMorris (his line editor), asking for an additional dozen copies to be billed to his royalty account, "but this book is exceptional in that I had expert help from quite a large number of people."[5]

When the books arrived in January he sent one to his brother Clare, "Capt. of Engineers who, by expressing a firm opinion in 1944, planted the seed of which this is the fruit," and another to Marsh Gurney, the Fourth-Year from Hell who had given him such a hard time of hazing in his Plebe Year at Annapolis.

He had run into Gurney at the Congress of Flight convention in Las Vegas earlier in 1959, where half the program was about space flight. Perhaps that was why Gurney was in Heinlein's mind. He inscribed this one: "To Marsh Gurney, '26 who made me memorize log tables, the Mary Gloster & beat my tail—and thereby shaped my character for the rest of my life. With thanks RAH '29."[6]

As the Heinlein family gathered in Kansas City weeks later, to bury Robert's father, reviews began appearing in newspapers across the country. One that must have stung was written by his old friend and comrade A. P. White for his "H. H. Holmes" review column in the *New York Herald Tribune,* calling it an "irate sermon with a few fictional trappings." This was exaggerated—with more hyperbole to come: "This author is so intent upon his arguments that he has forgotten to insert a story or any recognizable characters."[7]

As uncomfortable as it was, A. P.'s review was more or less fair: Except for the hyperbole of *no* story and *no* characters, it was basically within the bounds of legitimate criticism.

But in the review that appeared in the *San Francisco Chronicle* the same day (November 8, 1959), the reviewer, Robert McCrary, let his hyperbole slop over to outright misrepresentation:

> . . . someone should criticize Heinlein, not as a bad writer, but as a peddler of dangerous ideologies. The need is all the more acute because most of Heinlein's novels are aimed at teen-age readers.

Heinlein's philosophy, at least as expressed in his novels, is the cult of violence. If someone disagrees with you, kill him. Anyone who thinks disputes can be settled peaceably is a coward. You must obey Captain Queeg [of *The Caine Mutiny*], even if he is insane, because he is in charge.

This philosophy has turned up in previous Heinlein novels, but never in so blatant a form as in "Starship Troopers." This time the plot is less a foundation for a story than a framework on which to hang a tract . . . .

At other points he extolls the virtues of flogging criminals and executing the mentally ill. (I am not making this up.)

Through it all runs the basic philosophy: You must do what I say, because I am in charge. I am in charge because I am stronger than you. If you can kill me, then you will be in charge . . . .

Heinlein's talents as a writer are undeniable. His approach to morality is incredible. Don't we already have enough immature persons who think that the answer to problems is violence? Do we really need skilled writers to egg them on?

It was hard to believe that anyone who actually read the book could take this review in any way seriously—but apparently people, and specifically some of his colleagues in science fiction, were lining up behind some of the crudest of its misrepresentations.

Starship Troopers, already in its first month of release (the condensation of the book, "Starship Soldier," appeared in the October and November 1959 issues of *The Magazine of Fantasy & Science Fiction,* and the book itself was released in October 1959), had begun to generate discussion among science-fiction writers in a new fanzine-for-professionals, the bombastically named *Proceedings of the Institute for Twenty-First Century Studies*—PITFCS—edited by Theodore Cogswell. Poul Anderson wrote a longish letter of comment, disagreeing—intelligently—with a number of the book's postulates. Heinlein wrote a cordial, but private, reply to Anderson, stressing that he would *not* be joining in the public discussion (though shoptalk with a colleague was always in order).

Cogswell wanted to reprint the McCrary review along with Anderson's letter and some remarks of his own to generate a full, formal discussion among his subscribers. His own view of the book, he told Heinlein, was somewhat different from McCrary's: A soldier, himself, in two wars, he found it a fine book for adults, but he objected to "the presentation of the idea that war is basically an exciting athletic contest in which the best side (ours of course) always wins. This I consider to be downright immoral . . ."[8] Since Heinlein's book had started the controversy, Cogswell believed it would be appropriate to include Heinlein's commentary.

Heinlein agreed with the premises, but not the conclusions. This is what he had thought he was talking about:

> The central theme is expanded in many ways and many sub-propositions consistent with or corollary to the main one are shown: (a) that nothing worth having is ever free; it must be paid for; (b) that authority always carries with it responsibility, even if a man tries to refuse it; (c) that "natural rights" are not God-given but must be earned; (d) that, despite all H-bombs, biological warfare, push-buttons, ICBMs, or other Buck Rogers miracle weapons, victory in war is never cheap but must be purchased with the blood of heroes; (e) that human beings are not potatoes, not actuarial tables, but that each one is unique and precious . . . [sic] and that the strayed lamb is as precious as the ninety-and-nine in the fold; (f) that a man's noblest act is to die for his fellow man, that such death is not suicidal, not wasted, but is the highest and most human form of survival behavior[.][9]

How one could possibly get from what was in the book to "the idea that war is basically an exciting athletic contest in which the best side (ours of course) always wins" was beyond his power to understand. Through most of the book, he pointed out, the humans are losing the war. The story ends with the war still unwon, just before a major battle—"and the reader is intentionally never allowed to know which side won."[10]

Cogswell's complaint that he had "prettied up" war Robert found incoherent.

> Answering this summary criticism is a bit like fighting a feather bed. It implies first that my purpose was to give a full understanding of what war does to everybody, both ourselves and everybody else—enemy and innocent bystander . . . [sic] or, if that is not my purpose, then it certainly *should* have been my purpose and that I am lacking in not having served that purpose, whether I planned to or not.[11]

He tried to reason out what Cogswell might have meant by his criticism:

> Now, what is the nature of your condemnation of my book? Is it that my book has *reduced* the degree of appreciation of the meaning of war in human terms? If so, how?

Or do you mean that the book failed to preach this "wide appreciation of what actually is involved in human terms" (with the assumed, and for the moment, stipulated assumption that such was or should have been my purpose). If this is what you are condemning, will you please tell me where, *within the narrow framework of a first-person infantry-soldier story,* I failed? What should I have had Sgt. Juan Rico say, think, experience, or feel in order to satisfy your (undefined) requirement which you say I have not met. I do not ask this lightly, as it is entirely possible that you, an educated man and a veteran of two wars, can suggest [to] me a theme or proposition which would be valuable to the reader and which I might be able to patch into the story at its forthcoming revision . . .[12]

This thematic examination of why an unprepared young man would choose to place his frail body between home and war's desolation might help young men whose real-life experience left them no more prepared than Johnny Rico.

Every young American today is subject to military service; most of them, as shown by the Mayer Report, et al., are not prepared for it, either emotionally or by formal schooling . . . .

He doesn't see why he should expose himself to death; nothing in his experience justifies it. The whole thing is wildly implausible and quite unfair—like going to sleep in your own bed and waking up in a locked ward of an insane asylum. It strikes him as rank injustice.

And it *is* . . . [sic] the rankest sort of injustice.

My basic purpose, then, was to promote in that prototype youth-in-a-foxhole a better understanding of the nature, purpose and function of the ridiculous and dangerous predicament he found himself in.

There were various ancillary purposes but this was the main one . . . . I was forced to limit my scope to: "Why in hell should a young man in good health be willing to fight and perhaps die for his country?". . . .

I do not expect you to like the book, nor to speak approvingly of it, since you quite clearly do not like it and do not approve of it. But, in fairness, I ask that you, in published criticism of it, (a) read more carefully what I *did* say and not impute to it things which I did *not* say, and (b) judge it within its obvious limitations as a short first-person commercial novel and not expect it to unscrew the inscrutable with respect to every possible facet of an extremely complex philosophical question (i.e., don't expect of me more than you require of yourself).[13]

McCrary's piece was clearly dishonest, and Cogswell's letter was just as clearly sincere and honestly held opinion—that had nothing whatever to do with the book. It would be quite impossible to argue with him: Heinlein courteously declined to participate in a public discussion, marking all comments as private shoptalk. Reprinting McCrary's review would simply perpetuate its "lies and malicious distortions" in a community of his friends and colleagues, where it would be most embarrassing. He would regard it as an unfriendly act to do so, with or without ancillary comment—"But please do not hesitate to print any honest unfavorable comment. I expected this book to be controversial; I knew that I was disturbing quite a number of sacred cows . . . ."[14]

Denial of the concept of "natural rights" would also be unpopular—"likely to arouse anger, not logic."[15] The flogging, too, would raise hackles, though the story logic set the flogging against the concept of jailing, and sociologists had been concerned for some time that jailing a man simply imprisons him in a school of crime, whereas the milder punishment of flogging did seem to have some deterrent potential.[16]

Most of all, his treatment of the franchise would raise howls of outrage, just as it was intended to do: "To suggest that they owe some service to their country first before they are entitled to a voice in the destinies of that country—well indeed! Shocking!"

He, himself, was deeply shocked at conscription.

Poul Anderson pointed out to me that he rather doubted if this country could survive through purely voluntary military service.

Perhaps he is right. I care not. If there are not sufficient Simon-pure, utterly uncoerced volunteers to defend a country and save it . . . [sic] then let it go down the drain! And that applies just as much to my own beloved country as it does to the Roman Empire . . . The thought of a draftee being required to die that I may live is as morally offensive to me as that of galley slaves, chained to their sweeps, and drowning in battle not of their choosing.

If the United States goes under (as I am inclined to think she will), I will be inclined to blame it on moral decay rather than on the superiority of our enemies . . . [sic] and, to me, the gravest aspect of that moral decay lies in the fact that we have elected to depend on human slaves as cannon fodder.

But I suppose that my opposition to a democratically accepted and publicly approved social institution such as the National Selective Service Act—having the gall to label this flag-bedecked and chaplain-blessed custom "human slavery"—is still another of "Heinlein's dangerous ideologies," as seditious as my unspeakable notion that the franchise is not a "natural right" to be handed out as freely as favors at a children's party, but to be earned by toil and danger at great personal sacrifice.

Well, if my teachings are now to be indicted as "dangerous," tending to "corrupt the youth of the land," I will be in most noble and distinguished company. Pass the hemlock, please—[17]

Cogswell replied temperately, saying that his criticisms were based on his overall impression of the book as a juvenile sold to children's librarians—so he could agree with every specific point in Heinlein's letter, without changing the totality of his reaction.

And in the meantime, chico, relax. I don't know about the outsiders, but as far as the writers go you are warmly liked and greatly respected (though often disagreed with, and that is as it should be) and it should be obvious that no comments by a reviewer are going to change that.[18]

If you must take hemlock, he added, finish the Future History first!

Perhaps the review wouldn't matter—but the book was generating discussion among his colleagues, so off the point, seizing so much on incidentals and missing the main message, that Schuyler Miller, who had gotten more earfuls at that year's World SF Convention in Detroit than he could really tolerate,[19] took the opportunity of his review of *Starship Troopers* for the March 1960 issue of *Analog* (John Campbell had been gradually changing the name of *Astounding Science Fiction* over to *Analog Science Fact Science Fiction* over the last year, fading the old name down on the cover while the new name became more prominent) to remind people that what appeared in the story was not the direct reflection of the person. This was an aspect of provincialism, he wrote, "that refuses to remain provincial, a mark of naiveté that is apt to brand the most sophisticated."[20] He compared the reaction to the completely unjust vilification experienced by Kenneth Roberts, the writer of a 1940 historical novel, *Oliver Wiswell,* written from the viewpoint of a Tory in the American Revolution. The issues Heinlein raised in *Starship Troopers* were fit and relevant subjects for discussion: "Surely any writer has the right to choose an unpopular theme, and develop it with all his skill, without being condemned—without being identified with the thing he writes!"[21]

Cogswell went on to publish the McCrary review and many letters in the *Proceedings of the Institute for Twenty-First Century Studies.* Only one of them—

George Price—seemed to be able even to read the clear language of the book. Robert began to feel that his colleagues in the field—with a few exceptions— despised him.[22]

Even more disturbing was the pattern he was seeing coming together, the emergence of what we now call "political correctness." Three years later, Heinlein let his hair down in shoptalk with Ted Sturgeon:

> . . . I am still bugged by the quality of reviewing generally accorded science fiction. Or let's call it "speculative fiction" for a moment because one of the things that bugs me the most is that some critics seem strongly indisposed to permit a writer to *speculate*.
>
> It seems to me that the only excuse for the sort of fiction we write (whatever it is called) is *speculation,* as far-ranging and imaginative as the author can manage.
>
> But is this permitted? Don't make me laugh, it hurts. The usual critic drags in his Procrustean bed at the first hint of free-swinging speculation. There has grown up an extremely conservative orthodoxy in science fiction, spineless, boneless, suffocating. It is almost amorphous but I can sketch the vague outlines. It is do-goodish and quasi-socialist—but not Communist; this critic wouldn't recognize dialectical materialism if it bit him in the face. It is both "democratic" and "civil libertarian" without the slightest understanding that these two powerful and explosive concepts can frequently be in direct conflict, each with the other. It is egalitarian, pacifist, and anti-racist—with no notion that these concepts might ever clash. It believes heartily in "freedom" and "equality"—yet somehow thinks that "older & wiser heads" are fully justified in manipulating the human psyche to achieve these ends—after all, it's for their own good . . . [sic] and these new orthodoctrinaires are always quite certain that they *know* what is good for the human race.
>
> (Me, I *don't* know. I keep thinking about it—and speculating.) . . .
>
> This pious critic will allow any speculation at all, on any subject—as long as it conforms to the unwritten assumptions of the new orthodoxy.
>
> However his twin brother works just across the street—he believes in science fiction "for amusement only"—like pin ball machines.
>
> He will permit any speculation at all—as long as it is about gadgets only and doesn't touch people. He doesn't care what mayhem you commit on physics, astronomy, or chemistry with your gadgets . . . [sic] but the people must be the same plain old wonderful jerks that live in his Home Town. Give him a good ole adventure story any time, with lots of Gee-Whiz in it

and space ships blasting off and maybe the Good Guys (in white space ships) chasing the Bad Guys (in black space ships)—but, brother, don't you say anything about the Methodist Church, or the Flag, or incest, or homosexuality, or teleology, or theology, or the sacredness of marriage, or anything philosophical! Because you are just an entertainer, see? That sort of Heavy Thinking is reserved for C. P. Snow or James Jones or Graham Greene. You are a pulp writer, Bud, and you will always be a pulp writer even though your trivia is now bound in boards and sells for just as much as Grace Metalious' stories[23] . . . [sic] and you are not permitted to have Heavy Thoughts. Space Ships and Heavy Thinking do not mix—so shut up and sit down!

The rule is: Science Fiction by its nature *must* be trivial.

This of course rules out . . . a large fraction of my work—and all of my future work, I think. Because . . . I'm tired of writing about space ships and rather bored with gadgets. Oh, I've always dealt with philosophical problems, just as you have, but I usually sugar-coated them and packaged them to look like something else—*Methuselah's Children, Citizen of the Galaxy, Have Space Suit—Will Travel, Star Beast* and some others were just as loaded and explosive as *Starship Troopers* or *Stranger in a Strange Land*. But the packaging was a bit different and each had a bit more cops & robbers in it than these last two did.

But in the meantime this conservative orthodoxy has grown up and it becomes harder and harder to sneak in an original idea without being nailed for it by either the Pious Critic, or his brother the Just-for-Fun Critic—or both. So the hell with 'em both. I'm going to write what I please—about sex or love or duty or marriage or politics or epistemology or God. Probably somebody will print it. If not, at least I'll enjoy writing it—and I can't enjoy writing if I must always keep one eye on the Procrustean bed.[24]

He began to receive fan mail about the book. One "bumptious and argumentative" youngster,[25] about age fifteen, disagreed with some passing remark about the role of cosmic radiation in evolution—a perfectly orthodox speculation. And he seemed to assume that Dr. Teller's "a little radiation is good for you" implied a wholehearted endorsement of thermonuclear war. Heinlein tried to steer him away from his assumptions, to get him to think about the material instead of his preconceptions, but had little success. The boy wrote back—and again wrote later, long letters wanting to discuss politics and especially atomic energy policy and Communism. Apparently he had a great deal of time on his hands—time Heinlein did not have when he was trying to get back to work. He turned the correspondence over to Ginny. Ginny had been spending a fair amount of time on the new Broadmoor ski slopes and had a disagreement with a snowbank; she replied to the boy's next missive (and the next and the next) while Heinlein started another book. Ginny found the letters tiresome, too, "shrill and disputatious,"[26] "long letter after long letter, each one more argumentative and know-it-all than the last."[27] "Then we both got fed up with his manners and his illogic and stopped answering . . . [sic] and after a while he quit writing, to our great relief."[28]

That would not be the last time they would be troubled by Alexei Panshin.[29]

Heinlein pulled out the abandoned manuscript of *The Heretic* and took a fresh look at it. This book was supposed to be a satire, and he might have stalled earlier because he had just been too *careful* before, but he didn't want to pull his punches anymore.

He had tried a very conventional way of telling the story—the same way Olaf Stapledon had framed *Odd John*: A journalist tells what he sees and reports on the story's protagonist. But the *Man from Mars*'s journalist, Ben Caxton, may have been too much of a man-of-the-world personality, who kept the story moving away from the nurse and the Man–Martian. He switched over to another viewpoint character—the crusty minor character he had mentioned in passing in his very first set of notes in 1948, when it was still going to be the "Gulf" story.[30]

The change of viewpoint character probably was enough to rearrange the relationships and break the story loose from the *Odd John* storytelling model. Jubal Harshaw firmed up as the kind of older mentor Heinlein himself had always relied on:

> Some critics say that my stories always contain a wise and crusty old man who is my own concept of myself. Not true. They are all different and they are *not* self-portraits; they are many men who did indeed live and who were my mentors—and now they are all gone to whatever Valhalla there may be for such men . . . .[31]

This would be partly Arthur George "Sarge" Smith—with whom he had struck up an intimate correspondence[32]—and partly E. E. "Doc" Smith—and partly Hermann Deutsch (much of his physical appearance from Deutsch).[33]

Early in January 1960, Willy Ley wrote trying to interest Heinlein in a television show that was buying story outlines,[34] but the Heinleins were scheduled to leave in the spring, for a trip to Russia they had been planning for years, and Heinlein would be out of the country just when the TV work would be heating up. Ginny had tried several times to talk him out of the trip—she wanted to stay as far away from the Iron Curtain as possible—but Heinlein was determined to go, and she had finally agreed to it because there was an international summit meeting between President Eisenhower and Premier Khrushchev scheduled for the time they were to be in the USSR; the Russians would want to avoid an international incident while the talks were going on, so it might be reasonably safe . . .[35]

On January 5, 1960, Robert McCrary wrote offering him space for a rebuttal to McCrary's review of *Starship Troopers,* but the damage was done, and in any case Heinlein needed to write something saleable for himself and Ginny, instead of helping Hearst sell more newspapers. He began to write again on January 23, 1960, and his *Man from Mars* (re-retitled from *The Heretic*) flowed and flowed, and took on a life of its own. An ordinary book might take him three to four weeks, but this was not an ordinary book. He wrote "The End" on March 21, 1960, and had a stack of eight hundred pages of manuscript (compared to about three hundred pages for one of the juveniles)— not strictly science fiction, not like anything he had ever done before. Ginny was startled by it: "When he finished it, I finally got to read it all in one piece, and it was one of those 'what hath God wrought!' things to me."[36]

The long gestation period for this book had bridged from the postwar period (1948) into the Kennedy era, and American culture had changed and changed again in the interim. It was not publishable when conceived—and there was some doubt whether it was yet publishable in 1960:

> . . . I shan't be surprised if nobody wants it. For the first time in my life I indulged in the luxury of writing without one eye on the taboos, the market, etc.; I will be unsurprised and only moderately unhappy if it turns out that the result is unsalable."[37]

At least part of its "problem" was that the book did not cleanly fall within science fiction as it was in 1960: "This story is Cabellesque satire on religion and sex, it is *not* science fiction by any stretch of the imagination."[38]

In 1960, *The Man from Mars* was ahead of a curve that would become pronounced in mainstream fiction during the early 1960s. The perennial debate among literary critics about the "death of the novel" heated up again in the late 1950s, and there was speculation in the critical community that the possibilities of the realistic novel might be exhausted, and the next trend in prestige literature might be satires. Joseph Heller's important satire *Catch-22* was published in the same month as *Stranger in a Strange Land,* at which time the first of Kurt Vonnegut's satires of the 1960s, *Mother Night* (1961), was already in production.

The Man from Mars shows some significant sourcing that suggests Heinlein drew comfortably on mainstream sources. For example, from William Lindsay Gresham's *Nightmare Alley* (1946, filmed in 1947), as well as Philip Wylie's 1930 *Gladiator.*[39]

Gladiator has been grandfathered into science fiction (through the efforts of genre historian Sam Moskowitz). *Nightmare Alley,* the story of a con man who moves through several different underworlds and half-worlds, has no discernable connection to genre science fiction. It was a mix that was to become characteristic of Heinlein—and with which his genre readers were not always comfortable.

He just had time to correct the manuscript for *The Man from Mars* and send it to the typist before they left for the Soviet Union. Meanwhile, Shasta had finally given up the ghost, and Ted Dikty had offered to get Heinlein the printing plates for the three Future History books. It would have to wait until he got back. He just had time to write Schuyler Miller a thank-you letter for the "cool and analytical" review he had given *Starship Troopers* in the March issue of *Analog.*

They were scheduled to leave on April 18, stopping by Wiesbaden to see Freddie and Martha (King) Smith. Fred Smith was now a general, in charge of the American presence in the European theater. Rex wrote, asking to have his daughter Tish join them in Wiesbaden and for the trip, but Robert was very reluctant to put her in harm's way: As a brutal fact, the State Department would not be any protection for Americans traveling in Russia. She could join them for the "civilized portions" of the trip, Robert ruled—in Germany at the start and Scandinavia at the end—but not for the Russian middle.

Then their plans abruptly changed on them: The Russian visas came through marked ten days earlier than they had planned—ten days before the summit was to convene in Paris. They had to decide whether the additional risk was worth the trip—and they would have to go almost directly there.

THE WORKERS' PARADISE

On April 19, 1960, the Heinleins left Colorado Springs for New York. They pushed the European part of the trip to the end, after the Russian part. The Paris summit was to convene on May 16, so they would be safe enough during the preparatory period. They reduced their baggage to a minimum, but there was one item they did not skimp on for this trip:

> Ginny ordinarily does not carry jewelry outside the States, not from fear of losing it (insured) but because it is such a nuisance at customs. But when we went to the USSR, she carried with her about $6,000 worth of emeralds, in a chamois bag, pinned to the lining of an inner zippered compartment in her purse . . . not to wear, but as valuta . . . because when war breaks out paper money is suddenly worth nothing and travelers' cheques even less, whereas all through history it has been possible to bribe one's way across a border with precious stones.[1]

They flew to Frankfurt, gaining a day but losing a night's sleep. They were booked then on an Afghan-airline mixed passenger–freight flight to Prague.[2] Prague seemed gray-looking and dreary, the people moderately prosperous but subdued, numb, not yet recovered from the crackdown on Czechoslovakia.[3] The Heinleins flew on to Warsaw, along with politicians from the Mexican Senate on a junket, and found a city bombed nearly flat in the war, distressingly poor and still not rebuilt. "You would be hard pushed to find a Communist in Poland," Heinlein wrote to relatives of Sprague and Catherine de Camp, "and they hate the Russians with the same intensity with which they hate the Germans . . . Only in the captive Baltic republics do you see signs of the terror which a stranger can spot."[4]

On the last day of April, they boarded an Aeroflot flight to Moscow, when they got their first exposure to Russian consumer engineering: The seatbelts had only one side—they could not be fastened; there was nothing to fasten to. At Vnukovo (Grandfather) Airport, the customs officials were startled to hear Ginny speaking painfully correct Russian. The Heinleins were met by a car and driver, and their English-speaking guide, provided by InTourist.[5]

The ride to the hotel was . . . illuminating: Moscow appeared not to have suburbs at all: It went directly from rustic log cabin dachas to apartment blocks in the severe and bleak Russian Modern style.[6] The Hotel Ukraine was in that style—a thousand rooms and jammed with local political delegations from Africa and Asia and a dozen or so tourists. Possibly the crowding was due to the next day being May Day, the largest national celebration in the Soviet Union. Ginny found herself pressed into service as an impromptu translator for the *sedmoi etadz*—tourists who did not speak Russian—mostly making inquiries for blankets, schedules, and so forth.[7] Wherever there were Americans, they clung to each other as strangers in a very strange land.

Not knowing what kind of accommodation they would encounter, Ginny had booked them at Luxe class, the best, and also the most expensive. The suite they were given, at the end of a maze of corridors, was enormous, palatial—larger, in fact, than their entire house in Colorado Springs. But the locks were literally falling off the doors, and the parquet floors crackled when walked upon, the tiles popping up at odd angles.[8] These conditions obtained throughout the entire Soviet Union—in one hotel the tiles made a wooden flower blossom, coming up around the legs of the piano—possibly because they were wet-mopped incessantly and never cared for. Unskilled labor was never a problem in the Soviet Union, which had a full-employment policy, and makework was found for even the oldest and feeblest. Every floor had its own "dragon"—a concierge to whom they must surrender their keys when they went out (their passports were held at the front desk). The streets were swept by grandmothers with twig brooms, and even in the deep and otherwise impressive Moscow subways, they found a young woman at each landing whose only job it was to press the start button if the escalator stopped.

The food in Moscow—indeed, all over the Soviet Union—Robert and Ginny found indescribably bad. They lost several pounds each during their two weeks there. Alcohol was plentiful. Vodka and sedatives were a practical necessity, given the frustrations people were presented with on an hourly basis. "The most prominent sight in Moskva and everywhere in USSR is the passed-out drunk; he is everywhere . . . One freedom remaining in Russia is the right to get stinking drunk in public, any time, anywhere."[9] There seemed to be, Robert remarked, a drunk passed out in every washroom in the city.[10]

On May Day, the hotel had not reserved any viewing positions for its guests for the parade. Robert and Ginny took their heaviest coats, as the day was chilly—a special lightweight cashmere coat Ginny had bought for Robert that entertained them both by surprising the Russian coat-check girls, who always expected the usual Russian weight. Loaded up with cameras, including the heavy StereoReal-ist Ginny had given him for Christmas in 1954, they went over to the National Hotel, which had balconies overlooking the street. But Margaret Truman—former President Truman's daughter—was staying there at the time, and they could not get into the hotel. Instead, they found a spot on the street. The crowd built up as the parade began "with a series of huge rockets (on carriers) which we later learned were only mockups."[11] They gave way for a French Communist tour-ist who asked them to let grandmother through—a tiny woman—so she could see the parade. The rest of the family crowded in after her, and Robert and Ginny found themselves pushed back against the building. But Robert got some good stereo slides of the parade despite the conditions.

After the parade, Ginny got their guide Ludmilla—a sweet child but more a hindrance than a help in Ginny's opinion—to take them to Red Square. St. Basil's Cathedral was closed. Nor was the Kremlin open to the public. That left "Goom"—the huge central Soviet department store, *Glavnyi Universalnyi Magazin* (or GUM). "Nothing of any interest to a human being was on sale there."[12] They did get an exposure—somewhat horrifying—to everyday liv-ing conditions: Ludmilla wanted to buy some lipstick while she was there. They watched fascinated as she got in line at a counter and eventually told the clerk what she wanted. The clerk wrote up the purchase and sent her to another counter—another line—where she paid for the purchase and came back to the original counter to get the lipstick.

So much for shopping in Moscow.

They had three more days there, and the sightseeing ran out depressingly soon. They were able to obtain tickets, though, for Tchaikovsky's most fa-mous opera, *Eugene Onegin,* and for a Saturday matinee performance of the Bolshoi Ballet of a children's ballet, *The Hobby Horse.* The Russian practice was to not release tickets until the day of the performance, but a black market of scalpers existed, and they found they could get tickets for a performance of Chekhov's *The Cherry Orchard* at the Moscow Arts Theatre—the theater where Stanislavski had worked before coming to New York.

Robert encouraged Ginny to dress up for the Bolshoi, and she wore Chi-nese silks and emeralds—an obvious foreigner and an equally obvious capi-talist: During intermission a Red Army officer shoved her brusquely out of his way, gone before Robert could even react. His was simply the most overt of the various disapprovals they met with. Most Russians, they found, were warm and friendly—but there were exceptions.

Robert had picked up a cold on May Day, and he was glad to get out of town on May 4, headed to Alma Ata, near the border with Tibet and about a hundred and thirty miles from the border with Red China. This was the most remote part of the Soviet Union they could get to (they were not allowed into Siberia—in fact, the American consul in Moscow had been slightly faint at some of the places they planned to go). They had an overnight stay in Tashkent—more down-at-heels hotel luxury—and in the morning continued on to Alma Ata where their hotel had just been opened, though the decor literally dated back to Czarist days—crushed velvet curtains with ball fringes. When Robert closed the door for the first time, the entire locking assembly came away in his hand. He asked Ginny how to say "Good morning" in Russian, and then went to greet their floor's dragon at her desk, handing her the lock. She was quite startled.[13]

When the Heinleins came back from breakfast, they found a repairman trying to reinstall it, but, Robert said, he was complaining that the screws were too short. Robert had scarcely a word of Russian, and the repairman spoke no English—but somehow they communicated that to each other.[14]

Their InTourist guide took them to the Forty-Years-of-October collective farm where they received gifts of hothouse tomatoes and a bottle of the local raisin wine and were guests of honor at a special pageant presented in their honor by the local kindergarten class—recitations and songs. It was all very charming indeed, Robert said—but he wasn't following the actual words, the way Ginny was: When they got outside, she told him the recitations were the Life of Lenin and the Seven Year Plan, and the song was about preserving the October Revolution.[15] When their guides got them back to the hotel, they found a summons to the local InTourist office.

On May Day, while they were crowded on a sidewalk in Moscow, the Russian military had been able to shoot down one of the American U-2 spy planes making a high-altitude overflight to photograph military intelligence. That day, the Russians connected with Francis Gary Powers's plane over Sverdlosk, halfway into his flight from Pakistan to Norway, and he had to bail out when the plane began to break up. Powers survived the parachute jump but was promptly arrested by Soviet authorities. Premier Khrushchev delayed making the announcement of the capture of plane and pilot to make use of the propaganda opportunity. On May 5, 1960, the lid came off. Two days later, he let it be known that they had the plane's cameras and gear—and the pilot, who had survived and would be put on trial for espionage.[16]

Robert and Ginny were harangued by the local InTourist head about the incident,[17] claiming a moral high ground the Heinleins were certainly not going to concede. Robert had drilled into Ginny that she must *never* lose control of her temper while in the Soviet Union, but he lost control of his own, shoving the tomato and wine "gifts" across the man's desk.[18] Their guide, Mikhail, tried to keep up with him, translating. Ginny tried to maintain her own cool, answering in her best Russian,[19] but Robert losing his temper was very bad for her. She jumped in feet first, pointing out that a nation that kept slave labor concentration camps had no right to any sort of moral high tone. In 1960 the Gulag still did not officially exist, and the commissar denied it. Ginny began pointing out the location and name of the installations they had seen, supplemented with statistics they had deduced from stray facts picked up in casual conversation about how many slave laborers had been worked to death in each.[20] Robert took the opportunity of the stunned pause in the harangue to gather Ginny up and stomp out of the room, without being dismissed.

They went back to the hotel room, shaking: There was no telling what might happen to them. They were 3,500 miles inside the Soviet Union, at a place their State Department had specifically told them the United States could not reach to protect or rescue them. They stood a very good chance of being arrested and *disappeared*. They slept that night in their shoes, prepared for the five A.M. pounding on the door that meant Vorkuta[21] for them.[22] But they stood their ground. Summoned again to the InTourist office the next day, they refused to go. Eventually the InTourist commisar gave up on them and returned their passports and tickets for the next leg of their trip.[23]

But from that point on, Ginny remarked, it was as if a curtain had fallen over them. The atmosphere turned icy: No one was warm and friendly anywhere they went. Americans were officially disapproved.[24]

Their itinerary took them back to Tashkent overnight, and then on to Samarkand—another of Ginny's particular choices for this trip, and the reason, she said, she had agreed to go to Russia in the first place. Samarkand is a place of golden legend, in turn-of-the-century romantic literature. The tomb of Tamburlane the Conqueror is there.

The reality was not golden: Their hotel was standard-issue Soviet model, but so crowded with furniture it required forethought to move around in it. The bathtub was being repaired, and there was no hot water at all. No bottled water. No boiled water. Ginny quadrupled the halazone tablet dosage to purify the water, but it didn't do any good. Spit-baths for them—and another case of amebic dysentery for Ginny.

But the area itself was beautiful and romantic, the landscape littered with blue onion domes. Samarkand is in a predominantly Muslim part of the Soviet Union, and Ginny photographed women in the head-to-toe version of the *abaya*, with the burqa, the required "veil," with its curtain-window of gauze (*purdah*) to

see out (officially no longer permitted, but evidently tolerated). They were allowed to tour the tombs of Tamburlane's relatives, and finally even the Great
One's tomb, two stories underground and not lit at all. Robert got taken on one
of their huge boatlike swings rocked by a German girl from the Volga region.
He could not remember the Russian for "stop!"—urgently necessary for someone who gets seasick—and was badly shaken up.

That was the fun part of the trip. From there to Tblisi (unbearably hot), and
on to Kiev for a few days, where it was cold and damp and rainy. They were glad
for the opportunity to rest up, for Robert's cold contracted on May Day was
worse. Ginny told him to stay in bed while she went out to find a bookshop for
something to read. Kiev showed conspicuous signs of shelling left over from the
Great Patriotic War. She found just two books—something by Mérimée and
another book that had first been published in English in the eighteenth century.
In Russia, they publish books in limited editions and might or might not reprint
when the supplies become exhausted. Books of all types tended to disappear
rapidly.[25] Worse, she was coming down with Robert's cold—but found he had
used the last of the tissues they had brought from the United States.

They were gradually making their way north and out of the country. The
Paris summit was scheduled to start on May 16. From Kiev they went to
Vilno (Vilnius) in Lithuania. At the airport, they encountered at first hand the
"pravda" about the Baltic states: In a casual discussion with other American
tourists about their trip and their next destination, Ginny mentioned that Lithuania had been conquered by the Soviet Union during the Great Patriotic War. A
translator rushed over to contradict her with shrill indignation: "Mrs. Heinlein
was *lying*!—that Lithuania had *always* been part of the Soviet Union."

> The most ironical—and the most chilling—aspect of this incident was that
> she was *sincere*. She was certain that she was speaking the truth—and that
> Mrs. Heinlein was a liar, a capitalist aggressor liar, intentionally spreading
> false stories about her beloved country.[26]

Ginny shrugged, told her she was wrong, and turned her back on her.

Vilno was not particularly interesting, but they were there on Sunday May 15
when they encountered a group of Red Army Cadets boisterously celebrating the
manned launch of a Russian astronaut!

> One cadet asked if I had heard of their new spaceship? I had not, so he told me
> about it: it had lifted off that morning; he gave me the gross weight in kilos,
> the lift-off time, the period, the apogee and perigee—"And even now," he said,

making a sweeping circle with his hands, "a Russian cosmonaut is circling the globe!"

I congratulated them with a glassy smile, [and] hurried back to my hotel . . .[27]

But suddenly, official silence fell on the subject. By evening the launch had become *un*manned—the Vostok capsule being tested had carried dummies only. Reaching his hotel, Heinlein tried to get a fuller account from the Soviet Union's main newspaper, *Pravda*.

No *Pravda*—

No *Pravda* anywhere that day. I tried to listen to the Voice of America that evening; it was thoroughly jammed. I did listen to the Voice of Moscow, which reported a shot in exactly the same terms the Red Army cadet had used—but made no mention of the shot being manned.

Later that day my InTourist guide looked me up and carefully told me that the cadet had been mistaken.[28]

Reports a few days later said one of the retro-rockets had fired in the wrong attitude, and the ship could not be retrieved: It was outward bound from Earth—possibly carrying a dead cosmonaut to the stars.

They were approached in a corridor that day by a frightened man who identified himself as a dissident, wanting their help. This was fantastically dangerous for all of them, but they both memorized the message he wanted to get out, and the address, and then Robert burned the paper it was written on. Ginny then spontaneously embraced the man, told him soberly that he had nothing to fear from them. Robert embraced him also. And then he hurried away into the night, and they never learned anything more about the man or what happened to him.

There was nothing they could do but go on to Riga (Latvia), where they saw a church service that overflowed the chapel, with people kneeling in prayer on the sidewalks, and were entertained by the Soviet Writer's Union. Robert's request to unblock royalties for pirated stories published in Russian had never borne any fruit: His name was not even carried on the credit lists the Russians kept of their international piracies, under either of the two letters of the Cyrillic alphabet used to transliterate the initial sound of the name Heinlein (a factor that plagued them almost daily, as they could never be sure of finding their names or reservation on InTourist lists, whether as *gainlain* or *chaynlain*), but he was treated here as an honored fellow professional, at a borrowed Czarist palace rather than the union's headquarters building—a marathon, five-hour drinking bout traditional for such affairs.

One of the party acted as official toastmaker; others could amend the toasts, and then the entire group would toss back their cognac (rather than the more usual vodka)—just a largish thimbleful per toast, but there were *a lot* of toasts. Ginny quit early on, but Robert kept up with them, to uphold the honor of the profession in the United States. He kept up his end of the bargain, walking out unassisted.

Their next stop was Leningrad, and they arrived on May 16, 1960—the very day the Paris summit between President Eisenhower and Soviet Premier Khrushchev started. The first thing on the Heinleins' agenda was the Hermitage Museum—the collection of art assembled by Empress Catherine the Great in the eighteenth century. But it was closed that day, to wax the floors. Instead, they had a picnic lunch packed for a car trip to Zagorsk (sandwiches were, apparently, not in the repertoire of Russian chefs, but they could get bread and traditional appetizers—*Zakuski*—consisting of sliced meats and various pickled vegetables, so they made do). That night they were able to get tickets for another ballet performance—which impressed Ginny as mediocre. She had assumed that the standards of the Bolshoi were maintained everywhere in the Soviet Union and was disappointed to learn there was as much variation in performance standards there as in the United States.

They were lunching with some other Americans on their second day in Leningrad when a newcomer arrived with the news, still officially suppressed inside the USSR, that the Paris summit had collapsed: On the first day, while the Heinleins were still in Riga, Khrushchev had demanded an official apology from President Eisenhower for the U-2 overflight two weeks earlier. The president refused to offer an apology—the Soviets had as much or more spy activity in the United States as the United States had over the Soviet Union—and Khrushchev walked out, taking the whole Soviet delegation with him. There would be no summit.

Robert and Ginny looked at each other for a second and then, without discussion, stood up simultaneously, abandoning their lunch in mid-course. They went directly to the InTourist office and demanded the first flight out of Leningrad and out of the USSR. They would pay extra for it—whatever was needed.

Impossible! they were told: They must continue with their scheduled tourist activities until the planned conclusion a few days later. The two international flights out of Leningrad each week were booked solid for weeks in advance.

They talked the InTourist official into applying to the Moscow headquarters for permission for them to leave by train to Helsinki, in Finland.

The next day they were allowed to board the train at the old Finland Station (an irony that could not have been lost on them): They were reversing Lenin's route from exile in Switzerland to St. Petersburg in 1917.[29] The train was almost empty, except for one young Russian naval officer who conveniently spoke English and chatted amiably with them for the entire, rough trip. Ginny was morally certain he was keeping an eye on them for the Politburo.[30]

Russian trains operate on a different gauge than train tracks in Europe. They had to stop and literally change the wheels on the cars before proceeding into Finland. When that happened, Robert and Ginny finally felt the release of not having to watch themselves, anticipate problems, rein in their tempers. "[W]e heaved a sigh of relief, and felt human again."[31]

When they pulled into Helsinki, they stopped by the Hotel Carlton and soaked up wonderful double martinis. While Ginny called to advance their reservations at the Hotel Torni, Robert went to a newsstand and bought up every free-world newspaper he could find—French, American, British, German—and surrounded himself with them, browsing and luxuriating in uncontrolled facts.[32] They called Kristina, a friend in Helsinki, and she greeted them with flowers.[33]

They had both fallen in love with the northern countries on their earlier trips, but Finland (which does not consider itself to be "Scandinavian") was special even among them, with a national character of fierce resoluteness— *sisu*—that precisely suited their mood on this occasion. The Suomic "do what must be done" was the *only* attitude that a free people could possibly take, living next door to the Soviet Union. The Baltic states—Latvia, Estonia, Lithuania—did not have it, and they had been eaten up by the USSR.

Robert itched to tell about his experiences. All the typewriters Ginny could find had a Swedish keyboard, but he found one in the hotel Torni without the extra accents and, while Ginny finalized their local travel arrangements for a month-long bus tour north of the Arctic Circle, wrote a serious 9,000-word discussion of the Soviets' somewhat "flexible" attitude toward facts, "'Pravda' Means 'Truth'":

> . . . . the simple truth is a tactic not contemplated under Marxism-Leninism doctrines. Here we have the essential distinction between truth and pravda.
>
> Truth, to the West, consists of all the facts without distortion.
>
> Pravda is that which serves the World Communist Revolution. Pravda can be a mixture of fact and falsehood, or a flat-footed, brassbound, outright lie.[34]

When the draft was finished, they began by traveling north from Helsinki to Lahti to see the high school graduation of a foreign exchange student they had met in Palo Alto—one of Rex's contacts—Marjatta Lievonen. Lahti is best known for its winter sports, but while they were there, Robert and Ginny visited one of its many parks and sculpture gardens, a memorial to the dead of Finland's most recent war with Russia. A group of Russian tourists happened to come along at the same time. Ginny Heinlein remembered the occasion:

> Robert became incensed at their presence, and muttered something about a dog returning to its vomit, and he propelled me out of the park and down the street to a florist shop, where he made a purchase of flowers. We carried them back to the little park and elbowing our way through the Russians, laid them at the feet of the statue.[35]

From Finland they went to Norway, taking a steamer to the Lofoten Islands and a tiny boat through the Göta Canal. In Sweden, where his niece Lynnie was finishing up her year as a foreign exchange student, they stayed on a family farm north of Stockholm—a stopover long enough to sketch out another article, funny-ish, in a gruesome sort of way, an ironic how-to deal with InTourist. The first draft of "Inside InTourist" (subtitled "How to Break Even (or Almost) in the Soviet Union") was 2,400 scathing words ("The proper mood for the Soviet Union is that of the man who hit himself on the head with a hammer because it felt so good when he stopped . . . You can avoid the worst shocks to your nervous system by knowing in advance that you are not going to get what you have paid for," and so on).[36] Heinlein put it away and they continued with a motor tour through Denmark. They managed the side trip to Wiesbaden they had had to put off when the Russian leg of the trip was advanced by ten days, and visited their friend Fred Smith, Commander for the European Theater. General Smith took the Heinleins to Intelligence, and they were questioned minutely about what they had seen and heard: Firsthand reports of the interior of the Soviet Union were very hard to come by. Apparently the transcript of their debriefing circulated through the entire U.S. intelligence community: Even the Soviets must have had a copy before they got back to Colorado Springs.[37]

Nearly three weeks later, their agapomene with the North—all of it!—came to an end, and they flew over the North Pole to Anchorage, Alaska, where Robert stayed close to the hotel nursing his cold and Ginny judged the Miss Alaska contest, with cartoonist Shel Silverstein as a co-judge. And then they were debriefed again at Elmendorf Air Force Base (adjacent to Anchorage), leaving a little time for touring, visiting Point Barrow, the northernmost inhabited place in the United States—a tiny village with few permanent buildings in it. Chained dogs (for sleds) were in front of each building.

By July 20,[38] Point Barrow was as springlike as it was going to get. They arrived in time to see some of the local Inupiaq slaughter and skin a seal.

They acquired Eskimo sunglasses as souvenirs—ivory with slits cut into them—together with some large pebbles from the shore. Heinlein distinguished himself by falling into the Arctic Ocean—up to his ankles, at any rate. Fifteen years later, he wrote of the experience: "No real danger, plenty of help around, and I was taken indoors quickly. But I am still trying to get warm all the way through."[39]

They went on to Seattle. Ginny flew back to Colorado Springs to open the house while Robert went on to Palo Alto to bring fresh news of Lynnie to Rex and make his way back home by way of a nudist resort near Las Vegas, where he could bake in the desert sun and be really warm for the first time in three months. He got home around the middle of August, after four and a half months.[40]

Heinlein had several orders of business to attend to right away: E. E. "Doc" Smith had dedicated the Gnome hardcover publication of *The Vortex Blasters* to him, with an admiring inscription on Heinlein's personal copy. Dedications are always flattering, but this gave Heinlein an opportunity to tell Smith just how big an influence he had been on him:

> Doc, there is no easy way for me to tell you how honored and moved I feel at the printed dedication and your inscription. Perhaps it would be better for me to acknowledge in writing what I have told you orally years ago: the enormous extent of my literary indebtedness to you. I have learned from many writers—from Verne and Wells and Campbell and Sinclair Lewis, et al.—but I have learned more from you than from any of the others and perhaps more than for all the others put together . . . .
>
> For the past twenty years I've been trying to emulate you and any really astute literary detective could trace down hundreds of things in my stories which derive from your ideas, style, moral standards, et endless cetera. Plagiarize you I never did, at least not consciously; learn from you I always have, in every paragraph, and I am proud to acknowledge the debt.[41]

Lurton Blassingame was moving into that category, too—people he could unburden himself to and be confident their advice would be calm, balanced, and objective, and, even more important, impassioned in the right way.[42]

And the current work was moving forward: "'Pravda' Means 'Truth'" had already been picked up by *The American Mercury* but would require careful revision. He also needed to expand the "Inside InTourist" article—and collect *The Man from Mars* from his typist. It was time to see if he could remain a fiction writer at all on terms he could live with.

15

SCISSORBILL PARADISE

They were "debriefed" a third time in Colorado Springs, by someone from the CIA who tried to swear them to silence about anything they had seen and heard. "This is nonsense," Heinlein said, and handed back the secrecy form. Heinlein intended to tell anyone who would listen, as long as his breath held out. He had already been invited to speak to the Cadet Forum at the Air Force Academy—and Ginny got to be in some demand as an after-dinner speaker for her talks about the trip.[1]

The American Mercury magazine, which was, regrettably, no longer so cutting-edge or chic as when H. L. Mencken had edited it in the 1920s and 1930s, immediately recognized the timeliness and potential importance of the " 'Pravda' Means 'Truth' " article. The editor, Shields ReMine, wanted to rush it into the October issue—at half its length as written. Heinlein reedited some of the editorial opinions ReMine had inserted and got the galleys off to Blassingame on the last day of August 1960.

Both Robert and Ginny were reading proof on the typed manuscript for *The Man from Mars,* and both were in a state of exhaustion, but Heinlein decided to take time out to appear at the World Science Fiction Convention in Pittsburgh, Pennsylvania. *Starship Troopers* had won the Hugo Award for Best Novel of 1959—by what science-fiction historian Sam Moskowitz called "a decisive plurality."[2] "I had . . . been lured there by being told, just before the convention, and under seal of confidence, that I was due to receive a Hugo and wouldn't I *please* show up!"[3] Heinlein had become aware that a Hugo could mean substantial extra sales, if the publisher had time to put the announcement on book covers.[4] When he appeared suddenly at the Pittcon awards banquet, he received a spontaneous ovation—very gratifying, and somewhat unexpected, since the mail and notices he had received on this book so far were overwhelmingly negative. "I'm not sorry I made the effort—" he continued. "It's fun to get a Hugo and the Pittcon itself was fun. But I got there beat to the heels and should have been cremated at the end of it."[5]

The trip to Pittsburgh had a secondary benefit: He was able finally to meet Arthur George "Sarge" Smith in person—one of the older, wiser mentor-figures he so valued. They had been corresponding for a long time, and Heinlein considered Sarge Smith his best friend.[6] This particular occasion was also particularly appropriate for this meeting, as he had dedicated *Starship Troopers* to Sarge Smith.

Returning to Colorado Springs—he had let the euphoria of the convention trap him into agreeing to be guest of honor at the next year's convention in Seattle—Robert and Ginny got the *Man from Mars* manuscript to Blassingame on September 15. It was obviously too long at 220,000 words and would have to be cut, "but even the extraneous material is so interesting," Blassingame told him, "I would hate to see it go."[7]

Doubleday turned down *The Man from Mars,* and so did Scribner. When he found out it had been offered there, Heinlein instructed Blassingame explicitly not to offer anything to that house, ever again: Alice Dalgliesh had left Scribner, it was true—but Charles Scribner himself had participated in the shabby treatment given to the Patrick Henry campaign and to *Starship Troopers,* and to Heinlein personally. He no longer had any ambition to appear under the Scribner imprint.

Putnam's wanted *The Man from Mars* for their adult line and concurred that it was too long. Howard Cady, the line editor assigned to the book, began suggesting story points that could be cut or condensed. Heinlein initially misunderstood this discussion as a fundamental disagreement with the nature of the book. "We did not grok the whole last part of the book," Cady had told him, "in which religion and love become so completely associated on a physical level." Some of Cady's other ideas were even more troublesome: Cady was enthusiastic about the book, Blassingame told Heinlein, but the combination of sex and religion would probably hurt sales—and the miracles were weak sellers, too.

No sex. No religion—and none of the miracles that function as persuaders. That knocked the props out from the characters' motivation and destroyed the story, turned it into a "non-alcoholic martini."[8] This was not censorship of taboo material, Cady went on to assure Heinlein, but an inability to connect with the story on an empathetic level.[9]

Putnam's had already been exploring ways to cut the risk, by making a very early release to the Doubleday Science Fiction Book Club. An editor in the book club division insisted Putnam's cut the book almost in half, to 125,000 words (still very large for a science-fiction novel at the time). Cady passed this along as his own idea.[10]

The contract was signed on October 5, but Heinlein decided not to accept Putnam's advance until they had an approved manuscript. He took the opportunity to express his appreciation for Blassingame's effort in placing this very difficult property:

> Lurton, I do not think I have told you what a wonderful job I think you have done in placing this ms. I wrote the thing with my eye intentionally on the market with the other on the copy in this mill (yes, even when I disagreed with editors or producers). But I knew that I could never get away from slick hack work, slanted at a market, unless I cut loose and ignored the market . . . and I did want to write at least one story in which I spoke freely, ignoring length, taboos, etc.
>
> When I finished it and reread it, I did not see how in hell you could ever sell it, and neither did Ginny. But you did. Thank you.[11]

The lawsuit against the producers of *The Brain Eaters* was coming down to the wire, with a trial scheduled in December 1960. In almost all legal actions, the lawyers for each side put comprehensive sets of questions—"interrogatories"—to each other, ostensibly to establish the facts. A few days after sending his attorney, Fendler, his draft answers to interrogatories, Heinlein received a phone call from Roger Corman, who introduced himself as the producer of *The Brain Eaters*. This direct contact between litigants was highly improper, but Corman explained that he had read *The Puppet Masters* for this suit and was impressed with Robert's writing. If they could get this plagiarism suit settled quickly enough, he wanted to hire Robert to write a screenplay based on Jules Verne's *The Floating City*—a five- or six-week job for $3,000.[12]

Not tempted, Heinlein told Corman: That was about half what he would earn if he put the same effort into a boys' book.

The next day, Corman offered to mount a full production of *The Puppet Masters*—and maybe other Heinlein properties.

Heinlein was not born yesterday. This series of unsolicited offers was essentially an admission by Corman that he didn't have any real defense against the charge of piracy and was fishing for what it would take to get him to drop the suit entirely. Heinlein referred Corman to his lawyer and his agent, to see whether Corman could come up with some proposal that might actually tempt him. But the suit had essentially collapsed. By November Corman made him an offer he could live with: He had put together a co-development deal with an

English film group to do a full screen version of both *The Puppet Masters* and "If This Goes On—." The money end of the deal would be a complicated arrangement of cash and participation—$2,000 up front and an additional $2,000 in ninety days to secure the option on *The Puppet Masters*. An additional $6,000 would be deferred against revenues, secured by 15 percent of the net proceeds. In addition to this $10,000 (more than he had realized from *Destination Moon*), Corman would pay a $4,000 option on "If This Goes On—."

But it would mean a net loss: $2,000 to settle an infringement that had cost him a $10,000 sale of the same property.

Heinlein could live with that. It was three days before the scheduled trial date: The lawyers would agree to a ninety-day continuance (which cost them nothing, as the action was expected to trail until April, anyway), by which time Corman either would or would not perform on the agreement, and they could talk about dismissing the action at that time. The settlement papers were executed on December 27, with Corman's check in the lawyer's hands. Fendler would get 50 percent of the proceeds—his contingent fee. But Heinlein's $1,000 share of the first payment brought up a problem: What with the increasing foreign book contracts, and no expensive travel plans in mind, the cash was starting to mount up. Perhaps this is when Ginny started investing their surplus cash in stocks and bonds.

Interest in Heinlein's work had only increased recently, as a result of the publicity *Starship Troopers* was generating. On October 23, a radio program in New York City, Marion Selby's "Young Book Reviewers" on WMCA, had a debate-like discussion of the theory of government he had put into *Starship Troopers*, with a panel of high school teenagers from Teaneck, New Jersey. Heinlein did not hear about it until much later, but it represented exactly the kind of "best use" that could be made of the book, in his opinion: to provoke discussion, let people—especially young people—figure out just what it was they believed and why . . .

. . . and he was invited to join the Playboy Club as a charter member. In 1960, *Playboy* magazine was the height of cool, smart and trendsetting. The world had changed a great deal during his lifetime—and was changing still and would change even more. G. Harry Stine had seen in operation the Dean Drive that Campbell was pushing in *Astounding/Analog* and thought he had a mathematical model that might explain the apparent violation of Conservation of Mass-Energy. If it panned out, it might shake up physics and mechanics—overdue in Robert's opinion. He was skeptical of miracles out of *Astounding*, he told Stine—but you never could tell.

And Putnam's finally came to a decision about the target length for *The Man from Mars.* Cutting to 175,000 words would be relatively easy, Heinlein had told them; 150,000 would be difficult but doable. Cutting to 125,000 words would be *very* difficult and would probably take him months of work—"and the patient would probably die on the table."[13] They finally agreed to the 150,000-word cut.

Heinlein had not been able to work up any enthusiasm for either candidate in the 1960 presidential election. Vice President Nixon was—well, Richard Nixon. And he had no great expectations of John F. Kennedy, however bright he was (perhaps pro-fascist Joe Kennedy's boy was not the likeliest candidate he would have picked). "We are fiddling, waiting the outcome of the election," Heinlein told G. Harry Stine.

> If Kennedy gets in, I may just sit back and await the debacle while staying pleasantly drunk. Ginny feels about the same way—she is continuing Russian but neither of us can get really interested in anything, at least not until after 8 November.[14]

And to his brother, after the election, he wrote:

> . . . the difference between Nixon and Kennedy was much too small to be important. The only reason I voted at all this time is because I will always stand up and be counted—make a choice, even if the choice is bad and difficult. But the only satisfaction I take in this election is that Eisenhower is through, thirty days from now.[15]

Over the last several years, politics in America had been shifting around in a puzzling way. The people who were calling themselves "liberal" had taken on a bizarre kind of internationalist pseudo-pacifism, while he was finding liberals he could actually recognize, as he understood the term from his own liberal politics of the 1930s, billing themselves as conservatives and Republicans—including some New Dealers, such as Barry Goldwater.[16] Robert was a determined pragmatic: When Goldwater's *Conscience of a Conservative* came out in 1960, the Heinleins bought dozens of copies for friends and family. "Party no longer concerns me," Heinlein told his brother. "I simply want a President strong enough to stand up to the Russians. I guess I am an ex-FDR-liberal, i.e., I am more libertarian than ever."[17] He reflected on his ambiguous position respecting political parties.

Rex, I am not attempting to "make a conservative out of you." In the first place, I do not consider myself to be a conservative; I am an individualist with strong libertarian views, but my approach to both domestic economy and to foreign affairs is pragmatic, not doctrinaire . . . .

My approach is always pragmatic . . . . During the 'thirties I was an all-out New Dealer (even though I saw lots of things wrong with the New Deal). I am no longer a New Dealer *without having changed my basic evaluations.* Instead, circumstances have changed; the problems of the 'thirties are *not* the problems of the 'sixties . . . The central problem of today is no longer individual exploitation but national survival . . . [sic] and I don't think we will solve it by increasing the minimum wage . . .[18]

The first half of *The Man from Mars* was cut by January 2, 1961, and finished two weeks later. It was not going to be 150,000 words: He had cut it as much as he possibly could without damaging the story, and it was 160,083 words. He was geared up for battle: "I am tempted," he said, "to type those eighty-three excess words on a postcard."[19]

But Howard Cady replied calmly that if that was the length of the book, that was the length at which they would publish it—and agreed that promotion should be oriented toward the mainstream market; Heinlein's reputation would carry the SF readers' market without any help from Putnam's promotion department.

Heinlein was hit almost immediately by a sling—or possibly an arrow—of outrageous fortune: Samuel M. Moskowitz, a fan-turning-pro usually referred to in the fan press as "SaM," wrote that he had contracted for a series of biographical sketches of living science-fiction writers, and Heinlein's was to be the first of this new series. Due in three weeks.[20] Heinlein had enjoyed Moskowitz's sketches of historical science-fiction figures as they came out but told Moskowitz he had "no slightest wish to be the central figure in a fan dance while I am still alive."[21]

Nevertheless, it evidently was going to happen. "I would rather this article never appeared," he told Moskowitz, "but since you have already contracted to write it, I would prefer for it to be accurate."[22] He wrote a long and detailed response to SaM's questions, but he specifically withheld permission to quote from the letter: SaM could use the information to confirm or contradict any information he dug up from other sources, adding, "I wish to Christ that you would not discuss me, as a person, in print."[23]

In the meantime, *The Man from Mars* had moved from editing toward production—and marketing. In order to pitch it for a mainstream audience,

Heinlein suggested they eliminate "Mars" from the title—or any obvious appeal to the science-fiction audience:

> The book is not science fiction even though I have made use of two of the common devices of science fiction (i.e., space travel and a future scene, ca. 1990). But space travel is no longer science fiction, not in 1961 when it is on every front page . . . The story belongs in the same category as *Gulliver's Travels* and *Pilgrim's Progress*—philosophical fantasy—rather than with the works of Jules Verne.[24]

He suggested alternate titles: *All Who Grok, The Grokking Work, The Fallen Caryatid, No Sparrow Shall Fall,* or *A Sparrow Falls.*[25] Cady agreed with the general idea but wanted a title that would play better. *The Fallen Caryatid* was the best of that particular lot, but wouldn't entice a buyer in a bookstore.

Cady had for years been collecting unused titles as they occurred to him. He suggested one of these, taken from the Bible (Exodus 2:22): *A Stranger in a Strange Land.* That name appealed, and in a telephone call on March 22, the final title was set without the initial article. This book was a make-or-break test for him, he had told Lurton Blassingame:

> *The Man from Mars* is an attempt on my part to break loose from a straitjacket, one of my own devising. I am tired of being known as a "leading writer of children's books" and nothing else. True, those juveniles have paid well—car, house, and chattels all free and clear, much travel, money in the bank and a fairish amount in stocks, plus prospect of future royalties—I certainly shouldn't kick and I am not kicking . . . but, like the too-successful whore: "Them stairs is killing me!"
>
> I first became aware of just how thoroughly I had boxed myself in when editors of my soi-disant "adult" books started asking me to trim them down to suit my juvenile market. At that time I had to comply. But now I would like to find out if I can write about adult matters *for adults,* and get such writing published.
>
> However, I have no desire to write "main stream" stories such as *The Catcher in The Rye, By Love Possessed, Peyton Place, The Man in The Grey Flannel Suit, Darkness at Noon,* or *On the Road.* Whether these books are good or bad, they each represent a type which has been written more than enough; there is no point in my adding more to such categories—I want to do my own stuff, my own way.
>
> Perhaps I will flop at it. I don't know. But such success as I have had has

come from being original, not from writing "safe" stuff—in pulps, in movies, in slicks, in juveniles. In pulp SF I moved at once to the top of the field by writing about sociology, sex, politics, and religion at a time (1939) when these subjects were all taboo. Later I cracked the slicks with science fiction when it was taken for granted that SF was pulp and nothing but pulp. You will recall that my first juvenile was considered an experiment by the publisher—and a rather risky one.

Lurton, I have never written "what was being written"—nor do I want to do so now. Oh, I suppose that, if it became financially necessary, I could imitate my own earlier work and do it well enough to sell. But I don't want to. I hope this new and different book sells. But, whether it does or does not, I want my next book to be still different—neither an imitation of *The Man from Mars*, nor a careful "mixture as before" in imitation of my juveniles and my quasi-juveniles published as soi-disant "adult" SF books. I've got a lot of things I'd like to write about; none of them fits this pattern.[26]

A bonus materialized when Roger Corman made his second payment on the *Brain Eaters* settlement, though the co-production arrangements for "If This Goes On—" had fallen through, and he did not pick up the other option.[27]

Heinlein put off the next writing job to put a dam and catch basin in their arroyo, so they would not be so vulnerable to the area's periodic droughts. He added a decorative stonework pool—stonework was his favorite form of exercise (other than sex of course)—with a geyser-like fountain. Ginny marked her approval of the work and its progress by fixing a flower in his hatband. Working at stonework again took more off his waist.

I'm real purty. So is the pool, as I gave it a tumbled-boulders appearance with the engineering concealed, then used my irrigation pump to create a miniature jet d-eau, like the one in Geneve but only twenty feet high. I put spot lights on it at night. Total added cost: one shower head and ten feet of garden hose.[28]

Midway through "Project Stonehenge," Yuri Gagarin—a Russian cosmonaut—became the first human being to orbit the Earth, on April 12, 1961. Four years after Sputnik, the Russians were still making firsts in space—a prospect that could only be grim for mankind's future. It was not until May 1961 that Alan Shepard became the first American to orbit the Earth. Ginny continued lecturing on their trip to the USSR, and Heinlein was not entirely off the hook for public speaking. Even as galley proofs for *The Man from Mars* arrived for correction, Heinlein complained about his own obligations:

I have two speaking dates hanging over me—and I do mean "hanging over me." Despite the fact that I can and do speak in public and rather enjoy it at the time despite the fact that I used to, as a politician, speak in public half a dozen times a day, now that I am a writer I find that the anticipation of a speaking date hangs over me, interferes with the work in hand by monopolizing my imagination—I think about what I am going to say instead of thinking about plots.

. . . . every one of these overhead chores reduces the time I spend in original composition at this machine by exactly the amount of time lost; If I could avoid all correspondence and all public appearances I would at least double my real working time and have more time for fun as well.[29]

One of those engagements was his guest of honor speech for the Worldcon coming up in September, but the other was more immediate: On April 29 the Oklahoma State Library Association was to present him with the Sequoyah Award for childrens' literature, for *Have Space Suit—Will Travel*. Travel arrangements for that trip were inconvenient:

Alva [Oklahoma] turns out to be like the post office in Brooklyn; you can't get to it. No air service, other services impossible. Can drive, of course, but just far enough away to kill five days—three if we really knocked ourselves out, but neither one of us like to be on the highway when exhausted, especially at night.[30]

They wound up chartering a plane: "leave here after breakfast, speak at a luncheon meeting, home the same night. Only one day's work lost and, believe it or not, cheaper than driving, going by bus, train, or commercial air—quite a bit cheaper considering hotels, and enormously cheaper if my time is figured at any cash value."[31]

Starting in June, they had Jack Williamson as a temporary neighbor: He came to nearby Boulder, Colorado, to do ten weeks of coursework in preparation for his comprehensive doctoral oral examination in English literature (plus a class in Middle English).[32] The neighborhood was not quite as idyllic as it had been, though: By the time Williamson got there, construction had started on the Cheyenne Mountain Combat Operations Center, which would coordinate all the telemetry for NORAD (the North American Aerospace Defense Command). It also coordinated missiles and aircraft defense for the entire country.

The Colorado Springs area had seen a considerable military buildup in the previous ten years, particularly since 1958 when the Air Force Academy went in.[33] Overnight, NORAD would make Colorado Springs the number-one nuclear target in the United States.

Putnam's test-readers for *Stranger in a Strange Land* had been surprisingly enthusiastic about the book. The Doubleday Science Fiction Book Club released *Stranger* as its selection for June 1961—a month before the Putnam's release—and word of mouth started.

The early reviews were encouraging: *Kirkus Reviews* dwelled on the book's comic aspects. Baker & Taylor, the world's largest book distributor, compared *Stranger* (favorably) in the July 1961 *Book Buyers Guide* to "that best-seller of blessed memory," Pat Frank's *Mr. Adam* (1946). Putnam's was very pleased with the advance orders stacking up before their release in July.[34] It was beginning to look as though *Stranger* had a good chance.[35]

Sprague and Catherine de Camp came by train for a visit in July—mostly to see Jack Williamson this trip—with their youngest son, Gerry, and a cousin. Ginny set up an impromptu cocktail party for the de Camps in the garage, since Sprague was allergic to cat dander and couldn't spend any time in the house without breaking into alarming wheezing.[36] Later, Robert took the boys to a nearby animal park where they could pet the tame deer.[37]

Lucky Herzberger threw a fifty-fourth birthday party for Robert the next day. A few days later, the first fan letter arrived for *Stranger*: It was the best book—and the best science fiction—the fan had ever read.[38] This was a pleasing change from the negativity over *Starship Troopers*. Although many people didn't "get" what was going on in the book—including the reviewer Orville Prescott, for *The New York Times* (singularly clueless, even for a book reviewer: "A disastrous mishmash of science fiction, laborious humor, dreary social satire and cheap eroticism"[39])—the mail was overwhelmingly positive, and it apparently affected a lot of people very deeply. Heinlein was startled to learn, at the end of the month, that Putnam's planned to place $1,000 ads promoting the book.[40]

Two weeks after his birthday, Heinlein received an affirmation that he was making a real mark on working science. Some time previously, he had a short but satisfying exchange of letters with Harold Wooster. Wooster had noticed his coining of "xenobiology" in *The Star Beast* (1954), and they had a short etymological discussion comparing the Latinate "exo-" prefix used by some scientists for extraterrestrial subjects with the Greek root "xeno-" that Heinlein preferred. Wooster wrote a letter about their correspondence to the editors of *Science,* the weekly organ of the American Association for the Advancement of Science, quoting one letter almost in full.[41]

Other of Heinlein's coinings had become established over the years— "astrogation," for example, and related words like "astrogator" (and, truth be told, he wasn't absolutely sure he had coined "xenobiology" from scratch, though he was pretty sure of "xenic" for any extraterrestrial subject).[42] He had had a certain amount of influence in the missile field just after World War II— he hadn't been able to get his name attached (as the "Heinlein Grid"[43]) to the pole-to-pole, orange-slice orbit he had first described in 1947, but Robert Cornog had told him that his description of radio and radar-jamming techniques had been called the "Heinlein Effect" in in-house reports created by Northrup at Wright Field for Guided Missiles.[44] Neither of those had caught on, but "Waldo" was in use for remote manipulators, and this was an even more solid acknowledgment of influence among working scientists.

So he was in an expansive mood when Sam Moskowitz's "Robert A. Heinlein, Man, Myth or Monster" appeared in the June 1961 issue of *Amazing*— "a swell job," he told SaM (in spite of the ludicrous title the editor had given it)—the best and most level-headed job he could have anticipated. "You even managed to teach me some things about myself that I had not consciously been aware of . . . . I greatly appreciate the meticulous care you took not to invade my privacy."[45]

Reaction to *Stranger* inside the SF field—if *Stranger* was in any realistic sense "inside" science fiction—was coming in very mixed. The fan letters were overwhelmingly positive, and several of his colleagues (including dedicatee Philip José Farmer) wrote approvingly about the book's "experimental" qualities. Fred Pohl commissioned a correspondingly experimental extended review for *Galaxy* from Algis Budrys.[46]

Budrys began writing science fiction in the early 1950s. His 1958 Cold War novel *Who?* was adapted for the screen in 1973, starring Elliot Gould as Sean Rogers, and his 1960 novella "Rogue Moon" was nominated for a Hugo Award. When the review came in, it looked a little *too* experimental, a little too self-conscious a performance. Pohl queried Heinlein for a rebuttal.

Heinlein had managed to be a science-fiction writer for more than twenty years without ever saying a critical word about a colleague in public, and he was not about to start now. Furthermore, there just wasn't any *point* in trying to explain a book to someone who didn't get it from reading it. Budrys had managed to talk about the book for three thousand words, blathering on about reincarnation (a subject that was not actually in the book in any significant way[47]), without ever once noting that the central character was engaged in a quest—a religious quest—"and that he found his answer in sexual human love . . . [sic] I have just searched through his ms. word for word—and do you know, there is no word about, no inkling of any sort that Stranger has any sex in it."[48] Between Heinlein's comments and Pohl's own reservations about the review—whether it actually represented Budrys's views or was mainly a "performance piece"—Pohl decided not to run it.

Heinlein had a chance to meet Budrys in person two weeks later, at Sea-Con, the 1961 World Science Fiction Convention in Seattle, Washington. Budrys was a Lithuanian patriot, and Heinlein wanted feedback from him about the section of his guest of honor speech that was about the long history of Lithuania, crushed out of *pravda* = official truth inside the Soviet Union.[49] Harlan Ellison was toastmaster that year, which represented a chance to meet another colleague—and a very promising one—for the first time (he wrote Ellison a fan letter about *Final Shtick* when he got home).[50]

But shortly after arriving in Seattle, a case of the sniffles turned into influenza, and the flu was threatening to turn into something more serious: He had that "drowning from the inside" feeling that might presage pneumonia.

Alan E. Nourse, the fan Sprague de Camp had introduced him to in Philadelphia years ago, had become a doctor and a professional writer.[51] Nourse's fast action with hypo and pills kept Robert on his feet enough to give his speech on Monday, September 4.

Heinlein had given the committee an open-ended title, "The Future Revisited." That title played off his 1941 speech, "Discovery of the Future," but when he fleshed out the speech, just days before leaving for Seattle, he compared the jittery state of the world in 1961 with his prior guest of honor speech, given on the verge of World War II,[52] and then talked about the current situation in terms of the likeliest alternatives, concentrating on the nuclear war that everyone anticipated:

> . . . very few Americans are prepared to stay alive while the fallout cools down. Nor am I criticizing, please note . . . My wife and I have no fallout protection of any sort. I'm not proud of it, I'm not ashamed of it—I'm simply in the same boat as almost everybody else and have paid as little attention to the warnings . . . . This is how it *is*. We are not now prepared to live

through a heavy attack—and those figures of a third or maybe a half of us dead *stand*—unless we do prepare. If we do, and from what I've seen of American temperament I doubt if we will prepare.

The other part that makes up the ninety percent of all of our possible futures is simpler, slower—and just as deadly in the long run. In due course, with no more than minor brush wars unfelt by any but the poor blokes who get killed in them, the United States will find itself in a situation where the simplest, easiest, and safest thing to do will be to surrender . . . the idea is that the Kremlin will be giving the orders here rather than Washington. . . . The laddies who liquidated the trouble in the Ukraine [a "planned famine" in 1932–33 called the "Ukrainian genocide"] and used tanks on the school boys of Budapest [Hungarian Revolution, 1956] won't hesitate to liquidate the bourgeois mentality here . . .[53]

American history might be wiped out, the way Soviet pravda had wiped out Lithuania's. "Freedom and democracy we can lose . . . and then regain them in time. Not in your time and mine, probably—but when the human race needs these factors, we'll use them again."[54]

In order to deal realistically with the dangers, he urged them to "[t]reat the world the way a research scientist treats a problem—examine the data, try to organize, try to predict coldly and logically."[55] And the point that most clouds the picture is the picture of the enemy as *villains*:

Let me repeat it like a radio commercial: Communists are *not* villains!

They are devout, moral, very moralistic, kind, humane, and utterly convinced—by *their* standards! And they live by *their standards*! . . . . Until you learn this one thing about Communists, you have no chance of reading and understanding the Cold Equations.

Communists are nice people, almost all of them. They are sincere, they are true believers—and they won't be seduced by sirloin steaks.[56]

If the American people and in particular American political leaders took the trouble to try to learn the mind and methods and *high moral standards* of their enemy, we would not behave as foolishly as we do.[57]

Heinlein was given an ovation—but he was running a temperature and wasn't entirely sure he hadn't just lapsed into incoherence:

. . . all I remember of it is the room moving slowly around me like a turn table (and once almost falling off the platform) while I tried fuzzily to pull myself together and remember what it was I had intended to say and in what order—and then a horrid feeling when it was over that I had certainly forgotten the logical sequence . . .[58]

He invited the entire convention—three hundred fans—back to the suite he and Ginny had taken for an informal "at-home" reception and went to change, drenched with fever sweat.

It was a disturbing speech—deliberately, of course. And, of course, what most of the audience heard was "it's all over"—not what he said at all. F. M. Busby, one of the convention's organizers who was later to be a science-fiction writer himself,[59] was in the audience and told Heinlein, "You overestimated the ability of the audience to 'fill in the punchlines.'" Years later, Busby reported publicly on the reaction:

> It was pretty obvious to me that the speech was intended to have a deliberate effect and to rouse a specific response; I asked Heinlein about this, and in such a way as *not* to tip off my guess unless it turned out to be correct. As I'd guessed, his idea was to shatter complacency and to spark the listener to insist and act upon the third (unstated) alternative; that we *can* tough it out without either precipitating Atomigeddon or surrendering. About 10% of the audience responded in that fashion and not one of them seemed to realise that he was doing anything but refuting Heinlein.[60]

When Heinlein got back to his room after his guest of honor talk, he showered quickly and had just time before people started arriving to get on the long yellow corduroy bathrobe Ginny had made. He gave up the attempt to dress and rolled with the situation, receiving, like Thomas Jefferson, in his dressing gown.

They did have very nearly the entire convention in their suite at one time or another during the night, including Jerry Pournelle, a young engineer from Boeing—a very stimulating person—who wanted to quit his job and take up writing as a living. Later, Pournelle wrote that he was happy to see Heinlein introducing SF fans to "Grand Strategy."[61] Within a few years, Pournelle would be working with think tanks and policy wonks himself.[62]

Heinlein was also happy to renew his professional acquaintances, especially with Poul Anderson and his pretty young wife, Karen. Karen camped at his feet when he sat down, gazing up at "God in a yellow bathrobe."[63]

Somehow Heinlein got through the convention—enjoying himself though not getting nearly enough rest, in Ginny's opinion.

I conceive it to be the g. of h.'s job to make himself available and to be sociable, rather than necessarily attending the formal meetings—and everybody was nice to us . . . . and we had a wonderful time.[64] I had a good time in spite of being sick and getting sicker as the convention progressed. But I'm vague about what happened.[65]

He insisted on participating even in the Masquerade Ball, Ginny in cat costume as Vesta the Vegian from Doc Smith's *The Vortex Blaster,* while he—"I am depending largely on green grease paint and crepe hair to create a Charles Addams horror: Minister Plenipotentiary and Ambassador Extraordinary from Arcturus III."[66]

They got through the speech at the University of Washington the day after the convention ended and flew back to Colorado Springs, where Ginny caught Robert's flu and took to her bed.[67]

That speech he had given at the convention would not let him go: All the way back home, he thought about the potential hypocrisy involved in telling these young people they should invest their futures in fallout shelters.[68] One supercilious and ignorant "colleague" had already as much as accused him of hypocrisy in print, talking about (nonexistent) radiation proofing on his house in Colorado Springs.[69] That stung more than he cared to admit in public. He had considered building a bomb shelter, but the house was built on a granite outcrop, and there was no place to *put* a shelter.

Do you recall Carl Sandburg's anecdote in *The People, Yes* about the man who spread the rumor that they had struck oil in Hell . . . and spreads it so well that he sells the idea to himself—and leaves for Hell? Something like that happened to me:

I.e., in Seattle, in my talk, I told the audience that everyone, pacifist or fighter, should provide himself with a fallout shelter—and also noted that most Americans would not do so . . . with myself as a typical bad example of an American who, despite all warnings, had done nothing at all to protect himself and his family from possible atomic attack.

. . . I had a long string of excuses—no children and no overpowering desire to last through a fourth war in one lifetime, neighbors with children who had done *nothing* (and who would be certain to show up with their kids if I built a shelter—leaving me to sit outside and fry), the extreme expense of the thing, since my house has no basement and no attic and sits on a shelf of granite . . . no cheap and easy way to do it . . . .

Excuses—I had the money and I also had the strong conviction that the

USSR is less likely to attack the stronger we are . . . in particular, if most Americans did their best to render themselves as nearly immune from attack as possible (without waiting for the government to do it for them), then the Kremlin would *not* attack, because those babies bet only on sure things.

The fact that I still believed that the majority of Americans would sit, fat, dumb, and happy, and take no steps to survive, in no way relieved me of my obligation to make my small piece of America as strong as possible. So wearily I undertook to design and build a fallout shelter.[70]

He got some chores out of the way first—thank-you letters, including a thank-you ad in the progress report for the next WorldCon, in Chicago; he offered to put Algis Budrys in touch with some high-level people in Washington, D.C., who might be interested in some of A.J.'s ideas about the Lithuanian resistance movement. And then General Kuter,[71] from NORAD, invited him along to attend the Air Force Association meeting in Philadelphia on September 20 to 24.

Heinlein flew from Peterson Field in the General's private plane. This was his third such meeting: He had attended the first in Denver during the Patrick Henry campaign—depressing for its dispiriting sense of defeatism. This one was invigorating, energizing him with the implication that there were things that could be done to check the long, slow slide into surrender. He came back to Colorado Springs on Sunday evening, following the banquet.

16

SMOKING RUBBLE

Since it was going to be difficult anyway, Heinlein decided to take on all the difficulties at the same time and make not just a fallout shelter, but a blast shelter that could survive anything but a direct hit. Ginny insisted on a back-door exit, which made good sense from a survival perspective but complicated the design and engineering.

He started building a shelter by the first of October 1961, blasting a pit twelve feet wide, twelve feet deep, and twenty-four feet long—big enough to accommodate a seven-by-seven-by-fourteen shelter. The crew dug out the rubble and installed a reinforced steel frame to keep the surrounding rock from collapsing.

The roof was twenty-eight inches of reinforced concrete, "vibrated into place and cast over a heavy steel shell (to avoid the shrapnel effect of cracked concrete)."[1] When they got it installed, it was reached through a counterweighted door set flat into the house's east balcony, backed up by two submarine-type vault doors, to take the overpressure necessary to keep radioactive dust from seeping in. And for Ginny's bolt-hole, a concealed "escape tunnel" made of culvert steel, well stocked with tools and a concealed exit in the arroyo. The tunnel could also be used for food storage. Altogether, the shelter would keep two people alive for three months.

His example set off a burst of building among his neighbors, a little behind the national craze and too late to shore up the marginal shelter-supply businesses in the area that were starting to fail. He was able to pick up much of his initial stock and specialized equipment at going-out-of-business sales.

The shelter was completed by mid-November. But building the shelter was the easy part. The hard part was people. He knew what the "correct" answer was: Nobody in once the doors are shut. But he doubted he could carry it out that way: No matter what he "knew" intellectually, he would take in at least any children. That, he did not allow to be widely known: "Lots of people have seen our shelter . . . [sic] and far too many of them have said brightly, 'Gee, I'm glad you've built this! Now we'll know exactly where to go when the alert sounds!?'"[2] Chilling. Overwhelmed instantly; all die—and every single one of his neighbors was well-off enough to build shelters of their own. "Simple horse sense is so damned scarce in the human race that it is amazing that we took over this planet."[3]

Poul Anderson had been agonizing over the same dilemma. He had settled in the Bay Area town of Orinda, tucked away on the other side of the Oakland Hills from San Francisco. Heinlein commiserated and encouraged by mail:

> Each shelter built reduces our vulnerability to blackmail, increases our national chances if it comes to the worst. Neither you nor I nor any other individual can build a shelter that will take anything—but we most certainly can vastly improve our chances and, with that, our country's chances.[4]

The moral problems were hard—and could not be shared or divided, e.g., by the kind of public or neighborhood shelters that were available to city dwellers and suburbanites. In the end, it comes down, as it always comes down, to each individual human being doing what he—or she—must to live with himself/herself. ". . . In my opinion there is no such thing as an unsolvable moral problem . . . It is only necessary to know what your moral standards are, and why, and then have the guts to carry out the answers."[5] A very old and inescapable position: Epictetus had outlined it in the second century C.E.: "First say to yourself what you would be; and then do what you have to do." The whole project was an exercise in Epictetus: "Make the best use of what is in your power, and take the rest as it happens" is another well-known quotation from the *Enchiridion*.

Howard Cady at Putnam's was pleased with the fall sales of *Stranger*; they might even have to go into a second printing before the end of the year. Heinlein began casting around for another writing project. Putnam's had always wanted a juvenile from him, and he did have a stub juvenile in his files.

In 1958 he had started a freakish juvenile—freakish because it had a teenage girl protagonist, and girl-oriented science fiction was impossibly *outré*. He had a third of *Podkayne Fries: Her Life and Times* already written—a story about a teenaged Mars-colonist girl on an interplanetary cruise to Earth and Venus. By the time he was ready to work on it again, it had evolved: It wouldn't be the kind of girls' Wanderjahr he had originally planned. Instead, when he finished the writing on January 14, 1962, he had crafted an important message about "latchkey kids" and parenting in the age of Sputnik and orbiting missiles.[6]

And about that time he got a letter from an advertising agency, Carson/Roberts. They had developed an innovative ad campaign for Hoffman Electronics, thousand-word short-shorts by noted science-fiction authors, preferably illustrating some problem in electronics. A. E. van Vogt and Isaac Asimov had already done stories for them. Now they wanted Heinlein.[7]

He referred them to Fred Brown, who was a specialist in that sort of short-short—but Carson/Roberts's D. H. Steele was persistent: They wanted Heinlein, and they were prepared to pay a premium rate for him—double or triple the rate they originally offered. He finished *Podkayne*—retitled now *Podkayne of Mars*—and there really wasn't any reason he should not get in on the bonanza at an unheard-of sixty-two cents per word. But electronics was not a field he was comfortable with, and the correspondence with Steele continued until a couple of possible gimmicks occurred to Heinlein in March.[8]

Both he and Ginny were having troubles with their health in early 1962, Ginny's more serious than his. He had been suffering from throat spasms for some time, which was annoying but not essentially serious. A "soma compound" taken one tablet before meals gave Robert some relief.

Ginny was not so lucky. At a dance in January, she had suddenly doubled over in extreme pain, like nothing she had experienced before. The next day, Robert put her in the hospital (Ginny hated doctors and hospitals and almost always had to be coerced into them), with a shot of morphine for pain. A round of tests started. With a reaction that extreme, they feared cancer—advanced and widespread, metastasized and inoperable. Fortunately, they were soon able to rule out cancer. A shadow on an X-ray suggested an aytpical kidney stone. The doctors suggested trying to dissolve it by a strict diet, as an operation would probably destroy the kidney.

This started a cycle of yo-yoing in and out of the hospital, and Robert would get his dinner usually with Andy Ahroon and his family—his closest friends in Colorado Springs.[9] When Ginny wasn't in the hospital she was being worked over by "specialists" in this and that. Three days out of four, about dinnertime she would have an attack of acute, system-wide pain, for which injections of Demerol were prescribed. Robert learned how to give her the injections and put her to bed. Evening events became simply out of the question—which played havoc with their social life. After a while, they no longer had one.

In March, Ginny was back in the hospital again, and Robert had an attack of appendicitis, acute but also atypical, so the doctors decided to wait and see rather than operate. With both Heinleins hospitalized, the doctors began to suspect other causes than the obvious. They began by taking stool samples— and found to their amazement that Robert had no organisms to culture in his stool. "In other words," he chortled, "I produce 'pure crap.' This will come as no surprise to many literary critics."[10] By the end of March, the doctors settled on a diagnosis of amebic dysentery and put them both on an antibacterial regimen. It seemed to help. Ginny continued on Demerol nearly daily—for months and with no end in sight.

It was probably at this time that Heinlein also took the opportunity to discuss with the doctor something that had been bothering him:

> I was definitely slowing down in every way—and I have always been wor-
> ried about premature senility because my father became utterly senile when
> he was a year younger than I am now. He was a wreck, no pleasure to him-
> self and a nuisance to other people and unable to do any sort of work—a
> zombie and he never did pull out of it even though he stayed alive another
> quarter of a century.
>
> This is the only thing I have ever been afraid of—that I would go the
> way my father did. So when I started slowing down, I went to our doctor
> and insisted on some monkey glands in pill form.[11]

The doctor started him on oral Metandren, a synthetic testosterone pill.

Whether it was simple recovery of health or the Metandren was giving his energy a boost, by April Robert felt able to write again.

All of Robert's "first readers" loved *Podkayne of Mars*—except for the ending. Every one of them. And when it was submitted to Putnam's, Peter Israel joined the chorus (Howard Cady had left Putnam's in the interim, and Peter Israel was now Putnam's editor in chief). *Everybody* hated the fact that he killed Poddy off. Heinlein felt this was a misread of the text: *Podkayne* was not a juvenile, but a cautionary message to adult readers—to parents and po-tential parents "too busy" to parent their kids.

> *Podkayne*—as originally written, the title character was supposed to die
> and her brother was supposed to have the ending all to himself . . . with the
> story over when *his* character change was completed. I weakened—because
> my wife, my agent, and both my editors, serial and trade book, just couldn't
> stand to have me kill off such a nice little girl. The result was that practi-
> cally nobody understood what I was driving at.[12]

Podkayne's death was the direct result of her mother's failure to parent—and Clark's sociopathy, as well.[13] The last five words of the book—Clark's decision to join the human race—were intended to be the most poignant thing he had ever written[14] . . . and it was set up by Poddy's death.

Fred Pohl was interested—not for *Galaxy*, which couldn't use a teenage girl protagonist either,[15] but for *Galaxy*'s sister magazine, *Worlds of If*. Heinlein had not expected any serial sale for this manuscript and considered Blassingame's success in marketing it somewhat miraculous. He still didn't think the change of ending everybody wanted was necessary—but *everybody* wanted it, so he agreed not to kill Poddy off so definitely. Blassingame and Ginny and Peter Israel passed his compromise ending, allowing the possibility that Poddy might recover, and he was done with *Podkayne of Mars*.

Heinlein wrote the Hoffman Electronics ad short-short story, "Searchlight," in the last week of May, meeting the Carson/Roberts deadline, even with the unexpected rewrite on *Podkayne*.[16]

Lady Livia Gollancz wrote from London that the British publisher Victor Gollancz Ltd. wanted to put "Universe" and "Commonsense" together into a book for the British market, to be titled *Orphans of the Sky*[17] (one of the possible titles he gave them). This would have been the core of the fifth of Shasta's original Future History series—and he wouldn't need to write "Da Capo." The Doubleday SF Book Club picked it up for the American market, and they arranged publisher-to-publisher for Putnam's to issue the book for the American trade.

When his brother Rex taught electrical engineering at West Point (1942–53), he had introduced to Robert one of his students, George Scithers. Scithers was one of the "organized" science-fiction fans (a term that always strikes SF fans as either irritating or else inexpressibly funny because it so misunderstands the deliberately chaotic nature of their little subculture), and even published a fanzine, *Amra*, devoted to a narrow sub-genre of heroic fantasy designated (by Fritz Leiber) "Sword & Sorcery." In the early 1960s Sword & Sorcery was becoming popular. It was a highly conventionalized form, and not Heinlein's usual kind of thing—particularly the adventure-melodrama apparatus of clear-cut hero and black villain—but Scithers had said something in correspondence that kicked off a train of thought: What happened to the hero, he asked rhetorically, once the adventure was done?[18] A story began taking shape in Heinlein's mind about just that question—like *Stranger* a "Cabellian" story. What he evidently had in mind was the *story form* Cabell had used over and over again: The first act sets up the desired; the second is the search for the desired. And in the final act, either you do not achieve the desired, or else—and so much better—you do achieve it . . . and find out it doesn't make you happy. ". . . happiness, after all, abides a thought farther down the bogged, rocky, clogged, befogged, heart-breaking road, if anywhere."[19]

For that, of course, was Heinlein's answer to Scithers's provocative question: a Hero did not stop looking for his—or her—heart's desire. You set out on that "bogged, rocky, clogged, befogged, heart-breaking road"—the Glory Road—again. That's what Cabell had missed, himself: His heroes of romance all settled into domestic bliss and spent the rest of their lives yearning. That just wasn't in Heinlein's conception of the hero's psychology.

The apparatus of wizards and aristocrats didn't much appeal to Heinlein's democratic soul. Instead he made *Glory Road* a kind of "gay deceiver." Los Angeles SF fan Walt Liebscher had coined this term to describe fantastic stories that had mundane explanations—dreams, most often. The "fantasy" elements of Heinlein's new story would be high-level technology, applied mathematics mostly, and literary psychology, so that the fantasy would be science fiction in masquerade. Heinlein acquired a multivolume Encyclopedia of Magic and a copy of the Red Grimoire[20] for research purposes (grimoires are record books kept by working witches; a few have been published over the centuries)—and started *The Power and the Glory* on April 12, 1962.

He finished his book as *Glory Road,* at 106,000 words, three weeks later (May 4, 1962) and began strategizing with Lurton Blassingame about a big omnibus volume of his Future History stories.[21] Heinlein had placed reprint contracts for the three existing books with Gnome Press in 1959, since they had brought out *Methuselah's Children* in 1958. Although the *Methuselah's Children* issue was in many ways unsatisfactory,[22] Heinlein planned then to add a fifth book to the series, *The Endless Frontier,* for which he would write the capstone of the series, "Da Capo," to conclude the adventures of Lazarus Long. Although Putnam's was interested in putting out an omnibus edition of the Future History series as early as 1962,[23] the Gollancz/Putnam's *Orphans of the Sky* that year replaced *The Endless Frontier* and essentially put the Putnam's omnibus on indefinite hold.

After a brief contact in 1955, Mary Briggs—now Mary Collin—had written him—a *Stranger* fan letter—in 1961. That brought back cherished memories of 1929 and the vision she had given him of what it was possible for a woman to mean—a vision that had stayed with him ever since.[24] He had not seen her since before he married Leslyn, in 1932—but he had thought of her often over the years.

You have probably had more influence-per-hour on me than anyone I have ever known . . . We have actually been in each other's presence very little time indeed, much less than a week—yet you have influenced me and my thinking and most especially my attitudes toward women enormously more than many, many other people whom I have known enormously longer and quite intimately.[25]

Particularly when Ginny was in the hospital, Heinlein grew sentimental and wrote love letters to Mary, which he knew Ginny would read if she was interested when she was up and around again. He assured Mary that he was not "sneaking around" on his wife:

In any case Ginny and I *are* in love and are *not* jealous. With me it is an attitude I have had since I was a kid. With Ginny it is an attitude she has gradually grown into over the course of years, having started out with a quite conventional attitude. But I did not argue her into it—nobody *ever* argues Ginny into anything; she is as stubborn as a cat.

She reached more mature evaluations, in her own way and at her own time, as she grew up . . . .

Anyhow, we are both unjealous, each of the other. But not indifferent. Heavens, no! I would be shocked, shamed, and very much hurt if Ginny were to bed down with some man whom I did not like, admire, and respect in all ways. However, there is not the slightest chance of that happening; Ginny's standards are higher than mine, if anything. In a complementary fashion Ginny not only does not object but thoroughly approves of my adventuring on occasion into other pastures—but it had better by a damn sight be with some gal she likes and approves of herself.[26]

He had other distractions to relieve his excess of sentiment: Andy Ahroon had gotten him invited as a ride-along on a short (fifty-four-hour door-to-door) trip the Secretary of the Navy was giving for a visiting Canadian Air Vice Marshall (NORAD was an integrated American-Canadian command) over Heinlein's birthday, and Heinlein made arrangements for Ginny to get her shots while he was gone. Andy stayed behind entertaining the SecNav but loaned his plane to ferry the Air Vice Marshall and party to San Diego. In the morning they had breakfast on the sub tender *Nereus* and then spent the day under 115 feet of water in the submarine *Raton,* destroyers seeking them out by sonar to depth bomb them (simulated with hand grenades, concussive enough in a closed underwater box).

They were flown to an aircraft carrier to observe night and then day operations. That was a kind of reunion for Heinlein, the day before his fifty-fifth birthday, since the carrier was *Lexington* (CV-16). His *Lexington* (CV-2) had gone down in the Coral Sea in World War II, but the new Lady Lex was as high-tech for 1962 as his had been for 1929—its deck slanted to give a longer "runway" for the supersonic jets she was carrying now.

> It was a tremendous show. I had not realized how greatly carrier operations had changed—the last time I had landed aboard was in a T4M that came floating in at a relative speed of about 20 kts. An F3H screeching in, missing no. 4 wire and roaring off, is another matter. But I had to see it, *smell* it . . . [sic] to realize it.[27]
>
> It is tremendously exciting and the noisiest thing I have ever heard anywhere.[28]

Adding to the pleasure, Heinlein was recognized everywhere he went and asked repeatedly for autographs. He was greeted by an officer on *Lex* who wanted to interview him for the ship's paper—fitting turnabout for all the times he had pestered visitors to make fill-copy for his own days trying to cobble up the next issue of the *Lexington Observer*.

They left immediately after, flying back to Colorado Springs on July 7. About an hour into the flight, Captain Erwin handed Robert two letters he had been holding on to since they left two days before—birthday love and wishes from Ginny and another from Andy Ahroon's wife Lou—then broke out liquid refreshments and toasted his birthday. That was his first birthday party. There was another at the Ahroons' place later that evening, and a third the following day, this one a quiet evening at home with the Ahroons and Ginny.

Ginny's condition, though stable, was not improving. A trip to Bethesda Naval Hospital didn't offer any hope of substantial improvement or any way of avoiding an eventual hysterectomy. Robert wrote Earl Kemp that they probably would not make it to Chicago for the WorldCon that year. If they were able to travel at all, he said, Ginny wanted to make the Aerospace convention in Las Vegas instead, to which she had a special guest invitation. He could probably make an overnight trip to accept a Hugo Award, if he knew about it far enough in advance—even, perhaps, as late as the morning the presentation was to be made—but that was the only reason he would come. Kemp told him he would give him a tipoff one way or another, after the Hugo Award balloting closed on August 5.[29]

Luck intervened. Tom Stimson, who had done the *Popular Mechanics* article on the Colorado Springs house in 1952, called to say that *PM* had assigned him to do an article on the Gemini program, and Stimson wanted Heinlein to write it instead—it was right up Heinlein's alley. Stimson had made extensive notes for the story already which Robert could work from.[30]

Heinlein was not completely satisfied with the notes and anticipated a trip (at *PM*'s expense) to the new Manned Space-flight Center in Houston and the McDonnell facility near St. Louis where the new spacecraft was being built. "Truth is," he wrote to Stimson, "this is turning into more of a job than I had planned on, too—but I don't see how I can do this in living, breathing technicolor with wide-screen stereo and power glide[31] without getting much closer to the job than I am here."[32]

He let himself be talked into it: With a little canny advance planning, he could schedule the research trip for the end of August and then, if absolutely necessary, make an overnight trip from St. Louis to Chicago for the World Science Fiction Convention.

Blassingame found *Glory Road* "delightful" but some of the editors who saw it had mixed feelings. Avram Davidson at *F&SF* told Blassingame he wanted Heinlein to chop off the last hundred manuscript pages. Heinlein responded that the whole point of the book was in Oscar's dissatisfaction with the hero's reward, the "happy ever after" of domestic bliss. He did not object to the labor of cutting, but—"If I do this, what is left is merely a sexed up fairy story, with no meaning and no explanations. I do not want this story published in such an amputated form . . . It leaves the story without meaning."[33]

The message of sexual freedom was much too strong for *Analog*, John Campbell wrote him. He would have to edit out a lot of stuff he knew Heinlein did not want edited out. Too bad. The first half was a terrific saga—

. . . it marches. It sings! It's a hell of a yarn!
The last half sits down on its duff and meditates about the uncertainties of life . . . [sic] which is exactly what a Hero and a Saga don't do!
I thought I was getting a saga . . . [sic] and I got a sermon.
Nuts! . . . [sic][34]

This was basically the same rejection letter Heinlein had gotten from Campbell over "Goldfish Bowl" in 1941, and he was even less inclined now to accept the sacred inviolateness of an editor's—or reader's!—expectations of genre as a creative Iron Maiden. Surprising the reader with a shift was *entertaining*—to him at least—and if the mail he got could teach him anything, it was that it entertained his readers, too, no matter what Alice Dalgliesh or Learned Bulman or John Campbell thought they ought to like instead. *Glory Road* would sell.

Earl Kemp upped the ante for a trip to Chicago: Not only had *Stranger* won the Hugo, he told Heinlein in confidence, but the chief editor at *Playboy* magazine, A. C. Spectorsky, had specifically asked for him at a "symposium" of SF writers—a taped, closed-door session followed by an early morning party at the Playboy Mansion on the Sunday night following the banquet.[35]

That decided him. *Playboy* was looking at *Glory Road,* and it was a very high-paying market. Earlier in the month, Ginny thought she might be able to make the Chicago convention—until Robert pointed out that Kalamazoo, Michigan, was nearby and he might be able to see Mary Collin for a long-delayed reunion, for which getting reacquainted in bed was not out of the question. "Ginny looked just barely surprised. 'Oh—I hadn't realized that was a factor. All right, I'll stay home. Mary is a good gal and I approve of her, you know that.'"[36]

He called Kemp immediately, while Ginny was still in the room: He would come the night of the banquet, but he wanted it kept as low-key as possible, saying he didn't want to "take the shine off" his friend Ted Sturgeon, who was guest of honor that year.[37]

Ginny was improving slowly, so Heinlein decided to take the risk of being away. On August 30, he left for Dallas, scheduled to view engineering mock-ups in Houston then go to St. Louis to see the actual spacecraft under construction at the McDonnell facility there. He wrote most of the article "Appointment in Space" in a hotel room in St. Louis, while the experience was fresh in his mind, then flew to Chicago on Sunday, September 2, checked in to the convention hotel, and dressed in white dinner jacket for the Hugo Awards banquet. As the award for *Stranger* was announced and accepted in his absence by Betsy Curtis,[38] he entered the ballroom and strode to the head table, amid a shock wave of surprise that turned into a spontaneous ovation.[39]

This award can only have been particularly meaningful to him: As much as the Hugo for *Starship Troopers* two years before, it validated his decision to kick over the traces and slip the surly bonds of editors and children's librarians. He had a quip prepared: "My wife Ginny," he held the rocket statuette up to display it, "is getting tired of dusting these things." Again, as last year, he invited everyone back to his hotel room for an open house and again he "received" in one of the ankle-length bathrobes Ginny made for him—a blue and white mattress-ticking stripe this time, with cotton pajama bottoms. Tradition. And good theater.

Heinlein enjoyed this kind of thing, though the receptions were always wearing on him, and he would pay for it later with days of exhaustion or weeks of respiratory infections: Parties with wide-ranging and sometimes scintillating conversation with these fearsomely bright—though sometimes unworldly-naïve—young people, and of course the dress-down element of dress-up was a very theatrical counterpoint to the extreme formality of the awards ceremony. Heinlein might not yet have realized it, but this kind of thing might be an important experience to the fans, possibly even something akin to his own emotional attitude toward Doc Smith and Sarge Smith, older figures whose life wisdom he respected and sought out.

Heinlein could not have given these young people what his own mentors gave him: The slow development of a world view could only be done through long and searching questioning together. There were too many of them, the press of flesh and the press of time were too great. The very circumstances that made it possible made even the attempt impossible. The most one could do under these circumstances was to banter with a witticism. Sometimes that was enough.

Heinlein had, over the years, developed his own version of Captain—Admiral—King's "voice of command":

The "voice of command" somehow carries with it to the hearer the subconscious knowledge that its owner is used to being obeyed, has the power to require obedience, expects to be obeyed, and does not encompass any possibility of not being obeyed.[40]

With Heinlein it was something more inward, which George Scithers characterized as "quiet persistence and presence of command." Scithers related an incident he saw at a lunch counter, possibly at this very convention. Heinlein sat down nearby, and there was a paper at the other end he wanted; the waitress didn't seem inclined to put herself out to get it, but by the time Heinlein was finished with the contest of wills, she got the paper for him—and he tipped her accordingly.[41] It was more attitude than technique, something that came from inside. There was something primal about Heinlein that the fans wanted from him—they came to warm themselves at his fire.[42]

The *Playboy* Symposium interview, moderated by Murray Fisher, was held that night after Heinlein's informal reception, from midnight till 3:00 A.M., and included a dozen science-fiction writers from the convention (Heinlein said "several of us—Pohl, Paul [Poul] Anderson, Ted Sturgeon, Tony Boucher, etc."[43]) and followed by a dazzlingly chic party at the Playboy Mansion that didn't even get under way until the small hours:

This fabulous house illustrated a couple of times in *Playboy*—and it really is fabulous, with a freeform swimming pool in the basement, a bar under that with a view window into the pool, and all sorts of weird and wonderful fancies. Several "Playmates" were around here and there (clothed) and I saw my chum Shel Silverstein (much annoyed that Ginny wasn't with me and distressed to learn that she was ill) and I met Spectorsky (who expressed great eagerness to receive copy of mine but no mention of *Glory Road,* so I suppose it bounced . . . .)

I got into a long, drunken, solemn discussion with Hefner in the bar and stayed until 7:30 A.M.—much too late or early, both from health and from standpoint of proper behavior of a guest. I like Hefner very much—my kind of a son of a bitch. No swank at all and enjoying his remarkable success.[44]

Heinlein didn't get to Kalamazoo that trip: He went back to Colorado Springs, wiped out from missing two nights' sleep in three days.[45] The *Playboy* Symposium was published in the November and December issues of *Playboy* for 1962.

By September 20, 1962, they were in Las Vegas for "Ginny's" aerospace convention, the Air Power Council. They saw a thrilling firepower exhibit at the Indian Springs range—the Mach 2.5 F4H in flight. They also saw the DynaSoar X-20 mockup, and met Dr. Edward Teller, who had been so supportive of the Patrick Henry campaign, as well as one of Teller's colleagues, Herman Kahn. Heinlein's ears pricked up when he was introduced to this jolly, bearded fat man who looked, he said, more like a young priest than one of the sharpest minds in current political thinking.[46]

Robert Cornog had cautioned him, ten years earlier, to pay attention to this young man's career, reconstructing one of his seminars out of his eidetic memory. And Cornog had been absolutely on target: Kahn was one of the world's most important theorists of the change in the geopolitical realpolitik that was going on in the early 1960s. His just-published book, *Thinking About the Unthinkable,* Heinlein said every concerned person ought to become conversant with.[47] Kahn's *On Thermonuclear War* was one of the books Heinlein listed as having influenced him greatly, in response to a request by a librarian.[48]

Kahn was a science-fiction reader and most emphatically a Heinlein fan. And since Heinlein was developing a circle of friends who intersected with Kahn's circle developed at the Rand Institute and brought over to his new Hudson Institute, they would see more of each other in times to come.

Playboy bounced *Glory Road* as "too romantic," and Robert concluded that *some*body was confused about their editorial policy (the same editor had rejected "All You Zombies—" as too sexy). He could understand *Playboy* might be hypervigilant about sexual content; they had a tightrope to walk between chic titillation and smut, a line that was somewhat blurry at the time. "Apparently the word 'romantic' does not mean to me what it means to you," he wrote the editor, but "If forced to a choice, I would rather read *Playboy* than sell to it."[49]

On October 19, 1962, Tom Stimson forwarded a "slight re-write" of the "Appointment in Space" article for his approval.[50] It was cut nearly in half and so changed it no longer felt to Heinlein like his own writing.

But they got what they paid for, and he made no objection. The cut version was published in the May 1963 issue of *Popular Mechanics* as "All Aboard the Gemini."

OLD WORLD, NEW WORLD, OLD WORLD

The Cuban Missile Crisis erupted on October 22, 1962, and Heinlein spent all his time glued to the radio tuned to CONELRAD, poised to drop everything and get into the shelter on a moment's notice.

The most remarkable thing about this thirteen-day crisis was that it was a crisis at all. All through the 1950s, after Stalin's death, Nikita Khrushchev's Soviet Union had steadily gained the upper hand on the world political stage. By the time of Sputnik in 1957, when it was absolutely certain that the USSR had technical superiority in ballistic missile technology, it began to look to the Heinleins (and to many others, as well) as though there was nothing the "kindly old gentleman" in the White House would not permit the Soviet Union to get away with—a failure of national nerve on a scale that could wipe America, and with it Western liberal ideas, off the planet forever.[1]

In 1959, the weak and corrupt dictatorship of Fulgencio Batista on the island of Cuba, ninety miles south of Florida, fell to Communist forces led by Che Guevara and Fidel Castro. In 1960, the Castro government nationalized all foreign-owned property. The new Kennedy government responded with an economic blockade of Cuba, embargoing imports of Cuban sugar (the island's principal cash crop) and fine Havana cigars.[2] Cuba's huge tourism and casino industry also dried up. Overnight, Cuba went from a marginally prosperous nation to one of the poorest countries on Earth. An attempt to retake Cuba the following year, the Bay of Pigs Invasion, failed because of logistical bungling. Castro was desperate for economic and military help, to keep his revolution alive. Uncle Nikita (Khrushchev) stepped up—but his aid came with strings.

The Soviet Union had lost its lead in the missile technology race: By 1962, U.S. nuclear missiles could reach all of the USSR, but Soviet land-based missiles could reach only sites in Europe. In April or May 1962[3] Khrushchev closed a deal to put missiles along the coast of Cuba, to reach cities in the United States. Building of the emplacements began in the summer of 1962.

The crisis was at full boil for a week before President Kennedy made the public announcement. A U-2 reconnaissance overflight had photographed missile emplacement construction sites on October 15, and President Kennedy immediately organized a dozen of his most important advisers into EXCOMM, to work out the U.S. response—a naval quarantine around Cuba, physically preventing delivery of the intermediate-range missiles to the island (there were already nine nuclear missiles on the island and under Cuban military control). President Kennedy's public announcement of the crisis on October 22, 1962, made it clear that any launch from Cuba would be considered an act of war and demanded removal of all offensive weapons. He stepped up reconnaissance overflights to one every two hours and on October 25 raised U.S. defense readiness to DEFCON 2.

This was, of course, nerve-wracking—but Heinlein found in it reason for long-term hope: the crisis, Heinlein wrote in a record of a telephone call with Lurton Blassingame that day, "reduces the overall prospects of war but makes the chance of *any* war much more imminent—today, this week, this month."

On Friday, October 26, Khrushchev offered by private letter to remove the missiles in exchange for a guarantee the United States would not invade Cuba. The next day, Saturday, another letter demanded the United States also remove its Jupiter missiles from Turkey.

President Kennedy was prepared to agree to the terms of the first letter—and the second demand was literally nothing: The Jupiter missiles were ineffective in Turkey, and he had ordered them removed as very nearly his first act as president. But the new demand now placed him in the intolerable position of appearing to give in to Soviet blackmail. Also, it was not possible to determine whether this was a serious offer or a feint while buildup went on.

That morning, a U-2 was shot down over Cuba, and the pressure increased from Kennedy's military advisers for an air strike to destroy emplacements. Saturday evening, President Kennedy decided to pursue a two-pronged strategy: a formal letter to Khrushchev offering to guarantee no invasion of Cuba once the removal of missiles was verified—i.e., accepting the terms of the first letter—while backchannel private assurances were given that the Jupiter missiles would be removed from Turkey, but *only* on the basis of a secret understanding.

The following day, Sunday, October 28, 1962, Premier Khrushchev announced he would dismantle the Cuban missile installations and return the missiles to the Soviet Union. By November 20, the dismantling was verified, and the Cuban Missile Crisis was formally over. Heinlein wrote to a friend in England:

> This crisis has made me really proud of my country and my compatriots for the first time in some years. The crisis and the ultimatum came as a surprise to most civilians. It was a surprise to me, not because I did not know of the missile buildup—I did know—but because I did not think that Mr. Kennedy would ever stand up to the Soviet Union; I had thought that we had saddled ourselves with a Chamberlain . . . . The all-prevailing attitude was one of calm resolution—and I was proud to be an American.[4]

But President Kennedy was also building another legacy: The month before the Cuban Missile Crisis, a young Negro man, James Meredith, had attempted to enroll in the University of Mississippi—"Ole Miss"—but was physically restrained from registering by the university and the governor, Ross Barnett. President Kennedy sent in federal marshals to protect Meredith, and on the day the boy enrolled made a live television address on the subject to the American people. While he was speaking, riots erupted on campus and in the nearby town of Oxford. The president ordered the federal marshals to quell the riots, which injured three hundred and killed two before quiet was restored. Along with the "Freedom Riders" bus trip through the South in May 1961, testing enforcement of the recent desegregation rulings of the Supreme Court, Meredith's enrollment and the Mississippi riots are considered cornerstones of the civil rights movement.

On the very day the removal of Cuban missiles was verified, Executive Order 11063 banned segregation in federally funded housing. A little more than a year earlier, probably in response to the violence in Alabama surrounding the Freedom Rides, the Interstate Commerce Commission had banned segregated facilities for all interstate carriers. It was an uphill struggle against resistance—but there was visible progress, line by line.

And if Khrushchev had his way, all this would be obliterated (the treatment of minorities in the Soviet Union was as extreme as anything anywhere in the world). The progressive liberal values of Western civilization would go up like tissue paper in a nuclear fireball.

Podkayne of Mars began to run in November as a three-part serial in the bimonthly *Worlds of If* magazine. Judith Merril wrote saying that her marriage was breaking up and asking for a loan to beef up the fallout shelter arrangements she would be sharing with Kate Wilhelm and Damon Knight.[5]

Robert and Ginny would be delighted to help—as a gift, not a loan. They had very poor luck with personal loans, Heinlein explained. With just one exception, not only had the loans never been repaid, but the embarrassment of being in debt to them had led to resentment and to having their friends cut them. They wanted to avoid that if possible—but

> If all or most of the adult civilians in the United States emulated your example, it would be worth far more to the country than would another couple of squadrons of ICBMs—Russia would *never* risk war with us if all of us were equally determined . . . .
>
> Our political system, our freedom, is rooted in the idea that basic responsibility is lodged in the individual. If we abdicate that personal, individual responsibility, then we abdicate the very notion of freedom—and might as well surrender quietly to the lords of the Kremlin . . . .
>
> . . . I know that gifts rankle the recipient, too, and I fully expect that you will not like us quite as well in the future as you do now, if you accept it. But gifts do not rankle as much as loans, as the matter is over and done with. If you are willing to take it as a gift, then I expect you to be honest with us, with no mental reservations about how you will repay it someday . . .

They were doing well enough to afford the gift: *Stranger in a Strange Land* was still selling at high levels for a two-year-old book[6]—both in hardcover and in paperback.[7] Heinlein went on, reinforcing the point:

> It must be a clean transaction; all finished, with no emotional hangover, no feeling in the back of your mind that it is "really just a loan." Nor even a feeling that you "ought" to feel gratitude. I am sufficiently cynical that I do not believe that more than a very small minority of the human race is capable of this most unusual emotion. If you are sufficiently eccentric that you are capable of feeling gratitude, try to keep the feeling to yourself and, with luck, it will go away and cease to disturb our relationship as friends.
>
> Trying to feel gratitude when one "ought to"—but does not—is even more difficult than trying to feel passionate when one is not in the mood.[8]

But losing friends seemed to be in the cards, money or not. In a burst of unpremeditated concern, Heinlein had offered places in their shelter to Andy Ahroon's wife and three children. Andy himself was on active duty and would not need a shelter. Robert would give up his place in the shelter and take his chances fading into the bush, following the example of Mark Hubbard twenty years before. He had not consulted Ginny before making the offer—and she was not entirely certain she was up to taking care of a cripple (Lou Ahroon had an advanced case of multiple sclerosis) and the children, two boisterous boys and a girl who was at the rebellious stage.[9] But she would back him up—even though it meant they would have to sleep in shifts.

Robert worked on getting in real beds—cots—and improving the sanitary facilities. He also laid in another gun and doubled their supply of batteries. Ginny had been collecting an entire shelf of survival skills books; she discovered that they had forgotten to plan for water and began distilling water and storing it in plastic jugs.[10] When she was done, she had food and water to allow as many as six people to survive (in crowded discomfort) for one month.[11] They instructed the kids how to get into the shelter and how to use all the equipment.

But late in November they had a "social spat" with Andy and Lou. "It was a silly business, just a broken date but some feelings were hurt on both sides."[12] Andy mailed back the key to the shelter. Robert sent it back with a note to the effect that they shouldn't penalize the kids over a difference of opinion among the adults.

> Yesterday he sent the key back to me for the second time, and made it quite plain that he would rather have his kids exposed unprotected to atomic attack than accept any favors from us . . . . It is a weird problem. We'll deal with it as best we can.[13]

The details of the writing business continued to pile up and had to be dealt with. In December, Peter Israel wrote, after expressing satisfaction with *Glory Road* overall, that he, too, wanted to cut the "pointless" last hundred manuscript pages of the book.[14] Ultimately Israel agreed to accept Heinlein's "story sense" as controlling, and Putnam's printed *Glory Road* as written—as did *F&SF* when Robert sent Avram Davidson, on a take-it-or-leave-it basis, the edit he had prepared for Putnam's.

Soon after the holidays, Ginny saw a specialist about her illness. Since her doctors said it was an inoperable kidney stone, Robert had been looking for other urologists and found that Dr. Howard, who had literally saved his life in 1934, was still practicing in Denver. Dr. Howard took a history and performed an endoscopic examination. Ginny did not have a kidney stone at all, he concluded—but when she was young, she had probably had a case of childhood tuberculosis (quite common in the 1920s) that left scars that might *look*, on an X-ray, like a kidney stone . . . if you weren't particularly careful about what you were looking at. There were other problems—a calcified lymph gland that did show up on X-rays but her physicians had missed, an infected sphinc-ter polyp, which he removed, and what looked like a lingering case of amebic dysentery—again. This time they both took the cure simultaneously, hoping to wipe it out completely.[15]

The amount and frequency of Demerol Ginny was taking dropped al-most immediately.[16] On January 23, 1963, Heinlein made a page of notes for a new book, *Grand Slam* (his family would be playing Bridge, with a seven No Trump contract when they took a direct nuclear hit that blasted them into the future). This book brought together two important topical subjects that had been on his mind since the Cuban Missile Crisis in Octo-ber and November the last year:[17] What he put into the book was an atti-tude that, in a very strong sense, the struggle for racial equality was the very emblem of the Western liberal values that would be the main victim of a nuclear war. The only thing a rational man could expect was that humanity would revert to its "normal" behavior throughout history. The inheritors of the Earth would think . . . differently: slavery at the very least—institutionalized cannibalism was not so unlikely. It had happened at various times and places in Earth's long and unsavory history. He would thrust his "nuclear" family into a world that made their own "limousine liberal" racism a world-system, the chief administrator a mirror of his hero, with only the color values re-versed. Leon Stover reported, more than twenty years later that Heinlein told him:

> . . . it does no more than play on Mark Twain's prophecy of 1885, that within a hundred years the formerly enslaved blacks of America would turn things around and "put whites underfoot," unless racial attitudes were changed.[18]

Most of the material he drew from his own experience[19]—a scathing satire, with ironic inversions of all the standard justifications for racial bigotry. He raced through the book in twenty-five days, 126,000 words, retitled *Farn-ham's Freehold*, presumably to throw the focus back where it ultimately be-longs—in the individual action of the individual human being, where the future is made.

Ginny approved of *Farnham's Freehold*. It was better, she said, than *Glory Road*. While polishing the manuscript before sending it to Blassingame,

Heinlein took the opportunity to enlist a doctor's help—Dr. Alan E. Nourse—to make the birth sequence as gut-wrenchingly believable as possible. Nourse suggested a long and difficult delivery, followed by hemorrhage and death by "bleeding out."[20] Heinlein was so appreciative that he eventually dedicated the book to Dr. Nourse.

In June, Heinlein again renewed his and Ginny's membership in the American and Midwest Sunbathing Associations, though he hadn't used them in years (all their nude sunbathing was done at home nowadays). Both Robert and Ginny continued their memberships for years, apparently on the principle that the right to be naked and not to be ruled by Mrs. Grundy deserves financial support from anyone who believes in freedom.

At any rate, he was getting extra sun, nowadays,[21] unclogging silted-up catch-basins and improving their water-recovery system by running a siphon system directly from Ginny's tub to the garden, to save the strain on her wrists carrying gray water during droughts.[22] She was recovering that summer from wrist surgery for carpel tunnel syndrome. She was also back on Demerol more often than not, up from twice a week back in April.

Her local doctors had essentially given up on finding out what was the problem, simply renewing her prescriptions for Demerol, which bothered Heinlein: It was habit-forming. No good could come of this in the long run.[23] But—

> . . . a light gleam of light about Ginny's health—she decided tonight [August 8, 1963] to try another approach . . . (Some of our friends have been telling me for months that I must *make* her do thus & so—haven't they ever heard of the Emancipation Proclamation? Women are not chattels. Ginny does her own deciding.)[24]

To Bill Corson, he added:

> She finally fired the joker who has not been treating her but loading her up with habit-forming drugs, and on Monday she goes into the hospital again, with new doctor, new tests, new hope for both of us. She hates it—she is *not* a patient patient—but this is a glimmer of light, maybe.[25]

Ginny probably had agreed to the change because she had taken up a new political cause, and the spasms of pain that came on at night interfered with her fund-raising activities for the Barry Goldwater presidential campaign.

Heinlein approved of Goldwater, both personally and politically—a New Deal liberal who had evolved in a sensible way, responding to the actual political realities the country had found itself in after World War II.

Ginny was setting up a "Gold for Goldwater" fund-raising campaign with five other field workers—a grassroots organization, outside the somewhat hidebound local Republican hierarchy. "Spend what you think we can afford," he told Ginny. He had been disillusioned with party politics for nearly a decade, but this was a campaign worth fighting.

> One reason I hope he makes it (a personal, non-political reason) is that he is half Jewish. Since Ginny and I are half Jewish, too, it would please me personally to see a Jewboy make the big one . . . when I feel like kicking an anti-Semite in the teeth—an exercise I enjoy—I prefer to have it be a to-tally disinterested act, a blow for freedom). . . . [26]

Heinlein was between books, but fan mail was becoming a real problem. "Ginny thinks I ought to stop answering reader mail entirely—but I can't. I'm just not cold-blooded enough to ignore entirely a letter from a stranger in which he says that he enjoyed something I wrote."[27] Nor was mail the only interference with writing and the ongoing project of improving their water-recovery system. In addition to what sometimes seemed "hordes" each summer, of friends and relations coming through, an increasing number of strangers felt free to drop by unexpectedly. Working time was constantly being eaten up. "Da Capo" was not going to get written this year—or the 10,000-word story he was working up for *Boys' Life*—or a novel, or all three.

Earlier in the spring, George Pal had looked at *Podkayne* for the screen, though he had not optioned the property. Now Heinlein's Hollywood agent, Ned Brown, was contacted by someone at Screen Gems, a television production company. Heinlein had developed a strategy by this time for dealing with Hollywood types: He was not interested in spending his working hours stroking the vanity of any illiterate with a checkbook he might or might not see the inside of. He devised a simple acid test to sort the frivolous from the serious. Ginny Heinlein recalled:

> . . . Hollywood producers would call frequently. Somehow they would obtain our unlisted telephone number if they were anxious enough to get in touch with Robert. They would talk about something, some project they would have in mind, and Robert would listen politely and then they would

say "why don't you come out here, hop a plane and come out here, and we'll talk about it?" And Robert would say, "why don't you hop a plane and come here to Colorado Springs, and we'll talk about it."[28]

That was usually the end of that.

The gambit failed, however, when the producer for Screen Gems, Howie Horwitz,[29] agreed to fly out to Colorado Springs to continue the discussions for a new kind of science-fiction television series, representing also his writing partner, William Dozier. Horwitz was in Colorado Springs on September 5 and 6, 1963, and he turned out enthusiastic, knowledgeable about science fiction—and very persuasive. Screen Gems, Horwitz insisted, was looking for something completely different from any science fiction that had been on television so far—adult drama, not watered down at all, and "undiluted science fiction." To make it possible, the interference was minimized by taking on multiple sponsors so that no one sponsor could control things. The Horwitz-Dozier team[30] had two hit shows on at the same time: *Route 66* (1960–64) and *77 Sunset Strip* (1958–64). Screen Gems had given them a free hand to come up with their next big thing. The show was to be called *Century XXII,* since it was to be set in about 2160 AD. Furthermore, Horwitz and Dozier were the producers; there would not be any "Hollywood committee" sticking fingers in this particular pie.

The day after Horwitz left, Heinlein began working on *Century XXII.* His strong suit as an SF writer, he knew, was the "literature of ideas" end of SF. He decided to build the pilot script and the series proposal around "Gulf," the strongest story ending he had ever thought up.[31] The "Gulf" story would adapt nicely to the international spy thrillers that were popular at the time—*Danger Man* from the U.K., and *The Man from U.N.C.L.E.* and *I Spy.* Kettle-Belly Baldwin, reworked to a younger, more vital character (Horwitz had Robert Stack in mind for a major role), was the core character, MacLeod. The series would go from crisis to crisis as MacLeod's organization of superhumans guarded and guided humanity. The story of "Gulf," with its tragic sacrifices of a comparative new recruit and one of MacLeod's more experienced "children," would be the pilot story, expanded to a ninety-minute format.

Ten days later, Heinlein had the series proposal ready—thirty-seven pages, plus a thirty-four-page appendix on the world of 2163 AD. He sent this, along with the first fifty pages of script for the pilot—"*The Adventure of the Man Who Wasn't There.*"

FADE IN:

EXT. TITAN CITY SPACEPORT—NIGHT

1.   MINIATURE—SPACESHIP LANDING

1

A long, low-key shot of FIELD and SHIP, with SATURN
conspicuous in B.G.

A high wind blows snow, sound of storm is an eerie
ululation. The ship lands straight down, guided by
pencils of light. We see by saturnlight and by floods
which cover the snowy field; spot lights let us see what
we wish to see. As the ship lands it partly obscures
Saturn. CAMERA CLOSES IN as the ship lands. Ship
extrudes jacks which steady it, cargo ports open, cargo
skids float up to them. The ship starts discharging
cargo as a long transparent tunnel snakes out from
the largest dome, a dome surrounded by a control tower.
A transparent ladder snakes down from the lower part
of the great ship and locks onto the tunnel. A rumbling
noise matches these movements. The ladder is an enclosed escalator, the tunnel from the dome is a moving
walkway. A light at the control tower and one at the
ship's conn change from blinking to steady as linkup is
made. Passengers in a crowded stream begin disembark-
ing, animation to match use of escalator and slidewalk.

DISSOLVE TO:

2.   SPACEPORT FIELD   2

We look past the shoulders of THREE GROUND CREW in
heavy protective clothing with helmets at the stream
of passengers inside the slidewalk tunnel. CAMERA
FASTENS on one man, MOVES with him. It is Professor
NIKITA ZARKOV, a middle-aged, unworldly scholar, a sweet
and friendly man. He is dressed in a 2163 mode, shorts,
shoes, singlet, and pouch belt. He is smooth-shaven
and his hair is very short. He is towing by a short
lanyard a very large bag which floats—there is a
small bulge at one end which is its antigrav unit.

As the CAMERA picks him out, he turns his head and
looks at us.[32]

Six days later, he wrote "The End" to the script, at an overloaded 141 pages.[33]

> 209. RAISE FROM BLACK TO PICTURE AS MUSIC SWELLS
>
> EXT. MINIATURE—FLAT LUNAR SURFACE, RINGWALL OF MOUN-
> TAINS IN DISTANCE, BLACK SKY AND STARS ABOVE. IN
> MIDDLE FOREGROUND IS A MONUMENT, CONVENTIONAL.
>
> Music starts as a dirge, shifts mood and becomes less
> mournful as we pull in toward monument. It quickly
> fills frame and the inscription on it then fills the
> frame so we can read it:
>
> > TO THE MEMORY OF
> > MR. AND MRS. ANDREW GENRO
> > WHO, NEAR THIS SPOT,
> > DIED FOR ALL THEIR FELLOW MEN
>
> We hold on this for at least ten seconds.
>
> As we raise the CAMERA from the monument to the
> starry sky MUSIC SWELLS in volume and becomes trium-
> phantly exultant as it merges into THEME OF SERIES.
>
> As quickly as stars alone fill the FRAME, we match
> with footage from the opening and start traveling
> fast through the stars. MUSIC UP AND OUT AS WE:
>
> >   FADE TO BLACK

Horwitz and Dozier were having the contracts prepared, and he was going to have to go back to Hollywood to close the deal. He made the necessary final revisions on *Farnham's Freehold* while he waited for the call.

He and Ginny had planned to go out for dinner on their anniversary, as usual, but they got the call to Hollywood for a meeting the day after, so they packed up and had their anniversary dinner in the air.

The meeting went well. They talked out the series proposal, and Heinlein "pitched" the rest of the pilot story. He had expected some resistance to kill-ing off the episode second lead, but neither Horwitz nor Dozier raised any objections. When he got back home, he fiddled some with the pilot script and on Armistice Day sent the full script to Ned Brown. Brown discreetly let him know it was not filmable as it stood: Horwitz's comments—"notes," they are called in the industry—would give him the feedback he needed to rework the teleplay. But he had gotten the *story* down, and that was the main thing.

The same day Ned Brown's comments were written (November 18, 1963), Robert and Ginny gave a dinner party for a number of people from the Navy

League western regional meeting being held at the Broadmoor, including three of his Annapolis class—all admirals now—Ricketts, Brandley, and Loomis.[34] At this party, Robert somehow got these dignitaries on their hands and knees on the living room floor, as ships re-enacting a famous Pacific naval battle while Robert read the progress of the battle to them.[35]

Ginny was more healthy and energetic—and quite suddenly. Just weeks before, she had been "so low that she had picked my next wife and was deciding to whom to give her jewelry."[36] Near the end of September, she had taken on a new doctor who had gotten her off Demerol with no residual effects at all. ". . . Ginny is well at last. Well, and suffering from a bad case of cabin fever; she went down and got herself a complete new set of flight baggage, so I am sure we will be starting out somewhere before long."[37] Heinlein had been working very hard on the television series. *Popular Mechanics* had proposed sending them to Antarctica for an article on Little America, but Ginny was talking about lying on the beaches of Tahiti, soaking up sun while he froze for the readers of *PM*.

The day after their dinner party was the last of the Navy League meeting, and Heinlein almost skipped it because of the late-night party. The keynote speaker was Assistant Secretary of the Navy, Col. Ken BeLieu.[38] BeLieu surprised everyone by ripping up his prepared speech and giving a rousing "go Navy!" talk that said all the things the admirals would like to have said but couldn't. He was given a standing ovation.

In the receiving line afterwards, Col. BeLieu did a double-take when he heard Heinlein's name. He hung on to Heinlein's hand and blurted out, "The Green Hills of Earth!"—Heinlein told a friend about the incident, continuing: "and I sez, 'Huh? You read the stuff?'—and he sez, 'I've read everything you've ever published. I've been wanting to meet you for years.'"[39] Robert and Ginny invited the colonel and his wife back to their place for drinks, and a passel of brass invited themselves along, so they had another wingding, second day in a row. The assistant secretary was indeed familiar with all of Heinlein's writing—including the boys' books most adults never saw. Flattering—downright flabbergasting when the Assistant Secretary of the Navy told him his favorite was *Starship Troopers*!

The boost to his morale stood him in good stead. President John F. Kennedy was assassinated on November 23, 1963, and the national shock and grief filtered even into Colorado Springs. Heinlein kept working: Howie Horwitz visited on December 4, on his way to tour the Denver Mint, pleased with the project so far. Robert finalized the long-delayed revisions on *Farnham's Freehold* and got the completed manuscript off to his typist a few days before Christmas.

On December 30, Horwitz sent him, not notes, but a completely revised script. His cover letter was not encouraging: He had fiddled with it a bit, he said, to improve the drama for television purposes—"though at some expense to dialogue."[40]

This was the first indication that Heinlein and Horwitz were simply not talking the same language: Horwitz had not simply reworked the blocks of dialogue, he had completely gutted the story—and the worst of it was a new ending that fell flat, "killed the story."[41]

Heinlein wrote to Horwitz of his—their—warm personal regard for him, hoping their friendship could survive anything that became of the series—but:

> The new script does not merely have a handful of major faults which might be corrected by changing these few scenes either back to what they were, or by changing forward to something entirely different. This new script is bad all the way through, in endless ways. Characterization, motivation, and logical construction of plot have *all* been destroyed . . . .
>
> Every time you get your hands on his dialog you turn him from a superman into a schnook . . . . since I can't look inside your head, I'm not sure just what your "Kenro" is like—but from the external evidence of the dialog and actions in your script he seems to be a muscly young man, with quick reflexes, fairly slow mental processes, and difficulty in making up his mind about anything.
>
> But the worst thing you have done to the Kenro character in this scene is to divest him of any nobility . . . . he flunks the superman test . . . .
>
> I am saying that intelligence without compassion is the most viciously dangerous thing in the world—and that is the moral of this story and should be the moral, one way or another, of every story in the series. This is spelled out in my original presentation for the series; apparently you have forgotten it since now all you seem to want is an adventure story with exotic locale and characters.[42]

And the new ending was flatly unacceptable: The whole story had been conceived around the original ending, in which Kenro and Edith sacrifice themselves to save humankind. Without it, you had only disarticulated shards of story elements, people moving around without consistent psychological motivation.

Within a day or two, Heinlein learned that William Dozier had resigned from Screen Gems.

Horwitz—and Ned Brown—must have looked at Heinlein's letter with a sinking feeling. Heinlein just didn't seem to understand *anything* about television. All his story criticisms were perfectly valid, Horwitz told him, but the practical realities of making television in 1964 simply could not accommodate many of them.[43]

In retrospect, Robert Heinlein was absolutely the wrong person to approach for this kind of a project. Isolated in the mountains of Colorado, he had hardly watched television at all, and had no internalized "sense" of the dramatic textures of a television show.

They might have been able to come up with something workable if they had taken up Heinlein's suggestion in his first reply, to scrap the "Gulf" story entirely and make up a new one from scratch. "We have a group of undefined characters in search of a plot and some fairly juicy elements to play with in constructing one."[44] But Horwitz insisted the story was salvageable—so long as you chop up the action, remove the longish speeches that establish the characters' deep motivation, get rid of the symbols that back up the plot line, and remove any trace of moral position from the conflicts.

Heinlein was skeptical: "A properly constructed plot is as tight as a syllogistic sequence," he told his agent, Ned Brown. "If you change the premises, you change the result. This is what Howie has done—but he fails to see it."[45]

> I suppose a vaguely similar story could be written, using the same names for characters, most of the locales, and the futuristic stage dressing. But plot structure, motivation, characterization,—and of course dialog—would have to be changed throughout . . . and it won't be written by me. If I am told to change the ending, I will change it, collect my blood money, take my name off it, and walk off. Howie approved my ending in December, reversed himself, then again reversed himself over the telephone a couple of weeks ago and again agreed to let my ending stand, now has reversed himself still another time and now insists on changing it. I'm sick of it . . . .
>
> Ned, don't even suggest to me that I go along with them on this point (other than as a trained seal, to complete a distasteful contract). Don't. Or I'm likely to bite right to the bone.[46]

Heinlein contractually owed them one more script revision and was "willing to do any damn thing they ask me to do," but "Suffice it to say I don't think *Shakespeare* could have worked for Screen Gems—and I have grave doubts about my own ability to."[47]

Heinlein drove with Ginny to Hollywood for a working meeting with Horwitz scheduled for Monday, January 27, to be followed by an extended stay—as long as it would take to complete the obligation. While there, they renewed some old acquaintances, both long-standing friends in the Hollywood area and new ones met at recent fan conventions.

Heinlein completed his basic contract, delivering the revised script just before midnight on Valentine's Day—Friday that year—but the script was still not satisfactory. Heinlein continued working sixteen-hour days on a third revised script which he turned in on February 27.

Ginny's health had improved greatly, but her right knee was acting up. That was the deciding factor: It was time to go home. Two weeks later, Horwitz had not asked for a further revision. The contract was judged fulfilled, and they left for home on March 18.

He still had a career in print: While he was battening down with that last script revision, Fred Pohl had picked up *Farnham's Freehold* for *If* magazine. *If* had started out as a sister magazine of *Galaxy*; by dint of hard work and exceptional editorial skill, Pohl was turning *If* into a real contender, and a steady market.

Heinlein was reluctant to start a new book, since he might have to be back in Hollywood that summer for pre-production work on *Century XXII*—and Jack Williamson was coming out for a visit at the end of May 1964 for his graduation from the doctoral program at Boulder, so they would have a visitor to entertain. Heinlein began to catch up on his backlog of technical reading and plowed into the mail that had accumulated in their absence.

The process of answering fan mail became so time-consuming that he instituted a postcard-only policy. Heinlein worked out a division-of-labor deal, with Ginny taking over most of the routine correspondence.

One correspondent wrote to give them a heads-up that *Stranger in a Strange Land* was starting to take on some unusual significance: At a recent seminar given by Alan Watts (America's Zen expert), Watts had mentioned *Stranger* and gotten knowing nods from the audience.[48] The April 1 royalty statements came in from Putnam's, for the second half of 1963: *Stranger's* sales were respectable, but they didn't give any particular evidence of activity picking up—probably about twenty-five hundred sales of paperback and hardcover, combined, for the last six months—up from the November low last year of about six hundred.[49]

The Screen Gems deal was still technically alive, but Screen Gems was undergoing a major reorganization, Ned Brown told him, and had been managed by a committee for a time. Now the new director, former child star Jackie Cooper, was coming in like a new broom, with his own cadre of management. Howie Horwitz no longer had an office there: He was working out of his home. The *Century XXII* project was in limbo.[50] Development hell. Heinlein had his Hollywood agent invoice Screen Gems for expenses and per diem on the trip.

And the science-fiction universe demanded his attention again: *Glory Road* was nominated for the Hugo Award. Even if the screenwriting venture was not successful, his writing was.

The universe was apparently intent on driving the lesson home: He received a partial reimbursement of expenses from Charles Fries at Screen Gems, along with a very nasty letter accusing him of dishonesty as to the rest. Robert politely acknowledged the check but pointed out the grounds for casting doubt on his honesty were not at all accurate (to say nothing of personally insulting). He might have stood still for the chiseling, he told Ned Brown: "A man can cheat me (and several have) and I will hardly blink. But if he cheats me and at the same time accuses *me* of cheating *him*—then I take any and all action open to me."[51] Two weeks later, Fries sent him the remainder of the expenses he had claimed.

Heinlein's long-standing proposal for an omnibus volume of the Future History stories got a boost when Truman Talley at NAL offered to pick up the entire series if Robert finished the fifth projected book. Since that book was substantially done with the British and American publications of *Orphans of the Sky* (1962), the omnibus project was on track. A glitch had emerged in December, over the 1958 Gnome Press issue of *Methuselah's Children*. By March 1963, it was back on the table: Doubleday had reconciled themselves to a seven-hundred-page volume, but Blassingame entertained suspicions: Already Doubleday had established a history of dumping its trade editions—giving them no substantial promotion—so they could issue in the cheaper and much more profitable SF Book Club (with a reduced author royalty).[52] Earlier in 1964, Blassingame had negotiated a contract with Doubleday to bring out a Future History omnibus. The contract was prepared, and Willy Ley asked to write the introduction,[53] but Heinlein rejected the contract as unsatisfactory[54] and outlined the minimum conditions—"two nonnegotiable points, five subject to discussion"—he would accept in such a contract (among the latter: whether the books were to be issued separately again, or only in the large, omnibus format).[55] When Doubleday wanted to take over the paperback rights for the original volumes, Blassingame, on Heinlein's direct instructions, pulled the plug on those negotiations and reapproached Putnam's, who had both *Orphans in the Sky* and *Farnham's Freehold* in process.

Putnam's was ramping up to market *Farnham's Freehold* with scare tactics, and in the process the jacket blurbs tipped too much of the suspense factor in the book—while ignoring the important secondary themes:

> . . . survival under very adverse and widely varying circumstances and the ever-changing problems of right conduct on the part of a free individual

when faced with conflicts involving the equal rights of other individuals—problems involving the nature of democracy, the relationship between responsibility and authority, conflicts and tensions involving rate, sex, marital duty, miscegenation, family vs. outsiders, many others—and all of them based on the assumption that a man possesses free will and a never-ending duty to himself to behave always with full and impartial justice to everyone no matter how difficult the circumstances . . . .[56]

To a correspondent, Heinlein confided: "*Glory Road* and *Farnham's Freehold* are possibly the least 'escapist' (along with *Stranger*) of any of my stories and the three together are a trilogy. But all three of them are heavily allegorical—and I'm damned if I'll explain the allegories!"[57]

But by that time, he had received another kind of wake-up call. It had started early in June 1964, with what could only be termed a "routine" alarum-and-excursion (for a political campaign) at the downtown Gold for Goldwater headquarters—alarming for Ginny. William Scranton, the governor of Pennsylvania, was tossing his hat into the ring for the Republican nomination, which was splitting the Goldwater candidacy: It was, in fact, a "stop-Goldwater" movement. Governor Love of Colorado was going to defect—jumping on the Scranton bandwagon before the groundswell of support he expected—and the entire Colorado Goldwater organization might fall apart.[58]

Goldwater had already lost the active support of former President Eisenhower when the subject of the president's younger brother, Milton S. Eisenhower, running for the presidency this year was broached to him. "One Eisenhower a generation is enough," he had said. And that was that. Ginny was an experienced field worker—but this was entirely outside her experience. She asked Robert for help.

GOLD FOR GOLDWATER

Up to this point, Heinlein had been content to applaud from the sidelines.

> I had intended to take no real part in this campaign other than donation of money, while Ginny devoted practically full time to it. But I find myself in the situation of the old fire horse downgraded to pulling a milk wagon—a school bell rings . . . and milk gets scattered all over the street! Last week I found myself, for the first time in a quarter of a century, presiding at a political rally—co-opted without warning at the last minute. I must admit that I rather enjoyed it. And I find myself pulled in on many other political chores and devoting perhaps half as much time to it as Ginny does.[1]

The Goldwater situation was eerily similar in outline to Upton Sinclair's EPIC movement—a grassroots campaign not entirely accepted by the local party regulars—but on the Republican side this time. As with EPIC in the 1930s, Heinlein believed it was the right thing to do in the current circumstances. Since his disillusionment over Roosevelt's involvement in Pearl Harbor, he no longer regarded party affiliation as important: "I usually voted a split ticket. There wasn't enough difference between the two parties to matter, usually . . ."[2]

> I really do not think my own political opinion moved very far either to the right or to the left between now and thirty years ago. I have grown far more experienced, far more knowledgeable, and my opinions have sharpened thereby. But I was an individualist and a democratic constitutionalist then and I am now. I thought Jefferson had just about the right ideas then—and I do now . . . .
>
> From my point of view what has happened is not that I have moved to the right; it seems to me that *both* parties have moved steadily to the

left—until the [moderate] Republicans . . . occupied a position somewhat left of center whereas the Democratic Party had moved to the far left.[3]

"Left" does not mean the same thing as "liberal," though leftists have a vested interest in maintaining and promoting the confusion. Before the twentieth century, in fact, there was no "left" and "right" in American politics. Those terms of European politics *could not* apply in the United States because monarchism (the "right") was not a possible position on the U.S. political spectrum. There was a time when Europeans almost could not conduct a political dialogue with Americans, because they did not share the same vocabulary of political ideas.

Liberalism was a political philosophy that had a minor role in European politics, gradually displaced in favor of various strains of Marxist thought after the psychological shock of the failure of the European liberal/democratic revolutions in 1848. The progressive theories of class-collaborationist liberals like Henri de Saint-Simon[4] fell out of favor in Europe (though they were and remained well entrenched in America), thanks to the bizarre utopian accounting system of Charles Fourier,[5] and Babeuf's[6] "you must liquidate the ruling class" ideas from the French Revolution framed the basis of Karl Marx's thinking after he fled the failed revolutions in Germany to haunt the British Museum researching and writing *Das Kapital.* The Soviet Union's October Revolution, seventy years later, played in the cultural psychology of the twentieth century the same role that the American Revolution played for the political psychology of Western civilization in the nineteenth century.

Heinlein's training and experience in party politics took place at a time when "traditional" American radical liberals—Upton Sinclair and his EPIC group in California—were in an almost unrecognized struggle with the more left-leaning New Deal for the soul of America's liberalism. The conflict might ultimately have gone either way—Roosevelt often seemed to have sentiments rather than ideology—but the New Deal programs were often created and guided by hard-core leftists such as Rexford Tugwell.[7] By the time the division in the Democratic Party was actually noticed as anything more than the usual and traditional disagreements between the moderate and the radical wings of the party, it was too late.

Heinlein was—and always remained—a traditional American liberal, Jeffersonian—not left and not right. This explains, for example, why he could marry and live with an announced conservative: Ginny's core values were traditional American liberal, as well, and it is to them that he responded. As leftists took over the Democratic Party, a certain number of traditional American liberals migrated into the moderate wing of the Republican Party, and as the Republican Party itself moved to the left (a very traditional migration, as all political parties in the United States traditionally drew their evolution from the radical wing of the Democratic Party[8]), they migrated into the "conservative" wing of the party, which is where Ginny's position was—and Goldwater's. Although the association of religious fundamentalists with the Republican Party is very traditional in American politics—Abolition was an issue promoted and sustained in America's churches, after all, and the Republican Party was founded to be the party of Abolition—the rise of the "religious right" is a much more recent phenomenon.

In the years before "libertarianism" became associated with another radical-liberal political movement, itself ultimately fallen down the NeoCon rabbit hole, Heinlein defined his position using a then-standard terminology: "liberal" means "for freedom, above all."

We [he and Ginny] are libertarians—i.e., we believe in freedom and individualism to the utter maximum attainable at all times and under all circumstances. To some people "libertarian" spells "socialist," "anarchist," "crackpot" or "black reactionary"[9]—to us it simply means personal freedom in any and every possible way at all times—with meticulous respect for the other person's equal freedom. (And that, incidentally, is the only sort of "equality" I believe in; all other definitions of "equality" turn out to be fake—in my opinion.)

Freedom—This is how I feel about things—and all the too-serious critics who have tried to analyze my stories would find a continuing inner consistency if they spotted that one point. (But for Goddsake don't tell anybody! Let em guess. I *try* to write clearly; if I fail to make my point to the reader, I *won't* engage in long-winded apologia . . .[10])

This is why they favored Goldwater. This is the quality he and Ginny had seen in his *Conscience of a Conservative* book (and why they dedicated so much of their own fund-raising to buying and distributing this and the other campaign literature and books Goldwater had authored). The concluding paragraph of the first chapter of *The Conscience of a Conservative* narrows to focus on this single, overriding issue:

The delicate balance that ideally exists between freedom and order has long since tipped against freedom practically everywhere on earth. In some countries, freedom is altogether down and order holds absolute sway. In our country the trend is less far advanced, but it is well along and gathering momentum every day. Thus, for the American Conservative, there is no difficulty in identifying the day's overriding political challenge: it is *to preserve and extend freedom*. As he surveys the various attitudes and institutions and laws that currently prevail in America, many questions will occur to him, but the Conservative's first concern will always be: *Are we maximizing freedom?*

To an even greater extent than Upton Sinclair's gubernatorial campaign in 1934, this was a "campaign of books," and Goldwater seemed to favor freedom in all its forms more than any other candidate. "For *me*," Heinlein wrote,

being free is much more important than being well-fed—and I speak as one who has been miserably poor and painfully in debt and very hungry far from home, friends, or acquaintances, and no one to turn to—I still vote for freedom, and will wangle the maximum of it for myself no matter how strongly the majority may be against me—breaking any laws I can get away with breaking in order to achieve the highest personal degree of freedom I can arrange.[11]

Certainly Goldwater's voting record helped Heinlein to support him. It showed he had his heart in the right place—he had voted for the New Deal when it counted and very visibly had put his pocketbook on the line when he ordered his family's department store to begin hiring Negroes. When he was a city councilman in Phoenix, Arizona, Goldwater had also spearheaded the movement to desegregate Sky Harbor airport. "The key to racial intolerance," he had said, "lies not in laws alone but in the hearts of men."[12]

Heinlein had met the man outside the political context and years before the current campaign, while Goldwater was on a hunting trip in Colorado. "I like Goldwater as a person, too—but met him long after I had decided [in 1959] that he would make a good President."[13] Heinlein had no doubt that Barry M. Goldwater was the real deal. In fact, Goldwater's biggest political liability as a candidate came directly from the fact that he was the real deal: He said what he thought about an issue the moment the subject came up, colorfully and vividly, without weighing what might be the politically expedient thing to say. His political opponents said that Goldwater "shoots from the hip"—and he did occasionally come out with the kind of thing that might be floated in a think tank but was political death for a national candidate (using low-yield nuclear weapons to exfoliate the jungles in Vietnam, for instance).

This mattered less to Heinlein than that the opinions were sound and he always zinged his target.[14]

This somewhat countered Heinlein's natural suspicions of a man who won't drink coffee. In a Republican field that included Richard Nixon (who had declined to run this year), Henry Cabot Lodge, Jr., Governor Scranton, and Nelson Rockefeller, Barry Goldwater stood out. Heinlein wrote to his brother Larry:

I don't know whether Goldwater can be elected or not—or whether he can change things if elected. But I would like to see the United States make a radical change away from its present course. I'm sick of bailing out Kremlin murderers with wheat sold to them on credit and at tax-subsidized prices, I'm sick of giving F-86's and Sherman tanks and money to communists, I'm sick of undeclared wars rigged out not to be won—I'm sick of conscripting American boys to die in such wars—I'm sick of having American service men rotting in communist prisons for eleven long years and of presidents (including that slimy faker Eisenhower!) who smilingly ignore the fact and do nothing, I'm sick of confiscatory taxes for the benefit of socialist countries and of inflation that makes saving a mockery, I'm sick of signing treaties with scoundrels who boast of their own dishonesty and who have never been known to keep a treaty, I'm sick of laws that make loafing more attractive than honest work.

But most of all I am sick of going abroad and finding that any citizen of any two-bit, county-sized country in the world doesn't hesitate to insult the United States loudly and publicly while demanding still more "aid" and of course "with no strings attached" from the pockets of you and me. I don't give a hoot whether the United States is "loved" and I care nothing for "World Opinion" as represented by the yaps of "uncommitted nations" made up of illiterate savages—but I would like to see the United States *respected* once again (or even feared!) . . . [sic] and I think and hope that the Senator from Arizona is the sort of tough hombre who can bring it about.

I hope—

But it's a forlorn hope at best! I'm much afraid that this country has gone too far down the road of bread and circuses to change its domestic course (who 'shoots Santa Claus'?) and is too far committed to peace-at-any-price to reverse its foreign policy.[15]

Although Heinlein (mildly) preferred Lyndon Johnson over Alan Cranston among the Democrats, this year he went to work for the Colorado Goldwater campaign.

Heinlein's political experience had been gained in a Democratic Party that had recently tripled its size and was wide open, young, and vigorous. Moreover, his basic training was in an impoverished organization, not at first supported by the party establishment. Beating the bushes for money and exposure was second nature to him. His sudden emergence into the staid, long-established Republican organization in El Paseo County was not so much a fresh breeze as a hurricane. "His activities were a revelation," Ginny later remarked, giving as one example, "Instead of simply charging the price for a book, he set up a goldfish bowl, and asked for contributions, getting more out of each customer."[16]

He was effective, no doubt, but his style was an affront to the party hierarchy.

On June 20, he was invited to a strategy and planning meeting at the home of the county chairman, Robert M. Laura, Esq. Laura casually suggested something that got Heinlein's hackles up: He was going to retain a portion of the monies raised locally to fund the local office—not unreasonable in itself, but their fund-raising literature promised explicitly that anything they collected would be sent directly to the national campaign headquarters.

Just like Sinclair's EPICs in 1934, Goldwater Republicans in 1964 were viewed with suspicion by traditional Republicans, and many of the usual party fund-raising doors often remained closed to the candidate: The national campaign needed every cent it could raise. What Laura proposed was foul betrayal of the party hierarchy—a local organization usurping the goals of the party. But, Robert was the new man in this particular group, and no one else objected. He kept his misgivings to himself.

Instead, he turned to their immediate problem with the state organization, writing directly to Governor Love. The Scranton groundswell of support had never materialized, he pointed out: All Love could do now was to divide the party, on the eve of the nominating convention.

Lyndon Johnson's Civil Rights Act of 1964 had come to a vote just before the nominating conventions, and Goldwater had voted *against* it. Heinlein understood Goldwater was not voting against civil rights: He was voting against *federal* enforcement of civil rights.[17] In Senator Goldwater's opinion, it was a matter for each state to do, individually, for itself, and, even more importantly, it was, at heart, a matter of the attitude of individuals, which could not be legislated by state *or* federal government.

Goldwater's opinion was Constitutionally "correct." The U.S. Constitution had not specifically delegated this kind of power to Congress or the Executive, and it did reserve to the states any powers not specifically delegated. Lyndon Johnson, following the Kennedy brothers' lead, used federal forces for the pragmatic reason that some states—George Wallace's Alabama, for example—*would not* cede the rights of U.S. citizens unless coerced.

"States rights" is a conservative issue in American politics, going all the way back to the Federalist Papers. Goldwater was where he belonged, after all—and perhaps also where he could do the most good on net. Heinlein's notions on this issue probably remained more typical of a Democrat: How realistic could it really be to pretend that the United States was still a federation of sovereign states? And in any case, enforcement of a citizen's civil rights under the Constitution most assuredly *was* the business of the federal government. But it was an honorable disagreement over tactics, not over basic goals, and it meant that racism would become an issue in the campaign.

The Republican National Convention nominated Barry Goldwater on July 15, 1964. His acceptance speech articulated a position that was to become iconic: "I would remind you that extremism in the defense of liberty is no vice. And let me remind you also that moderation in the pursuit of justice is no virtue." But it was another campaign liability: The extremism charge had been raised earlier in the campaign by fellow Republican Nelson Rockefeller, who was standing up for the reactionaries in the party—but it allowed Lyndon Johnson, as activist a president as existed in American politics since Lincoln (and "the phoniest individual that ever came around," according to Goldwater, since Johnson had been lukewarm to civil rights prior to this), to position himself as a moderate and Goldwater as a lunatic extremist. Over a dirty-tricks television ad of a girl picking daisies over a countdown to an atomic bomb that goes off in the background, Johnson supporters turned Goldwater's campaign slogan—"In your heart you know he's right"—against him: "In your guts, you know he's nuts."

Ginny stepped up her work for the campaign. Heinlein stepped up his work, too, but he was still conflicted—and at another meeting at Bob Laura's house on August 1, he finally had more than he could take. Laura was temporizing over an offer of help Ginny had taken by telephone from a woman who identified herself as a Negro. He would take the matter up with his State Central Committee contact, Laura said, but his own reaction was: "Oh, they are free to go ahead and form *their own* committee."[18] Heinlein lost his temper for the first time in many years. He told Laura,

> They offered to stick their necks out; we should have shown instant gratitude and warmest welcome . . . . I can't see anything in this behavior but Jim-Crowism . . . . you were suggesting a Jim-Crow section in the Goldwater organization.

Mr. Goldwater would not like that. His record proves it.

Negroes are *citizens*, Bob . . . . It is particularly offensive, *this* year and *this* campaign, to suggest that Negro Goldwater supporters form their own committee . . . .

He then ticked down a list of Laura's administrative foul-ups, concluding:

—these faults can easily lose the county . . . [sic] and with it the state . . . [sic] and, conceivably, if the race is close, the Presidency itself.

. . . . So I'll try to refrain hereafter from offering you advice. But I think it's time for you either to behave like a manager, or resign.[19]

Laura apologized for his part in the altercation.

Ginny went into field work full time, and Heinlein agreed to handle an expansion of the county office now that the nominating convention was over and the campaign was ramping up in earnest. As Laura temporized on the Jim-Crow question, he gave Heinlein a personal criticism, not the first time he had heard it: "I know you don't believe that anyone could consider you a 'yes' man. I wonder, however, if you can conceive of another's opinion, differing though it may be, possessing any merit."[20]

On this issue, no: The opinion that a Negro volunteer should be treated differently from a white volunteer possessed no merit whatsoever—and if that was "intolerant" in Bob Laura's book, so be it. "I'm one of the most intolerant men I've ever met," Heinlein noted to himself. "I had thought that, simply because I had uncustomary responses as to what I liked and what I hated that I was 'tolerant.' I'm not. I'm not even mildly tolerant of what I despise."[21]

There were things more important than party unity in the Republican Party of Colorado.

Late in August, the political situation became very black-and-white for Heinlein: President Johnson made a broadcast address to the nation, timed to catch the evening news. Early in the month (August 2 and again on August 4), the U.S. destroyer *Maddox* was fired on by North Vietnamese forces in the Gulf of Tonkin. On August 7, Congress passed the Gulf of Tonkin Resolution, essentially putting war powers in the president's hands without a declaration of war. In his August 18 news conference[22] President Johnson told of an attack in progress—actually launched but not yet engaging the enemy.

This was an extraordinary—indeed, almost treasonable—violation of national security: giving away intelligence about an offensive before it happened.

As the results came in—one naval aviator dead and one captured—Heinlein's shock turned to raw, uncontainable fury.

> It was that hour and thirty-nine minutes of warning to the enemy—simply to catch the late evening east coast newscast!—that disgusts me. In civilian life we call this sort of thing "murder." Since we can't hang him for it, I intend to make every possible effort to see to it that he is retired to Texas where he can do no further harm . . . [sic] or at least will not be in command of men—and betray them.[23]

No matter what, Johnson must be defeated.

> Politicians bungle and military commanders are often stupid—but this is a depth of cold-blooded villainy almost unique . . . . But I do not drink my brother's blood—nor stand idly by while another does so—and *any* man who is defending my life with his is my brother and his safety is as much my personal concern as is that of our nephew. The least I owe him is to get rid of a commander who does not value his life and replace him with one who understands the responsibility of a commander toward his men . . . .
> We shan't spare any effort and will spend whatever money is necessary."[24]

Heinlein cancelled his planned trip to Annapolis for his thirty-fifth class reunion and got a second car so both he and Ginny could be mobile.[25] He began working full time at the county offices, setting up an expansion into a satellite office to handle the closing months of stepped-up campaign activity.

A wonderful fund-raising opportunity fell into their laps at the start of September when a wealthy party regular, Al G. Hill, volunteered to underwrite a fifty-dollar-a-plate dinner and open-bar cocktail party at the Garden of the Gods Park—an elegant, high-profile tourist destination, with spectacular towering red rock formations. The local party organization already had a similar fund-raiser scheduled in a more "traditional" venue,[26] but Heinlein saw this as an opportunity not to be missed: It could be marketed to the sort of people the party usually had a hard time getting contributions from— socialites and the resort crowd who normally contributed, if at all, in their home districts. This would be a social event—a gala—rather than a stuffy party function.[27] Heinlein got the preparations under way for September 26—a Saturday evening far enough in advance of the elections for the new money to do some good.[28] This new money was not tied to the county organization's campaign literature or the phony promise to send everything to the national headquarters: Heinlein got the proceeds earmarked to spend on uncommitted voters in El Paseo County.[29]

At an Executive Committee meeting on September 9, Laura tried to impeach him (Heinlein's notes are not clear on the issue involved) and eject him as a troublemaker. "I declined to be 'tried,'" he remarked dryly in his office journal, but made his regular report instead. Two days later, Weldon Tarter, Laura's contact with the state party organization, conducted what Heinlein's office notes call a "Drum Head Court Martial" of Heinlein, accusing him of rudeness, excessive brusqueness to the headquarters staff, and even a kind of personal violence, saying he had been observed throwing someone out of the office literally by the scruff of his neck and the seat of his pants (this latter was contradicted on the spot by an eyewitness).

Heinlein had tried to effect a change, get more out of the organization they had—and you can't change unless you actually, you know, *change* . . .

Heinlein demanded to be confronted by his accusers—or at least to know the details of these accusations, but Tarter ignored him. He would not even discuss any details.

"I said that I could not continue in Hq under such conditions," he noted in his office journal. Ginny and he withdrew completely from the formal party organization in the county until Tarter should give them a written statement of what their duties were. They never heard further from Laura or Tarter. Heinlein turned over all his outstanding files to Laura and put all the contracts he had been generating on hold until Tarter and Laura should make up their minds what to do with the new assets.

But Heinlein did keep one file: The Garden of the Gods dinner was less than two weeks off.

This fund-raiser had a lot of support even inside the county organization, where not everyone had taken the *ugadat, ugodit, utselet* vow ("pay attention, ingratiate yourself, survive"—the motto of the old Soviet bureaucracy). In addition to the $500 they had already donated, Heinlein was covering the minor overhead expenses out of pocket, so they could market it as any money raised being 100 percent donation to the cause; they had the enthusiastic and intelligent cooperation of the manager at the Garden of the Gods, and donations of labor and kind supplemented the underwritten cost of the dinner and the open bar.[30] Nearly every penny raised could be donated to the campaign. They were limited to a seating of sixty, so Robert felt it best to deflect any potential conflict with the traditional fund-raiser being organized by the local party by urging people to subscribe to the party dinner instead.[31]

The Garden of the Gods dinner was soon fully subscribed. Heinlein had sought out subscribed tickets for each local Republican candidate and wife and was able to secure the appearance of two-thirds of them. A special political guest, William Miller, the vice presidential candidate and Goldwater's running mate, was flying in for the affair. Heinlein told his sponsor, Al Hill:

> But there were still some candidates for whom I did not have subscribed plates. When Mr. Miller's advance man, Jack Cole, told me that Mr. Miller could be expected to attend the cocktail party, I phoned the remaining candidates and the officers of the County Central Committee and invited them to the cocktail party. You had not authorized me to invite any extras to the cocktail party but with the tough situation which does exist between the old-line Republicans and the Goldwater organizations, I felt that this was necessary.[32]

They raised $3,625—on a theoretical maximum of $3,000—all earmarked for local campaigning and not controlled by the county organization. A large part of it went to purchase campaign literature for precinct workers. Some of the money went to underwrite Senator Goldwater's television appearances, and for these Robert wrote three thirty-second spots:

```
"Communist opinion" 30-sec spot.
Heinlein 6 Oct. 1964
THEME SOUNDER
    When Goldwater was nominated, Radio Moscow said, "The
Republican Party has been taken over by some pirates led
by a sworn enemy of the Communist camp." But after the
Democrat Convention, PRAVDA, official Soviet newspaper,
praised the Democrat platform. Why?
    THE WORKER, official organ of the American Communist
Party, says: "STOP BARRY!"
    Why?
Why does every socialist, every Communist, every person
intent on overthrowing our free government, scream for us
to "Stop Goldwater!" Think it over.
In your heart you know he's right.
END SOUNDER
```

```
"Shooting from the hip" 30-sec spot.
Heinlein 6 Oct 64
THEME SOUNDER
SOUND EFFECT—three rapid gun shots.
    1ST VOICE (male or female, surprised and frightened):
```

He shoots from the hip!

2nd VOICE (male, confident, hearty approval): And he hits
the mark—every time!

3RD VOICE (female, confident): In this supersonic age,
fast, accurate decisions are a must! Goldwater knows where
he stands and doesn't have to waste precious minutes
looking it up. He flies supersonic fighter planes where a
man must have split-second correct judgment to stay alive.
He has more than four thousand hours as a military pilot.
Today . . . [sic] for us all to stay alive . . . [sic] the
man on that hot-line telephone must have fast and accurate
judgment. Vote for Goldwater! In your heart you know he's
right!

END SOUNDER

"Civil rights" 30-second spot.
Heinlein - 6 Oct 64
SOUNDER

  MALE VOICE: (Rising intonation, indignant unbelief)
Goldwater against Civil Rights? NONSENSE! Here's the truth:
as a Phoenix City Councilman, Goldwater voted to desegregate the city airport restaurant. As chief of staff of the
Arizona Air National Guard, Goldwater ordered desegregation. GOLDWATER's department store was the first major
employer in Arizona to hire Negroes on a regular basis.
Goldwater says: "The key to racial intolerance lies not in
laws alone but in the hearts of men." In your heart you
know he's right! Vote for Goldwater!

END SOUNDER

There is no evidence these spots were ever used. A week later, Heinlein
sketched out a campaign speech.[33] But by mid-October it was already clear
that Goldwater's chances were slim.

The last few weeks of the campaign were personally depressing for the
Heinleins. On September 24, Sarge Smith died of advanced lung cancer in a
Cleveland hospital. And on October 2 their cat Shamrock died delivering kittens: Ginny took time off from the campaign every few hours to feed them
formula.[34]

Robert and Ginny arranged to go directly from the voting booth to the
airport on November 2, 1964, flying out to Houston for an AIAA/NASA
Manned Spaceflight Conference. When that was over, they would board a
Danish freighter, *Hanne Skou,* at Mobile and travel in the Antilles and South
America. "A rest from politics will be welcome."[35]

After the Spaceflight conference, they went from Houston to New Orleans instead of directly to Mobile (freighters do not keep tight schedules, and they were delayed) and spent a few days relaxing as Hermann Deutsch's houseguests. Goldwater carried only six states and 36 percent of the popular vote. Goldwater said he would not have voted for himself if he believed everything that journalists had written about him.

They toured the Boeing plant in Louisiana, guests of the chief engineer and chief counsel—"and I beg to report that the Saturn is the most monstrous big brute imaginable," Heinlein wrote to Blassingame, "and I do not believe that the Russians can do things on the scale of our APOLLO project. I do believe we will have a man on the moon this decade; progress looks good."[36]

Ginny did not show her usual enthusiasm for shopping on this trip, but she did find one unusual item in New Orleans: A saluting gun—a brass cannon, about twenty inches long and four inches in diameter—from an eighteenth-century sailing vessel. It reminded her, she said, of that old joke about the man who retired and went into business for himself, polishing a brass cannon. They had their own brass cannon shipped to Colorado, where they could deal with it after they got back home.

They had only begun to unwind when *Hanne Skou* embarked from Mobile on November 9 for Jamaica, Aruba, Maracaibo, Porto Cabello, La Guaira, and Trinidad before heading back to Mobile on about December 5.

The Danish captain thought he would have a little amusement at their expense, assuming they would be conventionally racist: He invited them to his cabin one night while they were in Kingston, Jamaica, and they found the captain and his first officer with a couple of local girls, both quite dark. Robert and Ginny had drinks, and then it was suggested they go nightclubbing on the island. Ginny recognized the invitation as a challenge, and so did Robert. Naturally they accepted the gauntlet.

The first nightclub was a beautiful location high on a hillside, but nightclub entertainment is sparse, even in Jamaica, on a Monday night. They visited two more nightclubs. After this time, even at only one drink per place, the party was a little the worse for wear. Ginny recalled what happened next:

After the third club, one of the girls took the bit in her teeth, and gave the taxi driver an address . . . We arrived there and I immediately noted that there was a red light at the side of the building, but Robert did not see it, and we went inside the house. (I was, well, delighted—I'd always been curious about those places.) Inside there were a number of girls in various stages of undress lying and sitting around the living room. We went through and into a place that served as a bar, ordered drinks, and the Madame joined us there. She was furious at the fact that I was along, and talking it over later, we decided that was caused by the fact that my presence was losing business for her.[37]

The girls seemed ominously well acquainted at their next destinations, a succession of dives on the waterfront. Eventually the Heinleins turned in for the night, leaving the captain and FO—and their dates—to their own devices. Robert complimented Ginny on her excellent comportment in trying circumstances.

Back at home was back to the grind.

THAT DINKUM THINKUM

Around Christmastime, Heinlein began receiving angry or puzzled letters from a number of his friends saying this Alexei Panshin person was asking nosy questions about him. Shortly before New Year's, Panshin wrote to Lurton Blassingame, saying he had been commissioned by Earl Kemp at Advent to write a critical work about Heinlein: "I am in the need of information, advice, and quotable opinion."[1] Blassingame sent the letter on to Heinlein with an inquiry, but replied to Panshin, saying, "It's about time for a critical study of this sort."[2]

Betsy Curtis[3] told Heinlein that Panshin had winkled a file of Robert's letters to Sarge Smith out of his widow and was going to write a biography.[4] Heinlein placed a call to Earl Kemp within an hour of receiving Curtis's letter, and wrote also to Sarge Smith's widow, telling her he did not want Panshin having the letters—would prefer he never saw them at all. He recalled Panshin from fan mail following the publication of *Starship Troopers*—an arrogant, argumentative, and tiresome teenager. "Pee" (as Heinlein later came to refer to Panshin) had also, he later found out, written an arrogant and clueless article titled "Heinlein By His Jockstrap"[5] for a Los Angeles–based fanzine—claiming Heinlein was sexually naïve and puritanical, hypocritically pretending to sophistication.

Kemp's response was strangely evasive. Panshin had approached him, he said, not the other way around. Heinlein later said:

I told Kemp that I preferred not to have my total corpus of work evaluated in print until after I was dead . . . [sic] but in any case, I did not want a book published about me written by a kid less than half my age and one who had never written a novel himself—and especially one who had tried to pick a fight with me in the past. Why not ask someone nearer my age, one with a long experience in the field and with established reputation as a science fiction writer—such as de Camp, Knight, Merril, or Leiber?

When it finally became clear that Kemp was dodging and was firmly determined to get my name on his list by this means (since I would not write a novel for him), I wrote Kemp a registered letter[6] stating that, while I could not keep anyone from writing about me, I would not condone anything and I was reserving any and all legal rights and redresses if it should develop in the future that I had been damaged. (I did *not* "threaten to sue" as was widely claimed. There is a vast difference between reserving one's rights and uttering threats.)

But it did scare Kemp off.[7]

Mrs. Smith wrote to Panshin asking for the return of the letters, and he complied. There was nothing in them he found useful for his purposes, anyway, he said—which struck Robert as very odd when the remark was relayed to him: In those letters, Heinlein had bared his soul, including discussing much of the material that went into *Starship Troopers*. Biography or critical commentary, how could such a thing *not* be useful?

Matters that others might discuss on a couch to a psychoanalyst I took up with Sarge; he was my father confessor for years. If a competent critic wanted to delve into the inner Heinlein, that letter file would be a gold mine. But Panshin could not see it—possibly because what I had to say did not match Panshin's preconceptions. (I do not know.)[8]

If there was any doubt before, it was probably this remark reported of Panshin that took him out of the class of responsible professionals in Heinlein's mind and positioned Panshin as just one more toxic fan.

The unique problem of organized fandom is one that I have wondered about for many years. Here is a group made up largely of well-intentioned and mentally-interesting people—how is it and why is it that they tolerate among themselves a percentage of utter jerks?—people with no respect for privacy, no hesitation at all about libel and slander, and a sadistic drive to inflict pain . . . .

The situation was the same back twenty-five years ago—and I became so disgusted by the behavior of this minority that I had nothing to do with fandom for almost twenty years. Then I was urged back in, found it fun at first—but again began to run into the sadistic jerks.

Only now the jerks were of supposedly mature years.[9]

At just that moment, in fact, science-fiction fandom was tearing itself apart over the preemptive cancellation of the membership of a suspected pedophile by PacifiCon, the most recent world science-fiction convention, in September 1964.[10] This conflict might have passed the Heinleins by, except that the suspected pedophile was the husband of one of Heinlein's more intimate correspondents, Marion Zimmer Bradley. Heinlein never commented on the "Breen Boondoggle" publicly, but to Bradley Heinlein wrote:

> The fan nuisance we were subjected to was nothing like as nasty as the horrible things that were done to you two but it was bad enough that we could get nothing else done during the weeks it went on and utterly spoiled what should have been a pleasant, happy winter. But it resulted in a decision which has made our life much pleasanter already and which I expect to have increasingly good effects throughout all the years ahead. We have cut off all contact with organized fandom . . . . I regret that we will miss meeting some worthwhile people in the future as a result of this decision. But the percentage of poisonous jerks in the ranks of fans makes the price too high; we'll find our friends elsewhere.[11]

Fortunately, not all their fan contacts were so unpleasant. In December 1964, Jerry Pournelle, whom they had met in Seattle in 1961, and kept up a very stimulating correspondence with, attended one of Herman Kahn's seminars at the Broadmoor less than a mile away.[12] The Heinleins invited Pournelle home for drinks and a chance for extended conversation.

Ginny left them jawin' and yarnin' and went to bed early. Eventually the evening wound down. Before it should reach a state of total incoherence, Robert called a taxi to drive Pournelle back to his hotel. It was very late, and the Colorado winter had turned bitterly cold overnight. It was below freezing in the uninsulated garage, and the ground was slick with ice. When the taxi got there, Heinlein saw Pournelle out and shook hands and watched as the taxi got about thirty-five feet up the incline to Mesa Avenue and slid back, wheels spinning. It tried three more times, then called another taxi, which had exactly the same problems.

By this time it was after three A.M. Pournelle later recalled the incident:

> He took me inside and he said, "I am going to show you a secret which you will reveal not until after I am dead."
>
> Sir, I kept my word: I didn't tell anybody until now.

He unfolded some couches that were in the living room, and they turned into a bed. Below them he had stashed away stockings, underwear, t-shirts of various sizes, new pajamas, a new robe—all set up for visitors, except he didn't want anybody to know that he *could* have visitors.

And he said, "There's nothing for it but to reveal this secret, and you must never tell anyone." And I said, "Yes, sir."[13]

In the morning, Pournelle had to get back to the seminar so they were both up early. Heinlein apologized that he couldn't offer anything more than toast and coffee for breakfast (Ginny always made morning coffee for Robert—they liked the robust Navy blend sold in 3 lb. cans at PX's), but he had checked the larder last night and the cupboard was bare. Pournelle suggested they could buy some now—Robert's car had snow chains and could get up the hill. But when they got in the car, the engine turned over but it would not move. A little investigation revealed that the tires were frozen to the concrete. ". . . we went back in," Pournelle remembered,

and sat there glumly drinking coffee, at which point we smelled bacon and eggs cooking. Ginny brings out a platter of bacon and eggs, and Robert says, "There isn't any bacon: I looked." And she said, "Yes, I know: I went down and bought some."

And he said, "You couldn't have gone down and bought some; the car won't work. We tried it."

And she said, "Oh, there's nothing to that. You just—the steel lugs were frozen to the driveway. You go out with a pot of hot water and pour it on them; you melt them loose."[14]

She had simply boiled extra water when making Robert's coffee: two quarts, no waiting.[15]

Heinlein laughed: It was just as he always said—smarter than he and more practical.[16]

Pournelle got back to his seminar, and Heinlein began making notes on his new book. In the course of that evening, Pournelle had casually used an expression they had never heard before: TANSTAAFL. It was an acronym, Pournelle explained, that he got from his father, for the expression, still widely used in the American South (Pournelle had been born in Shreveport, Louisiana, in 1933): There Ain't No Such Thing As A Free Lunch.

Saloons used to advertise free lunches with drinks—anything from pickled eggs to elaborate buffet spreads. Of course, there was nothing "free" about the food. The cost was folded into the price of the drinks. Free lunches had disappeared from the American scene around the time of World War I. The acronym, collapsing the whole thing into a single word, was exactly what Robert had been looking for: "I was working on a novel into which it fitted perfectly,"[17] Heinlein later explained. He was working up a story background around *Economics in One Lesson,* and that one word, TANSTAAFL, functioned perfectly as a motto for that society. At the time he made a note of it on one of the three-by-five index cards he carried everywhere with him, for just such flashes of inspiration,[18] and it entered the mix that had been accumulating for some time. Virginia Heinlein later recalled:

> I suppose that all of this society in *The Moon is a Harsh Mistress* arose out of discussions that Robert and I had. What happened was that we held a number of discussions (and I remember them well) about ideal government.
>
> The problem with government is that, given some areas to make laws about, they move out into other areas, until all freedoms are gone.[19]

Before starting to write the book, he had a deadline to meet on an article on science fiction for the *Book of Knowledge* people, "Science Fiction: The World of 'What If?'" But by the end of January 1965 he turned in the *Book of Knowledge* article[20] and started organizing his outline, *Wyoming Schmidt: Notes for a Luna-Terra novel, 24 Feb. 1965.* The story was about a background incident in his unproduced *Century XXII* script—a woman who spied for a colonial revolution on the Moon, combined with the "gravity gauge" idea he had been talking about since at least 1948:[21] Anybody sitting at the bottom of a gravity well was vulnerable to missiles or even just rocks thrown from orbit or from a satellite. Heinlein also had an idea how money could be stolen to finance a revolution by a "dishonest" computer—and "it also describes how a libertarian revolution could go wrong in other ways."[22]

The *Wyoming Schmidt* version of the story organized itself around Wyoh's revolutionary comrades—Wells's "small and devoted elite."[23] Revolution, Wells had said, should not be the work of "thwarted pedants and unlicked youngsters . . . restless shop stewards and the sort of defectives who set fire to things."[24] In the process of unthwarting a pedant, Heinlein arrived at a somewhat Leninesque figure as one of his principals—but a charmer rather than a wasp—and a naïve young man for another, and the sentient computer became a practical joker—and Wyoh's role moved out of the center of the story. If Wells probably had Lenin and the Bolshevik revolution in mind, Heinlein's thinking naturally gravitated to the American Revolution.

I think this story has got to be from ca. 1774 through ca 1784—starting
not with secession but with complaints—which get no where. In fact we
might admit the parallel by having the Declaration of Lunar Independence
be dated July 4, 2176. Or perhaps July 4, 2192 . . . [sic] and intentionally
fudge the data to match.[25]

The computer was the missing piece of this particular puzzle, with everyone revolving around it. Heinlein began writing the story on February
27 as *That Dinkum Thinkum* and put "The End" to his 150,000-word manuscript—603 pages—on April 13. He typed out a fresh title page: *The Brass
Cannon*[26]: *Being the Personal Memoir of Manuel Garcia O'Kelly Davis, Free-
man, concerning the Lunar Rebellion: A True History.*[27]

If a person names as his three favorites of my books *Stranger, Harsh Mistress,* and *Starship Troopers* . . . then I believe that he has grokked what I
meant. But if he likes one—but not the other two—I am certain that he
has misunderstood me, he has picked out points—and misunderstood what
he picked. If he picks 2 of 3, then there is hope, 1 of 3—no hope.
All three books are on one subject: Freedom and Self-Responsibility.[28]

And years later, he was asked—yet again!—about the apparent dichotomy
between *Stranger* and *Starship Troopers* and replied that there *was no dichotomy*. A witness recalled his remarks as "They are both descriptions of objects
of human love. Loving his fellow men enough to be willing to die for them in
one, and the other—well, the whole book is about it."[29]

Heinlein then took a short break from the writing for a seminar Herman
Kahn gave at the Air Force Academy on his book of that year, *On Escala-
tion*.[30] Kahn urged Heinlein to come to one of his seminars as a personal
guest—but Heinlein could not clear his schedule that rapidly, as the manuscript required cutting (by about 20 percent, from 150,750 words to 125,000
words) that would take longer than the writing.[31] Regretfully, he passed—but
Kahn renewed his invitation in his bread-and-butter note.

Heinlein worked steadily, cutting the 603-page manuscript to under 500
pages. This time the cutting involved an unusual step: He converted his viewpoint protagonist's speech into a kind of polyglot Loonie argot.

Here we have a first-person story, which therefore must be told in something approximating the natural language of the imaginary narrator.
This can be done whole hog, as Mark Twain did it in *Huckleberry Finn* or

it can be done simply by suggesting the style and accent. I decided on the latter.

In deciding how he would speak it was necessary for me to define both him and his social matrix. . . . I concluded (assumed) that these people would speak a pidgin based largely on English but with both its vocabulary and its syntax strongly influenced by both Cantonese and Russian. But this pidgin (in view of the way they must live) would be loaded with technical terms—in English, since English is now the international technical language and bids fair to remain so.

But such a pidgin would be far too hairy for story purposes; I had to simplify it. . . . I attempted to suggest the Russian and Chinese sources by butchering the syntax, primarily by omitting those English structure words of no semantic content, which have no parallels in Russian or in Cantonese. . . . In the draft Mannie's spoken dialog was the only part, which invariably displayed this butchering; his narration was more or less Standard English. But in trying to shorten it I applied this pidgin rule to his narration as well.[32]

The cut was finished enough to send it to the typist by the middle of May. It was ready to go to Blassingame by June 21.

Playboy bounced *The Brass Cannon* within a week, saying they didn't want to take on a long serial. It was also too long for John Campbell—a darned shame, he said, "'Sa good yarn, too." But the complaints over the length of Frank Herbert's *Dune* meant *Analog*'s readers would not hold still for another *five*-part serial.[33] Blassingame sent the manuscript on to Fred Pohl.

Putnam's accepted the book for publication, even though the sales of *Farnham's Freehold* had dipped below his normal pull.[34] His editor, Peter Israel, did not like the title. Heinlein was used to the drill by now. Somehow in the process, it got changed to *The Moon Is a Harsh Mistress*.[35]

Herman Kahn's seminar on "The Next Ten Years: Scenarios and Possibilities" was held at his Hudson Institute in Tarrytown, New York, beginning on July 25. It was immensely stimulating—six and eight lectures a day and scenario discussion groups that might break up at midnight or later, with classes resuming early the next morning. If he hadn't taken special care, he would not have gotten more than five or six hours a night of sleep.[36]

This group was fearsomely bright—and, flatteringly, most of them knew of him already:

> . . . if I attend an ordinary cocktail party, perhaps two or three out of a large crowd will know who I am. If I go to a political meeting or a church

or such, I may not be spotted at all . . . But at Hudson Institute over two-thirds of the staff and over half of the students button-holed me. This causes me to have a high opinion of the group—its taste, I.Q., patriotism, sex appeal, charm, etc.—writers are incurably conceited and pathologically unsure of themselves; they respond to stroking the way a cat does.[37]

Ginny and he capped the seminar by going on to New York for business and for pleasure. Heinlein lunched with William Targ, his new editor at Putnam's (Peter Israel was taking off a year to write a novel), and met with Terry Carr at Ace to handshake the deal for a new collection Blassingame had rustled up, *The Worlds of Robert A. Heinlein*.[38] He agreed to provide the contents by September 2. He could hardly work up enthusiasm for the paperback original they intended to make it[39]—but it gave him an opportunity to put some of his orphaned children into print, and that was all to the good. He also ground out an update to the set of predictions he had made in 1950, to see where he stood, after fifteen years, as a professional prophet.

They had not been to New York since 1960, so they packed in a lot of shows: *Kismet* ("Froth, sure, but such superior froth"[40]) and a ballet performance of *Jacob's Ladder* by the Nederlands Ballet corps. Up to the Tanglewood Music Festival for an outdoor concert under the stars by the Boston Symphony Orchestra, where they tracked a satellite in the sky over the orchestra—and, best of all, a live production at Stratford, Connecticut, of Shakespeare's *Coriolanus*.

Here is a play almost never produced and which I read once over forty years ago and had forgotten completely. So, in effect, I was seeing a *new* play by Shakespeare—it could have been its first performance.

Well, it knocked me out of my seat! This boy writes a good stick. . . .[41]

They even got over to Connecticut to see Hank and Barbie Stine one night, and Robert spotted a copy of *The Sirens of Titan* (Kurt Vonnegut, 1959) on a bookshelf and borrowed it to read on the flight back to Colorado. On the plane he found himself seat-hopping to talk with interesting passengers—and forgot the borrowed copy of *Sirens of Titan* in one of the seat pockets. A sin! ("I might steal a man's wife, given opportunity; I would not steal his books.")[42] He hastened to replace it as soon as he got back, first priority. Good book, too, though he liked *Player Piano* (Vonnegut, 1952) better.[43]

This trip had done wonders for their morale—both of them, but Ginny especially. Heinlein wrote thanking Lurton Blassingame for the hosting, and added:

I don't know whether you realize it or not, but you are my closest friend. Ginny and I both tend to be rather lonely. About two friends here in town—but the other people we feel really close to are scattered around the country and around the world, from Finland to Singapore. But of those scattered friends you have long been the most important.[44]

They agreed they had gotten into a rut recently: They began talking about buying some land in Washington state, as the "excess" royalties came in from some of the new foreign sales Blassingame continued to place—always providing their health held up. Ginny started to feel ill again just a few weeks after they got back.

Heinlein was not doing so well, himself: For the last year or so, he had a slight, obscuring mist in his vision, both eyes, and his doctors had finally diagnosed cataracts coming on, for which he would eventually require surgery. Ginny had been researching the problem and found a discussion in one of Adelle Davis's books on nutrition. She started him on a program of riboflavin—Vitamin B2—50 milligrams a day in two doses of 25 milligrams each. A year later, the doctor didn't find even a trace of the clouding. By the time he was due to set up the surgery, every vestige of cataract had disappeared.

Doc Smith died suddenly in September 1965, not quite a year after Sarge Smith's death, and that was upsetting. Of his older, wise mentors, only Hermann Deutsch was left—and he was ill due to complications of old age. "So you take care of yourself, you hear me?" he told his friend Lurton Blassingame: "We can't spare you too."[45]

Ben Babb, the publicist friend Heinlein had made while working on *Destination Moon,* died two weeks later, after a long illness in a VA hospital in Houston. A little more than two weeks after that, Heinlein had a handwritten letter from Cal Laning: Their mutual friend from the Naval Academy days, John S. Arwine, died in New York of a sudden heart attack.[46] His generation of contemporaries were entering their sixties now.

Clifford Simak, a working newspaperman as well as a highly respected SF writer colleague, wrote for a quote, for a story he was writing on assignment from his paper(s), the *Minneapolis Star* and *Tribune*—what do SF writers write about, now that we have conquered space? That was somewhat premature, Heinlein wrote back, as Simak surely knew: The space age could barely be said to have started yet—and in any case speculative fiction was concerned with many other subjects than space.

I suppose I could say that I always write about politics, sex, and religion, three markedly non-scientific subjects . . . [sic] but three utterly unlimited subjects. But add these three subjects together and it spells "people." Which simply paraphrases the very old statement that "the proper study of mankind is Man." Man remains the oldest and closest of mysteries; until we solve the mystery of Man—where he came from, where he is going, and why—there can be no lack of variety in subjects for speculative fiction.[47]

About October 10, Ginny stopped him in the house with the first volume of their *Encyclopedia Britannica* in hand and read him a list of symptoms that matched up with her medical problems over the last seven or eight years. She had been reading up on anoxia, or "mountain sickness"—a pure guess on her part, but it made sense: When they were traveling—at sea level most of the time, since they went most places by ship and visited seaports—Ginny perked up and felt fine. But a couple of weeks after they got back home and back to seven thousand feet, she usually got sick again. The encyclopedia also said that, whatever else you might have, anoxia made it worse.

"So I went to the doctor," Ginny recalled, "and I said could this possibly be my problem? He said, why yes, everybody feels better at sea level."[48] A diagnosis in the usual sense was neither possible nor necessary. She sat down with Robert for a family conference, and within minutes they had reached a decision: If Ginny needed to be at sea level, it was time to abandon the baggage and git. "We were firmly entrenched in that house," Ginny said, "but it was getting a little small for us."[49]

Robert suggested they look at the coast near Tryon, North Carolina, where a friend of Blassingame's had settled happily some years before. But Ginny was not enthusiastic about anywhere on the East Coast—and the South was out because of the race problems. She had had more of the desert than she really liked—and she also didn't care much for the idea of California.[50]

One of their friends in the Seattle area suggested Sequim (pronounced "squim"), Washington, on Sequim Bay, an inlet of the Strait of Juan de Fuca that separates Washington from Canada. They would start there, and if that wasn't right, they could work their way down the coast, all the way to Mexico, if necessary. Blassingame could handle most business matters, as he had done for them in 1954, while they took what amounted to a long working vacation.

The phone rang one day while they were in the middle of packing, and Robert took the call standing up in the bedroom. They had gotten an unlisted number recently, to cut down on the random interruptions, and Heinlein was surprised when Harlan Ellison identified himself (probably Ellison had gotten the number from Damon Knight, who was busily getting together a new writer's guild for science fiction, Science Fiction Writers of America ("SFWA"). Heinlein's loyalties were still with the Authors Guild, but he had made a quiet donation under the table, to help get organized and pay the bills).[51]

Harlan Ellison is a living demonstration of $E = MC^2$—a solid mass of energy and nerves. His normal speaking voice—Ohio Valley with a slightly nasal quack—raised the energy level of any room, like a quick one-too-many shot of caffeine buzz. Ellison was putting together a new anthology—a new *kind* of anthology—of stories too unconventional or too challenging to find publication in the normal magazine venues. For this *Dangerous Visions,* Heinlein was the first name on his list when he planned the book.

> Go all the way. Say what you want to say. Pull no punches. Heinlein is known as a bootstraps man for openers; now he can do it in every subtle hue and color he's maybe had to personally dampen for gutless publications.[52]

Heinlein promised to think about it when he had time, complimented Ellison on *Paingod,* recently published—and went back to packing for the trip.

The Heinleins said good-bye—one last dinner with the Sencenbaughs, their best friends in the area—and left on their seventeenth wedding anniversary, stopping for the night in Gunnison, Colorado, at a motel that was graduating a class from the hotelier school for the Ambassador hotel chain. The next day, somewhat hungover with last night's celebratory champagne and dancing, they made their way to Utah.

By October 24, they were just over the state line into Oregon and spent the next night on the shore of the Columbia River. They were only a short drive, then, from Sequim, where they decamped at a motel.

Sequim had groceries and a good service station—and just one traffic light. Once they unloaded an unending mass of cameras and portable TVs and radios and gourmet cookbooks and the ton-weight atlas, Ginny got the service station man to flag the now-empty trunk with a tiger-tail hanging out behind.

Ginny had made a "spectacular" recovery of her health and energy. They rented a winter cabin called "Sea Echo," a hundred feet or so from the Strait of Juan de Fuca, where he had sweated through a difficult transit in fog more than thirty years before, and prepared to sample life in Sequim. "We sit at breakfast and watch the ocean liners go past our front door, sea gulls on our lawn, hundreds of ducks just down the bank below our post box . . ."[53]

The overcast was a little too continuous for Robert's taste, and the real estate costs were even more preposterous than he had expected: "Sequim does have a remarkable climate but it is a junky looking place, with abandoned houses, barns falling down, and scrapped automobiles cluttering up its woods—plus delusions of grandeur about the price of land."[54]

If Sequim did not suit, there were other locales nearby that might: A two-day excursion to Whidbey Island looked very promising. They were not going back to Colorado.

But Ginny went into a local bar without him one evening and was told Washington state did not permit women to order drinks at the bar. And that was that.

Wherever they went, the trip would be leisurely, with stops along the way, for Heinlein was correcting galleys for *The Moon Is a Harsh Mistress* and preparing the front matter even as its five serial installments came out in *If* magazine. Putnam's had delayed issuing this one so long that it was now doubtful they could catch the annual Christmas book-buying frenzy. Putnam's did not push this book. They did not even make a full print run, since the sales of his last book—*Farnham's Freehold*—had been, for Heinlein, lackluster (4,000 copies).[55]

They put the Colorado Springs house on the market by mail, giving it a top asking price for the area of $47,000—justified by all the features Robert had built into it (including the bomb shelter), and left for Port Angeles on December 15, 1965, making their way down the coast in easy hops—to a small town south of Portland, to Fort Bragg, to Novato, about thirty miles north of San Francisco. There, Ginny spotted a billboard ad for forty acres of redwoods near Watsonville, about 130 miles farther south. The big trees had always exerted a certain fascination for Robert, but even these smaller coastal varieties had their charm, they agreed.

They went on to Watsonville on the Monterey Bay the next day and got in touch with the real estate agent.[56] It was a beautiful, if somewhat remote, property, shaded—perhaps a little *too* shaded—in the "little" redwoods canopy only 150 feet overhead. California was Robert's obvious choice, but not Ginny's. "Ginny is somewhat averse to locating anywhere in California," Robert told Bjo Trimble, "for reasons of smog and traffic and too many people and high taxes." She was obviously thinking about conditions in Los Angeles—"But the first three can be avoided almost entirely since we have complete freedom to choose our location unconstrained by business necessities or schools—and high taxes might be a penalty we would have to pay to live where we want to live . . . ."[57]

Robert let the scenery make his pitch for him: They continued south through the spectacular Big Sur coastal route—which Ginny had never seen before—stopping overnight in San Simeon, within sight of the Hearst Castle. They talked that night about the property they had seen near Watsonville earlier in the day.

Ginny liked the site—and she was prepared by now to concede that Northern California was obviously not smoggy and not overcrowded the way Southern California was—though she was still dubious. But the main thing was Robert's obvious enthusiasm. He was already at least half in love with the place.[58] She wanted a night to sleep on it.

They reached Laguna, California, the next day, where they collected accumulated mail and sent a thousand-dollar deposit check to Harrah's, the real estate agent for the Watsonville property. As of December 21, 1965, they were owners of forty acres of redwoods, pines, and mixed oaks. That night they celebrated with champagne.

They made their planned overnight visit to Arcadia, three days before Christmas, to visit with Robert's mother and sister, then headed back up the coast to Palo Alto, forty miles north of Watsonville, to spend Christmas with Rex and Kathleen Heinlein. Two days later they were back in Watsonville and executed the purchase contracts. The next day they took an apartment there—the Cabrillo Arms Townhouses. They had a headquarters now. After the holidays—New Year's with Rex and Kathleen again—they would start to build in the redwoods.

HOUSE-BUILDING—AGAIN!

There were drawbacks to the Watsonville property: It was mostly dense growth; mail delivery would be a mile away and the nearest store five miles. The private road into the site was almost impassable and shared with six other parties, some of whom did not want it improved.

> It was the road that finally stopped us. We drove up after a rain storm and almost failed to make it although our car was equipped with new snow tires of the type with steel lugs set in the rubber. We slipped and skidded and had a terrible time and twice I thought we were going to slide right off the road into that rocky mountain torrent. Once we reached the top, I simply sat and shook uncontrollably for several minutes.
>
> That night I found Ginny sitting in the bath tub, crying—so the next morning I saw our attorney and told him we were not going through with it. It cost us, of course—we lost our down payment and the cost of the preliminary title search but our attorney managed to get releases and stave off a law suit. Then we set out again.[1]

That entire area on the north side of the Monterey Bay, from Watsonville on the east to Santa Cruz on the west, was redwood country and low, coastal mountains, well within Ginny's range. They told the local real estate agent, Mr. Zimmerman (Wilson Brothers), what they wanted—a property with its own water being the main requirement, though the redwoods were a consideration (and Robert had a whim of his own: He wanted to live in a town with a romantic Spanish name).[2]

Zimmerman said he thought he had something that might suit their needs. This property was smaller—only five acres—but situated on a county road, winding and hilly but not actually impassable, and with telephone and electrical right at the property line, with eight or nine redwood cathedrals and dozens of other kinds of trees.[3] The property had a spring—not a natural spring; someone had driven a pipe into a wet place in the hillside forty years before—with a slow but steady flow of seventeen gallons per minute of soft, pure, perfect water, being used as a neighborhood well. There was also, interestingly, an abandoned shed the real estate agent told them had housed a Communist spy ring during the 1950s. The FBI had spied on the spies from a neighboring house farther up the hill, just barely visible to the north.[4] And over the tops of the trees across the road there was an ocean view, just visible from the top of the hill that faced the road. That was where they would site the house.

Heinlein called the agent that night, January 11, 1966, and bought the property on Bonny Doon Road.[5] The next day they found a rental in Santa Cruz, twenty miles closer to their new property, at 115 Echo Street,[6] near the new university.

If they could sell the Colorado house at top of market, the proceeds would pay for land and materials and make a dent in the labor costs that had grown so enormously in the construction trades since 1950. The rest he would have to make up from royalties—which meant at least one new book to be written, soonest. *The Moon Is a Harsh Mistress* finished its five-part serialization in April, so he had nothing in the pipeline except the off-again, on-again Future History omnibus (off at the moment) that might not clear any major royalties at all if Putnam's had to issue it at the then-high price of $10.

Heinlein began the search for a professional architect and started making preliminary sketches for his own use, surveying the property himself and then working on the design to Ginny's specification that she wanted a round house.[7] He used many of the same design principles they had used for the Colorado Springs house—minimizing housework and bringing in light with a north-south-oriented clerestory. Ginny remembered that the design required nine drafts before they were satisfied with it.[8] They built the structure out of California slump stone, giving tribute to adobe, with a color scheme for the trim that would harmonize with the redwoods around them. There was enough room for a turning circle and porte cochere in the driveway, and there they would have their own flagpole. Heinlein also tried a trick he had picked up in a hospital—build the *vacuum cleaner* into the walls. You could plug in a hose wherever you wanted to clean, without carrying the noisy vacuum pump around with you (and frightening the animals!).

They did build a swimming pool. Ginny was initially dubious about this California innovation, since they were inconveniently far from repair services—but she quickly got used to the idea of going directly from gardening to pool, dropping clothes by the poolside and calling for a towel at her leisure.[9] Robert gave each of the bathrooms its own outside entrance, so he and Ginny would not have to track water into the house. This house was custom-made for their lifestyle—and expensive. It was an all-electric neighborhood in an all-electric era, with no gas lines available from the city. Ginny wanted two chest-type freezers, since they were forty miles away from major shopping. Robert brought in seven electrical circuits for just the kitchen alone.

Fortunately, Blassingame made more foreign sales, and a clutch of contracts turned up while they were getting ready to build. There were complex arrangements between the trade publisher and the British SF book club combining two of the Future History books into *A Heinlein Omnibus,* plus another issue under the same name that made a jumbo with *Beyond This Horizon.* And the American SF Book Club wanted to bundle *The Puppet Masters* with his old *Waldo & Magic, Inc.* collection as *Three By Heinlein,* which would be issued in England as *A Heinlein Triad.* Since Doubleday already had the plates for both properties, Heinlein didn't have to do any work putting that one together, except issue the permission. It was found money—at a time when he had a use for it.

The rented house in Santa Cruz had turned out a mixed blessing. Its location more or less on the edge of Santa Cruz gave them access to the town's services—and in 1966, Santa Cruz was still a "charming" coastal town. But the lot was very narrow, and Heinlein's study faced the house next door, less than ten feet away. The neighbors played loud rock music that made concentration next to impossible.

Proximity gave Heinlein a chance to observe the area's one exotic ethnicity at close range: the "beatniks" (Herb Caen had not yet popularized the term "hippies," though that would come later in the year—and Flower Children and the Summer of Love were still a year away). Heinlein said in 1967:

> They have a sort of informal headquarters, the Hip Pocket Book Store, right downtown directly across the street from our bank . . . It is quite a good book shop. Ginny won't go into it; the appearance of the beatniks make her ill—but I am studying their manners and customs and odd speech in their native habitat . . . [sic] and, anyhow, it is indeed a good book shop with a wide selection, plus of course all the books and pamphlets of the new left wing, the boys who are so far out that they regard the Russian Commies as counterrevolutionaries. The town also has a John Birch book store—haven't visited it yet, but shall—and the Congressman is a Goldwater conservative.[10]

On net he preferred a certain amount of distance while things worked themselves out. They obviously thought they were much farther along in developing a self-sustaining culture than they actually were—and with no historical consciousness of the long-standing patterns in American culture they were recapitulating, they might never develop into one:

> The hippy trend I find most interesting but I don't want them in my lap. I am wondering what permanent effect it will have, if any, on the total culture of the country. Hippydom is not itself a culture (as the hippies seem to think) as it has no economic foundation; it can exist only as a parasitic excrescence to the "square" culture. (I am aware of the "diggers"—there are two communities of them just up the mountain from me. Both are on the skids, going though the usual, historical economic collapse of anarchistic communisms. I know of several others that have failed the same way. Anarchism and socialism are both viable—but not together, it would seem. At least for humans. The diggers aren't the first to stub their toes on this; history is full of analogous cases.)
>
> I don't think the hippies are so much a vanguard of something as they are a complex result of social trends they had little to do with.[11]

And he was particularly skeptical of the claims made for psychedelics:

> LSD and pot? Marijuana has been readily available to anyone who wanted it throughout my lifetime and apparently for centuries before I was born. LSD is new but the hippies didn't develop it; they simply use it. But it seems to me that the outstanding objective fact about LSD (despite the claims of Leary and others) is that it is as much of a failure as other drugs in producing any results of any value other than to the user—i.e., I know of no work of art, essay, story, discovery, or anything else of value created as a result of LSD. When the acid-droppers start outdistancing the squares in *any* field, I'll sit up and take notice. Until that day I'll regard it just as I do all other euphoric drugs: a sterile, subjective, sensory pleasure holding considerable hazard to the user.[12]

There were other interesting bits of Americana to study—the first newspaper ads he had seen for whorehouses since the 1930s—in the *San Jose Mercury*! One place offered free parking as an amenity.[13]

They continued to plan the house, adding details to rectify some of the deficiencies of the Colorado Springs house. It must have been about this time that Heinlein hired a "water-witch" to dowse the property for the spring.

> I hired him for purely pragmatic reasons. I had a great deal of data indicating that this man, no matter how he does it, can indeed find water . . . Oh, he found the place, and then I tried it, and Ginny tried it, and the thing did for her; it wouldn't for me; I apparently don't have that power. He found the place and he drilled so many feet down and he told us about what we could expect out of it, nineteen gallons per minute, and he was dead on the nose.[14]

Robert added a guest cottage that could be kept cat-free for guests with pet dander allergies. That brought the structures on the property (once they added a pump house for the spring and protection for the wiring) up to nine.

Ginny also had some definite ideas about the interior design. In the house's main bath, she wanted to eliminate shower doors and curtains by installing a "nautiloid" spiral—arc-shaped—wall that would contain splashes very efficiently without much upkeep.

She had her heart set on one futuristic kitchen gadget she had been awaiting for more than a decade. They first saw a "radar range" microwave oven demonstrated at a housing show. Heinlein's brother Rex told them he had rigged one up in his physics class. On a shopping trip to San Francisco at the end of March 1966, Ginny saw a Tappan Radar Range offered for regular commercial sale, and she had her microwave.

It was on that same trip—in fact, just minutes later—that they found themselves plunged into a social change even more startling than the radar range.

> . . . we were walking to our hotel, reached a cocktail parlor on Market Street and Ginny decided that we were footsore and weary (we were) and needed a drink. So we stopped in. And I encountered for the first time the San Francisco "topless." It was a perfectly quiet, ordinary Madison-Avenue-type bar—but all of the waitresses (6 or 7) and the bartenders (2, female) were "topless"—i.e., they decidedly were *not* "topless"—their tops were on display from the waist up and most of them were unusually well endowed in the milk-gland department.[15]

Carol Doda, who had started the topless craze by climbing up on a white baby grand piano dressed only in a bikini bottom on June 16, 1964, set a high

standard in that area: Her original 34" bust was about to be surgically enhanced to 44" (and that kind of surgical enhancement was relatively new,
too).

> Their costumes varied from "Cretan Empire" dresses down to one little
> blonde who seemed to feel that the lower half of a bikini ultra-minimum
> was enough—and every variation in between. Their uniforms were "uni-
> form" only in that each one displayed these twin full moons. I found it all
> rather startling at first (there had been no warning outside) but in about
> five minutes it becomes commonplace (while remaining, in my opinion,
> pleasant).
>
> That evening we had dinner at the Playboy Club—the beautiful Bun-
> nies' beautiful costumes looked downright puritanical. Afterwards we went
> to one of the North Beach night clubs which features a "topless amateur
> night" (No, Ginny did not volunteer!)—and stayed only one drink as the
> "music" was the loudest I have ever heard . . . .
>
> San Francisco is a unique city, probably the most cosmopolitan city in
> the world—and I include New York and Hong Kong in saying that—and
> has far more art, music, ballet, and theater than anyone can possibly use . . .
> [sic] plus the wildest Honkytonk outside of Tokyo.[16]

Robert had been poking at individual minds on a retail basis for decades,
saying "wake up!" and think more, reader by individual reader. His timing
had been just right. The boys—and girls—he had been Horatio-Algering in
the 1940s and 1950s were now in their twenties and thirties—and in control
of their own pursestrings—and the generation coming up behind the crest of
the wave were impatient with their buttoned-down, repressed elders, whose
attitudes were a legacy of the Eisenhower era.

Heinlein had gotten out of children's lit just in time.

His big book on hypocrisy—*Stranger in a Strange Land*—was just coming into its own. He was starting to get all kinds of strange mail on that book:
A magazine of literary criticism wanted to use *Grok* for their title; Kerry
Thornley, the founder of a group called "Kerista," wrote saying that *Stranger*
was virtually the group's "Bible." Several people had already mentioned not
being able to find a copy anywhere. The royalty report in April 1966 showed
a startling $968.89 for *Stranger*—probably almost ten thousand copies sold in
the last six months, *five years* after the book was published—and Avon had
just issued a reprint of 150,000 in January 1966. Walter Minton, owner and
CEO of Putnam's, was bringing up the Future History omnibus again, since

the rights to *Methuselah's Children* had finally cleared from Gnome, so Heinlein braced them for a hardcover reissue of *Stranger*—or, failing that, a new paperback edition.

In mid-April, they found an AIA architect locally, Kermit Darrow, and he recommended a solution to their Echo Street problems: The former owner of the Bonny Doon property also owned a summer cabin nearby and consented to rent it to them. Once they were settled into this temporary accommodation, Heinlein was finally able to set up his typewriter and clear off some of the accumulations of minor work. He had received an inquiry through Blassingame for film rights for *The Puppet Masters* from an English producer (Orson Welles, they later discovered), but the option Robert had given to American International as part of the settlement of the lawsuit was still running, and Welles never followed up after Corman let it lapse.

Harlan Ellison prompted him again in May: It was "utterly necessary," he assured Heinlein, that the *Dangerous Visions* anthology have a Heinlein story—but his end-of-May deadline was approaching.

Heinlein had really not had time to think about writing at all in the last eight months. But he did have one story in his files that might fit Ellison's criteria of "rejected-for-being-too-unconventional," and he had pulled the file copy of "Three Brave Men" to bring along on the trip. This was a story he had written in 1946, from the anecdote his brother had told him when he came to Fitzsimmons Army and Navy hospital in 1933, about TB patients dying on the table of artificial pneumothorax. He revised and retitled it "No Bands Playing, No Flags Flying" and got it off to Ellison before the submission deadline.

But that story found another stool to fall between: Ellison had been looking for a "shocker." This story could be considered science fiction only by the most liberal possible interpretation of genre boundaries—but it just didn't fit in *at all* with the confrontational stories Ellison had been assembling, stories rejected by conventional markets precisely because they were too much in tune with the new style of political and cultural discourse that was just coming into being. Rejecting a Heinlein story, Ellison told Heinlein, made him a certifiable lunatic[17]—but it just wasn't right for this project. He returned it.

The architect was being difficult. The house was just *too different.* He wanted to scrap their eccentric designs and start over fresh. It was a frustratingly long process to convince him that they actually *did* want all the peculiar features they had specified. Ginny developed a sore shoulder from all the driving and carrying and wound up going to a local doctor. The same day, Robert collapsed in agony with a hernia, brought about by his own efforts. He was rushed to the hospital on June 1 and operated on the next day, the first of three hernia surgeries.

He was out in a few days (discharged on June 6), but did not bounce back: He was sleepy all the time, and it was a struggle to get even minimal paperwork done. "It is not unpleasant save that I am totally useless and the work piles up."[18]

With construction actually getting under way, the one thing they absolutely had to get done was to pump some action into their Colorado real estate agent. He seemed to have gone dead on them. Ginny located another agent and took the listing out of his hands. June Compagnon was more energetic.

One morning there was a *wolf* in the driveway, and that brought home to them that the local wildlife really was wild. Ginny had delighted in spotting wild deer on the property, usually in the early morning, before the banging and sawing started up. "She counts any day lost in which she does not see at least one deer—so far not more than two or three days of the last two months have been 'lost.'"[19] But they had to have a fence, for many reasons (the local deer thought Ginny's rows of miniature roses were a salad bar).

They must have been doing something Jungian and archetypal: A visitation by a wolf would have been a major omen in ancient Rome. But that was just the start of it: One morning, not too long thereafter, Ginny went to the cabin to make coffee for their construction crew. In the driveway, coming back to the construction site with a lunch pail, she was set upon by eagles—seven of them—stooping on her out of the sky! She skidded under some brush but was otherwise unhurt. Robert simply refused to believe it—until it happened to him, too.[20]

The plans Darrow, the architect, delivered were full of glaring errors, page after page of them. Robert gritted his teeth and corrected the mistakes. Darrow could sign off on them. Having to redo the floor plans was holding up the specifications—which were what Robert really needed.

While Darrow corrected the most serious mistakes, Robert discussed the Future History omnibus that was back on the table at Putnam's—this time, apparently, for good, as Walter Minton had worked out a tricky copublication deal with the Doubleday Science Fiction Book Club that would allow them to keep the price at $7.00—still high, but not absolutely impossible. Robert could take the opportunity to include "Searchlight" and "The Menace from Earth," the two Future History stories written since the last of the Shasta collections in 1953—and he might write some of the "unwritten stories" to fill out the concept—"Fire Down Below" if he could manage a research trip to

Antarctica; "Da Capo" definitely—the "final novel of the series" he had planned to write in the fall had been derailed by the move from Colorado.

For the introduction, Robert suggested A. P. White or Willy Ley. Minton counter-suggested Damon Knight, whom Minton had hired as a consulting editor for his newly acquired paperback line, Berkley Books. Knight's 1956 book of critical essays, *In Search of Wonder*, Heinlein had found very impressive:

> It is a job that both publisher and author should be proud of . . . You can imagine how delighted I was with his essays. I do not mean what he said about me; while it was pleasing I cannot pretend to be objective about anything so personal. I refer to what he said about others and about this field of writing in general. Either he is a great critic or it happens that his tastes and mine coincide.[21]

Minton also wanted some kind of "poetic" title, and Robert was fresh out of poetry at the moment. Targ apparently suggested *The Past to Tomorrow,* but Robert counter-suggested a tweak: *The Past* Through *Tomorrow.* That made the title something he could live with.[22] They sent the tearsheets for the stories to Damon Knight to read for his introduction.

One early story, " 'Let There Be Light,' " Knight suggested, was too different in tone and key from the others, clearly an inferior story even though it belonged in the canon, "&, if this is not an impertinence, I wish you would leave it out."[23] Targ and Marcia Magill, his sub-editor who was doing much of the legwork on this project, concurred, and Heinlein himself told Willy Ley that he felt the story was too weak.[24] The galleys were printed without " 'Let There Be Light' "—though " 'We Also Walk Dogs,' " a story that is completely inconsistent with the Future History, was left in. Robert did not have time to write "Fire Down Below" or "Da Capo." He had to turn over the galleys to Ginny to proofread by herself, while he dealt with an architect crisis.

The architect wanted to go on vacation in the middle of their construction— which is just not professional for a builder. Heinlein fired him and took over the job himself, holding up the last $1,000 payment for two very tense weeks until the worst of his errors was corrected so they could get the permit process under way. That same day, their water-system subcontractor came out and gave them a temporary tank and hook-up. Five days later, on the last day of August, Heinlein squared the cornerstone of the masonry, working together with his bricklayers, who had been hanging fire since February. The architect had cost them $4,000 in fees and four months of summer construction weather. They would have to hurry to get the bricks laid before the rains started in late October or early November. Heinlein also had to finish the floorplans Darrow had left undone, and create all the hundreds of specifications by himself. He worked on the plans at night, handling such writing business matters as came up in whatever time he could get away from the drawing board.

As rest from what was, after all, a tedious form of mechanical engineering, he helped his contractors with the cabinetry work and bricklaying.[25]

In the winter, when the building eased off, Heinlein read Jerry Pournelle's first novel and helped out with writerly advice (swearing him to secrecy, as he did not want to be deluged with requests for such critiques). Poul Anderson wanted him to run for the top office in SFWA when Damon Knight's term ran out, later that year.[26] Robert was very dubious about that: Not only could he not make time for the duties required of the presidency of a brand-new union, but,

> I think it would be unwise of me ever to stand for president. At some later time, if asked, I would seriously consider serving as secretary or as vice president—but I do not think it would be good either for me or for the organization for me to occupy the top spot.[27]

Several universities had written him recently, asking for his working papers (university libraries had recently begun to open archival collections of working writers and academics, to supplement the special collections they had for a very long time kept of classic figures)—flattering, but he couldn't imagine what a university librarian would want with several tons of junk papers. And, besides, he said, he kept this stuff because he was *using* it. His writing career wasn't over yet.[28]

As 1967 came on, he got three such requests. One was from Donald T. Clark, the university librarian at the nearby, newly founded (1965), University of California, Santa Cruz. Heinlein had met Clark in April and May 1966 while he was using the library there for some research. This request to establish the Robert A. Heinlein Archive at UC Santa Cruz was flattering in a more pragmatically practical way. He received Clark, along with Rita Berner, the young woman who had recently been named Head of Special Collections, a few days later in their summer cabin.[29]

The university was only ten to fifteen miles away from their new house site—and Clark assured him they could photocopy any document he needed to reference, usually on twenty-four hours' notice or less. That made it very practical. Even better, Heinlein could take a tax deduction on the gift in the year it occurred—which would help since the *Stranger* royalties were throwing his budget out of whack.

Early in 1967, *The Moon Is a Harsh Mistress* went out of print, and Putnam's ordered a second impression. The fan mail on *Stranger* continued to increase— and invitations to speak. Michael Murphy, at a place called Esalen, wanted him to colead a seminar on "Religion in the Space Age" with Alan Watts, America's Zen teacher,[30] and an Episcopalian priest, David Baar.[31] When interest plateaued in 1967, he was receiving speaking invitations on average twice a week. By the end of 1966, the complaints from readers about not being able to find copies of *Stranger* were becoming a chorus. Putnam's unwillingness to consider a reissue was becoming very odd, and Robert was getting fed up. Also, Ginny noticed a consistent pattern of small accounting errors in the royalty statements—always in Putnam's favor. By the end of the year, the errors totaled nearly fifteen hundred dollars—a very substantial amount in 1966 dollars.

This was becoming intolerable. They were reporting tens of thousands of sales for *Stranger* (Avon had only 15,000 left of its January 1966 issue of 150,000[32]) but simultaneously saying sales were too low to justify a reissue. After five years, most hardcover sales of most books were made to libraries— and libraries weren't buying *Stranger*; Minton thought it was because of two negative reviews in library journals early on. But this made no sense in terms of *Stranger*'s actual pattern of sales: "A California writer, who is dramatizing *Stranger* for the stage, recently drove across the country and tried in every city through which he passed to buy the book but was unable to find it anywhere."[33] But Putnam's was not willing to take the (nonexistent) risk of ordering a hardcover reprint. Avon could make a reissue when their stocks ran out.

At Avon they considered the resurgence of interest in the book a fad in the science-fiction community and planned a full reissue in July 1967. The demand would probably last only three or four months . . .[34]

21

STALLED

They had had Barry-the-cat shipped out from Colorado—heavily sedated—in October, when they thought they would have a home to offer him imminently. And they had just acquired a companion for him, a girl cat named Smoky that Ginny had adopted rather than see her sent on a one-way trip to the pound.

The rains came on in November, with the foundation in and the masonry walls only partly finished. They finished the walls and got the roof on in the middle of the rainy season and began using the Bonny Doon address on correspondence before the end of November.

Now that they had actual covered storage, it was time to pack up the contents of the old house in Colorado and ship everything to California. They had been making do with house-sitters—a pleasant young woman who had to leave for the World Figure Skating competition. It was time to push on the sale of the house.

The problem, June Compagnon told them, was not that the property was undesirable—or even that the real estate market was slow or the asking price was too high: Buyers had a hard time arranging financing for this particular property. Having the house free and clear of debt put a huge up-front burden on a new buyer. Money was tight and expensive.

What would probably work best, Compagnon told them, was a half-year lease (to keep the house occupied and to prevent deterioration over the winter—and to help defray expenses) while they looked into the possibility of mortgaging the property. A point or two under the going rate of 7 percent would be ideal. That would allow a buyer to assume a mortgage on attractive terms.

By January 2, 1967, June Compagnon had found a renter for them, one Marshal Herro—a skating mom. The Heinleins flew to Colorado Springs on January 4 for an anticipated four days of packing and were surprised and very pleased to be met at the airport by Pete and Jane Sencenbaugh—along with a new Chevrolet sedan with snow tires, for their use while there. Even better, they found a hot dinner—*service complet*—vodka, whiskey, and mixers on hand, and breakfast makings in the refrigerator. They were very touched: Warm and thoughtful friendships like that are an irreplaceable asset, and a life spent making that sort of relationship is well spent, no matter what else you do in the meantime.

All Ginny's medical symptoms came back, but she worked through the pain, sorting and packing. They wound up with eleven thousand pounds of books and possessions—seventy packing cases just of books—and gave away or junked as much more. Robert also thinned out his working files: About a quarter of the working papers altogether went up in smoke.

On Sunday, January 8, their new renter showed up unexpectedly—before they had even signed the lease—and demanded without preliminaries that they clear themselves and their possessions out *right now* as she intended to sleep there *that night.* The woman actually began threatening, and it took over an hour to get her out of the house. Robert and Ginny were speechless: Apparently, civility—even basic sanity—is not universal even among ice skaters.

The next day Robert went downtown to arrange with the bank for a mortgage.

> I arranged for us to be able to advertise it as "low down payment, buyer as-sumes 25-yr loan at 6%; owner will accept 2nd mortgage for balance." All very involved and I had to pay through the nose to arrange a 6% loan when the going price is 7% and up—but the house should sell now.[1]

While he was gone, Herro let herself in without knocking, and Ginny had to deal with her alone. This time, Herro told Ginny, she was not leaving under any circumstances: She had "taken counsel" and would get a court order if the Heinleins did not vacate immediately, and then have the sheriff throw them out.

Not likely.

This went on for two hours with much vilification and screaming, during which time June Compagnon arrived, extremely embarrassed, and then Robert arrived. Eventually the intruder left, and Robert immediately got a locksmith in to change the locks.

They flew out on Saturday, January 14, sending the movers on, to rendezvous the following Monday, January 16, at the Bonny Doon site. Rex and Kathleen met them at the San Francisco airport, and they spent the night in Palo Alto. The weather was clear and dry, and they had just gotten out ahead of a huge blizzard that blanketed the entire Midwest. They arrived at the Bonny Doon house to find that the windows had not been put in during their absence, or the doors hung: The factory would not even ship their double-glazed windows for another three weeks. Their belongings were delayed in the blizzard: The tractor unit broke down twice en route and did not arrive until Thursday, January 19—just before a typhoon that hit the Oregon coast and moved south, dumping ten inches of rain in two days.

The unfinished driveway (which would *not* take sealant, no matter how much plastic cement they poured in) became a cataract of mud—but the big van inched up to the doorway as the sky clouded over, and the packing cases were stacked neatly in what would one day be their dining room.

The water system was sabotaged the following night.

The contractor they had hired for the water system, and then fired for incompetence, had hired German students on a "profit-sharing" basis. One of them was threatening now to sue Heinlein for three months' back wages. Nobody could *prove* anything, but the saboteur knew how to avoid the "booby-trap" klaxon and spotlight alarm at the gate, knew how to find that particular pipe in the dark (not easy), and was not interested in the house. He went straight to the vulnerable part of the water system and wrecked it.

The damage to the water system was repairable, but this incident highlighted the fact that the house-building project was in a very vulnerable state at the moment, with piles of expensive building material heaped around and the house essentially wide open. The only real solution was to move over from the cramped, cold cabin so they could keep watch over the place themselves. And get that property fenced at the earliest possible opportunity, with a six-foot cyclone fence, topped with angled barbed wire. "We may wind up with a moat and drawbridge and portcullis," Heinlein wrote to Blassingame, "—and piranha in the moat. Ginny strongly favors the last although she is willing to settle for hungry alligators."[2]

The German "mechanic" lawsuit was coming up for a hearing on February 24, 1967, so they got together all their documentation to defend the ludicrous action. But the rainy season was nearly over, and Ginny projected they would stay out of the red: June Compagnon had found a buyer for the house in Colorado Springs—$36,000 cash.

On January 27, 1967, a fire in the Apollo 1 capsule killed astronauts Virgil "Gus" Grisson, Edward White, and Roger Chafee. The setback was stunning—the first fatality among America's astronaut corps—and put the program on hold until safety redesigns could be put in place.

And two more inquiries came in for film rights for *Stranger*—prompted,

Blassingame thought, by a mention in a *New York Times* book review on February 19. Putnam's finally started filling back orders on *The Moon Is a Harsh Mistress* in February, but Robert was fed up. He instructed Blassingame: No more sales to Putnam's.

Once they were actually *in* the house, they could begin unpacking the shipment from Colorado—if they could get any time to work on that. The clock was ticking on the tax deduction for a gift of his papers to the UC Santa Cruz library's Special Collections. Ginny had recovered her health immediately on returning to sea level, so at the end of January she took over supervising the construction: "Right now she is bossing the job," Heinlein wrote to Blassingame.

> I am officially ill, an acute attack of hypochondria in fact. This enables me to keep out [of] sight and tackle a mountain of paperwork while Ginny does some rawhiding over on the job as "lady boss." We both think that this is going to result in faster action—her idea[,] with which I agree. If the contractor comes over here to consult, he will find me in pajamas and robe, with three days of whiskers and a sad look. But for the next few days he is going to learn that it is far easier to hustle and give Ginny what she wants than it is to talk her out of it—my God, that gal of mine can be difficult when she puts her mind to it![3]

Heinlein spent eight days unpacking and inventorying a large batch of story files, creating a detailed set of accession notes (so detailed, in fact, that he assigned the accession notes their own opus number in his filing system). Donald Clark had told Heinlein—and his own lawyer had confirmed—that this constituted a valuable gift he could claim on this year's taxes if the gift were inventoried and at least some of the papers actually in the hands of the university before taxes were prepared and the tax laws changed, eliminating this deduction. What with the sudden increase in the royalties, he could use the extra deduction this year.[4]

He would have to get the whole lot appraised to get a firm figure, so in the spring he contacted Robert Metzdorf, a New York appraiser of book and manuscript collections—who told him it would take at least a year before he could schedule this work. But he was the best: Rita Berner told him Metzdorf's valuations had repeatedly stood up to IRS challenge.[5]

The work on the house was making visible progress, but they were not ready to move in until July. A sale of movie option to *The Door into Summer* that month, to Reed Sherman and Barney Girard, funded the rest of the material purchases.[6]

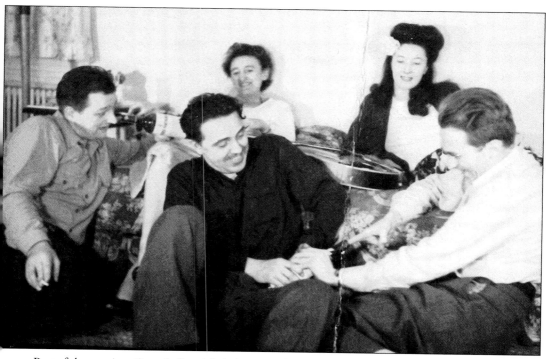

Part of the wartime Campbell social circle, around 1944. BACK ROW, LEFT TO RIGHT: John and Doña Campbell, Grace Dugan. FRONT ROW: Jerome Stanton and Theodore Sturgeon.

Courtesy of Grace Dugan Sang Wurtz.

The golden wedding anniversary of Rex and Bam Heinlein, 1949.
LEFT TO RIGHT: Bam and Rex Ivar Heinlein, MJ Lermer,
Louise Bacchus, Virginia Heinlein, Andy Lermer with son Andy.

Courtesy of Robert A. and Virginia Heinlein Prize Trust.

Robert Heinlein with
director Irving Pichel
on the set of *Destination
Moon*, 1949.
*Courtesy of Robert A. and
Virginia Heinlein Prize Trust.*

Virginia Heinlein with her *Destination
Moon* scrapbook, around 1950.
*Courtesy of Robert A. and Virginia
Heinlein Prize Trust.*

Ted and Irene Carnell, June 1953.
Courtesy of Robert A. and Virginia Heinlein Prize Trust.

Lurton Blassingame with his elk. Hunting trip with Robert Heinlein in 1956.
Courtesy of Robert A. and Virginia Heinlein Prize Trust.

Robert Heinlein at work condensing *Stranger in a Strange Land,* 1960. The "baby coffin" (silencer housing) typewriter on his desk produced the manuscript.

Photograph by Virginia Heinlein; courtesy of Robert A. and Virginia Heinlein Prize Trust.

Robert Heinlein posing with the *Starship Troopers* Hugo Award with Arthur George "Sarge" Smith at Pittcon in 1960.
Courtesy of Robert A. and Virginia Heinlein Prize Trust.

Robert and Ginny at the SeaCon masquerade, 1961. Heinlein described this one himself: "Ginny is 'Vesta the Vegian' from Doc Smith's *The Vortex Blaster*. I am depending largely on green grease paint and crepe hair to create a Charles Addams horror: Minister Plenipotentiary and Ambassador Extraordinary from Arcturus III."
Courtesy of Robert A. and Virginia Heinlein Prize Trust.

Robert Heinlein with E. E. "Doc" Smith and his daughter Verna (Trestrail) Smith, around 1960.
Courtesy of Robert A. and Virginia Heinlein Prize Trust.

Robert Heinlein at work on "Project Stonehenge" around 1961. The flowers
in his hat are Ginny's mark of approval.

Photograph by Virginia Heinlein; courtesy of Robert A. and Virginia Heinlein Prize Trust.

"God in a yellow bathrobe"—Robert Heinlein with Judith Merril at his Chicon room party after receiving the Hugo Award for *Stranger in a Strange Land,* 1962.

Courtesy of Robert A. and Virginia Heinlein Prize Trust.

Poul Anderson visits the Heinleins while construction is underway
on the Bonny Doon house, 1967.

Courtesy of Robert A. and Virginia Heinlein Prize Trust.

Bam Heinlein shortly before her death in 1976.

Courtesy of Robert A. and Virginia Heinlein Prize Trust.

Robert and Virginia Heinlein relaxing on board *Mariposa,* 1973.

Courtesy of Robert A. and Virginia Heinlein Prize Trust.

Robert Heinlein with Isaac Asimov, L. Sprague and Catherine de Camp. Poul Anderson is in the background (LEFT) with Norman Spinrad (CENTER), around 1976.

Courtesy of Jay K. Klein.

Robert and Virginia Heinlein with Ken Keller, chair of MidAmeriCon, 1976. Frank Robinson is seen in the background.

Courtesy of Robert A. and Virginia Heinlein Prize Trust.

Robert and Virginia Heinlein at MidAmeriCon, 1976.

Courtesy of Jay K. Klein.

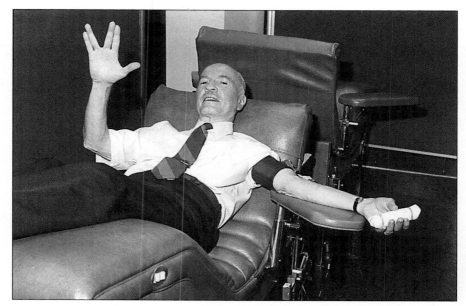

Robert Heinlein giving blood at SunCon in 1977.

Courtesy of Robert A. and Virginia Heinlein Prize Trust.

Robert and Virginia Heinlein at SunCon, talking with C. J. Cherryh (RIGHT) and Jerry Pournelle (CENTER), 1977.

Courtesy of Jay K. Klein.

Robert and Virginia Heinlein with Norman Spinrad and Fred Pohl
at a SunCon room party, 1977.

Courtesy of Jay K. Klein.

Robert and Virginia Heinlein visiting with Arthur C. Clarke
in Sri Lanka, March 1980.

Courtesy of Robert A. and Virginia Heinlein Prize Trust.

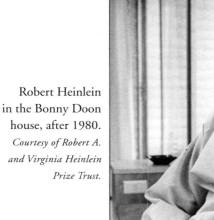

Robert Heinlein in the Bonny Doon house, after 1980.
Courtesy of Robert A. and Virginia Heinlein Prize Trust.

Autographing, after 1980. Due to a series of illnesses affecting his balance, Heinlein could no longer stand to sign books. Ginny would write inscriptions for him so that he could give more autographs.
Courtesy of Robert A. and Virginia Heinlein Prize Trust.

Leon and Takeko Stover at U. C. Santa Cruz in 1984.

Courtesy of Robert A. and Virginia Heinlein Prize Trust.

A Citizens Advisory Council meeting, about 1984. RIGHT TO LEFT: Jerry Pournelle (STANDING), G. Harry Stine, Robert Heinlein, Dr. Phil Chapman (retired astronaut), Greg Bear, Jim Baen.

Courtesy of Robert A. and Virginia Heinlein Prize Trust.

Robert Heinlein with "Honey"—
Rita Berner Bottoms, July 6, 1987.
This is one of the last pictures
ever taken of Heinlein.
Courtesy of Rita Bottoms
and Robert A. and Virginia
Heinlein Prize Trust.

Virginia Heinlein at the dedication of
the Robert and Virginia Heinlein Wing
of the Butler Public Library, 1990.
Courtesy of Robert A. and Virginia
Heinlein Prize Trust.

Poul and Karen Anderson dropped by the site on their way driving to Wester-con[7] in San Diego. That visit must have been virtually a campout, as the Andersons wound up leaving behind their air mattresses and drop cloths.[8] By the end of August, the Heinleins had their first real houseguests: Cal Laning and Robert Cornog both paid them quick visits, now that they were able to entertain after a fashion. On Labor Day *The Moon Is a Harsh Mistress* won a Hugo Award—his fourth Best Novel Hugo—more than any other science-fiction writer, ever.

"This one surprised me," he told Dan Galouye when congratulations started coming in early in September. "I had not known that my story had been nominated."[9]

The Hugo was flattering, of course. So, in an awkward way, was a bit of plagiarism—the second-sincerest form of flattery—that came to his attention that fall. Hollywood again. He was passing through what would become Ginny's office when the phone rang—not another supplier, but someone who identified himself as Gene Coon, one of the coproducers, with the creator Gene Roddenberry, of a television show that had been airing for about a year now, *Star Trek*. Heinlein knew about the show, but did not at that time own a television set; he had not seen it.

They had bought a terrific comic script from a brand-new young writer—his first sale, in fact—and it was not until production was actually under way that someone noticed a couple points of similarity with an episode in one of Heinlein's Scribner juveniles. Coon conceded the similarity, but—pulling out the violins—asked if Heinlein would not waive his claim, as it would throw people out of business and might even mean the end of *Star Trek*.

Heinlein was not naïve: He was reasonably certain that Coon and Roddenberry had already "taken counsel" and were trying to find out how hard-nosed he was going to be about the acutely serious (for them) matter.

But he had other things on his mind and did *not* want to get embroiled in another plagiarism suit—and the opportunity to give a new writer a boost probably weighed in as well. He agreed to waive the "similarity."

They sent him the script for David Gerrold's *The Trouble With Tribbles* a week later, and Heinlein realized he had been "overly generous, to put it mildly."[10] The "Tribbles" were his flat cats from *The Rolling Stones*. He was mildly conflicted because he knew he had created them fifteen years ago by "filing off the serial numbers" of Ellis Parker Butler's comic story "Pigs Is Pigs."[11] This might be unconscious plagiarism: Gerrold had not even reworked his flat cats—just given them a different name and exploited the same comic turns.

Robert let it go—and even wrote Gerrold a letter telling him not to worry about it. The episode aired on December 29, 1967. He was less pleased when,

after the show went off the air, Gerrold began selling stuffed fake-fur and ve-
lour Tribble dolls at science-fiction conventions, substantially the same as the
props used in the show, some of them with bladders to fake movement. That
kind of merchandising was *not* covered by his original waiver—and when
Gerrold printed the "permission" letter in another bit of gratuitous merchandising, a book for the series' rabid fans, Heinlein found it harder to maintain
a cheerful attitude.

> If the matter had simply been dropped after that one episode was filmed, I
> would have chalked it up wryly to experience. But the "nice kid" did not
> drop it; "tribbles" (i.e., my "flat cats") have been exploited endlessly.
>
> Well, that's one that did "larn me." Today if J. Christ phoned me on
> some matter of business, I would simply tell him: "See my agent."[12]

Dan Galouye's other news after the Worldcon was more disturbing: the
"liberal wing" of SFWA (the Science Fiction Writers of America) had started
circulating a petition opposing the war in Vietnam, with about seventy of
their colleagues' signatures so far. The petitions were going to be published in
several of the science-fiction magazines. Soon after, Poul Anderson wrote saying he and Dan Galouye and Sprague de Camp were thinking about a counter-
petition, supporting the war—temperate and concilatory in tone.[13]

The idea of the counter-petition distressed Heinlein, and he counseled
against it as promoting unnecessary—and ultimately futile—divisiveness
within SFWA.

> I am most sorry that this thing ever came up. It is not that I object to either
> side having their say, in print, or otherwise, and anywhere—I am for utter
> free speech and free press at all times without any reservations whatever.
> Nor am I afraid of the effect of your ad . . . [sic] it won't have the slightest
> effect on Mr. Johnson's decisions; he is a prisoner of his own policies and
> their political consequences.
>
> What I do regret is the effect it has already had on SFWA and the greater
> effect it is likely to have, and that is why I am trying to damp out the move-
> ment to answer it; it can only widen the split.
>
> If such ads could have any effect on National policy, I would not men-
> tion the welfare of SFWA in the same breath. But they won't . . . . [and] I
> hate like the devil to see it rent by a political schism.[14]

As to the war itself, the public news was "too distressing to discuss."[15]

No, I don't like this war. It's a proxy war, and I don't like proxy wars. It's a war fought with conscripts, and I don't like conscription at any time under any pretext . . . Slavery is not made any sweeter by calling it "selective service". . . .[16]

Nor was it possible to reconcile the conduct of this conflict with *any* concept of truth, justice, or national honor:

I can't stand the thumb-fingered way Mr. Johnson and Mr. McNamara run this war. What the hell do they think men are? Lead soldiers to be expended at a whim? What the devil are we doing fighting an infantry war in a rain forest . . . . [17]

I think Mr. Johnson has handled this war very badly. But I'm damned if I'll add to his troubles by public criticism—especially when my misgivings, if expressed publicly, could give some aid & comfort to the enemy. I took part in electing Mr. Johnson by voting against him; therefore I owe him full support during his tenure.[18]

Aid and comfort to the enemy, however, was a ship that sailed when the left-wingers' petition was published. The U.S.S. *Pueblo* surrendered to the North Koreans without a fight on January 23, 1968, becoming the first U.S. naval vessel to be hijacked by a foreign military power in 150 years. Student riots were hitting the news all around the world. Heinlein gave in and agreed to lend his name to Anderson's and Galouye's and de Camp's efforts, and underwrite whatever portion of cost of publishing the counter-petition could not be raised by subscription. As it happened, the support from traditional liberals—and conservatives, as well—to this anti-anti-war statement was more than sufficient to cover publication in *Galaxy*. Himself, he was "neither right wing nor left wing—I believe in freedom under the Constitution . . . [sic] as written and not as rewritten by Lord Warren. In short, I am obsolete—and if you don't believe it, pick up any newspaper." [19]

With winter coming on, and the house 95 percent done,[20] Heinlein was thinking about settling in to do some writing again.

I have not been able to write any fiction at all for more than two years . . . . Being unable to work has not produced a financial crisis—I've taken in more money each of the past two years than ever before in my life and this project is free of mortgage or debt. But it *has* produced a serious spiritual crisis; I have grown enormously frustrated at not being able to do anything with the story notes I am constantly making.[21]

The last 5 percent of the house-building went agonizingly, maddeningly slowly. They were able to purchase their own flagpole in February 1968,[22] and his insurance company demanded they put a locking gate on the fence to protect the swimming pool. It also helped keep out the deer.[23]

Heinlein continued to receive complaints by every post from readers who could not find copies of *Stranger*—and the university bookstore said the book was no longer even in Avon's—the paperback publisher's—catalog:[24] They had allowed it to go out of print in the middle of an incredible demand. But Putnam's had pulled the book from Avon and let it to Berkley Books, the paperback house they had acquired in 1965. Berkley brought out 250,000 copies in March 1968—the forty-third impression of the book.[25] It was gone almost before they could get it on the stands. And Putnam's still would not reissue it in hardcover:[26]

My real grouse against Putnam is not over the pbs but over their refusal to keep *Stranger* in print in hardback—damn it, if they would reprint, they could now sell copies to every public library and every college library in the country, plus many private purchasers, as I constantly get letters asking me *where* hardback copies may be found. (So far, I know of six college courses which use *Stranger*.)[27]

Willis McNelly was using the book to teach one of his college courses and had one hundred copies on back order for the winter term that year; the seventy-five copies he had bought for the last year's course were long gone, and he could not find any supplier.[28]

Heinlein's sister, Mary Jean, sent them a clipping from the UCLA *Daily Bruin* (in Los Angeles), showing a listing of an experimental class offered by Dr. Carl Faber on "Guru-ism," listing Heinlein with J. D. Salinger and Lawrence Ferlinghetti as "personal gurus." Salinger's name he knew, but not Ferlinghetti's (Ferlinghetti was the owner of City Lights Bookstore in San Francisco and a specialty publisher who kept Beat poetry and novels alive). But the idea that he was regarded as a "personal guru" made Heinlein absolutely livid: Guru was *exactly the opposite* of what he was trying to get across to these people.[29]

And yet—

And yet—

These people who were writing to him seemed to find in *Stranger* . . . certainly things he had put into it, things he had learned the hard way over the course of his life, and things that could not be found anywhere else. Drafted as a personal guru, he could refuse to serve. But *Stranger* out in the world seems to have been adopted as a voice for the "ethos of disaffiliation" from the conformist mainstream—the process Marxist social critic Herbert Marcuse called "the Great Refusal." Heinlein had his own continuing refusals to make, frustrating and wearing.

Some of them were relatively easy: When the fan letters started talking to him as if he were Jubal Harshaw, he could gently steer them away from it. To one boy, one of those who wrote him a long and rambling "poem of comment," he wrote:

> How does one answer a poem? With another poem? But, being "Jubal"
> quite as much as I am "Mike," if I wrote a poem, long habit would force me
> to sell it, rather than use it in a letter. Jubal, you may remember, did not
> fully approve of Mike's open-handedness (while going on being open-handed
> in his own cantankerous fashion).
> But I am also "Patty" of the snakes, who never wrote a line in her life.
> In fact, I am none of these, but simply myself, who knows as much as
> you do—but not a whit more—about the Martian rite of sharing water. If
> you are offering me friendship, then Asmodeus knows that, at my age, a
> man needs all the friends he can win. Thank you.[30]

Those were the easy ones. One request to define "grok" in seven words came from a student teacher, and it was possible to make a polite (but pointed) reply:

> Having neither "flappers" nor secretary I must answer your letter myself;
> 1.   I used ca. three pages to define "grok." Had I been able to define it
> in seven words I would have done so. See the discussion in the story.
> 2.   Any religious message you may find in the story is up to you—or to
> any reader. What I try to offer is entertainment, as that is what the cash
> customer pays me for. If he gets something more out of the story, that is a
> bonus not in the sales price.[31]

And to a Methodist preacher who offered extravagant thanks for the book—and wanted to talk theology:

Inasmuch as I am not a theologian but simply a writer of fiction I have most carefully refrained from trying to "Explain" *Stranger In a Strange Land*. My implied contract with my readers requires me to entertain him sufficiently to compensate him for the price he paid for the story . . . . if he gets six-bits worth of amusement out of the story, I have dealt honestly with him—I did not contract to save his soul nor to unscrew the inscrutable.

But this story is a fantastic allegory, more complex than a bang-bang cops & robbers; inevitably each reader reads it differently and what he finds in it depends as much on what he brings to it as on what I wrote into it. I have not tried to interpret the mysteries of the Universe for him nor solve the ancient problems of Good and Evil—at most I have tried to say that such questions are real and overwhelmingly important . . . [sic] and that they cannot necessarily all be solved by three o'clock this afternoon.

As to my own guesses, suspicions, or inner convictions as to the final problems I think I had best keep them to myself; I could so easily be wrong. Waiting is.[32]

But there were others; he patiently and earnestly answered cries for connection that went well beyond "fan letters." A young woman wrote to him about an argument the book had prompted with her (West Point cadet) boyfriend, who argued *Stranger* said sex brought people closer together—engendered love. Wrong, he told her. Her view was the correct one:

I ordinarily do not discuss my own stories in any fashion but your letter leads me to think that in this case there may be a very practical reason to bend that rule . . . .

It seems to me that it is made emphatically clear in *Stranger* that it is *your* viewpoint which is being expounded, not his. I am not going to stop to dig into my own writings in order to cite line and paragraph but in *every case* in that book the sharing of sex takes place after and only after the two persons already share love. Always.

Furthermore, the word "love" is precisely defined. It does *not* mean physical attraction . . . . If a male and a female each loves the other, it is almost a certainty that they will also feel physically attracted—in which case, if they choose to do something about it, the safest arrangement is contractual marriage, our society being what it is. Any other arrangement is hazardous, especially for the female. If a male truly does find that a certain female's happiness is essential to his own he will be very careful what risks he urges her to take in this cultural matrix we have today.

> Anybody who suggests *Stranger* urges sex as a way of attaining love hasn't understood what he has read.[33]

And on and on and on. One day Ginny answered the door to a young man who had travelled from Texas to confess to Robert that he had been having an affair with his minister's wife, and wanted Robert to shrive[34] him. Creepy and disturbing. Ginny wrote, "The whole thing was quite upsetting to both of us."[35]

You could not fume and storm when someone was in such deep spiritual distress and you could help. No good, either, to fume and storm when Blassingame received a postcard announcing the book publication of Alexei Panshin's "unauthorized biography," *Heinlein in Dimension.* Panshin had published fragments of the book in fanzines over the last several years, and Advent, now operated by George Price (Kemp had gotten himself in trouble with the postal authorities for mailing "pornography" as social criticism and was now in jail), was bringing out the book. Heinlein resented the commercial exploitation of his name in the title, he told Blassingame, though he would not do anything about it. He particularly asked Blassingame *not* to send him a copy of the book when it came out, as he would not read it, and "am particularly anxious that Ginny shall not read it; it would just make her froth and set this house in turmoil for days on end."[36] Blassingame skimmed the book and assured him there didn't seem to be anything actionable in it—not even anything that could be deemed an "invasion of privacy." He could relax and spend his money on the house instead of lawyers.

The threat to privacy coming just from the neighborhood was becoming a bother.

> Sure, I've known for years that I was a competent commercial writer. I have lots of check vouchers to prove it. But now I suddenly find I am an "Author" with my work taken seriously and used in many college courses—and the change from obscure pulp writer startles me . . . [sic] and while it's flattering, it's not very comfortable.[37]

But all was not completely irritating: Lee Atwood, the president of North American Rockwell, issued a warm invitation for them to view the Apollo Project equipment Rockwell was working on that March. Since it could coincide with a niece's wedding (Mary Jean's daughter, Kathy), they made a weekend of it. Atwood, they discovered, was an incorrigible check-grabber. He tried to pay for everything (but Heinlein outflanked him on the air tickets).

They were somewhat embarrassed to find that Atwood had saddled the head of the Space Projects division with them as escort-cum-valet, it seemed, giving them "split-second service everywhere."[38]

> Atwood took us to dinner the evening between the two days. We stopped at his home for drinks first, and I got him aside and asked him *why* we had received such extraordinary treatment. He looked thoughtful and said, well, he had read *Starship Troopers* . . . .[39]

They were barely able to see Kathy (now Petty) at her wedding reception, and had to go directly by taxi to the airport.

The next month they were in Berkeley for the West Coast version of SFWA's annual Nebula Awards banquet on March 16, 1968, at the Claremont hotel. The Nebula Awards are given by vote of the members, to honor their colleagues. In the 1970s, SFWA held one Nebula banquet each year in New York and a second somewhere on the West Coast. This was the first time since SFWA was founded in 1965 that Heinlein would be on one of the coasts at the appropriate time—and not tied up with house-building. He enjoyed meeting his colleagues again—though, sadly, A. P. White—"Anthony Boucher" to mystery and science-fiction fans—was dying of lung cancer and passed away on April 29, 1968.

Heinlein was contacted by David Gerrold on April 28: Gerrold had been hired to write a screenplay for *Stranger* and wanted to talk to Heinlein about the project. "You are personally welcome," Heinlein wrote Gerrold, but both his lawyer and his agent advised him not to discuss the script—or read it once written, unless specifically hired by the optioners, since to do so might prejudice his ability to re-option the property freely if they allowed the option to lapse—again.[40]

In any case, Heinlein didn't have time at the moment. His mother, Bam, had come up the coast from Southern California to visit with his brother Rex and with Robert and Ginny early in May 1968. She arrived at Rex's house in Palo Alto, and Robert phoned to make arrangements to come up to see her that day. While they were on the phone, Bam cut off in the middle of a sentence, and he could faintly hear moans of pain. After a moment, Rex came on the line and promised to call back—

The long bone in Bam's right leg, the femur, had snapped spontaneously, and she had collapsed to the floor. Bam was nearly ninety, and her bones had lost a great deal of calcium over the years. Dr. David I. Hull, one of the top orthopedic surgeons in the country, was at Stanford Medical Center. He operated that same day, securing the break with a metal pin and plate. Recovery at such advanced age, with such an advanced case of osteoporosis, would be long and slow—and problematical. She might eventually walk again, with a cane. She might not walk again—ever.

This hospital stay lasted three weeks, and Bam required skilled nursing for an indefinite period after that. They really had no other option but a geriatric nursing facility. Rex and MJ (Mary Jean Heinlein-Lermer's family nickname) argued about whether it would be in Palo Alto (close to Rex and to Robert) or in Pasadena (closer to MJ). Robert firmly stayed out of the argument.

Mortality. The old world was passing away that summer of 1968—a cousin wrote that Uncle Oscar's Heinlein Mercantile general store building had been torn down in Butler recently—and a new world was coming painfully into being. Martin Luther King and Robert Kennedy were assassinated. There were race riots in 125 cities across the United States that summer. Russian tanks rolled into Prague bloodily to suppress a relatively liberal reform movement in one of the Soviet Union's "buffer states." Lyndon Johnson declined to run for a second term as president, his entire social program for a second New Deal, the "Great Society," run aground on the anti-war movement that was growing in size and volume. "Hey! Hey! L.B.J.! How many kids did you kill today?!" The New Left turned to violence, and the old left responded in kind: Mayor Daley's notoriously corrupt Chicago police waded into anti-war protestors, mainly students, outside the Democratic National Convention—war of the government against its citizenry—as the convention nominated an anti-war candidate for president, Senator Eugene McCarthy. "Let's review the bidding," Heinlein wrote that summer to a friend in Colorado Springs:

—USS *Pueblo* was surrendered without a fight. Hanoi has agreed to negotiate the ending of all our aggressive acts against them. Mr. Johnson decided to be noble and statesmanlike and let Bobby have it. A Nobel Peace Prize winner [Martin Luther King] has been killed by person or persons unknown; today our leaders throughout the nation are beating their breasts and claiming the guilt for *you* and *you* and *You*. The White House is barricaded and the National Capitol is surrounded by machine guns. The United States has gone off the gold standard—except that it will continue to sell to France all it wants at $35/oz without being so rude as to mention 50-yr-old debts. We solemnly agree never to use space for warlike purposes and the FOBS[41] doesn't matter because we have a new radar that turns corners. And Stassen[42] and Dick Gregory[43] are running for President.

Did I miss anything?

Oh, yes, Hindu students are rioting. So also are Polish students British students South American students (several flavors) and California students and Howard students—each for different reasons, if you'll pardon the word.

I swear that I am not and never have been a member of the human race—and just as fast as I can report to the Intergalactic Council I shall recommend in the strongest of terms, using all tendrils, that this entire sector be placed OUT OF BOUNDS.

Further deponent sayeth not.

I'm damned if I'll make any comment on any of the above. After you are liquidated by a sniper while trying to put out a fire set by a looter somebody might go through your papers, find this, and I might face a People's Court for thinking forbidden thoughts. I'm glad old Sarge Smith died when he did.[44]

He who sows the wind shall reap the whirlwind. This was the late and bitter fruit of undeclared war, waged indecisively, the reckless spilling of treasure and blood.

I try to stay calm and not fret about things I can't correct. I find myself simultaneously angry at the Administration and even more angry at most of its critics—an attitude so complex that I try to avoid any political discussion with anyone but Ginny . . . [sic] who shares my views at a somewhat higher temperature.[45]

He decided to turn down all speaking engagements—except for librarian groups—"for the duration" and tried to follow Candide's advice. The rare letter he received from soldiers on the ground in Vietnam he valued as actual data. To a friend relaying data from a son in Vietnam he wrote:

I'm glad I'm too old to be doing the sort of things that Alex is doing. But I certainly do treasure these reports. I can't get *anything* out of the newspaper stories. Between the credibility gap, a conviction that we are fighting with one foot in a bucket for undisclosed reasons, and a dark suspicion that even the (presumably) uncensored "background" stories are heavily slanted, I just can't take the newspaper accounts. This private and straight tell right from the spot does far more for me than do the four newspapers we take.[46]

In the hours he was able to work, Heinlein continued to sort and catalog his working papers for the University Library. He had asked Special Collections to hold off making any announcement of the gift until his fence was up, but Robert Metzdorf, their selected appraiser, was ready to come to Santa Cruz and survey the papers already in the archive. The new tax laws that would take effect in 1969 were going to eliminate the "commercial value" of these gifts for tax deductions, leaving only the value of the paper and other materials.

Metzdorf arrived on November 5, 1968, just after the election (Richard Nixon was elected president, on a pledge to end the war in Vietnam—"victory with honor") and was with them to November 8. He valued the collection— the two consignments Heinlein had sent by that time, plus a third Metzdorf hand-carried to the University Library—at a staggering $30,230.00. Heinlein told Cal Laning he was shocked at the recent appraisal. He knew the papers had to be worth something because he had been asked for them by five or six universities—"but they were waste paper to me and had to thin them out constantly."[47]

They finished their guest cottage in December 1968, and that was the last of the house-building.

Chesley Bonestell had just moved from the Bay Area to Carmel, fifty miles around Monterey Bay from Santa Cruz, and had gotten in touch with the Heinleins. They invited the Bonestells up for Christmas dinner and also invited a couple of local friends—widowers both, who for one reason or another couldn't spend the holidays with family that year: Dr. Robert D. Calkins, lately president of the Brookings Institute and now vice chancellor at UC Santa Cruz, and Lionel Lenox, a retired banker, amateur photographer, and Ginny's gardening buddy.[48] Robert was glad to be able to show off the house. Bonestell, trained as an architect, was not impressed—and said so.[49] The house suited *them* and that's what counted.

It was wet and raining outside, but warm and dry inside the house. Ginny had spread herself for this feast, which featured a Swedish baked ham entree with this and that, and concluded with Crêpes Suzettes as they watched the launch of Apollo 8 on television.[50]

> [S]o by combining forces we turned what would have been a grim and lonely day into a merry one. So the end of the year finds us in good mood, both in good health, all construction completed (thank God), and ready to enjoy life to the fullest.[51]

22

PICKING UP WHERE HE LEFT OFF

On New Year's Day of 1969 the power went off in the middle of a winter storm. In an all-electric house, no power means no cooking, no heat—and no water, since the pumps from the spring are electric. Ginny built a big fire in the living room fireplace, and they moved into that one room for the duration. Robert was vexed because he had just started the new Allen Drury novel, *Preserve and Protect,* and couldn't stand to put it down. Five straight hours of reading by electric lantern exhausted all the batteries.[1]

The outage was fortunately not more than a day—this time. Next time they could move into the guest house, which had a propane tank for heating and cooking. "The cats won't like it, but we don't expect to consult them."[2]

In February Fred Pohl forwarded to them a cabled request for Robert to serve as an honored guest at a film festival late in March, in Rio de Janeiro. They would be screening *Destination Moon* as part of a tribute to George Pal. If he would give a speech introducing the film, the Brazilian Ministry of Culture would pick up the tab.[3] There are certainly worse things in life, in the middle of a Northern California winter, than an expense-paid trip to Rio.

Ginny figures it's a shopping trip. I pointed out that they had not offered to pay her expenses. She sez, "What's that got to do with it? Let's spend it before it inflates." So she's going. (I figure my tab comes out of my taxes anyhow, by way of the Alliance for Progress.)[4]

The weather continued to improve, and they held a big housewarming party on March 7. They invited Rex and Kathleen, as well as local friends they had made over the last two or three years—the McHenrys;[5] Dr. Calkins and Lionel Lenox, senior and junior (who had all three been with them at Christmas dinner); Dr. and Mrs. Richard Bronson;[6] Mr. and Mrs. Richard Kessell (their local lawyer who had been so helpful with all the legal matters in the house-building); Mr. and Mrs. Donald Clark and the Head of Special Collections and Archives at the university, Rita Berner; the Page Smiths[7] and Mr. and Mrs. Joel Schaefer.[8] They invited Frank and Beverly Herbert down from Seattle (where he was still a working journalist, *Dune* not yet earning enough for him to quit his day job). And Blassingame and his wife, Peggy, as informal guests of honor. This was, after all, "the house that Lurton built" by providing a steady stream of advances and royalty checks to pay the workmen.

Two weeks later Robert and Ginny were flying down to Rio on an all-expense-paid junket and on a plane full of science-fiction colleagues and celebrities such as Roman Polanski, for the "II festival internacional do film rio de janeiro."[9]

They were given diplomatic courtesies and entertained at formal receptions in various embassies, all in Rio's end-of-summer oppressive heat and humidity. Amid the floor-length gowns and Ginny's formal white gloves, there was a sprinkling of the British "mod" fashion given a South American twist: see-through blouses and micro-mini skirts, often worn with nothing at all underneath.[10] The festival viewings were held at the theater in the French embassy, and they also got to take in all the other films, new and old, at the festival (Robert recommended *The Lion in Winter*[11]).

At one of the embassy parties, Roman Polanski found Heinlein and introduced him to his wife, the stunningly beautiful Sharon Tate. She had been filming in Europe but had taken a break to join her husband at the festival. Ginny was off, circulating, as she usually did. Karma balanced: She had Dorothy Lamour (from the *Destination Moon* wrap party in 1950—see chapter 3 *supra*), and he had Sharon Tate in 1969.

At the festival, all the attention was on Pal, but Heinlein wanted to commemorate Irving Pichel's role in *Destination Moon* in his talk on March 28. He titled it after something Pichel had said to him once: "Creativity Is Indivisible."[12] *Destination Moon* worked, he said, because Pal had done with Pichel what Pichel had done with him: pick his man and let him work without interference. Pichel was able to craft a coherent filmic "vision" because of Pal's creative work in producing—in picking the right man and letting him do the job.

They had a very good time on the trip. They had ample sightseeing and shopping time and were speaking "tourist Portuguese" in a matter of days.[13] Aside from a bizarre incident with Harry Harrison trying to have a scuffle with Robert and crashing an embassy party,[14] only one other thing marred the trip: Ginny banged her head getting into a taxi one day and knocked herself out briefly. She seemed to get over it, with only a small cut on the outside

of her right eye, but soon she began to experience a ringing in the ears—
tinnitus—that would not go away.[15]

They flew back to New York, planning to spend time with friends there
and do a little business, but Heinlein caught a bad case of flu and was bedridden in the Tuscany hotel. Ginny decided to cancel all their plans and get him
home to Santa Cruz as soon as possible.[16] She had a thirty-five-year reunion
coming up at Packer next April; they could come back then and do what they
had failed to take in this year.[17]

The big trees of Santa Cruz were soothing after Rio, though the accumulated mail was not. The mail on *Stranger* was now a significant portion of the
total, and it tended to be different from the regular run of fan mail, repetitive
in its own way, but sometimes spiked with the unexpected—such as an article
in an academic literary magazine, *The CEA Critic,* by Willis McNelly, Ph.D.,[18]
at Cal State, Fullerton, "Linguistic Relativity in Middle High Martian."
McNelly talked about the Whorfian[19] underpinnings of the hypothetical Martian language of *Stranger in a Strange Land* that was both playful and serious.
The article pleased Heinlein very much—"so much so that there is danger of
taking myself seriously . . . [sic] but not too much danger so long as I remain
married to my Best Friend & Severest Critic. 'Cut to the chase!' is her motto,
and she keeps me reminded."[20]

But McNelly's article was anything but typical of the *Stranger* fan mail.
And now Heinlein was starting to receive thanks and congratulations on his
political writing in *The Moon Is a Harsh Mistress.* There was a slow resurgence
of interest in classic American individualist political philosophy. The radical
fringe of this new libertarianism tended to anarchist theory, and he couldn't
quite go along with that:

> I miss being an utter anarchist only by a very narrow margin[21]—i.e., a
> misgiving about the possibility of maintaining a complex society capable of
> mass production without a certain amount of sheer force, both internal and
> external. (I'm still searching for the libertarian philosopher who can ex-
> plain convincingly how this can be done—I haven't quite given up hope.)[22]

In a sense, he was too individualist even for these confessed radical indi-
vidualists, and some of that had leaked over into his portrayal of lunar society
in the first part of *The Moon Is a Harsh Mistress.*

Ginny offered to take over *all* the correspondence, to give him time to
write. At first he was reluctant[23]—but the alternative was to do it himself (in
which case he might never be able to write any new fiction at all) or quit an-

swering mail from strangers (which stuck in his craw). Ginny took it all over—business correspondence, fan mail, management of their finances (which she had been doing for nearly ten years by that time), and gradually, with decreasing amounts of oversight and participation on his part, the management of the business aspects of the writing, which left Heinlein free to do the writing aspects of the writing.

By the beginning of June 1969 he was wandering around with a glazed expression and bumping into things. Ginny told Willis McNelly that he was at the "horrid stage" of generating a story.[24] But he got no further than nine pages of outline notes dated June 18, 1969, for a novella aimed at *Playboy*—four years, two months, and five days since he had put "The End" to his last writing project. Possibly he was inhibited by the prospect of another trip that would have to be made in July.

The next Apollo mission, Apollo 11, was to land a man on the Moon, and Heinlein wanted to be there at Cape Kennedy on July 16, 1969. "I am going to see that shoot," he told Blassingame. "I've waited a lifetime for the first trip to the Moon and I am not going to miss it."[25]

But neither research nor pull could get them a room anywhere within a hundred miles of the launch site: And he would pay anything at all—anything!—for a reservation the night before the launch.[26] But he could not even get press credentials. He could go back to writing his "2-part serial intended for *Playboy*—Intended length ca. 30,000 words."[27]

Over the last eight years while he was out of the game, a sort of amorphous "movement" had started to show up in magazine science fiction, called—mostly by detractors—"The New Wave." The individual writers lumped together in this way—Harlan Ellison, Michael Moorcock, Norman Spinrad, Brian Aldiss, Harry Harrison, others—denied there was anything like a "movement" going on. There were publishers now that were sometimes willing to publish experimental writing—refreshing in a genre that could get pretty hidebound with formula. Most readers, most of the time, Heinlein had long since concluded,[28] don't want experimentation—don't want fresh, new material at all. They want more of what they had been getting all along—"mixture as before." It was his biggest problem writing particularly those children's books for Scribner. Heinlein was naturally sympathetic to experimentation; it kept the field fresh and growing—and a great deal of the new stuff was clearly trying out different storytelling conventions than the somewhat stale magazine story formulas that had dominated SF for decades.

Unfortunately, a lot of it just wasn't very *good* experimentation; too much of it was simply recapitulating the Modernist prosodic experiments made in the 1920s and 1930s—stuff that had by and large been abandoned because it made the reading harder work for the reader. On the other hand, some of science fiction's readers wanted to enshrine Campbell-era story conventions, and that wasn't the way to go, either.

Although Heinlein rarely discussed his process with the story that became *I Will Fear No Evil,* he seems to have been acutely aware of these developments. It was as if he was working on crafting a New Wave kind of story that worked as *story*—the kind of thing for fiction that Frank Lloyd Wright had done with the Bauhaus when he designed Fallingwater in 1935: Let a "washed-up" old-timer show the young turks how it ought to be done . . .

This new story he was working out had a foot in both worlds. He took two of the hoariest clichés in science fiction—the mad scientist and the brain transplant—and turned the ideas upside down and inside out and *shook* until something interesting fell out.

The immediate inspiration for this story came out of an article he saw in *Parade* magazine in 1968, about rare blood types and an astonishing one-man operation of volunteer rare-blood donors, the National Rare Blood Club.[29] He had clipped it at the time and found his thoughts returning to the issues it covered.

> Heart transplants were in the news then, so I extrapolated and did a brain transplant story and used blood matching as a gimmick, with this Club, as a minor plot gimmick.[30]
>
> We now have endless complications of identity, money, his-her marital status (she was married), sex complications (cf. Thorne Smith's *Turnabout*—and stay well clear of it!) as this new body is horny as hell—for men—and his old brain is still horny—for women—and he-she is AC-DC as Noel Coward . . . [sic] and he of he-she is terribly intrigued by female libido.[31]

Matching up an *old* man's brain and a *young* woman's body gave him a story about that other hot topic in the editorial pages, the "generation gap." So in an odd way it was echoing in story form his real-life dialogue with the field of science fiction—the old man learning from the new kids on the block, even as he teaches . . .

He was able to start outlining the story by June 18, 1969, and start writing "A Dirty Old Man" two days later. But he crossed out that working title and penciled in the pun "Now I Lay Me—." On June 24, he changed the title to a more explicitly Biblical quotation: *I Will Fear No Evil,* which continues "for thou art with me."

His female protagonist, Eunice Branca, was to be racially ambiguous, so he took clippings from two magazines—a sunny blonde and a stunning black woman, and posted them on the ledge over his typewriter, alternating looking at them, so he wouldn't unconsciously drift into racially stereotyped language.

Heinlein had always said he had a tough time getting started until he could hear the characters talking in his head, and then it took off on its own. This one took off and dragged him along with it: The character(s), it appeared, had no intention of confining themselves to a novella: The story kept unfolding and unfolding. The theme of what a modern young woman—the body—had to teach a ninety-year-old man—the brain—and conversely, what age and life experience could give to youth and beauty—ran away with the story, and it came to be about both kinds of life-wisdom, with the ironic twist that the transplanted brain goes slowly insane as it acquires this wisdom: The brain accepted Eunice's life experience, even while the Eunice body rejected the brain.

But there was another reason that contributed to this story running away with itself: Heinlein was not working purely within the conventions of science fiction, and not recapitulating the high modernist experiments either. He had always followed current general fiction, including the experimental writing that was occasionally published. Heinlein never made reference to *Ada or Ardor,* published that year, 1969, but Nabokov was clearly on Heinlein's radar (because of *Lolita,* 1955, 1958, which was referenced periodically in Heinlein's correspondence). A number of story figures in *Ada or Ardor* are suggestive—the merging of the incestuous couple into Vaniada and the extended meditation on death. Perhaps *Ada or Ardor* helped kick off Heinlein's train of thought.

Heinlein did not like to take long breaks once he got a piece under way, but this time it couldn't be helped: Exactly a week after his sixty-second birthday, his mother was having her ninetieth, on Bastille Day. On July 12 he stopped writing, 60,000 words into his 30,000-word story,[32] and flew with Ginny south to Arcadia, an eastern suburb of Los Angeles, where Bam was living with MJ and Andy Lermer.

In fact, this became a long and worthwhile interruption: Lee Atwood (who had hosted them so sumptuously in 1968) invited them to the Apollo 11 launch as his personal guests.

The sudden, unlooked-for prospect of it really coming to pass put Heinlein into a very strange emotional state. He watched with a sense of unreality as it took all four of the wives plus another miscellaneous relative to light the ninety candles on the cake simultaneously—

. . . at times during that whole period I had a dream-like quality to the effect that well, I'm going to wake up and discover that tomorrow morning I have to take a plane to Florida because it's about to happen . . . . it was not only a tremendous spiritual experience, but also, it still had a dream-like quality, I'd dreamt so long . . . . [sic][33]

This is how Robert Heinlein was, overwhelmed.

After Bam's birthday party on the fourteenth, they flew out to Orlando with Atwood and his stepsons in Atwood's private jet. They were ferried like royalty to a motel in Coco Beach.

They were taken to a quick succession of parties—first, one for the astronauts before they had to buckle down to the pre-liftoff checks, and then to a party of their science-fiction colleagues, where they talked with Hank and Barbie Stine and with Arthur C. Clarke and his wife, Connie. Then on to a dinner party, where Ginny finally got to meet Barry Goldwater in person.

The viewing stands, on the morning of July 16, 1969, were four miles away from the launch pad—and, in fact, it wasn't practical to get much closer anyway: The Saturn V was so gigantic that close up you couldn't take in the top of it.

There were more than a million people there, most coming on foot from the surrounding area. The traffic was snarled—the Reverend Ralph Abernathy, president of the Southern Christian Leadership Conference and Martin Luther King's immediate successor as leader of the civil rights movement, was conducting a small march of the Poor People's Campaign, to protest the money being spent on space exploration. Of course, not investing in growth is the best and easiest way to keep people poor—and the poor segment of the population growing. But this is not a truth Rev. Abernathy was ready to hear.

It became almost impossible to move. Heinlein almost didn't notice.

He recognized the feeling in the crowded VIP stands: It was the feeling you get in a midnight Christmas church service or at a Bar Mitzvah or such.[34] Politicians, engineers, everyone (even the Reverend Abernathy, who got caught up in the spirit of the thing), were welded into a spiritual community here.

When he was in high school, Heinlein had made a $10 bet that man would be on the Moon before his fortieth birthday. He had missed it by a full generation—he should look up the boy, if he were still alive, and pay him that sawbuck.[35]

It was worth the wait.

As 9:30 A.M. approached, the zero hour and minute, there was the familiar tension that any rocket launch inspires. It was not real—it could not be; it was his living dream . . .

. . . and yet it was real, it was as real as could be. The rumble in the ground, the rumble in the air, the smoke, the flame, the seeing that enormous big thing lift up and go up in the sky and *know* it was going to the moon . . . .

You know, when that thing went off, there was a dead silence. There was over a million people there, absolute dead silence. And then, spontaneous cheering. Cheering that rumbled over miles, just like the rocket did. And then, separation. The same thing, dead silence . . . [sic] and then this rumbling of cheering, all over the place.

. . . There was just nothing like it. The whole crowd was euphoric. Somebody would step on your feet and you'd smile, you'd step on somebody else's feet, and they'd smile. It had a dream-like quality, and yet it wasn't a dream . . . .

I don't know if seeing God is an appropriate comparison, but I do feel as if—not as if—I *know* that seeing the first moon ship take off is the greatest spiritual experience I've undergone in my life.[36]

It was in orbit around the Earth before they got back to the motel for lunch. That afternoon, Atwood's jet took them to Miami, and they caught a commercial flight to New Orleans, where Heinlein was interviewed for the New Orleans *States-Item*:

On a stay in the Crescent City this week, world-renowned science fiction writer Robert Heinlein had this to say: "The human race has passed from adolescence to manhood. July 16, the day of the moon launch, was New Year's Day of the Year 1.[37]

It was a message he was to repeat many times, in many places.

The next day they went on to Houston for an overnight research stop. CBS television had asked him to be on hand the following day at their remote facility in Downey, California, for color commentary when the lunar lander touched down in Mare Tranquillitatis. CBS had platoons of astronomers and specialists of every sort on hand. Among the luminaries they had gathered together in Downey—and a like crowd in New York—was Robert "RNS" Clark, Heinlein's closest friend on the *Lexington*,[38] now working with North American Rockwell. Clark told Heinlein:

Our brief reunion, under such interesting circumstances, brought back wonderful memories. I was proud to be associated with my old friend Bob

Heinlein—the good shipmate over all these years—who had the savviness and the gumption to make radical predictions about space exploration.[39]

Heinlein was in his element for the entire forty-one and a half hours, through "*Eagle* has landed" and the incredible moment of "One small step"—*televised*! For all the hundreds of science-fiction stories about a landing on the Moon, *no*body had thought it would be televised and broadcast live back to Earth.[40] A staggering one billion human beings gathered around televisions and radios over the entire planet—until *Eagle* lifted and Apollo broke out of lunar orbit. "Robert was euphoric at the time," Ginny later recalled.[41] At intervals CBS arranged to have everyone fed; Robert and Ginny got a three-hour nap at one point, then back on the air.

The Downey stage facilities were fairly basic—no complicated backgrounds to match to Walter Cronkite's anchor desk in New York, which he was sharing for much of the time with Arthur C. Clarke (who had certainly earned a front-row seat) as the main "color commentator." Asimov and Bradbury also appeared as commentators.

Robert envied Clarke his ease and composure on camera.[42] Cronkite was obviously charged up and a little manic. Ginny told Lucy and Bill Corson about the event:

Bob says he [Cronkite] never comes to a complete stop, ending every sentence with an—"and," and then continuing. The camera cuts to someone he's asked a question of, and Walter goes right on and answers it, leaving the answeree with a mouthful of teeth. He even talks during prayers, etc. Great talker.[43]

But Heinlein's politician reflexes were back online: He rearranged his three-by-five cards of notes[44] and must have studied the coverage the way a platform speaker sizes up his crowd. He countered Cronkite's manic style by taking a slow and deliberate approach, making Cronkite slow down to his speed.

When Heinlein's time on camera with Cronkite came, at 8:29 P.M.,[45] July 20, 1969, Cronkite mentioned the "science-fiction quality" of the pictures coming in from the Moon—and how much like Robert's imagined Moon landing twenty years earlier, in *Destination Moon*. Robert appeared calm and composed—certainly more than he felt! The main point was that this was a glorious, inspiring first step—but it *was* literally "one *small* step"—a *first* step.

"This is a great day," he told Cronkite.

"This is the first day! . . ." This is the greatest event in all the history of the human race, up to this time. This is . . . today is New Year's Day of the Year One. If we don't change the calendar, historians will do so. The human race . . . this is our change, our puberty rite, bar mitzvah, confirmation . . . from infancy into adulthood for the human race. And we're going to go on out, not only to the Moon, to the stars: we're going to spread. I don't know that the United States is going to do it; I hope so. I have . . . I'm an American myself; I want it to be done by us. But in any case, the human race is going to do it, it's utterly inevitable: We're going to spread through the entire universe.[46]

On several occasions, he ignored Cronkite's interruptions and continued speaking, to the secret delight of the CBS studio crew. "[H]e did cut across Walter Cronkite's bow a number of times . . ." Ginny told friends when they got home. "But he was darned well going to have his say . . . The CBS people were cheering about him cutting Walter out!"[47] At one point, Heinlein ticked off another index-card point and remarked that designers and engineers could achieve even greater performance by designing the Apollo equipment for an all-female crew—a suggestion that appears to have shocked Cronkite. "Women in space!! Never!"[48] Cronkite continued to splutter and Heinlein pressed the momentary advantage, unperturbed. Cronkite must have realized how he would come off and gotten his prejudices under control enough to let Heinlein's continued remarks pass without objection. When Heinlein's segment was over and the camera went back to Cronkite, the crew in Downey broke into spontaneous applause. "I think they had never seen anyone who could flap Cronkite before."[49] But it might have been a futile gesture. It was Heinlein's impression that they had simply junked the entirety of the taped interview with him, without airing any of it. Only a small portion of the appearance was recorded in the memorial book CBS published of the coverage.

By the end of the Downey coverage, on July 20, 1969, they had been up forty-one hours with only a brief nap. The Apollo capsule had a four-day trip back to Earth. They had one day and night in Los Angeles—and two parties that night—before returning to Santa Cruz.

Among the accumulation of mail they found a letter from a fellow SF writer, Frank M. Robinson, with six questions to kick off an interview for *Playboy.* Ginny wrote that Robert was involved in a new book and couldn't.

He would have made the effort for *Playboy,* except that five of the six were questions about his colleagues, which he wouldn't answer, or about his own stories, which he would not discuss either. But the *Playboy* editors came back with a new slant that made it doable: They wanted him to concentrate on the Moon landing and space in general, since an anti-space lobby was already ramping up.[50]

That was different. He was in the mood to take up the bully pulpit. He and Robinson settled on the date of August 9, two weeks away, for Robinson to come down from San Francisco to Santa Cruz with a *Playboy* staff photographer. On the same day (July 26), Heinlein composed an open statement to begin to counter the custard-heads—essentially a press release:

Anyone who honestly has the welfare of the human race on his mind should be pushing hard for us to go ahead with space exploration as fast as technology permits. Anyone who thinks we should "stop spending all that money" on space and spend it instead on such problems as pollution, poverty, etc., simply does not understand the situation.

. . . I am not at all certain that Mankind can solve on this planet the problems of population pressure, nationalism, pollution of atmosphere and water, destruction of natural resources—you name it. All of them add up to the simple statement that we are breeding ourselves to death. BUT PUT A FEW COLONIES OUT ELSEWHERE AND THE HUMAN RACE GOES ON.[51]

The interview with Robinson took two and a half days—coincidentally the very days on which Sharon Tate and her friends were murdered, as well as Leno and Rosemary LaBianca, though the reportage of the gruesome "ritual" style of the murders had not hit Bonny Doon by the time the interview was concluded.

Robinson cooperated in keeping the interview on track, and the subject did allow Heinlein to develop some opinions that were not exactly politic: He was still steamed about Billy Graham's arrogance in verbally slapping President Nixon's wrist for saying the lunar landing was the greatest day in human history, and that provided the starting point for the interview:

I'm talking here about the people who have been against space travel all along and who didn't believe in it and so forth. Now it's done and they now look like the fools they are and I'm tired of being polite to them. Half a century of being treated like a madman for believing what was perfectly evident all along since the days of Sir Isaac Newton is long enough for politeness. They are, and were, fools, and I now say so . . . . [sic] except that false prophets never *do* shut up. Their smugness, their conceit, their vested interests and things that they are, their basic stupidity and lack of imagination won't let them shut up. They are at a dead end and don't know it.[52]

Robinson transcribed the eight cassette tapes of interview himself—28,000 words. Heinlein went back to work on *I Will Fear No Evil*[53] but directed that the honorarium for the interview be sent directly to the Ed White Youth Center Memorial Fund in Seabrook, Texas (White was one of the astronauts killed in the Apollo 1 capsule fire in 1967).

The book reached the "gargantuan" stage—over six hundred pages of manuscript—and the characters were writing themselves without consulting him at all, which bemused him. In response to a query from Blassingame, Robert left Ginny a note:

Please tell him that I am anxious to learn what the new book is all about, too—especially the ending.

I seem to be translating *Giles, Goat Boy* [John Barth, 1965] into late Martian.[54]

He put "The End" to it on September 3, after struggling with the last chapter for days.

This time I am attempting the impossible, I am trying to bridge the "generation gap." All I can say about it at this point is that anyone I failed to offend with *Troopers* and *Stranger* I will probably offend with this one. It is a 360° traverse of skunk spray. With any luck it will be condemned both by the SDS[55] and the John Birch Society.[56]

I Will Fear No Evil had come out at 165,000 words—and it was so odd, so unlike anything he had ever done, that it was very difficult to cut. Part of the reason it had ballooned so uncontrollably might be that he had written his first postmodern novel, that plays with several metafictive levels of storytelling. The events might be "real" for the world of the fiction, or they might be a dream/hallucination/delirium of a dying man, wholly or in part—but there is no firm evidence as to where the delirium might take up. The operation itself might be a dream-fantasy. The metafictive levels interlocked in such complex and deliberately ambiguous ways that cutting around them was a difficult project. It was a pioneeering work guaranteed to be difficult, guaranteed to be rejected by anyone who wanted "more of the same" from him.

Three weeks after finishing it, Heinlein had made several brush-pen passes through the manuscript, eliminating excess qualifying phrases, tightening up the language, catching typos. He had cut twelve thousand words out of the story and hoped to get another twelve thousand out[57] before he gave it to the typist in October, taking pass after pass through the manuscript. Anything that was going to be done on this one, had to be done now, as he wouldn't be able to think about the book for a long while: The fortieth reunion of his class at the Naval Academy was coming up in October, and this he would not miss. Even 140,000 words was too much.[58] "In my opinion," he wrote later, "that novel is about 30,000 words too long."[59]

Shaking up any entrenched intellectual position was a good thing in and of itself, and a worthy goal for any professional clown (as Heinlein sometimes referred to himself).[60] In furtherance of this goal, he was glad to give permission to Paul Kantner of the Jefferson Airplane rock group in nearby San Francisco to quote lines and passages from some of his novels in their lyrics.

I am pleased by your courtesy in asking permission. Bits and pieces from my stories have been used by many people around the country—names of groups, names of songs, parts of songs, names of churches, endless buttons, decals, etc.—and it is rare indeed for anyone to bother to ask my permission.

I would like to ask two things of you: a) When and if you do make such use of bits and pieces of my material I would like to have typed copies and (eventually) platter or tape. These items would wind up in the vault of the UCSC Library in the Robert A. Heinlein Special Collection, as the University of California is my archivist. I hope this is not too much trouble; the University Librarian seems to want *everything*.

Item b) is just for myself: I would enjoy having a *Jefferson Airplane* platter the jacket of which has been inscribed by all the members of the combo. I now own *Surrealistic Pillow, Bless its Pointed Little Head, Jefferson Airplane Takes Off,* and *Crown of Creation.* I think you have several more titles; if you can lay hands on one for me, I will appreciate it. And please tell Miss Slick that even if I did not enjoy her singing (I do!), nevertheless she would be an asset to any group just through her smile.

Coincidence: Our college-student-gardener Gene Bradley tells me he knows Marty Balin.[61]

In the mail was a disturbing letter from a young woman in Inyo County—out by the Mojave Desert near Los Angeles—who asked him for help: She and her friends were being chased by police helicopters. It was a crazed letter—the margins filled with decorative drawn fancies—and yet there was something about this one . . .

Ginny's instincts went into overdrive. "Honey, this is worse than the crazy fan mail," she told him. "This is absolutely insane: *Don't* have anything to do with it."[62]

But he placed a call to the Inyo County Sheriff's office and found that the bare outlines of the woman's story—"Annette or Nanette or something"[63]— were accurate: The police were chasing down a group of young people, but in answer to Heinlein's question, the sheriff's office told him drugs were not the issue—and that was all they would say.[64]

The "Annette or Nanette or something" who wrote to him was probably Lynette "Squeaky" Fromme—a name that would later become chillingly familiar as the trial of Charles Manson and his "family" got under way the following year.

The cut manuscript of the new book went to his typist on October 17. Six days later, they left for the reunion in Annapolis.

The reunion itself was raucous, boisterous as only sixty-five-year-olds revisiting their youth can be. For Heinlein, the highlight of the experience was being able to carry a drink into Bancroft Hall. "Never thought I'd live to see the day that this would happen!" Ginny remembered him saying.[65]

After the reunion they were invited to Norfolk for a visit *en famille* with Commodore Trottier, the U.S. Naval attaché in Rio they had met at the film festival earlier in the year, with his wife Rebel, and Dorace, their daughter. From Norfolk they went to New York for a little miscellaneous business talk: The rumors of a new Heinlein book after four years were generating a lot of anticipation in the publishing world, and, Ned Brown had told Blassingame, in Hollywood as well.

From New York they flew to Houston, to the Manned Space Center, where George Trimble gave them a very special treat: They were taken to view a Moon rock, a sample of several pounds of gravel and dust sampled on the Moon and brought back to Earth by Apollo 11: "It was un-Earthly!" Ginny told Poul and Karen Anderson. "It had little inclusions or bubbles. I thought they looked silvery, Bob says they looked golden. Beautiful!"[66]

They were invited to a big party in honor of Sir Christopher and Lady Briggs, who were on their way to join Sir Edmund Hillary climbing Mount Everest. The Heinleins stayed over in Houston. If the Moon rock had put them back into July's dreamlike state, the party was more surreal yet. Sir Christopher had been knighted because he handled the protocol arrangements for Prince Charles's investiture as Prince of Wales in 1958, but the gentle knight and his lady paled into insignificance in the presence of their daughter, the Honorable Jane, a BOAC hostess dressed in glittering London Mod miniskirt and spangled blouse, neckline plunging to the waist and giving clear testimony she was not wearing a brassiere.[67]

Heinlein discovered that a goodly percentage of the women there were fans of his, and he rapidly collected an entourage of beautiful Texas blondes and spent the remainder of the party trailing clouds of glories. He and Ginny were introduced to astronaut Jim McDivitt, whom they found "very witty indeed."[68]

They flew out to New Orleans the next morning and went to their usual hotel, the St. Charles, and were startled and outraged when the hotel required them to present identification before they would check them in—an impertinence virtually without precedent in the days before 1985, when the United States for the first time required citizens to carry identification. Robert and Ginny shook the dust of the St. Charles off their feet and taxied to the Ponchartrain instead, where they unpacked and settled in. This incident was so matter-of-course that it is not even mentioned in Ginny's various descriptions of the trip, though Heinlein wrote about it to Blassingame.[69]

Ginny went out shopping—her first impulse any time she was in New Orleans—and Robert took an unexpected telephone call from Eberhardt Deutsch (Hermann Deutsch's older brother, a distinguished lawyer), who had tracked them down at their hotel. "What are you doing there, young man?" he demanded of Heinlein.

When Ginny got back to the hotel, Robert told her to pack up again: Deutsch insisted they stay in his penthouse with him, complete with hot and cold running servants. He presented Robert with a gold-plated key to the penthouse and insisted they stay there whenever they were in New Orleans thereafter. Eberhardt Deutsch's insistence was a hard thing to resist in any case, and they surrendered.

Getting back to Santa Cruz was like being dumped out of a warm bed and back into the cold realities. "Kids, I'm spoiled," Ginny told the Corsons. "I hated to come back to doing my own dishes, even with a dishwasher, and as for cooking!"[70] And the retyping of the manuscript, Heinlein found, had not even been started in the three weeks they had been gone. Their typist was sadistic, Blassingame told him.[71]

Xerox delivered a behemoth of a copying machine on Armistice Day—too big to fit in any room except the living room, which, even so, it overwhelmed—but no paper. There was a nationwide paper shortage that year, and their paper stocks were on back order. Heinlein had no manuscript and no paper to make the ten copies of a five-hundred-page manuscript the two agents were clamoring for. Ginny feared she would have to retype the manuscript herself.[72] The rental fees on the copier were horrendous—

But they would not be driven into the poorhouse by it. The October royalty statements had arrived while they were away: The three existing editions of *Stranger in a Strange Land* had earned Heinlein in the last six months nearly $13,000 (nearly half a million copies). The new Berkley issue had sold out completely at a staggering $2.75 cover price.

When he began sending correspondence to the Archive at UC Santa Cruz, Heinlein became concerned about privacy issues. There were some pretty frank opinions expressed in some of his letters, particularly in his correspondence with Blassingame. And some of the people talked about unflatteringly were still alive, even thirty years later. The best interim solution to the problem seemed to be a restriction on public access to the correspondence. Rita Berner Bottoms (she had married Tom Bottoms earlier in 1969) drafted language for a restriction during their lifetimes.[73]

The first half of the *I Will Fear No Evil* manuscript came back from the typist a month later—very badly done, with far too many typos for a clean submission manuscript. He would have to make do with it, but Heinlein found a new typist and sent the rest of the book to her six days before Christmas 1969.

TROUBLE, WITH A CAPITAL "P"

On January 6, 1970, the Heinleins attended a special dinner given by the chancellor of UC Santa Cruz, Dean McHenry, and his wife Jane, in honor of Robert's old EPIC cronies, Judge Robert and Susie Clifton. The next morning, Robert told Ginny he had not felt well during the night. He had a chill and was shaking so badly he was afraid he would bite right through the glass thermometer.[1]

Ginny put him back to bed and talked their local GP, Dr. Calciano, into making a house call, since Robert wasn't up to the fifteen-mile trip into town. Before Dr. Calciano got there (after his regular office hours), Robert had another serious chill, shaking alarmingly for half an hour.

Dr. Calciano did not examine Robert, but concluded he had some kind of "unknown virus" and prescribed Darvon for the abdominal pain and Bonine for the nausea. Robert would get better on his own in a few days, the doctor assured Ginny.

But he didn't improve, and in fact was barely lucid for days at a stretch. Ginny fretted—and called Dr. Calciano every day for instructions and her daily brush-off.

On January 8, the *San Francisco Herald-Examiner* published an unbylined piece on the front page, claiming that the Tate-LaBianca murders committed last August were directly inspired by *Stranger in a Strange Land*. "Manson's Blueprint?" the headline screamed. "Claim Tate Suspect Used Science Fiction Plot."

A few days later, the same story, slightly revised, went out over the UPI wire services, copyrighted by Robert Gilette, a science writer for the *Herald-Examiner*:

**SAN FRANCISCO PAPER SAYS MANSON PERHAPS APED
SCIENCE FICTION HERO**

This was a bandwagon everybody in the press saw was worth jumping on. *Playboy* immediately wanted a comment on the Manson issue to print with the interview.

Robert was in no shape to make any comment at all (though later he was "very incensed about it"[2]), and, besides, he had made it clear at the time of the interview that he did not, as a matter of policy, comment publicly on his own work—ever. Ginny wrote a "furious letter"[3] to Blassingame:

> Will you also please tell Mr. [Hugh] Hefner that the *only* reason Robert agreed to be interviewed was *not publicity* for himself, but the offer of a forum to boost the space program. Publication of this interview in an early issue might have helped. As it is, the space program is in ruins, and Hefner is attempting to make something of what might have been by the use of *Stranger* and the Manson case. We will not go along with this. He has not bought himself a tame rabbit by that contribution to the Ed White Memorial Fund. He can take his [magazine] and stuff it, having first folded it until it is all corners. Under no condition will we make any public statement about the Manson case and *Stranger*. We consider Mr. Hefner's suggestion very much out of line and an invasion of our privacy. It's not a matter of *reluctance* to discuss Robert's work, but a downright refusal to do so, which has been a policy of his for a very long time.[4]

Frank Robinson recalled, "Hefner then personally pulled the article from *Playboy,* where it had been previously announced. Heinlein sent back their check but A. C. Spectorsky, titular editor at the time, returned the check to him."[5]

On January 19, Ginny finally had enough of Dr. Calciano's long-distance brush-offs. By that time Heinlein was very ill indeed. "He couldn't even keep water down," Ginny later remembered. "I had been in touch with the doctor, and finally called him and told him that in my opinion, Robert belonged in the hospital, that the so-called 'unknown virus' had *not* gone away, and to please send an ambulance."[6] They went to the Dominican Hospital in Santa Cruz. Dr. Calciano went off on a ski trip, leaving Heinlein's care in the hands of a substitute doctor he designated.[7]

On that same day, *Time* magazine ran an article based on the UPI story, titled "A Martian Model":

> . . . Most madmen invent their own worlds. If the charges against Charles Manson, accused along with five members of his self-styled "family" of killing Sharon Tate and six other people, are true, Manson showed no powers

of invention at all. In the weeks since his indictment, those connected with the case have discovered that he may have murdered by the book. The book is Robert A. Heinlein's *Stranger in a Strange Land,* an imaginative science-fiction novel long popular among hippies . . . .

According to one of the attorneys in the case, Manson was compiling a Martian-style list of enemies to be murdered.[8]

The attorney the *Time* piece mentions in the last paragraph was probably Los Angeles County Deputy District Attorney Steven Kay, an assistant prosecutor. The lead prosecutor, Vincent Bugliosi, investigated the claim, he later said, but decided it was worthless.[9] The bullet points of similarities listed between Manson and *Stranger* in both the UPI press release and the *Time* piece don't match up to the book very well—and sometimes don't even match up to the factual foundation Bugliosi was laying for the Manson Family trial. The book Bugliosi wrote, *Helter-Skelter* (1974), does not even contain an index reference for Heinlein or *Stranger.*

Kay's description in his own book (cowritten with Ed Sanders), *The Family: The Story of Charles Manson's Dune Buggy Attack Battalion* (1972) sounds like a thirdhand retelling of plot elements from a book he had never read himself. He characterizes *Stranger* as: "The story of a power-hungry telepathic Martian roaming the earth with a harem and a quenchless sexual thirst while proselytizing for a new religious movement."[10]

Heinlein did not see the *Time* article, or the clippings their friends sent them of the *Herald-Examiner* article and the UPI press release: When he was not unconscious, he was delirious, and the doctors—none of whom Ginny had ever seen before—would not tell her anything.[11] She had to reserve her energy for arguing them into installing an IV drip to relieve obvious dehydration.

On January 23, after a week of tests, Dr. Calciano came back and told her they concluded he had pneumonia—because his temperature was quite high. This startled Ginny, because he had *not* displayed any respiratory distress. It was seventeen days after onset; he had not eaten anything since then, or had any liquid in almost as long.[12]

This pushed Ginny over the edge. Robert's brother Rex Heinlein had urged her to get Robert out of the deathtrap there and get him to the Stanford Medical facility.[13] When one of the Dominican doctors suggested he might be better off at Stanford Medical Center, Ginny called an ambulance herself and rode with him to Stanford, forty miles away, not even stopping to close the house or grab a toothbrush.[14] Mr. Kessel, their local lawyer, told them they had an excellent lawsuit against Dr. Calciano (and in fact, Ginny later said that Dr. Calciano was sued by another patient for a similar treatment).[15] Ginny was holding herself together with Valium,[16] and "[Robert] was out of his head at the time, so I had to decide for him."[17]

At Stanford, he was admitted as a staff patient[18] with Dr. Anderson as his primary care physician.[19] Dr. Anderson and his colleagues were shocked at Robert's condition.[20] They got him settled in and started their own battery of tests. The next morning, Rex took Ginny back to Santa Cruz to pick up her car, which was still in the parking lot at Dominican Hospital, to pick up a traveling kit of clothes and so forth, and to put the house in mothballs and kennel the cats with the vet. She stayed with Rex and Kathleen while Robert was at Stanford.

When she got back to the hospital that morning, it was the chief of surgery, Dr. Harry Oberhelman, who told her Robert had an advanced case of peritonitis, a major infection in his bowels. It had started out with a hole in his intestines—a "perforated diverticulum." By now, however, it had been untreated for seventeen days (in a hospital!), and his chills and fever were caused by flourishing bacterial infections—septicaemia—and consequent blood poisoning—toxaemia. Bluntly, he was dying.

He was so weak, and his system was so compromised, that they couldn't operate until the infection was under control. They started him on massive doses of the antibiotic Kanamycin, and scheduled exploratory surgery for the following Monday, two days later.

Heinlein came to twice during this time. The first time, he was under restraint with tubes going into him, and a mask being placed over his face. He recognized this: It was his description of Johann Sebastian Bach Smith in the book he had just finished—a very odd coincidence. And then he went away, unconscious again. The second time, he woke up while being wheeled into surgery and muzzily recited to himself the last scene of the book.

A writer is far gone when he identifies with a fictional scene—especially when it is factual in essence at that time. I was briefly lucid; I knew where I was, who I was, and what was about to happen . . . .

. . . in that lucid time just before surgery I feared no evil; I was simply happy to be privileged to die aware of what was going on . . . [sic] and much intrigued by the odd parallel with the ending of my last story. I do not hold any certainty of personal survival—at most a vague hope because I am so acutely interested in all of this strange world.[21]

They split him open from sternum to pubic arch, plus cross flaps for access.[22] More than a foot of colon—probably where the perforation had developed originally—was just gone, tatters of rotting flesh. Dr. Oberhelman performed a left colectomy,[23] removed eighteen inches of intestine, and sewed (resectioned) the ends together. During the course of the operation, Heinlein received blood transfusions collected from five anonymous donors. Since Robert had an uncommon blood type (universal recipient—Ginny had the even rarer universal donor type), it was almost certain that his life had been saved by the efforts of the National Rare Blood Club he had come across while researching *I Will Fear No Evil*.

While Heinlein was still in recovery, their primary care physician, Dr. Anderson, took Ginny aside to tell her Robert would need special nursing care, more than the usual floor nurses could provide—round-the-clock nursing care on top of the operation and two hospitalizations . . . this last big royalty distribution was gone already. "I told him to order anything necessary," Ginny later told a friend. "Round the clock special duty nurses cost in the neighborhood of $900 a week"[24]—a staggering amount in 1969.

Heinlein gained consciousness—sort of—and began visibly to improve. The incision looked huge, but it was gradually healing up, and his front would eventually look, Robert said, like a road map of New Jersey.[25] On January 30, they removed the surgical drain tube. He was lucid enough the next day to give Ginny an unlimited power of attorney, to make all medical decisions for him, as well as business decisions.[26]

And then he lapsed back into a mental state that looked lucid only part of the time. Ginny had not had time for her usual careful grooming in several weeks by that time, and the roots of her hair were coming in white. For several years, she had been tinting it with henna for Robert's benefit.[27] It was time to let that vanity go; she was fifty-four years old, and she had gray hair, and that was that. She let the roots grow out white, and Robert did not recognize this white-haired woman who was in his room.[28] He teased her about this for years, saying,

> "When I woke up, they told me this woman is my wife. My wife has red hair. This impostor's hair is white!"
>
> After listening to Robert carrying on in this vein for a while, Ginny turned to him and smugly pointed out: "I may not be your wife, but I still have your power of attorney."[29]

Ginny tried to get him to eat something. On February 3, a week after the operation, he finally managed to get a morsel down—and it promptly came up again. This was *not* according to plan—and in fact he didn't look right at all: The antibiotic had induced uremia, and his kidney function shut down. The doctors changed antibiotics (manufacture of Kanamycin was discontinued later that year), and Heinlein began improving rapidly. Six days later, he was able to eat some cereal without becoming nauseous, and that was a triumph.

It was also a rarity: During February, anything he was able to wrestle down, more than a bite at a time, came right back up. He could not even keep water down: Only the IV was keeping him alive. But he was "present" for longer periods now, and Ginny was sometimes able to get away for brief periods, to round up the mail and keep the business affairs going. She answered the mail by his bedside, while he was dozing.

Ginny had completed the gargantuan job of copying and hand-collating all the copies of the new manuscript and mailed them off back in January. Blassingame found *I Will Fear No Evil* intriguing and unusual and was shopping it around for serial and trade issue. It was closer to a mainstream novel, Ginny thought, than anything like conventional science fiction,[30] but *Galaxy* magazine picked up the serial rights.

One day, collecting the mail and tidying Robert's desk, she discovered a notecard he had written early in January: "I do not want any editor to cut this story because they don't know how it's put together. Any cutting that's done on it I want to do it myself."[31] So it could only go to publishing houses that would agree—in writing—not to make changes or cuts. "Stubborn certainly," Heinlein later wrote, "and no doubt stupid at times—but I won't be a trained seal for anybody, at any price."[32]

When Robert was awake and becoming alert, Ginny took him out in a wheelchair for a change of scenery, which meant girl-watching. Miniskirts were pleasantly abundant. Gradually his concentration improved, and when he felt up to reading she brought him a new book: Philip Roth's *Portnoy's Complaint.*

Ginny was extremely grateful at the time—and Robert was grateful later, when he understood it—when Dr. Alan Nourse flew down from Seattle[33] and went over all the surgical and postsurgical care records with the physicians. He then interpreted it for Ginny in layman's language. He could not have survived at all, Nourse told her, if he didn't have the constitution of an ox to start with.

Robert's improvement was gradual, but over the weeks, it did become visible. On February 26, he kept down a small serving of breakfast eggs. But that was it. Five days later—eight weeks and six days since it had started—he had lost forty-two pounds; his weight was down to 132 pounds. But the doctors said that if he would feed himself, he could go home.

Ginny bundled him into the car and drove the forty miles very carefully. They were coming to a cold house with no food, but it was a welcomed homecoming: ". . . He cried as we entered the canyon and said, 'I never thought I'd see it again.' "[34]

Ginny got him to bed, with blankets and hot water bottles nearby, and drove downtown to buy fresh supplies. She also bought some small, colorful, transparent plastic boxes. She had a plan: He could keep down a mouthful at a time, so they would go with that. She made his favorite foods and placed bite-sized bits in the plastic boxes, which she kept by his bedside, along with rich eggnog made with ice cream. Every ten minutes or so, Ginny would require him to eat a bite or so.

It worked: He gained back half a pound within a few days, five pounds by the end of the first week. But it was not until nearly the end of May that he could muster enough interest in food to ask for second helpings of anything. The only real downside of the program was that it kept her tied to his bedside as thoroughly as the hospital had.[35] Between this and keeping the business going, it was the hardest-working period of her life.[36] She stayed up nights to answer the business mail and the fan mail, keep the books, and prepare the income taxes.

By the beginning of June 1970, Heinlein was up and around for most of the day and enjoying the scenery again. When she was able to get a gardener's assistant, Ginny started repairing some of the neglect and made special flower plantings for the view out Robert's bedroom window. He began combining his trips to Palo Alto with visits to the dentist to repair some of the damage done by extended severe malnutrition. His weight was back up to 160 pounds, and he swam every day in the pool he kept heated to blood-temperature. He also picked up some light correspondence on his own and started studying Yiddish, working from Leo Rosten's delightful The Joys of Yiddish.

It wasn't over: The doctors had found a large gallstone, and he had the removal operation to look forward to, and his original (1966) hernia repair to finish with a separate operation,[37] but the doctors were optimistic about scheduling these surgeries in the near future: He was clearly on the mend. "So toward the end of this year, I should have a bright new Robert, all patched up and repaired and in need of a paint job. What color shall I use?"[38]

His mind was still not as sharp as usual for him—but it was sharp enough to participate in business again. He realized how messy his estate would have been if he had died in January and executed a temporary will on June 1, taking their new accountant's advice to set up living trusts and move some of their investment assets into Keogh plans. The trusts bypassed the expense and delay of probate and gave Ginny permanent direct control over the business aspects of the writing. The Keogh provided an income when he was no longer generating new books.

Heinlein also made changes in his lifestyle:

> . . . this hooptydo has changed my attitude and pace; from now on we do what pleases Ginny and me. I have had printed a checkoff form for fan letters to be used Procrustean Bed style on 99% of the mail—unless a letter is really charming . . . No more speaking engagements for any reason whatsoever. No more help with theses, term papers, dissertations, no more visitors whom we are not truly eager to see. Et cetera. In the past ten years people have been whittling away at my life—and I have at last realized that I have no obligation to give *any* of these golden days to anyone but friends. I realized in the hospital that, had I died in February, none of these things that people want me to do would have been done—so I'm treating it as a rebirth and intend to live life to the fullest and not get bogged down in donkey work that I don't want to do, and no one has any real right to demand of me . . . .
>
> . . . I'll write a story occasionally and we'll spend the rest of our time gardening, traveling, playing with the cats. I find I don't like being a "public figure" and I'm putting a stop to it.[39]

The arrangements for this last book had been settled while he was still mostly *non compos mentis*. *Galaxy* was prepared to issue the book without cutting, in five installments, which pleased Robert.[40] Putnam's wanted it for trade issue. Ginny recalled: "I stalled off the contract as long as possible, but he wasn't up to doing any cutting, so I finally signed the contract myself by power of attorney."[41] Robert confirmed to Ginny what she had found on that notecard: He didn't want any editor to try cutting it who might not understand how the story was put together—and she was prepared to insist on this.

Walter Minton made only two editorial notes to Heinlein, and both would involve fiddling with the text. First, the middle sagged so badly that his editorial readers found themselves skipping over parts—especially the sections of interior dialogue; and, second, they had trouble taking the end as credible. Minton himself thought—as Robert had—that the amalgamated Joan-Eunice character was going insane (though he tried to keep the other possibilities open),[42] but *none* of the readers read it that way.[43]

Heinlein worked at editing the master copy, but found he couldn't effectively edit it; he was only able to cut a few words from each page.[44]

And he lost two pounds while he was fussing over the manuscript. Ginny put her foot down: Regression was *not* an option.

Minton had already scheduled *I Will Fear No Evil* for a fall 1970 release and was reluctant to pull it from his lineup and move in anything else. He offered more than double the negotiated advance—a staggering forty thousand dollars (at a time when the highest advances for science fiction books were five thousand dollars)—if Ginny would allow one of his staff editors to cut the book.

That was a *very* tempting offer: With forty thousand dollars in hand, they could liquidate the hospital bills and use the big *Stranger* royalties to pay for the follow-up and the two new surgeries . . .

But Minton had as much as told them already that his editors *didn't* understand the book. Robert's wishes were very clear on this point: He couldn't cut it himself, and he didn't want an editor to cut it. It was either publish it as written or withdraw it and find a publisher who would. Money is money, but money was not the last word.

Minton paid out the smaller advance—still a sizeable advance in 1970— and had the book set up in type as is, including the notice Robert requested for the National Rare Blood Club—the very least he could do to "pay it forward." Robert requested a set of galleys in June, to see if he could edit it before he went back in for surgery. His sense of humor had returned with his energy:

So I have been tidying my affairs lately . . . In the course of it I attempted to do two things: leave my cadaver to Stanford medical school and replace the many units of blood that I had been given in January, February and March. (I had paid for the blood of course but there still remains the moral obligation to pay back the blood tissue itself, especially as I am a "rare blood" type—us vampires have our protocols.)

a.   Stanford refused my body. Seems their morgue is overcrowded and they are having to keep the overflow in the Coca-Cola machine.

b.   Rare blood or not, the hospital blood bank refuses to accept blood from me; I'm too old.

This caused me to write a magnum opus in lyric form. Title: "Dust Thou Art, to Dust Returneth—"

Poor old Wobert,
He's just mud;
They don't want his body,
They won't take his blood!

(Compadre, doesn't the pity-of-it-all getcha? Right there? No, a little lower down.)[45]

He didn't get to surgery that summer. Both Robert and Ginny were in the swimming pool one day in June 1970, when Robert had an itch on his shoulder and asked Ginny to look at it. Nothing was visible then, but the next morning there was a red patch that looked like poison oak or poison ivy.

They were lucky to have an extremely able allergist-dermatologist locally, Dr. Holbert, who had been practicing from an iron lung for twenty-two years. It was not poison oak, he ruled. By the next day, the rash was developed enough to identify it: shingles.

Herpes zoster, the virus which causes shingles, is the same virus that causes chicken pox and causes similar red wales and scabby sores. It stays permanently in the nerve cells—usually from a childhood infection with chicken pox—and can flare up whenever you undergo bodily stress. Robert's attack was intercostal—in a band around the ribcage—on the right side and affected the use of his right arm. The pain was severe, topping even Robert's high threshhold: He said it felt like a blowtorch applied to his bare skin.[46]

The infection spread uncontrollably, and a week after the first sign, Robert's temperature spiked. Alarmed, Ginny went into overdrive. Dr. Holbert couldn't admit his patients to the hospital, because he couldn't attend them (the main reason he had switched specializations from surgery to dermatology). And in any case, Ginny did not want Robert going back to Dominican. She called Dr. Oberhelman at Stanford and got permission to readmit him there.

The temperature, they discovered right away, was not caused by the shingles: He had also picked up a systemic infection of *Staphylococcus aureus.* Golden staph is one of those very hard-to-control bacterial infections that are a doctor's despair. They put him immediately into "reverse isolation," requiring everyone who came in to see him to gown up in scrubs (in the June heat!) and sterilize their hands going into and out of the room.

Robert's immune system was compromised already, and the Staph infection hit him harder than the shingles. Again he could not eat and so lost weight and strength for the ten days they struggled to control the infection. The antibiotics did help with the shingles—the skin part of it, anyway. Gallstone surgery was out of the question for the moment.

By the time he got back home, the first installment of *I Will Fear No Evil* was appearing in *Galaxy*'s July number. He was too weak even to pick at the galleys from Putnam's. Ginny finished up the front matter and all the exacting details that go into making a book.

The painkillers seemed to take all Robert's energy. If left to his own desires, he would stay in bed all day every day, moaning occasionally.[47] Ginny chivvied him out of bed, and they played games eight hours a day, sitting at the dining room table, for months, from July to December—Acey-Deucey, the Navy man's dice game, and Robert taught her how to play Cribbage, the navy man's card game. For variety they played Scrabble. As with the last bout of recuperation, Ginny handled the writing business and financial affairs, answering fan mail. The new form letter Robert had designed in the spring seemed too cold and impersonal for her, and she found herself adding long handwritten PS's— which defeated the purpose of the multigraphed form letter.

By August Robert was strong enough and oriented enough to cooperate on his own, and Ginny began taking him out with her on short errands that wouldn't tax his strength too much. The scabs had fallen off from the shingles, leaving not-too-prominent red spots—but unremitting pain.

It was about this time that a manufacturer in Hollywood sent him a complimentary water bed, "a child of your imagination," referring to the mentions of water beds (and "flotation beds" and "hydraulic beds" and "tank beds") in *Stranger in a Strange Land,* adding "Your prophecy is enriching man kind's mental state 100 yrs."[48] Unfortunately, the house's flooring wasn't engineered to take a ton of water in a four-foot-by-six-foot footprint, so the water bed had to stay in its shipping carton.

I Will Fear No Evil came off Putnam's presses on September 3, exactly one year to the day after he had put "-30-" to the draft (though they would not generally issue the book until November). The *Galaxy* serialization was in its third installment, and the mail was already starting to come in on it.

Heinlein was able to help a little with the writing business now, though insomnia and lack of appetite from the infections kept him at a very low level. He had another inquiry about *The Door into Summer* as a film property, and Reed Sherman was anxious to negotiate an extension to his option, even though his script was only half done. George Pal wanted to look at "The Roads Must Roll" as a film property. If Heinlein never wrote another word they could keep going for a while just on film options and royalties on the older books. Provided the medical expenses didn't bankrupt them first. He still tired easily and had frequent bouts of post-herpetic pain that continued for months, until the nerve sheaths had completely regenerated. It is not uncommon for post-herpetic neuralgia to continue for a year—and there was a chance the pain would never go away. But he did gradually improve.

While Robert's health was improving, Ginny's was declining. She was seeing an orthopedist now at Stanford Medical Center, about her feet. The bursitis that had plagued her since her basic training in World War II had gone from occasional twinges to continuous pain: She almost could not bear to stand on her feet or to walk. The orthopedist bound her feet tightly with adhesive tape into a kind of postmodern go-go boot. That helped ease the pain some, though it didn't seem to improve the condition. By November, they were giving her cortisone injections directly into the heels—10 cc at a time, which is a massive amount of liquid to take by injection. The bruised feeling in the heels lasted about ten days, but the injections seemed to help, while they lasted.

The reviews on *I Will Fear No Evil* were very mixed—a sign, he took it, that he had achieved his desired effect of shaking people up and challenging preconceptions. Some of the reviewers actually complained about a lack of graphic sex in the book, one calling him "the Victorian Mr. Heinlein."[49]

On the other hand, the book got glowing reviews in specialty publications for Women's Lib (as the feminist movement was casually called at the time), flower children, and libertarians, so the reviews were a wash—and the book sold well: In fact, it went into a second printing even before release.

They continued gradually to do more, a bit at a time, and by spring 1971 were able to entertain Violet Markham, the Hawaiian friend they had met shipboard in 1954, with a jaunt to San Francisco, taking her to the Playboy Club—quite daring and even in 1970 quite chic. A local bookseller in Santa Cruz held an open autograph party, and Robert signed books for two hours while it poured outside. Ginny watched over him like a hen with one chick: He had to tread a very careful line between being as active as his strength allowed and overdoing himself into a relapse.

Now that the big book was out of the way, Ginny had time to do more business planning. Scribner had hung on to the rights to most of the juveniles for decades, without getting them issued in paperback, and now that Mac Talley had left NAL, the half-dozen Signet books (for which Robert owned the rights outright) had been allowed to go out of print.

Ace had recently paid Scribner an enormous amount of money for a five-year paperback issue right—an illegal one, in Heinlein's opinion, not permitted by the original contract—and Ginny and Blassingame had been able to leverage that to pressure Signet to reissue them or they would void the contract and take them somewhere else: Ace was very happy to pick up the additional paperback rights for their line, and the issue was so successful that Ginny actually had to defer some of the royalties into the next tax year. She blessed their new tax accountant, George Coleman, a specialist in writers, for keeping track of these matters—and Alan Nourse for referring him.

They weren't out of financial danger yet—but knowing they had extra money coming in next April took a load off Ginny's mind. Robert no longer thought about such things unless forced to, even when he was healthy:[50] He relied on Ginny's judgment and abilities.

Around Christmastime in 1970, Heinlein took to working regularly at his desk—a good milestone, suggesting he would be strong enough for surgery in a month or two. Ginny would have to have foot surgery, probably, too.

The other cloud on their horizon was Robert's mother: Bam had suffered a stroke and was not expected to make any real recovery. Robert's sister Louise made a trip out from Albuquerque to Arcadia, to help out and take some of the responsibilities off Mary Jean and Andy Lermer, who had been caring for her for more than twenty years. The boys in the family had been covering Bam's living expenses by quarterly whip-rounds, but when her Medicare coverage and insurance ran out, the expenses would go up drastically, and the Lermers could not shoulder the financial burden of a convalescent home for her. Her mind was not at all clear anymore; she required constant supervision for the rest of her life. Robert wrote to Mary Jean:

> Rex and I and Mother's other children will always be in debt to you for this. Perhaps someday there will be circumstances in which we can repay in kind but in the meantime all I can do is to acknowledge that there is a deeper debt beyond money.[51]

Rex and Larry were retired and on fixed incomes—and Clare was a college professor, limited, too, in what he could do to increase Bam's financial support. With the sales of *I Will Fear No Evil* taking off—12,000 copies sold by the end of February of the initial print run of 13,500—and the new revenues from the Ace paperbacks coming in, Robert and Ginny were ready to pick up the slack when Bam's Medicare and insurance coverage ran out.

But she surprised them all: By mid-February, Bam was mentally oriented and mostly recovered from the worst effects of her stroke.

Early in March 1971, Arthur C. Clarke came through the Bay Area on a lecture tour. On the 16th he had a lecture in Hayward and went home that evening with Dr. Barney and Mrs. Priscilla Oliver, who brought him to Bonny Doon the next day and were invited in for an impromptu lunch. Clarke spent three days with the Heinleins, which gave them as good a chance to get reacquainted as one can in such a short time.

The weeks and months passed. Heinlein had extensive dental surgery done. Reed Sherman negotiated a permanent film option for *The Door into Summer,* so he wouldn't have to keep extending it from year to year. Poul Anderson sent them a copy of his new book, *Operation Chaos,* with a pleasing dedication. The novelettes that made up the book had been appearing in *The Magazine of Fantasy & Science Fiction* for several years. The recent ones made the connection to Heinlein's "Magic, Inc." even plainer, and his redheaded witch heroine, also named Ginny, made the homage much more pointed—though, as Anderson pointed out, that was just a happy coincidence: The first couple of stories were actually written before the Andersons had met the Heinleins in person.

By June 1971, two cancers were discovered in rough patches of skin on Heinlein's face. He had a nose cauterization, and the next day the cancers were surgically removed. He had had good luck up to now, but he was nearly sixty-four years old and had to make another lifestyle change: He could go out in the sun only with a hat and long-sleeved shirts from now on.

For Heinlein's birthday festivities in 1971, the entire Nourse family came down from Seattle for a visit. Just four days later, John W. Campbell, Jr., died. This rock, this anchor, ridiculed and ignored for years, cut everyone in the SF community adrift by his sudden absence. He and Heinlein had not passed more than casual correspondence in many years.

Heinlein gradually recovered the use of his right arm, and it became possible to contemplate some down time for Ginny. The cortisone shots weren't helping Ginny anymore, and the Stanford clinics had finally come to a definite determination that nothing would help the calcification in her heels but surgery—and that would incapacitate her for three months, it was estimated, from surgery to full recovery. With help, Heinlein could fend more for himself now, and he decided to postpone his own surgery. Although getting and keeping help of any kind that far out in the country was always a problem, they were able to hire a housekeeper-cook and an exceptionally good outdoor handyman-gardener's assistant at the same time—a minor miracle.

Ginny went into Stanford Medical Center for a simultaneous operation on both heels, on July 23, 1971. She went home on crutches in a week. Heinlein made up the first of the "multicopied" general reports on their health they used in later years and sent them out to about thirty-five of their friends.

Ginny was not a good patient. Initially, she occupied herself sewing and knitting. Their neighbors, Eve and Pete Agur, had been helping out with shopping and some minor errands, for which Ginny wanted to express appreciation with handmade needlework—placemats and napkins she hemmed herself. Left to her own judgment, she would overdo it and have to take more codeine, then when the pain subsided overdo it again. Robert designed—and Leif, their gardener-assistant, built—a bed table like a breakfast tray, able to hold the weight of a portable typewriter (though it sagged in the middle, even reinforced).[52] She could plan the day's meals for the housekeeper and the gardening for the day for Leif (plus another list for Robert). The accumulated mail she piled on the bed beside her.

And, of course, no bed-office setup would be complete without a supply of kittens to randomize the papers.

Heinlein had an entertaining new project to occupy himself: Don Ellis,[53] a rock composer who had been commissioned to write a modern jazz-rock opera for the Hamburg Staatsoper, wanted the work to be based on a Heinlein story. Heinlein had always ranged as widely as possible in his writing, with more or less success in different fields. He would not pass up the chance to do an opera libretto. One of their local friends suggested "The Green Hills of Earth" as a likely property. He started work on the libretto on August 23, "The Green Hills of Earth: The Story of Rhysling, the Blind Singer of the Spaceways," and completed seven pages of verse libretto before running into a snag: Ellis didn't want "The Green Hills of Earth." He wanted *The Moon Is a Harsh Mistress*.

This simply would not work: "It's just too involved a story," Ginny later told Leon Stover. "To cut it would ruin it."[54] But Ellis was adamant: He wanted *The Moon Is a Harsh Mistress*—or nothing.

Nothing it would be, then. Heinlein refused to release the rights to *The Moon Is a Harsh Mistress* for this purpose. And that was that.[55]

Heinlein had one last chore to do before he could have the gallstone/appendix/hernia operation he had been putting off for more than a year: Joe Sencenbaugh, son of their best friends in Colorado Springs, was in the Colorado University Engineering School now and asked for an interview-by-mail for the school's magazine, *Colorado Engineer.* Heinlein was glad to help, but the questions Sencenbaugh sent him were really too broad for the size of the interview he had in mind and would take a skilled writer investing a lot of effort to get the answers into a form compact enough for the magazine's scale.

But this would be worth something *post* his *mortem*: This was an opportunity to start building an estate. Their new tax adviser had told them royalties usually tapered off to nothing five years after a writer's death.

Since I have no insurance and can get none, it is imperative that I create an estate in other ways—real estate, tax-exempt bonds, and—especially—copyrights and common-law rights which may be turned into copyrights . . . [56]

This surgery was scheduled for October 21—their wedding anniversary. Heinlein went into the hospital for prep on October 20. Afterward, he got up from bed without being pressured or cajoled, though he tired easily and slept a great deal during his recuperation. Dana Rohrabacher and David Nolan wrote on November 8, asking him to be present at an organizational meeting for a libertarian political party. Ginny declined for him: He was still too weak.

By December 13, he felt up to writing letters.

DA CAPO AL FINE

The "Da Capo" story had been on Heinlein's professional agenda, in one form or another, for more than thirty years. In 1972, he wanted to put a grand cap on the Future History—close it off with the science-fiction version of the Solar myth, a return to Lazarus Long's origins—which were, roughly speaking, Heinlein's own.

Ginny urged him to write up an embellished-dinner-table yarn about the Midshipman Who Was Too Lazy to Fail ". . . the most interesting story in the way of personal history that I had ever heard."[1] The tale—a modified version of the real-life story of his Annapolis classmate Delos Wait—was really "about" life wisdom that ran across the grain of the "received wisdom" of the culture, and that was a vein Heinlein had been working for decades.

He had tried, before, to get across the most important thing, and it was always—*always!*—misread. He had just gotten an intriguing fan letter from one Tim Zell, who seemed to "get" that "Thou Art God" in *Stranger* was not a permission, but instead a token of ultimate personal responsibility. Heinlein wrote, rather carefully, that he was *not* hostile to *Stranger* spinoffs like Zell's Church of All Worlds, as the canaille among the organized fans apparently had it. But he wanted to be explicit: Zell had lumped him together with Ayn Rand and Robert Rimmer, and these two were, he felt, different *kinds* of writers than he, who made their stories fit their propaganda purposes:

I was asking questions.

I was not giving answers. I was trying to shake the reader loose from some preconception and induce him to think for himself, along new and fresh lines. In consequence each reader gets something different out of that book because he himself supplies the answers.

If I managed to shake him loose from some prejudice, preconception, or unexamined assumption, that was all I intended to do. A rational human being does not need answers, spoonfed to him on "faith," he needs questions to worry over—serious ones. The quality of the answers then depends on him . . . .

But anyone who takes that book as answers is cheating himself. It is an invitation to think—not to believe.[2]

That letter might have helped give shape to Heinlein's thinking about the new book—most likely what *not* to do with his men-like-gods theme—as he began pulling what amounted finally to eight hundred of the three-by-five index cards of ideas he had collected over the years.

What makes a god, ultimately, is the power of choice. Taboos are about things that human beings overwhelmingly desire to do—or would ordinarily wander into just because of the circumstances of living—unless they were sternly prohibited by custom internalized so intensely that people enforce their own mental "cages."

But adults don't need mental cages. Adults choose their behavior, sanely based on their circumstances, taking direct and full responsibility for their own acts.

Taboos are for emotional children. "One of Robert's ambitions was to break every taboo," Ginny later said.[3]

In addition to "The Man Who Was Too Lazy to Fail," Heinlein had some novella-length stories to tell, as well as "Da Capo," which had grown into a novel-sized return to the world of 1912 or thereabouts, his own golden age, when he was five. He carpentered all these stories together by setting up a *Tale of the Thousand Nights and a Night,* with the ironic twist of Lazarus Long (in the Scheherezade role) telling stories to entertain the Caliph of the then Howard Families—in exchange for the privilege of *dying.*

Heinlein did one other piece of professional writing before he actually got the book under way—his first, except for the aborted libretto, in two and a half years. Arthur C. Clarke and Chesley Bonestell were collaborating on a big picture book about the "Grand Tour" of the solar system NASA had proposed for a robotic spacecraft mission when all the planets were on the same side of the sun at the same time and would actually line up in the 1980s. Clarke was writing the travelogue and Bonestell was painting the images for *Beyond Jupiter: The Worlds of the Grand Tour*—and Little, Brown, their publisher, wanted an introduction from Heinlein.[4]

He was then able to start writing his book on March 13, 1972—*Lazarus Long: Being the Memoirs of a Survivor.* Heinlein was no longer able to work sixteen-hour days, but he spent the time he needed to, to get it exactly right—and did not stop until he wrote "The End," 119 days later, on his sixty-fifth birthday. The collection of aphorisms he called "the notebooks of Lazarus Long" involved particularly finicky work, reworking the sayings he had collected over the years as they occurred to him, to get the phrasing just right. He split the collection in two and placed half on either side of the centerpiece of the book, to give the reader a gently comic break from the pathos of his story about adorable Dora.[5] "He did not hurry it—" Ginny later remarked, "tomorrow was good enough. But no one really ever knew about that careful work. He tried to make it look easy . . ."[6]

The book was more of a virtuoso turn than anything Heinlein had done before—some of the finest pure writing he had ever done, and full of clever tricks: The opening of the book, for example, was an almost word-for-word retelling of a passage from *Caleb Catlum's America* (Vincent McHugh, 1936), one of the books he had used in the 1930s and 1940s as a compatibility touchstone for new acquaintances. There was a section of blank verse tucked away in prose form at the start of one chapter—a trick he had picked up from James Branch Cabell.[7] The "Dora" story—"The Tale of the Adopted Daughter"—is tremendously affecting.

Oddly, the more Heinlein engaged with the science-fiction genre, the more his last two books had turned out like "mainstream" fiction, as the SF fans called it. Heinlein had always kept up with what was being published currently in general fiction, and his writing came more and more to bridge between general fiction and the specialized conventions of science fiction. This one had migrated over to that corner of literature occupied by Izaak Walton and Laurence Sterne—and nowadays by John Barth and Philip Roth. During the 1960s, the "death of the novel" had become an issue in literary criticism, and some critics thought that the satire—or as critic Northrop Frye termed it, the "anatomy" (after Robert Burton's 1621 *Anatomy of Melancholy*)—might be the next prestige literary form. *Stranger in a Strange Land* (1961) had been part of the satire/anatomy movement in literature (and note that Burton's *Anatomy* was Jubal Harshaw's favorite book), flanked by Joseph Heller's *Catch-22* (1961) and *Giles, Goat Boy* by John Barth (1966)—as had *Glory Road* (1963) and *Farnham's Freehold* (1964). *Lazarus Long* returned to the anatomy form to organize its complex structure—while remaining core science fiction with its extension of the Future History twenty-three hundred years into the future.

The interlocking structure of the book was so complex he started his first cut on the manuscript while Ginny read the draft. In three weeks of concentrated work, Heinlein cut the book from 960 to 850 manuscript pages and changed the title to the "punchier" *Time Enough for Love*. Once the book was sent to a professional typist, he and Ginny took the vacation they both had been needing for some time. An opportunity fell into their hands for an interestingly different sea cruise.

Richard C. Hoagland was an energetic young man, a former science advisor for CBS at the time of the Apollo 11 coverage. At the end of July in 1972, Hoagland was promoting a Caribbean cruise in December to see the last of the Apollo missions launched. Apollo had achieved its purposes, and it was time to move on to the next goals—a permanent orbital station, a permanent lunar colony—perhaps a manned mission to Mars. This last Apollo launch would also be special because it was to be the only night launch in the program. Hoagland wanted to get a stellar group of scientists and journalists, science-fiction writers, and fans together, standing off the Florida coast when that Saturn V lifted off in the dark of night, the whole event surrounded by a seminar on space flight.

It was a grand idea—inspirational, educational, and in itself newsworthy. Arthur Clarke and Isaac Asimov both supported the venture, Asimov with a small cash investment. Hoagland wanted Heinlein as a speaker/lecturer, but Robert and Ginny decided to invest in the project, providing two thousand dollars in seed capital on September 6, 1972. After the launch, *Statendam* would go on to several ports in the Caribbean—and they would wind up in New York for Christmas and be on hand for the contract negotiations for the new book.

Early in August, Blassingame forwarded a letter from the Superintendent of the U.S. Naval Academy, Vice Admiral Mack, asking Robert to speak in April 1973 to the entire Brigade of Midshipmen plus faculty for the third annual series of public figure lectures inaugurated in honor of James Forrestal, the wartime Secretary of the Navy.

There could not be greater personal validation—particularly when Robert discovered that the Superintendent did not seem to be aware he was an Academy alumnus:[8] The request had come purely because of his status as a public figure. He said nothing,[9] but when the Admiral's assistant, C. M. Walter, wrote asking for a photo and bio, the cat was out of the bag. Heinlein regularized the situation by becoming a Life Member of the USNA Alumni Association.

Some of the luster wore off for him when he asked what subject they wanted him to talk about, and Commander Walter suggested he talk about how science fiction had changed over the years and its impact on the country.[10] Heinlein was "inside" the genre, and perhaps he could not appreciate what was plain to outsiders: Science fiction's conversation about technology of the future had become the vocabulary for how to think about science and technology in the now. Science fiction had even become an instrument of policy—probably why Herman Kahn had asked Heinlein to participate in his think-tank scenarios.

But still, Robert was not satisfied with the prospect of speaking only in his capacity as a professional clown. He would do as they asked—but he had a few miscellaneous observations to make in the leftover bits of time.

Robert and Ginny flew to New York, boarding *Statendam* on December 4. Holland America had put an announcement of the cruise in the Travel section of the November 19 *New York Times,* touting "a series of symposiums chaired by Capt. Edgar Mitchell,[11] and featuring such speakers as authors Arthur C. Clarke, Isaac Asimov, and Norman Mailer."[12]

It does not seem to have done the trick: There were, indeed, scientists and journalists and science-fiction writers aboard, but the ship was largely empty—only 100 paying passengers on a ship meant for 650. The conference administration was not as well organized as the ship: Meetings were called and canceled at a moment's notice, panelists were often unprepared, and the quality of the discussions ranged from incisive to whimsical.

Robert and Ginny socialized as much as possible, renewing acquaintance with friends and colleagues—Isaac Asimov, Marvin Minsky, Fred and Carol Pohl, Ben Bova,[13] Theodore Sturgeon and his wife. Television personality Hugh Downs was there acting as master of ceremonies.[14] Heinlein was granted courtesy of the bridge as an old Navy man. He was fascinated by the improvements in navigation technology since his day—since his last major cruises—particularly the real-time photoprints of weather satellite views.[15]

Norman Mailer and Katherine Anne Porter were on board as literary celebrities. Mailer had written a very arresting coverage of the Apollo 11 trip in 1969 and he was covering the last Apollo as well. He seemed also to have the same kind of remarkable memory Robert had, as he greeted Ginny by name, recalling them from a casual meeting years ago.[16] Unfortunately, some of the things he had to say were a little "out there": The Apollo missions might be disturbing the delicate vibrations of the "thanatosphere,"[17] he said, out beyond the biosphere. The reporters lapped up the drivel, and the *New York Times* report of the trip called him the "star" of the cruise—aside from the launch itself. When Mailer said that NASA had managed to make the most exciting event in human history boring, he may have had a point—but he did come down on the side of the angels: "I believe finally and fundamentally in the need and the necessity for us to voyage into space, for I think it is part of our human design, part of our inner imperative."[18]

Porter had been commissioned by *Playboy* to cover the night launch—somewhat unfortunately, as the journalists could not pass up unpleasantly whimsical references to her 1962 bestseller, *Ship of Fools.* Porter and Heinlein were distantly related through Daniel Boone, but the eighty-two-year-old writer was standoffish, and the fact that she had in her day been both a Communist sympathizer and a personal friend of Hermann Goering was not a combination that might have encouraged fraternization.

But they had the launch, and it was a glorious thing—"incomparably beautiful at night," Heinlein called it.[19] On December 6, *Statendam* anchored seven miles off Cape Kennedy. The launch was delayed two hours, but at 12:33 A.M. on the 7th, the flame flickered silently and illuminated from within the clouds of vapor venting from the launch vehicle, in flashes of brilliant white and orange. Slowly and silently it rose in the sky. "The lift off was every bit as fascinating as it had been for [Apollo] 11, but much much more spectacular! It was as if the sun had risen at midnight, but in the west, not in the east."[20] The Saturn V glowed golden and "lighting the night into a copper-colored semi-day,"[21] "making droplets of vapor glow like trillions of tiny stars."[22]

A full minute later, the roar of the rocket engine reached the ship like a physical blow, making *Statendam*'s hull drum with the sheer energy of it.[23] Porter talked about the experience in a newspaper interview: "I came out of a world so primitive you can scarcely imagine it. We barely had gaslight in New Orleans when I was a girl. When I saw them take off I wanted with all my soul to be going with them."[24] Amen. They had the earthbound next-best thing that evening in the ship's theater: a showing of *2001: A Space Odyssey.*[25]

The next day, *Statendam* lifted anchor and made for the Caribbean part of the cruise. Several new passengers and participants had joined the ship in Florida, and they picked up more in St. Thomas—including, particularly, astronomer Carl Sagan, with his wife Linda. Sagan brought with him poster-sized blow-ups of the photos that had just come in from the *Mariner* 9 mission that was mapping the surface of Mars for the first time.

Heinlein was scheduled to give an interview for Canadian television at the same time as Sagan's lecture, so Ginny went ahead to catch the first half. Heinlein joined her midway into the lecture, and they had a chance to talk with Sagan afterwards.

Things sorted themselves out socially on the ship. Ginny, who had the perspective of a passenger rather than a program participant, pointed out that the speakers tended to stick together in tight social groups, which meant that the paid attendees rarely got a chance to meet them. So Robert announced a mixer at about the halfway point of the cruise and undertook to make it happen, taking on the host role and breaking up the tight knots of speakers-speaking-only-to-speakers, and introducing the celebrities directly to the paying passengers. The atmosphere on board the ship changed as of that impromptu mixer, and the thing became an emotional success for everyone.[26]

With the launch behind them, the ship went on to San Juan, Puerto Rico, which was their principal Caribbean stopover. The seminars wobbled chaotically on. Heinlein's talk had been postponed until the 11th—the day the *Challenger* lunar module was to separate from the *America* command module in lunar orbit and land at Taurus-Littrow. His talk—listed in the program as "The Apollo Flights Viewed Historically"—was scheduled to start at 2:30 P.M., during the radio coverage of the descent, and he was asked while he was making his way to the platform to keep his presentation down to fifteen minutes. He had a prepared presentation timed for thirty to forty minutes: He had to cut and paste in his mind as he finished mounting the stairs to the podium. Small wonder Isaac Asimov characterized his talk as "wandering."[27] They broke for the radio coverage of the touchdown, and resumed afterwards.

Statendam made its way back up the Atlantic coast, docking in New York on December 13. The new book manuscript had not reached Blassingame's office yet, though the university copier in Santa Cruz had mailed it out on the 10th. The Heinleins were planning to be in New York for at least a couple of weeks, because they had found a gala way to go home: The P&O lines had a brand-new vessel on its maiden voyage in January, *Spirit of London,* for the Florida-to-San-Francisco route, going through the Panama Canal.

Challenger lifted off from Taurus-Littrow on December 14. It was scheduled to splash down in the Pacific on December 19—two days after the first copy of *Time Enough for Love* arrived in Blassingame's office. This book was so large—and, the editors agreed, so tightly written[28] that it could not realistically be cut—that they would have to issue it at an uncompetitive price. But Walter Minton, who was always eager to experiment with the newest technical methods, thought they could use computerized typesetting to keep the costs under control.

The immediate business concluded, Robert and Ginny then spent the remainder of their two weeks on the East Coast enjoying the decadent diversions offered by the Big Apple and environs (loosely defined), including a relaxed day with the Trottiers on the river in South Carolina and Christmas in New York. As Christmas presents, Ginny fed his recent interest in the immediate pre–World War I era by giving him a 1910 Sears catalog and a book about old—really old—cars.

In January they flew to Florida to catch the *Spirit of London* on its maiden voyage. Ginny was fascinated by the side jets that moved this brand-new ship *sideways* out of its slip. Robert was pleased with the ship's exceptional stability—and the same state-of-the-art navigation technology he had seen on *Statendam*.

The *Spirit of London*'s route took her through the Panama Canal. They had a little rough weather coming up the West Coast. Robert didn't succumb to seasickness, but he did pick up a case of the London flu. After clearing customs, Ginny got Robert bundled into a car and drove straight home, to a dismaying stack of mail and a dead garden (there had been a solid freeze, rare for the area, while they were away). Ginny promptly came down with the flu as well.

Heinlein had additional cause to be miserable when the galleys came from Putnam's: They were carbon copies, very odd, smudged and difficult to work with, and between the computer typesetting and a raft of errors added by a copy editor, Heinlein had to ask for page proofs to work with them at all. For this book he had to work very carefully. Clean manuscript, no revisions at all once it was in type, even though a limited number of revisions were permitted by contract. He studied Skillin & Gay's *Words into Type* and Putnam's house style sheet so he could anticipate the copy editor's objections and mark any variance from house style with "stet." When he was done with the galleys, they were the cleanest set he had ever seen.[29]

In February Heinlein began assembling his notes for the Forrestal lecture he had to give in two months. He had set himself a difficult task this time, because he did intend to comply with Cmdr. Walter's suggestion and talk about life as a freelance writer—but he had some things to get off his chest, some important ideas that had been percolating for decades.

In *Starship Troopers* (1959), he had tried to articulate the learning curve for a teenaged boy who went from mouthing platitudes to understanding deep within himself why his values might require of him that "last full measure of devotion." His "dead serious (but incomplete) inquiry into why men fight"[30] had used a style of argument he had probably picked up from Philip Wylie's wartime *Generation of Vipers* and *An Essay on Morals* (1947)[31]—one that starts with a factual observation instead of moral or religious explanations.[32]

Heinlein had gotten letter after letter from servicemen—in *all* the services—telling him they had found *Starship Troopers* personally very meaningful, that he had articulated something of what they felt emotionally about duty and personal honor and could not articulate for themselves. In the last few years, this mail had been taking a dismaying turn, of disillusionment. Robert traced this first to the demoralizing effects on the country as a whole of the undeclared and maddeningly inconsistently prosecuted "war"/"police action" in Vietnam—but also to the "liberalizing" going on now in the armed forces. He would give any help he could to these earnest young people, to help them recapture their sense of purpose and proportion.

It was hard to argue that the actual decisions under which these men operated were rational—or even sane!—but he could affirm for them that the task itself was worthwhile and that it made sense in the larger scheme of things. Perhaps he had at last worked out a way to articulate the thoughts prompted by a friend's comment on the "generation gap" four years earlier:

> "My generation was patriotic," she wrote, "but the present generation thinks patriotism is a joke."
>
> I think she may be right. Oh, I know young people who are fervently patriotic—and people even older than I am who are downright disloyal—but statistically she may have put her finger on the great difference. And the hell of it is that there seems to be no way to get through to them the idea that patriotism is not just irrational sentimentality but an indispensable survival factor as practical as good brakes and good tires—and that a nation that loses its patriotism is on the skids and headed for disaster.[33]

Patriotism is a social manifestation of a biological imperative, he went on to say, as useful and as finely honed by evolution as the opposable thumb or the camera eye. Patriotism is a pragmatic tool of evolution.

The first draft of the lecture was finished at about 8,300 words—more than twenty minutes over the time he had available. All the other business was shunted aside. Scribner was seeking some releases from him, and Heinlein was still steamed over the casually careless way they were treating him as a cash cow now that they had decided to get on the paperback bandwagon, after depriving him of the huge paperback market for decades. It would all have to wait until they got back—and he would have to handle it himself: When they got back, Ginny was going to start a long and painful course of periodontic surgery.

They arrived in Annapolis on April 4, 1973, the day before the lecture, and were put up at the Annapolis Hilton—except that they arrived late and found their reservation had been given away, despite a hold-for-late-arrival. They were directed to a motel on the main thoroughfare, with trucks rumbling by all night that kept Robert awake. Early in the morning, Ginny took him over to the Maryland Inn for breakfast. She rented a quieter room there and put him to bed to get some sleep. Later that day they made rendezvous with the Superintendent.

Robert's mind was, naturally, on his speech. He had memorized the text, but he had a printed manuscript with him, and he had made up three-by-five slips for his jacket pocket, with the bullet points of the speech, so he could recover quickly if he lost his place.

They took him to a huge outdoor tent, which was the temporary Field House. Half the interior was curtained off with canvas, and the four thousand plus seats were arranged in a horseshoe around the podium. He could not project enough to be heard—which meant he was tied to the microphone as well as the clock. The lecture was unofficially tape-recorded by one of the spectators.

The midshipmen seemed interested and applauded at the right places. In the first part, working into his subject, he was surprised at the cynicism he found in some of the responses from his young audience.[34]

> For example, when Heinlein asks the question, "Why are *you* here, mister?" a cadet on the tape can be heard to reply, "To get a free education." Heinlein replies with some asperity, "Better not let an officer hear you say that." In the transcription, this exchange is trimmed to "Don't answer that; it's a rhetorical question."[35]

The rot had set in, even here. But that made the second half of his message all the more urgent, and he trimmed what he could from the part about freelance writing.

The midshipmen were all on their best behavior, yet as he worked into his dithyramb on the evolutionary role of patriotism, and their important part in it, they did not catch fire as he expected.[36] As he built to his peroration, telling the story of the young stranger in Swope Park, when he was five years old, who sacrificed his life to save that of a young matron, he became caught up in the emotions of it: It was his own first encounter with the sublime, and powerful to him yet.[37] He was overcome and choked up as he delivered the closing lines of the story:

> *This* is how a man dies.
> This is how a *man* lives.[38]

He was blinded by his own tears as the applause broke. Cal Laning, who was by then so deaf he had not actually caught enough of the speech to follow its progression, came on stage to help him off. He thought Heinlein was bitterly disappointed at their audience "sitting on their hands" for his homily on evolution and patriotism, Darwinism and duty.[39]

The truth was somewhat different. Robert and Ginny later found out there had been a power outage and a serious breach of discipline in Bancroft Hall the night before—a race riot!—that had been hushed up so that nothing reached the papers.[40]

Sometimes seed was sown on stony ground, but you sow it anyway.

The next day they were given a private tour of the facilities. April was in the middle of instruction, and he got a chance to observe some of the teaching and to discuss the revised curriculum. Since his day, the USNA had changed over from a technical college to a first-rate academic institution. Heinlein was suitably impressed: "The present Brigade is now receiving a far better education than we got *without* neglecting the professional subjects necessary to an efficient junior line officer," he told his own classmates in his *Muster Notes* for the next year.[41]

The Superintendent's luncheon for them was much less formal than the prelecture dinner had been. One Lt. (Miss) Johnson told him she taught *Stranger* as part of her class in The Contemporary Novel. "That floored me," he wrote to a friend. "I know that book is all over the campuses but to find it being used in teaching at the N.A. I *never* expected."[42] He sat in on that class, that afternoon.

And then they went on for a week at Pennsylvania State University. One of Robert's publishers had arranged for a long interview to appear in the *New York Times Magazine* as a profile in the fall and had commissioned the work from Phil Klass—an esteemed colleague who wrote under the pen name of "William Tenn."[43]

Heinlein knew that the interest in *Stranger* was still peaking on campuses, and both he and Ginny knew he would be worn out after the Annapolis visit, so he had asked Klass to keep the meet-and-greet to a quiet minimum. But the invitations had apparently gotten out of hand: At one point he noticed some of the *gravitas* of the university sitting on the floor by his chair, literally at his feet.

Klass and his wife, Fruma, were greatly amused at Robert's characteristic gusto. "Would you like to hear the paper I read at Annapolis?" Heinlein offered, and immediately went on, "Of *course* you would!" Klass recalled that, as he read again his peroration, he was overcome again with emotion:

—tears were rolling down his face, I mean he was *sobbing* as he read about people who died doing their duty for the country.

And Fruma said to him at one point . . . "When you read that paper at Annapolis, did you cry, too?" And he said, "My dear lady, when *else* should a man cry?"

God damn it! He was such a huge figure. Such a huge—so much larger than life.[44]

The week at Penn State allowed them to get their bearings before moving on to New York for business. Putnam's intended to release *Time Enough for Love* in June 1973—and still no one was (very) nervous about the incest: It was the cover price they were worried about.

Publisher's Weekly commissioned another old colleague, Alfred Bester, to do an interview with him, which would come out as publicity for the new book. Bester was best known for his seminal SF novels *The Demolished Man* (1953) and *The Stars My Destination* (1956), but he had been in the business exactly as long as Heinlein.[45]

Ben Bova also called on them, socially, but it turned into a professional meeting when he heard about the Forrestal lecture and asked to read the manuscript. Bova had been hired to edit *Analog* after John Campbell's death. Intrigued by the Darwinian argument in favor of patriotism, Bova proposed printing the whole lecture as a "guest editorial."

Heinlein had never expected to have this particular piece of work published—but he would pass up no opportunity to get the patriotism/evolutionary message disseminated. He marked in by hand the additional cuts he had made on the fly and gave Bova the reading copy he had brought with him.

They were home before Easter. Ginny started her dental work. Her dental problems over the years had reached the point at which ordinary dentistry would no longer fix the troubles, even temporarily: Her jaw was crumbling and would not even take fixed bridges. Robert discovered, in a lightning round of research, that a new procedure offered hope: They could use bone transplants to rebuild the jaw, then bridgework would be enough to supplement the sound teeth that remained.

The main drawback was the four to six months of multiple surgeries at the University of Pennsylvania while the bone transplants "took"—but it turned out there was a capable periodontist in San Mateo, about fifty miles north of Santa Cruz. Experimental dental surgery, without insurance, is . . . *expensive*— and their medical expenses had been going *up* as Medicare kicked in, not down. In San Mateo, Ginny would have a team of three specialists. Drs. Robinson (periodontics), Burns (endodontics), and Jeffrey. Sometimes, if the procedure was not too complicated, the doctors allowed Robert to observe.

They were not able to get any real domestic help. Robert had to be house-keeper, chief cook and bottle washer, and lavender extraordinaire—bo'sun tight and midshipmite and crew of the captain's gig.[46] He struggled gamely with the details, instead of going to work on another book right away.

The first major surgeries were the hardest on her. Gradually, she was able to help out more and took over particularly the cooking—probably in self-defense. And just in time: After his bout with peritonitis, shingles, and gallstones, Robert's metabolism had shifted—not entirely surprising. It was something of a wonder, in fact, that it hadn't done so when he was in his fifties. Perhaps the hormones and glandular extracts had given him a few more years of middle age. But during the writing of *Time Enough for Love* his blood pressure had gone disturbingly high—180/130—and his serum cholesterol and triglycerides were way up, as well. For this, he was seeing a new internist, Dr. Colin MacKenzie, who put him on medication and a very strict diet.

This diet was even more of a headache than the food allergy regimen twenty-five years before. Literally *all* of Heinlein's favorite foods were off the menu—but Ginny figured out how to cope with the restrictions, exchanging tips and recipes with friends who had gone through much the same thing before them, planting berries and reading every book on the subject she could find. She even went on the diet along with him, and gradually their tastes adjusted. Within a very few months, his blood pressure was below the 120/70 magic numbers, his serum cholesterol and triglycerides were down to reasonable levels, and he had shed twenty-eight pounds. Heinlein was exultant:

> Chilluns, I feel healthier than I have for forty years. I feel *young*. Every bite of the skimpy, very limited diet I must follow tastes like gourmet cooking . . . I'm happy all the time and filled with vigor and find working from reveille to taps a pleasure—while being driver for Ginny to San Mateo 2 or 3 times a week and sometime nurse & cook & housekeeper & household shopper I am nevertheless working on 5 books and expect to see every one of them published and perhaps more to come—when I had been thinking since 1969 "Maybe this one is my last." But now I feel as if I could go on working forever.[47]

Time Enough for Love came out in June 1973 and within the first week of its release was on the bestseller lists in Seattle and Los Angeles—the first time he had ever hit the bestseller list for a hardcover initial release (*I Will Fear No Evil* was on the paperback list, and *Stranger* had been on the paperback list for years). By the end of the month, it was on the New York bestseller list.

Putnam's sold out the entire first impression, ordered a second and sold that out too, and was in the third reprint order—though, the lapse of time before the second printing could get to the stores caused the book to fall off the best-seller lists, and the slower, steadier sales after that never developed enough momentum to climb back on. Just before the initial release, *Analog* carried an excerpt from the book, "The Notebooks of Lazarus Long," as a special feature.

The book came out at about the same time as Arthur Clarke's book for 1973, *Rendezvous With Rama,* and the two books were reviewed in lockstep with each other. *The New York Times* gave them a midweek review as "Books of the Times" on August 22 that was curiously ambivalent about *Time Enough.*[48] A month later, the Sunday *New York Times Book Review* featured a complimentary and much more insightful review by Ted Sturgeon: "Remember, too, that it hurts a man to think through and past his own conditioning—but nothing will stop [Heinlein]—ever. I like his new novel less than the celebrated *Stranger,* but love it more."[49]

ON TO OTHER THINGS

Editors and publishers had always sent Heinlein manuscripts hoping to get a comment to use on the book jacket. Most of the time he was able to talk himself out of doing it, although sometimes a little treasure fell into his lap that way: He always appreciated Ted Sturgeon sending him the galleys for Edgar Pangborn's *Davy* (1964), for instance. For friends and acquaintances he often put a lot of work into technical critiques. One of their friends in Colorado, Dottie White, had written a novel in 1960 about an interracial marriage—from personal experience. Her Negro husband, George White, was a major at one of the local Air Force establishments at Colorado Springs. Heinlein had given her what advice and help he could, and tried to help her find an agent for the book. In 1973, Arthur Clarke's publishers wanted a puff for the paperback issue of *Rendezvous with Rama,* and he was happy to oblige with that one.

In June 1973, Jerry Pournelle sent him a *gigantic* manuscript for a science-fiction novel he had written in collaboration with Larry Niven, *Motelight,* and Heinlein girded up his mental loins for another job of analysis and technical critique. As he read, though, he found himself turning pages, getting involved with the characters and the story. But it had a major fault *as a book* that urgently needed to be addressed.

He spent three days going through the manuscript almost line by line, and finally, on June 20, sat down at the typewriter to frame his critique. His first note to the authors was:

"1. This is a very important novel, possibly the best contact-with-aliens story ever written . . . . (best aliens I've ever encountered, truly alien but believable and one could empathize with them, every ecological niche filled, total ecology convincing, etc.—grand[.])"[1]

With Pournelle, he knew he could be straightforward and even blunt—and there simply was no "delicate" way of saying some of the things he thought needed to be said—

> We are in a highly competitive market, battling each year against not only thousands of other new novels but also TV and a myriad other things . . . in the late XXth century one simply cannot use up 30,000 words before getting down to business with the main story line. . . .
>
> How to correct the major fault? I don't know. It's your story. But cutting the bejasus out of those [first] 100 pp would help. It is all featherdusting, not story, and you need to determine just what supporting data must be saved to keep the plot intact—then see how much of it can be tucked away into corners *after* page 100, and what is left that *must* be on stage before page 100—and what is left be told in such a way as to grab the reader and pull him along, not lose him.[2]

Heinlein's experience with this kind of hard-love advice was not encouraging: "People seldom take advice—and this advice you did not ask me to give. I shan't be offended if you don't take it; I hope that you will not be offended that I proffer it."[3]

He sent off the long letter to Niven and Pournelle and turned to another public-relations chore on June 26, 1973—another newspaper-article interview, this time by telephone. The interviewer, J. Neil Schulman, was a young journalist in New York, clearly one of the "New Right" libertarians *The Times* had been touting for the last few years, bright and curious, and thoroughly immersed in the movement literature—and in any case Robert felt the need metaphorically to walk up and down the Earth, and to associate with a stimulating wide variety of people and viewpoints.[4]

> [I]solated as I am in this study far out in the mountains, if I do not reach out through my typewriter to cultivate new friendships, I will inevitably grow old and crabbed and lose touch with the human race . . . and thereby become not only useless to myself but incapable of writing copy worth printing. If I am to stay young in my mind while my body grows older, I *must* seek out new human relationships.[5]

On June 26, Schulman phoned to discuss the interview, and Heinlein gave the most "personal" interview he had ever done—far more material than Schulman could use for his article, so he willingly granted permission to use any "left-over" material for a piece in *New Libertarian Notes,* one of the new libertarian magazines that had been springing up. One subject in the news at the time did not make it into this interview: That summer of 1973 the Nixon administration began melting down in scandal. Vice President Spiro T. Agnew was investigated for extortion, tax fraud, conspiracy, and for taking bribes while in office—on which latter charge he was criminally indicted (and later allowed to resign the vice presidency): "Agnew—English fails me, it would take Turkish or Russian or Yiddish to express my disgust. A slap on the wrist—for eight times as much as my recent ('38) opponent for the Legislature got sent to San Quentin for."[6] By the time of the interview, the Watergate break-in was being investigated by the Senate. Nixon, Heinlein said, had terrible judgment at picking his associates—but, he noted, "Watergate was a peccadillo (whether he knew about it or not); I had that and more done to me when I was an active politico."[7]

Many of the interviews he gave did not get published. Heinlein was not, therefore, unduly surprised when Neil Schulman reported a struggle with his editors to get "Looking Upward Through the Microscope" published.

Nonpaying chores were taking up more and more of Heinlein's productive time: There were two more major critiques that spring for writers just starting out, and Ginny finally extracted a written promise from him forswearing all such unindentured servitude.

Blassingame agreed—but gave him G. Harry Stine's *Third Industrial Revolution* to puff soon thereafter, so Ginny agreed to temper the agreement with generous exceptions, when and as appropriate.

Turning back to his own outstanding business, Heinlein came to a decision about the releases Scribner wanted from him. He instructed his accountant to return the $1,900 they had given him to quitclaim the dispute over outstanding royalties (they had used a different, and smaller, royalty percentage figure for the paperback editions than their original contract with Heinlein specified). There would be no new agreement with Scribner until and unless they made a reasonable offer at market rates.

In early August, Larry Niven and Jerry Pournelle surprised him with a revision of *Motelight.* He was shocked to see that they had taken his criticisms not merely in the *spirit* in which they were given, but as blueprints, even withdrawing the book while they reworked it:

I am pleased (and much flattered) that you took my comments on the earlier version seriously. I cannot remember this ever happening in the past (and for this reason I long ago quit commenting on other writers MSS; it is almost always a waste of time—but I tried once more because I liked almost all of the earlier version so well). I know all too well how dear to a writer are his brain children; most writers usually will not accept criticism—and usually should not, as creativity is usually not helped thereby.[8]

The writing business handed Heinlein new problems. One was a home-grown menace in Hollywood, the "fascinatingly terrible" television show *Starlost*.[9] Harlan Ellison had been involved in the show at the start and told the producers at Twentieth Century Fox that it was clearly based on an idea in Heinlein's "Universe"—the generation starship that has lost its purpose over the centuries and reverted to an agricultural society. But Fox ignored the information and sold the show to a low-budget Canadian developer who was busily gutting the concept—to say nothing of the copyright infringement. Ellison walked off the show—he had in fact been banned from the set—and required the new producer to take his name off the credits and substitute his "Cordwainer Bird" pseudonym. Ben Bova, hired as a science advisor for the series, also resigned in disgust but did not have the same contractual right to remove his name from the credits. Robert and Ginny missed the show's premiere, but they asked all their friends who had contacts in the industry to monitor the show as they put together the necessary documentation to pursue the copyright infringement.

The contracts and rights situation in England had gotten snarled in the last few years. The issue was brought to a head in 1973 when Sphere Books issued unauthorized paperbacks of an anthology assembled by Angus Wells and published by Sidgwick & Jackson in authorized hardcovers, *The Best of Robert A. Heinlein*. Heinlein's British agent, Innes Rose, didn't seem to have any concern about protecting the value of the rights—and in fact they understood that Rose neither liked science fiction nor had any particular special interest in or knowledge about marketing it.[10] He was a haughty Oxford man who despised anything American, but he handled all Blassingame's clients for English rights,[11] so they had kept their opinions to themselves. Their relationship with Rose and his agency, Farquharson's, dated all the way back to 1946, when Rose had initiated the unwanted Gollancz issue of *Beyond This Horizon*.

One of the book contracts Rose had let a few years ago, with Dennis Dobson, had never paid any royalties. Ginny raised the issue of nonpayment with Rose and was told she should get a lawyer and pursue the matter herself. They retained the London firm of Field Fisher and Martineau and spent a great deal of time for the remainder of 1973 preparing the finicky detail documentation a royalty suit requires—but they got into court early in 1974 and were awarded full back royalties, which Farquharson forwarded them, less their 10 percent agency cut. Requiring the client to do their job of enforcing the contracts, and then taking a cut, offended Ginny (and therefore Robert): not even the slightest suggestion that they share the legal fees (small in any case—a total of seventy-five dollars) or that their carelessness with their client's interests should in any way be acknowledged or mitigated.

There was a similar violation of paperback rights in Germany. All of Heinlein's juveniles had gone to Gebruder Weiss Verlag as they came out in hardcover; Gebruder Weiss was interested only in the juveniles, so the sales and therefore the royalty statements sagged over the years. Blassingame had reported struggles with Gebruder Weiss for years, going back to 1960, but in 1973 Robert and Ginny discovered Gebruder Weiss had made secondary contracts with a paperback house—not allowed by their contracts. The royalties were split fifty-fifty between Gebruder Weiss and the paperback house—and Gebruder Weiss simply did not notify them of subsidiary contracts or report those royalties at all. Blassingame's local agent found them a German law firm, and they instituted suit to get back royalties and declaratory reassignment of the rights back to them. It was to drag on for seven years.

Robert was developing a new skin cancer and wanted it taken care of at the superficial stage. He was given a new drug in the form of a salve—"Efuxed, or 5, fuschian, uracil." The treatment was no pleasure, since the salve stung going on and burned and itched while it was working—but it was a complete nonsurgical cure and didn't even leave a scar.[12]

In May 1973 Alexei Panshin wrote to Rita Bottoms, asking for access to the Heinlein Archive. Apparently he was getting ready to write more about Heinlein. Bottoms called Heinlein to discuss the matter on August 7, 1973.

As it happened, Panshin was on Heinlein's mind at the time. When Putnam's had announced *Time Enough for Love* in *Publisher's Weekly* in April, with no more information than the subject matter, size and price of the book, and the expected issue date, Panshin had written a recap of his view of Robert's psychology and guesses at what "more of the same" they might find in the new book—all wildly off the mark. This article had just appeared in the most important fanzine then being published, Richard E. Geis's *The Alien Critic*, no. 9.

Panshin's article was generating a lot of controversy already—which is, of course, meat and drink for the fanzines. Heinlein was professionally committed to ignoring such things:

I was hurt when the fanzines started panning me—after years of praising my work. It took me quite a while to realize that it proved I was on the right track . . . those fanzines don't even influence the organized fans enough to matter; I was awarded three of my four Hugos for "best novel" *after* the fanzines started panning me.[13]

When you write an adult story, he had concluded, the fanzines will always pan it—and that is good news, not bad news, he continued:

. . . even the organized fans who attend conventions and vote on Hugos are only a few thousand—while you are shooting for a market of millions . . . and I am only one of several writers who have proved that the general market will accept a well-written SF yarn quite as readily as any other type of fiction . . .[14]

Heinlein's feelings about Panshin made it difficult for him to be objective about the prospect of his coming to Santa Cruz. Ginny was alarmed and angry when she saw how disturbed Robert was over this. She got out her household miscellany and made Voodoo dolls of Panshin to stick pins in—to no apparent effect.[15]

Although such archives are normally open to the public with only minimal qualifications, that is a matter of practice rather than of policy: Bottoms had a certain amount of latitude in this case and a professional policy of not placing obstacles in the way of donors. When Heinlein told her Panshin was persona non grata with them, she wrote Panshin a brief and succinct reply: "I am sorry to inform you that the Robert Heinlein Archive is open by special permission and it is not being granted to you."[16]

Panshin naturally wrote back asking why permission was being denied him. This put Heinlein into an emotional tailspin, and he agonized over it for days. He even got out his copy of *Heinlein in Dimension* and read it. This was something, he decided finally, that he was not competent to decide: He drew up a long letter to Bottoms—eight pages—laying out his history with the Archive and his personal history with Panshin, and put the matter back in her hands.

To his credit, he acknowledged, Panshin had not published any fact about him not already in the public record. But, he concluded:

I do not like Mr. Panshin. I judge him to be neither a careful scholar nor a competent literary critic. I think he lacks judicial temperament and the proper scholarly coolness of approach. I know that he frequently misunderstands the clearest English I can write—then jumps to unfounded conjectures that he then treats as if they were proved conclusions.[17]

He concluded if it were anyone but Panshin, he would have allowed the access without a second thought—but he couldn't be emotionally objective in this case. He knew there was ample material to support the access: Panshin had a legitimate college degree and was both a published writer[18] and a member of SFWA. Heinlein withdrew his objection to Panshin accessing the Archive.

This does not change my opinion of Mr. Panshin as a man nor my opinion of his competence as a critic. But in fairness I must treat him in this professional matter exactly as I would treat a stranger having equivalent credentials . . . .

I urge you to ignore my personal animus and to do exactly that which you judge to be professionally correct—as if it had not been possible to consult me . . . you will never hear any objection now or later from me or Mrs. Heinlein.[19]

There were two "professionally correct" solutions: Accepting the gift bound the university morally as well as at law to abide by the donor's understanding of the terms of the gift: Panshin should be forbidden access. Yet the function of the Archive is to be a *public* repository: Panshin's access should be allowed. Bottoms reached a Solomonic decision: She wrote Panshin the next day, September 11, 1973, sending him Heinlein's letter and permission—but now Panshin was reluctant to make the trip to California, and Bottoms would not, as a matter of policy, copy and mail out any of her collections. Later, a researcher named Paul Crawford came to Special Collections, to research some of Panshin's questions.[20]

Ginny was ready to move into the "reconstruction" stage of her oral surgeries in mid-October. Before she went under the knife again, Robert had something to take care of: A scaly patch on his chest developed into an actual lump during the Panshin hoo-raw. Sensitized to skin cancers, Robert went to his doctor to have it biopsied. While he was anesthetized, they decided to remove the entire tumor, just to be on the safe side. The biopsy came back negative—it was a benign growth[21]—and it gave him opportunity to write teasingly for a few months, until the amusement palled, to various female correspondents, asking whether in view of his recent bout with "breast cancer" he should consider joining women's liberation or gay liberation. The sampling of opinion he collected thus lightly did not surprise him: theoretical agreement and aesthetic dislike of both. He agreed with one (female) correspondent: "I think I find Gay Lib distasteful for much the same reasons you find Fem Lib not to your taste: Each is raucous. Not that I am disdainful of either one; they are doing valiant fighting for personal freedom."[22] And to another, he wrote:

> Surely you know my views, as shown in *Stranger* in IWFNE and in TEFL: Anything at all between two or more freely consenting adults is good, and no damn business of government, of neighbors, of churches, or anyone else—but in the culture in which we live one has to be reasonably careful not to get slammed for some (utterly harmless) acts, and be especially careful not to harm the public reputations of others.[23]

But the lingering scar from his biopsy was the final straw. When the dressings came off, he made a conscious decision that his "practicing nudist" days were over, at least for "public" purposes. His scars would either frighten the children and horses, or else be used as a horrible example.[24] He allowed his and Ginny's already long-unused memberships in various nudist associations to lapse, one by one.

Vexations continued to accumulate. Copyright infringement was becoming an accelerating problem as his name and reputation grew outside of science-fiction publishing. Ignoring the new piracies created a presumption they could get away with more and more—and they did. He was doing the preparatory work for not less than *five* copyright infringement actions: "If I can work up just one cleancut one, I shall make the outcome *quite* public—as a warning. The money does not matter (I'll show a net loss anyhow, through loss of working time)—but I must abate this nuisance."[25]

"I'm not anxious to make money on infringements," he wrote to Walter Minton; "I just want to put one head on a spike at the city gates as a warning to others."[26]

Late in 1973, another egregious infringement hit the stands: A new science-fiction magazine was launched in large, glossy format, *Vertex, the Magazine of Science Fiction*. The first issue, dated April 1973, had an unauthorized reprint of Heinlein's 1941 guest of honor speech at Denvention. The editors at *Vertex* had contacted him for an interview, but he declined.[27] They contacted Forrest Ackerman on a consulting basis, and he gave them the transcription he had published (also unauthorized) in 1941.

Heinlein was furious: He had intended the "Channel Markers" editorial in *Analog* (January 1974) to be his highly publicized comeback to the SF magazines. This upstart had spoiled the publicity Bova could make of it. Heinlein wrote the *Vertex* editor, who offered to assign the copyright to him. That was satisfactory to amend their part in the piracy. Heinlein agreed to make up for their embarrassment by giving them an unpublished story for their second issue. The logical candidate was the "Three Brave Men" story he had revised and retitled after Harlan Ellison rejected it for *Dangerous Visions*. It had subsequently been rejected by another raft of magazines, and Blassingame had retired it again. The matter closed, he never dealt with *Vertex* again. He wrote directly to Ackerman in unequivocal terms: "You will not use that property again nor permit, encourage, or sell any 'right' to reproduce it. I will take any violation to court." He concluded, *"Keep your hands off my property."*[28]

Looking forward to the end of Ginny's surgery, they booked a cruise to the South Sea Islands. Their travel schedule for next year was already starting to fill up: the forty-fifth reunion of his Naval Academy class would take place in May 1974, and he had already lined up two speaking engagements in New York. Ginny's preparatory school, Packer, was having a reunion about the same time, and Robert wanted to see the institution that had put its mark on her.

Normally *Analog* comes out around the twentieth of the month preceding its issue date, but they got the January 1974 issue, with the Forrestal Lecture, on the stands early. Heinlein began receiving mail on it as early as December 2—and Ben Bova forwarded a letter of comment written for the letters column of *Analog,* "Brass Tacks," with a November 26 date, that called it "deeply moving." The sentiment was echoed almost unanimously in Heinlein's mail. Some said simply "Bravo!" or even just "thank you." The second half of the speech appeared in the tabloid *Human Events* as "Politics of Patriotism."[29] Almost immediately there were requests to both *Analog* and *Human Events* for offprints, which neither magazine could provide. Versions of "Politics of Patriotism" eventually appeared in several magazines. A broad range of people liked the piece and wanted to give it wider distribution: In addition to the usual places, it appeared in a *Star Trek* magazine, *Dimensions,*[30] a college paper enthusiastically titled *Right On!,*[31] and Heinlein granted permission to a group that made up flyers titled "Jesus to the Communist World."[32] He also made an extremely condensed, eight-hundred-word version, for *Family Week,* a Sunday-supplement magazine of the *Jefferson City (MO) News and Tribune.*[33] One State Farm insurance agency wanted to use excerpts in their monthly circular to policyholders.[34]

Over the next year, Heinlein was contacted by each of the service academies in turn, to reprint "The Pragmatics of Patriotism" (an alternative title

Heinlein had provided) for their own use—by the Army's Commandant of Cadets at West Point, by the Air Force Academy, and twice by the marines— the first time for reprint in the *USMC Gazette*; the second time to be printed in the service manual. At Admiral Mack's suggestion, Heinlein gave it to *Naval Affairs*.

Just before Christmas in 1973, Heinlein received a prospectus from Rowan Thomas, their friend and former lawyer in Colorado Springs. He had been investing in mines himself, as the price of gold and silver floated up again, and now he was putting together a mining limited partnership venture for Red Pine Mine in Montana. Robert looked over the prospectus—doubtless mindful of his disastrous experience with a Colorado silver mine in 1934[35]— and was impressed by Thomas's thoroughly practical plan.

The paperback for *Time Enough for Love* was going to be released in January, about six months earlier than usual—and in an issue of one million copies.[36] The extra income would probably push them into a higher tax bracket next year. They decided to take 5 percent of the mining investment as a hedge against inflation and as a tax shelter, as well.

Heinlein had never bothered with tax-avoidance planning before, content to pay whatever the government said he owed them that year. But since 1970 they had gone from living from royalty statement to royalty statement to having a plutocrat's income. The royalties from *Stranger in a Strange Land* continued high (though not at the peak they had achieved in 1970), and were no longer being eaten up by hospital stays and experimental periodontal work— and the "ripple effect" he had noted earlier, of people discovering *Stranger* and then seeking out his other books, had raised the level of royalties overall— just as Scribner finally allowed all his juveniles to go to the large paperback market. *Time Enough for Love* had earned as much in the first month of its release as each of his books had earned in total over sometimes decades. For the first time in his life "too much money" was not a mildly ironic joke.

The winter skies in the coastal part of Northern California are often clouded over or shrouded in fog, but driving back from one of Ginny's last dental appointments on January 2, 1974, they caught a glimpse of the comet Kohoutek for four minutes just after sunset, just over a cloud bank. And that was the last of relatively clear skies they had for a while. The next day, January 3, 1974, at about noon, the power went out over the entire area. And stayed out, day after day.

Winters around Monterey Bay tend to be rainy, rather than snowy, but without heating it gets very chilly. As the heat drained out of the house they moved into the living room, where they could use the Swedish fireplace. Robert wore a parka over layers of shirts and pants, over pajamas, while Ginny got out her Gore-Tex "Alaska pants." They brought in firewood, kerosene lamps, and sterno for their camping stove. Ginny cleared out the freezer and put a big iron pot of stew on the fireplace. By the fourth day, their firewood was running low. Fortunately, the telephone was still functioning, and they were able to order in another cord delivered. It was still piled on the front steps when the power came back on, after 124 hours and a bit, though the lights were flickering and the power supply not constant for yet more days. Stacking the cordwood gave them both backaches. The greenhouse was completely dead. Then there were decayed freezer contents to dispose of, and cleaning and disinfecting—and load after load of laundry.

They were so far behind they had to work doubletime to be ready to leave on February 4, 1974, for a now *really* much-needed vacation, a month aboard the ship *Mariposa* for a South Sea cruise. In fact, they missed *Mariposa*'s sailing date from San Francisco even though Robert worked fifty-two hours straight at the typewriter (on the documentation for the English copyright infringement matter) and had only a four-hour nap before they left the house. They were able to arrange a flight to catch up with *Mariposa* in Honolulu.[37]

They thoroughly enjoyed the cruise time, dancing every night, wonderful food, and an abundance of parties including dress-up and costume parties in which Robert took boyish delight. Ginny came to the Hat Party as Carmen Miranda, with real tropical fruit (heavy and awkward). At another costume party, they got an honorable mention when Robert came as the Ambassador from Arcturus in metallic green greasepaint and white dinner clothes, bearing Ginny as a Playboy Bunny on his arm. Robert spent as much time as he could in his favorite occupation—talking—or girl-watching by the pool. Ginny said she was a "shipboard alcoholic" since she rarely drank at home, and she engaged in some strenuous activities to keep her figure: dance classes, appearing in an amateur abridgement of *South Pacific,* and dancing in the chorus in a variety show on the way back. Robert played "pirate" in the King Neptune ceremonies crossing the Equator, harrassing the "pollywogs" at King Neptune's bidding.

This was their first visit to many of the South Sea Islands, and also their first actual contact with many of the Polynesian island cultures whose anthropology Heinlein had for decades been raiding for his fiction. The islands they found exotic and glamorous—but more dirty and squalid than they had expected. In Papeete, the main city on Tahiti, Robert bought Ginny a daring dress in shades of green that *almost* covered her standing, but slithered apart when she sat, scandalizing any jaybirds in the neighborhood. They visited Moorea, Rarotonga, and Samoa, too.

Unpleasant memories of their 1954 travels in Australia and New Zealand almost kept them on the ship, but Heinlein did go ashore in Auckland. Reporters were on the ship literally as soon as they docked, and Robert found himself giving newspaper interviews and submitting to be photographed before having his morning coffee. The invitations began to pour in. He gave a telephone interview on Radio I. Fans actually came on board the ship and sent gifts—quite overwhelming. They had very little time left to see anything of Auckland (but did get to the zoo).

The performance was repeated in Sydney, almost beat for beat—(and when they got to Fiji on the way back to Hawaii, they found waiting for them a package. On Auckland radio he had talked about meeting a baby elephant named Kashin at the zoo there and mentioned the elephant charm he used to tape to his wrist for fencing and which he had lost in 1930. One youngster had expressed him a tiny plastic elephant as a replacement!).

They left *Mariposa* at Honolulu and flew to Los Angeles, arriving after midnight on March 7, to be met by a passel of boisterous Cal-Tech students and ferried to the campus to speak at a seminar. They had hoped for a visit to JPL, but they were so much in demand that it was out of the question. And then, abruptly, they were home again, with just enough time to wade through the accumulation of mail before going off to Heinlein's forty-fifth reunion at Annapolis.

Time Enough for Love was nominated for a Nebula Award, up against Arthur C. Clarke's *Rendezvous with Rama*: the very complex and experimental poised against a book extraordinarily retro, with nearly all story structure sacrificed to mood. Heinlein didn't see the Science Fiction Writers of America honoring him with a Nebula under any circumstances whatever,[38] which made a win for *Rama* inevitable this year.

When it was suggested he might accept the award on behalf of his long-time friend—since Clarke, for a wonder, was *not* on an American speaking tour this April—Heinlein furnished himself with an extra copy of *Rama* to take to the awards banquet in Los Angeles.

Keynote and acceptance speeches at a Nebula Awards banquet can be a very mixed lot. This year, in the era of the Club of Rome report,[39] almost all were downbeat and depressing, even with the ever-entertaining Robert Bloch as toastmaster. As Heinlein was called to the podium to accept for Clarke, Ginny slipped him a note, "Give them hope," and so he opened his remarks with Pandora's Box and tried to find something cheerful to say about the future. Accepting the Nebula Award for *Rama,* he got all his colleagues to autograph it so he could send it as a souvenir to Clarke in Sri Lanka.

One colleague Robert had particularly looked forward to meeting at this Nebula Award banquet was Philip K. Dick. Dick was a long-established writer Heinlein had routinely kept an eye on because he was doing some interesting, though often uneven, experimental work. While they were away, Dick had written him a surprisingly shy and almost inarticulate fan letter:

> I am trembling as I write this, to address a letter to you, and I see that my typewriter itself is laboring under the weight of what I want to say but probably will not be able to. When you entered the science fiction field it was an infantile field, written so and appealing so. Those days are gone forever and because of you. You made our field worthy of adult readers and adult writers. I have long wanted to tell you that I know this, but I've been blocked in saying so; I don't know why. Perhaps there are some persons that one admires so much that one cannot even manage to express admiration—at least aloud. But my admiration for you and my enjoyment of your work has been in my heart for many years, unsaid. I want to say it now.[40]

Dick's Hugo-winning novel *The Man in the High Castle* (1962—the year after *Stranger* had won) was, he said, a "thinly veiled encomium" to Heinlein.[41] Heinlein wrote Dick a long letter of thanks and encouragement[42] and brought copies of some of Dick's books to Los Angeles. Heinlein asked Dick for autographs—which seemed to nonplus Dick.

The trip to Annapolis was coming up at the end of May, and to New York thereafter. In addition to his promise to give a talk at the Poetry Center at the Ninety-second Street YW-YMHA (Young Women's-Young Men's Hebrew Association), the National Rare Blood Club wanted him to speak at a banquet on June first, so he would be quite busy this trip. The Poetry Center was already publicizing the event, and Neil Schulman wrote that they were likely to meet Alexei Panshin there—a prospect they both viewed with distaste.

The reunion was leisurely this year, with parties each night, drinking and dancing too late. Ginny was excluded from some of the functions, but she did get to tour the facilities and saw that the Academy was now maintaining computer data storage for each of the midshipmen, on a vacuum tube computer they were timesharing with the Navy.[43]

Saturday, the second day of the reunion, they spent the afternoon sailing on the bay with Bob Kephart,[44] a small-boat enthusiast and energetic ship-handler who kept one rail or the other underwater so much of the time Robert said it was the only tall-masted submarine he had ever seen. They were late in getting back and covered with salt spray, and so missed dinner. In fact, they were permanently behind schedule after that and missed breakfast *and* lunch on Sunday.

In New York, they had several days at the Tuscany, to see friends and trans-act business. Richard Pope, an editor for *Encyclopedia Britannica,* contacted Heinlein through Blassingame to write a short article on the physicist Paul Dirac for the 1975 *Compton Yearbook*—an interesting project, since he had wanted to do some "catching up" in the sciences anyway, and Heinlein re-garded Dirac as one of the greatest mathematical physicists of all time. The fee was relatively small, but the perks made it very desirable anyway: A full set of the new *EBIII.* He accepted the assignment and went off to give a television interview about the National Rare Blood Club for the midday show and at-tend two other functions—a business lunch at L'Argenteuil with Blassingame and Robert Gleason and on to the Poetry Center at the Ninety-second Street Y, where they were fussed over by an elderly poetess who didn't quite know what to make of this science-fiction writer foisted on her.

Heinlein had not prepared a speech specifically for this occasion, since they would want him to talk about writing, and the freelance writing portion of the Forrestal Lecture would do for that purpose.[45] After the formal speech, he and the "hardcore fans" who remained retreated to a nearby room that had been set up with a table so he could autograph books, as at a bookstore signing. At one point, Panshin did try to introduce himself, but Heinlein refused to speak with him, saying just "Goodbye, sir!" several times and actually turning away.

This incident, mysterious to most of the fans who were present, and re-garded as so minor by the Heinleins that neither of them mentioned it in correspondence, was written up in fanzines and discussed at tiresome length as "The Shoot-Out at the Poetry Center"[46]—which could only have reinforced Heinlein's already low opinion of the social standards of organized science-fiction fandom.

While in New York, the Heinleins had habitually given "at-home parties" at the Tuscany Hotel, which had become their favorite home-away-from-home there. Two days after the Poetry Center, the Heinleins gave one of their "at-homes" with Herman Kahn and his family as guests of honor. The next day they moved to the Waldorf-Astoria. The National Rare Blood Club had fur-nished them with a suite in the same hotel where the banquet was being held that evening (June 1). The notice Heinlein had put into *I Will Fear No Evil,* publicizing the National Rare Blood Club had, he understood, doubled the donor base—a public-spirited achievement of which he was proud.

The suite at the Waldorf was staggeringly luxurious—as large as their entire house. The bathroom alone was the size of their living room—and had a huge crystal chandelier of its own. The Associated Health Foundation gave a small cocktail party in the suite before the banquet, and Robert and Ginny were introduced to Harry Hershfield,[47] who would be MC'ing that evening at the banquet. Hershfield was best known for his appearances on the *Can You Top This?* and *Stop Me If You've Heard This One* radio shows in the 1940s, but Robert remembered reading his newspaper comic strips in *1913*. At the age of eighty-nine, Hershfield was frail and wheeled around by nurses, but lively and witty and entertaining. He obviously knew his audience, too: Later he told Heinlein a string of dirty stories during dinner—some Heinlein hadn't heard before.

There were twelve hundred people at the banquet, all seated at their tables before they brought in the speakers. As Robert and Ginny came in and made their way to the table, the band struck up "Anchors Away," and everyone rose and applauded. Gradually it dawned on Robert that the ovation was for *him,* that he was not just *one of* the guest speakers tonight, but the *principal* honoree: He was being recognized as "Humanitarian of the Year." While he was still dazed, a spotlight picked out Ginny in black formal dress and jewels, and they presented her with a "gangster-size" sheaf of red roses, and Ginny cried. The program was a "This Is Your Life"–type presentation of Robert's life, with a large, blown-up photo—and an elegant, engraved glass presentation plaque.

When it was Robert's turn to speak, he told them how he had happened to place the notice in *I Will Fear No Evil*—and then fell ill and had his own life saved by five anonymous rare blood donors, and that the credit for this honor should go equally to the editors and publishers who got and kept that notice before the public—and he found in the audience and introduced Ejler Jakobsson, the editor of *Galaxy;* Blassingame; Walter Minton of Putnam's, with the editor Bill Targ; Targ's assistant Dorothy Rudo; and Col. Steve Conland, the president of Berkley Books.

The crush around the podium when the ceremony was over was overwhelming—more, even, than Robert's trick memory for names could keep up with. They adjourned to the suite for another party. "You need to have people around to help you climb back down from those high points, you know."[48]

The buzz was scarcely off three days later when Robert performed his last scheduled chore in New York—a taping for WOR radio of an interview with Patricia McCann for the National Rare Blood Club—and came back to earth and domestic matters in Santa Cruz. There was the usual accumulation of mail, including a big cardboard box with Ginny's birthday present for Robert this year—now too conspicuous to hide, so she presented it a month early: She had had a thirty-inch Mars globe made up from the Mariner 9 survey photos.

That June Robert enrolled them both in astronaut Edgar Mitchell's new Institute of Noetic Sciences, listing Ginny's experience with parapsychological concerns "enough to make her very receptive, none of evidential value by the strict rigor of methodology required for science." His own?

> None of any evidential value to anyone else . . . [sic] but quite a bit of strong evidential value to *me*. Examples: Ginny and I make limited use of telepathy between ourselves. I have both experienced and seen some minor telekinesis. I have had numerous and surprisingly accurate forerunners as to my own future. I have, on several occasions, been aware of deaths of persons close to me before the news reached me through ordinary channels—and on three of those occasions the event involved death by accident of persons in good health. I have encountered *idiots-savants* with "wild talents." And none of this is worth a hoot as scientific evidence.[49]

Ginny was having a run of forerunners: She would periodically get an intuition of an earthquake, which happen frequently enough in California to make a good test case. Robert encouraged her to write them down on three-by-five cards and seal them in an envelope. Her forerunners were surprisingly accurate as to timing and magnitude—for earthquakes in the news as well as those they experienced locally—though the information she got *about* the earthquake was almost uselessly variable.

A few of Ginny's prediction cards were preserved in the Heinlein Archive at UC Santa Cruz, along with items like Cal Laning's attempts to transmit telepathically while at sea during World War II. Heinlein might have closed out his teenaged Quest, with Laning and Allan Gray, in the 1930s, but he maintained a lifelong interest in disowned facts and the reality behind the reality that they represented.

26

MR. SCIENCE

The Dirac article occupied him all the summer of 1974, punctuated by concerns over his family's medical condition. His oldest brother, Lawrence, was frail though in no immediate danger, and Rex was at Letterman hospital breathing bottled oxygen. Bam fell again in June 1974. She fell again in July and broke the other hip (she had broken her right hip in a fall five years previously). She was in a convalescent hospital as a temporary solution, but she seemed to have lost contact with reality, inhabiting the world of her extreme youth. This hospital was appallingly dirty, careless, and understaffed—Bam had been allowed to fall again—and so Mary Jean was considering a permanent placement in a better facility, since it was not likely she would ever be able to come home. Ginny instructed their tax attorney to be prepared to take the full payment for the new convalescent home in Duarte as a deduction on their taxes that year.

Robert spent most of his time catching up on developments in physics since his days in high school. Dirac's antimatter led to quantum mechanics and speculative physics, and he found that the old nature-of-time argument that had been the hot topic when he was in high school was still going on. The players had different names, but J. W. Dunne's serial time thesis and Ouspensky's six-dimensional spacetime were still around, modified and cloaked in the lingo of quantum mechanics as "The Wheeler-Everett Many Worlds Hypothesis."

The Humanitarian Award was bearing additional fruit, too. Now that he was an "Authority," Heinlein's suggestion for a blood sciences article for the *Britannica* was quickly taken up by Mr. Pope, who commissioned a "rare blood" article for the 1976 *Compton Yearbook*.[1] At about that time, Heinlein was contacted by a Canadian hematologist, Denis Paradis, who wanted to put a Heinlein quote—Lazarus Long's definition of a zygote from *Time Enough for Love*—into his *Atlas of Immunohaematology*, a reference work that would be used by clinical researchers at the highest levels of blood science. Heinlein granted the permission, of course, adding "and besides, Lazarus may have stolen it himself—he would."[2] Paradis was a Heinlein fan as well as an authority in the blood field. He would be a valuable asset, since Robert had already decided to take the entire next year off to research blood science.

> . . . the principle article on "Blood" in EncBrit is by C. Lockard Conley, M.D., head of hematology division at Johns Hopkins . . . it is an excellent article, packed with information, with no attempt to be entertaining.
>
> *I* would never be asked to write *that* article . . . [sic] and Dr. Conley is not expected to do what I do. I am expected to *entertain* while *informing* and do both equally well. I am most emphatically expected to be scientifically accurate, but I am neither expected to be as detailed in treatment nor am I allowed as many words . . . .
>
> But . . . probably 90% of my readers range from 16 to 45, prime candidates to become repeat blood donors . . . I have no way of guessing how many future donors it will be the first incitement toward eventually becoming donors. Possibly none. But if (as I hope) it stirs out even a few hundred, my work will not have been wasted.[3]

Ginny pointed out he could have written another book—or two—in the time he was devoting to these projects, and it/they would certainly have brought in more cash—but what would be the point of that? Considering their tax situation already, the entire proceeds would have gone to the federal government and the California Franchise Tax Board.

Heinlein finished the draft of the Dirac article at four thousand words and cut it to twenty-nine hundred words for submission on July 30, 1974—two days before his August 1 deadline—and sent it off.[4] In fact, he was not yet done with the article, as he had to find and specify illustrations before 1 October.

Mr. Pope called it a "good article,"

> So I phoned him and told him it was like hell a good article as it had been cut from 4000+ words and all the juice and color squeezed out. He thought a moment and said, "I've already vouchered this for payment through your agent . . . [sic] but do you *want* to make it longer?"
>
> "I certainly do."[5]

He was given complete control over the copy and illustrations—the kind of freedom a writer is rarely given.

There was time even for a complete rewrite—which might be necessary, since he had discovered that Dr. Dirac was still alive and still working, in Florida at the moment. That was something like finding that Santa Claus was visiting your uncle or Albert Einstein had moved in next door. With this untapped resource, it would be a shame to let all the effort go to waste: He arranged for a telephone interview with Dr. Dirac—not a simple proposition, as Dirac despised telephones and would not use them at all.

Heinlein would chat with Mrs. Dirac, and she would take questions to Dr. Dirac—often outside in the garden—while Heinlein waited on the phone (Dirac wasn't uncooperative, just eccentric). Heinlein sent him two copies of the draft asking him to feel free to strike anything in error, anything he might regard as too personal. "Or objectionable for any reason whatever."[6] Knowing what a bane fan letters were to his existence as a writer, he carefully included a self-addressed, stamped envelope.

For the re-expansion of the Dirac article, Heinlein polished his original draft, but still this called for a full-out effort, can-to-can't, finishing up on the 14th of August, and then he slept for twenty hours straight. Dirac's daughter, Mary Collevaine, sent him a photograph of her father to be used in the article. A month after the first interview, he had a second telephone interview when Dirac was back at his permanent posting in Boulder, Colorado—and was flattered and flabbergasted when Dirac sent him a message through his wife that he was reading and enjoying *Starship Troopers*.

Mr. Pope had the article reviewed by one of EB's knowledgeable production editors, as well, Charles Cegielski, who questioned some of Heinlein's interpretations. This correspondence was very satisfying, since most of Cegielski's questions related to the assumptions underlying his interpretations, and he was forced to articulate just what he meant by some of the statements, to strike the exact nuance of belief and practice he lived by:

> The universe is what it is . . . [sic] but the returns from the upstate counties are not in; we don't *know* what it is in most of its major aspects . . . One *must* use assumptions in order to live, and I assume that the universe of my perceptions is real and behave accordingly, paying taxes, driving carefully, etc.—but I do not forget that it is an assumption, and this permits me to toy with solipsist notions in private . . . [sic] or sometimes on paper as fiction for profit.[7]

Other work was stacking up at the same time. Ginny handled an inquiry from Baird Searles, who was doing, of all things, a Cliffs Notes pony on

Stranger. Heinlein wrote to Philip K. Dick, who was in the hospital, having lost (temporarily) the use of one arm as a result of surgery. A get-well card would not do, so, as soon as the deadlines were met, he sent a long, chatty letter, talking shop and assuring him the injury need not seriously interrupt his writing and suggested an electric typewriter to cut down the sheer physical drudgery of writing.[8] Since freelance writers rarely have good medical insurance, he knew Phil and Tessa Dick would probably be broke, or next to it, so he bought and had delivered to them a good electric typewriter.[9]

There was another letter only he could handle: A naval officer, Commander Thomas B. Buell, had sent him an elaborate questionnaire about his time with then-Captain Ernest J. King. Buell was preparing a new biography of Fleet Admiral King for the Naval Institute Press and was routinely contacting all officers who had served with King.

Robert counted his time with King on board *Lexington* (CV-2) from 1930–32 as one of the formative experiences of his life. The things he noticed about King, and thought about then and in the years since, had created him as a person, as much as family and as much as any reading he had done. Master shiphandler, airplane pilot, submariner, and engineer-inventor, rigidly just and tempered with compassion, his intellectual processes sure and correct, King was Robert's idea (barring some nonsensical intra-service infighting after the war) of a perfect human being—not a model to be copied as to detail, but as an exemplar, to show how a self-aware human being can order the materials of his profession and his life. Heinlein wanted Buell to get it *right,* in a way that the recitation of biographical facts just cannot convey. He sat down at his typewriter with the questionnaire on October 3, 1974, and brought all his narrative skills into play to make King *live* for Buell.

> Ernest J. King was a man toward whom no one who knew him felt indifferent. He aroused either extreme dislike (often mixed with very grudging admiration)—or he inspired liking so extreme that his admirers tended (figuratively) to worship the deck he trod.
>
> I was of the latter group, so please take into account my bias . . . .
>
> I consider E.J. King to have been the most nearly perfect military officer I have ever known.[10]

And so on, forty-seven pages that day, then continuing on for a total of fifty-nine pages of reminiscences, speculation, polemical argument, and analysis— and then four more pages of officers who knew King well enough to humanize him for Buell, urging Buell to use Robert's name and the depth and intensity of his response to open up the personal memories of naval officers who might otherwise answer lukewarm.[11]

Heinlein found himself adopting this project as a personal enthusiasm, much as he had done the year before with *The Mote in God's Eye*. That correspondence was a cathartic act of confession for Robert, and he probably released in that letter the impulse to write a memoir, which he had been kicking around for a few years.

Shortly after Thanksgiving, Richard Pope sent galleys for the Dirac article, together with a set of layouts for correction and critique.

With that task at last out of the way, Robert and Ginny could go off on vacation—a working vacation, as Robert was already deep into the research on the blood science article. They booked passage again on *Mariposa*, back to Hawaii for an eighteen-day cruise beginning December 14 and returning to San Francisco on New Year's Day. They managed this time to catch the ship in San Francisco, loaded down with books and magazines.

The increasing complexity of their literary business demanded increasing vigilance. Their annual receipts continued steadily to grow, for the ninth year in a row—$158,745 for 1974—but just in time to meet increasing expenses. Bam's upkeep in the convalescent facility was costing one thousand dollars a month out of pocket, and by May 1975 it was clear that she would probably be there for the rest of her life. It was something they could afford, and no one else in the family was able to support Bam this way. The market for Heinlein's writing was strong now—but they had seen ups and downs in the market for science fiction before. Continued writing was the only way Heinlein could assure their financial situation would not collapse.

They were getting another useful tax deduction this year that would help: They had taken a 5 percent cash investment in the Red Pine Mine in Montana, through their old friend from Colorado Springs Rowan Thomas, and had increased their investment to 7 percent in the meantime. The investment was intended to be risk-capital with a tax deduction attached, and Thomas told them they could take a whopping $17,500 deduction for 1974 taxes. Between the increase in medical expenses and the venture capital deduction, they were just about covering the increase in taxes.

Heinlein was starting a project that would soak up a lot of that increased income. Perhaps it was sparked by a request they found in the mail from a daughter-of-a-friend in the publishing business for a letter to be published in a Candian high schoolers' civics magazine, *Canada and the World*. He wrote a 750-word letter/article to be published in their April issue: "A U.S. Citizen Thinks About Canada." The timing for this was particularly good: Robert had noticed that the vast majority of his research and reference materials on blood science were coming from Canada and England, and not the United States. Perhaps this was at least partly a reflection of the fact that Denis Paradis, from Montreal, was one of his primary sources of information, but he discovered that Canada and England—and all the Commonwealth countries, so far as he could tell—had much more efficient and better-organized blood collection services than did the United States. There were individuals with heroic dedication here, and he found the willingness to give of time and attention astonishing, but as he researched and wrote the rare blood article for the *Compton Yearbook,* 90 percent of the information he was using, and 75 percent of the support, was coming from Canada.[12]

That situation changed a little when they went to New York in April 1975. The Science Fiction Writers of America were honoring him with the SFWA's first Grand Master Nebula Award. Heinlein had quietly supported the SFWA during the lean years when it was in formation, actually paying the organization's bills with cash donations out of pocket, keeping it afloat until it should become self-supporting from member dues. Possibly no one but Joan Hunter Holly, the then-treasurer, knew about that, and that was just the way Heinlein wanted it.[13] He had let his membership lapse when Alexei Panshin became head of publications[14]—and would not, as a matter of stubborn pride, re-up while *Time Enough for Love* was still eligible for the Nebula. "I don't want any possible hint that I am arse-kissing," he told Philip José Farmer.[15] But now that was over, he quietly rejoined.

Jerry Pournelle was president of the SFWA in 1975. He had been outraged at the attitudes among some SFWAns about *Time Enough for Love* when it was up for Nebula consideration in 1974. Not only was the book outstandingly deserving of a Nebula (*pace* Clarke), but it was the organization's first, and possibly only, opportunity to honor one of the field's most influential writers, a generous and supportive colleague.

Pournelle found a way to rectify the manifest injustice by instituting a Grand Master Nebula, comparable to the Lifetime Achievement Oscar given annually by the Academy of Motion Picture Arts and Sciences. Heinlein was to receive this singular honor at the New York Nebula Awards banquet on April 26, 1975, at the Algonquin Hotel, the day after he and Ginny attended the Mystery Writers of America annual banquet and met Eric Ambler as he received his own Grand Master Award, then met Ross MacDonald and Phyllis Whitney afterwards. That afternoon Ginny had the fortieth reunion luncheon at her college prep school, Packer, and Heinlein attended with her. They kept a cab waiting while he looked around. Ginny had told him it was like nothing so much as *The Prime of Miss Jean Brodie* in her day, and she had giggled all through the play. In fact, it had been presented at Packer the previous fall—"with the girls playing themselves," Robert remarked dryly. Nor did they skip the ritual of having him autograph all of his books that were in the Packer library.

At a lunch with Robert and Ginny before the Nebula Award ceremony, Pournelle gratefully acknowledged all the help Robert had given him over the years. Remembering this moment for others, years later, Pournelle said:

> He helped me with my career a very great deal, and I once asked him, "How can I pay you back?" This is a little absurd from a young man, maybe thirty, thirty-five years old just getting started, just, to someone twice his age and who is very well established, and he said "You can't pay me back. But you can pay it forward." Something that I have attempted to do.[16]

When the SFWA Grand Master Award was announced, the crowd leaped to its feet and gave him a six-minute ovation. Robert was very moved:

> My brother, Major General Lawrence Heinlein, once told me that there are only two promotions in life that mean a damn: from buck private to corporal, and from colonel to general officer. I made corporal decades ago . . . but now at long last I know what he meant about the other. Thank you.[17]

He was given another three-minute ovation[18] as he stood at the table holding the Nebula for photographers.

He was able to meet and talk with several "new" colleagues at this event. One was Spider Robinson, whose "Callahan's Bar" stories he had read and enjoyed. He sought out Joe Haldeman, whose novel *The Forever War* had just been published in 1974,[19] and complimented him on his writing—which astonished Haldeman and several people in the crowd around him, as the book was widely viewed as critical of *Starship Troopers,* as indeed it is: Haldeman challenged some of the assumptions and developments in *Starship Troopers,* based on his experience in Vietnam. But this was not so much a "disagreement" as it was a fruitful "conversation," from which Heinlein could learn what he needed to know. Spider Robinson remembered the meeting as Heinlein interrupting the introduction by recognizing Haldeman as the author of "'*The Forever War,* of course,' Robert said, striding forward and thrusting his hand out. 'It is an honor to meet you, sir. That may be the best future war story I've ever read!'"[20] Heinlein always valued direct experience, and what

Haldeman had to say was in no way inconsistent with Heinlein's opinions as to what impact undeclared wars might have on the people who served.[21]

The day of the banquet was also the day that Thomas Clareson sent Heinlein an invitation to participate in a MLA (Modern Language Association) conference Christmas 1975 in San Francisco. The MLA is the most important and most prestigious organization for literary studies. Ginny declined the invitation for him, on the ground that they had no time free on the dates suggested—and in fact, it did fall into a time frame Robert had reserved for his long-delayed third, and hopefully final, hernia repair surgery. But Heinlein was also a little steamed about Clareson's apparently unconscious arrogance, asking for an unpaid public speaking engagement and, even worse, the event they wanted him for was to be chaired by Dr. David Samuelson, who had written a rather clueless article Robert referred to privately as "Panshin-like 'criticism' of my work."[22]

They had moved their usual holiday trip to after the Rare Blood article's deadline on July 1, 1975, and wrapped up arrangements for it while in New York for the Nebula Awards banquet in April and May. The Seattle Opera was giving the first U.S. performance of the entire *Ring of the Nibelung* in August, and Ginny wanted to see it. Robert felt he had already "done" the *Ring*. Ginny snorted: twenty years ago in Bayreuth! This was a music event of international importance, and she wanted to be there. Robert was mollified by part two—a sea cruise continuing to Alaska.

The prestige of the *Encyclopedia Britannica* opened doors, and Heinlein found the people involved in blood services a surprising lot like science-fiction fans: passionate rather than detached, and willing to devote astonishing amounts of their professional time to anyone truly interested in the work.

Heinlein took full advantage of blood science people's willingness to help, asking Dr. Harry Wallerstein at Jewish Memorial Hospital in the Bronx to brief him on technical issues. Dr. Wallerstein took an afternoon off and came to the Tuscany. Tapping him was like tapping a gusher—he came prepared with an "unhurried private seminar" going over all the fundamental issues of blood science: blood chemistry, types and functions of blood cells and plasma components, methods of testing, preparing, fractionating for refrigerating and for freezing. Wallerstein made notes and sketches and as he talked turned them over to Robert for his use, patiently amplifying any point when Heinlein interrupted (frequently) to ask a question.

Isaac Asimov had assured Heinlein it was essential for his article to get his foundation from the Race & Sanger manual *Blood Groups in Man*. The Drs. Race[23] had for thirty years been an international clearinghouse of blood science information, and *Blood Groups in Man,* first published in 1950 and now in its fifth edition, was the Bible of blood science. Ginny spent two days trying to track down a copy in New York, with no success: It was missing from all the libraries that had it in their catalog. The fifth edition was simply unavailable. It was, the director of the Irwin Memorial Blood Bank in San Francisco told Drs. Race and Sanger when they had met in Helsinki in March 1975, the book most likely to be stolen in America—more, even, than any pornography.[24]

But Heinlein's resources included an extensive network of his connections. "You have been exposed to my gauche tendency to yak to anyone about whatever is currently on my mind," he told his editor at *Encyclopedia Britannica.* He had talked about his problem of finding a research copy of Race & Sanger at a dinner party at the home of Martin Levin—the publisher of the Times-Mirror group.[25] The next day, Levin talked to Bob Tanner, a European book and author agent—and Heinlein's new agent for British rights. Tanner reached Heinlein the same day at the National Rare Blood Club and told him he could pick up a copy at the Times-Mirror offices. Levin and Tanner had deputized half a dozen people to hunt down copies of the book.[26]

Nor was that the end of it. When the Heinleins got home—a trip Robert weathered moderately well, as he only went to bed and slept thirteen hours straight but did not, as he often did, pick up some debilitating respiratory ailment—they found a copy of the Race & Sanger book loaned to them by mail by William M. Davis, M.D., Director of Hematology Service at the Western Medical Center of Massachussets.

It was their only copy, and Davis asked for it back in a week. Heinlein started swotting it immediately and found, as Asimov had told him, it was the basic foundation he needed—and the Wallerstein briefing had given him enough background to understand it properly. He asked Ginny to photocopy charts from the book for him on their 3M copier mornings when he slept in after working late into the night.

During the mornings, Heinlein availed himself of Dr. Wallerstein's offer and phoned him from California with questions as they arose, and always received the same patient, illuminating responses. Dr. Wallerstein's opinions were always carefully reasoned, even when they disagreed with the consensus, and Heinlein admired him for being a true scientist in a field so unexpectedly dominated by personal issues.[27]

By the time Dr. Davis's copy was due back in Massachussetts, the Levin/Tanner research combine had turned up another copy, same deal, checked out personally from the library at the Washington University medical school—and then a third.

Levin found a small lot of the fifth edition that were being pulled from distribution and snagged a permanent copy for Heinlein. They had been scheduled for pulping since the new edition would be out within the year. Better yet, Tanner had cabled Race and Sanger in England about Heinlein's problem, and they offered to send him page proofs early in June—just in time to make his July 1 copy deadline. There were, the doctors assured him, a number of important changes in this edition. It was an extraordinary courtesy but very consistent with the passionate advocacy Heinlein was finding throughout the entire community.

The unbound page proofs of the Race & Sanger sixth edition arrived on June 5, while houseguests from Finland were visiting. Heinlein raced through the book and immediately found the revisions, as the Drs. Race had told him, substantial and material. Without this book, his article would have been out of date the minute it was published. He finished the first pass of the article, incorporating the new information, and it came out to 9500 words—five times the length Pope had contracted for. Heinlein worked on this manuscript for days, condensing where possible and cutting where absolutely necessary. He got it down to just under three thousand words and stuck there. It was not possible to condense any further without relying too much on the technical language of a very esoteric science—and cutting *anything* further eliminated some facts that were essential to understand the subject. Nevertheless, he had made a contractual commitment, and he would make it. He cut the piece to the contractual limit of 1,990 words, and the result was so unsatisfactory that he struck out his own name and penned in a pseudonym, "Francis X. Riverside."[28]

A few days later, he called his project editor, Christine Timmons, and "tried to talk her into a longer version."[29] After additional meetings, he produced a clean manuscript of the 2,880-word version and sent it along, as well—with his own name on it. Pope and Timmons agreed this was much the better version and this was the one they would use. This time, the $1,000 fee went to the National Rare Blood Club.

Heinlein sent out copies of the 2,880-word version to his panel of experts, asking for the most nitpicking, close criticism. He explained to his editors: "I want it to be checked technically *savagely*, without mercy. I expect to be able to defend successfully every statement I have made . . . [sic] but I do not want *any* errors to find their way into print; the subject is too important . . . ."[30]

With the hard work done, they were able to leave for Seattle on July 14.

This production of the Ring cycle was much more satisfying to Ginny than the Bayreuth production had been in 1954 (though Bayreuth, she thought, had the better voices). This one was sumptuously mounted following as closely as possible Richard Wagner's original staging instructions. Robert found himself listening and watching the production as music and text in a foreign language, but as he became more interested, more immersed in the drama—

> Odd thing happened to me—My German is feeble . . . save that I learned Bavarian German at about five in the kitchen of a next-door neighbor—and forgot it. But it is buried somewhere deep down. I was listening and looking, entranced, when I suddenly realized that they were singing in English—whereupon they were singing in German. Then I again became bathed in the drama . . . and again they were singing in "English." I went through this several times. By the last day I was understanding all the lyrics . . . save for a couple of singers who did not articulate clearly.[31]

While in Seattle they renewed acquaintances, having dinner at the Nourses' home with F. M. and Elinor Busby and Frank and Beverly Herbert and the young writer Vonda McIntyre.

The cruise ship then took them to the Panhandle portion of Alaska, which they had never visited before. Once you got out of Anchorage and Fairbanks, there was more of the "Old West" there than they had found even in Arizona—wooden sidewalks, muddy streets, trading posts for trappers down out of the Yukon Territory—but it was Glacier Bay that arrested them and held them entranced on deck for most of the day, in the freezing weather:

> I've seen, oh, 20 or 30 or more, glaciers in the past—but never from this angle, never so close up, and *never* so active. Instead of a few inches a day Margerie Glacier moves *30 feet* per day—so it "calves" (gives off an iceberg) several times each hour. While I knew that glaciers give off icebergs, I had *not* realized how spectacular it is to see a cliff of blue ice break off and become a berg. And how *noisy* it is. A "white noise" rumble remarkably like that of a very large rocket.[32]

And back to the grind, and back, of course, to the usual stack of accumulated mail. They had offered Phil and Tessa Dick a loan in the summer, at the time Robert sent the electric typewriter, when they suspected the medical bills would swamp the Dicks financially, but Tessa had declined the offer. While they were in Seattle, she wrote reversing herself, apologizing that she simply couldn't juggle the bills anymore and asking for a loan to pay at least part of their taxes. Robert and Ginny sent off a chatty and supportive letter, together with a check for the full amount of the taxes.

And in the same mail was an invitation to be the first civilian passengers on the proposed space shuttle—which Ginny accepted for them with enthusiasm.[33]

The writing work continued on the rare blood article, as the critical comments began coming in from his experts. Most of the comments were lavishly complimentary about the article as a unit—it was "a literary coup,"[34] "a masterpiece of compression and information-loading,"[35] and "first rate for a young person's encyclopedia."[36] Isaac Asimov comically complained that, having driven all the science-fiction writers into the second rank, Heinlein was now driving the poor science popularizers (like him) into second place as well.[37] But the finicky accumulation of corrections required revision after revision—including an opportunity to take a swing at the racist stereotype of sickle-cell anemia being a Negro disease (the mutation occurs in all races; it's simply conserved only in places where malaria is endemic). Even as late as October, he was phoning in changes of wording, additions of a sentence or two to take new science into account, and a sudden change in federal law that required new handling procedures for reconstituted plasma.

He turned down a query from *Rolling Stone* magazine wanting to do a whole Robert Heinlein issue and let Blassingame handle the Avalon Hill people, who were doing a board game based on *Starship Troopers*. He began concentrating on blood services more than blood science.

Rivalry and factionalism was much more pronounced in blood services than in the pure-science end of the blood supply problem—but these people were passionate about something that actually mattered in the real world. That was something worth more than writing entertainments—worth dedicating your life and your treasure to. When he applied for membership to the American Association of Blood Banks (AABB) in December 1975, his strategy was already well advanced, building on the rare blood article as a start. The application asked him to state the nature of his interest:

Recruitment . . . When I started research for this MS [the rare blood article] I knew nothing about blood programs other than through my work in recruiting for NRBC. I now wish to recruit donors of *all* blood types for *all* legitimate blood programs: AABB, CCBC, American Red Cross, Canadian Red Cross, British Red Cross, etc., and I have the means to do it; this typewriter.[38]

He used all his politician's tact and fancy footwork to keep the dialogue going with the many scientists and scientist-administrators he had established relationships with—the same methods he and Ginny had used in Soviet Russia, turning their natural sociability to account:

> The magic words "Encyclopedia Britannica" got the Big Man on the line; now I must keep him there. I couch my question in technical terms of hematology plus blood bankers' argot . . . . then once I've established that I understand the language, I find opportunity to admit (with false modesty) that, No, I'm not a blood banker or an M.D. or anything of the sort, but a former aviation-structures engineer—however I have studied most carefully Race & Sanger's *1975* edition . . . . these blood people are all enthusiasts (fanatics, most of them) and they welcome a chance to pontificate at length to a layman who understands and appreciates their problems—they meet so few who do.
>
> If he shows any signs of slowing down, I use a banderilla: "Dr. Whoosis—" (some equally prominent hematologist as far from Santa Cruz as possible & who I know holds an opinion on a controversial issue diametrically opposed to that held by the man to whom I am speaking—and I usually do know, as I've been reading many pounds of the current literature and noting which side each one takes)—"Dr. Whoosis told me day before yesterday that, etc."
>
> He represses or sometimes fails to repress a snort of indignation. "Dr. Whoosis is a very learned man, a fine man, a close friend of mine—but between you and me he has a very narrow outlook on this matter. He fails to take into consideration the practical side of, etc."—whereupon I sit down, light a cigarette and listen and take notes.[39]

The proofs of the article were finally ready in December, two days before Heinlein went into the local Dominican Hospital for his third—and final—hernia repair surgery. This time he stayed awake for the whole thing, with a saddle block anesthesia, though the doctors irritatingly put a screen up so he could not watch what they were doing. Heinlein was released from the hospital on December 23, heavily sedated with Demerol so he would not be hurt by the winding mountain roads on the way home.

They were not "doing Christmas" that year, since Heinlein was restricted to bed rest until December 30, when he was able to totter around the atrium and the pain of getting into and out of bed was decreasing. He was particularly anxious to get back to work. His extra time in the hospital had given him a chance to indulge one of his sickbed habits: He read up on the history of the nun-nurses' religious order. That was an exceptionally productive read:

> I suddenly figured out something I had long wondered about: why nuns live so long but never grow old. It enabled me to put into words a truth that had been inchoate in me for many years. Hear me: One certain path to happiness lies in having the *opportunity* to work to the utter limit of your strength on some difficult task that *you* believe to be worth doing.

That was exactly the insight he needed for what he was about to undertake: "And a . . . corollary: Any time you can give someone the chance to work hard on something that *he himself*—no other judge!—evaluates as being worth doing, you are doing him a favor beyond price."[40]

Characters and personality types fall into and out of fashion, but they do not fall out of existence. Heinlein knew this character type; he was one, himself— and he had been writing for them, for more than thirty-five years.

27

"I Vant Your Blood"

As useful and important as the National Rare Blood Club was, it could not make even a dent in the problem of blood collection services in this country—appalling and an international embarrassment. Prior to 1976, most blood banks in the United States bought their blood stocks mostly from derelicts and the destitute—the population segment most likely to have untreated blood-borne diseases. Viral screening was almost nonexistent, and even bacterial and biochemical screening was limited and primitive.

The painfully obvious solution was to stop buying blood, and the American Blood Commission (ABC) was set up in 1975 to supervise the National Blood Policy Proposed Implementation Plan, changing over to an all-volunteer blood donor program, as many other countries had already done. The ABC expected the Big Three—the American Red Cross, the American Association of Blood Banks (AABB), and the Council of Community Blood Banks (CCBB)—to take the lead in developing the all-volunteer donor corps.

The blood banks had set about the project in the obvious ways—holding recruitment drives by placing notices of blood-mobile appearances in newspapers, and so forth. That, Heinlein concluded, was a souped-up way of preaching to the converted: "Donors do show up . . . [sic] but they are the same donors who showed up last time; such a notice rarely recruits a new donor."[1] What was needed—and what his casual polling of the blood-collection professionals led him to think they really hadn't grasped—was that they needed to recruit *new* donors.

And this is where Heinlein could put his shoulder to the wheel. He had found recruiting donors ridiculously easy on a retail basis. He had run a test of his ideas at their usual "at-home" at the Tuscany while they were in New York. That casual chat recruited Robert Erburu—president and chief executive of the Times-Mirror conglomerate—who was a Basque by heritage and therefore more likely to be in one of the rare groups. Heinlein had proved his suspicion, to his own satisfaction.

> . . . I think I've discovered the secret of recruiting donors. *Ask* him. Ask *him.* Some *specific* person . . . .
>
> I've recruited taxi drivers, strangers at parties, people I've just met. All it takes is to ask them . . . [sic] explain the need and ask. If he or she meets the requirements, the answer is Yes. Not one person in 50 is so unsocial, so little integrated into his tribe that he will say No to a direct request once he understands the need.[2]

Heinlein had some other ideas about activating volunteers, and he decided to run a series of experiments of his own, to see whether he could duplicate by intentional effort the incidental recruiting that had happened as a side effect of other activities.

He had already concluded that his initial focus on recruiting rare blood donors was misplaced. The true "rare" blood, from a practical point of view, was the one you need *right now* and don't have—which means the two *com-mon*est types—O/Rh+ and A/Rh+: Blood banks routinely run short of these on every three-day holiday weekend.

That means recruiting *any* healthy person, seventeen to sixty-six, for the entire United States.

His own circle of influence was principally in the science-fiction community—and he would work that source—but he had others, too: A note he wrote for *Shipmate* (the U.S. Naval Academy alumni magazine) turned up a surprising number of new recruits from his fellow alumni of the Naval Academy.

His hometown of Kansas City was hosting the 34th World Science Fiction Convention over the Labor Day weekend in 1976—"MidAmeriCon"—and they had asked him to be their guest of honor in the bicentennial year. He planned to use that as his place to stand.[3] The last time he had been guest of honor at a WorldCon, in Seattle in 1961, the convention had topped out at six hundred. Now they were talking about a possible attendance of more than *seven thousand*! It was an opportunity not to be missed. He kicked off his campaign with a full-page letter-ad in the convention's winter 1975 progress report, laying out his basic strategy:

> . . . I am especially anxious to meet personally every blood donor. . . . If you are not a donor simply because no one ever asked you to become one . . .

[sic] simply phone the Red Cross, any blood center, any blood bank, any hospital, your own doctor, or your local medical society and ask how and where—then donate a pint of blood. (Ask for written receipt as proof.) I want to meet blood donors because five of them, strangers to me, saved my life.[4]

With these arrangements, Heinlein could probably spend a few minutes with each donor . . . but the circumstances would have to be rigidly structured in order to make it happen at all. Blood recruitment was becoming his "job." He would have to put off another novel for at least a year.

He wrote two more ads—for the last progress report and the hardcover program book—and made arrangements with local blood services in Kansas City—and had special red-drop-of-blood donor lapel pins made up, to give out as premiums[5]—and then, since relations with the MidAmeriCon committee had turned rocky,[6] rented the necessary suite and function rooms himself. The sponsoring committee's change of attitude was inexplicable: Polite requests were met with incomprehensible refusals, and the chairman was not speaking to them anymore. Ginny asked Jerry Pournelle to step in as diplomat and things did smooth over: The problems were mostly misunderstandings, which he cleared up by being blunt where Robert had been overly polite.[7]

The *Compton Yearbook* came out in February 1976, and they were scheduled to leave for another South Sea cruise in March. The replies and correspondence and files of arrangements for MidAmeriCon took over the dining room, with piles and drifts of papers. Ginny saw that Robert was struggling to answer each letter individually with another letter, which was an impossibly cumbersome way to handle a project as massive as this was turning out to be. She sat down to help, starting by sorting the piles and drifts of paper into some more coherent order, and Robert snarled at her. Clearly he was overwhelmed. Gently, she told him he was going about it the wrong way—and after a while, he agreed with her. Ginny put her long-disused precinct-organization skills to work on the project and set up an invitation system, reducing the incoming mail to check-off lists: Anyone who had donated got an invitation automatically. Anyone who had tried to donate but was turned down also got an invitation.[8] That left only the usual, irritating assortment of time-wasters who tried to wriggle around the restrictions on the receptions—but since this was his pilot project, and coming out of his pocket, Heinlein did not feel the necessity of being nice to people who were not being nice to him.

They started out with three receptions to handle all the donors who RSVP'd.

And they had to add a fourth before the convention, each catered by the hotel with finger sandwiches and punch.[9] The expenses of these events made Ginny blanch. She was in charge of paying for things, and she was not allowed to say "we can't afford that," so she sometimes felt quite faint when the bills came in.[10]

The March trip was another working vacation—blood collection research in New Zealand and Australia. Just before they left to meet *Mariposa* in Honolulu, they got a pleasant, if frustrating, surprise: They would be at sea when Jack Williamson would be named the SFWA's second Grand Master at the Nebula Awards banquet in 1976. Heinlein wrote a warm and funny congratulatory letter:

> Two writers have influenced my writing most: H.G. Wells and Jack Williamson. But you influenced me more than Mr. Wells did.
>
> (I hope not too many readers noticed how much I've leaned on you. *You* spotted it, of course. But you never talk . . . .)
>
> I'm going to tell on myself just once. I took your immortal Giles Habibula, mixed him with your hero in *Crucible of Power* . . . [sic] and made another, after carefully filing off the serial numbers and giving it a new paint job. You invented the hero in spite of himself, the one with feet of clay, human and believable—and I knew a good thing when I saw it. The result? Lazarus Long.[11]

Mariposa ran two days behind schedule throughout the trip—which gave Heinlein more time for necessary study-prep. Blood-collection services in Australia and New Zealand were models the United States could use, and he had illuminating working discussions with the Secretary Organizer of the New Zealand Blood Transfer program in Dunedin.

The delay put them returning to Hawaii on Ginny's birthday, and the route took them zigzagging across the International Date Line and back as midnight passed, so that Ginny got two sixtieth birthdays. They docked in Hawaii, made a little time to visit, and flew back home: The MidAmeriCon project wouldn't wait—and the writing business was stacking up, too.

Ginny's friend Ward Botsford of Caedmon-Records had decided to offer spoken-voice disks and had set up Leonard Nimoy to read "The Green Hills of Earth" and "Gentlemen, Be Seated." Heinlein wrote a set of liner notes that gave him a chance to get Tony the blind machinist before the public: "My lead character is obviously not Tony—but without knowing Tony I could not have written it."[12]

And there was more travel: Ginny had been referred by Alan E. Nourse to a specialist in Seattle, to consult about the tinnitus she had picked up in Rio de Janeiro in 1969. She scheduled the doctor's appointment in July, to coincide with the American premiere performance of Wagner's complete Ring cycle. Robert felt topped off with Wagner. Instead, he wanted to go to Pasadena for the Mars landing. NASA was going to have live pictures of the landing.

This resulted in one of the few real conflicts of wills Robert and Ginny had over the years. Ginny wound up simply taking off for Seattle on her own on the thirteenth of July, Robert furious and not speaking to her. He left for Southern California on the sixteenth, staying with Larry and Marilyn (Fuzzy Pink) Niven in at their large home in Tarzana. Ginny joined him in Pasadena. They were both at the Jet Propulsion Laboratory in Pasadena the next night, which happened to be the seventh anniversary of the lunar landing—in the special lounge the NASA PR flacks had set up for VIPs. Jerry Pournelle had brought them even though there hadn't been time to get the proper press credentials: Heinlein was so obviously appropriate for this event that Pournelle thought nothing of it. According to an informal poll Pournelle had conducted, somewhere between one-third and one-half of the working scientists on the Viking Project told him they had been recruited into their careers by reading Heinlein—particularly the juveniles. But just before the lander was to touch down, they were approached by the senior NASA official at the Von Kármán Center, who told them Heinlein could not stay there, but should instead go up to the cafeteria where large television monitors had been set up for the general public admissions.

Pournelle was furious, but Heinlein would not let him make a scene, saying simply, "You will not do that." He took Pournelle by the arm, "and he essentially frog-marched me up the hill with him."[13]

They were just getting settled in—a very good view of the proceedings—when network news camera crews from NBC and ABC appeared and gathered around, cameras trained on Heinlein. They had followed them from the Von Kármán Center in order to interview Heinlein for first actual touchdown on an alien planet, leaving all dignitaries behind, including the governor of California and James C. Fletcher, the NASA administrator, wondering why no one was covering the event.

The first pictures of Mars started coming in around dawn the next day.

This event gave Pournelle an opportunity to talk with Heinlein about another project he was becoming interested in—the new L5 Society. In the 1970s Gerard K. O'Neill's space habitat concept—giant farmland stations in high Earth orbit—caught the imagination of some technically savvy young people, who had founded the L5 Society to put the ideas before the public. Getting the space message before the public was a subject Heinlein was always very interested in. Heinlein was on board with L5.

Ten days before MidAmeriCon, August 20, 1976, Robert's brother Rex died in Palo Alto. He had endured emphysema for years and had been struggling to stay alive for Kathleen, one breath at a time, as she suffered through chemotherapy on her own, ultimately losing battle for survival against metastatic lymphoma—cancer.

All his life, Rex had been the one Heinlein had to measure himself against—in a sense, he could mark when he became a man when he no longer had to compare himself to Rex and could come to like and admire his brother as a person.

Robert took on the sad but cathartic task of writing Rex's obituary. Rex was cremated at once, and his ashes were scattered in the Pacific Ocean. The Anglo-Catholic church Rex and Kathleen attended in Palo Alto held his memorial service:

> By the arrangements the priest had made, I read my brother's favorite psalm, the 23rd. Got up to the lectern and found that the revised Book of Common Prayer used a version worded quite differently from that of the King James Version. So I pretended to read while in fact quoting the King James Version, that being the one that I knew my brother knew and certainly preferred. It went off all right . . . when I had been much fretted by the unavoidable duty of taking part in this—when highly emotional I tend to choke up and can't talk . . . which I was, not from sorrow for my brother, as to him it was a victory and a release; his body was worn out and every moment was a pain-filled burden—no, *I* feel bereft; I shall no longer have his warm company and his wise counsel.[14]

MidAmeriCon was not what anybody expected. The committee's efforts to discourage attendance worked too well: Instead of the seven thousand that had been projected, on-site attendance was closer to two thousand, and a good many of them were disenchanted with the committee. This did not seem to lessen the numbers Robert and Ginny had to deal with, however: Almost *everybody* wanted into the receptions. They both were quite frazzled by the time the convention opened.

This was a very different experience from his last appearance as a World-Con guest of honor in 1961. This time, he seemed surrounded by a phalanx of committee people and rarely made contact of any sort with the convention attendees. Heinlein tried to keep a pleasant demeanor as they were whisked through back corridors and up and down service elevators, feeling isolated and sometimes a little disoriented, overworked and overcommitted. "The truth of the matter is," Ginny wrote after it was over,

> aside from the official events, Robert and I saw very little of the convention. Whenever Robert was in public he was busy signing books until his hand could practically no longer write. I did a lot of the inscriptions which people wanted and also some book-signing when I was asked. We did not go to any of the panels; there was always something else demanding our presence . . . Several days we got nothing to eat from breakfast until after midnight.[15]

Family commitments added to the pressure: Relatives he had, perhaps, not seen in years could not understand that he *could not* get away from the convention to have a reunion dinner and remember Rex with family. Robert and Ginny had invited Lurton Blassingame to spend the convention with them, and he was using one bedroom of the Truman Suite. They were not able to spend much time with him as it was.[16] Heinlein's brother Larry brought an entire suitcase full of his books to be autographed: It was either sign Larry's books or write his guest of honor speech.[17] He signed books for Larry; when the time came to give his guest of honor speech, he made up an impromptu speech using his accumulated repertoire of bits and anecdotes—and made it more interesting by using a gimmick of setting his watch's timer at the start of the speech and then simply chopping off in the middle of a sentence when the time was up. The speech—indeed many of the events of the convention— were "cablecast" in the hotel's in-house television network.[18]

The Community Blood Centers of Kansas City (whose Dr. Bayer was organizing the on-site blood collection at the convention) gave him an award plaque—as did the convention itself. Both he and Ginny were made honorary citizens of Texas, which was odd but pleasant. Heinlein was organizing three new groups at this convention: Science Fiction Blood Donors International, to take advantage of the worldwide attendance at WorldCons; The Future Donors of America and Canada (he had set this one up because some youngsters trying to donate had been brushed off when they should have been given deferral cards); and the SFWA Blood Club.

Making the arrangements for the special SFWA blood drive, he found the blood-donor proportions astonishingly high among his colleagues—*fourteen times* higher than the general public's rate. Dr. Bayer assured him, higher than the rate even among doctors and nurses. Heinlein took special pains to acknowledge his colleagues at this convention. He had been warmed to find that not only was he mistaken about the general attitude of his colleagues to him, but the fraternal feeling in the SFWA *in general* was much more pronounced than he knew—or could reasonably have expected.

After one reception, he had a chance to chat briefly with Spider Robinson in a receiving line. Spider stammered that "The Man Who Traveled in Elephants" was his favorite story. Heinlein looked surprised and leaned in to whisper that it was his, too—and no one had ever told him that before.[19]

On the last day of the convention, they had a book signing; Ginny intercepted books before they got to him, and wrote out the inscriptions so that Robert could just sign—and spend additional seconds chatting with people. Ginny flew back to Santa Cruz, leaving Robert in Kansas City for a few days to complete the blood-banking discussions he had started with Dr. Bayer. He made it home on September 11.

Ginny's wrists ached for days after they got back home, and she had to wear a wrist brace for weeks longer—but it was a wonderful experience, memories to be cherished and individuals met and to be cultivated. The blood drive was a terrific success; his pilot program worked out better, even, than he had expected.

Four days after he got back—September 15, 1976—Bam passed away. It was another "release," and a final cadence of sorts for the Heinlein family. She had been almost completely senile for the last five years. Her lucid periods showed that she was living in her youth; nothing after 1899 (the year of her marriage to Rex Ivar) existed for her, and she did not recognize her own children, not even MJ, who took care of her daily needs. Bam's body was shipped back to Kansas City; she wanted to be buried with Rex in the family plot. Robert and Ginny flew back to Kansas City for the burial.

Heinlein's appearance at MidAmeriCon had opened a floodgate, and invitations gushed in. He subscribed to Andy Porter's *Algol* for its reliable listing of science-fiction conventions, adding:

> If this is of any interest to your readers, let me add that Mrs. Heinlein and I intend to attend as many SF and/or ST [*Star Trek*] conventions that hold blood drives as possible—i.e., subject to health, strength, and conflicting dates while continuing to average three months per year for writing fiction (that being the average time I have devoted to fiction for the past 39 years) and while continuing our on-site investigation of blood services abroad (one or more months each year). But those restrictions will still permit us to attend many conventions; we are already signed up for seven in '77–'78, and each of us is in excellent health.[20]

They had set a policy to pay their own expenses, since they didn't want to be beholden to whatever deals the local sponsoring organizations were embroiled in. In October alone they were scheduled for a trip to Alamogordo, New Mexico, for the dedication of the International Space Hall of Fame, then to San Francisco for a blood bank convention. In 1977 they were scheduled for a *Star Trek* convention in Seattle and then across country to Atlanta for an important joint Red Cross–Community Blood Centers meeting on "The Human Element in Blood Services," specifically to discuss volunteerism in blood collection.

The blood bank conference in San Francisco was unusually productive for Heinlein. The blood professionals were struggling—floundering, really—with the volunteer donor concept. The regional director of the CCBC approached him to organize a Bay Area blood drive the following year, which he was delighted to undertake. Since Heinlein was a member of the American Association of Blood Banks—a "rival" blood banking organization—this was particularly welcomed as an example of cross-association cooperation.

He also took the opportunity to meet with David Gerrold and R. Faraday Nelson in their suite in the Hilton to set in motion the arrangements for the ongoing SFWA Blood Drive.

Local blood centers around the country had seen the rare blood article for the *Compton Yearbook* and were asking for offprints. The initial supply furnished by *Britannica* of one hundred offprints was soon exhausted, and they had to find a source of paper in order to fill those requests. But it was a high priority: That article was Robert's professional entre into the field, until such time as his work with volunteer donors earned the respect of the Big Three. He had been working closely with the Council of Community Blood Centers, and he had a certain amount of credibility built up with them; the American Association of Blood Banks and especially the Red Cross were going to be tougher: So far, they were *not* part of the solution . . .

The American National Red Cross was in charge of administering this joint conference with the Council of Community Blood Centers coming up in Atlanta from January 31 to February 4, 1977. What happened at that conference would affect what Heinlein would be able to do in the real world. But their application form stated bluntly that the conference was open only to *professional* staff members of the ANRC and CCBC plus *officially invited* guests. That left him out entirely, since the blood organization to which he belonged (AABB) was not part of the conference.

It was utterly ridiculous—but also utterly typical of the profession's failure to grapple with the realities—that the conference on "The Human Element in Blood Services" excluded "the human element" from their deliberations. Nevertheless, the Heinleins sent in their applications and prepaid the conference fees, including a special fee for a seminar scheduled early in the conference, on recruitment efforts.[21]

They did not receive even an acknowledgment of the application.

They left for a *Star Trek* convention in Seattle on Friday, January 28, 1977. The Red Cross had eventually come across with an official "invitation"—for Robert only, and only for the last two days of the conference, the CCBC meeting after all the Red Cross people had left.[22] Enough was enough. They dropped it from their schedule, canceled plane and hotel reservations for Atlanta, and concentrated on having a good time at the science-fiction and *Star Trek* convention in Seattle. Instead of visiting Atlanta, Robert now intended to let Ginny go home directly from Seattle while he took a dogleg side trip to inspect their investment in a Montana gold mine. Heinlein was interested in typical arrangements for blood supply when they were snowed in. The mine was too high for Ginny, at nine thousand feet.[23]

Seattle was their fifth blood drive since MidAmeriCon, but Robert found that working the blood drive didn't seem to take as much out of him as plain convention work. The example of these young people put as much—more— into him as the drain on his energy. He stayed in the recovery room, signing books and chatting, while he took the opportunity to observe closely how the entire process, as administered by the local Red Cross, worked.

It was a disillusioning experience. The professionals were . . . well, *professional*—competent, detached . . . and completely unprepared for any of the "new" donors they were getting. While Heinlein gave autographs outside the phlebotomy room at the Seattle blood drive, he saw a young woman sit down and collapse in on herself in a faint—a clear case of syncope. Feeling faint and woozy is a well-known side effect of giving blood. Experienced donors knew this syncope was not serious, knew what to do about it—slow down, eat something, wait it out. But no one here seemed to know what to do. Heinlein got her stabilized and took her back to her room with the help of a convention gofer, gently explaining to her exactly what had happened to her, why it need not happen, why it was *not* dangerous but merely unpleasant, how to avoid it the next time she donated—blandly assuming that she *would* donate again.[24]

The Red Cross—the *professionals*—weren't using even good sense in their setup, and the waste of human resources he saw offended him: The out-of-state medical people, who were not licensed to practice in the convention's state, could help out with care and feeding of the new donors. "A first donation *must* be a happy experience," he wrote, "or you have failed to create a repeat donor."[25]

Worst waste of all, though, was the volunteer donors simply turned away. With his recent insights about the emotional importance of the opportunity to be of service, Heinlein realized that this would have a deadening effect on the entire process. Instead, they should be allowed to serve in whatever capacity they could. He explained his thinking to the coordinator for the SFWA Blood Club:

> Since the blood centers can't supply the degree of T.L.C. a steady flood of first-timers needs, we must be prepared to supply it ourselves. Fortunately the job does not require medical professionals; any intelligent layman can be taught all he needs to know about what sort of trouble to expect, how to avoid it, what to do if something slips. But the job *must* be done or our new recruits will not become repeat donors. So we must do it ourselves.
>
> The rejected or deferred volunteer offers the best source of helpers in this—with the double bonus that this work not only creates repeat donors but also creates that other indispensable factor: enthusiastic, industrious, volunteer blood workers. Hurt pride has been healed by the chance to be useful.[26]

On Sunday night, the last day of the convention, they received a telephone call in their hotel room from William Kyler, the executive director of the Council of Community Blood Centers. He wanted them at the meeting in Atlanta.

By this time, Robert had certainly lost any enthusiasm for the conference—and he was getting fed up with the "professionals" anyway (Kyler personally was a special case; they were on a very friendly basis). He gave Kyler to Ginny and told him he would do what she decided. They talked for half an hour, and in the end she said "we go." They dropped by home late Monday evening to pick up some more clothes—and Ginny's ice-skates—and took a flight to Atlanta the next day, having missed the "recruiting seminar" they had paid for. But they were there for the plenary session, and what Heinlein saw there—[27]

> This learned group of truly intelligent people talked nonsense for hour after hour . . . [sic] and were not aware that they were talking nonsense . . . .
>
> Most of them seemed puzzled that anyone should question their right and their authority to make moral decisions about your blood and mine. They were the experts. "Father knows best." We were just so many milch cows who must give down when told to do so.[28]

They seemed quite offended when people didn't respond with enthusiasm. These people simply did not get the concept of volunteerism, and were sabotaging their own efforts by mismanaging the human resources they depended on. Now Heinlein understood how it could be that his and Ginny's minor but actual volunteer donor programs were flooding the blood centers every time they held a drive. He did now what he always did: pointed out the realities, bluntly: "In general, I made myself highly unpopular."[29]

After the session, the medical director of the Red Cross's largest blood center buttonholed Heinlein to set him straight, laying down the law. Robert would have preferred to let it go, since the prospect of public arguments always made him ill. But he was representing the "human element" here: He girded up mental loins and stopped the doctor in mid-sentence. "We do *not* have to take your instructions. *You* have to get along with us. If the volunteer workers and the volunteer blood donors walk out on you, *you . . . ain't . . . got . . . no . . . job!*"[30]

After the doctor indulged in a bit of face-saving bluster, Heinlein volunteered to make good the "misunderstanding" by not coming into his district to recruit, leaving them to their own devices, which would have been a disaster—for them. Once the implications began to sink in, Heinlein invited him up to their suite for drinks and to continue the discussion on a more rational basis.

The next afternoon, all the Red Cross people left for home and the CCBC went into its sessions. At first, general talk-talk focused on donor recruiting—the one subject always on the minds of blood professionals. Heinlein expressed an opinion, based on his experience in Seattle, that the ARC's methods left something to be desired. He was quite blunt, unaware that the senior vice president of the Red Cross was present—and deeply offended.

After that meeting, the local Bay Area director of the CCBC, who had approached him the previous November to set up a blood drive, sought him out with his medical director—to jawbone him about badmouthing the Red Cross.

"No problem. Don't give it another thought."

"You won't talk that way about the Red Cross?"

"I can't think of any reason why I would be talking about the Red Cross in your district. But that wasn't what I said. There is no problem because I won't be in your district; the drive is canceled."

"Now wait a moment! Let's discuss this."

"There's nothing to discuss. Did you really think you could tell an unpaid speaker what he must not say? I don't permit that even when I'm charging all the traffic will bear."[31]

They both took on worried expressions and went into a huddle. As he later told R. Faraday Nelson, the head of the SFWA Blood Club,

> I never intended at any point not to do that drive; it is still scheduled. But I was not going to let them tell me what to say . . . blood politics in this country are *very* complex, and no SFWA member should ever let a blood professional boss him. If you surrender one iota of your independence you are all too likely to find yourself being used politically. Blood professionals are a peculiar breed. They are almost invariably fanatically devoted to saving lives—and they fight among themselves just as fanatically. Let's not get involved in it.[32]

The blood professionals absolutely could not be permitted to perpetuate their current policy of sabotaging their own recruitment efforts. If you want things to change—then you have to actually *change*.

And then he helped them help themselves into an arrangement they could all live with.

But the experience was very wearing.

Atlanta was followed a week later by an appearance as Fan Guest of Honor at SpaceCon, at the San Francisco Civic Auditorium. The real headliners were cast members of *Star Trek*. SpaceCon was another lesson—as if he needed it—in the professionals sabotaging themselves. The drive, run by San Francisco's Irwin Memorial Blood Bank, ground to a complete standstill. Two volunteers, Sondra and Myrna Marshak, took charge, and things began happening.[33] The Heinleins also noticed that there was less sheer pressure on Robert at the *Star Trek* conventions than at science-fiction conventions:

> Robert can go around in a Star Trek convention without being bothered, buttonholed, and so on. It's wonderful! I don't think that we met a single rude, self-interested-only individual in the entire group. Everyone was so cooperative and helpful that I find myself stunned by it all.[34]

It was at this convention, in one of the blood donor lines, that they met and were enchanted by Nichelle Nichols, who played Lt. Uhura on *Star Trek*. They were scheduled for another *Star Trek* convention in March. Ginny started collecting material for a handbook on recruiting blood donors and holding blood drives.

Heinlein was having a hard time settling down actually to write a new book.[35] On the evidence of what he eventually did write, he wanted to do a

romp, revisiting the exciting fictional worlds of his youth—Oz and Wonder-
land, the Barsoom of Edgar Rice Burroughs, and the universes of the Lens-
men. Instead he wrote another "appreciation" letter for the next SFWA Grand
Master, Clifford D. Simak—another writer he had learned much from as a
young pup writer. Part of the letter he spent marveling at Simak's technique:

> Mr. Simak, I realize that you have done almost everything in newspaper
> work from printer's devil to publisher . . . but I know also that you have
> spent much of the past half century either on the beat, in the slot, or on the
> rim—then have gone home and written highly effective fiction that same
> day. *How* did you do it?
>
> That is a rhetorical question, as I would be incapable of understanding
> the answer and would continue to be amazed . . . .
>
> Let me close by saying that, since the earliest thirties, to read science fic-
> tion is to read Simak. A reader who does not like Simak stories does not like
> science fiction at all. So it gives me great pleasure to join in this celebration.
>
> With admiration and respect, I remain—
>
> —Robert A. Heinlein[36]

Heinlein had been "working on" his new book since the previous fall, but
he had barely gotten anything actually written down by the time they had to
pack up for the next blood drives. A major Science Fiction Exposition was
scheduled in Tucson, Arizona, early in June, and they had agreed to do two
blood drives in Phoenix before driving to Tucson, 120 miles south—numbers
six, seven, and eight for the year. One was a fee-arrangement: Robert agreed
to give an after-dinner speech for a meeting of the recently formed Libertarian Party, for a fee of fifty pints of blood—which they paid by a sheaf of donor slips put in his hand as he came into the hall.

Robert thought of himself as a libertarian-with-a-small-l—Judith Merril
had once called herself a democrat and a libertarian. "I think that describes
me, too," he told her—

> —still a democrat not because I love the Common Peepul and not because
> I think democracy is so successful (look around you) but, because in a life-
> time of thinking about it and learning all that I could, I haven't found any
> other political organization that worked as well.
>
> As for libertarian, I've been one all my life, a radical one. You might use
> the term "philosophical anarchist" or "autarchist" about me, but "libertar-
> ian" is easier to define and fits well enough. But I'm glad you didn't use the

term "liberal" which used to mean much the same thing and with which I once tagged myself. But today "liberal" means to me a person who wants to pass laws and use coercion to force other people to live in *his* notion of utopia—the word "liberal" no longer seems to have any connection with its root "free"—it always means "Pass another law! *Make* the bastard do it our way." Whereas my solution to almost everything is "Let's repeal that law" or, possibly, "Let's not do anything—let's wait."[37]

But he came this time to kick some over-upholstered butt. Most of these new converts had been brought in by Ayn Rand and suffered from a peculiar kind of mental arthritis. Robert had no use for theoretical doctrinaires, so he decided to play *advocatus diabolus* and took as his text the lifeboat problem: You are ship's officer in a lifeboat, in freezing, choppy seas, he posited, with the only gun. There are too many people for the boat's supplies to sustain, and more in the water. What do you do?

This was a good test problem, because it requires you to take a position on an extremely fundamental question: the moral relationship of the public and the private. "I find that if a man can face up to the 'lifeboat problem,' find a solution that makes sense, I can deal with him."[38] But the simplistic, doctrinally pure answers favored by this generation of libertarians gave no help.

> Any libertarian so doctrinaire that he cannot find a pragmatic solution to this problem deserves no tolerance from others. His opinions on "rights" in space are worthless; the rest of us are under no obligation to let him waste our time.
>
> Unfortunately a large percentage of those who describe themselves as "libertarian" are indeed that doctrinaire, and would thereby be a mortal danger to their shipmates.[39]

He would not let them change the terms of the problem, or tap dance out of it. One older man became so angry he cursed Robert and stomped out of the meeting; a younger man became so upset that he began to stammer and could not talk.[40]

His work there was done. On to Tucson.

The SF Expo was very badly conceived and executed. Instead of the thousands expected, only about five hundred showed up, and the blood drive (they had dragooned the young Michael Cassutt to run it) collected only thirty-five pints of blood. But if the Red Cross was happy, Heinlein was happy. He gave a television interview promoting the Red Cross to KGUN TV[41] and on a tour of a hospital at the University of Arizona, observed an experimental heart catheterization done on a dog, the fluoroscopic television monitor showing the tube moving up the dog's arteries to its brain where they injected an X-ray opaque dye. The dog didn't seem to mind, which was mind-boggling.[42]

Back at home, Robert went to work, writing. Ginny noticed that he was abstracted quite a lot of the time, which was usual while he was writing. But he also went off on talking jags sometimes, which was not usual at all.[43] By the end of June 1977, he was two hundred pages into the manuscript. Years earlier, as the projects got larger, Ginny had stopped reading the "dailies." Heinlein said he got more useful feedback from her if she read it all at once, when he was finished with the first draft.[44] This one was going slowly; when the manuscript reached five hundred pages, he told her it might take two years to write![45]

They had been contacted by David Hartwell for Gregg Press's line of hardcover science fiction for libraries.[46] Heinlein always was interested in keeping his books in hardcover—and knew they sold well to libraries. Despite a very small advance,[47] Heinlein and Hartwell contracted for two books to appear in 1978, *Double Star* (with an introduction by Joe Haldeman) and *I Will Fear No Evil* (with an introduction by Paul Williams, founder of *Crawdaddy*, the first U.S. magazine of rock music criticism).[48]

At the urging of Lloyd Biggle, Heinlein finally decided to accept an honorary Doctorate of Humane Letters from Eastern Michigan University on September 23, 1977. Ginny arranged three blood drives in conjunction with the trip to Detroit and Ypsilanti—to keep him busy while she made some stealth arrangements of her own: The artist Frank Kelly Freas had done a very sexy portrait of Nichelle Nichols as Lt. Uhura that was destined for the Smithsonian's permanent collection. Ginny wanted a copy—a duplicate painting, actually—to give Robert for his birthday. Freas was dubious about being able to complete it in time, but his wife, Polly, assured Ginny she would see to it. Ginny recruited Kelly to help out with the upcoming SunCon blood drive at the end of the month, sketching to entertain the donors waiting for the doctors.

For the ceremony Heinlein was decked out in academic regalia, with gown and mortarboard. President Brickley of the university gave the principal address:[49]

[H]is work has endured remarkably. In an era when a bestselling, prize-winning novel may be forgotten within a decade, virtually everything Robert Heinlein has written in the field of science fiction is still in print, still being bought and read with high praise, wherever people read books and in whatever language.

Doc Smith's daughter Verna Trestrail was there, and Betsy Curtis—and Denis Paradis came down to Detroit from Montreal, to meet in person for the first time. Denis noticed something "not quite right" about Robert's health, but could not put his finger on it exactly.[50]

SunCon, over the Labor Day weekend of 1977, plunged them back into big science-fiction conventions, so much more stressful than the *Trek* conventions. On the way to the registration desk, they were stopped half a dozen times by autograph seekers, and finally had to beg off, saying that because of Robert's medical problems with balance he could no longer sign standing up; he really needed a table set up to give autographs these days.[51] On another occasion, they were seated in the lobby talking with some friends, and Ginny looked up to realize they were surrounded by a ring of fans trying to listen in to the conversation. It was tiresome—and not a little creepy—to be so constantly on display.[52]

On one occasion, a bearded young man marched up to Heinlein in the middle of the hotel lobby, obviously having screwed up his courage to the act. His name was Jim Baen, he explained, an editor for Ace Books. He had noticed that Ace had just one Heinlein property, the old (1966) *Worlds of Robert A. Heinlein* collection, that had an unaccountably low royalty: 4.5 percent. He had persuaded the powers-that-be at Ace to increase the royalty rate, he said, to 8 percent. Heinlein had paid almost no attention at all to the royalty reports on this "bottom-of-the-barrel" collection, so he was surprised by the news, but properly grateful: He thanked young Baen, but before he could invite him to sit down and chat, Baen marched away, having successfully surmounted his personal crisis.

Between the blood drives, Robert kept plugging away at the new novel, *The Panki-Barsoom Number of the Beast.* Working on it one day, he had a brief moment of disconnect, and his vision doubled and went blurry. He sat quietly until it passed. He was overstressed, he knew—but he had too much lined up for the immediate future to take a break now. He did not mention the incident to Ginny at that time.[53]

On October 13 they flew to Salt Lake City for two blood drives in Utah. The first was in conjunction with a small science-fiction convention, Saltcon, where two local Mormon hospitals were collaborating on the blood drive. Just three weeks after the doctoral ceremony, he was obviously tired. At one point, Jerry Pournelle solicitously offered to help him getting down a stairway. "Of course I can get down the stairs!" Heinlein snapped. "I can always *fall* down!" He was articulate and witty in private conversation, but Karen Serassio (the chair of the convention) observed that the prospect of giving his public guest of honor speech seemed to distress him, and that he was nervous and ill at ease during the speech. She later heard audience members speculate that he was going senile.[54] The announcement that Bing Crosby had just died was in the news that morning, so he led off with a prayer. The high percentage of Mormons in his audience was obviously on his mind, but he was not articulating well. Ginny sat in the front row so she could prompt him, if necessary—and did when he said "LSD" instead of "LDS." At the end of his speech, he led the convention singing "Come, Come Ye Saints."[55]

The next leg of the trip, a blood drive in Logan, Utah, was disastrous. When they got to Logan, they found that *none* of the conditions on which they had agreed to come had been accommodated: The Red Cross did not want them there in the first place; the library told him to talk about science fiction—and refused to limit the audience to blood donors (which was an absolute condition so far as Heinlein was concerned).[56]

This was exactly why they made a policy of paying their own way: Heinlein told them bluntly that he would not be bullied by them, and he and Ginny went home a day early.

After they got home, they received a phone call from Judy-Lynn del Rey, in New York. Arthur C. Clarke was in town, and she had taken him and Isaac Asimov to dinner earlier in the evening. She had a brainstorm, talking with them in her living room, about getting all of "the big three" of science fiction together virtually, if not in the flesh, and phoned Robert at home. At one point, Asimov jocularly said, "Come on, fellows. We've been the *big three* now for decades, and people are getting tired of it. Don't you think, in order to give a break to the other writers, that one of you two (since you're older than I am) should step aside?" They all got a good laugh when Heinlein cut through the indirection: "Fuck the other writers!" he said.[57]

OctoCon, October 21 to 23, 1977, in nearby Santa Rosa (about 150 miles north of Santa Cruz), was the last SF convention blood drive of the year for them, and they were both tired but satisfied with the progress they had made in just a year and a little more. They were getting reports of repeat donors they had recruited early on, so it looked like they could count on the effort reaching a point where it would sustain itself.[58] They could go to Atlanta for an American Association of Blood Banks convention in November with a good report to make.

Heinlein was able to write "The End" on the new novel before the trip to

Atlanta. He finished it early one morning and left the completed manuscript on the kitchen counter for Ginny to read, as usual, and went to bed.

Ginny read through *The Panki-Barsoom Number of the Beast* with growing puzzlement. The story was straightforward enough—two newlywed couples fleeing across alternate realities from alien villains he called "Black Hats" (the Barsoomian name for these "vermin" was *Pankera,* pl. *Panki*). She put down the manuscript. While it was perfectly competent yard goods, it just wasn't a *Heinlein* novel.[59]

She knew what she had to do—and she could not bring herself to do it.

Over the years, Heinlein had always sat down at the typewriter wondering if he could pull it off one more time, and maybe he had just reached the point where he couldn't. This could be the end of his writing career. It would be devastating for him. It was "not best work," she told him.[60] "I took that responsibility very seriously," Ginny later said. "The idea that I just had to tell him not to try to publish it was—almost a death-knell for us."[61]

This was the first time Heinlein had to confront his faculties failing in some important way—and it meant more for him than simple old age. The possibility he would go like his father or his mother—mind gone for years, or flickering in and out—was disturbing. "We just thought it would be that way," Ginny said simply.[62]

There was absolutely nothing that could be done about it—except to accept the reality as he found it and adjust accordingly. He would carry through with the arrangements he had already made for that year, while he still had the ability. Neither of them said anything to anyone. Thanks to Ginny's careful management, their savings would be adequate to keep them comfortable, and even if he did not produce any new books, the writing business continued to expand.

The AABB presented him with an Award of Merit dated November 15, 1977. He had essentially accomplished with the blood drives what he had set out to do. They could be happy with the successful results of their efforts. The AABB and the CCBC were already taking his legacy seriously, and the Red Cross would come around in time, even without his direct supervision.

But for the first time in years, he caught a post-convention respiratory infection and spent time in bed. They took another South Sea Island cruise in mid-December—Heinlein was going to investigate the blood services situation in Papeete now that they had a hematologist reorganizing blood services on the island.

They were in Tahiti by the first of the year, and Heinlein visited the clinic on January 3, 1978. He had another of those "attacks" where his eyes went blurry for a second, but he sat down and waited it out, again not saying anything to Ginny.

The next day, he and Ginny took time off to walk the beach at Moorea, strolling the landing's road, enjoying the view. Robert turned to look at the mountain, and things went blurry. He didn't quite collapse, but he couldn't walk, either. Balancing on his left leg, he told Ginny: "I am very sorry, darling, but I must ask you to take me back to the ship. I have gone into double vision and I'm partly paralyzed on my right side."[63]

"Human Vegetable"

Ginny half carried, half dragged him back to the ship. She got him settled in their cabin and called the ship's doctor.

Dr. Armando Fortuna diagnosed a Transient Ischemic Attack, TIA—not a stroke per se, but a momentary blockage of blood to the brain that can be a precursor to a stroke, an early warning. Heinlein needed to make immediate lifestyle changes—starting with giving up cigarettes. He had an unlit cigarette in his hand at this exact moment: He had smoked for nearly sixty years—since the very first Armistice Day, in fact, November 11, 1918. He put the cigarette back in its pack and never smoked again.[1]

They spent the rest of the trip keeping quiet. Heinlein had numbness and tingling on his right side that came and went, even when his vision was clear. They were in Lahaina on January 11—and did not even let local friends know they were there. Nevertheless, he had another TIA in Hawaii.

Back in Santa Cruz by January 19, 1978, a round of doctor's visits commenced almost immediately. Dr. MacKenzie, their internist, took him off alcohol as well as tobacco and gave him an even more restricted diet than he had been following. He also ordered exercise. In March, Ginny told friends, "Robert has been taking daily exercise for about a week now. He hates it; but does it in the same spirit in which he flosses his teeth—do it and get it over with."[2]

MacKenzie sent Heinlein to Dominican Hospital for an MRI of his brain. Tomography—a series of X-rays combined and interpreted by computers—was a very exotic, high-tech procedure in 1978. The tomography revealed no tumors or evidence of strokes; Dr. MacKenzie said there was a 55 percent chance he could live another five years without a stroke—*if and only if* he reduced lifestyle stress to zero at once and permanently. "Act your ages," he told them. He specifically forbade any more conventions or blood drives.

Dr. MacKenzie suspected a blockage of the carotid artery, so a neurological specialist was called in, Dr. S. Allan Dorosin, at the Sutter Hospital in Santa

Cruz. Dr. Dorosin told them that their best strategy was to wait and see for six months, because the surrounding blood vessels might take up the increased load. He prescribed aspirin and Dipyridamole as blood thinners.

They tried to get on with their lives. Ginny began working on organizing the handbook on conducting blood drives for which she had been collecting notes.[3] She took to wearing earphones so that she could listen to the classical station on the radio all day without disturbing Robert, either because he was sleeping or because it was, as he said, "too emotional" for him to concentrate.[4]

Ginny had told a few friends and business associates about her husband's medical situation, enjoining them to keep quiet about it, as they would be flooded with mail and phone calls if word of his condition got out.

Even with the medication, Heinlein's condition continued to deteriorate. By the first of April 1978, his sense of balance was seriously impaired, and he had to hold on to the walls just to get around the house. Worried, Ginny called Dr. Dorosin just two months into the six-month waiting period: Robert wasn't going to make it at this rate.

Dr. Dorosin needed to get better information. He referred Robert to Dr. Wylie at the UC San Francisco hospital, who was a specialist in the operation that scraped out the carotid artery, reducing the plaque that accumulated on the walls of the blood vessel so that the blood flow could be restored.

Ginny did not tell Heinlein, because he had enough on his mind as it was, that Rowan Thomas, their general partner in the Montana mining operation in which they were so heavily invested, fell ill early in April and went into the hospital with a stomach ache. Four days later, he was dead of advanced metastatic cancer. He was fifty-five years old and apparently in good health, right up till he died.

Heinlein found himself on the other end of the process he had witnessed last year in Tucson, on a dog. The surgical staff positioned the television monitor so that he could see it as well, and he watched the catheter travel up his own veins for two hours on April 16, 1978. The only irritant was that the head of the team performing the angiogram (four doctors, three nurses) was a fan of his and wanted to talk about his stories. Robert mostly could ignore him, interrupting—frequently—for a medical question.

How many people ever get a chance to watch their own hearts beat? Utterly fascinating! I could see my heart beating, see my diaphragm rise and fall, see my lungs expand and contract, see the dye go up into my brain . . . [sic] see the network of blood vessels in my brain suddenly spring into sharp relief. It was worth the trip![5]

The flush of X-ray-opaque dye pinpointed the blockage, high in his skull, above the branching of the artery. The other tests ruled out problems with his heart and the rest of his circulatory system, but this blockage was too high in his skull for the reaming-out operation Dr. Wylie specialized in. Dr. Wylie came to his room while they were both there, and shook his head, saying nothing could be done about it. The prospect of going like his father, fading out for years, was now a reality.

A little later, though, Dr. Wylie stuck his head in the room: "There is one hope," he said. There was a relatively new operation—by chance it was featured in *Scientific American* that month, and Ginny had just read about it—called a "bypass"—in Heinlein's case a carotid bypass. They were mostly done in Zurich, but by chance the world's expert in this new operation, Dr. Norman Chater, was in San Francisco at the nearby Franklin Hospital. Dr. Wylie set up an interview.

The tests showed Robert's other arteries were in good shape: This operation would take a section from an artery servicing the surface of the skull on his temporal lobe and reverse it, joining the cut end to the main artery in the Sylvan fissure of the brain, and jumping around the obstruction (hence "bypass"). Dr. Chater gave him an 85 percent chance of improvement, but the risks were great: They would be operating through a hole in his skull, very near the language and creativity centers of the brain. And there was a 2 percent mortality rate.

He should think about it, Dr. Chater told him—but it should be done quickly; he was especially vulnerable to strokes right now, and any damage to the other blood vessels in a stroke would cut his chances.

This was risking everything on one throw of the dice.

"Well, Honey," he told friend and archivist Rita Bottoms, "it's either sit on a couch for the rest of my life as a vegetable, and never write again, or go through this and take care of it so I can write."[6] He asked Ginny what he should do, but she declined even to give input. There was a sizeable chance of losing him—and she wasn't ready to let go[7]—but, it was something he would have to decide for himself: She would go along with whatever he chose to do.[8] "Was it worthwhile?" Heinlein later wrote:

Yes, even [were] I [to die] at one of the four critical points . . . [sic] because sinking into senility while one is still bright enough to realize that one's mental powers are steadily failing is a miserable, no-good way to live . . . I was just smart enough to realize that I had *nothing* left to look forward to, nothing whatever. This caused me to be quite willing to "Go-for-Broke"—get well or die.[9]

They scheduled the operation for April 28, 1978, at the Ralph K. Davies Medical Center, Franklin Hospital, UCSF. Dr. Chater was a little apprehensive: He had done over two hundred of these operations, but he had never before had so prominent a patient. A few days before the surgery was scheduled, Heinlein contracted a cold. They were reluctant to put off the surgery, so he was "dried out" with antihistamines.

The procedure began with trephination: They peeled back a flap of the scalp and drilled a two-inch-diameter hole into the skull over the left ear, exposing the brain. Heinlein joked to Dr. Chater that a hole in the head was no handicap to a science-fiction writer—a line too good to use only once; he repeated that joke to others, for months. When the bypass was finished, without incident, the surgeons covered the hole with a plastic plate and replaced the scalp.

Jack Williamson had come to San Francisco for a visit, and Ginny took him in to see Robert the morning after the surgery. Even with his short night (there was a period of four hours when he was disoriented and could not speak—postsurgical aphasia—but it passed), the improvement was obvious. Williamson had seen him last in 1976, at MidAmeriCon, and was disturbed then by his "old man's walk and look." Now, "In bed, with a bandage around his head, he greeted us with a strong voice and a vigorous handshake."[10] Ginny put an index card in Robert's hand and told him to write his name: It was the first time in more than a year that his handwriting was legible. The recovery was instantaneous: "It was the difference between a light that's turned on and a light that's off."[11]

Medicare was not covering more than a fraction of the expenses. The supplemental insurance they carried paid only 20 percent of what Medicare paid—and the amount of bookkeeping required to get even that covered was staggering.[12] They were not destitute—but it must have been on Ginny's mind that Robert's retirement from writing might be permanent, and their accountant had warned them that reprint income tends to dwindle away once a writer goes out of production.

And nights, in the hotel, without mentioning it to Robert, Ginny was long-distance managing their Montana mining investment, taking matters into her own hands to prevent the whole thing from collapsing after Rowan Thomas's sudden death. Using Robert's proxy, she appointed a lawyer to represent them at the general partnership meeting and saw to it that the new general partner was an experienced lawyer with a background in mining. She made small, direct loans—a few thousand dollars—to keep the payroll current while probate tied up the funds. Rowan Thomas's widow, Barbara, called her several times, long and uncomfortable pleas to save the partnership by taking more of the investment. This, however, Ginny was not prepared to do: They could not even contemplate throwing good money after bad. The losses on the mining investment, together with the surgery, had wiped out their savings.

Some of the other limited partners called, too, with the same requests, but she rapidly reached the stage where she told them bluntly, "Don't be silly."[13]

"I know there's money in mining," Robert had told her: "We've put a lot into it."[14] And so they had. And that was enough: They had realized some tax benefits from the investment, at a time when they needed the write-offs to control their tax burden, and Ginny decided not to continue with risk investments.

They let him go home a week after the operation, on May 6, 1979. The following morning he resumed his normal schedule, coming into the kitchen to let Ginny know he was ready for breakfast. He fainted, falling against Ginny, hard enough to bruise her.[15] Alarmed, she caught him and wrestled him into a chair, putting his head between his knees until he recovered,[16] "and then he was all right, and he never fainted again after that, but that was a near thing."[17]

They found out immediately that they would have to make more adjustments in their living/working arrangements: Robert called for Ginny that day, and she couldn't hear him because she was wearing her earphones. She began carrying a walkie-talkie with her everywhere.[18]

Heinlein was anxious to get back to writing.[19] After only a few days of bed rest, he got out the manuscript for *Panki-Barsoom* and read it over. It was worse than bad, he told Yoji Kondo later that year: It was mediocre.[20] But he must have seen possibilities in it.

Heinlein had been interested in a specific technical problem for a very long time: multiple first-person viewpoint. Before his mind started to fade, he had drafted experiments with this sort of thing—fragments just to work on the technical problem—and shuffled them into what he called his "laboratory," a drawer in his desk where he kept his writing experiments. There was a lot of noncommercial stuff in his laboratory—including an entire shelf in his closet of porn he had written for his own amusement. Some time ago, he had written a letter of instructions to Alan Nourse, effectively making him their nonofficial literary executor in case they should both be killed while they were

traveling together. In the letter, he had told Nourse where their various concealed caches of money and such were to be found and asked him to dispose
of both the porn and the laboratory—use it for his own amusement if he
wished, but Robert would prefer he destroy it.[21]

John Masters had done something with multiple first-person in *Bhowani
Junction* (1954), but it wasn't quite right: Heinlein had for years been thinking about applying cinema technique—fast, rapid cuts, a kind of different
approach to stream of consciousness[22]—and he had learned enough by his
decades of private experimentation to give it a try.

He had moved, over the last decade, toward a more literary denseness of
structure, always keeping more or less within the bounds of science fiction.
For *The Number of the Beast,* he devised a test platform, an extended argument among his four viewpoint characters. In *Panki-Barsoom,* the character
Zebadiah had naturally gravitated into leading the little band of explorers,
but in *The Number of the Beast,* they had a rotating captainship, arguing out
the problems of command as they went along. The gestation period for *The
Number of the Beast* extended from May to October 1978.

Lurton Blassingame had recently been diagnosed with Parkinson's disease,
and he took on some junior associates and combined agencies with another
agent, Kirby McCauley, to take some of the workload off his shoulders. It was
only a matter of time until he would retire, bringing Heinlein's close association of more than thirty years to an end.

Blassingame brought Kirby McCauley out for a visit late in July 1978, to
introduce him in person. McCauley did not leave a good impression: Some of
the decisions he had made seemed overhasty to them[23]—and he simply could
not get it through his head that Ginny was the business manager for this
team. It grated on Ginny's nerves.

> We tried out Kirby I think for three or four months, and Robert told me
> that I would end up in tears after a conversation with him on the tele-
> phone. He had an attitude toward women that was Medieval. And you
> know: "There, there, little girl. Everything's all right. Now, you just do as
> I say" . . .[24]

She also found he was too careless with details—and their business affairs
were *all* details.[25] She found herself taking on more and more of even the most
minor tasks, and growing increasingly frustrated with trying to deal with
him. Robert told her bluntly they should change agencies, and Ginny began
asking discreetly around, finding out who had what agent.

There had been a sprinkling of academics publishing papers on Heinlein over the last few years: George Slusser, a literature professor at UC Riverside, had published two little monographs in 1976 and 1977.[26] A whole book of academic essays about him was about to be issued by Taplinger Publishing Company.[27] Many of the academic pieces they had seen simply misrepresented what he wrote, either ignoring or misconstruing the clear language of the texts. Now, another academic, H. Bruce Franklin, had written asking for an interview, but Ginny put him off.[28] Robert would not, Ginny knew, be enthusiastic about another academic, even though Franklin had a commission from Oxford University Press to do a book entirely about him—and Franklin had named Sam Moskowitz as a personal reference, which was a point in his favor. Ginny replied that Robert's health was uncertain, but Franklin could write again when he actually got to San Francisco later in the summer of 1978. Possibly by late August Robert would be up to receiving.

Dr. Chater was pleased with Heinlein's progress and discontinued his Dilantin. He was in good spirits, but tired easily, and sometimes the balance problems returned unexpectedly. Heinlein despised the daily exercise routine and said he got enough exercise attending the funerals of friends who did exercise,[29] but by mid-June he could walk up the steep driveway from the road in front of the house—a pull that sometimes winded Ginny—without stopping in the middle to rest. By the end of July, he seemed nearly recovered.

Heinlein was sticking to the regimen this year—no conventions, to keep the stress down; no flying at all. Ginny was going to fly to Phoenix this year for the World SF Convention, IguanaCon II. Blassingame had heard about her discreet inquiries for other agencies and had suggested, instead, that she give a try first to the younger associate he had taken on, Eleanor Wood.

They were already pleased with the new associate who was handling all the foreign business, Ralph Vicinanza: He was on top of the details of all their hundreds of foreign contracts (350 altogether, Ginny found when she went through the files and prepared status summaries for Vicinanza's use) and was even able to do what Ginny had not—get some movement on the Gebruder Weiss lawsuit that had stalled in the German courts. And when their English agent, Innes Rose, announced his retirement later that year, she and Vicinanza were able to move Heinlein's entire backlist to Robert Tanner, the former head of the paperback house New English Library (NEL), who had gone into agenting. Vicinanza swept through their entire list, making several changes, and new foreign contracts rose to startling numbers in 1979. Ginny concluded it was better for them if she did all the fiddling bookkeeping, leaving Vicinanza more time to market the properties.

Eleanor Wood was an unknown quantity—a younger, less experienced agent—but it was certainly worth trying, if for no other reason than to preserve the relationship with the new Blassingame, McCauley & Wood agency.

Heinlein was much better by August—"He's doing things which he hasn't done for several years," Ginny wrote at the time, "driving, working with his hands to make minor repairs, and so on."[30] He was even back at the typewriter, though not yet writing *The Number of the Beast.*

H. Bruce Franklin was in the Bay Area, and the problem of whether or not to give him the interview was now imminent. Heinlein made inquiries and found out two facts, which pointed to opposite conclusions: (1) Franklin was one of those very public academic Marxists—a Maoist, in fact, and (2) he was a former Strategic Air Command pilot and intelligence officer. Heinlein wanted to question him about actual conditions in SAC—but there was a genuine concern about how much usefulness could come out of any serious interaction with an academic Marxist.[31]

Franklin had contacted Rita Bottoms as archivist for Heinlein's papers at the University of California, Santa Cruz, and asked her to intercede on his behalf. Franklin was a respected scholar, currently at Rutgers University, though he had been dismissed from a tenured position at Stanford several years earlier because of his Maoist political activity. Bottoms presented the idea to Robert, and this kicked off nearly two weeks of soul-searching by telephone calls among Bottoms, Robert, and Ginny, much of it after hours. "Not fun," Bottoms remarked succinctly: "It was excruciating."[32] This, she sensed, was his "process"—a long and agonizing process, but something he had to go through to get maximum clarity on a difficult problem. What struck Bottoms about this dialogue was how very *principled* it was[33]—and so like him personally, working from principles to ethical behavior. Most of the time, the process was not so difficult. Heinlein felt something like an obligation to cooperate in Franklin's process of collecting the material from which his opinions would be framed. Against this, he did not like Franklin's confessedly Maoist politics.

If he had access to more detailed historical records, Heinlein might have been swayed more in one direction than another, for he was unknowingly enacting a historical crisis going on in American politics at the time—and playing the part of the traditional American liberal confronting the New Left. Franklin's expression of his political opinions was not confined to academic papers: He had founded the Vinceremos splinter off the SDS (Students for a Democratic Society) specifically to start terrorist acts now (rather than the fifteen years in the future that was the "mainstream" opinion in the SDS)—and

Vinceremos ultimately became the Symbionese Liberation Army, which had catapulted to national fame in 1975 when they kidnapped and "turned" heiress Patty Hearst. But that was years in the past by 1978, an occult detail of organizational history, and neither Heinlein nor Bottoms were aware of it.

The enactment played out with Heinlein just as it played out in American politics: If this was naïveté, it was the kind Americans specialized in, of granting goodwill and credence far beyond its rational due.

Finally, Heinlein outlined all the reasons he should give the interview and all the reasons he shouldn't—and then told Bottoms, "Honey, you decide."[34]

By that time, Heinlein and Bottoms had known each other for more than ten years and were on very friendly terms. She did some soul-searching of her own. Franklin's politics clearly bothered both Robert and Ginny—but Franklin had outlined an interesting "take" on Heinlein's work: Robert Heinlein was representative of America, in just the way that America was represented by science fiction. The title of his book would be *Robert A. Heinlein: America As Science Fiction.* There was too much possibility of good coming of this project: The very agony he put himself through meant Heinlein was exactly right as the focus of Franklin's thesis, Robert Heinlein as America as Science Fiction . . .

Bottoms told him in her opinion he should do it. That was enough: They arranged the interview for the afternoon of August 21, 1978. Ginny put a cold lunch in the refrigerator and left by the back door as Franklin came in the front; she would not stand in the way of this, but she also would not give assent by acting hostess for this Maoist in her house.[35]

A week later Ginny flew to Phoenix to meet Eleanor Wood and to oversee the WorldCon blood drive. Heinlein settled in to do some writing—"must find out whether or not they put all the pieces back when they closed my skull."[36] By August 31, Robert had taken the first 250 pages of manuscript from the fatally mediocre *Panki-Barsoom Number of the Beast* and set the situation spinning in a new direction. When Ginny returned from the Phoenix WorldCon—highly successful blood drive with 160 units collected—Heinlein drove to San Jose airport to pick her up, the longest trip he had made on his own.

During the summer, a fan named D. F. Vassallo had sent them a series of beautiful illuminated mottos from the "Notebooks of Lazarus Long" that Robert had put into *Time Enough for Love.* Ginny enjoyed them so much she sent them to Walter Minton for his own enjoyment—simply because she knew he liked such things. Minton wanted to publish them as a gift-book for the Christmas trade. He was getting ready to sell Putnam's to a conglomerate,

MCA, and this would be the last of the old-style publisher's way of developing a prestige line of books, to the highest standards.[37] The first printing came back for proofing with the first page cocked: Something was wrong with the registration on the print run—not bad enough to bother anyone but him, but he had the entire run destroyed, which astonished Ginny. It was printed again, straight this time, and went on sale just before Christmas.[38]

At about the same time, Heinlein got another big project under way. In September, Eleanor Wood had routinely forwarded to them a request from Donald A. Wollheim,[39] to do a Heinlein anthology for his paperback-original house, DAW—but Robert had another notion in mind, that might benefit many more people.

> #153 [*Worlds of Robert A. Heinlein*] is a property I had long since washed out of my mind as being of no importance; the added items are all out of the "dead" file so far as any intention to exploit them farther is concerned. Then we got some wild ideas: I decided that I could get Jim [Baen] to revert the contract, Ginny thought you [Wood] might like to try ren[eg]otiating it instead—then it occurred to me that I could use this putatively worthless property to establish SFWA's model pb contr[act].[40]

SFWA had drafted a "model contract" but had not yet been able to get any publisher to accept it. Robert realized he could get the SFWA Model Contract implemented for the first time, thereby setting a useful precedent (even though it meant taking a hefty reduction of his usual contract terms). At the same time, he could give a leg up to that young editor who had gotten his royalty rates raised at Ace Books. Ace had fallen on hard times and had been the subject of ongoing grievances on the part of SFWA for many years.

What Heinlein proposed was to create an expansion of *The Worlds of Robert A. Heinlein* for Ace that would turn it from a dead loss into a genuine producer. He still had a lot of unused material in his files, and he proposed to flesh out all the pieces in this collection with forewords and afterwords that would come as close as he ever did to autobiography—eighty thousand words of "new" material (some of it genuinely new), an entire new book's worth.

And to tie this package up with a big, red bow, he would do it only if Tom Doherty at Ace accepted the SFWA Model Contract. That would bring Ace into conformity with industry practices—which would, if they looked at it right, benefit them in the long run. This would be a complex negotiation for Wood to handle—an excellent way for her to cut her teeth.

> [L]et's discuss the probable points of resistance. But first let me stipulate
> that your prime purpose and Ace's prime purpose is profit . . . [sic] and
> profit has been my prime purpose for forty years—it just happens that
> today for this negotiation I can afford the luxury of a different purpose. But
> to succeed in my purpose I must cause the interests of all three, Ace, me,
> and my agent (you), to run concurrently . . . [sic] and this can be done only
> by maximizing $$$$$$$$$ for all of us—sales, profits, royalties.[41]

And if Ace didn't accept the deal, he instructed Wood to declare a cancellation of the contract and take it to another publisher. *Some*body would want a
new Heinlein collection.

Just then, one of the boutique publishers they dealt with asked casually if
they were considering retiring. Ginny just laughed: They were working harder
now than they were fifteen or twenty years ago. Their business affairs had
become so complex that literally *no one* else could manage them. They had a
tiger by the tail and could only hang on.[42]

By the beginning of October 1978, Heinlein was ready to begin writing his
new book. "He feels that he wants to do another just to prove to everyone that
he still can do it," Ginny wrote to a friend. "I think that he can, but novels are
pretty wearing on him when he's in the best of health, and he's been having
some trouble with sleeping."[43] But he did settle down to the writing he had
been planning out for the last six months.

The story he originally wrote for *Panki-Barsoom* started out, like the book
before (*I Will Fear No Evil*), with a science-fictional cliché: "He's a mad scientist, and I'm his beautiful daughter"—but he spun it differently this time,
writing a book just as experimental, just as different, as anything he had ever
done—only more so. Metafictive in a post-postmodern way, the distinction
between reality and the worlds of fiction was not just blurred, it was obliterated,
viewpoint among the protagonists shifting as often as they shifted from world
to fictional world, arguing about who should lead and who follow, and how:

> Tomorrow I will seven eagles see, a great comet will appear, and voices
> will speak from whirlwinds foretelling monstrous and fearful things—
> This Universe never did make sense; I suspect that it was built on govern-
> ment contract.[44]

And he enjoyed some other legendary writer's tricks, self-conscious and self-
referential. L. Ron Hubbard's "Typewriter in the Sky" had made the case
long ago (1940) that, so far as the characters in a story are concerned, the real

villain of the piece has to be the author, jerking them about and causing suffering for the sake of the story. It was a literary principle older than Hubbard, of course—it was in *King Lear*: "As flies to wanton boys, are we to the gods; they kill us for their sport."

The identity of their devil—The Beast—is given in anagrams in this great *jeux d'esprit,* starting with the first one, an academic: Neil O'Heret Brain— N.O. Brain—"Robert A. Heinlein" rearranged as an anagram (Ginny got in there, too, in various odd guises).

And at the end, there is a huge, idealized science-fiction convention that recapitulates the travelers' wandering across continua, into the worlds of fiction. All the worlds of fiction and all the realities, parallel and not so parallel, came to visit and mingle with Ginny and him and his friends in this "consensus reality." And here the writerly jokes become even more self-referential:

> In one running thread, the central characters keep confusing other Heinlein characters—Oscar Gordon for Zeb Carter, the Empress Star for Ishtar, and so forth. (A common criticism of Heinlein is that his characters tend to fall into narrow categories, becoming indistinguishable from each other.)
>
> In a second twist on reader assumptions, Heinlein keeps referring to "Robert, Isaac and Arthur." In science fiction, these names are usually taken to be those of the "big three" modern sf writers. However, it slowly develops that Heinlein is referring to Robert Aspirin, not Robert Heinlein; the Venerian dragon, "Sir Isaac Newton," not Isaac Asimov; and Arthur Conan Doyle, not Arthur C. Clarke.[45]

Heinlein finished *The Number of the Beast* early on the morning of December 17, 1978, completely worn out from working fourteen-hour days ("years ago," Ginny told a friend, "he said, 'If I could stay awake long enough, this thing would be done at one sitting.'").[46]

29

TRAVELING ROAD SHOW

The Number of the Beast was being cut and polished, and his typewriter was going to pieces. Heinlein had his eye on one of the new "word processors," and Ginny was convinced her personal millennium had arrived when she saw Marilyn Niven's Atari in operation—but Marilyn was a computer specialist, able to give it the almost constant servicing it required. The Heinleins were probably forty-five miles from the nearest service. It wasn't practical, yet, for them.

And while they were about it, could Heinlein get a replacement body? His balance problems were coming back, and his back ached frequently—from sitting and lying down too much. He had taken to using a cane to help getting around (though he hung it on his forearm much of the time).[1] He had insomnia most nights, and Ginny observed one night that he did sleep but was strangely motionless: He had slept through the entire night with a tray and glass of water balanced on his chest. In the morning, he was crippled up.[2]

Dr. Chater had a long phone conference with Heinlein's local internist, Dr. MacKenzie, and came up with a verdict: polycythemia: His bone marrow was overproducing red blood cells. The treatment was oddly old-fashioned: They bled him, taking a pint of his A negative rare blood, which would have to be thrown out since blood banks would not accept it on account of his age and health. Ginny used the waste blood to fertilize a Bird of Paradise plant. "[T]he following morning he came dancing into the kitchen. Enough sleep, loss of some red cells, and dramatically, he was in quite good health."[3] The leeching put him back to normal for a day or so at a time, but something had to be done about his general condition.

The early reports on *The Number of the Beast* were favorable, and Heinlein began sleeping easier: He had been quite worried about whether the brain surgery would affect his writing: "It's a great relief to him because he doesn't want to retire from writing."[4]

Putnam's had an option, but Eleanor Wood arranged for the book to go up for auction. Putnam's option would thus allow them the opportunity to meet the best price offered. Putnam's had been sold to MCA in 1975, and Walter Minton was removed as president in 1977, with Peter Israel succeeding him. Robert and Ginny had nothing against Peter Israel, other than the way Minton was being treated now—Heinlein had even given Israel's first book a puff after he had taken years off to write rather than edit—but their loyalty was to Walter Minton's Putnam's, not to MCA's.[5] A dozen publishers were invited to participate in the auction, and the "floor bid"—the minimum bid that would be accepted—was set at $500,000, with an as-is, no-edit condition. At first Heinlein was reluctant, but Ginny talked him into it: "Robert really didn't want to sign those big contracts. And I said, 'Don't be silly. Might as well. If they're offering that money to you for a book, take it.'"[6]

In January 1979 Heinlein wrote a letter to Ned Brown, his agent in Hollywood, asking why there had been no recent activity. The letter went unanswered for three months.[7] An independent producer, Hart Sprager, contacted Brown to discuss optioning a Heinlein property and received a reply letter so odd and so un-agent-like that he forwarded it to Heinlein directly. "The copy of Ned Brown's letter which you sent to us," Ginny told Sprager, "was a real shocker to us. You can see why, I'm sure."

> One, he doesn't even know the title of Robert's most recent book, and two, telling you to look in the library for a list! It looks as though Ned is getting senile or something. Not only that, but he goes off and turns down all kinds of things without notifying us. (Robert's had all kinds of interest expressed in his books, only to have Ned not listen to even a reasonable offer. We're disgusted.)[8]

"We've mistaken good manners for good management," Heinlein commented dryly[9] and severed professional relationships in March, literally in the same week that they changed English agencies from Farquharson to Tanner. And in the same week they signed with Eleanor Wood's Spectrum literary agency, from Blassingame, McCauley and Wood.[10] They had had settled relationships for decades, and the abrupt changes came all at once. For representation in Hollywood, they signed with ICM (International Creative Management), Bob Bookman handling their account.[11]

Also in January 1979, a fan in the east, Perry Chapdelaine, was planning a selection of John Campbell's letters and wanted permission to print some of Heinlein's to Campbell, since the discussions they had by letter were fascinating.

Chapdelaine was a friend of Robert Moore Williams and had let them know about Williams's death, so they had had prior contact with him. After Campbell's death in 1971, Peggy Campbell had essentially given Chapdelaine the entire file of Campbell's correspondence for this purpose, after removing the letters she thought of as "sensitive"—but Heinlein remembered the wrangling and the up-and-down stuff, particularly at the beginning of the war. Ginny wrote refusing permission to quote from Heinlein's letters to Campbell—and telling Chapdelaine in the strongest language she could muster that they would consider it an invasion of privacy to print any of Campbell's letters to Heinlein.[12]

With their accountant handling some of the audit the IRS had demanded for their 1977 taxes, the production work on the new book began taking up all their time: For this auction they had to make *forty* copies of the nine-hundred-page manuscript, each copy requiring two manuscript boxes. It was an exhausting process that took nearly a month, since each copy had to be laboriously checked page by page.

The American auction for *The Number of the Beast* was to be held on May 15–16, 1979, with another in England a few weeks later. By that time, Robert's year of travel restriction would be up, and they planned a quick trip to Chicago for a small convention: A group of fans of Gordon Dickson's Dorsai books had organized themselves several years before—at MidAmeriCon, in fact—as the "Dorsai Irregulars," to provide security for science-fiction conventions and had rapidly grown into a jolly social group that included Robert and Ginny Heinlein comfortably. This "relaxicon," Thing IV, was typically held near the St. Patrick's Day weekend, but this year it was in May. On May 10, 1979, they flew to Chicago, with a change of planes in Denver that revealed some of Heinlein's new limitations. He apparently had an altitude ceiling now that was lower even than Ginny's: He had to change planes in a wheelchair. But the convention made little demand, and they had a thoroughly enjoyable time for four days. Thing IV was held at the same time as a convention of gymnasts, which gave it a certain peculiar flavor. Robert and Ginny were startled one evening when the elevator door opened, revealing three girls, balanced in a pyramid, all upside down. The Dorsai Irregulars made them both honorary life-members and designated "slaves" of appropriate sex for each of them.

They flew back to San Jose on the day of the book auction, and Heinlein slept for sixteen hours. By the time he woke, they had a winner of the auction: Their floor bid had been met, and the CBS conglomerate would bring it out under their Fawcett-Columbine division label, in an illustrated trade paperback.[13] *Locus,* the premier publication for the business of science-fiction publishing, covered the auction in their June 1978 issue:

The new Robert A. Heinlein novel, *The Number of the Beast,* went up for auction on May 15. The auction, conducted by Heinlein's new agent Eleanor Wood, lasted two days. Fawcett Books, a division of CBS, was the winner with a complex half-million dollar bid. The only other bidder was Pocket Books. Both bids were counter offers to the original proposal by the agent. The advance payment will be spread over 10 years . . . .

New English Library exercised their matching privileges to buy British rights for $43,000. They also offered a high royalty rate plus higher royalties on earlier books . . . .

According to senior Editor Micheala Hamilton, the book will be used to launch the fiction part of Fawcett's new Columbine line of trade paperbacks. It will be heavily illustrated in full color.[14]

Once the English auction for *The Number of the Beast* was over (eleven publishers participating) they were able to place serial rights with *Omni* magazine for 10 percent of the book—about twenty thousand words—which was the amount suggested by the English publishers. Ben Bova, who had left *Analog* in 1978, was now fiction editor for *Omni* and would make the cut himself. Bova was already at work on an illustrated republication of "The Notebooks of Lazarus Long" for the August issue of *Omni.* *Omni* appeared likely to become in the 1980s as much a "home" for Heinlein as *Astounding* had been for him in the 1940s.

On June 29, 1980, Heinlein gave Bova an extended phone interview for the tenth anniversary of the Apollo 11 landing on the Moon.[15] Developments in that area bothered him.

Ben, I am terribly worried about the space program. With its current unpopularity (i.e., polls showing that ca. 90% of the voters feel that we are "wasting" too much money on space "stunts"), with a presidential election coming up and an incumbent [Jimmy Carter] who seems willing to do anything to hang on, with inflation rate now 13.2% and the 2nd differential increasing, with the Skylab fiasco blamed on NASA by the public (instead [of] blaming Congress—where the fault lies), I have a horrid feeling that, by the time Voyager 1 nears Saturn, no one will be watching. No money. NASA dismantled, its buildings and grounds turned over to other agencies or departments, its instruments old or mothballed or given to another department such as the new department of education.

Oh, we would still (I think) have ComSats and WeatherSats and LandSats—anything that is already a proved moneymaker (even to Proxmire!)—but no research organization for space. None.

Of course you and I and a very small minority realize that NASA is a "proved moneymaker" in *all* respects, and especially through its research.

Getting into space was only one of NASA's jobs: In addition to developing new technologies, it was supposed to be transferring those technologies into the American—and then world—economy.

But we are opposed by an overwhelming majority who do not understand research, don't want to, and are not merely ignorant but strongly *anti*-science.

With such people the only effective approach is to show him "What's in it for me"—and there is plenty in it for him, and his wife and his kids; NASA is one of the very few Federal programs of the past fifty years to show a whopping cash profit on the money invested in it.

But, through the truly incredible incompetence of NASA public relations, the truth has not reached the common citizens.[16]

The material was fresh in his mind, then, on July 2, when he received, forwarded from Blassingame, a letter asking him to testify before Congress on applications of space technology for the elderly and the handicapped—in seventeen days. Claude Pepper's Select Committee on Aging and Don Fuqua's House Committee on Science and Technology were holding a joint session later that month, to hear NASA's report given by its new (since 1977) head, Dr. Robert A. Frosch. "I don't know a thing about it," Heinlein told Ginny.

It would be a coup for him—a chance to follow in Mark Twain's footsteps again (Twain—Clemens—had testified before Congress in 1886 about copyrights). And, of course, anything to help the faltering space program. "You're in a very good position to find out," Ginny said.[17] And, indeed, he was.

Heinlein had developed a number of friends, and friends of friends, who could advise him on various subjects. As he tended to collect as friends people whose minds ranged widely in the first place, he could ask virtually any question about any subject and someone among his circle of "Baker Street Irregulars" (as Ginny and he called them informally, after Sherlock Holmes's network of street kids) would know the answer—or know where to find the answer. In this case, since time was short, he got on the phone with Alan Nourse, a doctor, the same day, and Art Dula, a lawyer who was specializing in space law, a discipline that barely had begun to have a subject in 1979.

Dr. Nourse began compiling notes the next morning, and Dula began gathering "strategic information" by calling on his contacts in Washington, D.C. Heinlein had been invited to speak on the first day of the two-day hearings, which he would share with Dr. Frosch, Hugh Downs, and Buckminster Fuller—to give the joint committee an overview of what had been done and what remained to be done in this field. The second day—the tenth anniversary of the Moon landing—would be given over to testimony among government agencies about expediting this kind of technology transfer.

Most of the "spinoffs" from NASA-developed technology were due to NASA's push to miniaturize all the components going on spacecraft—which amounted to a huge chunk of economic and moral "lift." (A Chase Econometrics study already being prepared, though not released until 1981,[18] suggested that for every dollar spent directly on space up to the Moon landing in 1969, NASA's technology transfer program returned *fourteen* dollars to the U.S. economy—and that was before the Silicon Valley boom, based on the microprocessor, started up.)

Dr. Frosch's testimony was to be narrowly focused and comprehensive[19]—a forty-eight-page, professionally produced booklet titled "Technologies for the Handicapped and the Aged" by Trudy E. Bell would accompany Frosch's oral testimony. Heinlein could be "demonstrative evidence"—a living example, to complement Dr. Frosch's comprehensive report, since he would not be alive now without those spinoffs.

The Heinleins had a tight schedule, but went to Pasadena to see the *Voyager 2* pictures come in at JPL (with the usual wearing assortment of television and radio interviews). They made it back with just four days to turn Heinlein's study notes into written testimony. He wanted to give his testimony from memory, if possible, not even referring to notes, as a further demonstration of just *how* recovered he was. Later he told Ben Bova:

> I spoke without MS or notes in order to *show* that the brain surgery had worked—had I read from a MS it would have proved merely that I was bright enough to read aloud . . . [sic] but it would not have proved that I myself had written the MS. (In fact Art Dula did prepare for me a formal written presentation . . . [sic] which reached me *after* my written testimony had been Xeroxed.[20]

Washington, D.C., in July is hot and muggy. Heinlein got only two hours of sleep the night before, and his stammer came back, as it often did when he was tired. The morning's testimony ran long, with Dr. Frosch barely audible.

Frosch also disappeared after his testimony, not troubling himself to greet and make nice with the other persons testifying—an obvious mistake, Heinlein thought, but a telling example of what was wrong with NASA's Public Relations: Common courtesy, let alone common sense, should have made it a priority for Dr. Frosch to welcome and thank members of the public who went out of their way to support his agency. But NASA had been under the gun for years, with budget cuts and public criticism, and the NASA administration, Art Dula observed, felt forced into a zero-risk strategy.[21] Testifying before Congress is always a risk.

> Frosch could have made two firm friends for life in thirty seconds just with a smile and a couple of hand shakes, a "Thanks for appearing," plus an invitation to drop into the National NASA offices and get acquainted (we could not have accepted but we would never have forgotten the offer).
>
> Ben, you and I can't offset that sort of clumsiness. But we can ignore it and go on beating the drum for NASA . . . [sic] until NASA goes down the drain . . . [sic] which is exactly where it is going and soon, unless NASA makes a fantastic reform in its public relations. I'm sorry to say that I think NASA is a terminal case, beyond the point of no return. But I intend to go on trying as long as NASA is still in business.[22]

Eleanor Wood and Ralph Vicinanza had come down from New York for the circus on July 19, 1979; they were able to discuss business over lunch. Heinlein was also able to introduce Dr. Yoji Kondo to Dr. Charles Sheffield, space scientists and colleagues as science-fiction writers. Sheffield was another client of Eleanor Wood's, and Heinlein's brother Lawrence had introduced Dr. Kondo by correspondence several years earlier.

Heinlein wanted to get his testimony into the expanded collection Jim Baen was preparing for Ace. Ben Bova had also asked to publish it in *Omni*. When the transcript of his testimony arrived in a few days, Heinlein was appalled at the slips and mangled syntax, the result of his lack of sleep and the long morning. He hand-corrected the transcript to something resembling his usual prose, cutting here and there to improve the reading quality.

Someone at *Omni*, he discovered, had made changes in the abridgement of *The Number of the Beast* after he had approved it.[23] That could not be permitted to happen to "Spinoff": The article was Congressional testimony; he couldn't have some editor making random changes in the manuscript. When he sent the manuscript to Wood, he told her, "Because of its nature *it cannot be edited*. It can be cut *by me and no one else* according to editorial instruction. If

I find myself unable to comply, then we withdraw it & try elsewhere—*Galileo* probably, then *Analog*."[24] He asked for proof sheets for "Spinoff"—not a usual procedure for a magazine publication.

It appeared in the September 1979 *Omni,* which made a clean sweep of the fall months, since the "Notebooks" was in the August issue and Ben Bova's abridgment of *The Number of the Beast* was to appear in October.

Waiting for the galleys, Heinlein started a long, fiddling household project he had been putting off: They had run out of shelf space for books and could not find anything anymore. Heinlein built some more shelves, using up the last uncovered walls in the house (close to the entranceway), and catalogued title and location of every book they had in the house.[25] And then he turned to the big project of putting together the rest of the manuscript materials for the new collection, *Expanded Universe.*

Ace, which had been acquired by Grosset & Dunlap in 1972,[26] had signed the SFWA Model Contract for *Expanded Universe* and then promptly renegotiated the deal upward, to make it conform to the customary terms Heinlein was then getting for book contracts. It had served its purpose.

Heinlein wrote a number of new pieces for the book in addition to providing file copies of unsold material. He also updated his 1950 predictions in "Where to?" as he had done in 1965 for *The Worlds of Robert A. Heinlein,* publishing the follow-ups together and so tracking his predictions over thirty years. A number of these pieces Baen wanted to publish in his quarterly "book-azine," *Destinies* (later titled *New Destinies*). But much of the new material consisted of forewords and afterwords to the various pieces. Baen called Heinlein, and they talked about the bits over the telephone, working out the language, which Baen then edited into typescript. Heinlein gave as close to a memoir of his long writing career in these forewords as he was ever to make[27]— and since there was a certain amount of Dutch Uncle/Cassandra talk in this "interstitial material" about the woeful state of things in the United States, he prohibited sale of the book outside the United States and Canada.

Robert's fiftieth class reunion was at Annapolis that October. Matters kept him busy right up to time to leave. The letter-essay Heinlein had worked up in the spring about the Future History series was published in the *SFWA Bulletin*'s fall issue (whole number 71)—the "keynote address" of the "SF Future Histories" special issue edited by John F. Carr. The Heinleins received an appeal from Sheldon Dorf, the founder of the San Diego Comic-Con, which had successfully and enthusiastically held blood drives for years. The convention's expense money had been stolen. Robert and Ginny sent a check to cover the shortfall.[28] An assistant professor of physics at L.A. State University, Peter

D. Zimmerman, showed up at their gate unexpectedly one afternoon in September, to court Heinlein's support for the John Anderson presidential campaign, because of Anderson's pro-space position. But he had not made an appointment—or, indeed, any prior arrangements—and Ginny had learned her painful lesson about drop-ins by now: She did not let him in the gate. Mr. Zimmerman left a letter-brochure, but Heinlein decided not to respond to it.[29] On the evidence, he was having second thoughts about politics at that time. Ronald Reagan was running for election, and it may be that Heinlein thought Reagan represented a new flicker of the same pragmatic willingness to address real problems that had drawn him to Goldwater fifteen years earlier. He switched his party affiliation to Republican with a $1,000 donation.[30]

And about then, Verna Trestrail asked him for an article-appreciation of her father, E. E. Smith, who had passed away in 1965. A small convention at the end of September in Moscow, Idaho—Smith was born in Idaho, in 1890—was honoring him, and Trestrail was going to be guest of honor to accept the posthumous citation for him. Heinlein wrote a thoughtful appreciation for the MosCon 1 program book, "Larger Than Life," that summed up what he thought about Doc Smith. It arrived just as Trestrail and her husband were leaving for Moscow, and had her, she said, in tears.[31]

Trestrail accepted for Heinlein, in absentia, an award given him by the convention, a wooden plaque with a pebbly stained-glass (plastic) insert representing a lambent Lens of Arisa, the Second Stage Lensman award.

Another chore Heinlein had moved up on the priority list was a persuasive letter for one of the small grassroots space organizations, which was quoted in a "guest editorial" in a *Star Trek* fanzine[32]—a usage he approved this time. Ever since Gerard O'Neill's imaginative invention of space-habitat colonies at the Lagrange points (stable points in any orbit), the number of just-folks people who were taking an active interest in practical space affairs was growing into a movement. They had not yet had cause to flex their political muscles—but the time was clearly on the horizon, and there was a good test issue: The space shuttle was due to begin operational flights in July 1980, after three years of testing, and environmentalists were mounting protests to prevent *Columbia* from flying.

Bjo Trimble, a friend and correspondent with Heinlein since 1961, had organized an astonishing letter-writing campaign among science-fiction fans in 1967 when *Star Trek* was to be canceled at the end of its second season. The campaign had been successful in getting a third season for *Star Trek*.

That mobilization of opinion was the essence of political clout, and Heinlein thought it could be turned to good effect here. A similar letter-writing campaign among Trekkers (the name preferred by *Star Trek* fans) had gotten the first shuttle named *Enterprise* (the one that, ironically, never flew), so it was likely Trekkers would take a personal interest in this issue. Heinlein wrote to Trimble:

> . . . The "environmentalists" are trying to put a stop to the space shuttle flights in So. Calif. I don't know what they base their theories on, but they are making an attempt. So this is in the nature of being an SOS . . . .
>
> . . . I think that it might be a good idea to get this story into the Star Trek papers, as soon as possible, and get a letter writing campaign started . . . . I intend to write to our local Congressman, and our two Senators, myself.
>
> I'm sorry that I have to spread this bad news, but I think that if the Trekkers get the word they can stop it from happening . . . .[33]

The most important job before they left for Annapolis, and for the round-the-world cruise they had scheduled for the winter aboard the S.S. *Rotterdam*, was the proof sheets for the English edition of *The Number of the Beast,* which was going to issue as a hardcover from NEL weeks before the American illustrated trade paper first edition. The English edition would be the "definitive" first of this book.

The book was getting a good reception from publishers wherever it was marketed,[34] but they were a little irritated by the glacial speed Fawcett-Columbine was making.[35]

30

New Beginnings

Rotterdam departed on January 23, 1980, and they planned to be back in Santa Cruz by the first of May. This would be the first time they had been away from advanced medical facilities for any length of time, and Robert's health was not perfectly restored, even yet: He still had problems with his balance and walked with a cane most of the time.

Rotterdam was almost a floating Chatauqua, with writers and artists and entertainers flown in for lectures and performances. The Apollo astronaut Wally Schirra was one of these. He and his wife were there for two weeks, much of it spent with the Heinleins. The Schirras were a very entertaining couple when they didn't have to be on display.[1] Taylor Caldwell was on that cruise as well, but did not connect with Heinlein. Ginny thought she was "haughty."[2]

In addition to Hong Kong and Manila (for their first time), they called at Singapore, and were astonished at how developed the places had become over the last twenty-five years—"like Manhattan now. With their lack of space, they must grow upward, or cease to exist, I suppose, but I don't have to *like* it."[3] The monkeys Ginny had once fed with bananas and peanuts at the Botanical Gardens had all been shot years before.[4]

By March they were on the other side of the world. They did not go ashore at India at all, remembering how they had both disliked the country the last time they were there—but they stopped in Sri Lanka for a couple of days to visit with Arthur C. Clarke. He chartered a plane and flew them over Sigiriya and Adam's Peak and then on to the Great Barrier Reef, where Clarke showed them the location of the sunken treasure ship he had found, and they bombed the diver-instruction center with toilet paper—in the grand old RAF tradition, Clarke said (the Royal Air Force being his own service during World War II).[5]

Ginny was never comfortable flying over the ocean, so they turned around and went back to Colombo and Clarke's home, which could only be described as a palace. In addition to his science (and science-fiction and film—and now television) activities, he was a formal consultant to the government of Sri Lanka and an important social and economic force on the island.

The trip did them both a great deal of good, and they needed all the stamina the long rest gave them for Robert A. Heinlein Day in Butler, Missouri, on April 17, 1980. It was like something out of Heinlein's story "The Man Who Traveled in Elephants": "[T]he entire town turned out to greet their favorite son, the SF world's first acknowledged Grand Master of the form."[6] The town council of Butler had installed signs on the main freeway entrances, north and south, boasting it was his birthplace, and a plaque at the site of his grandfather Lyle's house. There were receptions and a reviewing stand built right in front of the courthouse, and a parade with *two* bands and a run of antique cars, and a commemorative dinner.

> . . . [T]he chipper and jovial Heinlein privately began his day by visiting the Bates County Museum, then enjoyed a luncheon with relatives prior to speaking to students at Butler High School. He then sat in review while a brief parade consisting of a marching band, several theme floats and local groups wound its way around Butler Square to pay homage to their hometown hero, who accepted the tribute with smiles and applause, obviously pleased with the whole affair . . . . Following a semi-private dinner, the rejuvenated Heinlein attended a public meeting at the Butler Public Library, rounding off a thoroughly rewarding day for those lucky enough to have attended.[7]

A framed and illuminated version of the Missouri State Legislature's formal proclamation of Robert Heinlein Day was presented to him, and Butler's representative in Washington had it read into the *Congressional Record,* where it would be a permanent part of national history. And choicest of all, an article in a local paper headlined, "Top Hillbilly Author of Science Fiction Receives the John Glenn Parade at Butler, Missouri."[8] "Robert now says that he feels like a Hysterical Marker," Ginny remarked to friends.[9]

Back in Santa Cruz in May, they found the usual accumulation of mail. The New English Library hardcover of *The Number of the Beast* was already out. "I hear that the British sales are proceeding apace," Ginny wrote to friends, "and a friend told us yesterday that a dealer in Westwood [a suburb of Los Angeles] has imported 50 copies and is selling them at a round $25.00 each. Plus tax probably. It's illegal, and against our contract, but there doesn't seem to be anything to do about it."[10]

The Fawcett release was put over to August, with *Expanded Universe* coming out in October. Fawcett had stopped communicating with them—did not even send out author copies. Ginny found out about the release by seeing the listing in the trade journals.[11]

When it was released in August, the Fawcett edition of *The Number of the Beast* was on three bestseller lists—*Publisher's Weekly,* the *New York Times Book Review,* and B. Dalton's bookstore list, where it had debuted at number ten and jumped up to number three in its first week. By August 17, it was in its third printing, with 145,000 copies,[12] and a *New York Times Book Review* author profile based on a telephone interview designated it a bestseller, so that made it official.[13] Two weeks later, the count was up to fifth printing and 193,000 copies.[14]

Some of the initial reviews were unpleasant[15]—but that was par for the course; the fan press typically got into print before the professional venues, and Heinlein had decided over the years that if the fans didn't hate it, there was something wrong with it. They seemed disgruntled any time you didn't give them a comfortable formula—"mixture as before"—and *that* he was no longer willing even to pretend to do.[16]

The *New York Times Book Review* got into press with its major review of *The Number of the Beast,* by Gerald Jonas, on September 24 (*qualified* unpleasantness). In his opening paragraph, Jonas used words like "hubris" and "seems bound to destroy his own brain child," meaning science fiction—but followed by observations that did not actually seem to understand what was going on in the text very well.

> . . . this novel consists almost entirely of dialogue in which it is impossible to tell who is speaking. This makes it difficult to follow the plot. But such difficulties, like everything else in the book, dissolve at the end into a long solipsistic set-piece in which Mr. Heinlein makes fun of science-fiction conventions, science-fiction readers, other science-fiction writers and his own penchant for solipsistic fiction . . . "The Number of the Beast" fails because it plays with ideas that it ultimately fails to respect.[17]

The book was already number one on the Quality Paperback bestseller lists. By that time, Heinlein's fan mail—almost all very positive—had become "overwhelming"[18]: *Some*body seemed to like it. They always got a bump in the mail when a new book came out, but this was unprecedented.

And then in October, Ace/Putnam's issued *Expanded Universe,* without fanfare, and the fan mail took another jump: They could not believe the amount and kind of mail that was coming in. They were getting the kind of letters solicited in the book, from anyone who possessed more current knowledge about conditions in the U.S. military and also inside the Soviet Union. Fred Pohl wrote about his recent trip there, and a Russian emigre, Mr. Pazan, wrote also. Joe and Gay Haldeman wrote about current conditions in the Navy. These letters were more or less expected, from within "the community," though even the community contained surprises: L. Ron Hubbard wrote congratulating him on his rare continuing productivity (Hubbard himself had just finished a 450,000-word SF novel, he said, to mark his fiftieth year in science fiction).

The sheer quantity of mail was the least surprising thing about it: Many of these were from first-timers, with bizarrely detailed questions—about everything from economics to where Robert parted his hair. Clearly people were responding to the "interstitial" material much more strongly than anyone could have foreseen. They were responding to his voice and his public persona as they often in decades past had responded to him in person—coming to warm themselves in the fire of a personal charisma, helped along by an appeal to the reasonable and rational these readers found missing from their own lives as the gap between what we Americans actually *do* and what we allow to be said about it was widening again.

Ginny was in charge of answering this mail, but it was so overwhelmingly positive that she had to share it. Heinlein was "surprised and delighted" with the response.[19] Ginny was to spend most of the next two years answering *Expanded Universe*'s mail while Heinlein worked on another project, complex and demanding.

When Ronald Reagan was elected president in the November 1980 elections, Reagan's transition team commissioned a number of white papers. Heinlein was among thirty or so scientists, military men, policy wonks, and science-fiction writers invited to help form the Citizens Advisory Council being put together by Jerry Pournelle to come up with a strategic defense recommendation for the Reagan administration.

Ten years earlier, Pournelle had cowritten with Stefan Possony and Francis X. ("Duke") Kane a policy paper titled "The Strategy of Technology," one chapter of which ("Assured Survival") foresaw a strategic posture of defense, rather than of overwhelming aggressiveness. Such a defense posture was at last becoming technologically feasible—a way out of the ticking time bomb of Mutual Assured Destruction that had blighted the entire world since World War II.[20] The Truman and Eisenhower—and Kennedy and Johnson and Nixon and Ford and Carter—administrations had allowed themselves to be pressured into too many things that were not right for the American democracy: undeclared wars, "foreign aid" as almost naked bribery, and the revolting practice of propping up anti-Communist dictatorships in the third world. Self-sabotaging: These were the kind of *realpolitik* games you had to play if you wanted to be an imperial power on the world stage, but it left no room, either tactically or morally, for the much more important task history had charged America with, of being its pilot project in self-governance, of finding ways for a people to control their own lives without dictators or princes or prelates. That was a default twentieth-century America could never live down.

The first meeting was held at Larry Niven's home in Tarzana in December 1980—Newt Gingrich and Hans Mark attending by telephone—to work out a strategic recommendation. In the following months, a consensus emerged among this and other policy groups around the country that broadened their task well beyond the initial briefing and recommendation for the transition.

The Citizen's Advisory Council's main business was to produce a number of technical reports and policy recommendations. They formed several smaller groups to work on specific problems. The small groups each generated a document that became raw material for the final report, which would be written and edited by Dr. Pournelle, as the council's chair. Each paragraph of Dr. Pournelle's draft was read aloud and critiqued by everyone present at the council meetings.

From the second meeting on, General Meyer[21] brought in General Daniel O. Graham, the former director—now retired—of the Defense Intelligence Agency, who was informally advising on military matters. General Graham became the Washington "point man" for the strategy the council worked out.

But they had a second, and even more direct, line to President Reagan: The new national security adviser was Dr. Richard V. Allen—Dr. Possony's long-time colleague at the Hoover Institute. "Our papers went from Dick Allen direct to Reagan who read them all," Pournelle recalled: "One Page Summary, Executive Summary, Summary, and Support documents, the whole damned thing."[22] Phrases—even whole sentences—from those reports were used by the president in later speeches.[23]

Being in the company of the best brings out the best in one ". . . but in that company no one was going to stand out very far. Everyone on that team pulled his weight or wasn't invited to the next meeting. Robert was invited to all of the meetings."[24] He came: The possibility of an effective actual *defense* against nuclear weaponry was worth pursuing.

And, the more you do, the more you find you *can* do: Heinlein was writing again by December—a new novel, kicked off by something Ginny had said about "Gulf," written thirty years earlier: Kettle Belly Baldwin, she said, had been one of his juiciest characters, and he hadn't done nearly as much with him as he could have.[25] Heinlein seems to have combined that comment with a bit he had mentioned in passing in *Time Enough for Love,* about assembling people out of genes from many different sources: His protagonist was a composite of the genes of both Gail and Joe Green, who had never had a chance to procreate in "Gulf." His protagonist for *Friday* is a genetic composite of the best of humanity, in a balkanized United States, which symbolically reflects Friday's own genetic balkanization—a true human who is nevertheless a true superhuman and who gains interior unity by the end of the book. Friday naturally led back to the subject of bigotry—and in the era of the Equal Rights Amendment, who better to represent humanity as a whole and the damage done by bigotry—and the possibility of self-healing that had always fascinated him—than a woman, Friday.

His last several books had started off in dialogue with the small world of science fiction. This one started off from a base in general literature, with one of the "strong fabulist" fantasy worlds of English literature: *Robinson Crusoe.* His female protagonist was Crusoe's Friday—his hewer of wood and drawer of water—with a touch of Cunegonde from Voltaire's *Candide.*[26] Friday wanders around the world as Candide did, and gave Heinlein a kaleidoscope of situations to reflect back on his central problem. He made an elaborate timeline specifying the locations of each—and noted that there were a few locations he did not know directly: "Must visit Vicksburg, Winnipeg, & border below Winnepeg."[27] And late in the year, that is just what he did as research for the book: visit the places he did not know firsthand, traveling by himself for the first time in decades.[28]

He started writing in November 1980, while Ginny began researching the current generation of computers to replace typewriters and paper files. During the startup period, Heinlein dealt with a minor vexation: Ben Bova had commissioned Alexei Panshin to review *Expanded Universe* for the April 1981 issue of *Omni.* Bova sent them an advance courtesy copy of the review. Normally, Heinlein made a point of not paying attention to reviews ("reviews good or bad distract a writer's mind from current work"[29]). This Panshin piece, clearly polemical on its surface, extracted quotations and twisted the readings to make a case that Heinlein was a hypocritical bully. Disagreements and bad reviews were one thing—but this was simply malicious. Robert told Ginny, and she relayed to Ben Bova by phone, that this hatchet job was so pernicious, so dishonest on its face, that if Bova published it, Robert would never deal with him again.

Heinlein finished *Friday* in late March—just in time for the April 1981 issue of *Omni*. Bova had made his choice. Heinlein never dealt with *Omni* or Bova again.

Heinlein wanted to try copyediting his new book on a computer or word processor, and Ginny found the computer she wanted for both of them (they had already established the habit of buying duplicate typewriters and continued the practice with computers)—a Zenith Z89 with gargantuan 64 KB of internal memory (most personal computers at that time had 16 KB of RAM). It arrived on April 2—two huge boxes with a Sprint Qume printer and wires and cables and Magic Wand word processing software. This time of year, exactly forty-two years before, he was banging out his first commercial story on a rickety portable typer—manual. Once he had the computer set up, he retyped the current manuscript, entering it into memory, and edited it with Magic Wand. That first day, he had the search-and-replace function chug-chugging through the part he had already "input."[30] That kind of minor revision (changing a character's name throughout) would have occasioned a complete, tedious read-through and a full retype of the entire manuscript— literally a couple of months' work, providing he could hunt down a reliable typist in the first place, which was by no means certain. "This frees me from the tyranny of typists!" he exclaimed.[31]

Ginny concluded that the software that was available off the shelf would not be adequate for her purposes, so she threw herself into learning—at age sixty-five—computer programming, in CBASIC and MBASIC (and as preparation reviewed trig and calculus and boned Boolean algebra).

By the time the de Camps visited them in November—finally getting to use the guest house that had been kept free of cats for Sprague for nearly fourteen years—the Heinleins were experts and old hands at computers by virtue of a trial by fire: The new book, *Friday,* had been cut and edited, printed out, copied, and placed in their agency's hands by June. The Tandy Corporation was after them, wanting to market a computer game based on *Starship Troopers,* and gave them one of the new color TRS-80s. Ginny figured out how to operate it without referring to the instruction manual at all. She had a natural affinity, it seemed, for computers.

Holt, Rinehart & Winston were to bring *Friday* out in June 1982 (with a periodical appearance of a selection in the September-October "double issue" of *Science Fiction Digest*[32]). Heinlein had made no less than *thirty* dedications for this book—three columns that would have filled the page in a normal typesize, of first names of the women in his life and in science fiction—and every one of them was going to be sent an autographed and inscribed copy.

He also had to autograph five hundred copies of the first signature of the book he found on his doorstep in February for a luxury edition he had not known anything about.

The dedications took priority. Ginny's name, of course, led all the rest in his mind, for which reason he had given her last place in the list—"semper toujours," one of their private jokes. When he broke open the cases of author copies that spring, he made a small ceremony of presenting her with one of the specially reserved copies as her personal copy. It was a ceremony he was to repeat with each succeeding book. He never gave any particular reason for this, but "[n]o one outside this house can really know how fully she shares in everything I do."[33]

In April 1982, Heinlein attended a small convention Jerry Pournelle organized in Los Angeles to discuss space development matters. After the initial successful meetings of the Citizens Advisory Council, Jim Ransome, who had helped Pournelle put together the invitation list, talked Pournelle into doing a Space Development Conference, for which he then enlisted the aid of the local (Los Angeles Science Fiction Society) convention runners. Milt Stevens was the cochair of the conference, held over the Easter weekend of 1982.[34]

The Los Angeles Space Development Conference was more "public" than the Citizens Advisory Council and well attended. Following science-fiction convention traditions, the principal guest of honor was Apollo 13 astronaut Fred Haise, and Heinlein was the "fan guest of honor." General Graham was also one of the invited guests, and he was astonished by the warm reception he was accorded there, as opposed to the chilly reception his ideas were generally given in the national press.

It was a very productive conference, well attended by speakers from the Jet Propulsion Laboratory and space scientists from the University of Arizona, and other academics—and even the small but intense cadres of space development entrepreneurs that had already come into existence. It was also attended by the membership and board of directors of the L5 Society—which also had a very significant overlap with the Citizens Advisory Council.

Heinlein's fan guest of honor duties called for one formal presentation, and he also participated in a number of the informal discussions that took place and gave a number of book signings. At one point in general assembly, Heinlein stood up and essentially nominated attorney and space activist Arthur Dula to put on next year's conference in Houston. No one was more surprised about this than Dula:

One minute I was dozing quietly on stage as a useless L-5 board member (I was their lawyer—so I was essentially asleep), and the next minute I heard

". . . and you will do it, won't you Art?" From Robert. My response was "Yes sir, what was it you wanted me to do?" I had never heard of the conference and had ignored the discussion about it.[35]

Dula later took Heinlein aside and applied some of the moral leverage Heinlein had just given him, extracting a promise that he would be there in Houston.

The reviews on *Friday* were wonderfully divided, in a peculiar way: As with each book in the last ten years especially, the mainstream press received it as simply the workproduct of a master craftsman of the genre and went on from there. The *New York Times Book Review* review was by H. Bruce Franklin[36]—unsurprisingly jaundiced, and essentially a codicil to his Oxford University Press book that had been out for a year. Franklin managed to miss or ignore the *Robinson Crusoe* and *Candide* references carried by the rape of Friday and the balkanization of the United States—and all the irony and satire, and thus the implications of Friday's end-of-book *Il faut cultiver notre jardin.*

The genre press was absolutely schizophrenic about the book: Some parts of the story tickled the genre-readers' appetite for safe and familiar formula science fiction, and other parts could not be fit in with their preconceptions. It simply confirmed what had been obvious for years now: Heinlein's natural evolution as a writer had again taken him outside genre comfort zones—as it had with the *Post* stories and with the juveniles and with *Destination Moon* and with *Stranger in a Strange Land,* all rejected in their time by the fan press. Challenging preconceptions was what it was all about, then and now. All the disgruntled fan comments about "old Heinlein" and the bad, new Heinlein[37] can be summed up by Don Marquis's perceptive remark: "If you make people think they're thinking, they'll love you; but if you really make them think, they'll hate you."

Holt, Rinehart set up a special guest appearance for him at the ABA (American Bookseller's Association) in Anaheim the last weekend in May 1982, just before the book was formally published. It was already on the *Publisher's Weekly* bestseller list, debuting at number nine. Their flight was delayed, so they arrived late on June 2, 1982, and found that the convention management was holding the floor open past 5:00 P.M. just for Robert A. Heinlein—and for the long, *long* line of fans waiting to get an autograph. The entire floor of the huge convention burst into spontaneous applause as they entered, Robert on Ginny's arm, jaunty with his cane.[38] His name was on a gigantic poster in letters a foot high. They were both astonished—this was the first time Robert and Ginny had encountered anything like this.[39] He signed four *hundred* copies of *Friday* in the hour the convention management kept the door open for him.

The fan press might be qualifiedly disgruntled (less qualifiedly as time went on), but this experience was overwhelmingly positive feedback—from exactly the people he wanted to reach—that Heinlein was doing *something* right.

He was already contemplating another novel, and in the nature of things, this one would probably come out in 1984, an iconic year for science fiction: George Orwell's *1984* had been the gold standard for "literary" science fiction through most of Heinlein's career. But Ginny had proposed two longish trips, back to back, and there was fallout from the Citizens Advisory Council generating work, as well.

Early in June 1982, Heinlein received a telegram from Robert Himber, editor of *Survive!* magazine. They were planning for one of their fall issues a short exposition of General Graham's High Frontier concept.[40] The facts were covered: What they needed was something that gave the meaning and significance of it—the emotional dimensions of High Frontier. Jerry Pournelle had recommended they get in touch with him. They asked for it on an unfortunately short (ten-day) deadline.

Heinlein knew General Graham had a book on High Frontier coming out later in 1982, and it would be useful to keep the pot keeled. He agreed to write a short piece, on the condition it not be editorially changed:[41] There was simply no time in this telescoped schedule for an editing cycle.

Heinlein crafted a very careful performance piece, 611 words in letter form for maximum impact and aimed directly at the hardest-shelled status-quo-tarians:

> "High Frontier" is the best news I have heard since VJ Day.
>
> For endless unhappy years the United States has had no defense policy. We had something called a defense policy . . . [sic] but in the words of Abraham Lincoln, "Calling a tail a leg does not make it a leg" . . . .
>
> High Frontier places a bullet-proof vest on our bare chest . . . . It is so utterly peaceful that the most devout pacifist can support it with a clear conscience—indeed *must* support it once he understands it . . . [sic] as it tends to stop wars from happening and to save lives if war does happen.[42]

General Graham was so pleased with the piece that he asked to use it as the introduction for his book, *High Frontier: A Strategy for National Survival.*[43] A few months later, Heinlein made a short appearance on one of the High Frontier's informational videotapes.

The previous September, Ginny had booked an Orient trip on the Royal Viking Line—Japan, where he would get a chance to meet his publisher (Japan had already become one of his best international markets), Shanghai, Hong Kong, Manila for the first time, and Saipan (Ginny was less than thrilled about the dip into Communist China).

For decades, Robert had wanted to visit Antarctica, the last really unexplored continent left on Earth, barely touched by human habitation at all. There was one organization mounting tours, but they had suspended operations while Britain and Argentina were at war in the South Atlantic. Now a new tour group was being organized for ordinary people—somewhat inconveniently scheduled for the end of January 1983, just a couple of months after the Heinleins would be getting back from the Far East. But Heinlein was seventy-five years old: He seized the opportunity.

In the month remaining before the first trip, he finished up his research for his new book, reading in the Bible for weeks before starting to write.[44] Everyone else who was taking note of the date would probably be writing political sermons about 1984, which left sex and religion as topics offensive enough to offer the correct toes to be stepped on. He had done sex, but not religion for a while—and the cultural changes since 1961 offered a gigantic target, in the "family values" attempt to roll back the Enlightenment.

Something Isaac Asimov had written to him forty-three years ago provided the first kick of inspiration: ". . . you had better like this one," he wrote Asimov the next summer,

as you are its godfather. This is one of the best kept secrets in SF. Yes, you. Do you recall writing a letter to me in October 1939 (give or take a decade) in which you were discussing the fact that Jehovah had all the best press agents and that Satan wasn't getting a fair shake? That letter from you has been in the vaults of McHenry Library, U of Calif, these many years[45] but I did not need to refer to it; the subversive doctrine in it had been working in my mind all these decades and finally bore fruit in *Job*. All through these forty-odd years I had intended to write a story based on the idea you handed me. But it needed the right time, the right cultural milieu.[46]

He took a page from James Branch Cabell's multiple worlds of myth in *Jurgen* and wrote another Comedy of Justice, with a good Mark-Twainish visit to Captain Stormfield's version of The Heaven of Jurgen's Grandmother. Into the mix went the biblical book of Job and its trial of humanity, ironically inverted: He took another "righteous man, beloved of God," and let Jehovah put him through trials—and then turn the tables and have that self-righteous prig be judged by the Maker of Things As They Are for his conscienceless violation of the laws of esthetics.[47]

At the beginning of August 1982, he started writing, drawing on a religious rite that would probably sneak past most of his readers' censors—a fire-walking demonstration he and Ginny had witnessed on one of their South Seas trips in previous years. He left off writing on the last day of August. Ginny arranged with Denis Paradis's friend Paul Edmonds to come from Canada to house-sit for them from mid-January until they returned in March.

From San Francisco to Hawaii, to Japan, where they would have time to do a little exploring. Their stateroom was far forward, and the bow would come up occasionally and slap down on the next wave—noisy. But Heinlein found their forward port had a wonderful view: It was where the stewardesses sunbathed.

The Japanese publisher, Hayakawa Shobo, laid out the red carpet for them, and from the beginning the hospitality was more personal than professional—though there was professional stuff in abundance. They got to know Hiroshi Hayakawa's entire family.[48] On their first day in Yokohama, they were blinded by the continuous popping of flashes from the representatives of major Japanese news magazines. Japanese science-fiction writer Tetsu Yano had taken a room in their hotel, since he would function as their principal translator—very necessary, as Japanese was not among Ginny's languages.

That evening, they were taken to a very large wedding reception in Tokyo (over the extremely crowded toll road between Yokohama and Tokyo, at *rush-awa*, which gave Ginny the jim-jams. In the United States, "bumper-to-bumper" traffic still has some spacing between the cars; in Japan, "bumper-to-bumper" was almost touching, at 70 mph. She kept her eyes squeezed shut much of the trip.

This wedding was for the well-known illustrator and comic book artist Go Nagai. They take graphic novels very seriously in Japan. They take weddings very seriously in Japan as well: It was jammed. The entire function space of the hotel was taken over with samples of Nagai's work near the entrance and more than a thousand guests, with unending tables of delicacies and a bar at least twenty-five feet long. There were platoons of geishas, ravishing, dressed in brilliantly colored silk kimonos (matching the bride's mother, but not the bride, who wore, as did all the men in the wedding party, Western dress). Their personal geisha was elegant and made it her job to keep their plates filled with especially tasty things.

Many of the guests were science-fiction fans and writers, cartoonists and illustrators. Almost the entirety of the Japan Sci-Fi Writers Club was there to meet Heinlein.[49] All evening long he was politely buttonholed by earnest men, almost all over forty, who told him he was their "spiritual father." Odd and very touching.[50]

Dr. Yano had told his friend, the eminent Manga artist Osamu Tezuka (creator of the popular *Astro Boy* series), that the Heinleins would be at the wedding just two hours beforehand, and Tezuka made a special effort to be there and meet him. This is somewhat equivalent to being sought out by Walt Disney. Tezuka told Robert his books had spurred him on for forty years. When the evening ended, Tezuka loaned them his car and chauffeur for the drive back to the ship.

They went to Kobe and took the bullet train to Kyoto—160 miles per hour—to meet Yumiko Shibayama and Naomi Kameda. Heinlein had been corresponding with both for some years, and Ms. Shibayama, who described herself as Heinlein's number one fan, was the model for a character in *Friday,* Shizuko.

Ginny had reluctantly consented to visit Communist China now because they were in a period of "liberal" reform they were calling their "Second Revolution," and international tourists had been able to visit since about 1978. The goal was to achieve "The Four Modernizations" of agriculture, industry, science, and national defense. This was an old dance with many repeats and far too many off-with-da-capos—but it made travel there briefly possible.

They found Communist China quite as crowded as they had expected— Shanghai was jammed with traffic and bicycles—but surprisingly much more pleasant than the Soviet Union had been twenty years earlier.[51] They had expected to see poverty and misery and soul-destroying regimentation—but the Cultural Revolution did not seem to have done the same damage to the spirit of the Chinese that Stalinism had done to the Russians. They had not notified anyone they were coming to China, but word apparently got around the usual underground channels. The Shanghai Foreign Language Institute asked Robert to speak, and they got a chance to meet a host of Chinese science-fiction writers.

On another day, they were invited to give an informal talk at the Shanghai Institute of Science. There was one would-be defector there, and Robert and Ginny sat in a corner and talked with him, surprised at the frankness of his dissent from government policies. It gave them a strange sense of déjà vu, since the last time they had done something like this was skulking in an alley in Leningrad.[52]

Mainland China gave them a great deal to think about, and in too short a time their ship moved on to Hong Kong—"one vast shopping center"—that pleased some of their shipmates more.

The shopping in Manila was not so impressive—but Robert and Ginny were not there to buy clothing and fripperies. They took a city tour that ended up at the American Cemetery, among the graves of the nearly twenty thousand Americans killed during the Japanese occupation in World War II. "Both of us," Ginny wrote, "found ourselves in tears since we have always felt far closer to the war in the Pacific than we felt to that in Europe. Personally, I found myself recalling things I had read many years ago, and had a deep emotional catharsis."[53] Perhaps Robert had more than reading to fuel his own feelings: Mark Hubbard, his brother-in-law (through Leslyn, who had passed away in 1981, though Heinlein might not have been aware of this fact) was not there— he had been shot and burned alive in Bilibid Prison on Christmas Day of 1944.[54] Hubbard was another of those men who formed an example for Heinlein of what it means to be a human being. "This is how a man dies—this is how a *man* lives." Of Hubbard he wrote to Poul Anderson, "This is how a man gets to Valhalla"[55]—the warrior paradise of Norse mythology.

They had little time to assimilate this moving experience, though: With the Antarctic trip coming up in January, they could not dally on their way home. They barely had time to answer the fan mail that had stacked up. It was not possible to write to all their friends; instead Ginny wrote a single longish trip report—the first time she had tried this particular letter format—and sent it around to the various friends she would normally chat with about it. Heinlein went back to fiddling with the novel he had been putting together, though he had a hard time getting back into the swing of it—he was really too long away from it.[56] By mid-December Ginny had purchased the necessary heavy clothing for the trip, layered for warmth, and Robert had a new parka and felt-lined snow boots.

31

ENTOTIC

They boarded *Lindblad Explorer* in Punta Arenas, far in the south of Chile on the Strait of Magellan. It was the end of summer in Antarctica: They would be skirting the coastline in the Bellingshausen Sea and touching at the scientific station on the Ross Ice Shelf on the way to New Zealand and going home from Auckland. The crew used an unfamiliar adjective, "entotic," and it was a few days before Ginny realized that was the Australian pronunciation of "Antarctic."

They were almost immediately confronted with the fact this would *not* be a luxury tour ship: The showers had "minutieres" shutting down the water after a minute—barely possible. *Lindblad Explorer* was built specifically to be an "expedition cruising," passenger-cum-exploring vessel, "to take small groups of adventurous travelers to remote or inaccessible places."[1] They were not so much tourist-sightseers as they were being allowed limited participation in the scientific enterprise.

The Heinleins had to practice getting into their Arctic gear in the strait confines of their cabin. They found themselves in the immemorial dilemma of small boys onionized by their mothers in layers of bulky winter clothing, unable to bend far enough to get on their boots.

But this struggle was worth the effort when they hit the beach the first time. The excursions were conducted by a kind of rubberized-fabric-raft-with-frills called a Zodiac, the lineal descendant of the aircraft lifeboats Ginny had worked on in World War II—and nearly gotten herself court-martialed over.[2] The Zodiac had an engine and a lightweight wooden floor. Passengers sat on the flotation tubes and held on to loops of rope wound around the sides. Sometimes they could not land at all, but watched wildlife—whales, mostly—from the boats.

Their first beach was dark and rocky and smelly and indescribably noisy: They had come to see a rookery of Chinstrap Penguins that one of their ship's experts estimated held a *million* birds. And there were clusters of seals—males with harems, they were assured—on the fringes. The smell was very strong—fish (krill actually, tiny pink shrimp with huge black eyes that made up the majority of the penguins' diet) and guano.

Robert and Ginny made their way to the beach following the "outbound" lane of the double line of commuter penguins on their mile-long waddle to and from the ocean where they fed and caught krill for their young, emerging from the water with their white breasts stained pink by the krill caught in the feathers.

The birds were about knee-high. If you got down to their height, they might walk right up to you and inspect you. The next time they were out penguin-watching, Robert brought along a copy of *Friday* and propped it open in the snow. He got a series of photos of "penguin critics" inspecting the book, apparently reading it, then turning tail on it and waddling away.[3]

On another occasion, a pod of humpback whales surfaced nearby to feed on the same krill the penguins were eating. Each whale, weighing something like thirty tons, took in huge gulps of water, throats pouching out, then expelled it through their filter structures called balleen, seawater cascading from them. Curious as dolphins (their evolutionary cousins), they swam underneath the Zodiacs. The boats suddenly seemed frighteningly flimsy as they rocked in the whales' wake.

And then they went about their business, leaving the puny Zodiacs and their even punier human cargo to the seals and the ice floes in the Bay and the cormorants nesting on the surrounding cliffs. This trip was truly "primarily a spiritual experience rather than a physical one."[4]

From the Argentine zone near South America, they stopped by the stone hut the 1914 Shackleton expedition built for shelter after ice crushed their ship, then headed for McMurdo Sound and the Ross Ice Shelf in the American zone, arriving at the main American base at McMurdo Sound on the coldest day of the entire trip, 45 degrees below zero Fahrenheit with wind chill factored in.

There were about twelve hundred people at McMurdo Sound. Heinlein found many fans among the scientists there, and the "visit" continued for him even after returning to the ship: One of the scientists who happened to be sleeping when they were at Palmer Station discovered he had missed them and called the ship. Heinlein radiophoned him back. The route to Siple Station was not open at the time, but one of the men stationed there sent a letter and a gift sweatshirt.

On the way out from McMurdo Sound, the captain spotted two icebergs and gave them a slow cruise around the bergs. While they were watching, a huge wall of ice split off from one of the icebergs and fell into the ocean—an awe-inspiring sight.

Soon they found themselves in a field of about sixty icebergs—some of which might, they were told, be as much as a century old—and they put out for a Zodiac cruise among them. Once the ice mountains split off from an ice sheet or glacier, they assumed a flat, squared-off shape called "tabular" ("table-like"). At some point, after a certain amount of melting and sculpting by the winds, the tabular bergs would turn over in the water, underside exposed to the winds, which carved the ice into fantastic shapes called "Aeolean sculptures"—castles and dragons and fantasies of the imagination.

While they were out in the Zodiacs, some of the crew had landed on one of the tabular bergs and prepared a champagne party for them all, carving an ice chest out of the berg.

On the way back, they put in at several of the islands south of New Zealand and approached the South Island of New Zealand on its west side, coming in to Milford Sound and New Zealand's Fjordland, finding the Tasman Sea unexpectedly calm and glassy.

The rest of the trip was almost an anticlimax after the adventure of the Antarctic. They returned home to Santa Cruz in the middle of a "hundred-year storm." The ground was saturated with the heavy rains, and there were many landslides in the area. The aggravating hours and wheelbarrow full of money spent reengineering the swamp in the driveway years before, until it graded and drained properly, were effort well spent. They got their house-sitter, Paul Edmonds, back to Montreal safely by March 7, "full of superlatives about the Heinleins."[5]

Friday had been nominated for a Nebula Award that year. Heinlein was scheduled to go to the L5 Conference in Houston in April, so the Nebula banquet at the Statler in New York would not be possible for him. He spent time writing, offering a sympathetic shoulder to one correspondent who was depressed about the state of the world and, more pleasantly, writing a letter-appreciation for Jack Williamson, who was this year's guest of honor at Leprecon, a small science-fiction convention in Phoenix, Arizona, on Williamson's birthday. Heinlein totted up the numberless influences Williamson had had on him over the years, and wound up:

Your own life has been as romantic as your stories, I think—and not alone in returning, like Ulysses, after many years and much wandering, to the home of your youth, there to marry the sweetheart of your school days.

That tops it off, surely, but I do not mean that alone. How many settlers have migrated west by covered wagon . . . [sic] then lived to the age of space-ships?[6]

He also wrote a congratulatory letter to Brad Linaweaver, a young writer on the same Nebula Award ballot as he, for a novella, "Moon of Ice."

It's a good story and I hope you win the Nebula with it. It reminded me sharply how close we came to losing World War II. Some of the younger people today seem unaware that there was a long bitter time when every day was a new disaster and victory seemed most uncertain, ever.[7]

And on March 23, 1983, President Ronald Reagan made a major speech calling on the scientific community "to give us the means of rendering . . . nuclear weapons impotent and obsolete." In phrases and even entire sentences lifted from the Citizens Advisory Council papers, Reagan enunciated the new national policy that would come to be the Strategic Defense Initiative (SDI).[8]

There was, predictably, opposition from the press and from Congress, and SDI was soon dubbed "Star Wars." Soviet Ambassador Anatoly Dobrynin said SDI would "open a new phase in the arms race." It did indeed—a phase in which the faltering Soviet economy could no longer compete. The mere anticipation of a defensive research project—deployment was something indefinitely far into the future—threw the Soviets into paroxysms of fear and rhetoric. But Reagan never allowed SDI to be put on the negotiating table as a bargaining chip: All the Soviet rhetoric about "stability" meant keeping the Soviets' current military superiority and was not to be permitted.

The work of the Citizens Advisory Council continued as the policy debate ramped up and the most preliminary testing of the technology commenced in 1983 and 1984. But the great victory was already won, and the world had already shifted: The "unthinkable" again became unthinkable.

Heinlein continued to work with the Citizens Advisory Council, but this policy initiative was only a side issue for him: His real interest, all along, was space, and the defense-in-space was simply a pragmatic application of the more lastingly important task of getting a permanent presence off the planet.

It had gradually become clear that NASA was not going to accomplish that. The Space Shuttle program had already trapped NASA in military-industrial-bureaucratic amber, and the national legislature seemed disinclined to invest in the future (for that is what space exploration and exploitation really means), cutting NASA's budgets each year.

But there were hundreds of thousands of space-concerned ordinary citizens: More than two hundred thousand people turned up at Edwards Air Force Base in July 1982 to see the first Shuttle landings, and a good many of them signed up for further contact by the L5 Society. The grassroots space movement was just beginning to get its legs under it. There was an active segment of the general public—large enough, as Bjo Trimble's effort for the CAC had proved—to influence policy to some degree, at least, if properly mobilized.

And Heinlein had the means to do so at hand: He had been asked to join the L5 Society's board of directors several years earlier—not, initially, as an active director but as part of its "dignity committee."[9] Now that there was a new administration that seemed at least willing to hear the message, Heinlein decided it was time for him—and some of the other space advocates on the Citizens Advisory Council—to take a more active role in grassroots space advocacy.

He had already started putting his wallet on the line: When budget cuts at NASA threatened to close down the Earth-based telemetry receiving stations for the Viking probes on Mars that were still functioning, years past their design lifetime, astronomer-activist Stan Kent got up a grassroots Viking Fund to collect money from the general public to keep those receiving stations open. "Feed a Starving Robot . . . and a Starving Space Program" was the Viking Fund's motto. The effort to raise $1 million had been ongoing since 1979 by many organizations. Heinlein attended a small convention Kent organized at Ricky's Hyatt House in Palo Alto, in 1982, and contributed $1,000 to the Viking Fund. "He said," Kent explained, "he liked our philosophy of putting your money where your mouth was when it came to privately funding space exploration and he pulled out ten one hundred dollar bills and presented them to me."[10]

The Heinleins were also investors in (and Robert was a board member for) the Sabre Foundation, which was trying to cut through international red tape to get tax-exempt equatorial spaceports sited (though there seemed little progress on that front).

The 1983 Space Development Conference was every bit as successful as the first (in April 1982)—one thousand people at the Houston Astrodome Hotel, with a televised banquet for five hundred (and it even made a profit).[11] Heinlein brought two weeks of space-related activity to a close back in Santa Cruz, with a dinner bringing Richard Johnson of NASA Ames together with Jerry Pournelle and Larry Niven and Paul Bohannan.[12]

Heinlein needed to rest and recover—and get some writing done. He sent his regrets for the High Frontier meeting scheduled for May 1, saying that he was feeling "feebly." By 1983, his hands were stiff and painful with arthritis, his breathing was shallow and difficult, and his energy was not what it used to be: Often he could work only a couple of hours at a time before he had to lie down—and he might or might not get back to it for another couple of hours, later. On June 2 he finished the principal writing on *Job: A Comedy of Justice*— just as *Friday* came out in mass market paperback and went onto the best-seller lists.

Ginny was enthusiastic about *Job*: "It's as odd in its way as *Stranger* was in its own way. If you can understand that. But . . . I like it, so that's all that matters. This one will be controversial, I am sure."[13]

He had *Job* proofread and edited (three times) and printed out twice for the necessary corrections and revisions—and Xeroxed and mailed out to his agent—within two weeks of putting "-30-" to the rough manuscript. He recommended the word processor enthusiastically to Clifford D. Simak:

> I figure that it has extended my professional life practically up to the day I take to my bed for the last time—and that's the way I want it to be. I enjoy writing now . . . and writing had stopped being fun in late years. Now it's fun again, because the drudgery is gone. It does not wear me out.[14]

The timing was perfect: Lars-Eric Lindblad called to notify them that he was going to take the *Lindblad Explorer* next year to attempt the Northwest Passage—the fabulous ocean passage seventeenth- and eighteenth-century explorers sought from Europe to the Orient north of the Canadian mainland. The trip was scheduled for August, to give them the best chance of getting through. An end-of-summer passage would give them their widest choice of sea clear of pack ice—and cross fingers!

Heinlein's immediate reaction was "let's go—now, if possible!" but his health was a serious consideration. He was definitely growing feebler each year, and his breathing was becoming so labored, so often, that he was obviously in a race with the oxygen bottle and Chronic Obstructive Pulmonary Disease (COPD).

But he was not down until he was down. Ginny was up for it if he was, and he was ready to put down another round of betting against fate, for one last voyage of discovery and exploration, a real one, one for the record books.

But fate intervened: When he called back to make their reservation, Lindblad told them this voyage was already overbooked. The best he could do right now was to put them on the waitlist. There would be other voyages, later.

How much "later" might be practical for him was problematic.

Heinlein shrugged it off: What cannot be cured must be endured. Instead he started assembling his notes into a coherent story for his next book—a kind of wild *Don Quixote* (an early draft bears the title "The Reluctant Knight") goaded on by a Sanchette—set in the same universe he had built up for *The Number of the Beast*, but also referring back to his 1957 story "All You Zombies—."

Implicit in Heinlein's organization of *The Number of the Beast*, possibly not fully worked out as early as 1980, was a tantalizing notion that there might be such a thing as the grand story of the multiverse. The last three books he had done could all be viewed as component parts of that master story, in much the same way all the books in Cabell's Biography of the Life of Manuel were component parts of the same story.

It might be that *Job* brought this on. In *Job,* he had played around with world-switching; in this new book Heinlein followed H. G. Wells's advice to bring "the fetish stuff up to date and ma[k]e it as near actual theory as possible"[15] and upped the voltage on the quantum mechanics time-travel jargon to deal with *all* the different kinds of time travel science fiction had imagined over the years—single loops, multiple loops, switching from time track to time track, even isolated "bubbles" in time disconnected from their originating time tracks, bringing together quantum uncertainty and literary uncertainty—the Schroedinger's Cat paradox meets "The Lady or the Tiger" . . .

On November 8, 1983, he began writing his sardonic comedy of manners—a murder mystery titled *The Year of the Snake* for the ancient[16] tail-swallowing world-snake Ouroboros, since the Time Corps gimmick from "All You Zombies—," with its Circle of Ouroboros, had assumed such prominence in the story. Heinlein had often revisited his earliest themes later in his career—in some ways, for example, *Stranger in a Strange Land* was a revisit of the themes he had first explored in "Lost Legacy" in 1939. Both *Job* (1984) and *Friday* (1982) had revisited earlier themes, as well. In *The World Snake* (another working title) he imagined the world of *The Moon Is a Harsh Mistress* a hundred years after its war of independence and in the kind of bureaucratic decay Manny foresaw at the end of the 1966 book. He broke after Thanksgiving for a trip to Los Angeles to attend a Citizens Advisory Council meeting. He was back at work on it before Christmas, and kept at it steadily until February 1984, when Lars-Eric Lindblad called again: There were enough cancellations for the Northwest Passage trip to make berths available, if they were willing to pay the entire fee for the trip up front.

Heinlein wanted those berths.

He would not be able to attend the 1984 World SF Convention in Los Angeles: The Northwest Passage trip was taking off from Newfoundland just days before the WorldCon was scheduled to start. Instead he wrote a few paragraphs in letter form to promote their blood drive.

That February also, Mary Collin passed away after a short bout with pneumonia.[17] Her youngest daughter sent Heinlein Mary's last postcard to him, left uncompleted at her death. She was not quite two years younger than he. Over the years Heinlein had joked about outliving his enemies. But that meant outliving your friends, too, and that is no joking matter. They had never managed to get together after reestablishing contact in 1955 and again in 1961, but the memory of what Mary Briggs had meant to him in 1929 stayed warm and living.

For reasons not recorded, Heinlein left off work on the novel and turned his attention to other matters. When Frank Robinson had conducted that long *Playboy* interview in 1969—the one that was later (1972) badly chopped up for *Oui* magazine—Robinson had mentioned an academic Heinlein would probably like: Leon Stover. Now Dr. Stover contacted Heinlein for an interview: He was in the middle of a book on H. G. Wells for Frederick Ungar, and the publishing house had asked for a book on Heinlein. An anthropologist by training and China advisor to the State Department, Stover had published widely in fields as diverse as Chinese cultural anthropology, the development and meaning of Stonehenge, and a book in French on the cultural anthropology of science fiction. He was now at the Illinois Institute of Technology teaching courses in science fiction in which Heinlein figured prominently. He wanted to do a book more on Heinlein's role in intellectual history than biography or even literary criticism per se and would come to Northern California in June, if that were convenient—and he had a class argument to lay at Heinlein's feet to make it interesting. Heinlein decided to do the interview.

In April he attended the L5 Society's Space Development Conference in San Francisco. The Society had grown faster and larger than anyone could have foreseen after the successful lobbying effort to get the Moon Treaty taken off the table in Congress. The San Francisco group wanted the Society to start *moving,* preferably toward a space station.

Heinlein and Pournelle were not sure this was politically achievable with the capital and goodwill they had available to work with—which might be better spent pushing SDI. They had naturally assumed that the L5 Society would support the space aspects, at least, of the Citizens Advisory Council work on Mutual Assured Survival, but there was a sizeable faction on the L5 Society Board of directors who were deeply suspicious of anything military in space.

After forty-five years of struggle with "custard-headed pacifists,"[18] Heinlein was predisposed to see anyone who blocked the Society's active involvement in SDI as pacifists, but the situation on the L5 board was more complex than that: Much of the resistance was coming from a *tertium quid* who felt that L5 had a more useful mission doing practical political groundwork.[19] This is a very different thing from stubborn pacifism, but it was not something Heinlein was disposed to see at that moment.

At one point, Heinlein said to Pournelle, "Jerry, you're being nibbled to death by ducks. Let's let them get back to their games. We have better things to do." They resigned, though were persuaded to return so a compromise could be enacted.

Heinlein went home and wrote a congratulatory letter to Andre Norton (1912–2005) on the occasion of her fiftieth anniversary as a published writer. She was named SFWA Grand Master in 1983:

> It comes as no surprise to anyone and no one of us deserves it more richly than you do. Do you happen to recall a time when I telephoned you on a matter of SFWA business? Sunday evening 27 August 1978, it was. In the course of that conversation I suggested that you could expect this recognition in the near future.
>
> It was the easiest prediction I ever made.[20]

A few days later, June 9, 1984, Leon Stover visited in the afternoon with his Japanese wife, Takeko.

Heinlein must have found Stover quite an interesting fellow, with life experience and conclusions completely different from his own, but often complementary in stimulating ways. Stover himself was a kind of Johnsonian tory—a type not often seen anymore, an entertaining eccentric.

Heinlein rarely discussed his own stories at all except in shoptalk with another writer—but he made an exception here. In response to a question about "Coventry" and the "Calvinist" reading that had been advanced by George Edgar Slusser, he hardly needed to think about the problem. Stover and Slusser were both mistaken: They had taken different gambits written into the story that misdirected their thinking.

And then Stover did something that must have impressed Heinlein: He accepted what Heinlein told him at face value and integrated the new information into his mental picture. Stover was demonstrating a very rare intellectual quality: The potential for moving behind and beyond the superficial slogans Heinlein presented to the world—all, he judged, that most people could assimilate.

It was probably at that moment that Heinlein began to think of a possibility he had more or less abandoned a decade ago. This was a man who might be able to write a biography of him. He was not "opposed to memoirs per se. A person with a box seat at great events should record what he remembers."[21] Heinlein put it into the back of his mind to let it mature and picked up *The World Snake* again, with the prospect of several weeks clear—more than two months if he needed it.

Job was not due for release until mid-August, just days before they were to leave for Montreal and parts north, but the *Kirkus Reviews* got in an early and favorable review while Heinlein was working in the two-hour stretches that now constituted his personal "'can'-to-'can't'." He finished *The World Snake* two weeks and two days after his seventy-seventh birthday in July, and found you could get the computer to *count the words* for you—130,805 of them. He gave it a quick read-through for typos and grammatical errors—and then he put it away. He *might* be able to get it edited and finalized in the three weeks before they had to leave, but there was no hurry about it: Putnam's would not rush a new book into print until sales on *Job* had peaked. January or February would be the right time to hand over the *Snake*.

In the meantime, he got the newest high-resolution maps of the area north of the Canadian mainland. All the land there, north of Hudson's Bay, looked like nothing so much as a wet sponge. He sent off a series of letters to friends optimistically informing them to expect him in Japan at the end of September— and to Isaac Asimov to expect them in New York late in October.

Job was released by Del Rey in mid-August, debuting on the *New York Times* bestseller list at number fifteen (rising later to number nine). They flew out on August 19 to Montreal. The next day they flew on to St. John's in Newfoundland,[22] where they were able to board *Lindblad Explorer* just in time to cast off that same day.

The two-day passage to Greenland was taken up with orientation— surprisingly more intense than the orientation for the Antarctic. They were read frightening passages from G. W. Melville's account of the attempt by the *Jeanette* in 1880 to make the Northwest Passage, which stressed the deadly danger of the pack ice: Captain Lindblad wanted them more than wary this time—he wanted them *scared*.

At Jakobshavn in Greenland, the ship took on as much fresh water as it could hold, and even the ship's small swimming pool was filled with drinking water.

From Jakobshavn they made north along the southern (inner) coast of Greenland and into the Davis Strait, crossing the Arctic Circle. The Davis Strait led to Baffin Bay through a field of smallish icebergs, and to Baffin Island and another fjord—spectacle again, with cascades of glacial melt spurting from the tops of the high cliffs on each side. They continued into Lancaster Sound separating Baffin Island on the south from Ellesmere Island and the tight cluster of the Queen Elizabeth Islands on the north, pointed almost to the northern tip of the Boothia Peninsula, the northernmost connected part of North America.

They landed at Beechey Island, where members of the Franklin expedition had died in 1845 and 1846, interred in the solid ice.[23] This event made the international news, but by that time *Explorer* was on to Resolute on Cornwallis Island, which is almost the northernmost settlement on Earth.[24]

The Arctic is alive in a way the Antarctic is not. The Eskimos—called "Inuit" in Canada (actually there are dozens of cultures and peoples lumped together under either of those names)—lived there, though traditional lifestyles were being wiped out by the laws that made nomadic existence impossible: You can't send your children to a little red schoolhouse from a dogsled following reindeer herds. The wildlife of the Arctic is abundant, not limited to seals and seabirds. The ship's films and lectures this time expanded from geology and ice physics to the entire natural history of the area and extensive treatment of flora and fauna.

The fauna that drew the most attention were the polar bears. There was something almost magical about these beasts—and for just that reason the crew and scientific staff drilled the passengers relentlessly about the danger they represented. Bears are touchy under the best of circumstances, and polar bears found the ship's engines irritating and so were likely to become annoyed if they could not wander off to find someplace quieter. Any time they were ashore, the expedition leader would carry a rifle "loaded for bear," and if one were sighted on land, they would make back to the boats. As Heinlein often said, the best way to avoid trouble is not to be there when it happens.

They were able to get off the ship at Gjoa Haven[25] on King William Island—a tiny settlement named for Amundson's vessel from his 1903 expedition. Amundson had wintered there, taking shelter from the ice pack. The ground was tundra, soggy where the top melted over permafrost, hilly and hummocky and difficult for Heinlein to get around on. He was in good enough health, but he does not look strong in the pictures that were taken.

From Gjoa Haven they ducked underneath Victoria Island, keeping in sight of the Canadian mainland. As they got closer to the Beaufort Sea, they were joined by a Canadian ice-breaker, *Camsell*, that broke a path for them as the pack ice grew thicker. It was a slow process, but very interesting. If the pack ice was too thick to simply shove aside, *Camsell* would heave itself up on the ice and break it with its weight. The passengers had a "chipping party" one day, as ice accumulated on the deck of *Lindblad Explorer* and all hands turned out to chip it away.

Camsell and her little caravan left *Explorer* at the Canadian border, taking the Mounties with them and leaving *Explorer* to "long, lonely days in ice-filled ocean."[26] The pack ice was rafting up on them, but they were only a hundred miles from Point Barrow, and they had *Explorer*'s special ice-breaking prow.

They found Barrow modernized remarkably from their last visit in 1960. There were still no local industries, but instead of "temporary" structures, there were permanent buildings and even streets now. And Heinlein was found and entertained by his fans and readers, even there.

The hard part of the Northwest Passage was now behind them. This was essentially as far as most of the successes had gone, though the trip on to Japan, along the chain of Aleutian Islands and into the Bering Sea, was relatively less difficult. They were ahead of schedule, so they had a few additional unscheduled stopovers, visiting Eskimo settlements at Diomede and other islands in the Bering Strait. More than ten thousand years ago, during the Ice Age,[27] these islands were mountains on the Bering Land Bridge that is now on the bottom of the ocean, and the remote ancestors of the North American Indians walked across from Asia. Even today, Eskimos look enough like Japanese to be mistaken for them without the furs.

They made landfall at Little Diomede, an American island just two and a half miles from Big Diomede, a Russian possession. Little Diomede was so steep that the Heinleins stayed close to the landing, though some of the more adventurous passengers climbed a bit.

From Diomede it was a longish hop along the chain of Aleutian Islands and across to the Japanese Home Islands. They reached the northernmost, Hokkaido, and were greeted at the dock by newsmen and a television crew to record this historic event: Thirty-three ships before them had gotten through the Arctic ice, but all had originated in North America; the *Lindblad Explorer* was the first ship in human history to complete the passage from Europe to the Orient, the culmination of four hundred years of ambition.

They took their time in Japan this trip, visiting in Tokyo with friends made on the trip last year—Tetsu Yano, Hiroshi Hayakawa and family, and Osamu Tezuka. As October came on, the 55th reunion of the Naval Academy class of '29 was coming up. They flew back over the pole to the States, making the last leg of their trip to Annapolis by commuter train.

This year their numbers were greatly reduced, though many of Heinlein's special friends were still among the living. Bob Clarke was still alive, and Cal Laning—people who had bridged with him the era from cloth-winged biplanes, when rockets and spaceflight were "crazy Buck Rogers stuff," to the era of space travel come and gone while Doc Smith's "lambent rays" conducted space battles overhead (or near enough).

They went on to New York for a few days and caught up with the progress of the book while they were away. *Job* was performing very satisfactorily, Eleanor Wood informed him. Jerry Falwell had given the book an unlooked-for publicity boost when he condemned *Job* in his September *Moral Majority Report* newsletter,[28] which must have pleased Heinlein since this was the closest modern equivalent that could be managed to being banned in Boston—the ambition he had started out with, all those decades ago. And, of course, it was a heartwarmingly genuine *cri de bunion* satisfying in itself: He would probably have been puzzled and disappointed if this book hadn't stepped on some toes that badly needed stepping on from time to time.[29]

As was their custom, Robert and Ginny threw a party in their hotel suite on October 23, 1984. Heinlein might need a cane nowadays to keep upright, and he might be on the verge of an unwelcomed shotgun marriage to a Lindé bottle, but there was nothing wrong with his memory: He greeted and introduced every guest by name and without notes—even those not already known to him.

When they got back to Santa Cruz, they found news from Leon Stover about the book deal with Ungar—it had fallen through: They were only interested in a treatment of Heinlein as a genre figure, and that wasn't Stover's vision. Heinlein was more appropriately, in his opinion, classed as an *Americanist* than as a genre writer.

> Mark Twain was once regarded as a Frontier writer, and Herman Melville as a writer of Sea Stories. How long will it take the critical establishment to see that RAH is destined to shed his contemporary reputation as merely the best of SF writers? Something more there is in this, that places his work with the classics of American literature (not to say World Literature, if we stand the best of the boy's books up against the work of Robert Louis Stevenson).[30]

The project was not dead yet: Twayne might be interested in the book for its United States Authors series.

Heinlein turned his mind to the SDI struggle that was still going on. The Citizens Advisory Council had scheduled a meeting for December 8, at Larry Niven's home in Tarzana, again. Arthur C. Clarke had been invited to visit following anti-SDI testimony he had given before the Senate Foreign Relations Committee on September 17, 1984, and he showed up at about 11:00 A.M. A couple of years earlier, Clarke had written an article for *Analog* criticizing the strategic feasibility of some of the hunter-killer satellite ideas,[31] but he had made some arithmetic mistakes in calculating orbits, and his entire argument, which was conducted in very strongly worded terms (at one point in the Senate testimony he termed proposed SDI hardware "technological obscenities"), was off base. He also seemed to be criticizing the idea of a leakproof defense—which nobody on the Council was advocating, because nobody thought such a thing possible in the first place.

The essay had been reprinted in Clarke's collection of anti-SDI essays just released, *Spring: 1984.*[32]

Heinlein's steadfastly affectionate feelings for Clarke had cooled somewhat when Clarke started giving anti-SDI polemics on his speaking tours. At that time Britain's foreign policy backed the Russians' various ploys to get SDI removed from policy considerations, and the Soviets had given Clarke a Potemkin luxury junket. Robert and Ginny were disappointed that Clarke seemed to fall for the Red carpet treatment, but it was really the Congressional testimony—particularly when he was clearly wrong about his facts—that put him over the line:[33] "We both felt that Art was far too friendly with the commies in the S[oviet]U[nion] for our taste, and we resented him talking in public about such things."[34]

The rules of the Citizens Advisory Council do not permit any individual to be quoted; nevertheless, several accounts of this incident have been published, some of them quite inaccurate in both fact and in relating the emotional content of the confrontation that did occur.

As Clarke entered the meeting, Max Hunter and Lowell Wood kidded him about his erroneous technical assumptions and particularly the mistakes in orbital calculations. "Arthur's first words coming into the room were—'But Max, I learned everything I know about celestial mechanics from you,' to which Hunter replied, 'I didn't teach you enough, Arthur.'"[35] The group of about forty went over the technical issues together with Clarke. That unsettled Clarke, but he was an honest scientist, and he was grappling with the realization that he had made, not one, but a series of embarrassing and embarrassingly public mistakes. "He asked several questions," Jerry Pournelle told Clarke's biographer, "and at the end of it he admitted, 'I clearly was wrong.'"[36]

Heinlein had not participated in the technical portion of the briefing, but Clarke had tried to take a moral high ground against SDI, and Heinlein finally had enough of the arrogance of the Brit who sees no problem in telling other people how to run their country and told Clarke so directly, if politely—always, as Jerry Pournelle noted, politely, even when more heated than usual.[37]

Some of the other participants at the meeting suddenly woke up, as shocked as Clarke at the public remonstrance against an old friend. Gregory Benford summarized the incident for Clarke's official biographer:

> When Clarke stated his reservations about [the very idea of] strategic defense, Heinlein chose not to argue about it as a technical problem but rather to say something like, "Look, this is a matter of the defense of the United States, and you're not assisting the United States, and therefore you really don't have call to have an opinion about it."

Clarke's biographer goes on to summarize Benford further, adding, "Heinlein continued in that vein, saying that if he were visiting England or Sri Lanka, he would not tell those people how to run their country."[38]

Clarke was stunned: "'He accused me of typically British arrogance,' said Clarke, 'and he really was vicious. It really hurt me. I was very sad about it.'"[39] But it was Heinlein's position that Clarke's "moral doubts" about SDI were outrageously misplaced, since it was a move to make nuclear war technologically obsolete, and it was past bearing for Clarke to be shaking a moralistic finger at people who were trying honorably to work their way out from under the gun—a gun, moreover, not pointed directly at him and his.[40]

Heinlein figuratively turned his back on Clarke, who spent the rest of the meeting talking with others and trying to regain his equilibrium. "As the meeting broke up, Clarke approached Heinlein and said, 'I can't help the British [sic], but I'll try to do something about the arrogance.'"[41]

And in fact Clarke did change his position after that meeting (he still did think the "umbrella over the U.S." was silly and unworkable—but so did many of the CAC participants: that "perfect defense" was not on the technical agenda). He ceased speaking out against SDI.[42]

32

AFTER 1984

As soon as he got back from Los Angeles, Heinlein went back to work on *The World Snake*.[1] This book had turned out more complicated and possibly more confusing than most, because of the different time-travel methods all used simultaneously, and he took care with it.[2] There was no hurry to finalize the manuscript while the sales of *Job* were peaking; he spent five months revising the text and sent it off to New York in the first week of January 1985.

Leon Stover's proposal to Twayne's U.S. Author Series was approved for a book to come out in spring 1987. Both the Heinleins agreed to read Stover's manuscript, if he promised to tell no one. They feared being once again swamped with reading requests. "So let's keep it secret between us,"[3] Ginny wrote to Stover.

At the end of March 1985, Heinlein was formally diagnosed with emphysema—a progressive, degenerative lung disease in which the oxygen-absorbing tissues are destroyed. His lung capacity was hovering around 28 percent. It had been long enough coming that he was used to the idea and accepted it. More distressing, actually, was that Pixel had been diagnosed with feline leukemia around the same time. In the past, that would have been a death sentence. But he was getting treatment now. Pixel was such a character that he was a great comfort to them both—the most communicative and intelligent cat they had ever known.

They had acquired Pixel in 1982, when Taffy (Taffrail Lord Plushbottom) died—an eighth-generation descendent of Pixie, The Only Cat (feline hero of *The Door into Summer*) and the last of his line. Pixel was Shelley Pixilated Antarctica, a marmalade tom with tortoise-shell markings who looked like the original Pixie and was named for their guide in Shanghai and for the continent they had just visited. Pixel was a Robert's-cat, sleeping like the original Pixie in the crook of his arm or leaned up against him. For five years.

The World Snake sailed through the editorial process, except for one point: Eleanor, Ginny, *and* his editor at Putnam's, Susan Allison, all hated the "snake" in the title. *The Reluctant Knight,* a metaleptic reference to Don Quixote, didn't play well, either. Robert asked Ginny for help coming up with a new title. Pixel, who was a minor character in the book, was naturally on Ginny's mind at the moment.

> I said "how about 'he walks through walls?'" and Robert said, "No, but you've got an idea there," and he went into the study and he wrote and wrote and wrote. Finally came out with *The Cat Who Walks Through Walls.*
>
> And everybody said, "Don't you mean *The Cat* That *Walks Through Walls*? And he said, "no, I mean *The Cat* Who *Walks Through Walls.*[4]

Pixel was definitely a person.

Heinlein prepared a gummed label and fixed it over the title page instead of retyping it.

It was an unusually hot summer in 1985, and an unusually dangerous fire season. They kept emergency flight bags loaded in the car in case they had to evacuate. There was no birthday cake that year: Ninety-five degrees was simply too hot to bake. Instead he celebrated by making a $20,000 donation to High Frontier.

Heinlein was stirring up a new book, taking cards out of the idea files and shuffling them together. If what he came up with is an indication of his thinking at the time, he must have felt that the big meta-story of the World As Myth that had been shaping up for some time needed a parallel and complement to the Future History narrative, which was, after all, the master story (myth)—and which was also to some degree a myth of the America of the twentieth century. His new book was told through the eyes of a woman with enough perspective to be able to see it all—Lazarus Long's *mother.*

The basic story structure was probably coming together in his mind in mid-August 1985 when Jayne Sturgeon visited the Heinleins to ask for Robert's help.[5] Theodore Sturgeon had died on May 8, 1985. He had been working at a novel, *Godbody,* for more than fifteen years. The book was substantially finished but neither polished nor edited.[6] Jayne Sturgeon was a writer and professional editor herself, but she told Heinlein she could not get started putting *Godbody* in shape to send to its posthumous publisher, Donald A. Fine, though she urgently needed the money this manuscript represented.[7]

When Jayne mailed the *Godbody* manuscript[8] he read it over and was able to make suggestions about technical issues such as reworking the paragraphing.[9] Sturgeon had been playing with the same technical problem that Heinlein had been working: multiple-first-person. *Godbody* was something more along the lines of *A Night in the Luxembourg*:[10] A sylvan deity—a kind of Pan—touches the lives of eight people. It was regrettably poorly written in Heinlein's opinion[11]—though he would not say so to Jayne. He recommended some cuts and minor changes.

Jayne asked him to write an introduction for the book, and he wrote an affectionate and thoughtful memorial to the man, not quite three thousand words, August 30 to September 1, 1985: "Agape and Eros: The Art of Theodore Sturgeon."

> In *Godbody* he tells us still again, and even more emphatically, the same timeless message that runs through all his writings and through all his living acts—a message that was ancient before he was born but which he made his own, then spoke it and sang it and shouted it and sometimes scolded us with it.
> "Love one another."

Robert Silverberg, who was assembling the volume for publication, thanked Heinlein for an "absolutely perfect" introuction.[12] Jayne thanked him properly, and that was the compensation for this job—as he had planned.[13]

Heinlein started writing *Maureen Johnson: An Irregular Autobiography of a Somewhat Irregular Lady* in September 1985, passing the manuscript section by section as he wrote it, not to Ginny this time, but to longtime fan friend Betsy Curtis for an outsider's perspective.

—Just as Curtis finished up her first-reading, they received word that Judy-Lynn Benjamin del Rey had suffered a brain hemorrhage in New York. She did not die right away, but it did put to an end a brilliant career as an editor. She had shepherded the acquisition of Robert's remaining juveniles from Scribner in 1975 and 1976, getting them into paperback. Robert called frequently to cheer her up.[14]

The book business was changing drastically; all the book people were being replaced by bean-counters and button sorters. Heinlein was happy that the individuals who had taken a chance on him and stood by him during the time when his market was developing should have the benefit of the increased profitability—but when they were forced out and conglomerates took over, the sense of dealing with individuals as a small businessman disappeared.[15]

For decades now, Signet had been jiggering the reprints on their paperback issues to keep the market starved. Signet kept the automatic renewal options at the old, and very low, royalty rates. Heinlein's new contracts were offering royalties on the high end of the scale—10 to 12 percent—while the old contracts were paying the 1950s rates, 4 to 6 percent.

Mac Talley was long gone from Signet, and they had no debt of gratitude to whatever conglomerate held the stock in NAL this season. Ginny and Eleanor Wood finally had enough of it. When the next contract renewal came up in October 1985 they forced Signet/NAL into arbitration over the automatic renewal[16] and won their point for any contract that had a term clause—all of them except *Beyond This Horizon*. They were able to place the four Doubleday books with another paperback house right away, and that gave them a pile of galleys to check.

The Cat Who Walks Through Walls was released and hit the *New York Times* bestseller list on November 11. At the same time, the paperback release of *Job* was on the bestseller lists for both the B. Dalton and Waldenbooks chains. Since he couldn't do book tours of any kind anymore, due to his health, Heinlein wrote and recorded a short audio "Message to the Berkeley Sales Staff Concerning *The Cat Who Walks Through Walls*."[17]

Spider Robinson was the first to notice this book was part of a continuing story.[18] The *New York Times Book Review* review stressed Heinlein's iconoclasm, designating Heinlein "a master craftsman as he looks back over nearly half a century of labor, most of it in the fields of literature [there's the L word] rather than in its plantation house."[19]

The fan mail also started coming in. "[P]ractically every letter asks for a sequel," Ginny wrote to a friend. "I would have thought everyone would want Robert to bring Mike [the self-aware computer of *The Moon Is a Harsh Mistress*] back to life, but no, they're all interested in saving the kitten! A fictional kitten at that."[20]

Heinlein had, about that time, a letter from Keith Henson, one of the founders of the L5 Society, who had just moved to San Jose. Henson had been trying to interest him in cryonic preservation, because of the "cold sleep" he had written about in *The Door into Summer* (people were always assuming—and still assume—that Heinlein had a special personal interest in things he put into his stories, though it usually just meant he saw possibilities for a good story in them).[21] At a conference banquet, he had been overheard remarking to a dinner companion "How do we know it won't interfere with reincarnation?"[22] That was, of course, at least half facetious, but he had just enough leftover conviction from his childhood to treat it as a serious possibility. He didn't talk about it anymore, except, very occasionally, with Ginny. If it *were* true, he promised Ginny he would wait for her on the Other Side, just in case.[23]

L. Ron Hubbard passed away at Whispering Winds Ranch in San Luis Obispo, a few hundred miles to the south. His intimates withheld the news for a few days, but the *New York Times* obituary ran on January 28, 1986.

January 28, 1986, is one of those days that is etched into the memory of everyone who lived through it: the Space Shuttle *Challenger* blew up seventy-five seconds into liftoff. It was a great setback for NASA and the space program.

The publisher Jeremy Tarcher wrote on January 31 asking Heinlein to verify biographical details in a new Panshin book, *The World Beyond the Hill*. He declined. He and Ginny were reviewing Professor Stover's manuscript as it came in, chapter by chapter, and sending back comments. The impression Heinlein had gotten when the Stovers had visited, that this was a possible biographer, must have been growing stronger. There were things Stover got wrong[24]—but he was the first commentator in Heinlein's experience who seemed at all able to see some of the major thematic currents in his work, to understand even a little of who he was as a human being.[25]

Gradually, Heinlein was able to get back to his own work. He finished the first draft of *Maureen Johnson* early in March 1986, at 158,000 words—the longest thing he had written since *Time Enough for Love*.

As the Congressional hearings on the *Challenger* disaster wore on, the perennial arguments about "wasting money" in space surfaced again. When Heinlein was approached by the grassroots Challenger Campaign to underwrite an appeal to the American people, he enthusiastically donated money and the use of his name for a full-page "A Letter to the American People" ad that appeared in the Sunday *New York Times* on March 30, 1986, urging that NASA be encouraged to honor their memory by carrying forward the aspirations of these fallen heroes.

A trip to another Citizens Advisory Council meeting, on May 7, exposed Robert and Ginny to the "Russian flu" that was going around that year. Heinlein was not really up and around for three weeks: The influenza made his emphysema worse.

On his first partial day up he wrote a long autobiographical letter for Leon Stover. He had more "fiddling carpentry"[26] to do with the new book—fact-checking mostly. While he was down with the flu, he had decided to retitle the new book. Possibly taking a cue from that open letter "to the American People," he chose a title from Tennyson's "Ulysses"—about picking up and moving on, as humankind has always rolled on:

> *Come, my friends.*
> *'Tis not too late to seek a newer world.*
> *Push off, and sitting well in order smite*
> *The sounding furrows; for my purpose holds*
> *To sail beyond the sunset, and the baths*
> *Of all the western stars, until I die.*[27]

He titled the book *To Sail Beyond the Sunset*.

Robert's seventy-ninth birthday was spent quietly. He celebrated by making another $20,000 donation to High Frontier.

Ginny was up and around early in the morning July 26, 1986, getting her morning orange juice, when she heard a noise in Robert's bathroom. She went to investigate and found him in his pajamas, with blood flowing from his nose and down his chest. There was blood everywhere.[28] She went into overdrive and tried to stanch the flow. Robert told her he had simply turned over in bed, and the nosebleed started.

Ginny got his service to ring their local doctor on an emergency basis: She should take Robert to the Emergency Room at Dominican Hospital—while he called an EENT specialist to meet them there. Within minutes she hustled Robert into the car, still in his blood-soaked pajamas, with a box of Kleenex and an armful of Turkish towels (and a sack for the used tissue).

The drive took about forty-five minutes, and he was losing blood at an alarming rate (but an ambulance would have taken even longer). Robert was able to walk in under his own power. The specialist, Dr. Seftel, took charge of him.

Dr. Seftel positioned a balloon at the top of the nasal passage and inflated it, to put pressure on the artery that was bleeding, and then packed the nose. The whole procedure took about forty minutes.

Robert had lost a lot of blood—most of it on the bedroom and bathroom floors; probably two units, nearly a liter. He went directly to the Intensive Care Unit with an intravenous drip and oxygen and a battery of monitors. The bout of Russian flu might well have triggered this incident by inducing vascular fragility.

Later that afternoon, with a critical care doctor and nurse in the room, Robert's blood pressure began to drop precipitously. He could feel himself sinking, he told Ginny. She called out to the doctor and nurse as his blood pressure sank to 40/20. They got his head lowered, and Ginny tried to stay out of the way, while holding his hand.[29] He needed a transfusion.

Transfusions in 1986 were not the automatic thing they had been ten years earlier. The blood supply was known to be tainted, and there were risks—significant risks—of hepatitis and even AIDS.

When Ginny got back to the Bonny Doon house the next day, the bathroom looked, she said, like an abattoir, splashed with blood drying on the tiles.[30] Dr. Seftel tried to take out the packing and the balloon, and another massive hemorrhage started. Hastily Dr. Seftel reinflated the balloon and repacked the nose.

This was clearly going to require surgery—and Robert would once again need the surgical expertise at the UC Medical Center hospital in San Francisco. He was transferred the next day, in an ambulance. Ginny followed in the car.

They managed on July 28 to get the new hemorrhage under control and gave Robert two units of packed cells to replace the blood he had lost. By July 30 Dr. Crumley decided to give him a week of observation to regain some strength before surgery to tie off the artery on the right side of his face, top and bottom beside the nose, with silver rings.

On August 6, they actually got to the stage of prepping Robert for surgery. But about 12:30 that afternoon, Dr. Crumley found Ginny waiting in Robert's room and told her they wouldn't need to operate, after all: When the packing and the balloon were removed this time, the bleeding did not resume. A lucky stroke—the Maxillary Artery had closed itself off spontaneously.

If his blood pressure stayed stable, she could take him home.

On Thursday, August 7, they made the trip back to Santa Cruz. Ginny could not leave him unattended while she picked up his prescription in downtown Santa Cruz, so she called the local Visiting Nurses, just to have someone on hand to call an ambulance if needed—but the LVN they sent had a cold, and Ginny sent her away: They could not risk another respiratory infection for Robert. The pharmacist, who happened to live nearby, offered to bring the prescription with him that evening.

That was the most unpleasant and nerve-wracking day of Ginny's life. She fell into bed exhausted about 9:00 P.M. after rigging a "wake-me-up" cable tied to a radio with the volume turned up to full blast, so Robert could roust her out of bed if need be.

Two days later, Ginny wrote a circular letter to send out to all their friends, keeping everybody abreast of Robert's condition.[31] She was getting ready to mail out the second batch when the radio-alarm sounded. Robert was having another hemorrhage—his third. Back to Dominican, where Dr. Seftel installed a new balloon dam, and then back to San Francisco by ambulance, Ginny again following in the car with clean clothes and miscellanea.

This time, Dr. Crumley decided, they would perform the surgery no matter what. By the time Ginny found a hotel and got back to the hospital, about 11:00 A.M., they were already prepping him for the surgery.[32]

On the way up Ginny had noticed a flickering in her vision—like the "schlieren" refraction slips in the visual field she had noticed when she was studying microsurgical technique, years ago. It went away, and there didn't seem to be anything to be done about it; she did not mention it to Robert at all while he was sick.

The surgery went very smoothly, Dr. Crumley told her around 3:30 in the afternoon when they got him into post-op. By 6:30 that evening he was back in his room, cheerful and alert, though still weak, and of course his nose was bruised and painful. He needed two shots of Demerol that evening to get to sleep.

During several days of observation, Ginny occupied her time at his bedside checking the galleys for a new edition of *The Green Hills of Earth*. On Sunday the 17th of August, they were allowed to leave the hospital. The next day, Ginny wrote a continuation of her circular to their friends:

We came home in a very luxurious limousine; it gave Robert plenty of room for his legs, and he came through the trip very well. And is now back in his own bed. He's eating better than he did in the hospital, and seems to feel quite well considering that the operation is less than a week in the past. In fact, through many operations, I've never seen him come through so well. He's cheerful, cooperative, and seems happy to be home. And Pixel will be home soon, and will assist in nursing Robert . . . .

Now all there is to worry about is hepatitis and AIDS from the transfusions—wish us luck! I suspect that by this time the $25,000 nosebleed has reached around $50,000.[33]

Gradually they got back to their recuperation routine. The operation had left Robert with an ache on the right side of his face, for which he took codeine—which had given him a saintly and beatific demeanor, somewhat dreamy, but also seemed to confuse him and leave him unable to distinguish reality from his internal life[34]—alarming at first, but Ginny got used to him staring at the ceiling for hours at a stretch.

Heinlein's publishers decided to delay issuing *To Sail Beyond the Sunset* until his eightieth birthday—a longish delay, but justified considering how well *Cat* and *Job* were both still performing. In his lucid periods, Robert acknowledged it unlikely he would ever write again.

He never had the chance to bring his big vision for the World As Myth books to fruition—never even got his protagonists to the battle with the "villains" of the piece—even though he did get in Jubal Harshaw casting doubt on the whole idea of the villains.

By the end of August he was sitting up in bed and working—reading the galleys for *The Green Hills of Earth* that Ginny had read through while he was recovering in the hospital. He was even getting a little exercise: Ginny took him on daily walks around their atrium.

And now Ginny told him this business of being forty-five minutes from the closest hospital could not continue. She had turned seventy this past April and was feeling her age: She just couldn't take the anxiety of driving so long with him fountaining blood; they had to find a place closer to a hospital.

And she had been having eye trouble and needed to see an ophthalmologist.

She left it at that. Living in Bonny Doon depended on her being able to drive, since Robert had let his license lapse. She had learned well enough from him how to conceal the truth by telling the truth so that he did not pursue the details. Her vision had gone from schlieren to a nearly complete loss of vision in her right eye.

Ginny was fed up, she said, with the taxes and crowding in California, but Robert did not want to get too far out of the area. When he got some of his strength back, they would start looking in the Carmel area, twenty miles down the coast—probably in the spring, if he continued to improve. This meant he had to eat more, no more nonsense. He needed to get up and take exercise as soon as he reasonably could.

Heinlein improved gradually. As the doctors isolated side effects, the meds were replaced, one by one. And Ginny began fiddling with his diet, trying to tempt his palate—anything that would get him to eat was *ichiban*. Ensure milkshakes three times a day. He liked a molasses cake she could make within his dietary guidelines, and she was relieved when persimmon season came on and he would eat them with enthusiasm—another revenant from his boyhood: Persimmons are practically the state fruit of Missouri.[35] When the fall weather came on, and fresh, crisp apples started appearing in the supermarkets, she started making homemade applesauce, which he relished.

By the end of September, he was able to get up once an hour and do something for himself—anything. It was notable when he stood in the doorway one day in September and called for Pixel.[36] And now that Robert was off codeine, he was cheerful and working.[37]

By the end of October, *The Cat Who Walks Through Walls* was on all the mass market paperback bestseller lists. An article in *The Economist*—a magazine Ginny read religiously—said that one in ten novels sold nowadays were science fiction, almost directly due to Robert's influence, together with Clarke and Asimov.[38]

Heinlein had been saying for decades that science fiction for the mass market *could not* be the same as science fiction for a small and highly interactive readership of genre enthusiasts.[39] He began after World War II to pare away genre conventions. Over the years, his fiction moved toward a general audience and evolved away from standard genre science fiction, though nobody within the field seemed really to recognize it, and was moving toward something like the relationship H. G. Wells had with the contemporary fiction audience of his day. An academic in 1986, using *Friday* to ponder the literary/subliterary paradoxes of Heinlein's career, concluded simply he was "a leading contemporary novelist" without genre qualification.[40]

By December Heinlein was taking enough interest in things around him to read again. When Leon Stover phoned on Christmas Eve, he was surprised nearly speechless when Robert picked up the phone himself.[41]

Robert's oldest brother, Lawrence, died on January 17, 1987. Lawrence had always been his favorite big brother and an inspiration in a way he could not quite articulate. "They're all going," Robert told Ginny[42] and drew in on himself—which was not good for his recuperation.

Leon Stover had held off telling Robert his bad news: Stover's field editor for Twayne, Warren French, had arranged a session on Heinlein for the next year's Modern Language Association meeting in December 1987, at which Stover was to give a paper. The Modern Language Association is the premier academic organization for literary matters, and such a panel would represent a major step toward recognition of Heinlein as an American writer. Stover was not a member of the MLA, so would be there as a guest, with both Robert and Ginny. But, Stover told Ginny privately:

> You worried that Alexei [Panshin] might attend. That's the least of it, as it turns out. A greater enemy has stepped in to cancel the session, that Marxist s.o.b. whose name I retch to mention [H. Bruce Franklin].
>
> When he heard that the MLA had scheduled a special seminar built around a book sympathetic to RAH, he used his muscle within the organization to get it descheduled. And so it's off, just like that.[43]

It was his impression that Franklin thought there was too much risk of the MLA appearing to endorse a "fascist" writer and his "fascist" critic. "It would besmear MLA's liberal reputation," Stover told Ginny.

> You certainly judged aright the character of this SOB when he came calling at your place. Prof. French confirms to me that his [Franklin's] intentions were duplicitous from the start, which were to make RAH exemplary of everything wrong about America—Fascism, imperialism, racism, sexism, etc., etc. The usual Marxist nonsense. In warning the MLA program committee of the ideological error, he was acting as the defender of the One True Faith (and perhaps also to protect the preeminence of his own book).[44]

Heinlein gradually recovered his strength, and was able to perform an annual ritual: He called in to Jim Eason's regular fund-raiser for the Leukemia Society. Eason was a popular talk-radio host on station KGO News Talk 810. As Eason explains:

Every year, at some time during the broadcast, Robert Heinlein would call in, chat briefly, and pledge a large sum of money . . . .

He would identify himself to the producer when he called, but only to the producer, not to the audience. I would get a note that "A Robert Heinlein is on the phone." I would answer the same way I answered every caller, "Hi, this is Jim Eason, and you're on KGO."

I would hear a beautiful, clear, strong voice saying, "Hi, Jim, this is Bob." That was it—no showboating, no big deal, just a caller named Bob. We would chat for a couple of minutes, mostly about his health, how his wife was doing, what he was writing at the moment. He always ended the calls with a heartfelt pitch for listeners to pledge money to fight leukemia.[45]

The American galleys for *To Sail Beyond the Sunset* came in April, and Heinlein had to be chivvied into reading proof on them, though by the time the English galleys came, in June, he was interested enough to read proof without prompting. They cautiously began traveling on day trips down the coast to the suburbs of Carmel, to look for housing closer to hospitals.

After a false start with a co-op in Pebble Beach that rejected them because the condominium association didn't want anybody running a business from the condo (even a writing business), they found a place about a mile east of Highway 1 outside Carmel but within less than three miles of the Community Hospital on Highway 68—a ten-minute drive: "It's very pleasant, perched on a hill, with the most glorious view of the Pacific Ocean and Point Lobos. Robert will have the master bedroom for his study, which looks out on that view, as does the living room."[46]

The first purchase for the new house was a cat door for Pixel so he could come and go as he pleased.

They listed the Bonny Doon house with a real estate agent—in a depressed market, since the federal government was closing down so many nearby military installations. The first thing to do in preparing for the move was to collect all the bits of paper they had been holding on to for years, and send them on to the University Library for archival. On July 6, 1987, Rita Bottoms came with her assistant Paul Stubbs.

Bottoms had become a good friend over the years, virtually one of the family. Robert confided cheerfully that he thought Leon Stover would be suitable to write his biography, if anybody wanted a biography. On that occasion, they discovered that they both liked the song "Cool Water," and burst into song together, Robert croaking a little because of the emphysema but in good spirits.

Ginny was comfortable enough with Bottoms, too, to let down her guard from time to time. Coming into the kitchen, Bottoms was startled when Ginny suddenly sagged back against the closed door, obviously exhausted. "I just can't do this anymore," she said.[47]

The next day was Robert's eightieth birthday, and the publication date of *To Sail Beyond the Sunset*. The book had been on bestseller lists since June. Putnam's sent Robert balloons and chocolates to mark the occasion, and they received a congratulatory letter from President and Nancy Reagan. They had a rare social gathering, with in-person visits from science-fiction writer and veterinarian Jesse F. Bone and his wife, and Charles Brown, a fan friend who visited frequently (and was also publisher of *Locus* magazine). Yoji Kondo arranged for him to receive an honorary Judo Black Belt. Brown took pictures to memorialize the occasion.

Bottoms had let Heinlein know that they had gotten a number of requests from the general public over the years—for the Opus List in particular. Robert and Ginny decided it was time to tighten up the restrictions on what might be publicly accessible during their lifetimes. The Opus List would be made off-limits.

Bottoms had long ago drafted language for a seal on the correspondence, and on July 13, 1987, Heinlein made that seal a formal restriction on the gift of his papers—for twenty-five years, instead of the fifty years they had originally discussed. At the same time, he reversed a decision he had made ten years earlier: Originally he had marked what was left of the abortive 1977 *Panki-Barsoom Number of the Beast* for destruction after he was gone; instead, he put the manuscript box with the typewritten instructions among the material to be taken to the UCSC Library's Special Collections, with a fifty-year restriction.

The university was starting to send pleasant but very persistent functionaries angling for a big bequest. Perhaps it was becoming too obvious that he was getting old and had little time left. Over the years Heinlein had come to think that the money might be better spent in a donation to a smaller library—his birthplace of Butler, Missouri, for instance, had only a small county library. He had been talking with Ginny for some time now about donating enough money to them to build a really nice facility, and he told Bottoms that was what he was determined to do—the major bequest to the Butler library (though a smaller donation—say, on the order of $10,000—was still a possibility for the well-funded university).

It was probably all this thinking about his "legacy" that reminded him of Leon Stover, and Heinlein called on July 17, 1987, just to talk for an hour, ranging over this and that. One thing he made sure to get into the conversation:

"You've got it all wrong," he told Stover genially, about Stover's Calvinist interpretation.[48] There was still too much of it in the draft manuscript, but Heinlein
did not attempt to argue Stover out of it. Possibly he was satisfied that Stover did
get some of the important points others missed seeing—about him no less than
about the stories—and most of Stover's colleagues didn't even seem to be aware
of the background material Heinlein was moving around, or even of the history
of science fiction to which he was often reacting.

Stover wanted to position him with American writers such as Mark Twain,
rather than as a genre writer,[49] which was not altogether unreasonable. When
Gerald Jonas reviewed *To Sail Beyond the Sunset* for the *New York Times Book
Review* later that year, he observed that Heinlein had been migrating out of the
genre for some time, that "he now writes books that bear only the most superficial relation to either science fiction or the conventional novel."[50]

The house in Carmel went into escrow late in July, so they had about ninety
days to clear out twenty years of collected junk. Charles Brown came to help,
and Heinlein gave him some cover paintings for his earlier work and a pile of
some of the less valuable books—second impressions and book club editions,
mostly—sitting for hours on the living room banquette and signing book after
book, to increase their eventual sales value (the more valuable first editions were
to go to the Archive). He also sent his personal copy of one of his favorite books
to Leon Stover: Jerome K. Jerome's *Three Men in a Boat,* inscribed to Stover.[51]

Packing up his working desk brought up a matter that had been lying fallow
for decades: He got out the file of manuscript and notes and correspondence
about that first novel he had written in 1938 (*For Us, the Living*). Over the years,
he had mined it for story ideas—the whole trajectory of the Future History had
come from that book. It couldn't be anything more than a curiosity at this point.

Ginny agreed. "It wouldn't have done his reputation any good to publish it—
and I had begun to be aware that he had a reputation at that point, so I recommended that he chuck it."[52] They burned the entire file, together, all the copies he
had had made over the years, in the Swedish fireplace in the living room of the
Bonny Doon house.[53]

Toward the end of September, the house was bare walls and a pile of boxes.
Ginny asked him if he had any regrets—about marrying her, about having had
no children. He took a little time to think about the question: No regrets, he told
her. He had had a good life, and enjoyed almost every minute of it—and she had
been a big part of making it so, particularly these last decades, which he wouldn't
have had at all without her.[54]

And then the movers did come and cleared out the house to the bare walls.
Ginny had taken Pixel to a kennel, to spare him the upset of the move.

But Pixel accepted the new environment with only a few reservations. A few days after the move, they went back to the Bonny Doon house to clear out any leftover bits and get it in shape to turn over to the real estate agent. They stayed there for an hour or so. "It was sad, having to leave our home . . . [sic]. We both cried."[55]

Within a very short time they were more or less up and running in the Carmel house, with phone installed and Robert camping out in Ginny's way, at a breakfast bar between the office and the kitchen. He had decided it was time to use some of the contacts he had been accumulating and nurturing for the last several years and get back into politics: He started out with the SFWA Directory and the membership of the Citizens Advisory Council and worked hard to organize a candidacy for Jeane Kirkpatrick for the 1988 presidential campaign—when Ronald Reagan's second term would expire. He was pushing the campaign into funded existence by sheer force of will—but ultimately Ms. Kirkpatrick asked him to leave off and let her out of the commitment: Her husband had been diagnosed with a terminal illness and she wanted to retire to take care of him in his last days.

That Christmas they had a small tree, because Ginny didn't want to risk a ladder. Apparently Robert had packed some things she didn't know anything about. When she opened her main present from Robert this year, she found a largish, empty—almost empty—gold-colored and gilded bottle of men's cologne, King's Men, with the gilding wearing off. It was inscribed "Merry Christmas to Ticky, the queen of my heart." On the other side was one of his "Ticky pictures," with his perennial motto, "Semper toujours"—"always, ever."

This was the very bottle she had given him forty years and a few months earlier, when Robert had moved out of the house in Laurel Canyon and was living in motels in the San Fernando Valley. They had been driving on some errand and stopped at a drug store. She had bought this cologne for him then, and gave it to him when he got back into the car—just something to perk him up. He had scolded her then, for spending her hard-earned cash on something frivolous like that.[56] But he used it—used it up and saved the bottle, to give her forty years later.[57] It was a folly of sentiment—and so very like him.

It was a second answer, an *and I really mean it* to the question she had asked him a few months back at Bonny Doon—a question that really never needed to be asked, and for which no words could ever be sufficient, whether he regretted marrying her. "Cherish Ticky" was more than a family game between a married couple; it was their way of life.

LAST ACT

Shortly after Christmas 1987, Robert and Ginny were listening to KGO Talk Radio, an airwave institution in Northern California, when Dr. Dean Edell's regular medical advice program came on. This time, he had a report on a new surgery that could relieve emphysema. Heinlein's ears perked up immediately: He had been having more trouble breathing than usual since the move. This operation removed the small glands—the carotid bodies—on either side of the neck that control the breathing mechanism and caused panting. The breathing function was then taken over by another area of the brain.

This was not a cure: Nothing could repair the damage the lungs had already sustained—but it could greatly improve the quality of his life.

This was not precisely an "experimental" surgery; it was done frequently and even "routinely" in Japan—but it was controversial in the United States, almost certainly due to medical politics. There was just one doctor in the entire country performing this operation, Dr. Benjamin Winter at Doctors Hospital in Los Angeles. Heinlein called Doctors Hospital and got instructions for arranging this surgery. Ginny recalled: "And he said we're going to do it. And I said, 'Have you spoken to your doctor about it?' He said 'No. And I'm not going to. I'm just going to do it.' "[1] He probably didn't want to invest the energy in the argument that would inevitably ensue with his new doctor.

Since moving to Carmel, Heinlein had to find a new general practice physician, and he selected Dr. Lola Steinbaum—a graduate of Harvard who trained at Stanford Medical School.[2] The first time they saw "Dr. Lola" she asked if he was the Robert Heinlein who had written *Stranger in a Strange Land*—and then went to fetch her husband, Dr. Erickson, who was in practice with her in the same facility.

Heinlein had taken risks with surgeries before—wagering everything on one turn of the cards—and it had worked out well for him so far. "I tried not to interfere too much with what he wanted to do," Ginny later explained.

"Which was only good sense. You have to rely on the other person's good sense."[3] He had to decide how to manage his own risks, and she would support his decisions. He typed up the instructions Doctors Hospital gave him, with side comments for Ginny about timing and arrangements.[4]

New Year's was on Saturday that year. They rose at six o'clock on the morning of January 4, 1988, and had a taxi take them to the San Jose Airport, thirty miles away, for an anticipated stay of four days—not long at all for a surgery, but the doctor said he had his patients up and exercising the day after the surgery.

In addition to the traveler's checks they usually carried on trips, Ginny had gotten two cashier's checks to pay for the surgery. They had medical insurance, but the hemorrhages had run their insurance claims over $50,000, and they were reaching their claim limit.

Ginny was very uneasy about that prospect. Her careful planning and estate management could go up like paper in a flame—and it would, because she would liquidate every asset they had accumulated if it would keep him alive.

The next morning (January 5), Heinlein had the operation—under local anesthetic in theory, but he felt everything: The anesthetic, he later said, might as well have been normal saline. As soon as the first carotid body was removed, he felt some relief in his breathing: The sensation that he could not catch his breath lessened.[5]

Following the operation he seemed alert and cheerful. The next day the doctor had him walk briskly up and down the hospital corridor. He usually had his patients run a little, but Heinlein's ongoing problems with balance made that impossible.

The next step, if he wanted to take the next step, was one of the new heart-lung transplants, since the damage to his lungs could not be repaired, surgically or otherwise. But he did not want to take up that option. "One to a customer," he quipped.[6]

It was raining the day they were scheduled to return to the airport. They got Robert into the van while Ginny took care of the discharge papers. Hurrying to catch up, she slipped on the slick pavement, falling flat on her back, head bouncing on the curb.[7] She scrambled back up immediately, bruised and shaky, but insisted they continue on to the airport; they had a driver meeting them in San Jose, so she wouldn't have to face any demanding tasks.

Robert was exhausted—but that was normal for him following any surgery. Ginny got him into bed and when he was down took time to realize how much pain she was in. She remembered that she had some codeine tablets left

over from her last prescription and took enough of those to give her some relief. She put herself to bed and found herself taking codeine for the pain that
woke her every now and again.

Three days later her head cleared and she found she could move again—
with considerable pain, still, and extreme effort. She hadn't eaten or even gotten out of bed in that time. God only knows what Robert had done for himself.[8]
She was instantly consumed with guilt: What had she done!

Fortunately, she had dodged a bullet: He seemed normal for him, at this
stage of surgical recuperation, except for diarrhea. She tried to put her anxiety
out of her mind and cut back on the codeine.

Mary Jean and Andy Lermer wanted to help, and Ginny gratefully accepted
assistance with the shopping and so forth.[9] Ten days or so later, she was more
or less back on her feet and able to get out and around: They had been living
on microwaved TV dinners, supplemented with a little cooking of breakfasts
and lunches, so first priority was to replenish the larder. "We're leading a very
healthy life now—" Ginny wrote, "early to bed and up early too. I expect
within a month or so we will forget that we've had our current problems."[10]

Leon Stover's book on Robert was released by Twayne as part of its United
States Author Series, with a photograph of a young Heinlein taken by Bill
Corson almost fifty years earlier. The book immediately began selling briskly—
for Twayne: 759 copies in the first two months.[11] This is a number that would
be a dismal failure for any of Heinlein's works of fiction, but this was a scholarly series that sold almost exclusively to libraries, and their usual sale was a
thousand copies in toto.[12]

Three weeks after the operation, Heinlein was still bedridden, still diar-
rhetic, and obviously sinking. Alarmed, Ginny overrode his protests and got
him dressed for the first time since the operation and over to Dr. Lola's office
on February 1.

Dr. Steinbaum was shocked and horrified.[13] She immediately put Heinlein
into intensive care at the hospital for a week, as he was showing signs of con-
gestive heart failure—fluid filling the membrane that surrounds the heart.
She wanted to put Ginny in the hospital, too: Robert's uncounseled surgery
was bad enough, but she scolded Ginny particularly for neglecting to take
care of a back injury that could be permanently crippling.

At the very least, she lectured Ginny, she should not keep trying to do everything herself. Ginny arranged through a nursing agency for an LVN (Visiting Nurse) to help out since they would have to maintain a hospital routine
even after Robert went home from his second hospitalization in the first month
of the year.[14]

Robert continued bedridden and listless, though he could be coaxed out to take the amount of exercise the doctor recommended—and no more.[15] Ginny continued exhausted and overwhelmed. She feared her neglect when they came back from Los Angeles might have killed him . . . [16]

At first they had two shifts of nurses, but the second shift had virtually nothing to do, so Ginny cut back to one. That help, though, was a lifesaver, as it was often difficult to get help on the weekends.[17] They had family visitors occasionally—Kathleen (Rex's widow) came down from Palo Alto and Lynnie Ayers, their niece. Ten days later, February 16, 1988, Robert developed flulike symptoms, and it was back to the hospital for another week—the third time this year. And counting.

There was a new round of medications—and they hadn't gotten the last round balanced yet. The "hospital routine" they maintained at home intensified:

> Robert was on oxygen all the time, and the equipment kept breaking down, needing to be repaired, etc. The nurse fed Robert—he couldn't eat by himself—he did not sit up in bed, just lay there.
>
> I think that his vision was going bad—cataracts, possibly, because he did not read; I was busy with all the other things, and couldn't read to him. No time . . . I had my hands full.[18]

By the beginning of March, he began to sit up and take notice, which made things a little easier for Ginny, as she had some feedback to work with. She made an apple pie according to his strict diet, to tempt his palate, which seemed to work, as she was able to bribe him with it, to eat the entree. They watched some of the Winter Olympics ice-skating competition together on television.

He was still very weak; Ginny called Dr. Steinbaum on March 3 to say he could not make his scheduled follow-up appointment. Dr. Lola was going off on a trip for ten days and did not want to put off the examination. She made an unprecedented house call, and seemed satisfied with his progress.

The next morning, Robert hemorrhaged again. Dr. Lola's relief, Dr. Farrow, told Ginny to get him to the ER—a much quicker, much less stressful trip this time. The bleeding stopped of its own accord, but the hospital put him in the Intensive Care Unit for safety's sake. This was his fourth hospitalization in three months.

And the new heart specialist changed his meds again (the diarrhea he had been suffering from for months had apparently been caused by one of the medications). This time, Ginny was able to sleep at home, only a ten-minute drive from the hospital, instead of finding a nearby hotel.

At eight o'clock on the morning of March 12, Dr. Farrow's substitute, Dr. Grant (which made him Dr. Lola's substitute's substitute) called from the hospital: Robert had hemorrhaged from the nose again, and they had put him back in the ICU overnight, with a new transfusion. Robert was doing better now and would probably be moved back to the general population the next day—but Dr. Grant asked her about heroic measures.

They had talked about this, during the times when Robert could work up interest in anything. He did not want to live surrounded by life-support equipment, kept alive by main force. Fortunately, nothing "heroic" was needed this time.

Somehow Robert had picked up a bruise on his shoulder in addition to the other problems. It took major effort on Ginny's part, but she managed to get him to sit up some—it was bad for his lungs to lie down all the time—and even to walk a little, twice a day as the doctor prescribed. It was like pushing a dead weight, but that was her job, and gradually she could see improvement:

> This morning when I was in, Robert appeared more cheerful and more like himself than he had for a long time. For weeks, he'd been what I called withdrawn, but his doctor calls it apathetic. He even managed to eat some applesauce for me, and even asked for a piece of chocolate! I suppose things are looking up.[19]

By March 18, they were able to send him home again, though with a new battery of monitors to go along with the new regimen of meds. And he got out of bed by himself—the first time he had really walked in a long time. Ginny was working in her office. He got to her doorway and collapsed.

The nurse helped get him in the car and back to the hospital, where he was met by a CPR team. Fortunately, this was a false alarm. He was at home when Catherine Crook de Camp called, and they had a long, reminiscent talk, recapping, as she remembered, forty years of loving friendship.[20]

As the bills started coming in, Ginny really began to be afraid: One of the monitors he was on—and would be on for months, probably—rented for the staggering cost of $750 *per day*! And the nursing fees were not inconsiderable, either. It was an unpleasant fact, but it was inevitable: When their insurance ran out, they would be pauperized. She began planning what assets she could liquidate.

It was sheer good luck they had those assets in the first place—Robert's popularity well beyond the publishing enclave of science fiction—and careful management, learning over the years from her mistakes, that preserved it for just this time of need.[21]

In April, Robert was back in the hospital—though this was more like a "normal" hospitalization for him. His listlessness and depression were gone (Denis Paradis had gently suggested some of that depression might be caused by anxiety for her—not something she would have thought of, herself).[22] Much of his previous listlessness and apathy, it turned out, was caused by an undetected low-level urinary tract infection. Once that was taken care of, he was much more active. In this, his fifth hospitalization of the year, he had his own walker to help getting up and around—and even his physical therapist remarked on how talkative he was this time. He sat up for meals in his chair, at the room's deal desk. George Warren, a writer colleague who had become a close and sympathetic friend of both Robert and Ginny over the last nine years,[23] visited with them shortly before Ginny's seventy-second birthday.

> . . . I went to see him in the hospital a fortnight before his death. He was dying of emphysema and had tubes in his nose and he was below 100 lbs, and he was so weak I worried about him.
>
> So what did he do with his failing strength? He gave *me* a pep talk. I was changing markets, as he'd had to do when he moved from pulp paper to slick paper in the 1940's; he remembered how tough it had been. "Hang in there!" he said. "Outlast the SOBs!" He went on a bit in this vein, weak as he was. Heart the bolder, spirit the greater . . . .
>
> The advice he gave me cashed every bit as well as the check, too. "Treat people magnanimously if you can," he said, "It'll make you feel better. Expect nothing and you won't be disappointed. Do the decent thing if you can, but for its own sake."[24]

If Heinlein had to choose one capsule message to deliver, that would probably be it—the same message he had packaged for children in the 1950s and repackaged for the grown-ups those children had become in the 1960s, and repackaged again for the adults those children's children would hopefully one day become in the 1980s.

Ginny discussed his care with his doctor: The care he could get at home would be more than they could do for him at this stage. He was able to go home on April 21—by ambulance this time, so that he could be carried in, too weak to walk.

On April 25, Clifford Simak passed away.

Heinlein did continue to improve. Ginny made him a jelly omelette one morning for breakfast, trying to tempt his palate and get him interested in food. Normally, their "routine" was for him to call her in during meals, from another part of the house, and they would negotiate how much more he must eat at this meal. This time, he ate every bit of it and even asked for more. He was so lively that he played ironic word games with Spider Robinson. "I'd heard that reading had become a chore," Robinson remembered:

> I offered to read onto cassette some excerpts from the novel I'm working on, and when he heard it was about a whorehouse he expressed comically keen interest. I don't know whether he ever played the tapes. I hope so, but I don't mind if he didn't.[25]

But the improvement was short-lived. Soon his energy began to drop, and his labored breathing became more and more an effort. He was going downhill rapidly, and they went back to two shifts of nursing care. Gradually he became aware that it was time for his last acts as an adult.

"About two weeks before he actually died, he said to me when we were alone, 'I'm dying.'"[26] He seemed surprised to Ginny. "'Yes. I know,'" she said gently. "'And all I can do is make you comfortable.'"[27] So I got all the information I needed about what he would like. I threw away the diet that had been prescribed for him, and he ate whatever he liked. Including a blueberry pie I made for him."[28]

He gave Ginny his last wishes—not a burial; cremation. No memorial service, but a scattering of his ashes at sea—with military honors if possible. They subscribed to a burying service that would take care of the details.

There was more to say to each other, but they were both acutely aware they could not ever get any real alone-time together. "I kept a baby-tender by his bedside," Ginny wrote a friend,

> so that he could call someone at any time, and have someone come to him immediately. And there were things we never got around to saying to each other for lack of privacy. Oh, it was possible to turn off the speaking end in the bedroom, but I seldom did, because it caused the other end to howl. I was always conscious of the fact that someone else would be listening in to anything I said, and I think he was too.[29]

Sunday, May 8, was Mother's Day in 1988—a holiday that no longer had any personal meaning for either of them. Robert finished his breakfast and said he felt a little tired: He was going to take a nap—attended by the nurse on duty this morning. Ginny had her usual backlog of correspondence to do, so went to work at her office desk, answering fan mail.

After some time, the nurse came into the office and attracted her attention. "Mr. Heinlein doesn't respond." Robert had passed away during his morning nap—peacefully . . . but she had not been by his side when it happened, holding his hand.

Later, according to his wishes, she scattered his ashes into the Pacific Ocean from the deck of a U.S. naval vessel, with full military honors. Later still, she would join him on this final voyage, when her own ashes were spread upon the same waters.

> *Death closes all; but something ere the end,*
> *Some work of noble note, may yet be done,*
> *Not unbecoming men that strove with Gods . . .*
>   *Come, my friends,*
> *'Tis not too late to seek a newer world.*
> *Push off, and sitting well in order smite*
> *The sounding furrows . . .*

APPENDIX I

AFTER

It may be we shall touch the Happy Isles,
And see the great Achilles, whom we knew.
Tho' much is taken, much abides; and tho'
We are not now that strength which in old days
Moved earth and heaven; that which we are, we are;
One equal temper of heroic hearts,
Made weak by time and fate, but strong in will
To strive, to seek, to find, and not to yield.
Alfred Lord Tennyson, "Ulysses"

A little time after her husband's death, when Virginia Heinlein could move again, there were things that needed to be done. She called his sister, MJ, and the burying society. MJ and Andy Lermer were with her when they arrived to take the body away to be prepared and cremated. The death certificate was made out the next day.

From those two telephone calls, a spontaneous information tree developed, of people whose lives Heinlein's writing had touched calling others who shared their affection for him. Within an hour, hundreds of thousands of telephone calls were made, one person calling two or three others in a wave going in many directions, around the entire world, leaving in its wake grief more personal and more profound than the regard of a merely public figure—the kind of thing that had happened much more slowly in 1910, when Mark Twain passed away.

Robert Heinlein's books and stories had stirred people on an inexplicably personal level—because he had made it a policy to tell the disowned truths, things that people needed to have said, and repeated. The arrangements the Heinleins had made to preserve their privacy, to keep from being crushed by those who wanted only to be present in him, prevented them from truly grasping the magnitude of his personal influence, mediated through his fiction. Thousands of letters came to Mrs. Heinlein in the next few months—of people sharing what Heinlein had meant to them, of how he had influenced their career choices, of the comfort he had given them in personal darkness.

And the oddest thing of all: They were the same letters they had received every day of their working lives, steeped now in grief. Water divided is water multiplied.

Virginia Heinlein got through her personal grief and numbness by answering the thousands of letters of condolence that flooded in, as she had answered all the fan mail. In the end there was an entire filing cabinet drawerful of them, several thousand (which ultimately passed to the Robert A. Heinlein Archive at the University Library, UC Santa Cruz). On May 26 a Memorial Resolution was introduced in the California Assembly by Sam Farr. At Heinlein's instructions, over three days Ginny burned two file drawers' worth of his "experimental" writing in the small fireplace in Carmel, working in batches. She then began reading the forty-plus years of his accumulated correspondence, in preparation to compile and edit *Grumbles from the Grave,* which was issued the following year.

The Heinleins' tax advisor told her that long-term planning for the literary estate is not a high priority because typically current royalties dwindle to nothing by five years after a writer's death. The cash value of the entire estate at that time was about $1 million. She set in motion the Butler Library Foundation Robert had wanted her to create, with a cash endowment plus transfer of some of the literary properties and, eventually, title to the Bonny Doon house so that its sales proceeds added to the Foundation's endowment. These were the first acts of what became Virginia Heinlein's private and personal effort to preserve and extend Heinlein's legacy. In the midst of this first spate of legacy work, Mrs. Heinlein wrote a letter to her husband.

June 29, 1988

My beloved darling,

Now it's almost eight weeks that you've been gone. And I've been in a terrible emotional state all that time; sometimes it seems that I miss you so terribly, other times I wonder whether I'm not just feeling sorry for myself. Which one?

This house misses your presence, but I seem to feel you guiding me . . . [sic] can that be true? Now you know the answer to the great mystery, but I don't. Will you be waiting at the end of that tunnel, as you promised me, or is there just nothing out there? I remember vividly, when I landed in

Denver, you were there at the foot of the stairway of the airplane. Did I cry then? Or did we both?

And, when we were finally married, you cried all the way through the ceremony, and I cried at the end. Or was it the other way around?

We weren't separated very often after that, although you made a number of trips here and there and I made that one by myself to Seattle, and another to Phoenix.

One of the things that troubles me is the way you lay in bed, dying (I know now—you told me, but I wouldn't believe it) and I wondered and wondered what you were thinking about all those quiet hours. I didn't ask, and you didn't say. Were you reviewing your life, were you ever sorry that you married me? I wish I could be sure about that latter.

Kathy [Petty?] told me several times how patient I was with you, and she said that I spoiled you. I don't think I spoiled you, but perhaps I did. And Gale told me in a note that I had been a wonderful "nurse" to you, and that I gave you outstanding care. But I wonder whether there wasn't something more I could have done?

You know, I was always scared, despite the lots of money we had, that it would all go out and then what? I'd have spent it all on you, if it had been necessary, and I hope that you knew that.

The past almost-two-years have been so very difficult, and I have been so tired that it has been hard to know what to do. I miss you dreadfully. You were what made life worth while. But we had those few months of moving back last summer when we found this house and left Bonny Doon forever. The time when you tried to get Jeane Kirkpatrick to run for President, and the times when you were packing up your study for moving. When we got rid of the years of stuff we had pack-ratted away, I don't even know what left that house,[sic] I do know that you packed up lots of stuff in those plastic bags and got rid of it. But I found that you had saved my letters from so long ago, as I had saved yours. I've read them all over, and now I know that I loved you more when we parted, four weeks ago, than I did when we were so passionately in love (at least I think you were—I know I was!).

But one thing I want to say to you is that I'm surprised, although perhaps I shouldn't be, at the quantities of mail which keep coming in from people we loved, from some whose lives touched ours briefly, from others we never met. I have been, more or less steadily, at this computer trying to cope with that flood of mail. Four diskettes have already been filled with answers, and there are lots more still to go. It's more mail than came in over *Expanded Universe,* and heaven knows, that was a man-killer.

A couple of days ago I sent off a check to the Leukemia Society, for the usual amount, because I missed the drive while you were so sick. Via Lee Rodgers, in your memory.

Problems have come up since you left, which I would have liked to discuss with you before I did anything about them.

I sent off a number of keepsakes you cherished to members of the family. MJ has your watch—the last of the "little watch which Ticky gave me" series. And Clare has Gramp's chess set, to pass along to Jim. I sent Lynnie and Doug that emerald shaped paperweight which we admired so much, and Jennifer has the little bird's egg which was so beautifully decorated. William got the Apollo 11 things, and Ethan the B-1 airplane. Bill Bacchus and Mary have the Danish liqueur glasses you loved so well. And I sent Amy Baxter your "Curtsey to the Moon" vase as a reminder of our grandchild relationship. Kathleen wanted your sword, so I gave that to her. She will pass it along to one of the girls, I guess, along with her first husband's sword. Perhaps someday, someone in the family will wear it again, proudly.

And I am planning to set up a foundation for that Robert A. and Virginia Heinlein library in Butler. If it's done that way, and it can get a tax exemption, *all* the money we've saved over the years will go to that foundation, without a cut for Uncle Sam, and possibly California. I think you would have liked that!

A crew will be here one of these days to shred those papers you wanted destroyed. I know I promised to burn them but it just isn't possible in the fireplace here, so they will be shredded and taken away. The company which will do it, will do it *here* on the premises, so I will know that they're gone.

And I'm going to get the study whipped into shape—with all your awards displayed properly. Oscar did the obituary for *Shipmate* in proper form; I sent him a list of your awards, and he was very impressed with them. Somewhere in the masses of paper on my desk there's a letter from him about that. And get some pictures hung here and there. For some reason, you didn't seem to particularly like the Nichelle Nichols portrait, so I won't hang that. And get this place fixed up—the counters for the kitchen and study bath are ordered, and should be here soon. The kitchen ones are the yellow we planned, and the bath will be blue. And I'll get that floor and unfinished area around the bidet fixed up again. I told you that the pink curtains had been taken down, and some simple blue ones put in their place.

It seems to me that that takes care of all the requests you made. The funeral arrangements weren't turned into a circus—you were cremated and the ashes were strewn at sea, with military honors. Mostly, the obituaries have been kind to you, although several (which were take[n] from wire services mostly) had a number of items which weren't exactly facts. But the obits have come in from all around the world, and you know how newspaper people are.

I hid out, aided by the Coroner's office here, and Charles Brown. When they couldn't find me, they went to almost everyone associated with science fiction to get quotes. Isaac spouted off in his usual fashion, and so did several others.

How I miss you! You were the one fixed thing in my universe for over forty years. I never really appreciated how many, many people were affected by your ideas; now they're writing me, and telling me that it was your standards of honor and other virtues which affected so strongly their lives and their choices of careers and so on. Darling, I didn't realize it, but I did stop telling you to "sugar coat" those lessons you were giving them in the juvenile series. I do wish that you could read those letters, but perhaps you know? I certainly hope so.

This is my usual disorganized way of thinking. I'm sorry for any troubles I caused you, but I never, *never,* NEVER stopped loving you above all else at any time. You were my star, and still are, and I only hope that I will be able to meet you at that end of the tunnel we spoke about, only once, as I recall. Maybe you will be waiting for me there, as you were when I first landed in Denver, that time so long ago.

I'm lost without you. It's only answering all those letters that has kept my sanity for the past four weeks. Keeping busy, through my tears, has been the only thing that has kept me going. Pixel misses you too. He won't go into your bedroom—hasn't since you left, although he sometimes sleeps on my feet, rather inconveniently.

There are any number of small encounters which people tell me about that I hadn't realized had taken place. I must have been present on those occasions, but busy with other things. I know you haven't been up to it for a long time, but how much I'd give to work along with you on one of those blood drives again!

And our travels. Maybe I will do some travel again someday. But not now—I can't face being a widow on a cruise now—at least not for some time. But, if I ever do again, know that I will be looking at things with your eyes, for you.[1]

NASA arranged that October to make a posthumous presentation to Heinlein of its Distinguished Public Service medal in a ceremony at the National

Air and Space Museum on Capitol Mall in Washington, D.C. Dr. Yoji Kondo arranged a series of spoken memoirs by friends and colleagues.[2] For the occasion, Ginny read a transcription she had made of the "This I Believe."[3]

Soon thereafter (October 21, 1988—the Heinleins' fortieth wedding anniversary), the long process of the biography began with taped interviews made in the Carmel house with Leon Stover. Mary Jean and Andrew Lermer were also present for this occasion. In November 1988, Stover was granted special access to most of the sealed archival material at the Robert A. Heinlein Archive, Special Collections and Archives of the University Library, University of California, Santa Cruz. Over the next year, Stover undertook extensive research, both in the Archive and by personally interviewing (and in some cases establishing relationships with) many of Heinlein's surviving friends, including particularly Cal Laning.

A year later, increasingly concerned at the amount of rumor Stover was soliciting and not fact-checking with her, on November 19, 1989, Mrs. Heinlein revoked Stover's access to the sealed portions of the Archive, as well as permission to write an authorized biography.[4]

In rapid succession, Mrs. Heinlein arranged for publication of restored editions of three of Heinlein's books that had been mangled in original publication: *Stranger in a Strange Land* (Ace/Putnam, 1990), which Heinlein had cut in 1961 from 220,000 words to 160,000 for no reason other than that an editor at the Doubleday Science Fiction Book Club believed no one would read a 220,000-word book; *Red Planet* (Del Rey, 1990), which had been bowdlerized in 1949–50, particularly as to teenagers in a frontier setting using guns, at his Scribner editor's insistence; and *The Puppet Masters* (Del Rey, 1990), cut in 1950–51 from 100,000 words to 75,000 words for book publication by Doubleday, probably to weaken and constrain some of the book's horror elements.[5] These three restored books were issued in direct competition with the original as-published versions, as at that time, the entirety of Heinlein's work was in print with the temporary exception of the collection *The Unpleasant Profession of Jonathan Hoag*, which would soon be reissued. Quite remarkably, twenty-plus years later, all of Heinlein's works are still in print, and the restored editions (plus others issued later) compete successfully in the market with the original publications.

By 1990, Mrs. Heinlein's vision had deteriorated significantly. She was diagnosed with macular degeneration and a hole in her retina. The following year, Mrs. Heinlein gave up driving and moved from Carmel to Fleet Landing, a mixed-use retirement community for Naval personnel near Jacksonville, Florida. She continued to work on various legacy projects, endowing a Chair of Aerospace Studies at Heinlein's alma mater, the U.S. Naval Academy. The search for the first occupant of the chair was to take eight years; it was inaugurated in 2001 by Dr. Vincent Pisacane. Dr. Pisacane was succeeded in 2012 by Captain Kenneth S. Reightler, Jr. She also changed her will to realize a project she and Robert had discussed in the past: On her death the proceeds of all the remaining intellectual property of the estate would go to fund a Prize Trust for commercial space development—the Heinlein Prize Trust—a substantial cash prize inspired by and comparable to the Orteig Prize that motivated Charles Lindbergh's 1927 flight across the Atlantic Ocean.

Other of Mrs. Heinlein's legacy projects, brought to fruition in spite of her vision problems, resulted in the eventual publication of a significant amount of Heinlein's unsold file material, including the 1946 *How to Be a Politician,* published for the H. Ross Perot Presidential campaign as *Take Back Your Government!* (Baen, 1991)[6] and the 1954 travel book, *Tramp Royale* (Ace Books, 1992). She also informally assisted Dr. Yoji Kondo in assembling the book that became *Requiem: New Collected Works by Robert A. Heinlein and Tributes to the Grand Master* (Tor, 1992).

Having accomplished all of the major last wishes Robert left her with, Mrs. Heinlein regarded her memorial work as largely accomplished by 1992.

Robert and Virginia Heinlein had a very ambivalent attitude toward the commentary and scholarship about his work that came out during his lifetime, particularly starting with the contemporary comments about *Starship Troopers* published in the bombastically named fanzine for Heinlein's colleague science-fiction writers and editors, *Proceedings of the Institute for Twenty-first Century Studies* (Advent: Publishers, 1992). Alexei Panshin's commentary on the book, in particular, exasperated him, and as *Heinlein in Dimension* became embedded in the emerging scholarly commentary (science-fiction criticism accelerated in the 1960s and 1970s), his exasperation extended to the academic community in general:

> I find Panshin's opinions about that book [*Starship Troopers*], and about the books that followed it, repeated again and again in "scholarly" discussions of my works.
>
> It annoys me but I have found it useless to try to refute it—so useless that I have come to suspect that many and possibly most professors of English can't *read* English.[7]

Heinlein's opinion of the academic community's view of his body of work was somewhat justified: The scholarly work that existed by the time of his death was of generally dismal quality—"scholarship so faulty," one later commentator expressed it, "as to fail high-school Lit standards, much less those of any higher body."[8] Publication of Leon Stover's Heinlein book for the Twayne U.S. Author Series in 1987, despite its flaws, marked a genuine turning point in Heinlein scholarship, followed in 1993 by the doctoral dissertation of Marie Guthrie-Ormes, *Robert A. Heinlein: A Bibliographical Research Guide to Heinlein's Complete Works* and in 1996 by the doctoral dissertation of Philip Homer Owenby, *Robert A. Heinlein: Popular Educator and Philosopher of Education,* which had an extensive appendix analyzing and identifying much of Heinlein's philosophical underpinnings as deriving from the American Pragmatists. In 1997 *The Heinlein Journal* began publication to offer a venue for the new scholarship. In that same year the Heinlein Society was founded. Mrs. Heinlein began experimentally appearing in online group chatrooms in 1998, signaling that a genuine Heinlein community had begun to emerge online, and she assisted also with the early formation work of the Heinlein Society.

This trendline came to fruition in 2000 with the publication of *Robert A. Heinlein: A Reader's Companion* by James D. Gifford, which sought to establish an objective factual basis from which further academic and scholarly work could proceed. Other scholarly and academic works continue to emerge, many taking the work products of the new Heinlein scholarship into account.

The value of Heinlein's literary estate rose dramatically during the 1990s, as a result of Mrs. Heinlein's careful management. The Copyright Act of 1995 made it possible for her to terminate contracts and re-place them where they would generate increased income. The surplus she allowed to accumulate, to fund the Heinlein Prize Trust after her death. Late in 1994, a more-or-less faithful film of *The Puppet Masters* was released, starring Donald Sutherland, Eric Thal, and Julie Warner. Film options on *Stranger in a Strange Land* (Paramount) and *The Moon Is a Harsh Mistress* (Dreamworks SKG) were negotiated in 1995 and on *Orphans of the Sky* and *The Star Beast* (Disney) in 1996. Sony brought out a puzzlingly unfaithful production of *Starship Troopers* in 1997, directed by Paul Verhoeven.

On Thanksgiving Day in 2002, Mrs. Heinlein fell and broke a hip. She had been hospitalized twice earlier in that year. In the following months, Dr. Robert James, who had been in contact with Mrs. Heinlein researching Leslyn Heinlein's biography, found a surviving photocopy of Heinlein's unsold first novel, *For Us, the Living.* He put off discussing it with Mrs. Heinlein while she was in the hospital, but in fact she passed away in her sleep on the morning of January 18, 2003, and *For Us, the Living* (Simon & Schuster, 2004) was published by the Heinlein Prize Trust. In April 2003, a few days after what would have been her 87th birthday, her ashes were scattered at sea outside San Diego harbor by a small gathering of friends and family.

The value of the Heinlein estate had grown under Mrs. Heinlein's management from $1 million to $10 million.[9] She left a simple will, giving all the personal property, including a large amount of correspondence and other documents not already sent, to the University of California for the benefit of the Robert A. Heinlein Archive at Special Collections and Archives of the University Library at UC Santa Cruz. The investment accounts and the intellectual property (that is, those not already given to the Butler Library Foundation), endowed the Robert A. and Virginia Heinlein Prize Trust "to encourage and reward progress in commercial space activities that advances Robert and his wife Virginia's dream of humanity's future in space."[10] The first Heinlein Prize, in the amount of $500,000, was awarded to Dr. Peter Diamandis (Ansari X Prize, among many other accomplishments) on July 7, 2006 (Heinlein's ninety-ninth birthday); the second was awarded to Elon Musk (founder, CEO, and CTO of SpaceX—Space Exploration Technologies) on June 29, 2011.

On the three days before and including the centennial of Heinlein's birth, July 7, 2007, a conference and gala was held in Kansas City, Missouri, with an attendance of about 750 of "Heinlein's Children."

Learning Curve, the first volume of this biography, was published on August 17, 2010, with a trade paper issue in June 2011. An author site, www.whpatter sonjr.com, archives progress updates and corrections of errors and omissions incorporated into the trade paper edition.

"THE GOOD STUFF"

It is a truism of biographies that "all the good stuff" comes out after the first major biography is published. This is particularly true in the case of Robert A. Heinlein, as he was so protective of his personal privacy during his lifetime. His friends and family respected his wishes, for the most part, and did not discuss him or his life for public consumption. Even in such circumstances, though, when a biography is published, the bonds of privacy are loosed, and people become willing to share their memories.[1]

A good many of Heinlein's younger colleagues and friends did assist in the biography, and their kindness and generosity is acknowledged throughout, in the endnotes and elsewhere. However, the protracted process of the biography, through three starts over twenty-three years, had the unfortunate side effect of seeing almost all of Heinlein's contemporaries pass away, their recollections gone with them.

There was, however, one remarkable exception to this general rule: A comment on Facebook revealed that one of Heinlein's close friends acquired while in Philadelphia during World War II, Grace Dugan Sang (you met her as a character in chapters 27 through 30 of *Learning Curve*), still lived, now in her early nineties—was in the process of reading the biography—and wanted to correspond about various subjects therein once she was finished.

Sang—now Mrs. Howard Wurtz—was a very lively person in 2011, as lively and alive and full of beans as she was in 1945 through 1947, the time at which she and the Heinleins lived in close proximity. She generously gave her time in correspondence and digging through boxes of old documents and turned up some truly remarkable memorabilia (including the only known surviving full copy of Heinlein's 1938 campaign poster photograph, a full sheet of fragile, much-folded newsprint).

The process of first-pass revisions of this second volume of the biography was well under way by the time Mrs. Wurtz and I came into correspondence, but the generous fruits of her searches are reflected in endnote commentary and additions at various places in the second volume. Among the copies of letters she provided, however, were some items that could not be made to fit within the compass of the second volume, because they deal with events in the first volume. In a fragment of a letter written to her friend Theodore Sturgeon (she had been close with Jerome Stanton before knowing the Heinleins and ultimately marrying Henry Sang, and so came to know Sturgeon—Stanton's roommate—well, independently of the Heinleins), Mrs. Wurtz describes an occasion at which she was present, at which Heinlein for the only time spoke candidly of his breakup with Leslyn, which had then taken place only a few weeks before. At that time, tentatively fixed to mid-September 1947, Heinlein was "hiding out" in the San Fernando Valley (the Big Valley immediately north of Los Angeles), avoiding friends and getting ready to leave Los Angeles as soon as the divorce proceedings should be heard. The hearing was continued to September 22, 1947, after which he did leave the Los Angeles area entirely—with Virginia Gerstenfeld.

Much of the fragment deals also with details of Leslyn's erratic and unpleasant behavior before she left Los Angeles for Point Mugu (Leslyn was actually living in the same house as the Sangs at the time), but that portion, adequately documented, has been omitted here.

Fragment of a Letter
mid-September 1947
Grace Dugan Sang to Theodore Sturgeon

. . . .The next night we came home from dinner and a call came for us. Henry went upstairs and came down to ask, "How'd you like to see Bob Heinlein tonight?" Pierre Gordon had called earlier to say Bob was on his way over and wanted to see us and the Corsons to say good-bye, as he expected to go east when the divorce was granted. I was delighted, because I rather expected Bob's side of the separation to vindicate my cold and cr-u-el conduct [toward Leslyn] of the previous night. But I was surprised to find he had no intention of even mentioning Leslyn. (Unlike Leslyn, who describes Bob's conduct to everyone she meets.) From 6 to 12, he discussed everything in the world but his personal problem. At 12, we all left, bade the Gordons good-night, and went out to our cars. We were down to our final goodbyes, and everyone was thoughtfully avoiding mentioning Leslyn, but at the last moment, I couldn't stand it, and out of my horrid little mouth popped the words, "I'd gladly take a message to your ex-elect, except that

I'm not speaking to her." Bob came alive and looked like himself for the first time all evening. "What happened?" he asked and then, turning to the Corsons, and Henry, he said "Let's go some place and talk; I've got to hear about this." So you see, were it not for a doogan what has lots of guts we should never have heard Bob's side of the story. We went to a drive in, and Bob, Bill, and I sat together and talked for nearly two hours leaving Henry and Lucy Corson down the counter, dying to know what Bob was saying. His story was simple: that Leslyn has been an alcoholic for years, that she throws herself at terrified men and concludes that Bob is madly jealous when he rescues the men, at their request, and that she is getting more like her Donald,[2] every day: i.e., psychopathic, slightly nuts. Said Bob, he spent the best years of his life trying to get her to eat instead of drinking, but that she always had a way of sneaking in liquor and deceiving him, and if she did go on the wagon it was only for a few weeks, and then she'd be back at her tricks of hiding bottles around the place and sneaking quick nips now and then, until she'd have a mysterious collapse. But, said he, it never occurred to him that he wasn't forever responsible for her welfare, till Dr. Fink advised him not to throw away his life on her, that he had no moral obligation to see that she doesn't ruin her health. Ginny had nothing to do with it, he said, he'd had an affair with her, and it was nothing more than the other affairs which Leslyn had condoned. Bob agreed with us that Ginny was a queer sort, but said he hated to see her a scapegoat for Leslyn's wrath. No, he told us, he hadn't been seeing Ginny, or anyone—he was too upset by the whole thing, that divorce was the last thing he'd wanted, it just seemed the only thing to do. He was still terribly in love with Leslyn, he said, and he'd never have been able to stay away if she had not sold the house and thereby broken up the pattern he could so easily have returned to. Bill [Corson] at this point deplored Bob's taste in women, pointed out that Leslyn had never been able to forget her days at the Pasadena Playhouse, that she still felt herself a femme fatale, although with her skeletal frame and general repugnance no one would touch her with a ninety foot pole, unless he'd been 20 years in the south seas without seeing a white woman. Tho[ugh] Bob had been telling of the difficulty he had in indicating that to Leslyn that John Arwine and Fritz Lang and others were not interested in f[ai]r. wh[ite]. body,[3] he obviously resented Bill's saying this. He stiffened and declared that Leslyn was a very attractive woman, if she'd gain a little weight. Bill couldn't see it, and said so, with conviction. I thought Bob might rise up and smite him, in Leslyn's honor, but he desisted. He told us he was sorry he had dashed away without seeing any of us, but that he

found it sickening to go around to his friends, saying "And she's *another*!"
For, he said, she had assured him if he left her, he would have not a friend
left in the world, and she supplied him with elaborate quotations from all
his friends about his ugly faults. His plans were to go east for awhile and
then perhaps return to some isolated place in Arizona or New Mexico; he
hopes to marry again, he told us, but the girl must indicate that the very
taste of alcohol is sickening to her. And so we said good-bye to Bob—he
intended to go back into hibernation till his trek eastward—and he kissed
me with more abandon than ever before, and it was most interesting.

So there you have the thing, Leslyn's side, and Bob's side—you takes
your cherce. I'll admit I'm horribly prejudiced, but I think anyone must
admit that Bob's conduct has been more admirable since the separation.
Volumes, I suppose, could be written about the Heinleins, and their curious relationship, and no one would ever know what they were really like.

I had a plan for the reuniting of the Heinleins to save the rest of the
people who will meet them some day from the shock and confusion of
knowing them, but only Bernice [Hicks] supports it. Bill Corson is all for
Bob, and has always considered Leslyn a filthy influence, Pierre [Gordon]
feels about the same; Estill Hicks [Bernice Hicks's husband] likewise, while
Bernice agrees with me, and Henry feels they bring out the worst qualities
in each other and should remain separated, but he hopes to avoid both of
them. What do YOU think?

True to Bob's theory that is you leave anyone exposed to Leslyn long
enough, they will see why it's impossible to live with her—so there's no
need to explain, just give her a little time. It's certainly worked out in the
Hicks household, since we abandoned Leslyn and she became a full time
house guest. Estill is a nervous wreck from worrying about her smoking in
bed while plastered, and Bernice, who is hard to humiliate, has at least
been embarrassed at the way she staggers and tumbles around the house in
full view of the innocent daughters and fascinated visitors. She has made
passes at Estill, told him of her need for a MAN, and even tried to whisk
up a little misunderstanding between him and Bernice; she has lied to the
gals, telling them they needn't be shocked at her drinking, that their parents drink plenty, too, when they're not around. And meanwhile she has
drunk everything in sight, and found everything that's hidden away, from
plain beers to exotic liqueurs stashed away for special occasions. She has the
Corsons over a financial barrel of some sort; I don't know just what it is,[4]
but she uses their indebtedness as a goad to make them drive her to places
she's too wobbly to walk to. She had them take her to Laguna when sister

Keith was slugged and raped while drunk, and returned from Laguna in a taxi (the *rich* Mrs. Heinlein) so drunk that the cab-driver had to haul her inside the house. Pierre made the mistake of inviting her to a party which we accordingly avoided, and had to carry her home, and Bernice had to put her to bed.

Yet Leslyn may surprise everyone, for she came out of her stupor last week and got herself a job, editing some publication at the Point Mugu Navy experimental station up the coast. Bud Scoles (don't recall if you know him) got her the job, and everyone hopes to Christ she stays sober, since Bud just sluffed off his alcoholic wife a little while ago, and it would be just too much for the poor man. If she bounces back, Bernice plans to take her to a sanitarium and thence to the Valley A.A. people.

Anent Leslyn, last night Henry, Bernice and I had the most awfully embarrassing moment ever suffered, but I [end of ms.]

Mrs. Wurtz included a handwritten notation on the back of the second page of this fragment:

I don't have the rest of this, but this is the story: We had rented a room-and-bath from Bernice [Hicks] in her sprawling house in the canyon. The uppermost level is Seaview Trail, the lower level Woodland Lane. Our room had its own entrance on Woodland Lane. Leslyn was a house-guest, using daughter Dotty's room (Dot was away). Between our room and Dotty's was a little sitting room. Henry and I were there with Bernice. Leslyn had gone out for a walk, but after we'd talked a long time, the curtain between rooms was pulled aside, and Leslyn said "Did I hear my name mentioned?" !! Henry and I fled, leaving Leslyn to Bernice's wrath. B has no patience with eavesdroppers! (I don't think L went for a walk at all!)

As it happens, the main incident of this fragment, Heinlein's late-night meeting with friends, is mentioned in a letter Heinlein wrote to Bill Corson, on September 18, 1947:

I have been sorely tempted to take you up on your kind invitation, but don't think I will, despite the point about no discussion of my "domestic thing." The reason is that my emotional reaction to the last evening I spent with my friends—you and Mouse, Sangs, and Gordons—was intense and unfavorable. I went into the mulligrubs. I am able to stay on an even keel only by dissociating myself as completely as possible from my former life.

I plan to stay away from former associates and haunts until my emotional experiences have had time to age a bit, until I have become more or less indifferent to my Piglet. Even writing this letter brings up such emotions of sorrow that I can hardly control my tears. I have no doubt as to my course of action—my life with her had become intolerable—but I am by no means indifferent to her. No need to go on about it.

When I said good-by to you folks I honestly expected to be leaving Los Angeles within twenty-four or forty-eight hours and to be leaving California within the week. However the trial was delayed beyond the estimated date—it is now set for the 22nd [of September 1947]—and I did not dare leave California until my affairs were straightened up. So I found a court [trailer court] where I could hole up at the far end of San Fernando valley, about thirty miles from Hollywood. Not in Van Nuys—apparently Leslyn thinks I am in Van Nuys because I happened to mail two items to her on Ventura Blvd., I must have been in the V.N. postal zone. (I had to go to a bank to get a money order for her alimony payment; like a dope I mailed it at the time, instead of waiting until the next time I picked up my mail. Not that it matters, I suppose, but what you told me about her talk of detectives has made me jumpy. I've been meticulous in my conduct, continue to be, and am damn glad I have been. I've no way of guessing what she might do.)

(I have to hang around town because of her unpredictability. I don't want to find myself in the East, with my get-away money gone, when my next stop should be Nevada[5]—I've got to wait until she actually goes through with it. This stalling around has put the damndest pinch on me financially that I have experienced in years. And the waiting makes it hard to write decent copy.)

I may possibly look you and Mouse up after the trial and just before leaving, provided my emotions are in shape. I don't know, because I don't know just what the effect of the fait accompli will be on me. If it throws me into a tailspin, I'll want to sweat it out alone. You, more than any other person alive, know what is good about Leslyn and why I can't forget her—and you know also, better than anyone but me, what her characteristics were that finally made it impossible for me to go on any longer. I don't have to explain anything to you—and I *wont* explain anything to anyone else. I prefer being thought a heel to undergoing the disgraceful and undignified process of justifying myself by telling tales on my lost Pig.

My love to both of you,

Bob

Mrs. Sang also found a fragment of an earlier letter, also to Theodore Sturgeon or possibly to Jerome Stanton, which suggests how the "outsiders'" view of the breakup evolved over the summer of 1947. This letter appears to have been written in late July or possibly early August 1947—that is, before the events of the previous fragment, which took place in mid-September 1947. This summary of the breakup places the blame squarely on Ginny Gerstenfeld:

. . . . Leslyn resented and criticized her, the more Bob defended her. At last Ginny got Bob to turn agin Vida [Jameson], and Vida moved out. Then she began working to get herself moved in. Leslyn said no. Bob was irked, and finally Leslyn gave in, and invited Ginny to come live with them and be their love. Well, when the Snow Maiden got her skate in the door, things were different. Leslyn slept in the studio whilst Bob and the femme fatale cavorted in the master bedroom. Ginny was a virgin, but she learned fast. She and Bob drank and smoked a lot, but Leslyn was not to smoke or drink. One night when Fritz Lang was up, Leslyn kissed him when he was leaving, and Bob bawled her out for repulsive conduct. Leslyn's claim is that Bob had become very puritanical about her conduct, tho Bob had his harem, liquor, and cigarettes. Bob and Ginny left her home when they went skating (Ginny had given all the skating lessons to Bob, anyway, leaving Leslyn to cool her heels on the sidelines), and when all three went anyplace together, Ginny would cling possessively to him and paw him in public. At last Ginny decided she was tired of having Leslyn around and wanted Bob all to herself. Leslyn declined the suggestion that she move out, and Bob tried to keep things as they were, but Ginny was more and more possessive, and somehow Bob couldn't seem to concentrate on his writing any more. At last he said he thought they ought to go away for awhile, he and Leslyn, to some quiet place in Arizona where he could write.[6] When we moved in at the Hicks' house,[7] Leslyn was preparing for the trip, but a few days later I called and she was in tears because Bob told her he was only taking her along for appearance, that he intended to go off by himself for awhile, and she could go wherever she liked. This was too much, and Leslyn packed her bags and moved out to her cousin Marion Baird's house. A few days later Sam Kamens, their lawyer, called Leslyn and asked that she come to the office a certain day to discuss with Bob divorce arrangements. When she did so, she was offered a choice of getting the divorce herself with $30 a month[8] and the house being awarded her, or Bob's getting the divorce, keeping the house, and providing her with larger alimony. On Sam's advice, she chose the former.

Around the 4th of July Leslyn moved in here at the Hickses,[9] Dorothy Hicks having gone to Redondo Beach to fill a job teaching swimming for the summer. Bernice thought the Hicks household would be a gay and healthy atmosphere for Leslyn, and so Leslyn moved into Dorothy's room. About this time, I saw Bill Corson on Sunset one day and he expressed extreme sympathy for us on hearing that Leslyn was to be so cozily close to us. At the time, I thought this an extremely uncharitable attitude.

And so it began. We listened to Leslyn's endless accounts of how Bob carried on with Ginny and yet denied her both men and alcohol; we dried her tears and calmed her down when she threatened occasionally to charge adultery in the divorce and cite Ginny as correspondent or when she got sudden urges to wreak horrible revenges on Ginny, moods which would inspire Philip Wiley[10] to new tomes. But we tried to understand. We hauled her around in the car, had dinner with us every night, and let her drink all our beer.

Meanwhile we heard from Bob, after we had sent him a friendly note and cartoon at his accommodation address. My cartoon depicted a couple of earnest doogs (us) trying to persuade a belligerent squirrel (already under the influence of Bob's personality) to tell us whether Mr. H. were in, and Mr. H's residence was a hollow tree, of course. But he wasn't living in a hollow tree; he had a room on a ranch in Ojai.[11] He remarked in his letter that he was touched to hear from us in such an ordinary manner, all same like nothing had happened, that it was good to show he still had some friends left. "I had been far from sure," he wrote. And he hoped we could get together for dinner, but that he was sticking close to Ojai, being short of money.

Leslyn was writing letters to Bob at the rate of about two a week, and she showed me his replies which were businesslike but friendly, or perhaps I should say "not unfriendly." About this time, she sold the house at something like $11,000, and began talking about getting a job, the thought of which caused her to break down and weep now and then. She called Fritz Lang about a job, but nothing ever came of that. One day she went down town to be interviewed for a personnel job, wearing an outfit that was stunning in its lack of taste (white canvas sandals, a formal sort of ruffly black skirt, a striped tailored jacket, a jersey scarf in a tropical print, and a white straw hat made to look like an overseas cap with lace trimmings). I was sufficiently horrified to determine to get her into something easier to look at, so I dragged her down town next day, steered her away from bars, and finally got her to buy two gabardine tailored dresses that really fit her, some

shoes and a hat. But still she seemed to be turned down for personnel jobs.
Apparently a recently divorced female is not exactly what a firm needs to
pep up its employees.

Between interviews, Leslyn saw Dr. Fink, the psychiatrist and nerve specialist[12] whom both she and Bob were seeing right down to the last. I never
knew what Fink told Bob, but Leslyn gave us the impression that Bob was
unwilling to be helped and that Fink therefore had to give him up, which he
did just before Bob suggested going to Arizona alone. Leslyn's visits to Fink
after she and Bob separated never seemed to help her; she reported to us that
he merely told her to quit drinking, get a job, and "show" Bob, etc. [frag-
ment ends]

After the meeting with Heinlein at a diner, of course, Mrs. Sang knew what
Fink had told him.

The information in this sequence of letters may shed some light on an otherwise mysterious incident: Why did Robert instantly decide to separate and
get a divorce when Leslyn, confined to bed, told him she had tried to commit
suicide? In a general sense, something must have crystallized for him at that
moment. It is clear from these contemporaneous communications, even though
Mrs. Sang did not directly witness all of the events herself, that Dr. Fink's advice
to Robert Heinlein must have made a deep impression on him, and that ma-
nipulative admission of attempted suicide, added to the frustration and unhap-
piness that had, by Heinlein's own testimony, been building for years, must
account for what otherwise looks like an inexplicably abrupt decision.

1. Half Done, Well Begun (pages 13–29)

1. RAH, letter to Rip van Ronkel, 10/29/48.
2. RAH, letter to Doña Campbell, 12/03/48.
3. RAH, letter to Rip van Ronkel, 10/29/48.
4. Buddy Scoles featured prominently in *Learning Curve,* the first volume of this biography. Scoles and Heinlein had become friends while they were both at the Naval Academy (Scoles graduating in 1927) because they were both space and rocketry enthusiasts. Scoles had gotten Heinlein his wartime job at the Naval Air Materials Center in Philadelphia—which is how Scoles and Corson met—and then moved on to set up the Naval missile range at Point Mugu, and helped Leslyn get a job there after the divorce.
5. Bill Corson, letter to RAH, undated except "Sat. eve." but by context early in the spring of 1948.
6. RAH, letter to Lurton Blassingame, 09/27/48.
7. RAH, letter to Mr. McLean (otherwise unidentified), 11/06/73. John Campbell's letter containing his refusal of cash or credit has not been preserved in either Heinlein's correspondence or Campbell's, though Heinlein mentions it in correspondence with Lurton Blassingame.
8. John F. Dille, National Newspaper Service, letter to RAH, 10/06/48.
9. J. A. Byers with A & S Lyons, letter to RAH, 09/28/48.
10. Rip van Ronkel, letter to RAH, 10/12/48.
11. RAH, letter to Rip van Ronkel, 12/16/48.
12. RAH, letter to Rip van Ronkel, 10/29/48.
13. RAH, letter to Rip van Ronkel, 10/29/48.
14. RAH, letter to Bill and Lucy Corson, 11/10/48. The gold star chart was preserved in the Robert A. Heinlein Archive, Special Collections and Archives of the University Library, University of California, Santa Cruz.
15. RAH, letter to Virginia Gerstenfeld, 08/10/48, together with Virginia Heinlein's

commentary in Virginia Heinlein, taped interview with the author, Tape 12, Side A. In December 1948 (12/16/48) Heinlein wrote to Dr. Robert King, whom he had seen while in Hollywood, asking him to recommend a local (Colorado Springs) orthopedist.

16. Virginia Heinlein, letter to Denis Paradis, 01/06/79.

17. RAH, letter to Rip van Ronkel, 10/29/48.

18. RAH, letter to Rip van Ronkel, 10/29/48.

19. Virginia Heinlein, taped interview with the author, Misc Notes (9/4–9/8/01) Tape A, Side A and Tape 12, Side A. On the Misc. Notes tape, Mrs. Heinlein says only that she was unable to register to vote at all (since a one-year residency requirement was then in place). At Tape 12, Side A, she confirms that Heinlein had voted at his California residency by an absentee ballot. The absentee ballot is also mentioned in RAH, letter to Rip van Ronkel, 10/29/48.

20. RAH, letter to Virginia Gerstenfeld, 07/22/48, quoted in Virginia Heinlein, taped interview with the author, Tape 12, Side A (March 2000). Mrs. Heinlein had originally intended to destroy all the letters she and Robert Heinlein exchanged in the summer of 1948, while she was in New York and he in Hollywood, and so historically relevant extracts were read into the taped interview for use in the biography.

    For one reason or another, Mrs. Heinlein did not destroy the box in which she kept these letters (although she left instructions for this to be done); however, the other side of the correspondence—Heinlein's original carbon copies of his letters, together with all her replies—were found in a pile of papers on Mrs. Heinlein's working desk that she knew would go to the RAH Archive. Sometime between the first taped interview in February and March 2000 and her last hospitalization after Thanksgiving in 2002, Mrs. Heinlein made the fuller set of this correspondence available for use after her death in January 2003.

21. Virginia Heinlein, letter to the author, 03/04/00.

22. Alice Dalgliesh, letter to RAH, 10/06/48.

23. As is detailed in *Learning Curve,* 465–6, Heinlein had a potentially serious accident while suit-diving off the California coast in the early summer of 1948.

24. Virginia Heinlein taped interview with Leon Stover, October 1988, Tape 3, Side A, page 5 of transcript in RAH Archive.

25. RAH, letter to Jack Williamson, 02/18/49.

26. RAH, letter to Lurton Blassingame, 11/18/48.

27. Virginia Heinlein taped interview with the author, Tape 7, Side B.

28. Andre Norton, Preface to "The Long Watch" in *Grand Master's Choice,* 1989. Anyone who has walked in Bancroft Hall at the campus of the United States Naval Academy knows exactly where this sense of human process enforming acts of deathless heroism comes from: the Naval trophies displayed on its walls, and

the lore about them passed from midshipman to midshipman communicated to Heinlein just what he labored to communicate to others, nowhere more obviously than in "The Long Watch."

29. Virginia Heinlein, letter to Reginald Bretnor, 04/08/79. "The Long Watch" became part of Heinlein's Future History when he incorporated his series of "Luna City" stories written for the "slicks." Thus, the juvenile novel *Space Cadet* is also connected to the Future History by the Cabellian tapestry effect Heinlein devised as early as 1939. The impulse to connect story to story, therefore, does not rise suddenly after 1980 with the World As Myth books, but is present *from the very start* and throughout his writing career.

30. Virginia Heinlein, letter to George Warren, 02/28/79.

31. John W. Campbell, Jr., letter to RAH, 08/26/48; RAH, letter to Lurton Blassingame, 09/21/48.

32. In a letter to Campbell dated 12/3/48, Heinlein says they have just returned from Talmaine's, which fixes the date. They began to arrange the ham radio conversation in Heinlein's letter to Campbell of November 14, 1948.

33. Several different versions of this anecdote were encountered in different places. In most of them, the "time-travel issue" is Campbell's idea, and he approaches Heinlein to write "Gulf" without any prior context. None of these versions make reference to source material, so it was impossible to trace these recountings back to their source(s). However, in a letter to the author, Mrs. Heinlein recalled that the arrangements were made during a scheduled ham radio conference, at which she was present, at the end of November or beginning of December 1948. "So Robert suggested that they do the time-travel issue, and he was in for 'Gulf.'" (05/31/99). The correspondence shows that Heinlein and Campbell had been discussing his return to *Astounding* off and on since August 1948.

34. Heinlein's correspondence with Campbell about the "Gulf" story starts on December 3, 1948—just after the ham radio conference—saying that the "Gulf" story would relate to the Gulf of Mexico and suit diving "perhaps at the center of an underwater culture"—i.e., the abandoned (or postponed) *Ocean Rancher* material. Very shortly thereafter (though the specific date has not been recorded) he scheduled a formal "story conference" with his new wife, at which both the story that would become "Gulf" and the story that would become *Stranger in a Strange Land* were generated. At that time, he was engaged in putting together the story of *Red Planet*. Late in January 1949, Heinlein outlined to Campbell the Martian story as "Gulf," and he mentions the Martian story for that title as late as an April 15, 1949, letter to Dr. Robert S. Richardson. He apparently stalled in the writing, as he mentions in a May 13, 1949, letter to Rip van Ronkel during the negotiations for his consultancy for *Destination Moon* that he had been "egg-bound" on

the novelette for a month—with a fixed and unmoveable June 4 submission deadline looming. He wrote the superman story for the "Gulf" title between May 13 and May 28, 1949, the date on which he mailed the manuscript to his agent, Lurton Blassingame. No documentation of the change of story appears to exist. The Heinleins were busy packing for the trip to Hollywood during this period—a process complicated by the fact that they would also give up their rental in Colorado Springs.

35. Virginia Heinlein, taped interview with the author, Tape 10, Side B.

36. Virginia Heinlein, letter to the author, 11/07/99.

37. Virginia Heinlein, letter to Leon Stover, 03/17/89.

38. RAH, letter to John W. Campbell, Jr., 01/27/49.

39. Virginia Heinlein's recollection in *Grumbles from the Grave* that he came down the stairs the next morning with sixteen (or in another telling, eighteen) pages of notes is a rare reworking of her memory; the sheaf of notes eventually did total eighteen pages, but most of the notes were written in one or two working sessions years later. Based on typographical and format differences among the sections of the sheaf, he probably made two or three pages of notes on this first occasion. See Bill Patterson, "Early Chronology of *Stranger*," *The Heinlein Journal*, no. 6 (January 2000): 4–6.

40. RAH, letter to Frank Robinson, 09/18/69.

41. Virginia Heinlein, editorial note in *Grumbles from the Grave*, 52.

42. As late as April 1949, Heinlein was still planning to write his Martian Mowgli story as "Gulf," with a June 4 submission deadline looming and, by that time, a move to Hollywood also in the first part of June, to oversee the making of *Destination Moon*. See, for example, RAH, letter to Robert S. Richardson, 04/15/49. There is in all of Heinlein's papers no recounting of the origin of the spy/superman story for "Gulf" beyond the information given here. Even Heinlein's 1967 and 1968 Accession Notes (The Virginia Edition: The Definitive Collection of Robert A. Heinlein, vol. xxxvii, *Nonfiction 1*) contain no information that bears on this question.

43. Heinlein refers to the revision and retyping of the *Sixth Column* manuscript as taking place at the time of his letter to Lurton Blassingame, 12/04/48.

44. RAH, letter to Mr. McLean (not otherwise identified), 11/06/73.

45. Erle Korshak, letter to RAH, 12/04/48.

46. RAH, letter to Erle Korshak, 12/14/48.

47. RAH, letter to John Arwine, 01/27/49.

48. RAH, letter to John W. Campbell, Jr., 01/27/49.

49. Rip van Ronkel, letter to RAH, undated except "Jan. 1949" in Heinlein's hand.

50. RAH, letter to Forrest J. Ackerman, 02/19/49.

51. Forrest J. Ackerman, letter to RAH, 02/23/49.

52. Postwar food rationing in England was in some respects more severe than war-time rationing: Bread, which had been unrationed (though of reduced quality) during the war, was rationed from 1946 to 1948, and potatoes were rationed from 1947. Rationing was not lifted in England until 1953, when sugar and other sweets became available again. The transition was completed in 1954 when meat became freely available, but some industries, such as cheese production, were affected for decades.

In the United States, a small industry grew up of companies that would package and ship foodstuffs that were in short supply in England, such as canned meats and candies, particularly chocolate. The Heinleins sent such shipments to the Carnells as often as they could.

53. RAH, letter to Forrest J. Ackerman, 02/25/49.
54. RAH, letter to L. Ron Hubbard, 02/19/49.
55. RAH, letter to Lurton Blassingame, 07/13/49.
56. RAH, letter to Rip van Ronkel, 03/05/49.
57. Cal Laning, letter to RAH, 01/31/49.
58. Bill Corson, letter to RAH, 11/15/48.
59. RAH, letter to Bill Corson, 02/21/49.
60. They had purchased the Lookout Mountain house in 1935 for $3,000, using a mortgage that was paid off in 1940, and they had added a second lot to the property. Leslyn received the house and its contents in the divorce settlement and sold it in the summer of 1947, for $10,000. Virginia Heinlein, letter to Leon Stover, 03/29/89.

Leslyn's current broke state, however, was not due to profligacy; she had married for a very short time. In an undated letter to Heinlein from this period, Bill Corson remarked:

> From other sources, we gather that her marriage was to a piano-playing jerk greatly her junior, as bottle happy as she. He got every cent she could lay hands on. She says she has moved to Tortilla Flats section of Hueneme and is very infatuated with getting money. Her Navy Bob, it appears, is still in the picture and divine, and *he* has a family and children and wife.

61. RAH, letter to John Arwine, 02/18/49.
62. RAH, letter to Erle Korshak, 02/09/49. "Da Capo" is an instruction in music-Italian to go back to the "capo," meaning "head" or "beginning." The story-title "Da Capo" had been in Heinlein's story notes since his first set of story ideas written down in 1939 (when it started out as a reincarnation story and therefore a fantasy). By 1949 it apparently had shifted over to time travel, still nominally regarded as science fiction, rather than fantasy.

63. Lawrence Heinlein, letter to RAH, 03/28/49.

64. RAH, letter to Lawrence Heinlein, 03/29/49.

65. See *Robert A. Heinlein in Dialogue with His Century*, Volume 1, *Learning Curve*, 437–8.

66. RAH, letter to Claire Glass, 03/18/49.

67. RAH, letter to John W. Campbell, Jr., 08/19/48.

68. Claire Glass, letter to RAH, 03/10/49. Miss Dalgliesh had only laughed at the idea of a man writing girls' stories.

69. This second story conference, which seems to have stretched over several days, cannot be dated precisely but must have taken place in late February or early March 1949, as a letter from Erle Korshak to Heinlein dated March 8, 1949, acknowledges that Heinlein is *currently* working on the novella. Mrs. Heinlein at one point recalled it taking place in late April or early May 1949, but that cannot be correct; in a letter to Lurton Blassingame dated 03/12/49, Heinlein says that he is "about half finished" with the story.

     In his 1967 Accession Notes, Heinlein states that "The Man Who Sold the Moon" was written during "three weeks in March 1949." If March 12 is taken as the halfway point, then the writing likely stretched from about March 2 to about March 22, and the story conference would have been concluded enough for him to begin the writing no later than March 2—which suggests a late February/early March timeframe.

70. RAH, 1969 interview with Frank Robinson, 6 of submission draft; The Virginia Edition, vol. xxxvii, *Nonfiction 1*, as "Playboy Interview," 549. Heinlein's actual words, in response to a question as to whether he was surprised that the Apollo 11 Moon Landing was undertaken by the government, were: "I had it done by private industry [in *Destination Moon*] primarily for reasons of budget on the movie." The single-stage Moon ship in *Destination Moon* was also done for budgetary reasons—and for the look of the rocket.

71. RAH, letter to Stewart Rose, 05/30/47.

72. Virginia Heinlein, taped interview with Leon Stover, Tape 3, Side A (1988).

73. Virginia Heinlein, taped interview with the author, Tape 8, Side B. The Mississippi Bubble was a speculative boom in 1719–20 in which the promoter of the Mississippi Company, trying to raise investment in Louisiana, became the French Controller General of Finances and issued vastly more bank notes than could be redeemed. The French economy heated up briefly, then collapsed—an early demonstration of twentieth-century monetary practices.

74. The specific communication and date of the Scribner rejection of *Red Planet* has not been preserved or recorded, but Heinlein mentions dissatisfaction with his editor's response in a letter to Rip van Ronkel dated March 1, 1949, and in a letter

to Lurton Blassingame dated March 4, 1949, he complains about the terms of the rejection. The rejection must, therefore, have come to Heinlein at almost the same time as the story conference on "The Man Who Sold the Moon"—i.e., end of February/beginning of March 1949.

75. RAH, letter to Alice Dalgliesh, 03/04/48.

76. RAH, letter to Lurton Blassingame, 03/04/49.

77. RAH, letter to Lurton Blassingame, 03/15/49.

78. Margaret C. Scoggins, report forwarded by Alice Dalgliesh to Lurton Blassingame, 03/18/49.

79. Alice Dalgliesh, letter to Lurton Blassingame, 03/18/49.

80. Heinlein had received these comments about each of his juveniles for Scribner, but they were particularly pronounced about *Space Cadet,* just out. Just before Dalgliesh made this remark, and then again shortly after, Heinlein had correspondence from Robert Warwick (address not recorded) reporting he could not find a copy in any bookstore. On April 18, 1949, Warwick wrote Heinlein that he had been told by Scribner that the book went out of print (i.e., exhausted its initial print run) within two weeks of its release—that is, in September 1948.

81. L. Ron Hubbard, letter to RAH, 03/03/49.

82. RAH, letter to Lurton Blassingame, 03/04/49.

83. RAH, letter to Lurton Blassingame, 03/15/49. Heinlein viewed that he had a "standing order" from Scribner, and in any case they had a "handshake deal" once the outline was approved, so Heinlein had commenced work on the theory that the paperwork—including the contract and the advance—would catch up later.

84. RAH, letter to Lurton Blassingame, 03/24/49.

85. RAH, letter to Robert S. Richardson, 04/25/49.

86. RAH, letter to Lurton Blassingame, 05/01/49.

87. Lurton Blassingame, letter to RAH, 05/16/49.

88. RAH, letter to Lurton Blassingame, 03/24/49.

89. RAH, letter to Lurton Blassingame, 03/24/49.

90. Erle Korshak, letter to RAH, 03/29/49.

91. RAH, letter to Lurton Blassingame, 04/02/49.

92. RAH, letter to Lurton Blassingame, 04/02/49.

93. RAH, postcard to Erle Korshak, 04/02/49, quoted in RAH, letter to Lurton Blassingame of even date.

94. RAH, letter to Rip van Ronkel, 04/03/49. "Tomato juice . . . peed in" is a reference to one of Heinlein's favorite anecdotes about Hollywood, which Virginia Heinlein explained in her taped interview with the author, Tape 8, Side A: Two producers dying of thirst in a desert find a cache of tomato juice, but one won't let the other drink until it has been peed in "to make it better."

In an earlier letter to Bill Corson (03/24/49) he had been more humorous and less exasperated: "I am now engaged in rows with two publishers: one cannot get it through his head that it is not the principle of the thing, it is the money, and the other can't understand that it is not the money, it is the principle of the thing. I suffer."

95. Erle Korshak made this remark the first time in his letter to RAH, 04/18/49, but made the same remark on other occasions as well. "It grated each time you used it," Heinlein later told Korshak. "I ignored it because it was evident that you did not know any better; you intended to be persuasive. Your letters are filled with such unwitting bad manners" (RAH, letter to Erle Korshak, 04/15/51).

96. RAH, letter to John W. Campbell, Jr., 04/25/49.

97. Mrs. Heinlein recalled that he was looking for a manuscript for a reprint requested of him (taped interview with the author, Tape 10, Side B; Virginia Heinlein, letter to Leon Stover, 03/29/89), but Heinlein may have been searching for the manuscript for one of the stories to be collected into *The Man Who Sold the Moon,* as no other likely anthology contract was made conveniently close to the mid-April 1949 timing of this anecdote, whereas Heinlein was making revisions to stories for this collection during the month of April and into May.

Later, in 1952 and 1953, when L. Sprague de Camp was putting together *The Science-Fiction Handbook,* Heinlein told him about Ginny's opus system as a perfect way of organizing a writer's files. De Camp included it, then, and years after that Ginny passed it on to Beverly Herbert for Frank Herbert's use. Herbert then wrote it up for the *SFWA Bulletin.*

98. Virginia Heinlein, letter to Leon Stover, 03/29/89.

99. RAH, letter to Lurton Blassingame, 04/18/49, identifies the organization as ongoing at that time.

100. John W. Campbell, Jr., letter to RAH, 02/10/49. "Don A. Stuart" was a pseudonym Campbell had used for his experimental "mood stories" in the 1930s; in any case, Street & Smith discouraged Campbell from writing (or more specifically selling) stories either for *Astounding* or for other science-fiction magazines.

101. Robert and Leslyn Heinlein's visit to Los Alamos on the way from Philadelphia back to Los Angeles in August 1945 is detailed in *Learning Curve,* chapter 26, "Dangerous New World," 359–61.

102. "Sworn Statement of Robert A. Heinlein Concerning Robert Cornog," [mis]dated 05/17/45 (should be '49).

103. See, e.g., RAH, letter to Cal Laning, 11/26/50. The year following Cornog's investigation, Cal Laning proposed that Heinlein seek a security clearance, and Heinlein wrote in detail about his own contacts with Communists during his

political activity, a subject which is just alluded to in his recommendation written for Cornog. Heinlein concludes this letter to Laning with an indictment of the current "security" apparatus:

> Two things are very evident from the newspapers, that mistakes are being made *both ways*. Spies have had access to top secret information, and loyal men are being prevented from working where they can do the most good through "guilt by association" and other methods having roughly the scientific accuracy of witch smelling. It's ridiculous! It does not matter very much to the country, or, at this late date, to me, whether I am cleared for secret work or not. For myself, I've learned to live under a cloud, secure in my own heart; for the country, well, I'm not a top-rank physicist, my talents can be spared. But, goddam it to hell—we need better methods, quicker methods, more accurate methods. The present methods could have been used by Julius Caesar. If *anyone* in the security business can be interested in the idea of checking on a case by some other method than questioning his former employers and finding out whether or not he has ever bet on the horses or gone to a nudist camp (I've done both!), then I'm their boy.
>
> On the other hand, if they want to check me by methods which have already proved to be too cumbersome, too expensive in manpower, and too inaccurate to protect us against the communist apparatus, then I will be happy to cooperate in any way available to me. I know I'm loyal; no factual evidence can possibly be turned up to the contrary.

Heinlein revisited these comments years later, in RAH, letter to "Okie" [Harold J. O'Connell], 07/09/58: "It seems to me a hell of a note that I should be turned down while a guy like Alger Hiss gets by for years . . . . But I also know that investigating a man takes time, effort, and tax money."

Cornog's efforts, with the help of J. Robert Oppenheimer and Luis Alvarez, as well as that of Heinlein and others, were eventually successful: In December 1949 the Industrial Employment Review Board admitted his clearance had been improperly withdrawn, though it took another two years (1951) before the clearance was actually restored. Robert Cornog, "Discovery of Hydrogen Helium Three" in Trower, W. P., ed. *Discovering Alvarez: with commentary by his students and colleagues.* Chicago, Ill.: University of Chicago Press, 1987, cited in Higgins, William S., "Robert Cornog, Heinlein's Ambassador to the Atom," English language offprint provided by Mr. Higgins of a chapter he prepared for *Solution Non Satisfaisante: Heinlein et l'Arme Atomique,* Éric H. Picolle (who translated it into French) and Hugo Bellagamba. Paris: Editions du Somnium, 2010.

2. Hooray for Hollywood! (pages 30–36)

1. RAH, letter to Rip van Ronkel, 04/01/49.
2. RAH, letter to Rip van Ronkel, 05/04/49.
3. RAH, letter to Rip van Ronkel, 05/12/49.
4. RAH, letter to John Arwine, 05/16/49.
5. Quoted in RAH, letter to "Ernie" [Voigt?], 05/25/49.
6. RAH, letter to Rip van Ronkel, 05/13/49.
7. John Campbell's reaction was immediate and enthusiastic:

   > The mss. on "Gulf" arrived very much okay. It was very much okay as a
   > yarn, too—a lovely little dilly of a piece. Your post-war return will, as it
   > should, open with a bang. And that closing scene is a nasty piece indeed!
   > One item that I regretted; your hero didn't have a chance to clean out the
   > items in his "Personal" file, under "Bichos to be slowly eliminated."
   >
   > But a nice, nasty piece of work "Gulf" is. The boys'll love it.

   John W. Campbell, Jr., letter to RAH, 06/06/49.

   Over the years, the feedback Heinlein received from readers led him to the
   conclusion the ending of "Gulf" was the best he had ever conceived, which opinion he set down in RAH, letter to Howie Horowitz, 01/01/64, discussing the
   pilot he was writing for a television series derived from "Gulf."

8. RAH, "Author! Author!" letter-profile in *The Fanscient,* ed. Donald B. Day (Fall
   1949): 32–38.
9. RAH, letter to Jinny Fowler, 06/11/49.
10. RAH, letter to Lurton Blassingame, 06/14/49.
11. Several recent biographies of Mr. Bonestell, both in print and on the Internet, have
    suggested wrongly that Bonestell was actually attached to the project before Rob-
    ert Heinlein, and in one case, in an online article by Block and Rubin accessed in
    2001 but which has apparently since been taken down, that the film actually derived
    from Bonestell's *Life* magazine paintings in 1944. Without minimizing Mr. Bon-
    estell's quite substantial role in the success of *Destination Moon,* this is not the case.

    It is entirely possible that Fritz Lang may have had Bonestell in mind during the
    period when he was exploring the idea of a film, but this project came into specific
    existence when Robert Heinlein put his *Rocket Ship Galileo* property up for adapta-
    tion and suggested Bonestell in the early discussions with Lang. *Rocket Ship Galileo*
    has an A card for the picture (i.e., acknowledgment as the source of the story) because
    it is the originating point for *Destination Moon,* not Bonestell's Saturn paintings.

    Bonestell was certainly the most suitable man for the job—at that time he
    was *the only* possible candidate—and so it is not surprising that he should be
    considered by anyone contemplating such a project.

12. RAH, "Creativity Is Not Divisible," Guest of Honor Speech at Rio de Janeiro film festival honoring George Pal, March 1969, printed in *Requiem* (Yoji Kondo, ed.). The title of the speech is a play on the title (as well as the contents) of Irving Pichel's 1945 article for *The Hollywood Quarterly,* "Creativeness Cannot Be Diffused."

13. For the suggestion of the cartoon in the treatment, see Brad Linaweaver, "Destination Freedom," *The Heinlein Journal,* no. 9 (July 2001): 11–12; for Pal's relationship with Walter Lanz, see Gail Morgan Hickman, *The Films of George Pal,* 45. Heinlein's treatment for *Destination Moon,* along with much other material, is incorporated into the Virginia Edition, vol. xliv, *Screenplays of RAH 1.* The Pal/Heinlein/Lanz/Woody Woodpecker cartoon did boost the film's public exposure and made an immense impression—but the cartoon was destined to have a life of its own, as it was used in classrooms through the 1960s to introduce schoolchildren to the basic concepts of ballistics and the physics of rocket flight. Graphic novelist (and Eisner Award winner) Rantz Hosely, in a note to the author in May 2013, confirmed the importance of this cartoon: "In discussing the cartoon over the years (including the final shuttle launch STS 135) almost everyone I encountered or discussed it with had that cartoon serve as *their* first introduction to rocket physics." Heinlein's influence as a teacher of the young was broader even than his popular series of juvenile novels for Scribner.

14. Heinlein told L. Ron Hubbard about the shooting on *Rupert* preceding shooting on *Destination Moon* in a letter dated 06/20/49, whereas the subject of a production delay is not mentioned in Heinlein's letter to L. Sprague de Camp dated 06/14/49 about a forthcoming trip to Hollywood.

    At the time, Heinlein and Hubbard were in frequent contact, sharing intelligence about Shasta's business practices. Hubbard had been approached by a New York-based independent filmmaker to make one of Hubbard's Ol' Doc Methuselah stories into a film. Somehow (Heinlein's correspondence is not clear on this point), Hubbard became associated with the *Rocket Ship X-M* production, though he is not listed in cast and crew credits.

15. In her taped interview with the author, Tape 7, Side B, Mrs. Heinlein could not remember the name of the other couple.

16. RAH, letter to Harlan Ellison, 09/06/61; another recounting (Laura Haywood newspaper clipping, undated in the RAH Archive, but 1995) attributes the straight line to C. L. Moore and the witticism to Henry Kuttner.

17. This sarcastic term is never defined, even though it is still widely, if erratically, used in the industry ("Moom picture" is used occasionally also). It is thought to be a mocking imitation of Walter Winchell's pronunciation of "moving picture." The best inference I have been able to draw is that it refers to a full, serious production—as opposed to a short, documentary, cartoon, or other

less-than-full production. Thanks to Phil Paine and David Hartwell for clarifying the derivation.

Hubbard was exaggerating slightly: His Moom Pitcher he later identified as *Rocket Ship X-M,* which reported to have had a budget of only $94,000 (though Dalton Trumbo wrote the script, uncredited). Hubbard's name is not listed anywhere in the final credits for the film.

18. RAH, letter to John W. Campbell, Jr., 08/01/49.

19. RAH, letter to L. Sprague de Camp, 06/14/49.

20. Cal Laning, *Shipmate* "Class News" December 1988, 78–79.

21. Virginia Heinlein, letter to Leon Stover, 03/17/89.

22. Just when—and why—Pal talked about turning *Destination Moon* into a musical comedy is not fixed by the correspondence, except that it was before a passing comment made to Forrest J. Ackerman in August 1949—which would have been while O'Hanlon was reworking the script. See also RAH, letter to Lurton Blassingame, 05/21/51. This was not as odd, in 1949, as it now seems to us: the most recent commercially successful science fiction film was a musical comedy: *Just Imagine!* (1930)

23. Virginia Heinlein, letter to the author, 11/28/01.

24. Virginia Heinlein, taped interview with the author, Tape 8, Side B.

25. Virginia Heinlein, letter to the author, 11/28/01.

26. Virginia Heinlein, taped interview with the author, Tape 8, Side B (February 27? 2000).

27. RAH, letter to Lurton Blassingame, 07/13/49.

28. RAH, letter to Lurton Blassingame, 07/26/49.

29. RAH, profile for *More Junior Authors,* 1957. Heinlein does not mention it, but the terraforming of Ganymede in *Farmer in the Sky* may also owe something to an article titled "Morphological Astronomy" which CalTech astronomer Fritz Zwicky published in *The Observatory* (August 1948). Zwicky took up not only altering individual planets, but also the hoary science-fiction trope of moving them, even whole solar systems.

30. Virginia Heinlein, letters to the author, 11/07/99 and 12/11/99.

31. Virginia Heinlein, taped interview with the author, Tape 9, Side A (February 27? 2000).

32. This working title, *Ganymede,* is found on the Opus List index card, and Robert Cornog, who reviewed the manuscript for Heinlein in October 1949, uses *Ganymede* rather than *Farmer in the Sky.*

33. RAH, letter to John W. Campbell, Jr., 10/01/49.

34. The O'Hanlon script is preserved, with Heinlein's pencil markup, in the *Destination Moon* file of the RAH Archive, UC Santa Cruz, and is available for down-

load from the heinleinarchiveonline website. Heinlein wrote an exasperated critique of the O'Hanlon script, beginning "This screenplay, as it stands, is an unintegrated piece of nonsense," thirty-eight pages in double-spaced draft, which he sent to both Pal and Rathvon. Much of the detail given in this paragraph is derived from, or synthesized from, this critique.

35. Virginia Heinlein, letter to the author, 05/31/99.

36. Heinlein's production memo critique of O'Hanlon's script, page 3 of the draft in the RAH at UC Santa Cruz and available online through heinleinarchive .net.

37. Archive manuscript of RAH critique of O'Hanlon script, 35.

38. Brad Linaweaver, "Destination Freedom," *The Heinlein Journal,* No. 9 (July 2001): 14.

39. RAH, letter to Virginia Fowler, 09/08/49.

40. RAH, letter to Mary Cole Lincoln, 09/13/49.

41. RAH, letter to Lurton Blassingame, 09/24/49. This letter is the only mention of this occasion, and it does not fix the date, except to say he had forgotten to mention it in his last letter to Blassingame, which is dated 09/22/49.

42. Gladys English, letter to RAH, 09/27/49.

43. Neither the commissioning letter nor the manuscript has been preserved; Heinlein's archive file consists entirely of clippings of the first publication of "The Historical Novel of the Future" in an unidentified digest-sized magazine's "Bookshop News" Department for February 1950.

3. Hollywood Shuffle (pages 37–44)

1. The first mention of Irving Pichel as director of *Destination Moon* is in Heinlein's letter to Lurton Blassingame, 09/24/49.

2. This conference is not dated in correspondence or file notes, but must have taken place toward the end of September, as a letter Heinlein wrote to Alice Dalgliesh and Virginia Fowler at Scribner on 10/26/49 speaks of Pichel's controlling influence as an accomplished fact.

3. Not only did Heinlein continue to have a warm and friendly correspondence with Pichel for the remainder of Pichel's life, his recollections of Pichel—at a function honoring George Pal in 1969—were warm and respectful of his professionalism and artistic sense, the very elements Heinlein found fault with in the O'Hanlon script. See, "Creativity Is Not Divisible," Heinlein's 1969 speech at the Rio Film Festival, in *Requiem and Other Stories by the Grand Master,* ed. Yoji Kondo (New York: Tor Publishing, 1992), 203; and in the Virginia Edition, vol. xliv, *Screenplays 1.*

4. RAH, letter to Alice Dalgliesh and Virginia Fowler, 10/26/49.

5. RAH, letter to Lurton Blassingame, 10/01/49.

6. 7729 Hollywood Boulevard, on the corner of Hollywood and Courtney Avenue, just as it winds up into the Hollywood Hills. Courtney Avenue is four blocks east of Fairfax Avenue, in the outskirts of Hollywood, about two and a half miles from the Paramount Sunset-Gower studios.

7. Virginia Heinlein, taped interview with the author, Tape 1, Side B. See also, Virginia Heinlein, taped interview with Leon Stover, 1988, Tape 3, Side A.

8. *LA Times West Magazine*, 03/29/70, "This Place Looks Familiar—Hollywood left the moon to NASA and truth proved not so strange as fiction," by Gabe Essoe, quotes George Pal saying he needed the cracked lunar landscape to give forced perspective on the small sound stage. Pal's comments are also quoted in Gail Morgan Hickman, *The Films of George Pal*, 42–43.

9. In his 1957 lecture published as "Science Fiction: Its Nature, Faults, and Virtues," Heinlein remembered that he "sent for a photograph of one of the space suits Sprague de Camp had helped develop, and we copied it as closely as we could for the movie." The essay was part of *The Science Fiction Novel: Imagination and Social Criticism* in 1959 and is reprinted in the Virginia Edition, vol. xxxvii, *Nonfiction I: Miscellaneous and Juvenilia*.

10. RAH, "Creativity Is Not Divisible" as "Guest of Honor Speech—Rio de Janeiro Movie Festival, 1969" in *Requiem*, ed. Yoji Kondo, 203; and in the Virginia Edition vol. xliv, *Screenplays*.

11. Heinlein's initial estimate for the cutting of *Farmer in the Sky* for serialization in *Boys' Life* as "Satellite Scout" was two weeks (RAH, letter to Lurton Blassingame, 10/01/49), but the cut was not actually finished until "shortly after the New Year" (RAH Accession Notes, 1967). Heinlein had intended to draft the book at 40,000 words and then cut and expand for the different publications, but there is no 40,000-word draft in his files and no record of his being engaged in an expansion; the novel-length manuscript must have been his first draft.

12. RAH, letter to Robert Cornog, 10/05/49, and Robert Cornog, letter to RAH, 10/17/49.

13. The four freshmen who interviewed with Heinlein on this occasion were Carl Schwerdtfeger, Sam Horey, Stewart Gothold, and Stephen Ginn, together with their teacher, Mr. Stanton Presnall. *The Eagle*, 10/14/49.

14. RAH, letter to Irving Pichel, 02/27/50.

15. RAH, letter to Lurton Blassingame, 11/07/49.

16. RAH, letter to Lurton Blassingame, 11/20/49.

17. Ackerman did some freelance reporting for various radio and television outlets and was considered part of the Hollywood press corps for specialized (science-

fiction) film projects, as well. He was, for example, at that time promoting two projects directly to George Pal—Hugo Gernsback's *Ralph 124C41+* (which did not get made) and the Wylie/Balmer *When Worlds Collide* (which did).

18. Heinlein says only that this took place "around 1949" when he was in Hollywood. RAH, letter to *Vertex* magazine, 11/08/73. It is possible that the incident happened around August 1949, when the magazine came out, but work on *Destination Moon* slowed down during the filming of *The Great Rupert* and picked up again in October and November. There were many more opportunities for it to have taken place at this time.

19. RAH, letter to *Vertex* magazine, 11/08/73.

20. RAH, letter to *Vertex* magazine, 11/08/73.

21. Forrest J. Ackerman, letter to RAH, 07/22/49.

22. Virginia Heinlein, e-mail as "Astyanax12" to the author, 10/18/01. I believe this was intended to mean something like "she didn't let the right hand know what the left hand was doing."

23. Dry wit combined with lively intelligence seems to have been a Heinlein family trait. When the current generation of Heinleins decided to have their family reunion in conjunction with the Robert Heinlein Centennial (July 5–8, 2007) in Kansas City, the author had an opportunity to chat with them singly and in a group. This gathering included many of Heinlein's nieces and nephews, and the experience felt much like a taste of what family dinners might have been like around the greater Heinlein menage.

    That Centennial was also visited by Dorothy Martin Heinlein, then aged 94, wife of Heinlein's brother J. Clare Heinlein, Ph.D. Coverage of the Centennial program, and Mrs. Heinlein's participation, was included in *The Heinlein Journal*, no. 22 (January 2008).

24. Virginia Heinlein, letter to Miriam De Graff, 01/16/97.

25. Virginia Heinlein, taped interview with the author, Second Series, Tape B, Side A.

26. The estrangement came about in about 1939 because Rex thoughtlessly woke Leslyn while retrieving a trunk. The incident is detailed in the first volume of this biography, *Learning Curve*, at 244–5.

    See also, Virginia Heinlein, taped interview with the author, Second Series, Tape B, Side A. In that interview, Mrs. Heinlein maintained that Rex always thought Robert had made more over the 1939 incident with the trunk than the occasion merited, and that Robert came to the conclusion that Leslyn had a habit of fanning the flames. He often in these early years praised Ginny's policy of taking the high road as having practical good results for him.

27. RAH, letter to Rex Ivar Heinlein, 05/17/48.

28. Virginia Heinlein, taped interview with the author, Second Series, Tape B, Side A.

29. Gail Morgan Hickman, *The Films of George Pal*, 44.

30. Probably "cherry." The old sequence of colors for revision pages is white, blue, pink, yellow, green, goldenrod, buff, salmon, cherry, tan, gray, ivory. (Information provided by screenwriter Steve Tymon.)

31. John T. Abbott, Wright-Sonovox, Inc., letter to RAH, 12/01/49.

32. Robert B. Pitkin, letter to RAH, 12/16/49.

33. RAH, letter to Mr. H. A. Rossmeisl, 01/18/50.

34. Even before the Heinleins left Colorado Springs for Hollywood, Heinlein was talking about buying a house there or building one (RAH, letter to Doña Campbell, 12/03/48). By the summer of 1949 this had become a firm intention, mentioned in several contemporaneous letters, but see for example RAH, letter to Lurton Blassingame, 6/14/49.

35. Virginia Heinlein, letter to the author, 11/28/01.

36. Virginia Heinlein, taped interview with Leon Stover, Tape 3, Side A.

37. RAH, "Creativity Is Not Divisible" as "Guest of Honor Speech—Rio de Janeiro Movie Festival, 1969" in *Requiem*, ed. Yoji Kondo, 204.

38. L. Ron Hubbard, letter to RAH, 12/30/49.

39. Heinlein complained to Korshak many times about his business methods, but see RAH, letter to Erle Korshak, 04/07/51: "Being 'Korshaked' produces a nervous reaction much like that of being dumped out of a warm bed into a tub of ice water in the dark."

40. The Hubbard-Heinlein correspondence about Erle Korshak and Shasta started with a letter from Hubbard to Heinlein, 04/21/49 (when Hubbard is already at work on the book that will be released the following year as *Dianetics: Evolution of a Science*—and confidently expects an endorsement from the American Medical Association), and continues through May and June. By October, however, Heinlein is asking Campbell what had become of Hubbard.

41. RAH, letter to L. Ron Hubbard, 01/18/50.

42. Rogers Terrill, letter to RAH, 01/05/50.

43. A "treatment" is a narrative description of a film story used as part of the development process.

4. Rent or Buy or Build? (pages 45–56)

1. Virginia Heinlein, letter to the author, 11/28/01.

2. Virginia Heinlein, letter to the author, 11/28/01.

3. This house was at 1825 Cheyenne Boulevard.

4. RAH, letter to Harry Hinkle, 02/23/50.

5. Irving Pichel, letter to RAH, 02/25/50.

6. Alice Dalgliesh, letter to RAH, 01/31/50.

7. RAH, letter to Robert K. Willis, 12/08/65. "Arroyo" is a Spanish word commonly used in the American southwest, meaning a deep gully across a watercourse; Heinlein uses the term interchangeably with "canyon," another Spanish word that means a steep gorge, typically formed by a watercourse—as in the Grand Canyon.

8. Virginia Heinlein, letter to Leon Stover, 03/28/89.

9. Virginia Heinlein, editorial note in *Grumbles from the Grave,* 114.

10. Virginia Heinlein, letter to the author, 12/14/99.

11. RAH, letter to Robert K. Willis, 12/08/65. Most of the detail in this paragraph is taken from this description Heinlein wrote for his first real estate agent, when they decided to sell the Colorado Springs house after moving to California.

12. RAH, letter to Robert K. Willis, 12/08/65.

13. RAH, "If You Don't See It, Just Ask: A Preview for Playboys." This long and lively article, about the lifestyle options available to mid-century Americans, was written on spec in mid-1963. The article was never contemporaneously published, even though Heinlein later marked it up for submission to markets other than *Playboy.* It was first published in the *Robert A. Heinlein Centennial Souvenir Book* (2007) and, in a slightly different edit, in the Virginia Edition, vol. xxxvii, *Nonfiction 1: Miscellaneous and Juvenilia.*

14. Discussing the *Argosy* offer for the novelette, Heinlein said in passing, "I need the money for house building." RAH, letter to Lurton Blassingame, 01/02/50, and in another letter to Blassingame, 04/24/50, he said baldly, ". . . I need money so bad that I can taste it . . ."

15. RAH, letter to Mrs. Douglas, 08/10/49.

16. RAH, letter to Virginia Fowler at Scribner, 04/13/50.

17. RAH, letter to Alice Dalgliesh, 03/11/50. Heinlein never did understand why it was that so many of his readers wanted to know him as a person, why they were psychologically so warmed by the fire of his personality that filtered out through the conventions of his writing—and why this very same phenomenon generated so much critical piffle over the years.

18. For a time, no intact copies of this press book for *Destination Moon* were known to have survived. A copy used for David Hartwell's 1979 *festbuch* for Gregg Press, *Destination Moon,* was later water damaged beyond recovery. Until 2006, the Robert A. Heinlein Archive at U.C. Santa Cruz had a nearly pristine copy in a map case in the Archivist's office, but at the time the entire RAH Archive was put in non-call storage while the McHenry Library building was shut down for construction next door, this copy was lost. Two other copies have surfaced in the market since that time.

19. These pre-screenings of *Destination Moon* "in suburban sites" presumably took place in June 1950. The screenings were reported without identification of sources

in "Destination Moon: Robert A. Heinlein, Filmwriter" by Christopher Schaefer, *New Libertarian,* no. 187 (undated but 1999), 61.

> Two sneak previews in average suburban areas were used to test the box-office appeal. Survey results from these two previews showed that 64.4 percent felt the film was OUTSTANDING (or) EXCELLENT. Another 32.12 percent rated the film as VERY GOOD (or) GOOD. And 94.5 percent said they would recommend the film to their friends.
>
> Comments and reactions from audiences in these two pre-release screenings were all positive. Here's a sampling of typical comments from the audience that illustrates the enthusiasm with which the film was received:
>
> "The entire picture was remarkable, unusual . . ."
>
> "Very good!!! Excellent!!! Outstanding!!!"
>
> "Should be a nominee for the Best Picture of 1950. Fine acting."
>
> "I can sum it up in one word—outstanding!"
>
> "We need more pictures like this."
>
> "Movies are better than ever!"
>
> "Greatest picture ever seen! Exceptional music background."
>
> "This picture is in a class by itself . . . totally different. Most interesting picture I've seen."
>
> "I would like to see a sequel."
>
> "Your picture was the best I've seen in years!"
>
> "It's a top 4 Star picture in my opinion . . . it should get an Oscar."
>
> Eagle-Lion released *Destination Moon* with the ad lines, "Adventurers Conquer Space With Passenger-Carrying Rocket!"

When contacted in October 2013 about the source documents he used in this article, Christopher Schaefer said these comment cards and such were in the *Destination Moon* files at the main library of the Academy of Motion Picture Arts and Sciences, now on La Cienega Boulevard in Beverly Hills, California.

20. In L. Ron Hubbard, letter to RAH, 12/30/49, Hubbard says he is working simultaneously on a Western and on the "Dianetics book—will send along when it's done."

21. RAH, in fact, never discussed his reaction to Dianetics with Hubbard directly. Hubbard obliquely expressed disgruntlement about Heinlein's silence on the subject in a July 14, 1950, letter: "I guess you waited so long for the book that it just plumb wore out its welcome. If you knew the amount of pressure I had to put on the publisher to get you an advanced copy, you would appreciate it more."

Heinlein did mention his unsettled disappointment at vagueness and lack of demonstrative rigor to John Campbell, even before *Dianetics* came out publicly:

Your letter was most interesting re Ron's forays in therapeutic psychology. I have heard from him several times about such activities and am much interested and have asked many questions—but *your* letter has been a dern sight more informative than *his* letters. But he has promised me galleys of his book. (RAH, letter to John W. Campbell, Jr., 08/01/49.)

Nevertheless, Dianetics remained a subject much of interest and discussion among Heinlein's colleagues. Campbell, in fact, carried through the psychological experimentation he learned from Hubbard even after leaving the Dianetics movement.

After reading *Dianetics: The Modern Science of Mental Health* (1950), Heinlein commented to Campbell:

Dianetics—I wish to the devil that I knew a lot more about it. Your letters are persuasive but sketchy; Ron [Hubbard]'s book, despite its size, is remarkably vague when he gets right down to cases. I am troubled by the Great Schism and by the spectacular nonsense that accompanied Ron's troubles with Sara; I am troubled by the number of Simon-pure screwballs that I see associated with it, especially in Los Angeles . . . . (RAH, letter to John W. Campbell, Jr., 08/15/51).

A flavor—though not historically accurate—of what Heinlein may have meant by "Simon-pure screwballs" is depicted in the recent film evocation of the early Dianetics-movement, *The Master.*

22. Sara Hubbard, letter to Robert and Virginia Heinlein, 05/02/50.
23. RAH, letter to Robert Bloch, 11/30/50.
24. Virginia Heinlein, letter to the author, 06/04/99.
25. RAH, letter to Robert Bloch, 11/30/50.
26. John W. Campbell, Jr., letter to RAH, 05/27/51.
27. RAH, letter to John W. Campbell, Jr., 08/15/51.
28. RAH, letter to Lurton Blassingame, 03/08/50; RAH telegram to Irving Crump, 04/05/50.
29. Lurton Blassingame, letter to RAH, 04/21/50.
30. RAH, letter to Lurton Blassingame, 04/24/50. The relevant portion of this letter was also included in *Grumbles from the Grave,* 59.
31. RAH, letter to Lurton Blassingame, 04/24/50.
32. Lurton Blassingame, letter to RAH, 02/02/50. In his draft Answers to Interrogatories in the *Puppet Masters* plagiarism suit against Roger Corman and *The Brain Eaters,* dated 10/13/60, Heinlein recalled that the germ of the story was jotted down on one of the blank index cards he carried with him "sometime shortly after

the end of World War II—probably during 1946. The working title was INVA-SION BY E.T." That jotting concerned the image of a mountain lion ridden by what he then thought of as a Martian invader, and was concerned with the damage a large carnivore might do when intelligently controlled—a very *Astounding*-esque notion. "I recall that I toyed with the idea of having first contact with the invaders be between a hunting party in the rockies . . . But the hoorah over 'flying saucers' gave me a new notion which I added to the growing plot . . ."

33. RAH, undated story notes for *Between Planets* in RAH Archive, UC Santa Cruz. Don Harvey is caught up in interplanetary war and joins first the Venus rebels and then his parents' conspiracy of scientists. Interestingly, the initial workup for the story is focused on a dynamic space captain, based on L. Ron Hubbard— "Captain Dianetic" in Heinlein's notes. The character completely disappeared from the book when written, as Don took over as the main character.

34. RAH, undated story notes for *Between Planets* in RAH Archive, UC Santa Cruz.

35. RAH, letter to Lurton Blassingame, 03/08/50.

36. RAH, letter to Forrest J. Ackerman, 04/16/50.

37. Virginia Heinlein, taped interview with the author, Tape 8, Side B.

38. RAH, letter to Ben Babb, 06/06/50.

39. RAH, letter to Lurton Blassingame, 05/15/50.

40. RAH, letter to Lurton Blassingame, 03/25/53. In this letter, Heinlein is discussing Montgomery as the source for a character in *Starman Jones,* drawn from life.

41. Virginia Heinlein, IM with the author, 06/01/02.

42. Virginia Heinlein, letter to the author, 11/09/01.

43. RAH, letter to Lurton Blassingame, 07/09/50.

44. RAH, letter to Dick Mandelkorn, 11/08/73.

45. RAH, letter to Laurie MacDonald, 07/28/73.

46. RAH, letter to Forrest J. Ackerman, 06/13/50.

47. Forrest J. Ackerman, letter to RAH, 06/27/50.

48. Kendall Crossen, letter to RAH, 06/27/50; Forrest J. Ackerman, letter to RAH, 06/27/50.

49. RAH, letter to "Mr. Donelan, Jr.," 06/15/50.

50. RAH, letter to "Mrs. Donelan, Sr.," 07/13/50.

51. Virginia Heinlein, IM with the author, 11/09/01.

52. RAH, letter to Lurton Blassingame, 08/05/50.

53. RAH, letter to Lurton Blassingame, 08/05/50.

54. RAH, letter to Lurton Blassingame, 08/14/50.

55. Virginia Heinlein, letter to Mr. Ed Pippin, 02/27/79.

56. RAH, letter to Lurton Blassingame, 11/26/50.

57. RAH, letters to Lurton Blassingame, 11/04/50, 11/26/50, and 12/18/50.

58. Ben Babb, letter to RAH, 06/05/50.

59. Philip Wylie and Edwin Balmer cowrote *When Worlds Collide* (Stokes, 1933) and the sequel, *After Worlds Collide,* in 1934. Both were serialized in *Blue Book* magazine before the books were released.

60. *Aviation Week,* July 3, 1950.

61. Jinny Fowler, letter to RAH, 07/28/50.

62. John W. Campbell, Jr., letter to RAH, 07/27/50.

5. Alien Invasions (pages 57–74)

1. RAH, letter to Lurton Blassingame, 09/13/50.

2. RAH, letter to Bill Corson, 09/13/50.

3. Dorothy Shanahan, "Heinleins' Push-Button Home Is Model of Convenience," Colorado Springs *Gazette-Telegraph* (09/30/51) illustrated report, 1, Section B.

4. RAH, letter to John W. Campbell, Jr., 09/19/50.

5. Memorandum of conversation of author with Virginia Heinlein, 09/08/01.

6. RAH, letter to Bjo Trimble, 11/21/61.

7. Virginia Heinlein, taped interview with Leon Stover (1988), Tape 1, Side B.

8. RAH, letter to Bjo Trimble, 11/21/61. An image of *Medusa* (Lorraine Bergess) was found online on several auction sites, but the auctions contained no information about the artist or date of this 12"x16" lithograph.

9. RAH, letter to Forrest J. Ackerman, 08/04/52.

10. Virginia Heinlein, taped interview with the author, Tape 6, Side A.

11. Virginia Heinlein, taped interview with the author, Tape 3, Side A.

12. In a letter she wrote to Fred Pohl on 05/08/53, Leslyn herself called this medical crisis that started on July 4, 1950, a "series of strokes" followed by a coma. Dr. Robert James asked Dr. George Agzarian, associate professor at UCLA Medical School, to review the reported symptoms. Dr. Agzarian suggested he thought it more likely there could have been a subdural hematoma brought on by hitting her head in the midst of an alcoholic stupor or collapse. Robert James, Ph.D., "Regarding Leslyn," *The Heinlein Journal,* no. 9 (July 2001): 29.

13. RAH, letter to Henry and Cats Sang, 01/31/53.

14. In a letter to the author undated but late in February 2011, Grace Dugan "Cats" Sang Wurtz mentioned this incident: "Somebody had called me (a distant cousin, I think) who wanted to find out where her relative was spending her old age." The "distant cousin" was Marian Beard (sometimes, confusingly, spelled Marion, the masculine version of the name), a cousin who had grown up with Leslyn but had since lost contact. Mrs. Wurtz's telephone call to Heinlein's mother was inconvenient for Heinlein, but it was not unreasonable, as the Heinlein family liked Leslyn and might have kept in touch.

In an undated letter to Heinlein in late 1952 or early 1953, Cats Sang explained the situation:

> As it happened, everyone turned over to me the task of trying to find the surviving relative, Marion Beard, so the body wouldn't be shipped to you. I was the logical one, because as the only *declared* un-friend of Leslyn, I was least likely to be the recipient of her misplaced gratitude should she recover. I got in touch with Bob's mother, and together we tried to locate Marion (Mrs. H. had already been working on it), without disturbing you two with the unpleasant business. We called Sam Kamens, thinking he might have Marion's address. He had already talked to you. If someone made a sentimental appeal to him, it wasn't I. Am I pardoned?
>
> Cats

Leslyn did recover from this crisis, though she had a very unhappy life for a period of several years.

15. "Silly Season" is old newspaper slang for the later months of the summer, which is usually a slow news period. Newspapers would print insubstantial material they would not even notice in more active times of the year—just to fill pages.

16. RAH, letter to Cal Laning, 11/26/50.

17. Decrypted KGB files made public after the fall of the Soviet Union have confirmed the guilt of both Hiss and the Rosenbergs.

18. This is a sentiment Heinlein voiced many times in correspondence, but see particularly RAH, letter to Rex Ivar Heinlein, 09/29/64. William A. P. White, letter to RAH, 08/24/50, was probably the first time Heinlein personally noticed the country's postwar shift to the left.

19. In RAH, letter to Larry and Caryl [Heinlein], 07/19/64, Heinlein lists the Hiss case as one of many contributing factors to his "transition from 110% New Dealer to the black reactionary I am now."

Heinlein's personal sense of "liberal" is quite different from the contemporary usage. Before about 1969, many strains of liberalism were recognized; after the New Left, and continuing into the twenty-first century, the term is taken as synonymous with "progressive" and "left-wing."

The term "left-wing" was not regularly used in American politics until some time in the 1930s: It is a term of European politics that had no close parallel in American politics. The left-right dichotomy originated in the French National Assembly, where monarchists sat in a bloc on the right side of the center aisle, and small-d-democrats—i.e., liberals in the classic sense—sat on the left side of the aisle. In the American Revolution, all Tories (the English term for, roughly, their monarchist party) fled the country (or were driven out), so *all* American parties (at the time, Democrats and Whigs) were left-wing—except that we had then, as now, a third, unacknowledged party, a powerful holdover from seventeenth century politics in the theocratic conservatives descended from the Massachusetts Theocracy.

In Europe, after the democratic revolutions of 1848 failed, left-wing democratic liberalism faded and was replaced, ultimately, by Marx's "scientific socialism." A German historian at Arizona State University once noted in a lecture a political evolution that illustrates how the changeover took place, though different countries had different specifics: After the failed democratic revolutions of 1848, the German liberal movement shifted focus to unification of the 300+ minor German principalities into a single Pan-German state as its core issue. The declaration in 1870 of the First Reich decapitated the German liberal movement—at exactly the moment that Marx and Engels were eviscerating the European Workingmen's Movement. Marxists were able to step into a vacuum not only of power, but of foundational party issues.

But a different evolution took place in the United States, with liberals taking up first Abolition, then the American strain of native socialism (called, sarcastically by Marx, "utopian") that led eventually to Upton Sinclair and his EPIC program. This is Heinlein's idea of liberalism—intense Jeffersonian Americanism combined with "social justice."

After the Russian Revolution of 1917, American native socialism gradually faded away, and American radical liberalism became compatible with—and was gradually absorbed by—European Leftism. The international United Front Against Fascism of the 1930s appears to have been the entering wedge. By 1950 this evolution was beginning to be evident.

20.   RAH, letter to John Arwine, 04/17/50. Heinlein's disgruntlement with postwar Communists is not overstated: The Hitler-Stalin pact in 1939 had caused a shock wave of disillusionment in international Communist circles, since the party had been positioning Communism as the principal antagonist of Nazi Germany. The sudden alliance with Germany was widely viewed as rank and cynical hypocrisy on Stalin's part.

Judith Merril comments in her posthumous 2002 autobiography (assembled and partly cowritten by her daughter Emily Pohl-Weary) that her (liberal) high school fellow-classmates were already disillusioned in the late 1930s by the Soviet Union's show-trials of the mid-1930s.

21.   RAH, Discussion Notes for University of Chicago Lecture given on February 8, 1957 and published as "Science Fiction: Its Nature, Faults and Virtues" [in Basil Davenport, ed., *The Science Fiction Novel: Imagination and Social Criticism* in 1959 and reprinted in *Turning Points: Essays on the Art of Science Fiction* (ed. Damon Knight, Harper & Row, 1977)], Opus No. 129, in the RAH Archive, UC Santa Cruz.

22. RAH, Discussion Notes for University of Chicago Lecture, Opus No. 129, in the RAH Archive, UC Santa Cruz.

23. RAH, letter to H. L. Gold, 11/27/50; Lurton Blassingame, telegram to RAH, 11/27/50.

24. Lurton Blassingame, letter to RAH, 12/01/50.

25. RAH, letter to H. L. Gold, 11/27/50.

26. H. L. Gold, letter to RAH, 12/06/50.

27. "The Bulletin Board" did not sell to *Senior Prom,* perhaps because its theme is a little darker and more "realistic" than the previous two Puddin' stories: Maureen and Cliff engineer a party for a wallflower at Maureen's college, after which she is not a wallflower. The story was first printed in *Requiem* (Yoji Kondo, ed.).

28. RAH, letter to Lurton Blassingame, 05/06/51.

29. Lurton Blassingame, letter to RAH, 12/19/50.

30. Lurton Blassingame, letter to RAH, 12/29/50.

31. RAH, letter to Lurton Blassingame, 01/05/51 and RAH, letter to Alice Dalgliesh and Virginia Fowler, 01/05/51.

32. Heinlein did receive reports on *Tom Corbett, Space Cadet* from friends in Los Angeles and New York, but he did not see an episode until November 1951 (that is, a year later), when the producers brought some kinescopes to the Broadmoor for an advertiser's conference (a kinescope is a film made of the television monitor as the show is broadcast—the only TV recording technology available until videotape was introduced in 1956).

33. RAH, letter to Alice Dalgliesh and Virginia Fowler at Scribner, 01/05/51.

34. RAH, letter to T. E. Dikty, 01/10/51.

35. RAH, letter to T. E. Dikty, 01/10/51.

36. RAH, letter to Lurton Blassingame, 01/15/51.

37. RAH, letter to Lurton Blassingame, 01/15/51.

38. Virginia Heinlein, taped interview with Leon Stover, Tape 1, Side B (October 21, 1988).

39. RAH, quoted by Virginia Heinlein, in taped interview with Leon Stover, Tape 3, Side A (October 21, 1988?).

40. RAH, letter to Doña Smith, 02/03/51. Heinlein made a file of Leslyn's letters when her "poison-pen" barrage to all of his friends and business contacts started up, but the file was probably destroyed to save on tonnage of paper when they moved from Colorado Springs to Northern California. This communication in 1950 and 1951 is discussed in RAH, letter to Robert Cornog, 08/03/56.

41. The Campbells' marriage had broken up in February 1950, when Doña Campbell

abruptly moved to Boston, taking P.D. and Leslyn Campbell with her. John Campbell retrieved the girls to New Jersey (John W. Campbell, Jr., letter to RAH, 03/09/50). Doña married George O. Smith probably in late August 1950, as Bill Corson mentions in a letter to Heinlein dated 09/02/50 that Henry Kuttner had received a wedding announcement by postcard.

42. Forrest J. Ackerman, who met with Leslyn in Northern California a few years later, noted the same thing:

> My wife and I had a lunch with Leslyn, and the table was set for four. The chair that was empty was not empty. It was filled with hatred for Heinlein. She practically had him there at the table with us, and every other word was about what a miserable man he was and how much she hated him, and on and on and on with this hatred.

Forrest J. Ackerman, interview with Robert James, Ph.D., 06/09/00.

43. RAH, letter to Doña and George Smith, 02/03/51.

44. RAH, letter to Doña Smith, 02/03/51.

45. John W. Campbell, Jr., letter to RAH, 03/06/51. Although Campbell was Heinlein's best source of information about the Dianetics movement through this period, he heard from L. Sprague de Camp (East Coast), often by postcard, who seemed to delight in deflating Hubbard's pretensions. Others added to the confusion, which continued for quite some time. Robert Cornog (West Coast) wrote Heinlein as late as November that year (Campbell consistently misspelling Sara Hubbard as "Sarah"):

> News about Ron and Sarah is hard to come by. Rumor hath it that Ron is paralyzed on one side and in a hospital in the Midwest. Sarah is alleged to be receiving $200 a month support, and living in the Los Angeles area in semi-retirement. Also writing western stories for the pulps . . . The "Hubbard Dianetics Foundation" is no longer listed in the Los Angeles telephone directory. The Messiah must not only promise deliverance and salvation, but he must also avoid acts which lead to "loss of altitude" to paraphrase el Ron Hubbard (11/08/51).

46. RAH, letter to Alice Dalgliesh, 04/11/51.

47. David Hartwell, personal communication with the author, April 2013.

48. Truman Talley, letter to RAH, 08/10/51. Most of Heinlein's direct correspondence was with Talley of Signet, rather than with Pohl or Merril (who were going through a painful divorce at the time). Here is a sample of Heinlein's "work" on the anthology, written to Talley (he had already turned in his Preface):

I have just received your letter of 28 August, with copy of your letter same date to Frederik Pohl and enclosing copies of "Absalom" by Kuttner and "The Last Martian" by Fredric Brown . . . .

In order to save time copies of this are going to Fred & Judy, and to Walter Bradbury; all that follows is for all of you. I've just read "Absalom," found that I had read it five years ago but had forgotten the title, and I vote emphatically for it. It passes my first test of giving pleasure on rereading; therefore it rates hard covers. As for emotional impact, in my opinion it is only a shade less horrible than "Coming Attraction" and has the added advantage of being a plot story, a solved conflict, whereas "Coming Attraction," strong as it is, is a vignette incident. It contains, I believe, a minor mistake in the mathematics but one which in no way invalidates the story. As for the rest of the science aspect it's in a field so esoteric and concerning which so little of really hard fact is known that it is impossible (I think) for an expert in that field to say, "This could never happen." Hank himself is a thorough student of psychiatry and psychology; I think he handles those two *very* fuzzy subjects very well indeed.

I think "The Last Martian" is a strong story and I would be more than willing to see it included. I strongly doubt the possibility of Fred's thesis, but here we are in complete *terra incognito*; my opinion is merely philosophical, with no data back of it.

49. RAH, letter to Erle Korshak, 04/07/51. In RAH, letter to Lurton Blassingame, 04/07/51, Heinlein also says, "What worries me still more is the amount of your time these jokers take up. You have been very nice about it, but I want to put a stop to it."
50. This piracy was mentioned only briefly in Erle Korshak, letter to RAH, 02/15/51.
51. RAH, letter to Lurton Blassingame, 03/25/53—i.e., at the time the paperback contract was being negotiated.
52. See, e.g., RAH, letter to Marty Greenberg, 05/04/59; RAH, letter to Lurton Blassingame, 07/29/64.
53. RAH, letter to Lurton Blassingame, 05/15/50.
54. RAH, letter to Lurton Blassingame, 01/05/51.
55. "Hi-yo, Tom Corbett!" *Newsweek,* 80 (04/02/51).
56. Lurton Blassingame, letter to RAH, 07/25/51.
57. RAH, letter to Lurton Blassingame, 04/07/51.
58. RAH, letter to Lurton Blassingame, 05/20/51.
59. Campbell's relationship with Hubbard and Dianetics featured in Campbell's correspondence with Heinlein over a period of a couple of years, from about 1950 to

about 1952. Following is a mild sampling of Campbell's analysis, from his letter to RAH dated 11/20/51:

> It is extremely difficult to give, in compact compass, the explanation of our work that would be required to make it clear . . . Ron's failure was to publish before he was ready to withstand the outrageous slings and arrows of psychiatric fortune. The heat was on him, and he didn't have his self-cooling asbestos underwear ready. He's now operating in a not-so-good condition, with a conviction that Joe Winter, I, and the others who originally backed him, are his worst enemies. Reason: we are loyal to his original ideal, and not to his fixed idea. His original concept of Dianetics required considerable ammendation and expansion. Joe Winter and I are particularly active in trying to do that; we'll back Ron 100% so long as he will go in that original direction. It would have been vastly to Joe Winter's advantage to claim complete separation and independence of Ron's Dianetics—so the MD's are mad at him, and Ron's mad at him because Joe came up with modifications of Ron's original ideas.
>
> I've been trying to make him see that the best way to get somewhere is to throw out ideas to as many individuals as possible and let those individuals do the real development work. Ron, unfortunately, wants to do it all.

Extracts from this entire correspondence, suitably edited to minimize Campbell's repetitiveness, are available in the Virginia Edition, vol. xxxix *Letters 1: Correspondence of John W. Campbell, Jr., and Robert A. Heinlein.*

60. Isaac Asimov, *In Memory Yet Green,* 625. The remark is dated to May 25, 1951, when Campbell told Asimov of the split.

61. The grant of adaptation rights is recorded in Heinlein's Accession Notes for *Red Planet* as of 06/04/51. The 121-page playscript itself was preserved in the Heinlein Archive and can be downloaded from www.heinleinarchive.com, for a nominal fee.

62. RAH, letter to Lurton Blassingame, 06/21/51.

63. Heinlein wrote Blassingame (12/14/48) that he had met Mark Reinsberg in 1940—which suggests they met probably in Chicago when Heinlein was attending the Democratic National Convention and then a General Semantics Seminar. After World War II, Reinsberg helped form Shasta Press with Korshak, but gave up the business.

> Mark is a quiet, intellectual young man . . . He parted amicably with Korshak [in 1948] because Mark is temperamentally not suited to Korshak's high-pressure, frenetic business life. Mark and his wife are here [in Colorado Springs] taking their master's degrees, she in psychology, he in lit.

64. RAH, letter to L. Sprague de Camp, 08/16/51.

65. Lurton Blassingame, letter to RAH, 08/22/51.

66. RAH, letter to Lurton Blassingame, 08/20/51. "Columbus Was a Dope" was the first fiction Heinlein wrote after WWII, in 1946, and aimed at the "slicks." Bar patrons denigrate the importance of exploration and scientific discovery—and a twist ending shows that they are in fact in the fruits of that exploration and discovery. All the slick markets passed on the story—which Heinlein himself called "feeble"—and it was published in the May 1947 *Startling Stories,* the last time the "Lyle Monroe" pen name was used.

67. RAH, letter to Lurton Blassingame, 08/20/51.

68. RAH, letter to Lurton Blassingame, 08/03/51, mentions the Corsons are preparing to leave. The visit itself, and its many unpleasantnesses, was the subject of a long letter from Heinlein to Corson, 08/07/51, and a subsequent correspondence on the subject.

    In this correspondence, Heinlein wonders at remarks Corson made in his first rejoinder:

> "I went to Colorado with the absolute determination to get along with her, come what might." Bill, the implications of this disturb me . . . The last time we saw a lot of you, before this last summer, was during the last period when Lucy visited her folks—a period in which Ginny invited you over for dinner more nights than not . . . [sic] so often in fact that I complained to her that she was inviting you too often during a period when I was trying to write a novel. (Not that I didn't enjoy your company, it was just that I was too busy for quite so much social life.) I know that Ginny liked you very much; not only did she say so, but she certainly would not have been suggesting that we have you over for dinner night after night if she hadn't. From your manner and from your statements to me, you liked her very much. If so, why in the world would it have been necessary to grit your teeth and be "absolutely determined to get along with her, come what may"? What the hell, Bill? This doesn't make sense. (RAH, letter to Bill Corson, 03/15/52.)

    And, indeed it does not. Remarks made by Cats Sang (Heinlein's and Corson's mutual friend and wife of Henry Sang) in correspondence with the author after the first volume of this biography was published, suggests:

> Everyone who had known him [Heinlein] in his earlier days in Laurel Canyon immediately assumed that Ginny was getting rid of his old friends. Corson (who probably *adored* Bob more than *anyone*) had declared that he, Corson, was *not* going to be discarded. But I think even *he* gave up in time

and adopted Henry Sang and me. (Grace Dugan Sang Wurtz, letter to the author, undated but late February 2011.)

The unpleasantness, thus, was probably a fossilized remnant of the divorce in 1947.

This incident (five years after Corson refused to be "discarded") did damage the long-standing friendship—however not to the extent Ginny suggested in Virginia Heinlein, letter to the author, 11/09/01, "The friendship dwindled off after that visit. We saw little of them in the future."

The Corsons may not have visited the Heinleins again—possibly due in part to the fact that once the Corsons moved from Los Angeles, they and the Heinleins never again happened to be in the same place at the same time—but in fact Heinlein and Corson continued to correspond frequently and cordially, peaking during the construction of Heinlein's bomb shelter a decade later and then tapering gradually off.

69. Dorothy Shanahan, "Heinleins' Push-Button Home Is Model of Convenience," Colorado Springs *Gazette-Telegraph* illustrated report (09/30/51), 1, Section B.

70. Virginia Heinlein, taped interview with the author, Tape 3, Side B.

71. RAH, letter to Stanley Stark, 08/10/71. In this letter Heinlein says that he started writing in July 1951 but put it away to perform "more pressing work." Virginia Heinlein, however, pointed out that this was an extremely unusual thing for Heinlein to do: "With the single exception of *Stranger,* I never saw R[obert] start a book or a shorter piece, and not finish it up as best he could do at the moment. He *always* finished what he began, no matter how terrible he felt it was." (Virginia Heinlein, letter to the author, 02/11/00.)

72. I have been unable to identify this book. Heinlein acknowledges receipt of the book in RAH, letter to Robert Cornog, 10/05/49. The book was not preserved in Heinlein's personal library catalog as of 1975 (this catalog is published in the Virginia Edition, vol. xxxviii *Nonfiction 2*), which probably means only that he returned the book to Cornog. Edward R. Dewey and Edwin F. Dakin published a book on economic cycles in 1947 titled *Cycles: The Science of Prediction,* but that book does not meet Mrs. Heinlein's description of dealing with "not economic, but other sorts of cycles." Leon Stover, taped interview with Virginia Heinlein, Tape 3, Side A, p. 7 of transcript. The only other likely candidate is not a book: In Heinlein's letter to Cornog of 10/26/49, he intends to order a paper recommended by Cornog, "The Analysis of Economic Time-Series," several parts of which were published in 1953 by the *Journal of the Royal Statistical Society.*

73. RAH, letter to Rogers Terrill, 01/01/50.

74. RAH, letter to Lurton Blassingame, 09/13/51.

75. RAH, letter to Lurton Blassingame, 10/13/51.

76. RAH, letter to Lurton Blassingame, 08/20/51.

77. RAH, letter to H. L. Gold, 10/02/51.

78. For several years Heinlein and H. L. Gold had an ongoing correspondence and spoke periodically by telephone—less usual then than now, but Gold was an agoraphobe and conducted his entire personal and professional life by telephone from his apartment. The correspondence was superficially cordial, but Heinlein expressed irritation in letters to his agent, about what might be thought of as "secondary costs" of doing business with Gold, of which unreasonable demands for extensive rewrites was one. Heinlein also felt pressured by Gold to write up ideas he regarded as substandard (see RAH, letter to Lurton Blassingame, 08/21/52).

79. *Tomorrow, the Stars* was a separate contract and didn't count against Heinlein's four-book deal with Doubleday negotiated at the time of the sale of *The Puppet Masters* in 1950.

80. Alice Dalgliesh, letter to RAH, 01/31/50.

81. Ruth Harshaw, letter to RAH, 08/23/51.

82. This must have been a very fast production cycle, as Heinlein's Accession Notes show the sale of the television right to CBS on 10/19/51.

83. Undated cover snowflake message, Ted Sturgeon to RAH, subsequently dated to March 1951.

84. RAH, letters to Lurton Blassingame, 08/08/51 and 09/11/51.

85. Lurton Blassingame, letter to RAH, 09/17/51.

86. RAH, letter to Lurton Blassingame, 10/13/51.

87. Knox Burger, letter to Lurton Blassingame, 12/21/51.

88. Although Heinlein had already run into H. L. Gold's acceptance of his *Cosmopolitan* article and Martin Greenberg wanting "Columbus Was a Dope" for a Gnome Press anthology, he did not yet realize that the standards of what constituted acceptable science fiction were changing—due in part to the emergence of *Galaxy* and *Fantasy & Science Fiction* as leading science-fiction magazines of the 1950s. It was probably the fact that his stories did sell to both the general fiction magazines (e.g., *The Rolling Stones* to *Boys' Life,* "Delilah and the Space Rigger" to *Blue Book,* "The Long Watch" to *American Legion*) and to the genre-specialist magazines—several of his juveniles wound up in either *Astounding* or *The Magazine of Fantasy & Science Fiction*—that gradually convinced him that *both sides* of advice he had received from Will F. Jenkins ("Murray Leinster") quoted in his 1947 theoretical essay, "On the Writing of Speculative Fiction" were true: "*Any* story—science fiction, or otherwise—if it is well written, can be sold to the slicks." Increasingly to the SF magazines, as well.

89. A few years later, John W. Campbell developed an interest in psionics, but in

1951 it apparently did not occur to either Heinlein or Blassingame that Campbell might have some special interest in "Project Nightmare," and the story was not shown to *Astounding*.

90. Virginia Heinlein, letter to the author, 06/06/00.

91. RAH, Accession Notes, 1967; comment follows *Between Planets* (Op. No. 88) and *The Green Hills of Earth and Other Stories* (Op. No. 87).

92. RAH, letter to Lurton Blassingame, 11/03/51.

93. RAH, letter to Robert Cornog, 11/14/51.

94. John Arwine, letter to RAH, 10/04/51.

95. "By the 1920s, psychoanalysis had become wildly popular in America (a country Freud visited only once and hated). Jazz age sophisticates held 'Freuding' parties at which they told one another their dreams." Lev Grossman, Janice Horowitz, Andrea Sachs, "Talk Therapy: Can Freud Get His Job Back?" *Time* magazine (January 20, 2003). Available online at http://www.time.com/time/magazine/article/0,9171,1004088,00.html#ixzz1hleMVwkQ (accessed December 28, 2011).

   See also Steven G. Kellman, *Redemption: The Life of Henry Roth* (2005), 127: [In about 1930] "Freudianism rivaled Marxism as the official local language of the Village [Greenwich Village], and 'Freuding parties,' in which guests found entertainment by probing one another's psyches, were a fad."

96. Virginia Heinlein, taped interview with the author, Tape 9, Side A (February 28?, 2000).

97. Virginia Heinlein, letter to Laura Haywood, 12/02/73. "Robert tells me that I really made a writer out of him stylistically speaking. I used to write comments in the margins of the copy, 'Unclear.' 'awkward.' etc."

98. RAH, letter to Lurton Blassingame, 12/01/51.

99. Virginia Heinlein, taped interview with the author, Tape 9, Side A.

100. Virginia Heinlein, taped interview with the author, Tape 9, Side A.

101. RAH, letter to Alice Dalgliesh, 01/08/52.

102. RAH, letter to Lurton Blassingame, 12/31/51.

6. Reality Bites (pages 75–89)

1. Fred Pohl, letter to RAH, 01/04/52. "Beyond Doubt"—a comic political fantasy set in ancient Mu—was written in 1939; Pohl had published it in one of the magazines he edited, *Astonishing Stories,* in April 1941 as by "Lyle Monroe" and Elma Wentz.

2. Alice Dalgliesh, letter to RAH, 01/10/52.

3. Passing mentions of Heinlein's recovery from surgery are scattered throughout his correspondence in January and February 1952, but see RAH, letter to Lou

Schor, 01/12/52: "Forgive crummy typing and my irritated tone—I am still very weak from surgery and can't sit up but a few minutes at a time."

4. "M.O.W." is television slang for "movie of the week," meaning any feature-film-length production for television.

5. RAH, letter to Lurton Blassingame, 01/10/52. The negotiations for this TV adaptation of *Between Planets* were discontinued in March 1952.

6. RAH, letter to Irving Pichel, 04/04/52.

7. RAH, letter to Lurton Blassingame, 01/15/52.

8. RAH, letter to Lurton Blassingame, 02/12/52.

9. RAH, letter to Lurton Blassingame, 02/12/52.

10. James D. Russell, President & Gen. Mgr. KVOR Radio, letter to RAH, 01/25/52.

11. RAH, letter to Irving Pichel, 01/27/52.

12. The Australian publisher bundled it with Stanley G. Weinbaum's "Parasite Planet" and put it out as a *Fantasy Fiction* pulp magazine, though the format is also somewhat reminiscent of comic books of the era.

13. Lurton Blassingame, letter to RAH, 02/07/52.

14. RAH, letter to Lurton Blassingame, 03/08/52.

15. See, e.g., RAH, letter to W. A. P. White, 03/27/57. A scissorbill is any of several species of skimming bird, of which some are common on seacoasts of the southern United States, but the derogatory usage comes from the labor movement of the early part of the twentieth century, generally referring to a disliked or contemptible person, but more particularly to workers who refuse to join a union or who take the side of management. Heinlein once referred to John W. Campbell, Jr., as a "supreme scissorbill" because of Campbell's rationalization of Street & Smith's more retrogressive rights-purchase policies. (RAH, letter to Lloyd Biggle, 09/30/76.) Discussing Marx's concept of class warfare and social classes in the United States, Heinlein once gave a fuller explanation of the usage:

> According to Marx, it is necessary to have a dispossessed proletariat before the revolution is achieved. This country has no proletariat! Oh, we have the economic classifications in this country used by Marx—but Americans don't behave according to those classifications because they are not aware that they are members of such classes. Being a member of a social class is much more a psychological matter than an economic matter. Well over ninety percent of Americans belong to the social class of "scissorbill." By the old Wobbly definition a scissorbill is a "Capitalist with very little capital." (RAH, letter to Fritz Lang, 05/02/46.)

16. RAH, letter to Bill Corson, 02/15/52.

17. In RAH, letter to Bill Corson, 08/07/51, Heinlein points out that all of his neigh-

bors are Republicans and that political conversation must be kept light for this reason.

18. RAH, letter to Ed and Olga Gordon, 02/15/52.

19. I.e., for Pogo. Bill Corson, letter to RAH, undated but late June 1952.

20. RAH, letter to Lurton Blassingame, 03/08/52.

21. Alice Dalgliesh, letters to RAH, 03/10/52 and 03/20/52.

22. RAH, letter to Alice Dalgliesh, 03/17/52.

23. RAH, letter to Alice Dalgliesh, 04/03/52.

24. RAH, letter to John Ciardi, 04/23/52.

25. John Ciardi, letter to RAH, 06/05/52.

26. RAH, letter to Lurton Blassingame, 04/26/52.

27. In her taped interview with the author, Virginia Heinlein says they looked at new as well as used cars and contemplated taking out a bank loan, but RAH indicated as early as a letter to Lurton Blassingame, 04/26/52, that he intended to buy a recent-model used car.

28. RAH, letter to Irving Pichel, undated but mid-May 1952.

29. RAH, letter to Poul Anderson, 07/21/61.

30. RAH, letter to Lurton Blassingame, 05/22/52.

31. RAH, letter to Irving Pichel, 04/04/52.

32. Robert A. Heinlein, "This I Believe," *Requiem* (Yoji Kondo, ed.).

33. Gladys Chang, letter to RAH acknowledging receipt of script, 05/27/52.

34. Virginia Heinlein, taped interview with the author, Second Series, Tape C, Side A.

35. Virginia Heinlein, letter to the author, 02/11/00.

36. Neil McAleer, *Visionary*, 60.

37. L. Sprague de Camp, postcard to RAH, 07/01/52.

38. RAH, letter to Lurton Blassingame, 07/16/52.

39. RAH, letter to George O. Smith, 08/05/52.

40. RAH, letter to George O. Smith, 08/05/52.

41. This is not the current Science Fiction Writers of America, which was founded in 1965, but an earlier and abortive attempt to organize a guild of science-fiction writers.

42. Forrest J. Ackerman, letter to RAH, 07/18/52.

43. RAH, letter to Forrest J. Ackerman, 08/04/52.

44. RAH, letter to Forrest J. Ackerman, 08/04/52.

45. Heinlein recognized a dilemma with regard to Ackerman; he felt professionally committed to stopping the multiple Hollywood representation that was only muddying the waters there, but acknowledged that the word he was getting back from his other Hollywood contacts was that Ned Brown would negotiate anything that came to him, but was not actively promoting him, whereas Ackerman

was (RAH, letter to Lurton Blassingame, 08/21/52). He therefore was faced with a promoter who was business-incompetent and a business-competent representative who was not promoting him. In the end Heinlein opted for business competency. "His [Brown's] representation may be sort of feeble but it is a good businesslike office," RAH, letter to Lurton Blassingame, 09/04/52. See footnote 35 of chapter 4 *supra*: "I wouldn't let Ackerman negotiate on my behalf for latch key to Hell; I'd be afraid he would louse it up."

With respect to Ned Brown's lack of energy, a few months later, when Brown was drawing up contracts for Seaman's *The World Beyond* project, he included a formal agency contract. Heinlein pointed out that he could not agree to the draft contract as written because it deauthorized Lurton Blassingame to negotiate or receive benefits for negotiating anything other than print rights for Heinlein:

> As they now read, literary publication rights are reserved for Lurton, but all other matters are reserved for MCA. This is not right, as Lurton has been extremely successful in selling rights other than literary rights for me during the three-year period, which your agency has been equally free to sell such rights, but has been totally unable to do so. Lurton has sold for me radio, TV, commercial, comic book, comic strip, dramatic, and other secondary rights during that time to the amount of about $30,000—in addition to his regular service in selling magazine and book rights. It would be neither reasonable nor ethical for me to place such rights now exclusively in another agency's hands . . . .

Heinlein continued, attempting to prompt a more energetic representation from Brown:

> Ned, you are an extremely busy man and science fiction is a specialized field. I don't expect you to have time to become a specialist; you haven't the time, it is too much to ask. There do happen to be two agents in Hollywood who know this field well, but I tell you frankly that I would never consider leaving you for either one of them (although they have each repeatedly urged me to do so)—as I like your business methods and I don't like theirs. But do you have an associate who knows science fiction, likes to read it for pleasure, and who could take hold of my stuff under your supervision and push it? If there were such a person, someone slightly less busy than yourself, Lurton and I could provide him with a complete file of my published works and I could work in close cooperation with him. If he thought that "By His Bootstraps," for example, merited a screen treatment or even a master-scene screenplay, he could tell me so and I could see what could be done about

putting it into a more salable form. I know the damned stuff is hard to sell. I don't expect you fellows to go out and make me rich without cooperation from me. (RAH, letter to Ned Brown, 10/21/52.)

However, this state of dissatisfaction with his Hollywood representation was to continue for some time.

Heinlein's experience echoes that of Hollywood insiders generally. There is a fundamental "disconnect" of expectations between an agent's clients—particularly writers—and the agent. The agent sees his job as to prepare and keep track of the appropriate paperwork for contracts and so forth—to protect his client's interest with respect to the studio or production company—whereas the writer (and this is generally true of Hollywood's "creative types") wants someone who will actively promote their work, get new work for them. Promotion does happen in an agent's daily activities—but usually only incidentally.

46. RAH, letter to Ned Brown, 08/23/52.
47. RAH, letter to Lurton Blassingame, 08/21/52.
48. RAH, letter to Ned Brown, 09/19/52.
49. RAH, letter to Ned Brown, 09/19/52.
50. RAH, letter to Mildred Frary, Editor, *Bulletin of the School Library Association of California,* 08/20/52.
51. The California *Bulletin* version is complete, and it is this version that was republished in the Virginia Edition, vol. xxxvii *Nonfiction 1.* This article for librarians is notable for containing the first public reference to "a Martian named Smith."
52. Virginia Heinlein, taped interview with the author, Tape 9, Side A. The Iditarod dogsled race commemorates this incident, as does a statue of Balto in New York's Central Park. Balto was the husky who led the team on the last leg of the anti-diphtheria serum delivery to Nome. In 1995 Stephen Spielberg produced a combination live-action/animation film about the dog, titled *Balto.*
53. RAH, letter to Ned Brown, 09/19/52.
54. RAH, letter to "O'Donnell," 10/04/73.
55. Virginia Heinlein, taped interview with the author, Tape 3, Side B.
56. Virginia Heinlein, taped interview with the author, Tape 3, Side B.
57. RAH, letter to Ned Brown, 09/19/52.
58. Janet Taylor, Rockhill Radio, letter to Lurton Blassingame, 09/30/52.
59. RAH, letter to Tom Stimson, 10/04/52.
60. RAH, letter to Tom Stimson, 10/04/52.
61. Virginia Heinlein, taped interview with the author, Tape 9, Side A.
62. RAH, letter to Ned Brown, 03/16/53. The treatments for "Home Sweet Home"

(about a bratty kid sabotaging an automated house) and "The Tourist" (about an alien visitor sampling Earth's culture as he possesses a space traveler) are printed in the Virginia Edition, vol. xlv *Screenplays 2*.

63. RAH, letter to Lurton Blassingame, 12/05/52.
64. Undated three-by-five card in RAH's hand.
65. RAH, letter to Ted Carnell, 10/28/52.
66. RAH, letter to Ted Carnell, 10/28/52.
67. RAH, letter to Lurton Blassingame, 10/28/52.
68. Lurton Blassingame, letter to RAH, 10/23/52.
69. RAH, letter to Willy Ley, 11/04/52; RAH, letter to Bill Corson, 12/29/52.
70. RAH, draft letter to Gregory Benford, 11/08/73.
71. Alice Dalgliesh, letter to RAH, 12/10/52.
72. RAH, letter to Bill Corson, 12/29/52.
73. RAH, letter to Jack Seaman, 05/04/53.
74. Virginia Heinlein seems to have thought that Heinlein did not know about the decision to turn "Ring Around the Moon" into a feature film, but this cannot be so, as a separate contract was negotiated for the film version—at Heinlein's insistence—and Heinlein himself did the additional writing to expand the script from a one-hour television production (i.e., 44 minutes of screen time, since television commercials take time away from story) to 63 minutes of screen time for a film (including opening and end titles).

   Project Moonbase was an obvious cheapie, with production values embarrassingly out of touch with standards for films in the early 1950s. But *Destination Moon* had kicked off what was virtually a craze for space movies, and Karl Johnson and Jack Seaman had decided between themselves to cash in on the craze, apparently hoping that a successful film release would help the series get picked up for broadcast.

   Although Heinlein was dubious about this reasoning, his handler at MCA thought it would do his career and reputation good to have another screen credit at that time. (Malcolm Stuart, MCA, letter to RAH, 01/28/53.)

   Project Moonbase was released in mid-1953 and had a very short run, disappearing into the attic trunks of Hollywood until it was revived for its camp value on VHS and DVD in the 1990s.

75. RAH, letter to L. Sprague de Camp, 12/15/52.
76. RAH, letter to John W. Campbell, Jr., 03/28/53.

7. Out and About (pages 90–100)

1. Virginia Heinlein, taped interview with Leon Stover, Tape 3, Side A, p. 10 of transcript in RAH Archive, UC Santa Cruz.

2. Virginia Heinlein, letter to the author, 11/07/99; Virginia Heinlein, taped interview with Leon Stover, Tape 3, Side A (October 22?, 1988); Virginia Heinlein, taped interview with the author, Tape 9, Side A (March 1?, 2000); RAH Accession Notes (1967) for *Starman Jones*.

3. In RAH, letter to Bill Corson, 12/29/52, Heinlein notes that he has the next boys' book on his professional agenda, with no indication that he has a story at this point; but he began writing, according to the Opus cards that contain his working history for each project, quoted in Marie Guthrie-Ormes's doctoral dissertation, on February 2, 1953. Given that Heinlein typically began writing as soon as a project was fully clear in his mind, the principal part of the layout of the book must, then, have come together in January 1953.

4. RAH, letter to Annette and Mick McComas, 08/26/53.

5. J. Francis McComas, letter to Lurton Blassingame, 03/01/53.

6. John W. Campbell, Jr., letter to RAH, 02/03/53.

7. The lawsuit was apparently threatened in a 1952 letter by Leslyn to Lurton Blassingame, which is no longer extant (apparently Heinlein destroyed the file he was collecting, as it never was received by the RAH Archive). He also received and acknowledged a similar letter sent on to him by Doña Smith. RAH, letter to Doña (Campbell) Smith, 02/18/52. On the same day, Heinlein wrote to his lawyer-friend Sam Kamens (who had represented both him and Leslyn in their divorce action—a practice that is still common when the break-up is cooperative and more or less amicable), saying that the current batch of letters was so over the top that he no longer thought even the most hungry lawyer would be persuaded by them to bring an action.

8. John W. Campbell, Jr., letter to RAH, 03/24/53.

9. RAH, letter to John W. Campbell, Jr., 03/28/53.

10. Lurton Blassingame, letter to RAH, 03/24/53.

11. RAH, letter to Lurton Blassingame, 03/25/53. Extracts from his letter were published in *Grumbles from the Grave* at 67.

12. RAH, letter to Lurton Blassingame, 03/25/53.

13. RAH, letter to E. J. Carnell, 05/08/53.

14. "Project Nightmare" was actually purchased by Howard Browne in May 1952 for the fantasy magazine *Fantastic,* but the magazine folded before the story could be published. The details of how the manuscript was acquired by *Fantastic*'s Ziff-Davis sister magazine *Amazing Stories* were not recorded.

15. Lurton Blassingame, letter to RAH, 05/03/53.

16. RAH, letter to Robert Moore Williams, 05/21/47.

17. Virginia Heinlein, taped interview with the author, Tape 4, Side B.

18. RAH, postscript to George O. Smith, undated but 1953:

V. V. himself is all over his nervous mannerisms and exudes the charm and self-confidence of W. C. Fields about to sell a sucker a gold brick. I liked him much better than I did four years ago, but that left plenty of room to increase liking without wanting to kiss him.

Four years previously would have been 1949, presumably when Heinlein was in Los Angeles working on *Destination Moon.*

19. RAH, letter to George O. Smith, undated but around 05/10/53.
20. RAH, letter to George O. Smith, undated but around 05/10/53.
21. RAH, letter to John W. Campbell, Jr., 03/20/53.
22. Van Ronkel's letter has not been preserved, but Heinlein's reply to van Ronkel, 05/17/53, conveys his shock, analyzes the possibilities (as given in the text), and concludes that any payment to Schor can only have been a bribe to conceal from them the difference between 10 percent of the production (which is what they thought they were negotiating for) and 10 percent of the producer's share (which is how the paperwork was drawn up). As Schor was a lawyer who practiced in entertainment law before becoming an agent, Heinlein concluded Schor "took a dive" and went on to say the matter was so distressing he could hardly stand to think about it.

    To Lurton Blassingame (letter of 05/17/53), Heinlein wrote in summary:

    Rip and I have a dirty, dark suspicion that he was handed this piece of the picture for working against the interests of his clients in the negotiations. It would explain a hell of a lot of things about his behavior and about some of the very real faults of the contract. I had thought he was just stupid; now I am tentatively of the opinion that he is dishonest.

    Of course, he may have some legitimate explanation as to how he got a piece of the picture—but what the hell could it be? And why has he concealed from Rip and myself that he had an interest much greater than his interest in his clients—and concealed it for three years? I just can't see any explanation other than that he sold us out.

    But neither Heinlein nor van Ronkel had access to hard data, and so it remains only a speculation. As Ginny Heinlein remarked, "That was never confirmed, and I don't know whether it is true or not. Robert considered that a part of the Hollywood treatment and felt that almost everyone on the film had betrayed him . . ." (Virginia Heinlein, letter to the author, 12/10/99.)

23. Twain's late book *Christian Science* (1907) predicted that Christian Science would have the United States in a theocracy within forty years.
24. Author's note of a dinner conversation with Virginia Heinlein in early March 2001.

25. RAH, letter to Irving Pichel, 05/29/53. Fifteen thousand words into the story is about where Secretary-General Douglas interviews Mike while still in the hospital and tries to get him to sign away his problematical Larkin Rights.

26. RAH, letter to Lurton Blassingame, 06/10/53.

27. RAH, letter to Lurton Blassingame, 07/05/53.

28. Virginia Heinlein, letter to the author, 07/07/99.

29. Virginia Heinlein, letter to Leon Stover, 04/08/89.

30. Rex Ivar Heinlein was diagnosed with Involutional Melancholia in, probably, 1938. This matter is treated in Volume 1 of this biography, *Learning Curve*, 202–4.

31. RAH, letter to Rex Heinlein (brother), 10/25/53.

32. Rex Ivar Heinlein (father), letter to RAH, 08/03/53. The note suggests just how difficult and awkward this visit must have been:

> Just want to repeat that I appreciate your efforts to make us enjoy our stay with you and Ginny. I especially appreciate the time Ginny spent playing Samba, since it seems she does not like the game . . . . Might have stayed a few days longer, but you seemed to feel that it wasn't fair to the rest of you for us to stay longer here than we did at your home. Besides we are beginning to feel that it will be nice to be in our own home once more.
>
> I am sorry that there were a couple of unpleasant episodes, and I hope time will efface some of the recollection of these . . .
>
> As to belittling Ginny's service, such was not my intention. I did not know that the service women carried rifles and drilled. It doesn't make sense. The war in which I had a very small part [the Spanish-American War, 1898–99] was of course a little one but just as big as any other to those who lost their sons. It also led to the United States being lifted up to a first class power in the world and give her a place in the world, good or bad, which she hadn't enjoyed before . . .
>
> I am sorry if Ginny considers herself an outsider. We have always tried to feel and make the new members feel that they were truly members of our family. I think it is true with the rest and I hope Ginny will come to feel that way also.
>
> I sincerely hope you and Ginny can come to see us before too long, since it is not possible that we will ever again make such a trip as the one we are soon to complete.
>
> All in all it has been very pleasant and will always be remembered that way.
>
> Love to both of you

33. Ned Brown, letter to RAH, 07/28/53, forwards a clipping from *Variety* about distribution being picked up for *Project Moonbase*.

34. Quoted in "Destination Moon: Robert A. Heinlein, Filmwriter" by Christopher Schaefer, *New Libertarian* 187 (undated but 1999): 63.

35. RAH, *Tramp Royale,* 2. The Heinleins contemplating building a rental property is not mentioned elsewhere in correspondence. It is always chancy to take as factual such a statement in so mannered a book as *Tramp Royale,* but in this case it is so plausible an idea that I elected to treat it as factual.

36. RAH, *Tramp Royale,* 4. The tenor of Heinlein's remarks about Ginny in his correspondence and to a certain extent also in *Tramp Royale,* written the following year, sound insensitive and patronizing to our ears but were considered merely "humorous" at the time and were intended as ironic playing with "little wife" conventions then current—expected possibly because of the age difference between them.

37. RAH, letter to Dorothy and Clare Heinlein, 09/23/53.

38. RAH, letter to Mick, Annette, and Tony McComas, 08/26/53.

39. RAH, letter to Annette and Mick McComas, 08/26/53.

40. RAH, letter to Lurton Blassingame, 10/24/53. A petition to adopt is not otherwise mentioned in the correspondence. A mention of being too old legally to adopt in Heinlein's letter to Greg Benford, 11/08/73, may conflate two different incidents some time apart, as he mentions Ginny's "plumbing problem," which occurred much later, but says she was then thirty-six, which would place it in 1954—although they are still actively considering adoption in 1955. RAH, letter to Bud Bacchus, 04/15/55, also mentions being too old to adopt by the laws of the State of Colorado.

41. RAH, *Tramp Royale*, 29.

8. World Travelers (pages 101–113)

1. Virginia Heinlein, letter to Reginald Bretnor, 12/09/79.

2. This incident is recorded in two places: RAH, *Tramp Royale,* 48; and in slightly different detail in Michael J. Patritch, "One Hundred and Fifty Minutes into Forever: A Meeting with Robert A. Heinlein," *Thrust SF & Fantasy Review,* no. 33 (Spring 1989): 10.

3. Heinlein's discussion of his challenged assumptions and the conclusions he drew from his exposure to South American lifestyles and politics are scattered through chapters 2 through 6 of *Tramp Royale,* and Heinlein touches on them again in the concluding chapter.

4. RAH, letter to Robert A. W. Lowndes, 03/13/56.

5. RAH, letter to Robert A. W. Lowndes, 03/13/56.

6. RAH, *Tramp Royale,* 63–64. These sentiments and conclusions appear at various

places in *Tramp Royale,* sometimes somewhat repetitively, including Heinlein's summation at the end of the book, of what he had learned by his travel.

7. RAH, *Tramp Royale,* 368–9.

8. RAH, *Tramp Royale,* 133.

9. RAH, letter to T. B. Buell, 10/03/74.

10. The title is taken from Rudyard Kipling's "Sestina of the Tramp-Royal" (1896)—a poem which Heinlein has said he often reread (RAH, letter to "Mr. and Mrs. Collier," 12/08/76). Mrs. Heinlein could not remember in her interviews with the author in 2000 and 2001 why the book title had the hyphen omitted and a rogue final *e* added.

11. RAH, *Tramp Royale,* 93. Many of Heinlein's remarks in *Tramp Royale,* especially about Ginny (he calls his wife "Ticky," one of their pet names, throughout the book) are crafted to be funny and endearing, as she is treated as a viewpoint character for the travelogue. Nevertheless, at least some of them may be taken as factual, in one degree or another. This remark, about Ginny not being able to contain her disgust for the Perón fascist regime in Argentina, comports with other reported behavior later in the trip, as well as with Heinlein's chosen persona for *Tramp Royale.*

12. Virginia Heinlein, letter to "Doc & Mimi [Knowles], Lucky & Art & Barby [Herzberger]," 12/13/53. Heinlein repeated this sentiment in *Tramp Royale,* 108.

13. Virginia Heinlein, letter to Robert and Vivian Markham, undated but by internal evidence about 12/15/53.

14. In the Argentinian newspaper reports, Heinlein found the reporters had simply made up answers to questions he would not answer (boasting about how much money he earned stuck in his craw, though it seemed to be ordinary and expected in Argentina). The questions might be odd and even offensive by his admittedly parochial standards, he concluded—but reporters are the same everywhere.

15. RAH, *Tramp Royale,* 112.

16. RAH, *Tramp Royale,* 136.

17. Virginia Heinlein, taped interview with the author, Second Series, Tape D, Side B.

18. From a clipping in RAH supplemental notes to the draft bibliography for his 1975 "Are You a Rare Blood?" article for *Encyclopedia Britannica,* Op. 175 file, "MISCELLANEY *Haptoglobins in Tristan da Cunha* - H. Harris & E.B. Robson— *Vox Sanguinis* AABB 8 (1963): 226–30. RAH Archive, UC Santa Cruz.

19. RAH, *Tramp Royale,* 151.

20. RAH, *Tramp Royale,* 171–173.

21. RAH, *Tramp Royale,* 180–181.

22. RAH, *Tramp Royale,* 180–181.

23. RAH, *Tramp Royale,* 190; Virginia Heinlein, letter to George Warren, 03/09/79.

24. RAH, letter to Bjo Trimble, 09/06/61. If the photograph mentioned was preserved, it has not yet been identified in the Heinlein Archive at UC Santa Cruz. Curiously, it is difficult to find information about this Ntuli, as the reputation of his son Pitika Ntuli, also a sculptor as well as painter and poet, has eclipsed that of his father. Pitika Ntuli was born in 1942 and was, therefore, only eleven years old when the Heinleins visited *their* Ntuli.

25. RAH, *Tramp Royale,* 228.

26. Virginia Heinlein, letter to Janet Crawford, 02/26/78.

27. RAH, *Tramp Royale,* 208.

28. RAH, *Tramp Royale,* 210.

29. RAH, *Tramp Royale,* 210.

30. Dell Comic Book *Tom Corbett, Space Cadet,* 8 (November–January 1954). Marked on first page in RAH's hand "purchased in Raffles Hotel, Singapore 28 Jan 54." *Space Cadet* file, RAH Archive, UC Santa Cruz.

31. RAH, letter to Poul Anderson, 09/06/61.

32. RAH, *Tramp Royale,* 230.

33. RAH, letter to J. E. Pournelle, 05/19/63.

34. RAH, *Tramp Royale,* 233–4.

35. RAH, *Tramp Royale,* 197–8. Pichel was to die a few months later, on July 13, 1954, of heart failure.

36. RAH, *Tramp Royale,* 208.

37. RAH, *Tramp Royale,* 252.

38. RAH, *Tramp Royale,* 254. Nevertheless, koalas do scratch and bite if annoyed.

39. RAH, *Tramp Royale,* 255.

40. RAH, *Tramp Royale,* 257.

41. RAH, letter to Alice Dalgliesh, 03/12/55.

42. RAH, *Tramp Royale,* 276. American magazines were also embargoed.

43. Lurton Blassingame, letter to RAH, 02/07/52.

44. Virginia Heinlein, letter to Robert Bloch, 11/10/73.

45. Virginia Heinlein, letter to Robert Bloch, 11/10/73.

46. Virginia Heinlein, taped interview with the author, Tape 6, Side A. When the Heinleins finally got home, they found a complaint from one of those teachers that a postcard was a skimpy reply to a child's effort to compose a letter. The teacher had discussed this serious matter in class and decided to let him eat his own books if they were so important to him.

47. Brian Finch, secretary on Futurian Society of Sydney stationery, letter to RAH, 03/31/54. Inquiries made to Australian fans in 2003 and 2004 were unable to turn up copies of tape recordings made at the time.

48. RAH, *Tramp Royale,* 299–300.

49. RAH, *Tramp Royale,* 315–6.

50. RAH, *Tramp Royale,* 309.

51. This summary brings into one place Heinlein's several observations scattered throughout his narrative about the New Zealand trip. He also made a (short) summary in *Tramp Royale,* 327–8 and again at 341–2.

52. RAH, letter to Robert A. W. Lowndes, 03/13/56. Heinlein was to revise this opinion in subsequent trips.

53. RAH, letter to Mr. and Mrs. Collier, 12/08/76. The quote is from Laurence Binyon (1869–1943) "For the Fallen."

54. This is essentially a paraphrase of the concluding chapter of Heinlein's travel book about this trip, *Tramp Royale.*

55. Virginia Heinlein, letter to Leon Stover, 03/17/89.

56. Modern, and especially post-60s leftism has hardly anything in common with Enlightenment-era liberalism. Even though it appears to be a canon of faith among modern leftists that there is great continuity between, e.g., Jeffersonian thought and modern progressivism, such continuity doesn't actually seem to exist in the historical record. For a big-government central-planning, urban-oriented progressive to try to claim the mantle of Jefferson is puzzling and disconcerting, since Jefferson's maxim "he governs best who governs least" is well known, and his vision for America was as a land of yeoman farmers.

    Heinlein's political positions in succeeding decades can only be understood by referring his various positions to *Heinlein's* idea of his own liberalism, which is closer to classical liberalism than to modern progressive leftism—though so individualist that it fits comfortably within neither extreme of this spectrum.

57. RAH, letter to W. A. P. White, 04/20/54.

9. Some Beginnings of Some Ends (pages 114–124)

1. Alice Dalgliesh, letter to RAH, 05/06/54.

2. "The Big Secret of Pearl Harbor: Roosevelt 'Invited' Attack, Admiral Says," *U.S. News & World Report* (April 2, 1954): 21.

3. *U.S. News & World Report* (April 2, 1954): 48, *et seq.*

4. Introduction to "The Final Secret of Pearl Harbor," *U.S. News & World Report* (April 2, 1954): 48.

5. R. A. Theobald, *The Final Secret of Pearl Harbor* (Devin-Adair Publications, 1954).

6. Virginia Heinlein, letter to Leon Stover, 04/23/89.

7. In his correspondence, Heinlein spoke of his disenchantment with Roosevelt, and Virginia Heinlein testifies that the Theobald Report was the first of at least three critical incidents that bear on his later political positions and activities

(the others being, in her opinion, Sputnik late in 1957 and the Patrick Henry campaign in 1958, although Heinlein also mentions other incidents as being critical to his evolution. In a letter to his brother Lawrence Lyle Heinlein, July 19, 1964, Heinlein says specifically:

> My change in opinion has been a gradual one in most ways but there have been some sharp break points, too. One was the day on which the full story on Pearl Harbor finally came out—and I've had no use for FDR since. Another was a day in Jugoslavia when I watched American tanks being handed over to Tito. Oh, there have been many other things—the Alger Hiss case, Operation Keelhaul, our forgotten Korean War prisoners, Castro and our State Department, Aid to Dependent Children and the "professional" relief client, many things.

But there is a logical gap between disenchantment with a former leader of the party and making a break with his life-long political party. Heinlein never discussed his resignation from the Democratic Party, but that the break happened at this time suggests that it was tied up with his recent experiences. I have here lined up some of the elements not often visible in the documentation, which I estimate went into Heinlein's taking stock of "the entire situation."

8. Heinlein's letters discussing the New Deal and EPIC, scant though they are (several discussed and cited in *Learning Curve* when dealing with the period), make no distinction between EPIC and the New Deal, except on the basis of differing tactical approaches to what are assumed to be the same political and social goals.

9. RAH, letter to Robert A. W. Lowndes, 03/13/56.

10. RAH, letter to Rex Heinlein, 09/29/64. Heinlein had advocated voting the party-plank in his 1946 book, *How to Be a Politician,* but he abandoned the practice when he became a single-issue voter after World War II, over the internationalization of atomic weapons.

11. RAH, letter to Rex Heinlein, 09/29/64.

12. L. Sprague de Camp, postcard to RAH, 05/24/54.

13. Per itinerary titled "Schedule for Trip East" and dated 05/21/54, preserved in the RAH Archive, UC Santa Cruz.

14. The anecdote is given in Isaac Asimov's autobiography, *In Memory Yet Green,* at 74.

15. Per itinerary titled "Schedule for Trip East" and dated 05/21/54, preserved in the RAH Archive, UC Santa Cruz.

16. RAH, letter to John W. Campbell, Jr., 03/28/53.

17. RAH, letter to John W. Campbell, Jr., 03/28/53.

18. Heinlein did not record any information about this session contemporaneously; several months later G. Harry Stine wrote to Heinlein asking for his side of the

complaints Campbell was making to him in letters. To set the context of his response, Heinlein provided all the background given here. The letters to Stine are cited as they occur.

19. RAH, letter to G. Harry Stine, 07/27/54.

20. RAH, letter to G. Harry Stine, 07/18/54.

21. RAH, letter to G. Harry Stine, 07/27/54.

22. RAH, letter to G. Harry Stine, 07/18/54.

23. RAH, letter to G. Harry Stine, 07/18/54.

24. There is no specific information about when "their last round of fertility testing" took place. The most recent time the subject came up, even obliquely, was in 1952, probably in connection with Ginny's false pregnancy after their National Parks road trip.

      This was probably the occasion when the subject of fertility surgery for Ginny came up because of "a minor malfunction that might have been corrected with estimated 25% success through prosthesia involving a laparotomy for her." Heinlein goes on to note: "I did not like those odds for her as she was then 36 when we pinned it down—and I was too old for a legal adoption—so we accepted the situation . . ." (RAH, letter to Greg Benford, 11/08/73).

      That was probably the event that triggered their exploration of adoption.

25. Virginia Heinlein, IM with the author, 01/01/01.

26. G. Harry Stine, letter to RAH, 06/23/54. Stine literally said: "He should not be belittling you because of your approach to problems. And vice versa." The "vice versa" must have been preemptive; since this was the letter in which Stine informed Heinlein that he had received the letter from Campbell, there had not been any "belittling" on Heinlein's part.

27. RAH, letter to G. Harry Stine, 07/27/54.

28. Walter Bradbury, letter to Lurton Blassingame, 06/24/54.

29. RAH, letter to G. Harry Stine, 07/18/54.

30. Heinlein asked for the return of the manuscript for *Tramp Royale* by letter to Lurton Blassingame, 08/30/54—after the summer visits were over.

31. RAH, letter to G. Harry Stine, 07/27/54. In this letter he also talks about the typewriter's "silencer housing." This typewriter and its housing was preserved among the "realia" in the RAH Archive, UC Santa Cruz.

32. The sales contract for the Model 12 Silent Underwood typewriter is in the RAH Archive, UC Santa Cruz, and shows a purchase price of $513.57, whereas book advances from Scribner were running around $500.00 at that time. The contemporary equivalent therefore, would be about $20,000.

33. Virginia Heinlein, letter to the author, 11/09/01.

34. Karen Heinlein (Kilpatrick), letter to Robert and Ginny Heinlein, 09/11/54.

35. RAH, letter to John W. Campbell, Jr., 08/30/54.

36. Learned Bulman, letter to Alice Dalgliesh, 08/30/54.

37. RAH, letter to Lurton Blassingame, 10/05/54.

38. Scribner had published *From Here to Eternity* in 1951, and the book came under attack (including boycotts of bookstores) by the Catholic group National Organization for Decent Literature because of its coarse language and sexual content. What Heinlein could not know at the time was that *From Here to Eternity* had its own prepublication censorship troubles with Scribner's editors in which Jones cut back on some of the expletives and removed some references to soldiers engaging in casual homosexual prostitution. The book was filmed in 1953—the year before Heinlein's exchange with Dalgliesh—with its iconic scene of Deborah Kerr and Burt Lancaster clinching on a beach in the incoming surf. The movie won six Oscars.

39. RAH, letter to Alice Dalgliesh, 09/07/54.

40. Alice Dalgliesh, letter to RAH, 09/13/54.

41. RAH, letter to Alice Dalgliesh, 09/15/54.

42. RAH, letter to Alice Dalgliesh, 09/15/54.

43. The year in which *Tunnel in the Sky* was written, 1954, was also the year of the Supreme Court's seminal decision in *Linda Brown v. Board of Education* (357 U.S. 483) overturning the "separate but equal" doctrine that permitted segregated schools. Separate but equal had been standard doctrine throughout much of the United States since 1890. The Civil Rights Act of 1964 eliminated separate but equal from all areas of public accommodation. The idea of racially integrated high school classes would have been shocking in 1954.

44. Alice Dalgliesh, letter to RAH, 03/16/55.

45. RAH, letter to Virginia Fowler, 01/07/55.

46. See, for example, Richard Lingeman, *Sinclair Lewis: Rebel from Main Street* (New York: Random House, 2002).

10. Vintage Season (pages 125–144)

1. Thirty-six thousand words is about the point in the story at which Jill has removed Mike from the hospital and decides to take him to Jubal Harshaw—possibly at the scene in which the Secretary-General's wife consults her astrologer about the Man from Mars.

2. Page 148 of Heinlein's earliest manuscript has our first view of Jubal Harshaw and his menage. At the bottom of the page, Jill arrives with Mike.

3. RAH, letter to Theodore Sturgeon, 02/11/55.

4. RAH, letter to Lurton Blassingame, 02/23/55. Fifty-four thousand words would be close to page 200 of ms.—around Mike's first demonstration of his "Martian powers" to Jubal, and also around the point at which Jubal Harshaw tells Jill that Caxton has probably been kidnapped.

5. RAH, letter to Lurton Blassingame, 02/13/55.

6. RAH, letter to Theodore Sturgeon, 02/11/55.

7. Two of these ideas Sturgeon did turn into stories, "The Other Man" and "And Now the News" (both published in 1956). "And Now the News" is widely regarded as one of Sturgeon's finest stories, and it became the title story for its volume (9 of 13) of the North Atlantic Books series *Complete Short Stories of Theodore Sturgeon*.

   Sturgeon told how the story came to be in his guest of honor speech at the 1962 Chicago World SF Convention, Chicon II, and the speech was reprinted in *The Proceedings of Chicon II*, Earl Kemp, ed. (Advent: Publishers, 1963). Sturgeon also told the anecdote in his story introduction for "And Now the News . . ." in his last collection, *The Golden Helix* (1979).

   "The Other Man" was collected into *The Worlds of Theodore Sturgeon* (1972). Heinlein's letter was published in *The New York Review of Science Fiction*, no. 84 (August 1995).

8. Virginia Heinlein, taped interview with Leon Stover, Tape 3, p. 11 of transcript in RAH Archive, UC Santa Cruz.

9. RAH, letter to Michael J. Harrington, 07/25/61.

10. RAH, letter to Lester del Rey, 04/19/57.

11. RAH, letter to Bud Bacchus, 04/15/55.

12. In a later letter, Heinlein cites the worsening headlines as a supplementary reason for giving up the idea of adopting. RAH, letter to "Herbert and Ginny" (Kee), 09/20/58.

13. RAH, letter to Larry and Caryl Heinlein, 07/19/64.

14. Probably to Frankfurt, although their immediate destination is nowhere recorded in the documents.

15. Virginia Heinlein, taped interview with the author, Second Series, Tape C, Side A.

16. RAH, letter to Stan Mullen, 07/15/55.

17. Virginia Heinlein, taped interview with the author, Tape 10, Side A.

18. In 1891 Mark Twain attended the Bayreuth Festival with his wife and family, and saw *Parsifal* (twice), which he said he enjoyed in spite of the singing, *Tannhaeuser,* and *Tristan und Isolde.* Twain wrote up his Bayreuth experience for the *Chicago Tribune,* appearing on December 6, 1891, as "Mark Twain at Bayreuth." The piece has been republished several times, sometimes under the title "At the Shrine of St. Wagner," and is available online at http://www.twainquotes.com /Travel1891/Dec1891.html (accessed 05/01/11). Of Wagner's music, Twain quipped that it was better than it sounded.

   Heinlein made little contemporaneous comment about the Ring at Bayreuth in 1954. Later he said that he became a fan of the Ring cycle after the Seattle production in 1975. After commenting that Seattle could not command the quality of the voices heard at Bayreuth, he went on to say: ". . . now I am a Wagner fan, as the Seattle Opera Company production followed as closely as possible the old man's explicit stage directions." (RAH, letter to Tessa Dick, 08/03/75.)

19. Ted Carnell, letter to RAH, 08/25/55.

20. RAH, letter to Alfred Bester, 10/17/55.

21. Virginia Heinlein, taped interview with the author, Tape 3, Side B.

22. The exact date of the Heinleins' departure for Colorado Springs is not mentioned, but in his bread-and-butter note to Lurton Blassingame, 09/23/55, Heinlein mentions seeing the devastating Hurricane Ione off to one side on departure, which places the date at 09/19/55, when Ione was at its 120 mph peak over North Carolina.

23. Virginia Heinlein, taped interview with the author, Tape 9, Side A.

24. This outline was in 2006 made into a complete novel titled *Variable Star* by Spider Robinson. As of this writing (2011) three sequels have been contracted for.

25. Lurton Blassingame, letter to Oscar Friend, 11/03/55.

26. RAH, letter to Lurton Blassingame, 12/13/55.

27. *Double Star* is widely regarded as one of the best science-fiction novels of the 1950s and was a choice by Library of America for its American Science Fiction series, *Classic Novels 1956–1958.*

28. Howard Browne (1908–99) assumed editorship of *Amazing Stories* in 1949, after Ray Palmer left Ziff-Davis. In 1952 he founded a companion magazine for *Amazing* in digest format called *Fantastic.* Response to this stylish magazine was so positive that Ziff-Davis resurrected an earlier, abandoned plan to change *Amazing* from pulp to digest format starting with the April–May 1953 bimonthly issue.

   Pulp magazines were usually published in a 7" × 10" format on rough pulp paper; the "digest size," presumably named after the famous *Reader's Digest* magazine, was smaller, typically 8¼" or 8½" × 5½", which typically used a higher grade of paper. A larger third standard magazine size, called "bedsheet," was adopted by many of the prestige "slick" magazines (such as *Life* magazine and *The Saturday Evening Post*) 9¾" × 12". Some of the pulp magazines used this format as well: the first SF magazine, *Amazing Stories,* was printed in bedsheet size from 1926 until the 1940s, and *Astounding,* too, flirted briefly with this format in 1942 and 1943, and again in the mid–1960s.

29. By the time the April issue of *Amazing* rolled around, Bridey Murphy was a household name and national cause célèbre for fakery. Robert found himself explaining over and over that he hadn't intended any special advocacy:

   I used the Bernstein book as a kick-off for some fancy speculation about possible future trends in research, much as I used the flying saucer craze as the kick-off in *The Puppet Masters* . . .

On the whole Bridget Murphy business I am as open-minded as a rainstorm. Insufficient evidence, highly entertaining, excellent basis for fiction—but I probably would not have made my reference to Bernstein and his subject quite so definite had I guessed what a furor was about to burst. You see, I wrote that piece for *Amazing* . . . about two months before the Bernstein book was published. I had had an advance look at the book and had known about Bernstein's researches for a couple of years—but I simply did not guess that the book would make such an outstanding splash. (I guess I'm really a wash-out as a prophet!) I remember thinking as I wrote those two sentences that probably not one reader in a thousand would know what case I was referring to, but that nevertheless it made a nice hook on which to hang the speculation. Had I been able to look three months into the future I would have picked another case (there are many much better ones that can be cited), but I used the Bernstein-Murphy case because it was recent in time and local in space and I hoped that some readers would recognize it.

RAH, letter to T. N. Scortia, 05/07/56. Heinlein had to explain that he was *not* a Bridey Murphy advocate for years. See, for example, Heinlein's letter jointly to Fred Pohl and Algis Budrys, 08/19/61:

[Quoting from 3 of "Bench Mark":] "It's useful to remember that five years ago, in a brief article for *Amazing Stories,* Heinlein declared that the Bridey Murphy case proved reincarnation and the persistence of essential personality."

I won't argue about the accuracy of the paraphrasing, although it does overstate the matter; what grouses me is that it here has been hauled out of context and there is no slightest suggestion that the original is part of a fictional "prophecy."

But I had done precisely the same thing I had done in *Puppet Masters,* made use of an item currently in the news to create a temporal tie-in with a future scene, give verisimilitude, lend empathy.

30. Heinlein's outline notes for *The Door into Summer* in the RAH Archive, UC Santa Cruz, contain most of the important elements of the story, except the unifying element of Petronius the cat and his engineer's affection for the cat.

31. Virginia Heinlein, taped interview with Leon Stover, Tape 3, Side A, 12 of transcript in RAH Archive, UC Santa Cruz; the anecdote is also given in Heinlein's Accession Notes (Opus No. 157, 11/05/68, 10), also in the RAH Archive. The full set of both letters which constitute the Accession Notes are published in the Virginia Edition, vol. xxxvii *Nonfiction 1.*

David Hartwell argued in his introduction for the Gregg Press reprint of *The Door into Summer* an inheritance from H. G. Wells's *The Sleeper Wakes* (a speculation Heinlein approved), but there are also turns from *Looking Backwards* ironically inverted. Suspended animation had a long literary tradition, and Heinlein was certainly aware of and used it.

32. RAH, letter to Lurton Blassingame, 03/09/56.

33. On January 14, 1957.

34. Virginia Heinlein, IM with the author, 01/31/02.

35. RAH, letter to William A. P. White ("Anthony Boucher"), 03/27/57.

36. None of Leslyn's 1956–57 poison-pen letters survive in the RAH Archive, UC Santa Cruz. Heinlein probably destroyed the file once the need for the letters disappeared, probably in 1968 (that is, ten years later) as papers he would otherwise have to cart from Colorado Springs to Santa Cruz. However, both Leslyn's letter to A. P. White and White's letter to Heinlein mentioning it are also missing from White's archive of personal correspondence at the Lily Library in Bloomington, Indiana. Only Heinlein's reply to White's letter is extant.

Here is a sampling from a prior (1953) round of poison-pen letters which was preserved in Fred Pohl's papers. Leslyn's bile is not reserved for Heinlein alone, but is spread around liberally.

> I'm amused also to hear you [Pohl] use his [Heinlein's] own term for his abcessed genitalia troubles. "his plumbing reamed out." I put up with periodic celibacy during most of our 15 years of marriage due to his urethral and urinary difficulties.
>
> If the guy would ever keep his "pride and joy" inside his pants for 24 hours at a stretch, and give it a rest—he might be able to dispense with the luxury of hypochondria!
>
> Vida [Jameson] is making out all right. Thoroughly selfish critters always seem to do so. Cleve's first wife was another of the same breed. And so is Heinlein and Virginia Gerstenfeld Heinlein.
>
> And Cleve, like me, is better off free of his illusions. Sometime Cleve will meet a woman who will appreciate and love him. Inasmuch as lil' ol' me could meet two adorable REAL MEN after Heinlein—I'm sure that Deity, Mother Nature, or the Law of Compensation has someone worthy in store for Cleve (1 - if you're a Deist, 2 - if you're a Theist, and 3 if you insist on being a scaredy-cat materialist).

And so on. Leslyn Heinlein Mocabee, letter to Fred Pohl, 05/25/53 (from Pohl's Archive in Red Bank, New Jersey).

37. RAH, letter to Robert Cornog, 01/16/57.

38. The entire paragraph, Lurton Blassingame, letter to RAH, 10/01/56.

39. RAH, letter to Lurton Blassingame, 10/09/56.

40. RAH, letter to Clare and Dorothy Heinlein, undated but datelined "Nogales, Arizona," and so therefore around the end of February 1957.

41. For these and similar sentiments about President Eisenhower (and about Adlai Stevenson), see, e.g., RAH, letter to Lurton Blassingame, 11/25/57. Stuart Symington (1901–88) was the first Secretary of the Air Force (1947–50) and recently (1953) elected Democratic Senator from Missouri. Symington served in the Senate until 1976.

42. Virginia Heinlein, taped interview with Leon Stover, Tape 3, Side A (1988), 12 of transcript.

43. RAH, letter to Lurton Blassingame, 03/09/56.

44. In Heinlein's file for *Citizen of the Galaxy* there are two story outlines of "Notes for a Boys' Novel," one that uses the *Arabian Nights* background and another, "Notes for a Novel," that explores the tramp commercial spaceship family. Heinlein occasionally did combine two or more story ideas into a single book.

45. Stanley I. Greenspan and Stuart G. Shanker, *The First Idea: How Symbols, Language, and Intelligence Evolved from our Primate Ancestors to Modern Humans.* (Cambridge, Mass.: Perseus/Da Capo Press, 2004): 82. Greenspan and Shanker summarize the extended life stages of the Eriksons in seventeen stages, of which this young adulthood stage is "Stage 12—Stabilizing a Separate Sense of the Self":

> The standards of one's caregivers . . . are not simply their values and judgments, but, through their good offices, the history of their culture as well as one's own—that is, one's heritage. There is . . . greater independence from daily reliance on one's nuclear family, greater investment in the future . . . and greater ability to carry one's past inside oneself as part of a growing sense of self and internal standard.

46. Author's notes of oral conversation with Virginia Heinlein, February 26? 2000.

47. RAH, letter to Robert Cornog, 01/16/57.

48. RAH, letter to Robert Cornog, 01/16/57.

49. Scribner offered to pay part of the expenses of this trip, so he could combine it with a taping of Ruth Harshaw's *Carnival of Books* radio program on *Time for the Stars,* and they could write it off as publicity (Doubleday picked up the remainder of the expenses), but Heinlein was leery of becoming indebted to Scribner for favors and declined the offer.

50. Curiously, literary critic Edmund Wilson had disparaged H. P. Lovecraft in *The New Yorker* magazine in November 1945.

51. Gary Westfahl argues, in *The Mechanics of Wonder: The Creation of the Idea of Science Fiction* (Liverpool, UK: Liverpool University Press, 1998) that Campbell's theorization of science fiction, although it is usually presented in *distinction* to Gernsback's, was actually a *development* of Gernsback's theorization, and that Gernsback's theorization constituted an inciting poetics of science fiction. Later scholarship—see, e.g., Ashley, Michael and Robert A. W. Lowndes, *The Gernsback Days: A Study of the Evolution of Modern Science Fiction from 1911 to 1936* (Holicong, Penn.: Wildside Press, 2004)—suggests that the editorship of David Lasser of Gernsback's *Wonder Stories* represented an important intermediate stage between Gernsback and Campbell. Lasser is not mentioned in Westfahl's book.

    This matter of the theorization of science fiction and Heinlein's pivotal role in the process was taken up in a conference paper by the author for the Science Fiction Area of the Popular Culture Association joint annual meeting with the American Culture Association in 2011, "The Role of Robert Heinlein in the Theorization of Science Fiction" and published in *The Heinlein Journal*, No. 23 (July 2013). Heinlein's was the first systematic attempt to theorize science fiction, and his two essays are at the root of all modern SF criticism through Joanna Russ's (1937–2011) seminal 1975 paper, "Towards an Aesthetic of Science Fiction," which repeated Heinlein's argument, point by point *but without mentioning Heinlein's name,* so that Heinlein's pivotal role in the theorization of SF has been erased from academic SF critical theory.

52. The two books cited as the start of formal science-fiction criticism in the authoritative four-part study and review of science-fiction criticism by Arthur B. Evans, Gary Westfahl, Donald H. Hassler, and Veronica Hollinger, "A History of Science Fiction Criticism," *Science Fiction Studies,* no. 78, vol. 26, part 2 (July 1999).

53. RAH, letter to Ruth Robinson, 03/12/55.

54. RAH, "Science Fiction: Its Nature, Faults, and Virtues" (1957) published in Basil Davenport, ed., *The Science Fiction Novel: Imagination and Social Criticism* (Advent: Publishers, 1959).

55. Alice Dalgliesh, letter to RAH, 01/18/57.

56. The transcript of Heinlein's remarks about *The Puppet Masters* was not included in *The Science Fiction Novel,* but his notes for this session were preserved in the lecture's Opus file in the RAH Archive, UC Santa Cruz. After setting the scene—"house unfinished, law suit prevented financing, much in debt—sheetrock over

boxes while G painted 4 coats—necessary to turn out some copy I could sell and use the advance—tired out and worried"—Heinlein gave a rare view of his opinion of the novel (rare, because as a rule Heinlein refused to discuss his own work):

> My prime purpose was to turn out a piece of entertaining fiction, a story that would leave the reader feeling that he had had his money's worth—I have a holy horror of cheating the cash customer. So I tried very hard. I am happy to say that it has been well received—serial sale, trade book, book club, pocket book, and has been translated into nine foreign languages. It is still making money—but my motivation at the time was a pressing need for a check to pay income tax and construction bills.
>
> What do I think is good, or bad, about *The Puppet Masters*? It has a tired plot and was hastily written; its literary merit is negligible. I strove hard to make characterization, scene, and incident have a feeling of reality and to entertain while doing so; the mail I have received seems to indicate that I succeeded.
>
> These virtues and defects are those of the professional juggler and clown, the entertainer—which is what I think a fictioneer should be first of all. If the book has any permanent merit it must lie in its theme, which is a thinly-disguised allegory, a diatribe against totalitarianism in all its forms. Each writer has his personal philosophy; included in mine is an intense love of personal freedom and an almost religious respect for the dignity of the individual—I despise anything which reduces these two and have, in many stories, explored the attendant problems. The trick in sermonizing through fiction is not to let your sermon get in the way of the story, to cause the story to make your point for you. Apparently I succeeded well enough in *The Puppet Masters* not to annoy most readers, so, despite the novel's obvious literary faults, I am reasonably content with it.

57. RAH, letter to A. P. White, 03/27/57.
58. RAH, letter to Alice Dalgliesh, 03/16/57.
59. RAH, letter to Dr. Hans Wynberg, 03/24/57.
60. Blish's argument is highly detailed and with many parts, but his thesis is stated early on in "The Door into Heinlein" (*SF Forum* I:1, March 1957, 38–40): "To the unskilled writer . . . first person is a trap. It becomes an exercise in autobiography; that constantly recurring word 'I' irresistibly leads the writer back to himself, and away from the kind of narrator the story being told needs." Blish

maintains this is particularly true of *The Door into Summer,* which "proved to be so closely tied to the problem of viewpoint that its failure to solve the problem killed the story." Since *The Door into Summer* is one of Heinlein's most beloved stories, it is difficult to understand what Blish means by the first-person narrator "killing" the story.

61. RAH, letter to Lester del Rey, 04/15/57.

62. RAH, letter to Lester del Rey, 04/15/57.

63. RAH, letter to Lester del Rey, 04/15/57.

64. This list of first names designates editors of current science-fiction magazines: Horace [Gold—*Galaxy*], Tony [Boucher—*F&SF*], Larry [Shaw—*Infinity* and *SF Adventures*], John [Campbell—*Astounding*], Bob [Mills—*F&SF* and *Venture*].

65. RAH, letter to Lester del Rey, 04/15/57.

66. John W. Campbell, Jr., letter to RAH, 04/05/57.

67. RAH, letter to John W. Campbell, Jr., 05/17/57.

68. John W. Campbell, Jr., letter to RAH, 05/22/57.

69. RAH, letter to John W. Campbell, Jr., 06/12/57. The text serialized in *Astounding* was, for this reason, slightly different (and a few words longer than) the text published in hardcover.

70. Alice Dalgliesh, letter to RAH, 04/25/57.

71. RAH, letter to Alice Dalgliesh, 04/29/57.

72. RAH, letter to Lurton Blassingame, 05/02/57.

73. Handwritten draft and cards with notes preserved in the manuscript file for *Citizen of the Galaxy* in the RAH Archive, UC Santa Cruz.

74. RAH, letter to Lurton Blassingame, 05/02/57.

75. RAH, letter to Lurton Blassingame, 05/17/57.

76. RAH, letter to Lurton Blassingame, 05/02/57.

77. RAH, letter to Alice Dalgliesh, 05/03/57.

78. Virginia Heinlein, IM with the author, 06/14/02.

79. Ben Bova, telephonic interview with RAH, 06/29/79. Although this interview was never published in *Omni,* for what reasons Mr. Bova was unable to recall, the transcript, lightly hand edited by Heinlein, is published in the Virginia Edition, vol. xxxvii, *Nonfiction 1.*

80. The title of *Have Space Suit—Will Travel* was not given after the Western television show that was airing then, *Have Gun—Will Travel,* but on an old ad series that had appeared in *Variety* years before, itself after a common theatrical advertisement of the Vaudeville era—"Have Tux, Will Travel" (also, for much the same reasons, the title of Bob Hope's 1954 autobiography, which was ghost-written by sports journalist Pete Martin).

81. Virginia Heinlein, taped interview with the author, Tape 9, Side A.

82. Virginia Heinlein, taped interview with Leon Stover, Tape 3, Side A.

83. RAH, letter to Lurton Blassingame, 09/03/57.

11. Going Off a Bit (pages 145–157)

1. RAH, letter to Bud Scoles, 10/09/57.

2. RAH, letter to Bud Scoles, 10/09/57.

3. RAH, letter to Bud Scoles, 10/09/57.

4. RAH, letter to W. A. P. White, 10/25/57.

5. Telegram, Margaret Sanger to Robert and Virginia Heinlein on board the S.S. *President Monroe*, 11/20/57.

6. Virginia Heinlein, taped interview with the author, Tape 2, Side B.

7. Virginia Heinlein, taped interview with the author, Tape 2, Side B.

8. RAH, letter to Alice Dalgliesh, 12/24/57.

9. RAH, letter to Alice Dalgliesh, 12/24/57.

10. In October 1957 a civil war broke out in Indonesia as a Sumatra-based military coup attempted to reform the Sukarno "Guided Democracy" reforms instituted in February and March 1957 under the slogan "nationalism—religion—communism," effectively bringing to an end a period of Western-style democracy in Indonesia. In December 1957 the Dutch were leaving Indonesia.

11. RAH, letter to Alice Dalgliesh, 12/24/57.

12. RAH, letter to Lurton Blassingame, 12/23/57.

13. Virginia Heinlein, letter to the author, 07/27/00.

14. Virginia Heinlein, letter to the author, 10/17/99.

15. Virginia Heinlein, taped interview with the author, Tape 2, Side B.

16. Virginia Heinlein, taped interview with the author, Tape 2, Side B (February 27? 2000). Mrs. Heinlein also mentioned that the Arabic inscriptions inlaid in the walls of the Taj look to her unpleasantly like graffiti.

17. Both quotations are from RAH, letter to Bjo Trimble, 11/21/61.

18. Anecdote told by Cal Laning to Leon Stover. Leon Stover, letter to Virginia Heinlein, 06/13/89.

19. Virginia Heinlein, taped interview with the author, Tape 9, Side A.

20. RAH, letter to Daniel F. Galouye, 10/02/57.

21. Ackerman maintained he had never received Heinlein's Hugo Award trophy and could not understand why Heinlein was angry at him. In "Through Time and Space with Forry Ackerman," part 4, *Mimosa*, 16-19 at 17 (and elsewhere), Ackerman published an elaborate explanation that centered on the factoid that the Award statuettes (which are often referred to as simply "the Hugos") were not ready at the time of the convention, so none were given out there.

This "explanation" is puzzling on many levels, because there are a number of pictures taken at the convention (NyCon II in 1956) of the winners with their Hugos. There is no mention of the award statuettes not being ready in any account of NYCon II, including convention chairman Dave Kyle's own, though he does discuss the fact that the hand-tooled trophies made for the first Awards could not be obtained, and they made the Hugo that year out of a car's hood ornament with wooden backing. The Hugos *were* ready at the convention, though no one seems able to recall what happened with the Best Novel Hugo.

This was only the third time Hugo Awards had been given out, and many of the traditions now associated with the Awards had not yet been developed. For example, although the Hugos are now given out the year following publication, the Locus Index to SF Awards shows the eligibility years for the 1956 Hugos as 1955–1956. It has also become customary for an author who cannot be present to accept his award to designate a proxy to receive it, but in any case, Heinlein did not know *Double Star* had even been nominated.

In the absence of facts, the most charitable speculation could be that, perhaps, Toastmaster Robert Bloch announced the award without handing off the Hugo, and it was inadvertently stored with the convention's effects until someone got around to shipping it out—after being prompted, possibly by this incident between Heinlein and Kornbluth—which leaves only the question of why Kornbluth would say such a thing in the first place.

In e-mail discussion about the biography with editor David Hartwell, and then with the author, Robert Silverberg (who has a photograph of himself taken at NyCon II with the Hugo) said that he was sitting next to Kornbluth during an early round of balloting for the Hugo, and Kornbluth told him he was anxious for his 1955 novel, *Not This August* to win. Silverberg thinks it quite likely that he was severely disappointed when he did not. (e-mail Robert Silverberg to David Hartwell, 02/18/14; e-mail Robert Silverberg to the author, 02/21/14)

So there is a possible motive. Kornbluth and Ackerman also had a long history of antagonism: perhaps Kornbluth was simply taking the opportunity to create trouble for both Heinlein *and* Ackerman.

22. Heinlein did not record the dates of these trips or the reason for the side trip to Washington, D.C.

23. RAH, letter to Lurton Blassingame, 06/18/58.

24. Ed Emshwiller, letter to RAH, 04/29/59.

25. RAH, letter to Lurton Blassingame, 02/23/55.

26. Searching for a reason that Heinlein might have stalled on *Stranger*, and then was able to resume, is a highly problematical project. Since the development Heinlein did write was to drop his journalist, Ben Caxton, out of the narrative,

the choice of viewpoint character seems significant. Of all the literary models Heinlein might have taken for the journalist-reporting-on-a-phenomenon (e.g., Upton Sinclair's *What Didymus Did*, London, 1954, *It Happened to Didymus*, U.S. 1958, has been characterized as a projection of a book of the Apocrypha into modern Hollywood), probably the strongest was Olaf Stapledon's 1935 *Odd John*, a book that recurs frequently in his correspondence. In this storytelling model, the subject abuses and tricks the reporter, using his credulity or amiability for his own ends. This would have implied a much greater degree of crafty self-awareness than Valentine Michael Smith can exhibit in the early part of the story. Keeping the reporter would have implied a quite different kind of story than Heinlein had in mind. The solution he eventually arrived at was to write Ben Caxton out of the story and give Valentine Michael Smith a satisfactorily crafty foil, Jubal Harshaw—a character, recall, which Heinlein developed out of Kettle Belly Baldwin of "Gulf"—the executive secretary for an organization of activist supermen—and gave the name of a *radio* journalist of whom he highly approved, Ruth Harshaw. By the end of *Stranger,* this is the role Jubal Harshaw assumes.

27. If Robert Heinlein was not a morning person, Ginny was just the opposite, repulsively cheery and energetic in the early mornings—when the house was quiet and she could develop perfect concentration—needing only a jolt of sugar in the form of orange juice to get herself going.

28. RAH, letter to Lurton Blassingame, 04/05/58.

29. Virginia Heinlein, taped interview with the author, Tape 9, Side A.

30. The picture Heinlein gives of this process, in his introduction in *Expanded Universe* to "Who are the Heirs of Patrick Henry," is that the ad was generated immediately on reading the SANE ad; however, a letter written that day to Lurton Blassingame (April 5, 1958), shows that although Ginny has already suggested a Patrick Henry campaign, Heinlein is at a loss as to how to proceed and is looking for an already-existing committee or political group to join.

    But the Heinleins's ad was published on April 12 and therefore cannot have been placed with the *Gazette-Telegraph* later than April 11, and is more likely to have been placed on April 10. The reaction may not have been instantaneous, but it was nevertheless very rapid.

31. The entire text of the Patrick Henry ad is contained in Heinlein's *Expanded Universe* collection, which is still available in paperback, but also published intact in the Virginia Edition vol. xxxi.

32. Virginia Heinlein, taped interview with the author, Tape 9, Side B (March 1? 2000).

33. RAH, letter to H. L. Gold, 05/06/58.

34. Lurton Blassingame, letter to RAH, 04/17/58.

35. RAH, letter to Alice Dalgliesh, 04/29/58.

36. In his June 18, 1958, letter to Lurton Blassingame, Heinlein says, "We were convinced of this [the campaign was a failure] a month ago, from the poor response. But we tried to keep going a while longer and searched frantically for some way to make ourselves effective because of two letters, one from Admiral Strauss just before he resigned as chairman of AEC and one from Dr. Teller." Mid-May 1958 would be about four weeks after the start of the Patrick Henry Campaign.

37. Quoted in RAH, letter to Lurton Blassingame, 06/18/58.

38. Quoted in RAH, letter to Rex and Kathleen Heinlein, 05/17/58. General Alfred Gruenther was the American Supreme Allied Commander in Europe from 1953–1956.

39. Hermann Deutsch column in the *New Orleans Item* (May 8, 1958).

40. RAH, letter to Kathleen and Rex Heinlein, 05/17/58. Heinlein typically kept his itineraries and speaking schedules when traveling in this way, but for reasons unknown no such record was found in the RAH Archive, UC Santa Cruz among the "Patrick Henry Campaign" papers. It is not impossible that those records were destroyed rather than moved from Colorado Springs to Santa Cruz—but similar records from 1964 were preserved. Lacking such detailed records, it is not possible to reconstruct his out-of-town trips for speaking engagements, except as they are mentioned in other sources, such as letters.

41. RAH, letter to Lurton Blassingame, 06/18/58b. He was also pleased with the response of Truman Talley at Signet.

42. RAH, letter to Lurton Blassingame, 06/18/56b.

43. RAH, letter to Lurton Blassingame, 06/18/58b.

44. RAH, letter to Alice Dalgliesh, 04/24/58.

45. The quotes are taken from two undated notecards apparently written contemporaneously with panels at the "Astro Symp. Denver 58." The symposium took place at the end of May 1958, but the dates are not clear from Heinlein's mentions in letters, and this specific symposium was not found in records searches.

46. RAH, letter to Lurton Blassingame, 04/26/58.

47. To Lurton Blassingame Heinlein wrote a fuller explanation:

Our personal mailing list includes, of course, many people in the writing and publishing business and many people who are mutual acquaintances of yours and mine. Let me tell you of some of them.

Shining out like the names of Rodger Young are yours, Victor Weybright, Mac Talley, and Marty Greenberg. Also Fredric Brown, Philip José

Farmer, Erik Fennel, Margo Fischer, Ruth Harshaw, Earl Kemp, Alan E. Nourse, Thomas N. Scortia, Harry Stine, and Jack Williamson. A very few of those names you may not recognize but they are all connected with the writing business.

But that is our corporal's guard—fourteen people. Of the couple of hundred writers and editors whom I know most refused by failing to answer even the follow up; the rest refused overtly. Stanley Mullen simply ignored it (and this case is personally very distressing to me). Lew Tilley signed and contributed to the "Sane Nuclear Policy" ad—and when I asked Lew about it, I learned (for the first time in years of knowing him) that he is a pacifist and regards people like myself with contempt—how far can hypocrisy go? He said to me, "Bob, I knew you were a reactionary but I preferred to ignore it." Ned Brown answered me by sending it back unsigned with no comment. Horace Gold jittered in seven different directions and asked me *please* to drop the subject—this I could forgive, as I know that Horace is a sick man . . . but I dropped Horace along with the subject. Tony Boucher and J. Francis McComas both failed to answer personal letters (something neither has ever done in the past) and this I expected, for each is pink as hell, tending toward pacifism, and strongly inclined to the anti-anti-Communist attitude—you know; the man who can forgive Alger Hiss but never Whittaker Chambers. John W. Campbell wrote a long letter agreeing that atomic tests should continue but not signing the P. H. letter—instead he expounded a complex theory about how democracies were innately incapable of making correct decisions. (He may be right but it's the only game in town; I had to file him under "Fence Straddlers.")

Robert Bloch turned out to be a pacifist. Miss Dalgliesh wrote me a confused letter, agreeing with me on every important point, but firmly refusing to sign a P. H. pledge—privately, I think the old gal is scared silly of World War III and hopes that she can close her eyes and have it go away. Jinny Fowler ignored it . . . Charles Scribner himself simply ignored it—maybe he thinks he is God but I think that if I were a publisher and I got a letter from one of my writers, whose books had earned my firm a profit in excess of a hundred thousand dollars, I would at least grant him the courtesy of an answer. The hell with him—I'm sorry to find it necessary to do business with Scribner's.

I did get a good solid pleasing answer from one of the editors of the *SatEvePost* and if you have been reading their editorials, you know that they are as solid on this as you are or I myself. Maybe I will again put most of my effort into trying to write for the *Post,* let Marty Greenberg have the trade book, and leave pocketbook with Mac Talley. I might not make much money with that routine but at least I would have the satisfaction of doing business with patriots.

What do you know of the political bias of the trade-book houses? Harper's I know is pinko; I wouldn't be caught dead in the place. But that is the only one I know about—and there is no point in jumping from the frying pan into the fire.

I must shut up; this letter is morbid. (RAH, letter to Lurton Blassingame, 06/18/58.)

48. RAH, letter to Lurton Blassingame, 06/18/58.
49. RAH, letter to Hermann Deutsch, 07/09/59.

12. Waiting Out the End (pages 158–177)

1. RAH, letter to Mrs. Omer E. Warneke, 06/19/58.
2. RAH, letter to Erle Korshak and T. E. Dikty, DBA Shasta, 06/17/58.
3. Dikty later told Heinlein he had not been formally partnered with Korshak since 1956. T. E. Dikty, letter to RAH, 01/14/59.
4. RAH, letter to T. E. Dikty and Erle Korshak, 06/17/58.
5. Heinlein is probably referring to White House Chief of Staff Sherman Adams (1899–1986). Adams was forced to resign in 1958 in a scandal over a bribe of a vicuña coat and an oriental carpet from a Boston textile manufacturer who was being investigated by the Federal Trade Commission.
6. RAH, letter to Hermann Deutsch, 07/09/58.
7. RAH, letter to Hermann Deutsch, 07/09/58.
8. RAH, letter to Alice Dalgliesh, 04/28/58.
9. RAH, letter to Hermann Deutsch, 07/09/58.
10. "I'm My Own Grandpa" was a novelty song written by Dwight Latham and Moe Jaffe and performed by Lonzo & Oscar in 1947. The gimmick of this song was that by a bizarre and unlikely combination of marriages a man becomes stepfather to his own stepmother—thus his own [step]grandfather.
11. Ray Russell, *Playboy* executive editor, letter to Lurton Blassingame, 07/24/58.
12. RAH, letter to Marty Greenberg, 05/04/59. The book had been issued in 1958, though Gnome did not include any copyright information.
13. RAH, Accession Notes for *Podkayne of Mars,* 11/05/68.
14. RAH, letter to Larry Heinlein, 10/26/58.

15. Virginia Heinlein, letter to the author, 11/07/99. In other letters, Mrs. Heinlein explains the context of her decision to study Russian:

> We were in a period of appeasement of the Russians. . . . a thing neither of us wanted to see.
>
> It further affected our actions—I took classes in the Russian language, Robert turned away from it, and wrote . . . He despaired of showing his friends the folly of appeasement.

Virginia Heinlein, letter to the author, 03/12/00. In an e-mail to Dr. Robert James, 09/05/02, she explained that she was studying Russian after the failure of the Patrick Henry campaign, ". . . *Starship Troopers* . . . was written at a fever pitch, following the abortive lack of success of our Patrick Henry business . . . At that time, I was studying Russian, and he surprised me by proposing a trip to the USSR."

The failure of the Patrick Henry campaign was probably only the final incident of a sequence that included the abortive Hungarian Revolution in 1956 and Sputnik in October 1957. Heinlein expressed the opinion that the Eisenhower administration's failures to take action to contain what looked like an unstoppable momentum for Nikita Khruschev's USSR would result in the United States effectively surrendering its sovereignty within the foreseeable, near-term future. Ginny did not record her specific reasons for taking up Russian, but it is easy to guess that she wanted to be prepared for Russian hegemony during her lifetime.

Looking backward through knowledge of what actually did happen in the next several years, this position, very understandable at the time, is no longer obvious to us. It was the best prediction that could be made at the time, given the data available to the Heinleins in 1958.

16. The Air Force Academy north of Colorado Springs had just begun operations in August 1958; the first graduating class, the class of 1959, had been training at Lowry Air Force Base at Denver, Colorado, since the facility at Colorado Springs was not yet finished when they were sworn in.

17. Lurton Blassingame, letter to "Mr. Siegel" of the Fender law offices, 06/29/59.

18. Payne (1912–89) reported that when he had first approached Universal for a *Puppet Masters* film in 1953,

> The head of the studio listened attentively, was very favorably inclined, and then read the book. There was silence for several days, and I then got a message that he was letting his wife read the book. A week passed, and

then, in a meeting with him, I got this reaction. It was an engrossing piece of material, he was unable to put it down, his wife read it, and was unable to sleep for several nights. This equated to the fact that the picture was too fearsome to make. It was unfair to scare an audience that much.

Of course, it is funny, but it is ordinary thinking in this strange racket. It made me sure, however, that I was right about the material.

Payne had also optioned Alfred Bester's *The Demolished Man* and Cyril Korn-bluth's *Not This August*, which he intended to package together with *The Puppet Masters* for film (John Payne, letter to RAH, 07/23/59).

The option offer for *The Puppet Masters* was still on the table when *The Brain Eaters* was released; Payne later suggested reopening the negotiations when the piracy matter was settled, after floating a counter-offer through a third party. Lurton Blassingame, letter to RAH, 06/30/59. The matter is covered in greater detail in the 1959 portion of this biography.

19. Lawrence Lyle Heinlein's promotion was not announced publically until May 1959—see LLH telegram to RAH, 05/19/59—but backdated to November 1958. It may well have been a family news item at the time *Starship Troopers* was being planned.

20. RAH, letter to Bud [Lawrence Lewis] Heinlein, 10/29/59.

21. Undated index card note in the *Starship Troopers* manuscript file, RAH Archive, UC Santa Cruz.

22. From the second series of *Barrack-Room Ballads*. The quotation of "Danny Deever" in the book may be a kind of metaleptic reference, as "Danny Deever" is in the first series of *Barrack-Room Ballads* (1892).

23. Edward Bellamy, *Looking Backward, 2000–1887* (1888). Boston: Houghton Mifflin Company (1926 Riverside Library edition with introduction by Heywood Broun), 189.

24. RAH, letter to Laurie A. MacDonald, 10/14/68.

25. RAH, letter to Ted Sturgeon, 03/05/62.

26. RAH, letter to Alice Dalgliesh, 02/03/59, marked "Never Sent."

27. RAH, letter to Judith Merril, 11/01/67, marked "Never Sent."

28. RAH, letter to Lt. Sandra Fulton, 08/07/65.

29. It is possible that Heinlein started with the "Shoulder the Sky" title as a direct reaction to Ayn Rand's *Atlas Shrugged,* which had been published in 1957.

30. When Heinlein finished the manuscript for what was still at that point *Sky Soldier,* he told Blassingame that he anticipated trouble with Dalgliesh but would not change the book to suit her (RAH, letter to Lurton Blassingame, 11/22/58). When he finally did send the manuscript to Dalgliesh, he notified Blassingame, saying he might as well "get the row over with." RAH, letter to Lurton Blassingame,

01/10/59; and in Virginia Heinlein, taped interview with Leon Stover, Tape 3, Side A, 14 of transcript in RAH Archive, UC Santa Cruz: "We both knew she wasn't going to like it, right from the scratch—and it was no great surprise to us when she advised him to put it on the shelf for a year and then redo it."

31. RAH, letter to Alice Dalgliesh, 02/03/59.

32. Undated three-by-five index card in Virginia Heinlein's hand inserted into RAH's file copy of *Starship Troopers*.

33. Michael Garrett, "Johnny Rico's Nationality," *The Heinlein Journal*, No. 5 (July 1999).

34. RAH, letter to Lurton Blassingame, 01/02/59. In Heinlein's draft Answers to Interrogatories in the *Puppet Masters* plagiarism suit against Roger Corman and *The Brain Eaters*, dated 10/13/60, he says bluntly: "So many of the details are essentially like those in the book that there can be no question of co-incidence; this is a deliberate piracy."

35. RAH, letter to Lurton Blassingame, 01/10/59.

36. RAH, letter to Lurton Blassingame, 01/10/59.

37. Lurton Blassingame, letter to RAH, 01/21/59.

38. Alice Dalgliesh, letter to RAH, 02/11/59.

39. RAH, letter to Lurton Blassingame, 01/22/59.

40. The original letter from Miss Dalgliesh to RAH seems not to have been preserved, but there are enough remarks about it by Heinlein in other correspondence to reconstruct, at least partially, its contents. Virginia Heinlein mentioned in an editorial note in *Grumbles from the Grave* that Dalgliesh had suggested it be marketed as an adult serial or else put away for a while.

    Starship Troopers was clearly intended from the start for Heinlein's juvenile audience, and based, he said, on his theory throughout the writing of the series, that "intelligent youngsters are in fact more interested in weighty matters than their parents usually are." Once again, he had centered the story in a young man crossing from adolescence into adulthood, coming to know his values from the inside-out, so it was following the thematic lines of his last several juveniles. But by the time the book was finished (and even before it was submitted to Scribner), he conceded that it was not a juvenile in the usual sense of the term. (Both remarks, RAH, letter to Lurton Blassingame, 01/10/59.) Indeed, it is difficult to understand how the first chapter, with its (by the standards of children's literature in 1959) hyperviolence could be marketed at all to teenagers of the duck-and-cover generation—not that *they* would not accept it, but the librarians who made up what Dalgliesh thought was the major segment of purchasers of Heinlein's juveniles would not.

    The opinion of Alice Dalgliesh and the entire editorial board of Scribner—though based on what turned out a false premise (that the "boys do not want that [social commentary]")—was only partly the kind of personal squeamishness to which Heinlein had objected over and over in the editorial process for his last several books for Scribner; it was also at least partly a business decision—and one which Heinlein probably should have been pragmatically able to anticipate.

41. Walter I. Bradbury, letter to Lurton Blassingame, 02/24/59.

42. RAH, letter to Betty Jane Babb, 02/04/59.

43. RAH, letter to Alice Dalgliesh, 02/17/59.

44. RAH, letter to "George," 02/03/59. I have not been able to identify this person in historical records.

45. George McM, letter to RAH, 02/10/59.

46. Alfred Bester, letter to RAH, undated except "Monday."

47. RAH, letter to Alfred Bester, 04/03/59.

48. RAH, letter to Lurton Blassingame, 04/05/59.

49. Tom Swicegood, letter to RAH, 01/24/59.

50. Information from Tim Kyger by e-mail, 10/02/06.

51. RAH, letter to Tom Swicegood, 02/21/59. A *"series bible"* is the document that first sells the television series to a production company and explains the basic concept, as well as all the details a writer would find necessary to work on the show: background, characters, ongoing storylines, if any. Series bibles also typically contain brief outlines of several of the early episodes.

52. *Crater Base One* series bible, page 2, preserved in the RAH Archive, UC Santa Cruz. Heinlein's letters to Swicegood are published in the Virginia Edition, vol. xlv, *Screenplays 2*.

53. RAH, letter to Tom Swicegood, 02/21/59.

54. RAH, letter to Tom Swicegood, 02/28/59.

55. Tom Swicegood, letter to RAH, 01/24/59.

56. RAH, letter to Tom Swicegood, 02/21/59.

57. Tom Swicegood, letter to RAH, 03/06/59.

58. RAH, letter to Tom Swicegood, 03/12/59.

59. *The Menace from Earth* collection contained "The Year of the Jackpot," "By His Bootstraps," "Columbus Was a Dope," "The Menace from Earth," "Sky Lift," "Goldfish Bowl," "Project Nightmare," and "Water Is for Washing."

60. Misc index card in RAH's file, probably organizing memoirs in the mid-1970s.

61. RAH, letter to Tom Swicegood, 03/11/59.

62. Harold A. Fendler, letter to Lurton Blassingame, 04/24/59. The Fendler & Lerner law firm no longer exists.

63. RAH, letter to Lurton Blassingame, 07/28/59. Curiously, a complete collected works existed in a Russian language edition long before the Virginia Edition in the original English.

64. RAH, letter to Lurton Blassingame, 07/28/59.

65. The contents of *Unpleasant Profession* were: "The Unpleasant Profession of Jonathan Hoag," "The Man Who Traveled in Elephants," " 'All You Zombies—,' " "They," "Our Fair City," and " '—And He Built a Crooked House.' " Interestingly, " '—And He Built a Crooked House' " was long considered by Heinlein and others such as A. P. White a Future History story rather than a fantasy per se. It was in fact the first story in the first volume Erle Korshak outlined as Shasta's proposal for the Future History book series in a letter to Heinlein on 12/04/48.

66. Holographic letter, unaddressed, by Virginia Heinlein, 06/23/59.

67. RAH, letter to Lurton Blassingame, 07/28/59.

68. See, e.g., Virginia Heinlein, taped inverview with Leon Stover (1987) Tape 1, Side A.

69. Virginia Heinlein, letter to the author, 03/12/00.

70. Tom Swicegood, letter to RAH, 04/10/59.

71. Heinlein's script for "Nothing Ever Happens . . ." is published in the Virginia Edition, vol. xlv, *Screenplays 2,* along with the full critical and analytic correspondence referenced in the text. While Swicegood was never specific about what "requirements for a television show" were absent from Heinlein's script, two features of the script do suggest themselves: First, there are no minor climaxes for commercial breaks at natural places in the story (a feature that television writers learn to craft the story around); and, second, the entire last act, the earthquake and aftermath, are unusually poor in action visuals. Heinlein's last act is written as a succession of talking heads.

    Having no substantive experience at all of television, it is not surprising that Heinlein would be an inexperienced television writer.

72. Tom Swicegood, letter to RAH, 07/31/59.

73. Tom Swicegood, letter to RAH, 06/23/59. Swicegood's "Moonquake" script was apparently returned to him, as it was not found in the RAH Archive, UC Santa Cruz. Heinlein marked up some of Swicegood's changes in pencil on his own script, but the version of Heinlein's script published in the Virginia Edition, vol. xlv, *Screenplays 2,* is restored to Heinlein's original.

74. RAH, letter to Jim Doherty, 07/24/59.

75. Tom Swicegood, letter to RAH, 07/31/59.

76. But *Men Into Space* did air thirty-seven of the thirty-eight episodes filmed and was later acclaimed the most accurate "hard" SF series ever to appear on television. The same review (Ed Uthman, IMDB user, 01/30/00; http://www.imdb.com /title/tt0052493/usercomments, accessed 05/25/11) credits the show for following the lead of Heinlein's *Destination Moon*. Heinlein never saw it.

77. Virginia Heinlein, taped interview with Leon Stover (1988), Tape 3, Side A, 14 of transcript.

78. See, e.g., RAH, letter to Lurton Blassingame, 09/16/60:

> Based on my own royalty records I conjecture that my books have netted
> for Mr. Scribner something between $50,000 and $100,000 (and grossed
> a great deal more). They have been absolutely certain money-from-home
> for his firm . . . and still are. Yet after years and years of a highly profitable
> association Mr. Scribner let me be "fired" with less ceremony than he would
> use in firing his office boy . . . not a word out of him, not even a hint that
> he gave a damn whether I stayed with them or not. I submit that this is
> rudeness, unpardonable in view of the long association.

79. Walter J. Minton, published letter to *Publisher's Weekly,* copy cut off, but read-
able part is 3/4/__. *PW* has not responded to a request to help identify the letter.

80. William McMorris, letter to RAH, 04/10/59.

81. The precise timing of this final choice was not preserved in the correspondence;
but on August 10, 1959, McMorris suggested *The Capsule Troopers,* to which
Heinlein objected that "capsule" implies something miniature. By an August 30,
1959, letter from Heinlein to Lurton Blassingame the title was changed again to
one of his working titles, *Shoulder the Sky*—a title McMorris rejected on September 3 as having previously been used. Some time that September, in a fax
whose date-stamp is partly illegible, but during the period Heinlein was staying
at the Shelbourne Hotel, McMorris offered two titles acceptable to Putnam's
Sales and Promotions director (unnamed): *Soldier of the Stars* or *Starship Troopers.* The book is not referred to in correspondence after this presumably late-
September facsimile, and the book was issued just a few weeks later as *Starship
Troopers.* Perhaps Heinlein telephoned his assent.

82. William McMorris, letter to RAH, 04/28/59.

83. John Payne, letter to RAH, 07/23/59.

84. John Payne, letter to RAH, 07/23/59.

85. Irwin O. Spiegel, Esq., letter to Lurton Blassingame, 07/01/59.

86. John Payne, letter to RAH, 08/04/59.

87. Daniel F. Galouye (1920–76) was a New Orleans native who had been seriously
and permanently injured as a Navy test pilot in World War II (in a letter to the
author, 04/06/00, Virginia Heinlein said he "went through the firewall of an airplane he was driving"). A newspaperman, Galouye was a well-regarded, though
minor, writer of science fiction starting in the 1950s. His first novel, *Dark Universe*
(1961), was nominated for a Hugo Award. His 1963 novel *Simulacrum 3* was the
basis for a German television miniseries directed by Rainer Werner Fassbinder in
1973, *Welt am Draht* (*World on a Wire*) and for the 1999 film *The Thirteenth Floor.*

88. RAH, letter to Hermann Deutsch, 04/03/60.

89. Eckard V. Toy, "The Right Side of the 1960s: The Origins of the John Birch Society in the Pacific Northwest," *Oregon Historical Quarterly* (Summer 2004).

90. Later, in a letter to Bjo Trimble, 02/17/64, Heinlein remarked: ". . . happens that Bob Welch of the John Birchites is one helluva good boy to get drunk with—as I have with him, more than once—and I think Bob is cracked."

91. The association started off well enough, with Welch circulating drafts of suggested letters to their representatives in the House and Senate, but the Heinleins very soon discovered that Welch would not tolerate any kind of deviation from his own odd take on the political situation—and his take did not coincide with either of theirs. He would not even listen to divergent input. *American Opinion* very rapidly lost what edge it had. A year later (1960), Heinlein wrote, ". . . we both feel that he has been getting steadily worse, losing his judgment, this past year, and we are not renewing our subscription." This kind of "fascist organization" was not something they wanted to be associated with, so they asked that their names be removed from the membership rolls. Robert was upset enough that he gave Ginny a rare dressing-down about it: "He didn't want any part of it. . . . It was the wrong kind of anti-Communist organization." Virginia Heinlein, taped interview with the author, "Misc Notes (9/4–9/8/01)," Tape A, Side A.

 Of Welch and McCarthy, Heinlein said they were both best judged by the enemies they made:

 > It is a shocking commentary on the state of the Republic that the job of weeding Communist traitors out of our public life should have gone by default to these two men, each of questionable judgment, while responsible major public officials, from presidents on down, have almost unanimously ignored the problem and swept it under the rug (as with Roosevelt and Truman) or gave it lip service and then did nothing about it, as with Eisenhower.
 >
 > . . . . I think Bob Welch's methods are puerile and I do not find it worthwhile to support him. But if I am ever forced to a choice between the John Birch Society and its enemies, I know which side of the barricades I belong on. I'll be on the same side the John Birch Society is on—because my enemies are on the other side.

 RAH, letter to Dorothea Faulkner, 07/27/61.

92. RAH, letter to Fraternity Snoqualmie, 09/16/59.

93. Lurton Blassingame, letter to RAH, 02/26/59.

94. Lawrence Lewis Heinlein.

95. October 23, 1959.

96. RAH, letter to Bud Heinlein, 12/03/59.

97. This period is detailed in chapter 30 of *Learning Curve,* the first volume of this biography, starting on 439.

98. RAH, letter to Bud Heinlein, 10/29/59.

99. Bud Heinlein, letter to RAH, 11/30/59.

100. Bud Heinlein, letter to RAH, 12/02/59.

101. It would be cumbersome to reference and cite the letters individually, but Virginia Heinlein summarized the entire sequence in a letter to Lawrence Lewis Heinlein (Bud), dated 12/03/59. In this letter she also mentions the alienation of Bud's mother, Alice, and Alice's subsequent attempt to find a construction job for Bud. Ginny referred specifically to "psychological instability." We would probably assume some sort of bipolar disorder now, or, even more disturbing, borderline personality disorder.

About a year later (01/07/61), Bud Heinlein seems to have come out of his emotional tailspin. He wrote a very apologetic letter, saying that the exchange should never have taken place, and that he was not sane when he wrote the letters. Going in for abdominal surgery for the second time in six months, Bud was not in good physical condition and felt an apology was necessary:

> "Debts are paid. Debts are always paid." [A quotation from Heinlein's *Citizen of the Galaxy* (1957)] I am trying to pay the moral debt I owe you, though you cannot know it. The financial one will be paid as soon as the medical load is off my back. I'm trying to pay the moral one by following your precepts—thinking of the girls and Donna before myself, trying to raise the kids to be the high-calibre individuals that they are capable of being.
>
> Bob, there is little more I can say. If, by chance, this business should be fatal, I must say that it has been my great privilege to know you and have your friendship and guidance thru most of my life. It is also my great sorrow that, thru my own stupidity and mental fuzziness, I threw away the friendship. If you can find it in your heart to forgive, I will be, to use a trite phrase, eternally grateful.

Although Lawrence Lewis Heinlein was still alive in 2011, he made no response to queries through family routes (i.e., by the late Bill Bacchus).

102. RAH, letter to Alice Heinlein Pemberton, 12/03/59.

103. RAH, letter to Bud Heinlein, 11/27/59.

104. RAH, letter to Gerry and Nan Crook, 11/23/59.

105. RAH, letter to Ray and Kitty Heinlein, 11/18/59.

106. Rose Elizabeth Heinlein, Heinlein's youngest sister, was thrown from a car Rex

was driving in 1926 and killed. The incident is detailed in chapter 5 of *Learning Curve,* the first volume of this biography, 72–73.

107. Much of the first volume of this biography returned over and over to Heinlein's relationship with his older brother, Rex Ivar Heinlein—his parents' all-too-obvious favorite.

108. RAH, letter to Ray and Kitty Heinlein, 11/18/59.

13. "My Own Stuff, My Own Way" (pages 178–189)

1. *The Kirkus Reviews,* October 1, 1959.
2. *The Kirkus Reviews,* October 5, 1959.
3. RAH, letter to William McMorris, 11/07/59.
4. Undated list of copies to be sent out in the RAH Archive, UC Santa Cruz. The list includes the inscriptions as well.
5. RAH, letter to William McMorris, 11/07/59.
6. The Marsh Gurney material is told in *Learning Curve* chapter 5, "Plebe Year," 67–68.
7. H. H. Holmes, "Science and Fantasy," *New York Herald Tribune* (November 8, 1959).
8. Theodore Cogswell, letter to RAH, 11/29/59.
9. RAH, letter to Alice Dalgliesh, 02/03/59, but marked "Never Sent."
10. RAH, letter to Theodore Cogswell, 12/04/59.
11. RAH, letter to Theodore Cogswell, 12/04/59.
12. RAH, letter to Theodore Cogswell, 12/04/59. No revision appears to have been made.
13. RAH, letter to Theodore Cogswell, 12/04/59.
14. RAH, letter to Theodore Cogswell, 12/04/59.
15. RAH, letter to Theodore Cogswell, 12/04/59.
16. RAH, letter to Theodore Cogswell, 12/04/59.
17. RAH, letter to Theodore Cogswell, 12/04/59. A few years later, shortly before conscription ramped up for the Vietnam War, Heinlein expressed just the same revulsion for conscription in a letter to Theodore Sturgeon, 03/05/62:

> I hate conscription. I regard it as human slavery of the vilest sort and do not think it can be justified under any circumstances whatever. To those who say: "Yes, but without the draft we could not defend the United States" I answer violently, "Then let the bloody United States go down the drain! Any nation whose citizens will not *voluntarily* fight and die for her does not deserve to live."
>
> I despise jails and prisons almost as much, and for the same reason, and I am contemptuous of punishment by fining because it is basically unjust,

being necessarily uneven and discriminatory in application—e.g., there is a reckless driver in this neighborhood who is quite wealthy. A $500 fine to him is nothing at all, less than nothing. To me it is an annoyance and one which might well cut into my luxuries and spoil my plans. But to my neighbor across the street, a cook with two children, a $500 fine would be a major disaster.

Yet $500 is what our local courts would charge any of the three of us for drunken driving.

I suggest that ten lashes would be equally rough on each of us—and would do far more to deter homicide-by-automobile.

Both of these ideas, opposition on moral grounds to conscription and to imprisonment, are essential parts of *Starship Troopers*. So far as I know, no reviewer noticed either idea.

18. Theodore Cogswell, letter to RAH, 12/09/59.
19. The Detroit World Science Fiction Convention was held over the Labor Day weekend in early September 1959, whereas the book was not released until October. Possibly the first serial installment, in the *Fantasy & Science Fiction* issue dated October 1959, was already available. A continued or renewed discussion between Robert Mills and Alfred Bester in a public place, such as a hotel bar among other colleagues, might also have been enough to create the buzz.

Much of the early commentary in the PITFCS publication continues to deal with the reduction that appeared in *The Magazine of Fantasy & Science Fiction*, months after the full text appeared in book form.

20. P. Schuyler Miller, "The Wiswell Syndrome" in "The Reference Library" Department of *Analog* (March 1960): 155–9, at 156.
21. Miller, "The Wiswell Syndrome," 158.
22. Heinlein used almost exactly this language in a letter to J. F. Bone, dated 03/12/77: "There was a period of almost fifteen years when I had strong reasons to feel that (save for a very small number of staunch friends) most of my colleagues in science fiction either disliked me or actively despised me." The *terminus ad quem* of this fifteen-year period was the start of blood drives in 1976, which pushes the *terminus a quo* back to 1961–62, the peak of negative intramural commentary about *Starship Troopers* and *Stranger in a Strange Land*.
23. Grace Metalious (1924–64) was the author of *Peyton Place* (1956), a kind of soap opera, frank for the time about sexual matters, almost forgotten now.
24. RAH, letter to Ted Sturgeon, 03/05/62.
25. RAH, letter to Mrs. Thomas V. Bottoms, 09/10/73.
26. RAH, letter to John and Sherry Jackson, 12/10/68.
27. Virginia Heinlein, letter to Willis McNelly, 06/03/69.

28. RAH, letter to Mrs. Thomas V. Bottoms, 09/10/73.

29. Alexei Panshin's earliest correspondence does not seem to have been preserved either in the general correspondence files or in the special "Panshin" file of the RAH Archive, UC Santa Cruz, so exact dating of this sequence has not been possible. Apparently the special "Panshin" file was begun in 1965, long after this time.

30. The origins of the entangled stories of "Gulf," *Stranger in a Strange Land,* and *Red Planet* are told early in chapter 1 of this volume.

31. RAH, letter to Laurie A. MacDonald, 12/12/73.

32. RAH, letter to Bjo Trimble, 11/21/61.

33. RAH, letter to Hermann Deutsch, 07/19/61.

34. Willy Ley, letter to RAH, 01/04/60.

35. Virginia Heinlein, letter to the author, 11/12/99. Discussing the moment inside the Soviet Union when she and Heinlein got word that the international talks had broken off, Mrs. Heinlein remarked, "That summit had been the only reason that I agreed to go to the USSR."

36. Virginia Heinlein, letter to the author, 05/29/99.

37. RAH, letter to Lurton Blassingame, 10/21/60.

38. RAH, letter to Lurton Blassingame, 10/21/60.

39. Both *Gladiator* and *Nightmare Alley* have carnival sections, and much of the carny material in *Stranger in a Strange Land* appears to be derived from *Nightmare Alley. Gladiator* is the story of a superhuman who is irretrievably out of place among ordinary mortals. During Hugo Danner's time working for a carnival, he suggestively meets a commercial artist named "Valentine"—who runs off with his (Hugo's) inconvenient lover.

14. The Workers' Paradise (pages 190–200)

1. RAH, letter to Nancy and Temple Fielding, 04/24/64.

2. RAH, letter to Gerry and Nan Crook, 10/11/60.

3. Virginia Heinlein, letter to the author, 11/07/99.

4. RAH, letter to Gerry and Nan Crook, 10/11/60.

5. Aside from the comments found in "Inside InTourist" and "'Pravda' Means 'Truth,'" Robert Heinlein rarely commented in detail about their experiences inside the Soviet Union. Nor did either Robert or Virginia Heinlein write contemporaneous letters to friends about the trip. Perhaps they both were overexposed and tired of the topic due to the public speaking done after their return to the United States. However, in a series of letters to the author late in 1999 and into 2000, Virginia Heinlein poured out her recollections. This correspondence, together with some comments to friends over the years, provides most of the available detail about the trip inside the USSR.

6. Virginia Heinlein, letter to George Warren, 02/28/79.

7. Virginia Heinlein, letter to George Warren, 03/09/79. The expression Mrs. Heinlein used, *sedmoi etadz,* is not a general Russian term and was probably a localism for *sedmoi etazh,* meaning seventh floor—apparently the Hotel Ukraine placed English-speaking tourists on its seventh floor.

8. Virginia Heinlein, letter to the author, 11/07/99.

9. RAH, letter to Gerry and Nan Crook, 10/11/60.

10. Noted in Virginia Heinlein, letter to Mr. Pazan, 09/27/80.

11. Virginia Heinlein, letter to the author, 11/07/99. Dozens of StereoRealist slides of the May Day 1961 parade are preserved in the RAH Archive, UC Santa Cruz.

12. Virginia Heinlein, letter to the author, 11/07/99.

13. Virginia Heinlein, letter to the author, 11/07/99.

14. Virginia Heinlein, taped interview with the author, Tape 6, Side A (March 1? 2000).

15. RAH, "The Future Revisited," Yoji Kondo, ed., 168–97, at 190.

16. Powers (1929–77) was tried in a Soviet court in August 1960 and sentenced to ten years' imprisonment for espionage. A digital file of his final plea in the trial is available online at www.history.com/speeches/powers-makes-final-plea-before-moscow-court#francis-gary-powers-released-by-soviets (accessed 03/04/2014). Eighteen months later (February 10, 1962), he and an American student were exchanged at the Glienicke Bridge between East and West Berlin for Soviet spy KGB Colonel Vilyam Fisher (Rudolf Abel). Although criticized for his handling of the matter, Powers was later absolved of any wrongdoing. He cowrote a book about the incident, *Operation Overflight: A Memoir of the U-2 Incident,* published in 1970. While working as a traffic helicopter pilot for a local news station in Los Angeles, he died in a helicopter crash in 1977, age fifty-eight.

17. David Hartwell recalled from a conversation with the Heinleins that took place "at some point in the 1970s" that they said they were sitting alone in a restaurant when the announcement about the U-2 incident—stressing that the United States was spying on the USSR—was piped in over the music system: "I recall Robert saying that they looked at each other and both stood up and sang the National Anthem. And then left. 'What else could we have done but that?' was the way he ended the anecdote." David Hartwell, e-mail to the author, 06/27/12. Perhaps the Heinleins were summoned to the InTourist office from their meal—or perhaps Heinlein has conflated this with the later incident at which they received the news that the Paris summit had collapsed, *infra.*

18. Virginia Heinlein, taped interview with the author, Misc Notes (9/8/01) Tape B, Side A.

19. Portion marked 8 November 1999 of Virginia Heinlein, letter to the author, 11/07/99.

20. Except as otherwise noted, information in this and the following paragraph from RAH, letter to Hermann Deutsch, 07/19/61.

21. Virginia Heinlein's expression. Vorkuta, a coal-mining town north of the Arctic Circle, in the Siberian region of Russia, was founded around one of the most "public" of the Gulag installations (*Gulag* is a Russian acroynm for the phrase "Main Administration of Correction-through-Labor Camps"). Here Mrs. Heinlein means Vorkuta as synecdoche for the entire Gulag system.

22. Portion marked 8 November 1999 of Virginia Heinlein, letter to the author, 11/07/99.

23. RAH, letter to Hermann Deutsch, 07/19/61.

24. Portion marked 8 November 1999 of Virginia Heinlein, letter to the author, 11/07/99.

25. Virginia Heinlein, letter to "Mr. Pazan," 09/27/80.

26. RAH, "The Future Revisited," in *Requiem*, Yoji Kondo, ed., 168–97 at 189.

27. Portion stricken from Heinlein's original draft of "Appointment in Space," significantly cut and published in *Popular Mechanics Magazine* as "All Aboard the Gemini," September 2, 1962.

28. Portion stricken from Heinlein's original draft of "Appointment in Space," significantly cut and published in *Popular Mechanics Magazine* as "All Aboard the Gemini," September 2, 1962.

29. Lenin had been exiled from Siberia to Switzerland in 1900.

30. Virginia Heinlein, letter to the author, 11/12/99.

31. Virginia Heinlein, letter to the author, 11/12/99.

32. RAH, "The Future Revisited," in *Requiem*, Yoji Kondo, ed., 168–97 at 190.

33. Virginia Heinlein, letter to the author, 11/12/99.

34. RAH, " 'Pravda' Means 'Truth,' " *The American Mercury* (October 1960); *Expanded Universe* (1980). The Virginia Edition vol. xxxi, 375, 377.

35. Virginia Heinlein, letter to the author, 05/27/00.

36. "Inside InTourist" Heinlein expanded to 8,800 words when he got back to Colorado Springs, but the article never found a commercial publisher. In 1979, Heinlein cut the piece to about 5,000 words for inclusion with " 'Pravda' Means 'Truth' " in *Expanded Universe*. Although in most instances the fullest version of articles were used for the Virginia Edition, *Expanded Universe* was taken into the series as vol. xxxi, without any changes, as it was found impossible to edit the book or break out its contents because of the surrounding commentary Heinlein wrote. Consequently, the original 8,800-word version has never been published anywhere.

37. Virginia Heinlein, letter to Leon Stover, 04/05/89.

38. The exact date of the visit to Point Barrow was not recorded, but a newspaper article, *Fairbanks Daily News* clipping written by Jay K. Kennedy, "Author of Science Fiction Visits Pt. Barrow Region," *Fairbanks Daily News* (07/27/60), says simply "returned last week from Scandinavian countries with Wine Alaska Airlines."

39. RAH, "A U.S. Citizen Thinks About Canada," *Canada and the World* (April 1975).

40. The exact date of Heinlein's return to Colorado Springs is not recorded; however, a letter written by Virginia Heinlein to Lurton Blassingame does not mention Heinlein's presence on August 9, 1960, and Heinlein's own next letter, also to Lurton Blassingame, is dated August 16, 1960.

41. RAH, letter to E. E. "Doc" Smith, 08/15/60.

42. Blassingame was an exception to the general rule, as Heinlein told Walter Minton at a time when Minton, too, was moving into the status of intimate (after a somewhat rocky start to their relationship):

> Lurton Blassingame is a special case; he and I are the same age near enough not to matter and we have been partners so very long that we are twin brothers in many ways. I was speaking of where I must look to find new friends to replace, in part, the older mentors I can never replace in full. (RAH, letter to Walter Minton, 12/31/73.)

15. Scissorbill Paradise (pages 201–216)

1. Virginia Heinlein, taped interview with the author, Misc Notes (09/08/01), Tape B, Side A. Aside from a few mentions in correspondence, the speaking engagements about the trip to Russia were not memorialized, so it is not possible to be more specific.

2. Sam Moskowitz, "Robert A. Heinlein," *Seekers of Tomorrow* (New York: The World Publishing Co., 1966), 189.

3. RAH, letter to Earl and Nancy Kemp, 09/09/61.

4. In a letter to Lurton Blassingame, 09/19/60, Heinlein discusses publishers' exploitation of the Hugo Award.

5. RAH, letter to Earl and Nancy Kemp, 09/09/61.

6. RAH, letter to Bjo Trimble, 11/21/61. In this letter, Heinlein said "a long, long time," though precisely when and on what occasion they began corresponding is not preserved. Smith was then archaeology curator of the Firelands Museum in Ohio.

   References to Sarge Smith begin showing up in Heinlein's correspondence with others only in 1960 and 1961. The entire discussion of Smith in the letter to Bjo Trimble is as follows:

> Do you remember Arthur George Smith, at the Pittcon? "Sarge" Smith, an elderly man with a bald head, a big, fat belly, and a most remarkable "Grand Duke Alexander" beard, bifurcate—the biggest beard among many beards there. Sarge is my closest friend, is the man to whom I dedicated *Starship Troopers,* and any resemblance between him and Jubal Harshaw is no accident.
>
> But, although he has held that supreme status with me for a long, long time, I met him in the flesh first at the Pittcon and have been in his presence a total of no more than six hours. But my file of Sarge Smith letters would weigh down a small pony. Neither of us is a good typist, neither of us likes to type . . . and neither of us really has time for much correspondence. But our association must needs be by mail, so we write each other long-winded letters as time permits . . . broken by long gaps when I write stories or when he is busy with his lecture series or his sorting of ancient bones.

Heinlein's file of his correspondence with Sarge Smith was kept separate from his general correspondence, presumably because of its intimate nature, and the file was lost some time after Heinlein's death. (Archivist Rita Bottoms remembered seeing it in the RAH Archive, UC Santa Cruz, around the time Virginia Heinlein put together *Grumbles from the Grave* in 1988 and 1989.) The Sarge Smith file containing his copies of the correspondence was destroyed in a family fight.

This is also the file Alexei Panshin obtained in 1964 and 1965 from Sarge Smith's widow, and which resulted in Heinlein's permanent anathematizing of Panshin, as will emerge later in the narrative.

7. Lurton Blassingame, letter to RAH, 09/20/60.
8. RAH, letter to Lurton Blassingame, 10/21/50. The relevant portion of this letter is excerpted in *Grumbles from the Grave* at 227.
9. Howard Cady, letter to RAH, 10/14/60.
10. Thirty years later, long after Walter Minton had left Putnam's—and after Heinlein's death—Minton told Virginia Heinlein that the severe cutting had been imposed by the Doubleday Science Fiction Book Club. "I never knew that the cutting on *Stranger* was required by the Doubleday science-fiction editor," Mrs. Heinlein replied to Minton.

> Nor, I think, did Robert. He was given specific instructions by Mr. Cady, and followed those instructions. Probably he wouldn't have been so eager

to let the SF Book Club publish it, if he had known." (Virginia Heinlein, letter to Walter Minton, 10/29/90.)

11. RAH, letter to Lurton Blassingame, 11/10/61.

12. Handwritten record in Robert Heinlein's hand, of telephone call with Roger Corman, 10/16/60, stapled to two-page typewritten memorandum to Lurton Blassingame and Harold Fendler.

13. RAH, letter to Lurton Blassingame, 11/10/60.

14. RAH, letter to G. Harry Stine, 10/28/60. Stine's work on the Dean Drive came to nothing, his son William Stine told the author in telephone calls and emails in October 2013.

15. RAH, letter to Rex Heinlein, 12/04/60.

16. In 1960 and 1961, Ronald Reagan was still a Democrat. He switched party affiliations and became a Republican in 1962.

17. RAH, letter to Rex Heinlein, 04/03/60.

18. RAH, letter to Rex Heinlein, 12/04/60. The term "libertarian" was a general descriptor in 1960 and had not taken on the specific ideological coloration it would acquire in the 1970s.

19. RAH, letter to Lurton Blassingame, 01/27/61; a portion of this letter is published in *Grumbles from the Grave*, 232.

20. Sam Moskowitz, letter to RAH, 01/22/61.

21. RAH, letter to Sam Moskowitz, 01/25/61.

22. RAH, letter to Sam Moskowitz, 01/25/61.

23. RAH, letter to Sam Moskowitz, 01/25/61.

24. RAH, letter to Howard Cady, 02/21/61.

25. RAH, letter to Howard Cady, 03/06/61.

26. RAH, letter to Lurton Blassingame, 10/08/60.

27. Harold Fendler, letter to RAH, 03/21/61.

28. RAH, letter to Hermann Deutsch, 07/19/61.

29. RAH, letter to Lurton Blassingame, 04/10/61.

30. RAH, letter to Lurton Blassingame, 04/10/61.

31. RAH, letter to Lurton Blassingame, 04/10/61. No publication of Heinlein's remarks on this occasion has been found.

32. Jack Williamson, letter to RAH, 07/03/61.

33. The Air Force Academy's first class (Class of 1959) started training at Lowry Air Force Base in Denver in 1955, but in 1958 they moved to the newly completed Colorado Springs facilities.

34. Lurton Blassingame, letter to RAH, 06/21/61.

35. Howard Cady, letter to RAH, 07/06/61.

36. L. Sprague de Camp, *Time and Chance: An Autobiography* (Hampton Falls, New Hampshire: Donald M. Grant, 1996), 285.

37. Catherine Crook de Camp, "The Robert A. Heinlein I Knew," *Locus* (July 1988): 40.

38. Terry Sproat, letter to RAH, 07/10/61.

39. August 4, 1961.

40. RAH, letter to Howard Cady, 08/29/61.

41. Harold Wooster, letter titled "Xenobiology" in *Science* 124 (07/21/61): 223, 225.

42. RAH, letter to "Howard" [possibly Harold Wooster], 03/23/61.

43. See, e.g., RAH, letter to Cal Laning, 04/20/47, and RAH, letter to Cal Laning, 07/17/47.

44. Reported in RAH, letter to Cal Laning, 01/19/46: "Two major fields of research are the controls and guidance of G[uided] M[issiles], and the jamming of such controls and guidance. (The so-called "Heinlein Effect" he [Cornog] tells me has been incorporated into Northrup reports on GM . . .)"

45. RAH, letter to Sam Moskowitz, 07/22/61.

46. Algis J. Budrys (1931–2008), born in Königsberg, East Prussia, was a son of the Consul-General of Lithuania. The family was sent to the United States in 1936. Lithuania was conquered by the USSR in World War II, though the United States recognized only the Lithuanian government-in-exile.

    Budrys had yet to begin the reviewing which would ultimately earn him recognition as an important science-fiction scholar (and recipient of the Pilgrim Award for contributions to SF scholarship).

47. One character, Mrs. Douglas, dies and then "reincarnates," but this is given as a situation-driven divine choice (since Mrs. Douglas, too, is God) for a heavenly "field agent," not a natural or even common pathway for souls.

48. RAH, letter to Fred Pohl, 08/20/61 (cover letter to Pohl dated 08/19/61).

49. RAH, letter to Algis J. Budrys, 09/06/61.

50. RAH, letter to Harlan Ellison, 09/06/61.

51. Alan E. Nourse, M.D. (1928–92) wrote science fiction professionally while going to medical school, which included the well-regarded juvenile novel *Trouble on Titan* (1954). While in private practice from 1958 to 1963, Nourse continued to write science fiction, including what is perhaps his best-known science fiction novel, *Star Surgeon* (1958), and then branched out to nonfiction books. After retiring from medicine in 1963, Nourse produced a contemporary-scene novel, *Intern* (1965), written as "Dr. X," and a monthly column of medical advice for *Good Housekeeping* magazine.

    In 1974 Nourse wrote another well-regarded science-fiction novel, *The Bladerunner,* which provided the title for the 1982 Ridley Scott film *Blade Runner* (the story was prominently sourced from elements in Philip K. Dick's 1968 novel *Do*

Androids Dream of Electric Sheep, but an intermediate screenwriter, Hampton Francher, used a 1979 William S. Burroughs screenplay of Nourse's book in his revisions to an earlier script and kept the name).

52. RAH, "The Future Revisited" in *Requiem,* ed. Yoji Kondo, 177.
53. RAH, "Discovery of the Future," *Requiem,* ed. Yoji Kondo, 173.
54. RAH, "Discovery of the Future," *Requiem,* ed. Yoji Kondo, 196.
55. RAH, "Discovery of the Future," *Requiem,* ed. Yoji Kondo, 172.
56. RAH, "The Future Revisited," *Requiem,* ed. Yoji Kondo, 175.
57. RAH, "The Future Revisited," *Requiem,* ed. Yoji Kondo, 176.
58. RAH, letter to F. M. Busby, 09/06/61.
59. F. M. Busby (1921–2005) began writing short science fiction in 1957 while still best known as a prominent fan and publisher/editor of *Cry of the Nameless,* a fanzine that won a Hugo Award in 1960. He began writing novels in the 1970s. Of his nineteen novels, the best known are his Alien Debt series, with Bran Tregare and Rissa Kerguelen.
60. F. M. Busby, "The Science Fiction Field Ploughed Under," *Speculation* II:12 (September 1969): 29.
61. Postcard from Jerry Pournelle to RAH, undated but from context some time in September 1961.
62. Jerry E. Pournelle, Ph.D. (Psychology and, in 1964, Political Science) (1933–) did take up writing for a living, achieving considerable success, particularly in his writing partnership with Larry Niven and as an early and longtime contributor to *Byte* magazine. Pournelle remained a friend of the Heinleins for all the remainder of Heinlein's life, and features periodically in the remainder of this biography.
63. Karen Anderson is reported to have coined this phrase at SeaCon in 1961, but its appearance in print is obscure. Both Poul and Karen Anderson used the phrase as late as their (separate) appreciations in Yoji Kondo's *Requiem* (1992), and Charles Brown (founder of *Locus* magazine) is reported by Ed Meskys to have disseminated the phrase:

> When Charlie Brown was still a fan he traveled to Worldcons and took numerous pictures and would have slide shows on his living room wall in the Bronx. I remember him after returning from Seacon in 1961 showing slides of RAH in a yellow bathrobe holding court and referring to him as "God in a yellow bathrobe." I think it was meant with awe . . .

(Ed Meskys, letter to *No Award,* no. 11 [2002]: 18.) Meskys goes on to speculate that the phrase might be a play on L. Ron Hubbard's phrase "God in a dirty bathrobe" in "Typewriter in the Sky" (*Unknown,* 1940), a metaleptic novella about the uneasy relationship of an author and his character. If so, the phrase gained ironic weight after 1980 when Heinlein began writing his quasi-postmodern, metaleptic World As Myth novels, that imply our consensus reality is the creation of a strong fabulist existing in another dimension.

64. Several correspondents including at least one of the convention's organizers wrote after the convention to express appreciation for Heinlein's accessibility at Seacon. Cf. Dirce Archer, letter to RAH, 10/09/61:

> You made a decided hit at the con from reports, and if you were the right sex could be elected Miss America by con members. I've often wondered just why those being honored by a whole convention should think they had to *hide,* and hope you have started a new trend. . . . It was so very good to hear that for once a GoH acted as if he was being honored!

65. RAH, letter to Earl and Nancy Kemp, 09/09/61.
66. RAH, letter to Judith and Dan Merril, 08/21/61.
67. RAH, letter to F. M. Busby, 09/06/61.
68. RAH, letter to Bruce Pelz, 10/17/61.
69. Jim Harmon, letter published in *The Proceedings of the Institute for Twenty-First Century Studies,* no. 137 (October 1960).
70. RAH, letter to Bruce Pelz, 10/17/61.
71. Gen. Laurence S. Kuter (1905–79) was in 1961 the commander in chief of the NORAD facility at Cheyenne Mountain. Kuter is best remembered for advocating to the Eisenhower administration a nuclear defense of Taiwan against Communist China in 1958. Construction on the NORAD facility had gotten under way in June 1961.

16. Smoking Rubble (pages 217–229)

1. RAH, letter to Robert K. Willis, 12/08/65.
2. RAH, letter to Poul Anderson, 12/13/61.
3. RAH, letter to Poul Anderson, 12/13/61.
4. RAH, letter to Poul Anderson, 12/13/61.
5. RAH, letter to Poul Anderson, 12/13/61.
6. The term "latchkey kid" had been coined in 1944—that is, during World War II —as a result of children being left alone and unsupervised while both parents were working (or a single mother was supporting the family while the father was in the armed forces). Children routinely left without parental supervision and both the restrictions and the feedback parents can provide often develop behavioral problems as a result of greater susceptibility to peer pressure in their teen years. Podkayne's younger, sub-teen brother, Clarke, was already a behavioral

problem, and Podkayne's poor judgment Heinlein attributed also to her parents' self-absorption in their own careers.

7. D. H. Steele, letter to RAH, 01/02/62.
8. RAH, letter to D. H. Steele, 03/22/62. Heinlein's two ideas were (1) to use a combination of radar and RF frequency-modulated laser to locate a man lost on the Moon and (2) using infrared to locate a missile or a ship hidden in the debris that collects in the Trojan points. By letter dated 04/05/62, Mr. Steele passed on to Heinlein approval by Hoffman Electronics of the laser idea. Steele suggested a four-to-six-week deadline (late May). The story "Searchlight" was written in late May and early June 1962, around the time the rewrites were being done on *Podkayne of Mars.*

    It is notable that, even in such a restricted compass, Heinlein complicates his basic idea, making the lost victim blind, a young girl, and giving her perfect pitch.

9. RAH, letter to Charles Ho, 07/11/62.
10. RAH, letter to Poul and Karen Anderson, 06/22/62.
11. RAH, letter to Lurton Blassingame, probably 02/23/67 though misdated as 02/03/67.
12. RAH, letter to Marion Zimmer Bradley, 08/08/63.
13. It was not yet obvious to the public at large—though it appears to have already been a matter of concern to Heinlein—that "parenting" had completely collapsed in the United States during the 1950s, largely as a secondary consequence of the flight to the suburbs, which took the commuting breadwinner essentially out of the picture as a parent and trapped the children in an impoverished environment—at the same time (and at least partly for the same reasons) that education was collapsing as well. Antisocial self-involvement has become an endemic problem in this country as a result of this ongoing crisis.
14. RAH, PSS to Ginny letter to Laura Haywood, 12/02/73.
15. Lurton Blassingame, letter to RAH, 03/19/62.
16. "Searchlight" was published in the August 1962 *Scientific American* and the following month in *Fortune.* A year later, "Searchlight" received an award, a "Certificate of Merit" from the Annual Exhibition of Advertising and Editorial Art in the West.
17. Lurton Blassingame, letter to RAH, 07/09/62.
18. At science-fiction conventions, George Scithers (1929–2010) many times remarked on Heinlein's ability to write an entire novel from a dropped remark and cites his own question to Heinlein as the incitement for *Glory Road.* The author heard Scithers tell the anecdote in 2001 at the Millennium Philcon in Philadelphia, where Scithers was the guest of honor.

The specific letter in which Scithers made the remark has not been preserved—perhaps it was kept in a desk file later inadvertently destroyed. But Scithers had been sending *Amra* to Heinlein since at least 1959, and the magazine is mentioned periodically in Heinlein's correspondence with fans.

19. James Branch Cabell, "Epistle Dedicatory" to *The Lineage of Lichfield*. If Heinlein made any written notes before writing *Glory Road*, they are not preserved in the RAH Archive, UC Santa Cruz; but the Cabellian story form—which Cabell called the "Cabellian comedy"—is immediately recognizable as the inspiration for the story form, from Heinlein's later resistance to his editors' desire to cut the last hundred manuscript pages—Oscar Gordon after the adventure of the Egg.

20. Heinlein had mentioned the Red Grimoire in 1940 (in the context of "Magic, Inc.") as an actual book in the Library of Paris, but whether copies of this particular grimoire exist could not be determined. However, "Red Grimoire" blank books are sold at occult supply stores. Heinlein may have at some time acquired "a" Red Grimoire rather than "the" Red Grimoire. Virginia Heinlein remembered the encyclopedia of magic:

> Between juveniles, Robert did books for adults—something much more to his taste. He enjoyed doing Glory Road and such things. I think that it was at that time that he got the Magic encyclopaedia. I don't know where the Red Grimoire came from—he could have had that earlier. Books would come into his order, and I would unwrap those and turn them over to him. Mostly I did not have a chance to read those.

Virginia Heinlein, letter to the author, 11/07/1999b.

21. RAH, letter to Lurton Blassingame, 06/22/62.

22. RAH, letter to Martin Greenberg, 05/04/59.

23. See, e.g., Lurton Blassingame, letter to RAH, 07/30/62, in which Peter Israel's involvement in negotiations with Doubleday for the ombnibus is mentioned; and Lurton Blassingame, letter to RAH, 12/18/62, in which the Gnome Press issue of *Methuselah's Children* will complicate a Putnam's omnibus issue.

24. The incident is detailed in chapter 9 of the first volume of this biography, *Learning Curve*.

25. RAH, letter to Mary Collin, 03/06/62.

26. RAH, letter to Mary Collin, 08/06/62.

27. RAH, thank-you letter to Capt. H. D. Hilton, USS *Lexington*, 07/09/62.

28. RAH, letter to Bam Heinlein, 07/11/62.

29. Earl Kemp, letter to RAH, 07/21/62.

30. Tom Stimson, letter to Robert and Ginny Heinlein, 06/22/62, and confirmation of arrangements made by telephone, 06/29/62.

31. "Powerglide"—also sometimes "Power Glide transmission"—was the first gener-
    ally available two-speed automatic transmission used on Chevrolets and some
    Pontiacs from 1950 through 1973. Ford did not introduce its own automatic
    transmission until 1974.

32. RAH, letter to Tom Stimson, 07/14/62.

33. RAH, letter to Lurton Blassingame, 09/30/62.

34. John W. Campbell, Jr., letter to RAH, 08/12/62.

35. Earl Kemp, letter to RAH, 08/16/62. Kemp had told Heinlein about the Hugo
    win, in highly coded language (". . . the condition is GO. Or to be more appro-
    priate, COME HERE. Pack the big harp, please, you will be expected to play a
    brief but strange Martian melody") on 08/06/62.

36. RAH, letter to Mary Collin, 08/06/62.

37. This telephone conversation was overheard by Virginia Heinlein and related in
    2000 as part of the taped interviews in preparation for this biography. Six months
    or so later, Alexei Panshin web-published a set of "memoirs" by Earl Kemp. Some-
    how not wanting to "take the shine off," Sturgeon was remembered as a demand
    for a follow-spotlight—something that would have been next to physically impos-
    sible in any case, though Kemp also says Hugh Hefner demanded a spotlight for
    his own entrance. A follow spot in one room for a limited occasion would not be
    impossible, but there is no evidence that such was actually ever done. Surviving
    photographs of the event show no evidence of a follow-spot.

38. Betsy Curtis was a fan friend. Virginia Heinlein remembers, "I believe it was fol-
    lowing the publication of *Stranger* that Betsy wrote to Robert, asking whether he
    would like to have a list of 100 reasons why she liked the book so much. . . . The
    correspondence continued for some years. . . ." (Virginia Heinlein, letter to Leon
    Stover, 04/07/89.) Indeed, Ginny was still receiving a kind of daily written blog
    from Betsy Curtis in 2000, and the file of correspondence from her amounts to
    several reams of paper in the RAH Archive, UC Santa Cruz.

39. Alexei Panshin gives a slightly different order and interpretation of events:

    > One for-sure example of egotistical game-playing (self-dramatisation?) I
    > can give where Heinlein and Chicon are concerned is Heinlein's Hugo ac-
    > ceptance. He hung around out of sight, dressed to the nines in a white
    > jacket and black tie, while the awards were made. Then, after Betsy Curtis
    > had accepted his Hugo for *Stranger,* he made an out-of-breath entrance.
    >
    > According to the convention proceedings (edited by Earl Kemp!), Hein-
    > lein said:
    > "I've been here about four minutes and, having asked Betsy to accept
    > for me, I just held back for a minute. Just call me the late R. A. Heinlein.

"I have been down in Texas at the Manned Space Flight Center, flew up to St. Louis to see the hardware for the project I've been working on and worked until 5 a.m. this morning in order to get here at all. As you know, Operation Skyshield stopped the planes this afternoon and I have spent the afternoon and evening getting across Illinois from St. Louis. I am glad to have gotten here at all. I didn't expect to.

"My wife is complaining about dusting these things.

"Having just this minute gotten off the train and checked in I have no prepared speech. In fact, I thought this would all be over with by the time I got here. I am very happy to be here and I am going to stay through the rest of the Convention and hope to see a lot of all of you."

Panshin goes on to point out that much of this business was disingenuous and self-dramatizing (i.e., knowing about the Hugo Award in advance, he had ample opportunity to prepare a speech). Alexei Panshin, e-mail correspondence with the author, 11/11/05. One may view it as Heinlein's view of "good theater" rather than disingenuousness—but, of course, Heinlein himself did not always make a clear distinction between the two.

40. RAH, letter to T. B. Buell, 10/03/74.

41. George Scithers, incident related orally at the Millennium Philcon, 09/02/2001.

42. There are, of course, psychological downsides to the qualities that bring about that kind of self-assurance. Henry Sang, writing just after decamping from the Heinleins' home in 1946 and 1947 (fifteen years before the 1962 Chicon), described some of these qualities:

> In spite of our great liking for the Heinleins, living there was a strain because of Bob's emotional condition . . . the hard work of catering to his exacting needs or rather requirements. As friends and hosts the Heinleins had two principal faults so far as I was concerned: whether the fault lies in them or in me is not clear to me. (1) Example: When Dugan and I planned our trip to San Francisco . . . To avoid coming in at all hours, since we weren't going to be living with them any more anyway, I said that we would stay in a Motel in Hollywood when we returned but Bob would not hear of it and said that we should stay there with them. When we arrived after our long drive, at seven in the evening, we had to stay up until 2:30 a.m. because Bob was using our bedroom for his writing and cannot be disturbed when he is at work. We went to sleep on the floor upstairs until he had finished. I considered this thoughtless, and typical of the strange mixture of great generosity and cruelty that the Heinleins sometimes show. (2) I could never quite get used to the Heinleins' attitude that their consid-

ered judgment on any social problem was the final word. They are certainly as intelligent as anyone I have ever known, but they regard Bob as "God"—they even use the word—ostensibly in fun—to describe him, and they have developed a way of talking about their friends—everybody, in fact—as if they were indeed sitting on a cloud and passing judgment on people.

This fragment was preserved in Henry Sang's files and provided by Grace Dugan Sang Wurtz, who dated the fragment 03/29/46 (actually 1947).

43. RAH, letter to Lurton Blassingame, 09/12/62. However, the list is quite incomplete—and "Anthony Boucher" (William A. P. White) did not participate in the *Playboy* Symposium, though he may have been at the party. The *Playboy* Symposium participants were: Arthur C. Clarke, William Tenn, Poul Anderson, Heinlein, Ray Bradbury, Isaac Asimov, James Blish, Theodore Sturgeon, A. E. van Vogt, Frederik Pohl, Rod Serling, and Algis Budrys.

44. RAH, letter to Lurton Blassingame, 09/12/62.

45. RAH, letter to Lurton Blassingame, 09/12/62.

46. RAH, letter to Dorothy and Clare Heinlein, 12/03/62.

47. RAH, letter to Dorothy and Clare Heinlein, 12/03/62.

48. RAH, letter to Frank Deodene, librarian at Lebanon (PA) Community Library, 02/21/65.

49. RAH, letter to A. C. Spectorsky, 10/10/62.

50. Tom Stimson, letter to RAH, 10/19/62.

17. Old World, New World, Old World (page 230–246)

1. There was one notable exception to the Eisenhower administration's unnerving international passivity: the 1955 Formosa Resolution, which guaranteed the Formosa Strait islands of Quemoy and Matsu would not be ceded to the People's Republic of China. The Formosa Resolution, together with the Soviet Union's unwillingness to come to China's aid, probably forestalled a hot war between Communist China and Chiang Kai Shek's Formosa—which could only have ended with Formosa being conquered and absorbed into China, at a minimum. At worst, it might have ignited World War III.

2. Pierre Salinger, then President Kennedy's press secretary, later said that he was sent out to buy up twelve hundred Cuban cigars just before the embargo went into effect. Salinger told the story at a Cigar Association of America annual meeting in 1987. The incident is mentioned by cigar authority Richard DiMeola in http://www.bocaratontribune.com/2011/07/retired-cigar-man-takes-a-light-look-at-the-industry/,accessed 03/04/2014.

3. The NSA archives say April, but Khrushchev's memoirs say May.

4. RAH, letter to Ted Carnell, 11/14/62.

5. Judith Merril, letter to RAH, 11/04/62.

6. Leon Stover, in *Robert Heinlein* for the Twayne U.S. Author Series, says *Stranger* appeared on the *NY Times* bestseller list in 1962 (45), which would be at the time of the first paperback issue. Other sources give 1963 as the date. That *Stranger* was the first science-fiction book to appear on the *Times* bestseller list is also widely mentioned, especially in reviews of the uncut version of *Stranger* published in 1990. The various online versions of the bestseller lists, however, are organized in ways that make it difficult, if not impossible, to confirm any of these references (the list maintained by *The Times,* for instance, lists only hardcover appearances and is not searchable in any case).

   Although *Stranger* sold well by science-fiction book standards, it is not likely that it would have appeared on any bestseller lists as early as 1962 or 1963. The period of the book's exceptional sales did not commence until 1967.

7. Years later, Heinlein reviewed the book's publication history for a mutual friend, who reported that *Stranger in a Strange Land* had "flopped":

   > "—and flopped." Hrrumph! Ginny is now so spoiled that she thinks a book should always earn at least $40,000 the first year of publication, or I'm slipping. I forced her to look at the records (her own work), which show clearly that SIASL was the most successful book in *every* way in its *first* year of all the books I had written up to that time: Publisher recovered his full investment including my advance in less than six months, hardcover sales at list price 1st cy ra. 6700, hardcover bookclub sales over 32,000, gross to us 1st 12 months $4,694.70—and the book took the Hugo. But what she remembers is that it took ca. 3 more years for the general public of *non*science-fiction readers to discover it . . . [sic] then the pb sales took off like a rocket . . . [sic] and all of my books have sold to the general public ever since, with a result that quintupled our income ahead of taxes. "Flopped—" I pause to shudder in indignation.

   RAH, letter to Laura Haywood, undated but marked "ca. Dec 73" in RAH's hand.

8. RAH, letter to Judith Merril, 11/07/62.

9. Virginia Heinlein, taped interview with the author, Misc Notes (9/4–9/8/01) Tape A, Side A.

10. Virginia Heinlein, taped interview with the author, Misc Notes (9/4–9/8/01) Tape A, Side A.

11. RAH, letter to Poul and Karen Anderson, 11/18/62.

12. RAH, letter to Judith Merril and Kate Wilhelm, 11/17/62.

13. RAH, letter to Judith Merril and Kate Wilhelm, 11/17/62.

14. Peter Israel, letter to RAH, 12/18/62.

15. RAH, letter to Mary Collin, 03/04/63.

16. RAH, letter to Mary Collin, 03/04/63.

17. Heinlein's outline for *Grand Slam* (*Farnham's Freehold*) in the RAH Archive,
     UC, Santa Cruz, begins: "Story starts ca. 1963 or any year shortly thereafter dur-
     ing a Cold War crisis similar to Cuban Crisis 1962." Although the notes deal
     only with the characters of the book and never reach plot details, racial attitudes
     are included in character descriptions, and in a three-page discarded opening
     dated 31 January 1963 and marked "False Start," they are one short of two tables
     for Bridge after a dinner party, and "Hubert" hesitantly suggests to another guest,
     "Ace Connolly," that they ask Joseph to sit in as fourth for the second table:

     > Connolly looked still more surprised. "You're saying that that . . . [sic] col-
     > ored man . . . [sic] plays contract?"
     >
     > "He plays. I haven't suggested it to him tonight. He may wish to, I don't
     > know. He may need to study."
     >
     > Connolly blinked and looked at his wife. She said, "It's up to you, Ace."
     > He said slowly, "Why, I suppose there's no harm in it, but—well, look, you
     > know I don't like to play unless there is a little something up, and we
     > couldn't very well play for our usual stakes, now, could we? I mean to say,
     > suppose I win some money off him. All I can say is, 'That's all right, boy.
     > Forget it.' See what I mean?"
     >
     > "Yes, I see. Joseph and I can play as a team."
     >
     > "Meaning you'll pick up his losses?"
     >
     > "Meaning my arrangements with Joseph won't be your problem. We'll
     > play a set game against you and Babe if you like. You're used to each oth-
     > er's play."
     >
     > Farnham's son broke in. "Ace, you're being set up as a sucker. Don't un-
     > derrate that dinge Pop's got in the kitchen. He's got trumps up his sleeve and
     > aces in both shoes, every time. You're about to help pay off the mortgage."

     The themes of atomic attack and racial politics thus appear joined on the first full
     page of the book. The conclusion(s) that (a) these themes had been on his mind
     for some time as the story was generated and (b) that the themes are to be devel-
     oped together (in the way that both religious hypocrisy and sexual hypocrisy had
     been developed together in *Stranger in a Strange Land*) seems inescapable.

     Furthermore, that the themes are to be dealt with in *ironic inversion* is suggested
     by the story materials, since they will be at ground zero of an atomic attack but

are unharmed. The later inversions displaying racial attitudes ranging from "country club liberalism" to plantation slavery are thus foreshadowed on the first pages.

18. Leon Stover, *Science Fiction Between Wells and Heinlein* (Macfarland, 2002): 126.

19. Although Heinlein never mentioned reading Philip Wylie's *Triumph* (*Beyond Armageddon*), the book was serialized in *The Saturday Evening Post* in October 1962, just as the Cuban missile crisis got under way. Resemblances of *Farnham's Freehold* to *Triumph* are rather superficial, and they are quite different *kinds* of books, as *Triumph* is a straightforward novel with some pulpish overtones, while *Farnham's Freehold* is a satire—but it is not impossible that Wylie's serial might have started the train of thought that led eventually to Heinlein's book.

If *Triumph* was an "influence" it is not for the alcoholic wife in both books, but for the mixed-race grouping and the observation:

> . . . people below the equator should come through in good shape! The air doesn't exchange across the equator fast enough to endanger them. What I mean is merely the USSR will be a graveyard. Europe, too, undoubtedly. The North Temperate Zone pretty much clear around the globe. Except where people can hold out in shelters comparable to this, or in certain military bases underground. And so on. Submarines. They will be safe (61–62).

20. Alan Nourse, M.D., letter to RAH, 04/02/63.

21. RAH, letter to Peggy Blassingame, 07/23/63.

22. RAH, letter to Marion Zimmer Bradley, 08/08/63.

23. RAH, letter to Marion Zimmer Bradley, 08/08/63.

24. RAH, letter to Marion Zimmer Bradley, 08/08/63.

25. RAH, letter to Bill Corson, 08/09/63. Corson had offered to make Heinlein a loan to finance Ginny's treatment. Heinlein thanked him, saying, "I think this is the first time in my life that anyone ever offered to lend me money."

26. RAH, letter to Bjo Trimble, 02/17/64.

27. RAH, letter to Marion Zimmer Bradley, 08/08/63.

28. Virginia Heinlein, taped interview with the author, Tape 5, Side B.

29. Howie [given name] Horwitz (1918–76) was the uncle of future science fiction and fantasy writer Alan Dean Foster. Foster's first sale was to August Derleth in 1968.

30. William Dozier (1908–91) was actually the senior member of the producing partnership, but all of Heinlein's day-to-day dealings were with Howie Horwitz. Television writer Mike Cassutt spoke with Dozier about this project in 1989, and ". . . he said he knew 'Robert' but didn't actually work with him on the project, suggesting again that it was Howie's baby." Mike Cassutt, e-mail to the author, 09/22/05.

31. In RAH, letter to Howie Horwitz, 01/02/64. That observation was written by Virginia Kidd ("Blish" at the time) in a fanzine review of "Gulf" titled "A Gaudy Notion," the manuscript of which is preserved in the Opus 73 file of the RAH Archive at UC Santa Cruz, with no indication of where it was published: "... two hundred words of pure and calculated artistic excellence built briefly into the best goddam climax of any science-fiction story I ever read, bar none."

32. RAH, pilot script, *The Adventure of the Man Who Wasn't There* for the series *The Twenty-Second Century*. RAH Archive, UC Santa Cruz and the Virginia Edition, vol. xlv, *Screenplays 2*.

33. Nominally scripts are supposed to run one minute of film for each page of script, forty-four minutes per hour, leaving time for commercials; Heinlein's 141-page script would imply a three-and-a-half-hour run time. Heinlein's original script is published for the first time in the Virginia Edition, vol. xlv, *Screenplays 2*. Heinlein's December 1963 cleanup, following the first set of producer's notes he received, was 97 pages. Between the first draft and the December revision, the protagonist's name went from Genro to Kenro.

34. Claude V. Ricketts (1906–64) was the Class of 1929's first four-star, and he had been gunnery officer on board USS *West Virginia* during the attack on Pearl Harbor. Ricketts Hall on the USNA campus is named for him. Later he was the Vice Chief of Naval Operations. Aside from the fact that Rear Admiral Buck Brandley was a flyer with *Lexington,* little is known about him. He was still living in 1973 when Heinlein recommended Admiral King's biographer contact Brandley. Similarly, all that is known about "Al" Loomis is that he was on the Naval Academy's fencing squad at the same time as Heinlein.

35. David Hartwell, e-mail to the author, 06/27/12. Hartwell concludes: "Ginny expressed great admiration for Robert's ability to get his friends to play such games." It was, indeed, an astonishing feat of persuasion—comparable in some ways to their memorable "bikini party" in 1955 (covered in chapter 10 of this volume), in which Heinlein had persuaded all the women to try on Ginny's imported bikini swimsuit—while he photographed them all.

36. RAH, letter to Marion Zimmer Bradley, 12/25/63.

37. RAH, letter to Sarge Smith, 12/22/63. This letter was fortuitously preserved in Heinlein's "Story Notes" file.

38. Kenneth E. BeLieu (1914–2001) was Assistant Secretary of the Navy from 1961–65, when he became Under Secretary of the Navy. Interestingly, BeLieu originally enlisted in the Army and fought in World War II and the Korean War (in which he lost his left leg below the knee). BeLieu retired from the Army in 1955 with the rank of Colonel and served as a professional Senate staff member for the Committee on Armed Services. He was appointed Assistant Secretary of the Navy

by President Kennedy. After working in the private sector, BeLieu was appointed Under Secretary of the Army by President Nixon, from 1971–73. He retired from the government in 1979 and became a professional consultant.

39. RAH, letter to Francis Ware, 11/21/63.
40. Howie Horwitz, letter to RAH, 12/30/63.
41. RAH, letter to Howie Horwitz, 01/01/64.
42. RAH, letter to Howie Horwitz, 01/02/64.
43. Howie Horwitz, letter to RAH, 01/06/64.
44. RAH, letter to Howie Horwitz, 01/08/64.
45. RAH, letter to Ned Brown, 01/17/64.
46. RAH, letter to Ned Brown, 01/17/64.
47. RAH, letter to Howie Horwitz, 01/01/64.
48. Eric Clough, letter to RAH, 01/27/64.
49. These are "guesstimates" based on the amount of the royalty payment, since Putnam's royalty statements did not detail by unit sales, or even by issue, but combined all formats together, so that a single number was a composite of an author's royalties for hardcover sales, Putnam's share of paperback sales, and Putnam's share of Doubleday Science Fiction Book Club sales for the period. The SF Book Club royalties in this period were about five cents per unit, whereas paperback royalties might have been as much as (half of) six or seven cents per unit, and the diminishing number of hardcover sales probably about twenty-five cents.
50. Ned Brown, letter to RAH, 05/05/64.
51. RAH, letter to Ned Brown, 06/04/64.
52. Heinlein complains specifically of this set of practices in his analysis to Blassingame of the proposed Doubleday contract on 07/29/64: ". . . Lurton, I have been trying to tell you for years that Doubleday scamps the trade edition, then milks the subsidiary rights, all to the disadvantage of the author . . ." In this contract, the extent to which Doubleday proposed to "negotiate" terms with its own subsidiaries and present them as fiats to the author scandalized Heinlein:

> At the moment I am so vexed at their unreasonable demands—the fashion in which that contract has been rigged throughout to clip the Author without ever quite telling him *how* he is being clipped—that I am strongly disposed to reject it in toto and withdraw the properties. Therefore I shall let it sit a few days until I have cooled down on the subject. . . .
>
> Here are a few of the many things I object to:
>
> In several places it says that the publisher can negotiate with *himself* (i.e., with a subsidiary division or affiliate of Doubleday) and decide how much profit to show on some right or permission—then I have to accept

50% of that rigged profit as my compensation. Lurton, this is as ridiculous as it would be for Ginny and myself to negotiate between ourselves as to what the return would be, then announce it to Doubleday—and Doubleday would have to pay me whatever we decided.

I will not accept any such blind provision, whether it be for the Science Fiction Book Club, the Dollar Book Club, or any other of the various front names for Doubleday. Either each such contract must be negotiated with me later, on terms agreeable to me—or the exact nature and terms of the sub-contract must be incorporated into the main contract *now*. I will *not* give blind permission for Doubleday to negotiate with Doubleday, and thereby bind *me*—at *my* expense.

Doubleday puts in a paragraph under which Doubleday may at any time (even immediately after publication) cease publication of the trade edition, remainder any stock—below cost and at no royalty to me, if they so choose—and again "negotiating" such sale with a subsidiary part of themselves!—and *nevertheless* retain forever all subsidiary rights!

I won't hold still for any part of this! I will not permit remaindering in less than two years after publication; any less time than that means they haven't tried. Nor will I agree that they can remainder by selling to *themselves* "below cost"—and thereby cut me out. But in particular I will *not* permit them to retain any rights whatsoever if they choose to let the trade edition go out of print.

And so on. Editor David Hartwell commented (in a marginal note to this manuscript, ca. mid-2012) that he knew of Doubleday's practices as of 1967, a few years later: "Doubleday would print, fill all advance orders and then pulp anything left upon sale to the book club—in all the genres where they ha[d] a library subscription program."

53. RAH, letter to Willy Ley, 07/23/64.
54. RAH, letter to Lurton Blassingame, 07/29/64.
55. RAH, letter to Lurton Blassingame, 08/10/64.
56. RAH, letter to Peter Israel, 06/15/64.
57. RAH, letter to Sandy Fulton, 09/24/65.
58. RAH, letter to Don and Andy Panda, 06/11/64.

18. Gold for Goldwater (pages 247–260)

1. RAH, letter to Lurton Blassingame, 06/15/64—possibly misdated from August or September 1963.
2. RAH, letter to Rex Heinlein, 09/29/64.
3. These quotations from RAH, letter to Rex Heinlein, 09/29/64.

4. Claude Henri de Rouvroy, comte de Saint-Simon (1760–1825) was an early French theorist of socialism. Saint-Simon fought in the American Revolution, taking part in the siege of Yorktown under General Washington.

   Saint-Simon returned to France and devoted himself to developing a class-collaboration brand of socialism distinct from Babeuf's class-warfare socialism of the French Revolution. Saint-Simon's theory called for society to be organized into an integrated industrial machine, directed by scientists. His ideas influenced his secretary, Auguste Comte (who invented the word "socialism") and after him Marx. His ideas formed part of the intellectual underpinnings of science fiction through H. G. Wells.

5. François Marie Charles Fourier (1772–1837) was one of the leading socialist theorists contemporary with Saint-Simon, though not, apparently, much influenced by Saint-Simon. In Kent Bromley's preface to Kropotkin's *The Conquest of Bread,* Fourier was designated the founder of the libertarian branch of Socialist thought. Fourier worked out the ideal infrastructure of what are now called "utopian" communities (his "phalanxes") based on notions of "passional attraction." That is, society could be self-organizing because different people are attracted to different professional and social functions. Fourier was influential enough in European politics to be condemned by Frederick Engels in the *Anti-Dühring* (1878).

   Fourier's first book, *The Theory of the Four Movements,* was published in 1808 and became the basis for wave after wave of socialist experimental communities in America through the nineteenth century. He also wrote up a fictional utopia called "Harmony" which might well be a source for Heinlein's Howard Families, since they remained sexually active into advanced old age. Fourier also coined the term "feminism."

6. François-Noël Babeuf (1760–97) was a French agitator and journalist (using the pseudonym "Gracchus") during the French Revolution. He originated class-warfare socialism with the idea that the aristocracy must be liquidated before the revolution could succeed. A partisan of the Terror, after Robespierre's death he organized an unsuccessful counterrevolution and was guillotined. His ideas were later developed by Karl Marx.

7. Rexford Guy Tugwell (1891–1979) was an agricultural economist who became part of President Franklin Roosevelt's "Brain Trust" developing the policies that would become Roosevelt's "New Deal." Tugwell served as assistant secretary (and then undersecretary) of the Department of Agriculture and was instrumental in creating the Agricultural Adjustment Administration ("AAA"), the Soil Conservation Service, and the Federal Food, Drug, and Cosmetic Act. Tugwell resigned from the Roosevelt adminsitration in 1936, accused of being a Communist.

8. This is a position articulated prominently in a book that deals specifically with late-nineteenth-century and early-twentieth-century sex radicalism: Hal Sears,

The Sex Radicals: Free Love in High Victorian America (Lawrence, Kan.: Regents Press of Kansas, 1977). The discussion in this book was highly illuminative of Heinlein's attitudes toward both sex and politics.

9. A few years later, it was quite startling to many historically-aware people within the nascent libertarian movement when the *New York Times Magazine* profiled libertarianism as a "new right" ideology ("The New Right Credo—Libertarianism," by Stan Lehr and Louis Rossetto, Jr., 01/10/71, 24–25). Libertarianism is a radical liberal position, with a strong emphasis on individualism. It is only the historical accident of a pervasive adoption of collectivist ideas on the left that later made a working political alliance of libertarians with American conservatives politically possible—and necessary. But a small Movement of the Libertarian Left continues to exist within libertarianism.

10. RAH, letter to Bjo Trimble, 02/17/64.

11. RAH, letter to Bjo Trimble, 02/17/64.

12. Quoted in RAH television spot for Goldwater Campaign, titled "Civil Rights 30 Second Spot," October 6, 1964.

13. RAH, letter to Bjo Trimble, 02/17/64.

14. Heinlein went on to write three radio commercials for the campaign, apparently never used. One of them dealt specifically with the "shoots from the hip" charge and used the "real straight shooter" language. The radio spots are published for the first time in the Virginia Edition, vol. xxxvii, *Nonfiction 1*.

15. RAH, letter to Larry and Caryl Heinlein, 07/19/64.

16. Virginia Heinlein, editorial note in *Grumbles from the Grave*, 212–13.

17. And these are much the same thoughts that later motivated Goldwater's scathing denunciations of Jerry Falwell and the "Moral Majority."

18. RAH, letter to Robert M. Laura, 08/02/64.

19. RAH, letter to Robert M. Laura, 08/02/64.

20. Robert M. Laura, letter to RAH, 08/04/64.

21. Undated index card in RAH's hand, in Safety Deposit Box documents, RAH Archive, UC Santa Cruz.

22. Heinlein is probably referring to President Johnson's news conference on August 18. In August 23, 1964, letters to Lurton Blassingame and to his brother Rex, Heinlein refers to the incident as "recent." President Johnson's next news conference was not until August 26, 1964. A list of President Johnson's news conferences is contained at http://www.presidency.ucsb.edu/news_conferences .php?year=1964 (accessed June 29, 2011).

23. RAH, letter to Rex, Kathleen, Karen Heinlein, 08/23/64.

24. RAH, letter to Clare Heinlein, 08/23/64.

25. RAH, letter to Lurton Blassingame, 08/23/64.

26. RAH, letter to Al G. Hill, 09/28/64.

27. RAH, letter to Al G. Hill, 09/28/64.

28. The first entry in Heinlein's office journal for the "Garden of the Gods dinner" was on September 6, 1964.

29. For example, some of the Garden of the Gods dinner collections went to purchase Goldwater's books, *Victory* and *The Conscience of a Conservative* for local distribution, per Heinlein's Goldwater Campaign Log, Garden of the Gods subfile, entries for 9/10 and 9/11/64.

30. RAH, letter to Al G. Hill, 09/28/64.

31. RAH, letter to Al G. Hill, 09/28/64.

32. RAH, letter to Al G. Hill, 09/28/64.

33. The campaign speech is published in the Virginia Edition, vol. xxxvii, *Nonfiction 1.*

34. Virginia Heinlein, interview with the author, Tape 4, Side B.

35. RAH, letter to Lurton Blassingame, 10/14/64.

36. RAH, letter to Lurton Blassingame, 12/11/64.

37. Virginia Heinlein, letter to the author, 06/12/00.

19. That Dinkum Thinkum (pages 261–273)

1. Alexei Panshin, letter to Lurton Blassingame, 12/31/64. Panshin has posted many of the documents, including correspondence, relating to the preparation and publication of *Heinlein in Dimension,* and other matters, on his "Abyss of Wonder" website particularly in the "The Crities Lounge" page, http://www.panshin.com /crities/lounge.com.

2. Lurton Blassingame, letter to Alexei Panshin, 01/05/65.

3. Betsy Curtis was a fan friend, who had at Heinlein's request accepted the Hugo for *Stranger in a Strange Land.*

4. Panshin's letter to Sarge Smith, answered by Smith's widow, is dated January 6, 1965.

5. Republished on Alexei Panshin's website as "Sex in the Stories of Robert Heinlein." Panshin gives a narrative of how the article came about in his prefatory "Introduction: Sex in Heinlein's Stories" at http://www.panshin.com/critics -/Heinleinsex/sexintro.htm (accessed 03/04/2014).

6. The registered letter to Earl Kemp in Heinlein's files is dated 02/02/65; Alexei Panshin gives the date in his web-published "The Story of Heinlein in Dimension" as 02/16/65. The entire essay is accessed through http://www.panshin.com /critics/StoryHiD/HiDcontents.html (accessed 03/04/2014).

7. RAH, letter to Lloyd Biggle, 09/03/76.

8. RAH, letter to John and Sherry Jackson, 12/10/68.

9. RAH, letter to Marion Zimmer Bradley, 07/15/65.

10. A good short discussion of the "Breen Boondoggle" can be found at "Dr. Gafia's

Fan Terms." This glossary of "fan-speak" discusses the Breen Boondoggle as one of three "Exclusion Acts" that all drew negative response from fandom at large:

> [In 1964] the Pacificon Committee chose to ban Walter Breen; the committee announced their intention before the Worldcon was held, explaining that they had been advised that they might be held liable if Breen were to seduce an underage male fan there, but also plunging all of active fandom into war. At around the same time, he was blackballed by the 13 members of FAPA [the Fantasy Amateur Press Association] needed to drop him from their waiting list, but within a very short period of time more than half FAPA's 65 members over-rode it and voted to reinstate him (the argument being that, whatever his sexual orientation might be, Walter was unlikely to seduce anyone in a organization whose activities take place via the mails) . . . Despite protests and even outright boycotts by some, Breen was not allowed to attend the Pacificon. Worldcon Chairman Bill Donaho outlined the committee's actions, detailing incidents which had been observed regarding Walter that fell short of seducing youths but nonetheless gave some people pause, in a pre-convention fanzine called *The Boondoggle.* The resulting fandomwide War is thus often referred to as the Boondoggle or the Breen Boondoggle . . . Breen did write the authoritative book on man-boy love and ultimately died in prison a convicted pederast. But even 40 years after the event, the sole point fans on both sides can agree upon is that the resulting feud had long-lasting effects, tore the fabric of the microcosm beyond repair and led to a proliferation of mutually exclusive private apas ["amateur press associations"] where the opposing forces retired to lick their wounds and assure themselves that they had been undeniably right while the other side had been unmistakably wrong.

http://fanac.org/Fannish_Reference_Works/Fan_terms/Fan_terms-03.html (accessed 07/01/2011).

11. RAH, letter to Marion Zimmer Bradley, 07/15/65.
12. It is very likely that the Heinleins were attending as well, though there is no direct evidence to this effect.
13. Transcription of Dr. Jerry Pournelle's presentation at the October 8, 1988 NASA Distinguished Public Service Awards Ceremony—from videotape provided by Virginia Heinlein. The videotape of the presentation is considerably more extensive than Dr. Pournelle's published remarks in *Requiem,* ed. Yoji Kondo.
14. Transcription of Jerry Pournelle's presentation at the October 8, 1988, NASA Distinguished Public Service Awards Ceremony—from videotape provided by Ginny Heinlein.

15. This anecdote is also told in Virginia Heinlein, letter to Leon Stover, 12/26/85; see also Virginia Heinlein, taped interview with the author, Series III, Tape B, Side B (March 27, 2001).

16. Jerry Pournelle, e-mail to the author, 10/12/05.

17. RAH, letter to Herb Caen, 06/22/76. Pournelle's visit was in December 1964; Heinlein's earliest outline-notes for *The Moon Is a Harsh Mistress* are dated 2/24/65. It is impossible to say just how long Heinlein had been working up the basic ideas: By the time he wrote notes about a story, he had been working at synthesizing his background for some time already. Heinlein's working records typically deal only with actual writing on the projects, not with the prewriting development process. The making of such written outline-notes is often, in fact, the very last stage of the development process, and it is not unusual to see him begin the actual writing during the outline, whole passages of dialogue and suchlike. Typically if he reached this stage during the outline, he would leave off the outline and simply begin the manuscript.

18. From Heinlein's draft Answers to Interrogatories in the *Puppet Masters* plagiarism suit against Roger Corman and *The Brain Eaters,* dated 10/13/60:

> I keep with me at all times 3 x 5 file cards on which I make notes—at my bedside, in my bath, at my dining table, at my desk, and everywhere, and I invariably have them on my person whenever I am away from home, whether for fifteen minutes or six months. An idea for a story is jotted down on such a card and presently is filed under an appropriate category, in my desk. When enough notes have accumulated around an idea to cause me to think of it as an emergent story, I pull those cards out of category files, assign a working title, and give it a file separator with the working title written on the index. Thereafter, new notes are added to the bundle as they occur to me. At the present time I am filing notes under sixteen categories and under fifty-three working titles.
>
> A story may remain germinating for days only, or for years—two of my current working titles are more than twenty years old. But once I start to write a story the first draft usually is completed in a fairly short time. Thereafter I spend time as necessary in cutting, revising, and polishing. Then the opus is smooth-typed and sent to market.

One of those long-standing working titles must have been "Da Capo," which was not actually written until 1971. Heinlein's file of idea index cards filled two long file trays by the time of his death, and the cards pulled for the last novels sometimes might exceed five hundred in number.

19. Virginia Heinlein, e-mail to David Wright, Sr. (cc. the author), 01/03/01.

20. Later, the editor at *Book of Knowledge* chopped up the "expert" piece they had commissioned and rewrote it. The original encyclopedia article as Heinlein wrote it is published in the Virginia Edition, vol. xxxvii, *Nonfiction 1.*

21. Heinlein had talked about the gravity gauge—i.e., the advantage enjoyed by anyone at the "top" of a gravity well—in his May 1948 talk at the Book Breakfast of the [Los Angeles] County Librarians' Association. See *Learning Curve,* 455.

22. RAH, letter to Mr. John Zube, 10/08/71.

23. H. G. Wells, *Phoenix: How to Rebuild the World: A Summary of the Inescapable Conditions of World Reorganization* (Girard, Kansas: Haldeman-Julius, 1942), 6. Heinlein never referenced or specifically mentioned reading this book, but the shape of the Future History Space Patrol (which did not exist in the prewar Future History stories) may have been suggested by *Phoenix*—and in any case Heinlein's thinking was so generally Wellsian that he may have arrived at these Wellsian notions independently.

24. H. G. Wells, *The World of William Clissold* (1926), 189.

25. Heinlein's draft notes for Opus. 152, RAH Archive, UC Santa Cruz.

26. The *Brass Cannon* title was inspired by the brass signaling gun Mrs. Heinlein had bought on their recent visit in New Orleans, and specifically for an old tall tale of which Heinlein was fond. Jerry Pournelle recalled Heinlein's telling of the story when he visited in 1964:

> I look over at the fireplace, and pointed at me was a cannon. And I said, "Robert, what is this?"
>
> And he said, "Well, don't you know the story?"
>
> And I said "No."
>
> And he said, "Well, there was this fellow once who had been a—had a sinecure. He had a political job. He was someone's brother-in-law, and they gave him the job of polishing the brass cannon on the courthouse steps. And he got paid on the order of $100 a week for doing this, and he did this for years.
>
> "And one day he came home and he said to his wife, 'Dear, I have quit my job.'
>
> "And she said 'You quit your job? How could you—You're too stupid to do anything else. What do you mean, you quit your job?'
>
> "And he said 'Well, I didn't see any future in it so I bought my own brass cannon and I'm going into business for myself.'"
>
> And Robert pointed to this thing and said, "That's the cannon."
>
> And I said, "Could you point it in a slightly different direction?"
>
> And I went to sleep, and I slept pretty soundly.

NOTES 583

Transcription of Dr. Jerry Pournelle's presentation at the October 8, 1988 NASA Distinguished Public Service Awards Ceremony—from videotape provided by Virginia Heinlein.

27. Mrs. Heinlein designated the gun to be bequeathed to friend and science-fiction writer Brad Linaweaver, and after Mrs. Heinlein's death Linaweaver had it reconditioned and fired in honor of Robert and Virginia Heinlein for the Heinlein Centennial celebration in 2007. A short (nine-minute) video of the test firing a few weeks before the Centennial is on YouTube as "Brad Linaweaver presents Robert A Heinlein's Brass Cannon" at http://www.youtube.com/watch?v=iZVauT_rZdk (Accessed 10/01/12).

28. RAH, handwritten index cards kept in his own safety-deposit box by his wife after his death and delivered to the RAH Archive by Art Dula on February 5, 2003.

29. The occasion was Heinlein's appearance at Young Men's/Young Women's Hebrew Association in New York on May 29, 1973, and the witness was Tom Collins, who recorded his impressions in his fanzine, *Transient* #31 (1974?) as "Tonight I Met Heinlein." The article has been web-published by Alexei Panshin on http://www.panshin.com/critics/Showdown/tomcollins.html (accessed 03/04/2014).

30. RAH, letter to John Conlan, undated but after 05/25/73.

31. RAH, letter to Walter Minton, 04/19/64.

32. RAH, letter to Peter Israel, 07/13/65.

33. John W. Campbell, letter to RAH, 07/06/65.

34. Walter Minton, letter to Lurton Blassingame, 02/20/67.

35. There is no indication in the correspondence how the new title came to be; on July 15, Heinlein opens discussions with Peter Israel about a new title; on August 5, his new editor, William Targ, refers to it by the *Harsh Mistress* name. Since Heinlein was lining up a trip to New York in the last two weeks of July 1965 (in connection with the Herman Kahn seminar on "The Next Ten Years"), possibly the new title was arrived at by telephone, or in person, instead of by correspondence.

36. RAH, letter to Karen Heinlein, 08/06/65.

37. RAH, letter to Lt. Sandra Fulton, U.S. Navy, 08/07/65.

38. Heinlein's editor at Ace is never specifically mentioned in the correspondence, but in a letter to Lurton Blassingame dated 06/21/65, he says Terry Carr is being too fussy about a paperback anthology he has no enthusiasm for, having rejected "Three Brave Men" as not-science-fiction. It is presumed this anthology was *Worlds of Robert A. Heinlein* (Ace, 1966), because there were no other anthologies in process at this point.

39. RAH, letter to Lurton Blassingame, 06/21/65.

40. RAH, letter to Peggy and Count (Lurton) Blassingame, 08/06/65.

41. RAH, letter to Karen Heinlein, 08/06/65.

42. RAH, letter to Lt. Sandra Fulton, USN, 08/07/65.

43. RAH, letter to "Sandy" Fulton, 09/26/65.

44. RAH, letter to Lurton Blassingame, 08/09/65.

45. RAH, letter to Lurton Blassingame, 09/11/65.

46. Cal Laning, letter to RAH, 10/09/65, reporting that Arwine had passed away "yesterday."

47. RAH, letter to Clifford D. Simak, 10/05/65.

48. Virginia Heinlein, taped interview with the author, Series 3, Tape B, Side A (March 27, 2001).

49. Virginia Heinlein, taped interview with the author, Series 3, Tape B, Side A (March 27, 2001).

50. RAH, letter to Lurton Blassingame, 11/10/65.

51. Virginia Heinlein, IM with the author, 4/19/00.

52. Harlan Ellison, letter to RAH, 10/19/65.

53. RAH, letter to Bjo and John Trimble, 11/30/65.

54. RAH, letter to Lurton Blassingame, 11/30/65.

55. Walter Minton, letter to Lurton Blassingame, 02/20/67. In this letter Minton said they originally ordered seventy-five hundred copies of *The Moon Is a Harsh Mistress,* of which only seven thousand were actually printed and bound. Putnam's was afraid *Harsh Mistress* would also be passed over for young adult markets because of the "rather unusual family system."

56. RAH, Journal, "The Road to Bonny Doon," 12/19/65.

57. RAH, letter to Bjo Trimble, 11/30/65.

58. Virginia Heinlein, taped interview with the author, Series 3, Tape B, Side A (March 27, 2001).

20. House-building—Again! (pages 274–284)

1. RAH, letter to Lurton Blassingame, 02/01/66.

2. Virginia Heinlein, e-mail to the author, 05/21/00.

3. Redwoods grow in concentric rings and their litter makes the soil in the center of the ring so acidic that only highly resistant plants can grow there. The walled-in spaces are called "cathedrals." Nothing competes with redwoods for sun.

4. Virginia Heinlein, taped interview with the author, Tape 6, Side B.

5. RAH, Journal, "The Road to Bonny Doon," 01/11/66.

6. RAH, Journal, "The Road to Bonny Doon," 01/12/66.

7. RAH, "The Heinlein Interview." *The Robert A. Heinlein Interview and Other Heinleinana,* J. Neil Schulman, ed., 166.

8. Virginia Heinlein, letter to Michael J. Cronin, EVP of Productivity Systems Division, Computervision Corporation, 03/11/79.

9. Virginia Heinlein, letter to the author, 10/20/99.

10. RAH, letter to Lurton Blassingame (second letter of the same date, continuation), 02/01/66.

11. RAH, letter to Elisabeth Price, 11/21/67.

12. RAH, letter to Elisabeth Price, 11/21/67.

13. RAH, letter to Lurton Blassingame (second letter of the same date, continuation), 02/01/66.

14. RAH, telephone interview with Ben Bova, 06/29/79.

15. RAH, letter to Peggy Blassingame, 04/06/66.

16. RAH, letter to Peggy Blassingame, 04/06/66.

17. Harlan Ellison, letter to RAH, 07/25/66.

18. RAH, letter to Lurton Blassingame, 07/01/66.

19. RAH, letter to Lurton Blassingame, 07/01/66.

20. While the author was consulting at the UC Santa Cruz library in 2003–6, he frequently experienced small birds stooping to pluck his hair, presumably for nest-building. Perhaps something of the sort was happening to Ginny Heinlein—a local Santa Cruz phenomenon.

21. RAH, letter to Earl Kemp, 01/20/57.

22. Many years later, talking in a general way, critic Fredric Jameson suggested that science fiction achieves a historical consciousness through projections of futures. Fredric Jameson, "Progress versus Utopia: or Can We Imagine the Future," *Science Fiction Studies* (July 1982).

23. Damon Knight, letter to RAH, 10/06/66.

24. RAH, letter to Willy Ley, 04/05/68.

25. RAH, letter to Lurton Blassingame, 09/04/66.

26. Poul Anderson, letter to RAH, 09/23/66.

27. RAH, letter to Poul Anderson, 10/09/66.

28. RAH, letter to Lurton Blassingame, 09/04/66; Virginia Heinlein, letter to Leon Stover, 03/28/89.

29. Author conversation with Rita (Berner) Bottoms, April 2004.

30. Michael Murphy, letter to RAH, 10/11/66.

31. Rev. David Baar, Bishop of California, letter to Michael Murphy (RAH is cc'd), 12/06/66.

32. Walter Minton, letter to Lurton Blassingame, 01/01/67.

33. Lurton Blassingame, letter to Walter Minton, 12/22/66.

34. Peter Mayer (Avon), letter to Walter Minton, 02/01/67.

21. Stalled (pages 285–299)

1. RAH, letter to Lurton Blassingame, 01/23/67.
2. RAH, letter to Lurton Blassingame, 01/23/67.
3. RAH, letter to Lurton Blassingame, 01/23/67.
4. RAH, letter to Lurton Blassingame, 04/18/67.
5. Rita Bottoms, conversation with the author, May 2006, in discussion of her oral history.
6. RAH, letter to Ned Brown, 07/06/67.
7. "Westercon" is the Western Regional Science Fiction Conference/Convention, the largest regional SF convention in the Western United States, held over the Fourth of July weekend each year and alternating between northern and southern regions.
8. Karen Anderson, postcard to the Heinleins, 06/28/66.
9. RAH, letter to Dan Galouye, 10/02/67.
10. RAH, letter to Harlan Ellison, 12/29/67. The dates of the stages in this matter were nowhere recorded in the correspondence, but may have been as late as October 1967.
11. Poul Anderson, memorial in *Requiem*; Virginia Heinlein, taped interview with the author, Tape 9, Side A (March 1?, 2000).
12. RAH, letter to Harlan Ellison, 05/24/75.
13. Poul Anderson, letter to RAH, 10/27/67.
14. RAH, letter to Judith Merril, 11/01/67.
15. RAH, letter to A. E. Wilson, 11/19/67.
16. RAH, unsent letter to Judith Merril, 11/01/67.
17. RAH, unsent letter to Judith Merril, 11/01/67.
18. RAH, letter to Lurton Blassingame, 12/06/67.
19. RAH, letter to Robert Moore Williams, 04/06/68.
20. RAH, letter to Barbara Herzberger, 12/21/67.
21. RAH, letter to Temple and Nancy Fielding, 04/02/68.
22. The invoice for the flagpole is dated 02/07/68.
23. RAH, letter to John Conlan, 04/06/68.
24. RAH, letter to Lurton Blassingame, 03/22/68.
25. Virginia Heinlein, taped interview with the author, Tape 5, Side B (February 25? 2000).
26. Mrs. Heinlein said *Stranger* had appeared briefly on the *New York Times* bestseller list in 1968, but there were not enough copies available to sustain it there. Virginia Heinlein, taped interview with the author, Tape 9, Side B (February 28? 2000).

This is not likely, as the *New York Times* bestseller lists for 1968 show only hardcover issues, and by that time *Stranger* was available only in paperback. It may be she is thinking of some other bestseller list, such as the B. Dalton List or the Waldenbooks list, which did show paperbacks (as a separate category), but there are too many such lists to check them one by one.

27. RAH, letter to Lurton Blassingame, 11/21/68.

28. Willis McNelly, letter to Alvin Wrobel, Circulation Mgr. at Berkeley, 11/04/68.

29. Virginia Heinlein, letter to the author, 12/24/99.

30. RAH, letter to Pat Gallner, 10/14/68.

31. RAH, letter to "Mrs. Hollingshead" (not otherwise identified), 12/29/68.

32. RAH, letter to Rev. Paul Wilkinnson, Asbury Methodist Church, 12/29/68.

33. RAH, letter to Marie Browne, 12/18/68.

34. Shrive = hear confession, assign penance, grant absolution.

35. Virginia Heinlein, letter to the author, 12/20/99.

36. RAH, letter to Lurton Blassingame, 03/22/68.

37. RAH, letter to Cal Laning, 12/17/68.

38. RAH, letter to Lurton Blassingame, 04/28/68.

39. RAH, letter to Lurton Blassingame, 04/28/68.

40. RAH, letter to David Gerrold, 05/28/68. The *Stranger* script project thereafter disappeared down a rabbit hole.

41. FOBS = "Fractional Orbiting Bombardment System," an orbiting missile base specifically forbidden by the Space Treaty of 1967. The Soviet Union launched FOBS 12 in April 1968.

42. Harold Stassen (1907–2001), former governor of Minnesota (1939–1943) and a perennial candidate for president, losing the Republican nomination eight times between 1948 and 1992.

43. Dick Gregory (1932–) Black comedian and social activist, one of the first to perform successfully before both black and white audiences.

44. RAH, letter to John Conlon, 04/06/68.

45. RAH, letter to "Buddy" Col. A. E. Wilson, 11/19/67.

46. RAH, letter to Pat Carroll, 12/17/68.

47. RAH, letter to Cal Laning, 12/17/68.

48. RAH, letter to L. Sprague de Camp, 12/28/68.

49. Virginia Heinlein, letter to the author, 10/20/99.

50. RAH, letter to Jane and Pete Sencenbaugh, 12/28/68.

51. RAH, letter to L. Sprague de Camp, 12/28/68.

22. Picking Up Where He Left Off (pages 300–315)

1. Virginia Heinlein, letter to Harry and Barbara Stine, 01/07/69.

2. Virginia Heinlein, letter to Harry and Barbara Stine, 01/07/69. The cuts were not allowed in the dunder-free quest house.

3. Fred Pohl, letter to RAH, 02/27/69, forwarding a cable from José Sanz.

4. RAH, letter to Wes Posvar, 03/04/69. The Alliance for Progress was a 1961 pro-
    gram initiated by President John F. Kennedy to counter increased influence of
    the Soviet Union, by increasing U.S. appropriations for South American eco-
    nomic growth. The goal Kennedy articulated in his proposing speech:

    > Let us once again transform the American Continent into a vast crucible
    > of revolutionary ideas and efforts, a tribute to the power of the creative
    > energies of free men and women, an example to all the world that liberty
    > and progress walk hand in hand. Let us once again awaken our American
    > revolution until it guides the struggles of people everywhere—not with an
    > imperialism of force or fear but the rule of courage and freedom and hope
    > for the future of man.

    President Kennedy's speech, "Preliminary Formulations of the Alliance for
    Progress, 1961," was given at a White House diplomatic reception on March 13,
    1961 and is archived online at: http://www.fordham.edu/halsall/mod/1961kennedy-
    afp1.html (accessed 03/04/2014).

5. Dean E. McHenry, Ph.D. (1910–98) was founding chancellor of the University
    of California, Santa Cruz. Chancellor McHenry and Heinlein also had in com-
    mon that they had both been EPICs in the mid-1930s, Heinlein in Los Angeles,
    McHenry while working on his doctorate at UC Berkeley.

6. One of Ginny's endodontists, in San Francisco.

7. Charles Page Smith (1917–95) was an American historian best known for *A People's
    History of the United States* (McGraw-Hill, 1976–1987). He was also an activist
    for the homeless in Santa Cruz.

8. I have not been able to identify Mr. and Mrs. Joel Schaefer.

9. For years a bizarre rumor has circulated in the community of science-fiction
    writers that Ginny had a "health crisis" immediately before the Rio trip in 1969—
    by which is meant a recent miscarriage.

    The rumor appears to have been the result of a misinterpretation of an un-
    pleasant exchange in the plane between Heinlein and another science-fiction
    writer/invitee on the way to Rio: Mrs. Heinlein was carrying a large handbag,
    and one of the other invitees asked what she was carrying, adding "a dead baby?"
    Heinlein is reported to have told the offending person something like: "If you say
    anything like that to my wife again, I'll kill you."

    At that time Mrs. Heinlein was nearly fifty-four years old—and in any case
    Heinlein was medically sterile. The conclusion that she had had a recent miscar-
    riage was based on no actual information at all—only on a supposed special
    sensitivity to the subject of dead babies.

10. Virginia Heinlein, letter to Bill and Lucy Corson, 08/03/69.
11. RAH, letter to Bill and Lucy Corson, 06/10/69.
12. A transcription of the speech was published in *Requiem,* ed. Yoji Kondo.
13. RAH, letter to Bill and Lucy Corson, 06/10/69.
14. Virginia Heinlein, letter to Leon and Takeko Stover, who were friends of Harrison, 03/13/89:

> We were attending a film festival in Rio, as guests of the Brazilian government—HH [Harry Harrison] was there too. An invitation came to us from one of the officials of the U.S. Embassy, a small dinner party at his house. Robert and I were dressed to go, waiting for a taxi, and Robert was carrying a box of flowers for our hostess, when HH came along with several others, and demanded to know where we were going. Robert refused to tell him, and HH tried to grab the box from Robert. It was a rather horrid scene, there on the sidewalk in front of the hotel.
>
> The taxi appeared. We left. And presently, after we'd had some drinks with our hosts and other guests, dinner began. Then, in walked HH and two other people (I can't even recall their names.) They weren't expected— it was obvious. Somehow they had found out where we were going and crashed the party.
>
> I was very upset about the matter, and don't remember it very well, but I was so disgusted with HH that I never wanted to even see him again. . . . I am sorry that I must relate these seamy matters, but I would just as soon never hear mentioned HH's name again.

15. Virginia Heinlein, letter to Dr. Roger Lindeman, 07/03/76. The tinnitus was with her for the rest of her life.
16. RAH, letter to Alfred and Rolly Bester, 06/14/69; Virginia Heinlein, letter to Virginia Fowler, 08/17/69.
17. Virginia Heinlein, letter to Virginia Fowler, 08/14/69.
18. Also as "Linguistic Relativity in Old High Martian" (*The CEA Critic,* XXX[6] [March 1968]: 4, 6). Willis E. McNelly, Ph.D. (1920–2003), English professor at California State University, Fullerton, best known for his 1984 *Dune Encyclopedia.* In 1971 he assembled, with his colleague Jane Hipolito, an anthology of Marsiana, *Mars, We Love You,* that contained the "Linguistic Relativity" essay, as well as an extract from *Double Star* (a practice Heinlein did not encourage but nevertheless sometimes allowed).
19. Benjamin Whorf (1897–1941) was a chemical engineer who became interested in linguistics and defined the "Whorf-Sapir" hypothesis of linguistic relativity

(Edward Sapir was Whorf's teacher at Yale University)—that language shapes what can be thought. Heinlein used this idea in *Stranger in a Strange Land*, and he knew of Whorf because of John Campbell's enthusiasm for Whorf's "Languages and Logic" article in 1941 (which came up in their discussions during the creation of *Methuselah's Children*—see the April 1941 correspondence of Heinlein and Campbell in the Virginia Edition, Vol. xxxix, *Letters 1: Correspondence of John W. Campbell, Jr., and Robert A. Heinlein*), but Heinlein first encountered the ideas in his studies of General Semantics with Alfred Korzybski. Comparing Whorf's ideas and Korzybski's, he wrote,

> . . . language is a barrier—but not nearly the barrier that culture can be. However, I am not discounting the language barrier *where the languages are essentially different in structure,* which is (usually, perhaps always) a situation in which the language difference mirrors a basic (and possibly insurmountable) difference in culture . . . Whorf has pointed out many of these cultural differences imbedded in syntax; Korzybski pointed out that the fashion in which a man thinks is constrained by the *unconscious* assumptions of the grammar of his native language. (RAH, letter to Howard Cady, 04/09/61.)

20. RAH, letter to Willis McNelly, 05/15/68.
21. A *very* narrow margin. Shortly after the publication of *Starship Troopers,* Heinlein set out as his own thought the core observation on which modern individualist anarchism is based. After remarking that he was against conscription and against confinement, he goes on to say:

> The only thing common to all forms of government is *force.* It was rude of me to say so, in an era when euphemisms of all sorts are customary. But there it is—force. . . . I am not objecting to this. I am simply saying: all government is force. The sole difference between one sort and another is: *who exercises that unlimited force?*

RAH, letter to George Scithers, 11/23/59.
   The modern definition of a state in libertarian theory, following a long debate over the notion of "competing governments" in the late 1960s and early 1970s, is an entity or organization which claims to control the exercise of force and violence within a given territory.

22. RAH, letter to Poul and Karen Anderson, 06/22/62.
23. RAH, letter to Lurton Blassingame, 06/04/69.
24. Virginia Heinlein, letter to Willis McNelly, 06/03/69.
25. RAH, letter to Lurton Blassingame, 06/04/69.
26. RAH, letter to Lawrence Heinlein, 06/09/69.

27. RAH outline notes for *I Will Fear No Evil*. RAH Archive, UC Santa Cruz.

28. This sentiment is voiced in several letters, but with particular direction to the juveniles, see RAH, letter to Lurton Blassingame, 03/10/62.

29. "The Rare Ones: How They Save Lives," *Parade* magazine (06/23/68).

30. RAH, letter to William S. Kyler, CCBC, 11/13/75.

31. Heinlein's outline "Notes for a 2-part serial intended for PLAYBOY" 18 June 1969 in the RAH Archive, UC Santa Cruz, first paragraph.

32. Heinlein's composition record, kept on his "opus" file card. The card file is still in use by the Heinlein Prize Trust in managing Heinlein's literary properties.

33. RAH taped interview with Frank M. Robinson, 08/09/69 (raw transcript). The unpublished *Playboy* submission format of the interview is published in the Virginia Edition, Vol. xxxvii, *Nonfiction 1*.

34. These sentiments Heinlein expressed in the Frank Robinson interview. The words specifically applied to the atmosphere in the Downey studio a few days later, but they were the ripened essence of the spiritual experience that began four days earlier, at the launch.

35. Frank Robinson, *Playboy* Interview file, UCSC Special Collections. Heinlein does not identify the person he made the bet with. Heinlein's closest friend in 1919 would have been Isidore Horoshem.

36. RAH, taped interview with Frank M. Robinson, 08/09/69 (raw transcript). The order of the remarks has been slightly rearranged for effect, as the questions and answers in the raw transcript were not in strict sequential order and were rearranged (in a different way) for Robinson's submission manuscript, which is published in the Virginia Edition, Vol. xxxvii, *Nonfiction 1*.

37. "N.O. Scientists React: 'A Step Into Manhood' or 'A Waste of Money'?" New Orleans *States-Item* (07/21/69), 10.

38. RAH, letter to T. B. Buell, 10/03/74.

39. R. N. S. Clark, letter to RAH, 07/26/69.

40. It was not generally remembered, even within the science-fiction community, that a televised Moon landing had in fact been predicted in a comic book at about the time *Destination Moon* was being written. Jay Rudin pointed out in the alt.fan.heinlein newsgroup on September 6, 2007, that it appeared in *Real Facts Comic* no. 15 (July/August 1948).

41. Virginia Heinlein, letter to the author, 06/14/99.

42. Virginia Heinlein, letter to Stevie and Ken Stone, 08/03/69.

43. Virginia Heinlein, letter to Lucy and Bill Corson, 08/03/69.

44. The index cards of Heinlein's notes for the lunar landing broadcast are preserved in the RAH Archive, UC Santa Cruz.

45. The time is recorded in a photo essay (screen captures) section of *10:56:20 P.M.*

7/20/69: The Historic Conquest of the Moon as Reported to the American People by CBS News over the CBS Television Network (New York: CBS, 1970), n.p. Much more video was taped than was used.

46. CBS News, *10:56:20 P.M. 7/20/69: The Historic Conquest of the Moon as Reported to the American People by CBS News over the CBS Television Network* (New York: CBS, 1970), 107.

47. Virginia Heinlein, letter to Stevie and Ken Stone, 08/03/69. Mrs. Heinlein believed the cheers and applause in the studio were for Heinlein's performance in discomfiting Cronkite (and that may well have been a factor), but it is just as likely the applause was for Heinlein's message—and for Heinlein himself.

48. Virginia Heinlein, letter to Leon Stover, 01/10/86. This exchange was not on the preserved portion of the interview tape; nor was it included in the CBS commemorative book. Stover's "outtake" in his book *Robert Heinlein* for the Twayne U.S. Author Series (at 122, fn. 2) is an almost word-for-word transcription of Virginia Heinlein's memory, as follows:

> The exchange which I recall so vividly between Robert and Walter Cronkite went something like this:
>
> R. About one third of the weight of this Apollo ship could have been saved by having an all-female crew.
>
> C. Women in space!! Never (words to this effect).
>
> R. Eventually whole families will go into space. But in this particular instance, if we'd sent someone—say Peggy Fleming—on this mission, the entire project could have saved a great deal of money, etc. Because women weigh less than men, and the engineering on the Saturn rocket would have been simpler and cheaper. An athlete like Peggy Fleming could have learned all the things she needed to know, and done what was necessary.
>
> C[ronkite] continued to splutter at the idea of women in space, and these days he would find himself a candidate for lynching if he said some of the things he said then.
>
> Robert continued with other considerations, and interrupted C[ronkite] again and again.

Stover added (at 123):

> What makes this exchange interesting is that it dramatically reverses all the usual cliches about these two men. While the media critics dub Cronkite the great "liberal" commentator of the TV airwaves, critics of Heinlein attack him for being illiberal, sexist, and antifeminist.

49. Virginia Heinlein, letter to Leon Stover, 01/10/86.

50. Frank M. Robinson, letter to RAH, 07/25/69.

51. Statement by Robert A. Heinlein, "26 July 1969." This statement was apparently not circulated or published anywhere at the time, but was incorporated in the Virginia Edition, vol. xxxvii, *Nonfiction 1.*

52. Robert Heinlein, taped interview with Frank M. Robinson, Tape 1, Side 1 (p. 1 of transcript, crossing over to 2).

53. Heinlein's opus card records: "resumed writing reading MS + notes in prep to resume writing on Ms 28 July 1969, 1250." The meaning of "1250" is obscure—perhaps the time at which he began the review of his previous work, i.e., ten minutes before 1:00 P.M.

54. Virginia Heinlein, letter to Lurton Blassingame, 08/28/69; *Grumbles from the Grave,* 178.

55. SDS = Students for a Democratic Society, a radical left-wing student organization, sponsor of the 1962 Port Huron Statement, a prominent manifesto of the New Left through the 1960s until SDS disbanded after their 1969 convention.

56. RAH, letter to Frank M. Robinson, 09/18/69.

57. RAH, letter to Frank M. Robinson, 09/27/69.

58. Undated letter, apparently a personal postscript or addendum by Heinlein to a multigraphed status letter sent to Ted Carnell in 1971.

59. RAH, letter to Rita Bottoms, 09/10/73.

60. See, e.g., RAH, letter to Ted Carnell, 11/14/62:

> If the audience does not laugh, the fault always lies with the clown. This is an axiom that writers should never forget. We are in the clown business, first and foremost, and if, in our pride, we forget this even for a moment, the results are disastrous—to the clown. Not to the audience.

61. RAH, letter to Paul Kantner, 09/18/69. Kantner later remembered the incident with a somewhat different slant:

> During an interview for David Gans' Grateful Dead Hour a couple of months ago, [Paul] Kantner [of Jefferson Airplane] told me this story: "When I was making *Blows Against The Empire,* I wrote a letter to Heinlein because I got his address. He lived down in Santa Cruz, in Bonnie Doon, actually, where my first girlfriend lived, so I thought 'well, this is propitious.' And I sent him a letter asking permission to use some of his words and some of his concepts out of his novels in *Blows Against The Empire.* He wrote me back saying, 'My god, this is staggering'—something like that—'you people have been ripping off my ideas and words for like 30 or 40 years and you're

the first person who's ever had the decency to ask for permission.' And he said, 'P.S. Oh by the way my gardener says he went to high school with Marty Balin, who is your lead singer right now, and sends his best.' That was a cute letter."

http://www.metafilter.com/48658/Specialization-is-for-Insects. Accessed by Bill Mullins 05/26/06 and reaccessed by the author 07/11/11.

62. Virginia Heinlein, taped interview with Leon Stover, Tape 2, Side A (October 21, 1988).

63. Virginia Heinlein, letter to *Locus* (July 1988).

64. Virginia Heinlein, taped interview with Leon Stover, Tape 2, Side A (October 21, 1988). A joint task force of National Park rangers, California Highway Patrol, and the Inyo County Sheriff's Office had raided two ranches to which members of the "Manson Family" had moved after Manson's arrest in August 1969—before the connection between the Tate and LaBianca murders had been publicly announced.

65. Virginia Heinlein, letter to Jane and Pete Sencenbaugh, 12/06/69.

66. Virginia Heinlein, letter to Poul and Karen Anderson, 12/06/69.

67. Virginia Heinlein, letter to Lucy and Bill Corson, 12/07/69.

68. Virginia Heinlein, letter to Art and Lucky Herzberger, 12/08/69.

69. RAH, letter to Lurton Blassingame, 11/12/69, the relevant portion of which is quoted in *Grumbles from the Grave*.

70. Virginia Heinlein, letter to Lucy and Bill Corson, 12/07/69.

71. Virginia Heinlein, letter to Poul and Karen Anderson, 12/06/69.

72. Virginia Heinlein, letter to Lurton Blassingame, 12/04/69.

73. Rita Bottoms, handwritten note to Donald T. Clark, 12/10/69; incorporated into Donald T. Clark, letter to RAH, dated 01/06/70. Rita Bottoms desk file.

23. Trouble, With a Capital "P" (pages 316–331)

1. "History of Robert's illnesses," Virginia Heinlein, letter to the author, 09/20/00.

2. Virginia Heinlein, taped interview with Leon Stover, Tape 2, Side A (October 1988?).

3. Virginia Heinlein, letter to Leon Stover, 03/17/89.

4. Virginia Heinlein, letter to Lurton Blassingame, 01/16/70.

5. Frank M. Robinson, e-mail to the author, 09/12/05.

6. Virginia Heinlein, letter to George Coleman, 03/17/71.

7. "History of Robert's illnesses," Virginia Heinlein, letter to the author, 09/20/00.

8. *Time* magazine, unbylined, "A Martian Model," (January 19, 1970): 44–45.

9. "In an interview almost twenty years later, he [Bugliosi] said that he had seri-

ously considered the allegations, investigated them, and then dismissed them," Leon Stover, "The Heinlein-Manson Hoax," *The Heinlein Journal,* no. 2 (January 1998): 2.

10. Steven Kay, Ed Sanders, *The Family,* 27.

11. Virginia Heinlein, letter to Violet Markham, 02/27/71.

12. Virginia Heinlein, letter to the author, 09/20/00; Virginia Heinlein, taped interview with Leon Stover, Tape 2, Side A (October 1988?).

13. Virginia Heinlein, letter to the author, 09/20/00.

14. This incident was retold several times in Virginia Heinlein's correspondence and in interviews; in some of the tellings, Dr. Calciano suggested Stanford Medical Center; in others it was a doctor at Dominican Hospital. At one point in the Stover interview of October 1988, and also in the "History of Robert's Illnesses" written for the author, she implies she made the decision on her own.

15. Virginia Heinlein, letter to George Coleman, 03/17/71. Mrs. Heinlein never specifically identified which "Dr. Calciano" she meant, but she might have meant Dr. Anthony J. Calciano, a cardiology and internal medicine specialist who began practicing in 1965 and is still in 2012 practicing at Dominican Hospital in Santa Cruz. It has not proved possible to trace Dr. Calciano's malpractice history— not unusual, as nondisclosure agreements are typically part of settlement negotiations.

16. Virginia Heinlein, letter to Lucy and Bill Corson, 08/20/71; Virginia Heinlein, letter to Lucy and Bill Corson, 08/30/71.

17. Virginia Heinlein, IM with the author, 01/20/00.

18. Virginia Heinlein, letter to the author, 09/20/00.

19. Virginia Heinlein, letter to George Coleman, 03/17/71.

20. Virginia Heinlein, letter to Violet Markham, 02/27/71; Virginia Heinlein, letter to Leon Stover, 03/28/69.

21. RAH, letter to Mrs. Thomas V. (Rita) Bottoms, 09/10/73.

22. Virginia Heinlein, letter to Dr. (Lloyd) Biggle, 03/12/77.

23. Dr. Harry Oberhelman, e-mail to Francesco Spreafico, 04/05/01.

24. Virginia Heinlein, letter to George Coleman, 03/17/71.

25. Virginia Heinlein, letter to Dr. (Lloyd) Biggle, 03/12/77.

26. RAH, letter to Robert Bloch, 10/11/71. Heinlein probably meant "durable power of attorney," as an ordinary general power of attorney ceases to be effective if the grantor ceases to be able to handle his own affairs, whereas the language which creates a durable power of attorney survives the grantor's incapacity.

27. RAH, letter to Mary Collin, 07/08/62.

28. Virginia Heinlein, IM with the author, 09/26/01.

29. Karen Serassio anecdote, undated, but after 1977.

30. Virginia Heinlein, letter to Lurton Blassingame, 02/12/70; *Grumbles from the Grave,* 180.

31. Virginia Heinlein, taped interview with Leon Stover, Tape 2, Side A (October 21, 1988).

32. RAH, letter to Robert Bloch, 10/11/71.

33. The time of Dr. Nourse's trip was not fixed in the correspondence, but must have been in February or early March 1970. Heinlein memorialized it in a letter to L. Sprague and Catherine de Camp, 06/04/70:

> Alan Nourse did the most wonderful thing for us in taking the trouble to make a trip just to look me over, talk to my doctors, read my chart, then talk to Ginny and explain it all to her. It gave her morale a great boost when she needed it badly—which in turn gave my morale a shot in the arm.

34. Virginia Heinlein, IM with the author, 01/20/00.

35. Virginia Heinlein, letter to the author, 09/20/00.

36. Virginia Heinlein, letter to the author, 12/14/99.

37. Virginia Heinlein, letter to Violet Markham, 02/27/71.

38. Virginia Heinlein, letter to Jan Lister, 05/21/70.

39. RAH, letter to Nancy and Temple Fielding, 06/05/70.

40. Virginia Heinlein, letter to Lurton Blassingame, 03/31/70.

41. Virginia Heinlein, taped interview with Leon Stover, Tape 2, Side A (October 1988?).

42. RAH, letter to Miss Hewey, 12/13/71.

43. Walter Minton, letter to RAH, 04/07/70.

44. Virginia Heinlein, letter to Walter Minton, 04/13/70.

45. RAH, letter to Robert Bloch, 06/04/70.

46. Virginia Heinlein, letter to Walter Minton, 08/13/70.

47. Virginia Heinlein, letter to the author, 07/05/00.

48. Per Timothy J. Hamilton, Share Water Bed, letter to RAH, 08/22/70.

49. Virginia Heinlein, letter to Lurton Blassingame, 11/20/70. Perhaps she is referring to the review by James Gunn in the *Kansas City Times* (the morning edition of the *KC Star*) on that date, "Heinlein Rocket Veers Off Course," in which Gunn remarks of *Stranger* (rather than *I Will Fear No Evil*): "His treatment of sex, though liberated and nonpornographic, reads like a youngster trying to demonstrate his freedom from a Victorian upbringing."

50. Virginia Heinlein, letter to the author, 12/14/99.

51. RAH, letter to Mary Jean and Andy Lermer, 02/26/71.

52. This bedside table, together with the high bed, came into the possession of the Heinlein Society after Mrs. Heinlein's death and was sold at auction in 2013.

53. Don Ellis (1934–78) was a jazz trumpeter, band leader, composer, and drummer best remembered for his film scores for *The French Connection* (1971) and *The Seven Ups* (1973).

54. Virginia Heinlein, taped interview with Leon Stover, Tape 1, Side B (October 1988?).

55. Virginia Heinlein, letter to Lucy and Bill Corson, 08/30/71; in Virginia Heinlein, taped interview with Leon Stover, Tape 1, Side B, she says she suggested "The Green Hills of Earth."

56. RAH, letter to Pete Sencenbaugh, 10/01/71.

24. Da Capo al Fine (pages 332–345)

1. Virginia Heinlein, e-mail to the author, 10/11/00.

2. RAH, letter to Tim Zell, 01/20/72. This letter was somewhat edited by Virginia Heinlein for the end of *Grumbles from the Grave* and published as from "a Reader"— possibly to assure the material would be received as a general philosophical comment, rather than as specifically addressed to Zell's neopagan Church of All Worlds.

3. Virginia Heinlein, IM with the author, 05/28/00.

4. Ultimately, NASA decided against the unmanned Grand Tour, and the book was revised to a general survey of the solar system. The introduction was very tightly tied to the NASA Grand Tour, so Little, Brown dropped the Foreword, and it was eventually published as the last item of the Virginia Edition, vol. xxxvii, *Nonfiction 1*.

5. Virginia Heinlein, taped interview with Leon Stover, Tape 3, Side B.

6. Virginia Heinlein, letter to the author, 12/14/99.

7. One of the earliest critical works about Cabell took its title from these sections of verse disguised and scattered through Cabell's prose, *Cabellian Harmonics* by Warren A. McNeill (1928). It is probably worth noting, as well, that verse inclusions in prose works can be read as a marker for Northrop Frye's Anatomy genre.

8. Virginia Heinlein, letter to Dorace Trottier, 11/05/72.

9. Virginia Heinlein, letter to Dorace Trottier, 11/05/72.

10. Cdr. Walter, letter to Lurton Blassingame, 09/01/72.

11. Neither Capt. Mitchell nor Arthur C. Clarke made the cruise.

12. "Notes: Offshore View of Apollo 17 Liftoff," *The New York Times* Section X, Travel (11/19/72): 19.

13. Isaac Asimov, *In Joy Still Felt*, 621.

14. Isaac Asimov, *I, Asimov*, 358.

15. RAH, letter to T. B. Buell, 10/03/74.

16. Virginia Heinlein, IM with Ron Harrison, undated but February 2000.

17. "Thanatosphere" is a neologism coined by Mailer—a spherical shell around the Earth, something like a second atmosphere, comprised of the souls of the dead. Mike Lennon of the Norman Mailer Society provides the information that Mailer discusses the concept first, without using the term, in *A Fire on the Moon* (1970) at 109 and coined the term in a *Christian Science Monitor* article on January 3, 1973. Mailer also coined the term "factoid."

18. Quoted in Tom Buckley, "Caribbean Cruise Attempts to Seek Meaning of Apollo," *The New York Times* (12/12/72): 53.

19. Quoted in Tom Buckley, "Caribbean Cruise Attempts to Seek Meaning of Apollo," *The New York Times* (12/12/72): 53.

20. RAH, letter to Nancy and Temple Fielding, 01/28/73.

21. Isaac Asimov, *I, Asimov,* 358.

22. *The New York Times* (12/12/72): 53.

23. *The New York Times* (12/12/72): 53; Isaac Asimov, *I, Asimov,* 358.

24. Katherine Anne Porter, quoted in *The New York Times* (12/12/72): 53, based on interview conducted 12/08/72.

25. *The New York Times* (12/12/73): 53.

26. Virginia Heinlein, letter to Arthur C. Clarke, 01/22/73.

27. Isaac Asimov, *In Joy Still Felt,* 624. Asimov has the date wrong, as the cruise was over by December 14.

28. David Hartwell, acquiring editor of this biography, commented during the editing of this volume in 2011 that he was the science-fiction editor of Putnam's at the time and he did not agree with this assessment but was ordered by Walter Minton not to suggest cuts.

29. See, e.g., Virginia Heinlein, taped interview with the author, Tape 10, Side B. Heinlein himself made similar remarks in contemporaneous correspondence with the author.

30. RAH, letter to Tim Zell, 01/20/72.

31. That Heinlein read and greatly admired *Generation of Vipers* is documented (in the first volume of this biography); that he read *An Essay on Morals* is presumed on the basis of some slight convergence of content.

32. For a nineteenth-century example of the "genealogical" style of argument, see F. W. Nietzsche's *On the Genealogy of Morals: A Polemic* (1887). The genealogical style of argument was devised as a counter to the then academically standard method of arguing from religious propositions as first principles. Gradually in most academic disciplines religious arguments went out of favor, but they were—and still are—very prominent in casual or popular settings, as the continuing "debate" over various forms of "creation science" demonstrate graphically.

33. RAH, letter to Dorothea Faulkner, 12/28/68.

34. RAH, letter to Cal Laning, 10/17/73.

35. Tape-recording quoted with author comments in James D. Gifford, *Robert A. Heinlein: A Reader's Companion* (Citrus Heights, Calif.: NitroSyncretic Press, 2000), 69.

36. RAH, letter to Cal Laning, 10/16/73.

37. This powerful memory from Heinlein's childhood was confirmed by David R. Bayard and Joel Davis, who researched the matter in 2011 and found that this story is likely based (at least in part) on an incident that took place in Elizabeth, New Jersey, on April 17, 1911. The report was also carried that date in the *Kansas City Times* (the morning edition of the *Star*) as "Fast Train Killed Three." The facts are not quite as Heinlein recalled them—it was an elderly woman and her daughter, and the man trying to help them was the baggage master of the station.

    The report of this incident may have been a matter of discussion among the adults, rather than something Heinlein experienced directly. He would have been three years old at the time.

    It is possible also that he conflated this with an incident that took place several years later in Chicago but which was reported in the *Kansas City Star* on September 3, 1919 as "Which a Father's Duty? Should Tanner have lived for children or died with wife? Chicago Debates the Question While Paying Tribute to the Heroism of Husband at Grade Crossing." This story not only has the thematic thrust of Heinlein's recollection, its details are much closer to his story: a husband and wife crossing railroad tracks; the wife's foot is caught in the tracks, and a flagman and the husband working together to free the woman as the train bore down on them, ultimately killing the husband and wife while the flagman was sideswiped by the train. This item was found by Bill Mullins in 2013 and published on the Heinlein Society's NexusForum "Woman Killed by Train" thread.

    If either or both of these items were his source, Heinlein has added details of his own (the hobo, for example) and his own interpretation of the meaning of the incident. It made a good story—one of the best.

38. RAH, "Channel Markers," *Analog* (January 1974).

39. Leon Stover, "The Forrestal Lecture," *The Heinlein Journal*, no. 4 (January 1999): 5.

40. RAH, letter to Cal and Mickey Laning, 10/16/73.

41. RAH's self-written profile for the 1974 *Muster Notes*, 61.

42. RAH, letter to Hap, Rebel & Dori Trottier, 04/18/73.

43. Heinlein and Klass did conduct the interview that was to provide the raw material for this profile, but for reasons Prof. Klass could not recall in 2004, when he was guest of honor at the NoreasCon World SF Convention in Boston (see remarks and quotations in "Textual Comparison of Three Versions of Robert Heinlein's

Forrestal Lecture," ed. Bill Patterson, *The Heinlein Journal,* no. 15 (July 2004): 6, the profile was never written. Of this incident, Mrs. Heinlein told Leon Stover in 1988:

> We made very special efforts to get to State College so he [Klass] could do this interview with Robert. It was at the behest of some publisher or something, who was anxious to get it into the *New York Times.* And he never got off the dime with all this material. He got so bemused by Robert's periodic sentences that he never got them written down or something. . . . he never wrote it down in publishable form, at least. And presently, it being topical, why, it was no longer useful.

(Virginia Heinlein, interview with Leon Stover, 1987, Tape 1, Side A.)

Prof. Klass was quite frail in 2004, but his wife and daughter both concurred that the reel-to-reel tapes of the interview had been placed in their basement storage and were probably still there. But to date they have not been unearthed or made available. Prof. Klass died in 2010.

44. Except as otherwise noted, all quotations from Phil Klass excerpted from transcription of taped hall conversation with Mr. Klass, Robert James, and the author, at NorEasCon III, September 5, 2003, as quoted in "Textual Comparison of Three Versions of Robert A. Heinlein's Forrestal Lecture," in *The Heinlein Journal,* no. 15 (July 2004): 6.

45. In fact, Bester had "won" the pseudo-contest that got Heinlein writing pulp in the first place, and his first story ("The Broken Axiom") appeared in the April 1939 issue of *Thrilling Wonder Stories* just as John Campbell was accepting Heinlein's first story, "Life-Line." That is, the notice of "writing contest" (that was actually a call for amateur writers to become professional science-fiction writers) originally appeared in *Thrilling Wonder Stories* in October 1938, and "The Broken Axiom" was written in response to that notice. The matter of the *Thrilling Wonder Stories* notice and Heinlein's start in writing is detailed in chapter 17 of *Learning Curve,* 213–35.

46. Sir William S. Gilbert, "The Yarn of the 'Nancy Bell'" (1966).

47. RAH, letter to Dick Mandelkorn, 11/08/73. Of the five books he had in process, none (probably) was actually completed and published, though one title, *Grumbles from the Grave* (originally intended to be a memoir) was recycled by Mrs. Heinlein for a posthumous selection of Heinlein's letters. Mrs. Heinlein was less enthusiastic about this project: The amount of kicking around he planned to give people in his memoirs would anger some people—and leave her with the pile of lawsuits. He fiddled with this project for many years, collecting dozens of three-by-five cards with notations of memorable events in his life. The index

card notations are somewhat cryptic, as the 1974 card demonstrates: "Sidg. & Jack. Marymon SS Dirac '29 Am. Human award. Mariposa xmas." Cf. also the 1975 card: "Mariposa home (Islands). Canada & World. Rare Blood EB Ring Cycle - Monterey - Alaska - Rare Blood."

Heinlein probably lost interest in a memoir after the quasi-autobiographical "interstitial notes" he did for *Expanded Universe* in 1979. Another of the five was to be a book on writing, comparable for the 1970s to Jack Woodford's *Trial and Error*. Mrs. Heinlein worked on that project after Heinlein's death, trying to bring together selections from his letters and so forth, but was unable to bring it to fruition.

The other three projects have not been identified, but it is possible he was beginning to assemble the earliest selection of material that would become *The Panki-Barsoom Number of the Beast* in 1977 and *The Number of the Beast* in 1980.

48. Joint Review by J. Leonard in the "Books of the Times" department of *The New York Times,* titled "Two Tales for the Future" (08/22/73): 35. Leonard is simultaneously insulting and complimentary throughout, as is illustrated by this comment late in the review:

> Really, besides being the sort of compulsive aphorist you can only shut up with a knuckle sandwich, Mr. Heinlein is a dirty old man, part goat and part Petronius. If it doesn't matter—and to me it doesn't—that all his characters sound and behave exactly the same, it's because the man is a master of beguilement. He pulls so hard on the dugs of sentiment that disbelief is not merely suspended; it is abolished. A great entertainment. I envy everybody who hasn't read "Time Enough for Love," because you can do so and I've already finished.

49. Theodore Sturgeon, "If . . ." *New York Times Book Review* (September 23, 1972): 38.

25. On to Other Things (pages 346–361)

1. RAH, letter to Larry Niven and Jerry Pournelle, 06/20/73. This is a fascinating letter, full of hard-nosed and useful advice, writer to writer, but much too long to quote extensively here. Heinlein's letters about *The Mote in God's Eye* to Niven and Pournelle are published in the Virginia Edition, Vol. xli, *Letters 3* [1960–87].

2. RAH, letter to Larry Niven and Jerry Pournelle, 06/20/73.

3. RAH, letter to Larry Niven and Jerry Pournelle, 06/20/73.

4. Heinlein said as much to the author when they first corresponded in 1973.

5. RAH, letter to Walter Minton, 12/31/73.

6. RAH, draft letter to John Conlan, undated but after 05/25/73. Heinlein is referring to Charles W. Lyon, the incumbent in the 1938 Assembly District 59 race covered in *Learning Curve,* chapter 16, "Party Animal," 201–13. Lyon was convicted of grand theft and conspiracy in a liquor license scandal in 1954 (i.e., graft) and served eighteen months of a five-year sentence at San Luis Obispo Men's Colony, when he was pardoned by Governor Goodwin Knight in 1958 and thereafter became a lobbyist. He died in 1960 of cancer.

7. Both quotations from RAH, letter to John P. Conlan, draft—undated but after May 25, 1973.

8. RAH, letter to Larry Niven and Jerry Pournelle, 08/26/73.

9. Virginia Heinlein, letter to Robert Bloch, 10/13/73. It is unclear whose opinion she was quoting; the Heinleins had not been able to see the show.

10. Virginia Heinlein, letter to the author, 07/10/00.

11. Virginia Heinlein, letter to the author, 07/10/00.

12. RAH, letter to Clare and Dorothy Heinlein, 07/07/73. Heinlein is probably mangling the skin cancer salve/drug Efuxed (Fluorouacil), also named, as he says, "5 FU."

13. RAH, letter to Greg Benford, 11/08/73. The bracketing of "three of my four Hugos" implies 1959 and the publication of *Starship Troopers.*

14. RAH, letter to Greg Benford, 11/08/73.

15. Virginia Heinlein, letter to Jerry Pournelle and Larry Niven, 09/19/73.

16. Rita Bottoms, letter to Alexei Panshin, 08/10/73.

17. RAH, letter to Mrs. Thomas V. [Rita] Bottoms, 09/10/73.

18. Panshin and *Heinlein in Dimension* had won the Hugo Award for Best Fanwriting in 1967 and his *Rite of Passage* won the Best Novel Hugo in 1968.

19. RAH, letter to Mrs. Thomas V. [Rita] Bottoms, 09/10/73.

20. Paul Crawford's letter to Panshin dated 10/29/73 found the visit "frustrating. I was able to gather some interesting information, but most of the precise information we needed [about the dates on which specific works were written] remained just beyond my grasp." Heinlein's accession notes had been removed from public accessibility by that time, and Crawford apparently did not realize that virtually all the information about composition dates and sales are stored with the manuscript files he looked at—and which he termed "uninteresting."

21. RAH, letter to Margot Fisher, 11/21/73; RAH, letter to Tom and Audrey Hollyman, 10/18/73.

22. RAH, letter to Laurie MacDonald, 12/12/73.

23. RAH, letter to Christine Floyd, 12/03/73.

24. RAH, draft letter to Philip José Farmer, 11/21/73.

25. RAH, letter to Howard de Vore, 10/01/73.

26. RAH, letter to Walter Minton, 12/31/73.

27. Forrest J. Ackerman, taped interview with Robert James, Ph.D., 06/09/00.

28. RAH, letter to Forrest J. Ackerman, 11/17/73.

29. RAH, "Politics of Pragmatism," *Human Events: Your Weekly Washington Report* (01/26/74).

30. Rennie McCoy, letter to RAH, 06/04/74.

31. Terry Quist, letter to RAH, 11/24/74.

32. Request dated 02/14/74.

33. 09/15/74. This version is reproduced in "A Fourth Version of the Forrestal Lecture" by William H. Patterson, Jr., in *The Heinlein Journal*, no. 16 (January 2005): 4–5.

34. David N. Grant, letter to RAH, dated 12/04/74.

35. The silver mine incident, with the Sophie and Shively lode, is detailed in chapter 13 of *Learning Curve*, at pages 168–70.

36. Virginia Heinlein, letter to Caryl and Larry Heinlein, 12/28/73.

37. RAH, letter to Ann A. Hancock (ed. Viking Press), 06/23/74.

38. Cf. Philip José Farmer, letter to RAH, 06/13/73:

> The voters of the SFWA would never nominate it [*Time Enough for Love*], but then what else would you expect from those finks? (I hasten to add that some of its members are among the greatest people on this earth, but for the majority I have an attitude bordering on contempt[)].

And Virginia Heinlein, letter to the author, 11/07/99:

> We were aware that Robert would never win the Nebula. His brothers in the craft did not want him to. And they also used the Australian balloting to keep him from getting one . . . Oh, yes, his colleagues did not like him!. . . . I do not think that the SFWA people thought in those terms [corrupting the balloting] when they set down *Time Enough for Love*—they just did not want him to win a Nebula. And those are much prettier awards than the Hugos—honor or no.

The Nebula Award is a block of clear lucite with some science-fictional device and a spiral nebula (galaxy) of glitter embedded in the lucite. Each is handmade, and each is a unique work of art.

39. The Club of Rome was a global think tank formed in 1968. In 1972 it issued a report titled *Limits to Growth,* a Malthusian examination of the consequences

of continued population growth and resource depletion, and predicted economic and social collapse in the twenty-first century. *Limits to Growth* had a profound effect on futurist thinking and particularly within the science-fiction community.

40. Philip K. Dick, letter to RAH, 02/11/74.
41. Philip K. Dick, letter to RAH, 05/10/74.
42. Heinlein's letter to Philip K. Dick was not preserved in his Archival PKD file.
43. When Mrs. Heinlein got back to Santa Cruz, she asked her bank about renting a terminal for her own use in keeping their accounts, which were becoming more and more complicated. Unfortunately, the price they quoted was a little steep for their needs: ten thousand dollars a month.
44. Robert Kephart (1934–2004), libertarian entrepreneur, philanthropist, and publisher of *Human Events,* founder of *Libertarian Review* and *Books for Libertarians.* In September 1973 Robert and Virginia Heinlein were informed by Lurton Blassingame that *Books for Libertarians* had obtained a tape recording of the Forrestal Lecture and was selling it commercially, without having obtained copyright—which would prevent the *Analog* appearance of the lecture. Kephart not only apologized and corrected the error immediately, he became a friend of the Heinleins, with whom he had a great deal in common.
45. A fan who was present, Tom Collins, reconstructed Heinlein's talk from memory as the first part of "Tonight I Met Heinlein" by Tom Collins, first published in *Transient* #31 (1974?), web-published by Alexei Panshin at http://www.panshin/critics/Showdown/tomcollins.html (accessed 03/04/2014).

First, I'll try to recollect what he said, then I'll get into what he did and what I thought and all that.

He said an ancestor of his, Peter Heinlein, invented the escapement for watches, and that watches were a wonderful invention because that way you didn't have to shoot the speaker to make him stop talking.

He said a word about taking creative writing courses: Don't.

He gave the five rules for writing (the major rules; there are also minor ones like always use a black ribbon, and throw it away when only half used because all editors suffer from eyestrain). The rules were laid down by him years ago, and are something like write, don't revise, keep writing, keep submitting what you do write. I didn't write them down. They're in print already.

He said he had used eight different pen names, and that whole issues of some pulpzines were by him. (Just like Randall Garrett, I guess—and how many others?) He said those editors, then, "didn't want it good, they wanted it Wednesday." He said he had stories on the stand while he still didn't know how they would end an installment or two later.

He said Katherine Anne Porter, whom he seemed to admire, had written the enormous novel *The Ship of Fools* as a 20,000 word novella, but that it kept growing and the characters were living lives of their own that she couldn't interfere with. Shakespeare killed off Mercutio because he was stealing the scenes. Mark Twain dropped them down wells only the well got filled up (a reference, though he may not have known it, to that odd twice-told tale *Pudd'nhead Wilson,* where that happened literally).

He said he wrote his notes for stories on file cards and accumulated cards perhaps for thirty years until, after shuffling they can be arranged into something like a story, after which he goes where the characters take him. All good literature happens that way, with the author dragged along.

"My wife says she knows I'm about to come down with a story when she finds my shoes in an icebox." That's the stage when the fictional reality is supplanting the other reality. He starts getting bad-tempered and blaming things on her. Shortest time he ever did a book was 13 days, *The Door into Summer.* The cat actually existed, and is buried in Colorado where they used to live at 7000 feet before they had to go to sea level for health reasons. Petronius the Arbiter—Pete—was Pixie in real life and "the toughest goldarn cat I ever saw." One winter after the first snow it went around to all the doors with his wife, then with Heinlein, looking at the snow and complaining. She said, "He's looking for the door into summer," and he vanished into his study, with what result we know.

The longest time was 100 working days, but it was a much longer story. It was written straight through with one day out for the dentist. After talking about it he mentioned the name almost as an afterthought, *Time Enough for Love.* It had to be long; it involved twenty-four centuries. It had to be episodic also because there could be no way to make such a story unified. "There were too many characters and they all wanted center stage and there wasn't anything I could do but sit back and let them take over."

Halfway through *I Will Fear No Evil* he fell desperately ill. The story was all written, but the cutting wasn't done yet, the paring to the bone that it needed. He and his surgeon both thought it would be a posthumous book, and he signed over a power of attorney to his wife, which she still has, making an X from his bed with nurses for witnesses. (Mind you these "quotes" and summaries are the product of my hasty and incomplete notes, and of my all-too-faulty memory.) That novel was never cut.

He won't comment on the work of living writers, but did mention Rostand who wrote s-f, Wells, M. Jules Verne (he pronounced it in French) whom he has "extremely high respect for" but Verne dealt more in gadgets and

Wells in people; Heinlein thus preferred Wells because he (RH) also was more interested in people.

About the space program, "I feel sure it will go on but I'm not sure in what language. I'm amazed at the dexterity of the public relations department of NASA that turned something so wonderfully romantic into something as dull as dishwater . . . Sure, sure, we're going out into space. There's no reason the human race could not go on indefinitely out and out" as in Asimov's stories.

"Writing is the best way I know of to have fun and make a living without actually stealing."

He told about a writer of mild porn for lending libraries [Jack Woodford] who began a book with the sentence, "Naked, Elaine stood at the front window and watched Tom come up the walk."

He said, "My stories are very short on tragic endings and very short on villains. I don't believe in villains." He said he never met a villain who thought of himself in those terms; they were not villains to themselves. "I never intentionally offered the market what I thought of as a story with an unhappy ending" though sometimes the lead character did die off at the end. "I see no reason why stories should be written about anti-heroes doing unpleasant things among unpleasant people." He doesn't like reading about them and he doesn't like writing about them.

He quoted a "schoolboy Latin" tag from Time Enough and Washington Irving, which he translated as "All is well without punishment, the time has come for fun; the time has come for laying books aside." He added, "I like Latin for the sound of it, though thank God we've got one that has fewer declensions." He digressed to say his wife has eight languages and that he "masticates French" and has some "cantina Spanish" picked up in Central America in the service. He says his wife has "absolute pitch."

He talked a good deal about the writer competing for beer money, for the money a person has to spend after the necessities are paid for, that he has a choice on. He said his ideal reader was a guy with 95 cents who wanted to buy his book. (That in response to a question.) He said anyone who tries writing to see his name in print will never see his name in print—a debatable hypothesis it seems to me. He said the way to learn writing was by studying everything else but. He used the image of the storyteller in a village talking along hoping for the chink of some coins in his bowl. He spoke always in terms of money, rewriting to an editor's demands for pay, choosing to write s-f (as opposed to something else) because it sold, etc. He consistently refused to take any responsibility for his creations.

Could you name some of your mystery stories we might find? I could but I won't. They're strictly from hunger. What happened to Mike in *Moon Is a Harsh Mistress*? No, I don't know what happened to the computer. How would I? Nobody told me. What is the future of s-f? I don't know any more about it than you do.

Would you name some favorite character of yours, or a favorite work of yours? My favorite is always the work I'm on at the time, always the characters I'm working with when I'm asked.

He said he was in the best shape he's been in in forty years, and has the weight and blood pressure he had when he graduated from Annapolis.

He said *Fear* [*I Will Fear No Evil*] was more popular than *Stranger,* selling better and faster, and that *Time Enough* may sell the best of all. Reason: he's not writing for an in-group where references have to be explained, but to the general public. There are kinds of stories that can be written today that couldn't be written before; that's why he is writing a different kind of book than he was 10 or 15 years ago; there's a different market.

"To grow old involves a process, if you're not going to let your mind go into deep freeze, of unlearning things you used to believe."

He said when his older brother took him out once to see an eclipse and to explain it, that gave him his interest in the heavens. He called his brother Maj. Gen. Lawrence L. Heinlein. He said his kid brother is teaching at the same school as Professor Armstrong, Neil Armstrong, that is. He always used the most formal and elaborate name possible for anyone. After the eclipse "I never from that moment to this lost my feelings of wonder and joy in the heavens."

He talked about his place at Santa Cruz, without mentioning the exact location, the town, etc. He said they were far enough from neighbors that when they shut the lights out they were in the dark under the stars with "nothing to keep you from getting dizzy with the glory of it."

Asked about slang, he said the current stuff doesn't last long enough so he invents neologisms to fill the need to keep characters from sounding like term papers.

He called Asimov one of the few Renaissance characters around today. "If Isaac doesn't know the answer, don't go look it up in the Encyclopedia Brittanica because they won't know the answer either."

Asked about an apparent dichotomy of worldview in *Stranger* and *Starship Troopers,* he said, "They are both descriptions of objects of human love. Loving his fellow men enough to be willing to die for them in one, and the other—well, the whole book is about it." Which left undefined what he thinks the book is about. Said he wrote *Troopers* whole in the middle of writing *Stranger* on either side of it. He keeps a log of his working time and can thus keep track. *Stranger* was actually written in four different years, but the ideas came about ten years earlier. He spoke with evident satisfaction of the people who said they could spot the break in the book, and so far all such people had been wrong. He said he saw no dichotomy in them because he wrote the two in alternation.

He said he has written engineering articles, engineering reports, "some of them classified," teenage love stories in the first person singular, adventure stories. . . . What is the greatest influence on your writing? "Money."

His books are in about 28 different languages. He sees no dichotomy between the romantic and the realist. "The real world is a romantic and wonderful place. Anyone who doesn't think so writes fantasy, and dull fantasy at that." He urged people to "run, do not walk" to their nearest library or bookstore to read Archy and Mehitabel and rehearsed at great length the story of the parrot who knew Will Shakespeare, who wished he had time to be a poet instead of writing pop pap.

He said when he was ill, when he wasn't in a coma more than half of what he thought he saw didn't happen—hallucinations.

Will Lazarus and Andy Libby be in a novel set just after *Methuselah's Children*? Any chance of that? "All I can say to that is I'm not dead yet."

46. For example, see Gary Farber's letter about the incident in *The Alien Critic* no. 10 (August 1974), with interlineated commentary by Richard E. Geis and Alexei Panshin. Another description, "A Show of Hands," was published by Guy Lillian, in *Transient* 34 and in *Spiritus Mundi* 22, both in 1974, and again in 2007, in his Hugo-nominated fanzine *Challenger* 26.

47. Harry Hershfield (1885–1974) was an American comic artist, who began publishing newspaper cartoons in 1899 and was a frequent guest on radio and television programs in the 1940s and into the 1950s. Hershfield passed away on December 15, 1974, just a few months after Heinlein met him.

48. Virginia Heinlein, letter to Laura and Bill Haywood, 06/07/74.

49. Robert Heinlein, letter to Edgar D. Mitchell, 06/11/74.

26. Mr. Science (pages 362–375)

1. Richard Pope, letter to RAH, 03/31/75; see also RAH PS to form letter to Denis Paradis, 07/20/74.

2. RAH, PS to form letter to Denis Paradis, 07/20/74.

3. RAH, letter to Dr. Harry Wallerstein, 12/03/75.

4. RAH, letter to Richard Pope, 07/30/74.

5. RAH, letter to William Rotsler, 08/23/74.

6. RAH, letter to Mrs. Paul Dirac, 08/20/74.

7. RAH, letter to Richard Pope and Charles Cegielski, 09/18/74.

8. RAH, letter to Philip K. Dick, 08/22/74.

9. Heinlein apparently had the typewriter sent directly from the seller; there is no correspondence dating the purchase and gift; however, it is mentioned by both Theodore Sturgeon and by Spider Robinson [291] in their appreciations of Heinlein collected in *Requiem*, Yoji Kondo, ed. Dick himself mentioned the loan and the gift of the typewriter in his introduction to his short story collection *The Golden Man* (1980).

10. RAH, letter to T. B. Buell, 10/03/74.

11. Heinlein's relationship with then-Captain King is detailed in the first volume of this biography, *Learning Curve,* in chapter 11, 126–43.

12. RAH, letter to Richard Pope and Carol Timmons (marked "never sent"), 07/12/75.

13. Virginia Heinlein, IM with the author, 04/19/00. Mrs. Heinlein, whose screen name was "Astyanax12," remarked: "SFWA would have vanished if Robert hadn't paid their bills and no one except Joan Hunter Holly knows about it. Knew about it—I think she's dead now too. . . . Actually he swore her to silence. But I knew about it. He must have sent her a lot of money—from our joint account!" Joan Carol Holly (1932–82) wrote science fiction under the pseudonym "J. Hunter Holly" from 1959 to 1977. Ms. Holly's papers are archived at the University of Kansas, Lawrence.

14. RAH, letter to Jerry Pournelle, 07/14/73.

15. RAH, letter to Philip José Farmer, 11/21/73.

16. Transcription by the author of Jerry Pournelle's presentation at the October 8, 1988 NASA Distinguished Public Service Awards Ceremony—from videotape provided by Virginia Heinlein.

17. In Joe Haldeman's remembrance in *Requiem*, 274.

18. The times of the two ovations were given by Joe Haldeman in *Requiem*, 274.

19. Confusingly, even though *The Forever War* was published both in serial and hardcover formats in 1974—and so ought to have been eligible for a Nebula at the 1975 ceremony in New York—it was instead voted best for the year 1975, so Haldeman received the Nebula at the 1976 ceremony in Los Angeles—the same year the book received the Hugo and Locus awards.

20. Spider Robinson, "Robert," *Requiem*, Yoji Kondo, ed. (New York: Tor, 1992), 315.

21. In an e-mail to the author dated 06/18/08, Herb Gilliland (English Dept., USNA) mentioned speaking with Haldeman about Heinlein's opinion.

> I asked Haldeman Saturday in Kansas City [at the Heinlein Centennial, in 2007]. He said, yes, there had been a slight followon. Some time after the first encounter, he and Heinlein were at an autograph table at some convention (with, he said, Heinlein's throng stretching off toward the horizon while Haldeman had two or three people), and Heinlein said something like, "I read your book again, and I like it even better."

Haldeman is probably referring to MidAmeriCon (1976), though it might have taken place at a blood drive at SunCon in 1977.

22. RAH, handwritten note on Thomas Clareson's invitation letter dated 04/26/75. Heinlein referred to this work by Samuelson as "a thesis on me (for his master's degree, I think) in which he picked up Blish's theory about 1st-person stories" (RAH, letter to Lloyd Biggle, 08/30/76). This seems to rule out Samuelson's best known Heinlein essay, published as "Frontiers of the Future: Heinlein's Future History Stories" in *Voices for the Future,* Thomas Clareson, ed. (Bowling Green University Popular Press, 1976), and as "Major Frontier Worlds of Robert A. Heinlein: The Future and Fantasy" in *Robert A. Heinlein,* Joseph Olander and Martin Harry Greenberg, eds. (New York: Taplinger Publishing Co., 1978).

23. Dr. Ruth Sanger was married to Dr. R. R. Race.

24. RAH, letter to Editors *Compton Yearbook* (marked "never sent"), 08/31/75. The reference to pornography may be obscure: Before pornography was legalized, some libraries kept locked reference collections of pornographic and other "unacceptable" literature.

25. RAH, letter (marked "never sent") to editors of *Encyclopedia Britannica,* 08/31/75.

26. No further mention is made of a copy obtained in New York; it may well be that the language of Heinlein's memorandum of the Levin dinner and subsequent book hunt with Tanner is unclear and what Tanner was actually communicating was that *when Levin's team located a copy* it would be available at the *Times-Mirror* office. But the Heinleins left New York within a few days.

27. RAH, letter to Dr. Harvey Wallerstein, 12/03/75.

28. This "Francis X. Riverside" pseudonym is unique; it is possible that it invokes Francis X. Bushman (a silent-era cowboy movie star) and the "John Riverside" name under which "The Unpleasant Profession of Jonathan Hoag" had originally been published in *Unknown* in 1942.

29. Three-by-five index card in RAH's hand clipped to 1,990-word version of manuscript, 07/03/75.

30. RAH, memo to Richard Pope and Christine Timmons, 07/06/75.

31. RAH, letter to Tessa Dick, 08/03/75.

32. RAH, letter to Tessa Dick, 08/03/75.

33. Dr. Robert Hecht-Nielsen, letter to RAH, 08/13/75.

34. Dr. Eloise R. Giblett, letter to RAH, 09/26/75.

35. Alan E. Nourse, letter to RAH, 09/19/75.

36. Charles Huggins, M.D., letter to RAH, 09/24/75.

37. Isaac Asimov, letter to RAH, 09/26/75.

38. RAH, application for AABB membership, 12/11/75.

39. RAH, memo to Richard Pope and Christine Timmons (marked "never sent") 08/31/75.

40. RAH, letter to R. Faraday Nelson, 02/07/77.

27. "I Vant Your Blood" (pages 376–395)

1. RAH, letter to William S. Kyler, Executive Director of CCBC, 11/13/75.

2. RAH, letter to William S. Kyler, 11/13/75.

3. RAH, letter to Dr. Harvey Wallerstein, 12/03/75.

4. RAH, open letter to "Dear Friends," written 11/26/75, in the MidAmeriCon Progress Report for Winter 1975.

5. Virginia Heinlein, taped interview with the author, Series 3, Tape B, Side B (March 27, 2001).

6. Virginia Heinlein, taped interview with Leon Stover, Tape 1, Side 1 (10/21?/88).

7. In an e-mail discussion with the author on August 19, 2011, Dr. Pournelle commented on this liaison:

> At some point I told the [MidAmeriCon] Committee "Do you think I am a bit old fashioned and fuddy duddy and hard to deal with?" They all grinned (well this was by phone so I infer the grins). "He graduated from the Naval Academy before I was born," I pointed out. Robert was very old fashioned in some of his beliefs about proper etiquette, and pretty damned rigid in his expectations.
>
> It all worked out but it cost me more time than I think either Robert or Ginny realized. I sure took pains to see they didn't know.

8. Virginia Heinlein, taped interview with the author, Series 3, Tape B, Side B (March 27, 2001).

9. Virginia Heinlein, taped interview with the author, Series 3, Tape B, Side B (March 27, 2001).

10. Virginia Heinlein, taped interview with the author, Series 3, Tape B, Side B (March 27, 2001).

11. RAH, letter to Jack Williamson, 03/20/76. This letter in its entirety is published in the Virginia Edition, vol. xxxviii, *Nonfiction 2*.

12. Heinlein's meetings with Tony Damico are told in *Learning Curve,* the first volume of this biography, at 316 and 344.

13. Transcription of Jerry Pournelle's presentation at the October 8, 1988, NASA Distinguished Public Service Awards Ceremony—from videotape provided by Ginny Heinlein. A somewhat shortened version of these remarks were included in *Requiem,* ed. Yoji Kondo.

14. RAH, letter to Garth Danielson, 08/25/76.

15. Virginia Heinlein, letter to Morning Glory Zell, 09/14/76.

16. Virginia Heinlein, taped interview with Leon Stover, Tape 1, Side A (October 21? 1988).

17. Virginia Heinlein, taped interview with the author, Series 3, Tape B, Side B (March 2001).

18. The videotapes made for the MidAmeriCon closed-circuit cablecast represent the longest video of Heinlein that exists, as every television appearance the author has been able to check was destroyed over the years. Even the original tapes of the appearance with Walter Cronkite and Arthur C. Clarke for the Moon landing in 1969 have been recycled. A screen capture of the public broadcast portion of the interview and commentary was preserved on a videotape presented to Virginia Heinlein, which is now in the RAH Archive, UC Santa Cruz. Digital copies of the somewhat age-degraded videotape were made for Mrs. Heinlein by the author in 2001 and 2002, and by special permission the Heinlein Society shows the CBS tape at some science-fiction conventions. The MidAmeriCon videos, also somewhat time-degraded, were given to the Heinlein Centennial by MidAmeriCon chairman Ken Keller for exhibition and have also been digitized.

19. Spider Robinson, "Robert," *Requiem,* Yoji Kondo, ed., 316–17.

20. RAH, letter to Andrew Porter, 01/15/77.

21. RAH, letter to R. Faraday Nelson, 02/07/77.

22. RAH, letter to R. Faraday Nelson, 02/07/77.

23. RAH, letter to Vikki Gold, 01/17/77.

24. RAH, letter to R. Faraday Nelson, 02/07/77.

25. RAH, letter to R. Faraday Nelson, 02/07/77.

26. RAH, letter to R. Faraday Nelson, 02/07/77.

27. RAH, letter to R. Faraday Nelson, 02/07/77.

28. RAH, letter to R. Faraday Nelson, 02/07/77.

29. RAH, letter to R. Faraday Nelson, 02/07/77.

30. RAH, letter to R. Faraday Nelson, 02/07/77.

31. RAH, letter to R. Faraday Nelson, 02/07/77.

32. RAH, letter to R. Faraday Nelson, 02/07/77.

33. Virginia Heinlein, letter to Sondra and Myrna Marshak, 02/14/77.

34. Virginia Heinlein, letter to Sondra and Myrna Marshak, 02/14/77.

35. Virginia Heinlein, letter to Jeannie and Alex Campbell, 04/12/77.

36. For the installation as Grand Master in April 1977; Published in NESFA chapbook of *Creator* in 1984 and again in the Virginia Edition, vol. xxxviii, *Nonfiction 2*.

37. RAH, letter to Judith Merril (marked "never sent"), 11/01/67—but note, this is more than a decade after he gave up his Democratic Party membership, and four years after working for Barry Goldwater's election. Heinlein is clearly a small-d democrat as well as a small-l libertarian.

38. RAH, letter to Prof. David Friedman, 08/05?/78.

39. RAH, letter to Joseph Martino, 04/15/85.

40. RAH, letter to Prof. David Friedman, 08/05?/78. Heinlein's relationship to libertarianism is quite complex and nuanced. Although he does not seem to fit comfortably within any of the common and named libertarian traditions, he seems to come closest to the radical individualism ("Egoism") typified by Max Stirner—a position that sets both Marxists and orthodoctrinaire libertarians on edge, as it acknowledges neither "natural law" nor the pseudoscientific Marxist "laws of history."

41. Tucson television news reporter Forrest Carr researched the KGUN9 Archives at the Arizona Historical Society in 2011 but was unable to find any record of this interview. Like most of Heinlein's television appearances, it appears not to have been preserved.

42. RAH, "Some Applications of Space Technology for the Elderly and the Handicapped," Congressional Testimony given on 7/19/79.

43. Virginia Heinlein, letter to Greg Hagglund, 06/12/77.

44. Virginia Heinlein, letter to Robert Forward, 07/24/77.

45. Virginia Heinlein, letter to Dr. and Mrs. Passovoy, 08/01/77.

46. The Gregg Press science-fiction line was founded in 1973 by Editor Thomas T. Beeler, to be run by Hartwell, who was his fellow grad student and friend in the English department of Columbia University. David Hartwell, e-mail to the author, 08/08/11. Hartwell goes on to add that he had also been an editor at Putnam's from 1973 to 1978, and as such was in direct contact with the Heinleins and their agent, Lurton Blassingame, about book projects and for that reason was also a part of the Heinleins' social and business circles and was invited to the Heinleins' "at-homes" at the Tuscany when they were in New York.

47. Hartwell indicated in an e-mail to the author, 08/08/11, that the advance for all the Gregg Press books was $100.

48. Altogether, Gregg Press published eight Heinlein books, five in 1979 and the last in 1981. Gregg Press ceased publishing in 1985, having issued 252 books.

The *Destination Moon* compilation edited by Hartwell was part of the Gregg Science Fiction and Film series and published in 1979. It contains Heinlein's novelization of the original movie script, an article Heinlein wrote for *Astounding* in 1950 about the film, and a selection of publicity material, including the contents of the press package designed by Heinlein's friend Ben Babb.

The remaining seven issues are as follows:

1978: *Double Star* (1956)	Intro: Joe Haldeman
1978: *I Will Fear No Evil* (1969)	Intro: Paul Williams
1979: *The Door into Summer* (1956)	Intro: David Hartwell
1979: *Glory Road* (1963)	Intro: Samuel R. Delany
1979: *The Puppet Masters* (1951)	Intro: James E. Gunn
1979: *Waldo & Magic, Inc.* (1950)	Intro: Charles N. Brown
1981: *Beyond This Horizon* (1942, 48)	Intro: Norman Spinrad

49. Program dated 09/23/77 in Denis Paradis binder of documents, RAH Archive, UC Santa Cruz.

50. Denis Paradis, letter to Virginia Heinlein, 05/03/78.

51. Virginia Heinlein, letter to the author, 12/11/99.

52. Virginia Heinlein, letter to the author, 12/11/99.

53. Heinlein had had the first of a series of Transient Ischemic Attacks—warning signs that a stroke is imminent. The timing of this TIA is not dated with specificity. Mrs. Heinlein mentioned only that he had had a TIA earlier, while writing. Virginia Heinlein, letter to the author, 09/20/00 and Virginia Heinlein, taped interview with the author, Series 3, Tape A, Side A (March 1?, 2001).

54. David Lee Powell, "Robert Anson Heinlein, Grandmaster One, 1907-1988," http://archive.is/rxOfD (accessed 03/04/2014).

55. Virginia Heinlein, letter to George Warren, 03/09/79.

56. Virginia Heinlein, letter to George Warren, 03/09/79.

57. McAleer, *Visionary* (2010), 223, quoting Asimov's recollections.

58. Virginia Heinlein, letter to Judy-Lynn del Rey, 10/25/77.

59. In taped interviews with the author in 2000 and 2001, Mrs. Heinlein claimed not to remember any specifics about the book or her initial experience of reading it, except that she told Heinlein at the time it was "not best work." But she did say that the author's reactions to the manuscript, reading it in 2002 when it was still sealed, "validated" her opinion. "Competent yard goods" and "not a Heinlein novel" was the language used in the author's report to Mrs. Heinlein, which prompted the "validated" remark in Second Series, Tape B, Side B.

60. Virginia Heinlein, letter to the author, 07/14/00.

61. Virginia Heinlein, taped interview with the author, Series 2, Tape B, Side B.

62. Virginia Heinlein, taped interview with the author, Tape 10, Side A.

63. RAH, letter to L. Ron Hubbard, 07/14/78.

28. "Human Vegetable" (pages 396–407)

1. Virginia Heinlein, taped interview with the author, Tape 4, Side B.

2. Virginia Heinlein, letter to "Ginger and Roger," 03/15/78.

3. The blood drive handbook was never finished, but it was put into publishable form for the Virginia Edition, vol. xxxviii, *Nonfiction 2*.

4. Virginia Heinlein, letter to W. G. Hagglund, 02/10/78.

5. RAH, "Spinoff," *Expanded Universe*, 507.

6. Rita Bottoms, Oral History, online in PDF format, at http://digitalcollections. ucsc.edu/cdm/compoundobject/collection/p265101coll13/id/3650 (accessed 03/04/2014). "Honey" was their private nickname for Rita, who had become a very good friend, not a patronizing characterization.

7. Virginia Heinlein, taped interview with the author, Second Series, Tape B, Side B (September 10? 2000).

8. Virginia Heinlein, taped interview with the author, Third Series, Tape A, Side A (March 27, 2001).

9. Robert A. Heinlein, full text of "Some Applications of Space Technology for the Elderly and the Handicapped" presented before the Joint Session of the House Select Committee on Aging and the House Committee on Science and Technology on July 19, 1979. An edited and somewhat condensed form of this testimony was published in *Expanded Universe* as "Spinoff."

10. Jack Williamson, "Who Was Robert Heinlein?" *Requiem*, Yoji Kondo, ed.: 335. The incident is also mentioned in Jack Williamson: "On Heinlein's *Friday*," *Science Fiction Digest*, I:4 (Sept.–Oct. 1982): 26.

11. Virginia Heinlein, taped interview with the author, Second Series, Tape B, Side B (September 10? 2000).

12. Virginia Heinlein, letter to Denis Paradis, 05/10/78.

13. Virginia Heinlein, taped interview with the author, Tape 10, Side B (March 2? 2000).

14. Virginia Heinlein, taped interview with the author, Third Series, Tape B, Side A (March 27, 2001).

15. Virginia Heinlein, letter to Denis Paradis, 05/10/78.

16. Virginia Heinlein, letter to the author, 09/20/00.

17. Virginia Heinlein, taped interview with the author, Tape 10, Side A.

18. Virginia Heinlein, letter to Denis Paradis, 05/10/78.

19. Heinlein left no direct testimony about his process going from *Panki Barsoom* to *The Number of the Beast*, but speaking of Heinlein's final illness, Mrs. Heinlein

remarked that "always before" he had been eager to get back to writing. Virginia Heinlein, taped interview with the author, Third Series, Tape A, Side A (March 27, 2001). The truth of this is suggested by the speed with which he began working on the new manuscript—mid-May, just two weeks following the surgery.

20. RAH, letter to Yoji Kondo, 08/30/78.

21. Heinlein's desk-drawer "laboratory" was probably among the material burned at the time of the move from Bonny Doon to Carmel in 1987. The shelf of porn was apparently also destroyed at some time, as none of it came to the RAH Archive (which received, by Virginia Heinlein's will, all of the Heinleins' personal property). A brief description of one such story, written by Heinlein for Leslyn before their divorce in 1947, was given by Grace Dugan Sang Wurtz in a letter to the author, 03/07/11:

> Did you know that Bob Heinlein was also a writer of *porn*?
>
>   I say *that* to get your attention. He didn't *sell* porn stories but he wrote at least a couple soft porn stories for Leslyn. When Henry Sang and I were living with Bob and Leslyn on Lookout Mountain [in spring of 1946], Bob and I were often left our own devices while Leslyn was at work with Henry trying to make his stories marketable. They worked in the back of the house on the porch, and Bob and I spread things out on the dining room table, and did our sketches and readings. Bob also had written a cutesy-pie story about Willis (more about him later) a baby possum, who lived in Bob's navel. The porn story I remember had to do with a three-some involving a man, his young wife, and his mother-in-law. It was the older woman who was the hottest participant. Was this maybe to introduce the idea of a younger junior wife?

22. This material is taken up in chapter 10, Vintage Season, *supra,* which deals with the mid-1950s.

23. Virginia Heinlein, letter to Margo Fisher, 08/04/78.

24. Virginia Heinlein, taped interview with the author, Tape 10, Side B.

25. Virginia Heinlein, letter to Margo Fisher, 01/05/79.

> To be very blunt about it, we can't stand Kirby McCauley—he's always away and often very careless about things . . . I know many people who swear by Kirby McCauley, but I've found his carelessness too difficult to put up with . . .

26. George Edgar Slusser, *Classic Years of Robert A. Heinlein* (1976) and *Robert A. Heinlein: Stranger In His Own Land* (1977). Both Riverside, Calif.: Borgo Press.

27. Joseph D. Olander and Martin Harry Greenberg, eds. *Robert A. Heinlein* (New York: Taplinger Publishing Company, 1978).

28. H. Bruce Franklin, letter to RAH, 06/01/78; Virginia Heinlein, letter to H. Bruce Franklin, 06/12/78.

29. Virginia Heinlein, letter to Denis Paradis, 01/20/79.

30. Virginia Heinlein, letter to Margo Fisher, 08/04/78.

31. Rita Bottoms, personal discussions with the author, supplementing her oral history materials, from September through November 2005.

32. Rita Bottoms, personal conversation with the author on January 25, 2006, supplemented on January 28, 2006.

33. Rita Bottoms, Oral History, 62.

34. Rita Bottoms, Oral History, 61.

35. Virginia Heinlein, letter to the author, 05/31/99.

36. RAH, letter to Cpl. Suzanne Deladrier, 08/30/78. David Silver, onetime president of the Heinlein Society, has argued that the interview with H. Bruce Franklin shaped and to some extent motivated all the writing that was to follow for the rest of Heinlein's life. It gave him, Silver claims, a vision of his antagonist—not Franklin himself, but the whole complex of ideas that were taking his society down. David Silver: "Blame It All on H. Bruce Franklin," *The Heinlein Journal*, no. 16 (January 2005); "The Lonely Silver Rain," *The Heinlein Journal*, no. 17 (July 2005).

37. The author's observation, not Mrs. Heinlein's. In a manuscript note by the editor of this biography in about April 2011, David Hartwell mentioned that he was an editor at Putnam's at the time *The Notebooks of Lazarus Long* came "over the transom," and Minton told Hartwell he published this quality paperback as "a favor to RAH." Hartwell wrote the introduction.

38. Mrs. Heinlein mentioned this incident several times in the first series of taped interviews with the author: Tape 3, Side A; Tape 4, Side A; and Tape 9, Side B (last few days of February 2000). It was also memorialized nearly contemporaneously in Virginia Heinlein, letter to Balls Clipping Service, 12/19/79 (a year after the initial publication).

39. Donald A. Wollheim (1914–90) was a leading editor and publisher of science fiction (as well as a writer); he had edited the very first paperback anthology of science fiction in 1943. Afer leaving Ace in 1971, he established DAW Books, the first mass-market specialty science fiction and fantasy publishing house.

40. RAH, memo to Eleanor Wood, marked "W's Pending File," 09/25/78.

41. RAH and Virginia Heinlein, letter to Eleanor Wood, 09/24/78.

42. Virginia Heinlein, letter to "Ginger and Richard," 09/24/78. The name of the small press is not referenced in the correspondence, but their acquaintance may

have been made in conjunction with the blood drives, as correspondence to and from them begins appearing in 1977.

43. Virginia Heinlein, letter to Denis Paradis, 10/03/78.

44. RAH, *The Number of the Beast* (London: New English Library, 1980), 14.

45. James D. Gifford, *Robert A. Heinlein: A Reader's Companion*, 137–8.

46. Both quotation and information about Heinlein being worn out from working fourteen-hour days from Virginia Heinlein, letter to Denis Paradis, 12/17/78.

29. Traveling Road Show (pages 408–417)

1. Virginia Heinlein, letter to Denis Paradis, 01/20/79.

   In 1975, Heinlein had written a kind of short-story/letter of thanks to George Zebrowski and Thomas N. Scortia, the editors of *Human Machines,* an anthology of cyborg stories, who had dedicated the book to him. It was a fictional complaint to the manufacturers of his body. The story is published for the first time as "Complaint," the concluding work of the Virginia Edition vol. xxxiv, *New Worlds to Conquer: The Short Fiction of Robert A. Heinlein 1942–1975.*

2. Virginia Heinlein, letter to Denis Paradis, 01/06/79.

3. Virginia Heinlein, letter to Denis Paradis, 01/20/79.

4. Virginia Heinlein, letter to Dick Mandelkorn, 05/07/79.

5. Virginia Heinlein, letter to George Warren, 03/15/79; Virginia Heinlein, letter to Margo Fisher, 02/11/81.

6. Virginia Heinlein, taped interview with the author, Tape 10, Side A (February 27? 2000).

7. Virginia Heinlein, letter to George Warren, 03/07/79.

8. Virginia Heinlein, letter to Hart Sprager, 10/13/79.

9. Virginia Heinlein, letter to George Warren, 03/08/79.

10. Virginia Heinlein, letter to George Warren, 03/09/79.

11. There was hardly any improvement, though, in the quality of representation. In August Heinlein received two letters, a copy of a letter from Art Cabot to Bob Bookman, 08/08/79, complaining of delays in responding to a query about availability of rights for "Project Nightmare" and from Vic Smith to Mr. Heinlein, also 8/9/79:

    > In your letter of June 5, 1979, you advised me to contact Mr. Bob Bookman of International Creative Management regarding the purchase of film rights to your novels Star Beast and HSSWT.
    >
    > I have sent letters and made phone calls with no response. On my most recent phone call the secretary asked, "Heinlein, who?"

12. Virginia Heinlein to Perry Chapdelaine, 02/16/79. Chapdelaine did continue with his project, bringing out two volumes of Campbell letters, which were a *suc-*

cess d'estime. Mrs. Heinlein did print excerpts from some of the Heinlein-Campbell correspondence in *Grumbles from the Grave* (1989)—without, it appears, obtaining permissions from Chapdelaine as the intellectual property rights holder.

Midway into the production of the Virginia Edition, Geo Rule, on behalf of the Heinlein Society, re-established contact with Chapdelaine, and an agreement was struck with the Heinlein Prize Trust, as owners of the Heinlein intellectual property rights, to bring out a volume of both sides of the Heinlein-Campbell correspondence as the first of the Virginia Edition's three volumes of letters, volumes xxxix (*Correspondence of John W. Campbell, Jr., and Robert A. Heinlein*), xl (*Letters 2* [1923–60]), and xli (*Letters 3* [1960–87]). Those volumes were issued in 2011.

13. David Hartwell, editor for this biography, was a participant in the *Number of the Beast* auction and indicates the auction was not quite the triumph Ginny represented (saying that the invited publishers were falling all over themselves to bid—Virginia Heinlein to George Warren, 03/09/79). Hartwell was at that time working for the Pocket Books division of Simon & Schuster and placed a bid for the science-fiction line that would, in 1981, be named "Timescape" Books. In Hartwell's recollection,

> The manuscript was generally received poorly and Putnam's had no interest in paying the price, which was why it went to auction. Still, then, no one else came to play until I bid because it was generally assessed as a bad book and/or uncommercial. I knew that was not the case . . . it would be a bestseller because there was a five million person Heinlein audience who still read new work by him in the late 1970s because they grew up reading him (I did my own math). Fawcett bid because I was very credible and if I bid, then they should too. This has happened to me a fair amount in my career. Their editor, whom I knew, knew nothing about Heinlein or SF and was assigned the book.

E-mail from David Hartwell to the author, 08/05/11, 2:41 P.M. Hartwell also recalled a "no edits" condition. The amounts of the bids were identical, varying only in the terms for paying out the amount. Hartwell (same e-mail): "I was very frustrated when my boss required a long payout to a writer who was ill."

Eleanor Wood, who conducted the auction suggests a different recollection. In the first place, it was not, strictly speaking, an auction:

> Heinlein had gotten grossly undervalued advances . . . I don't call it an auction, in that I didn't take a floor.

It was simply a multiple submission, with what we hoped to receive. We didn't get it, so took the next best offer. Nothing really out of line. And I can't recall including the "no edits" in any submission letter.

(Eleanor Wood sequence of e-mails with the author, 08/12/11.)

Earlier in the same e-mail discussion sequence, Mrs. Wood explained: "As I recall, I asked for a million dollars, which Putnam refused to pay, so I then made a multiple submission. The asking price presented to Putnam's was $1 million." She also commented, "An auction, at least in the past, had very specific rules, and this wasn't as formal as an 'auction.' I don't mind it being called that, but someone might step forward and complain it wasn't a 'real auction.'"

In the second place, Hartwell might or might not have known that Fawcett had already submitted its bid.

David's was definitely not the first bid. Arlene Friedman [of Fawcett] made the first bid. Then I waited—I can't recall exactly how long—until David finally got approval to offer the same amount of money with less advantageous terms.

I think the deal was no edits without the author's approval, but perhaps I'm not remembering correctly on that point.

(Eleanor Wood sequence of e-mails with the author, 08/12/11.)

"No edits without author's approval" would be much more in line with Heinlein's usual practices.

14. *Locus* magazine XII:5, whole number 222 (June 1979), at 1: "Heinlein $$ set record."

15. This interview seems never to have been used or even finalized (Mr. Bova was not able to recall in 2010 why this was the case). A corrected raw transcription of the interview was found among Heinlein's papers and was published in the Virginia Edition, vol. xxxviii, *Nonfiction 2*, as "Telephone Interview with Ben Bova."

16. RAH, letter to Ben Bova, 07/27/79.

17. Virginia Heinlein, taped interview with the author, Tape 10, Side A (February 28? 2000).

18. Chase Econometrics Associates, Inc. "The Economic Impact of NASA R&D Spending: Preliminary Executive Summary" (April 1975).

This report subsequently came under methodological attack (see, e.g., "NASA Technological Spinoff Fables" http://www.fas.org/spp/eprint/jp_950525.htm, accessed 08/10/11), though some of the critical arguments seem more questionable than the study's original methodology, examining only some categories of direct spending, omitting consideration of technology transfer effects differentiating between NASA spending and other sorts of government spending, and also omitting to consider secondary economic effects (an example of a secondary economic effect would be an increase in NASA's share of the market for medical computers that comes about because of the NASA-driven medical telemetry developed for astronauts).

Whether one can legitimately account the microprocessor market to NASA technology transfer (the base market came from Defense investment) seems to be an arbitrary matter of where one draws the line in a cascade of secondary effects—when it is the existence of the cascade that is the significant point.

Heinlein spoke directly to this point in his testimony:

But this I *must* say: NASA's presentation is *extremely* modest; it cites only 46 applications—whereas I *know* there are hundreds. Often one bit of research results in 2nd, 3rd, and 4th generations; each generation usually has multiple applications—spinoffs have spinoffs, branching out like a tree. To get a feeling for this, think of the endless applications of Lee de Forrest's vacuum tube, Dr. Shockley's transistor.

Here is an easy way to spot space-research spinoffs: If it involves microminiaturization of *any* sort, minicomputers, miniaturized long-life power sources, highly reliable microswitches, remotely-controlled manipulators, image enhancers, small and sophisticated robotics or cybernetics, then, no matter where you find the item, at a critical point in its development it was part of our space program.

(Official transcription of Heinlein's Congressional testimony, 07/19/79, later cut and revised for "Spinoff.")

And in any case, the Chase Econometrics study was the best evidence at the time of Heinlein's Congressional testimony.

19. Art Dula, letter to RAH, 07/06/79.
20. RAH, letter to Ben Bova, 07/27/79.
21. Art Dula, letter to RAH, 07/06/79.
22. RAH, letter to Ben Bova, 07/27/79.
23. RAH, postcard to Eleanor Wood, 09/21/79.
24. RAH, postcard to Eleanor Wood, 09/21/79.
25. This catalogue of the Heinleins' personal library is published in the Virginia Edition, vol. xxxviii, *Nonfiction 2*.
26. Grosset and Dunlap was then acquired by G. P. Putnam's Sons in 1982. In 1996, the Putnam Berkley Group was acquired by Penguin Books.
27. In an interview conducted by David A. Truesdale on April 17, 1980 (Robert

Heinlein Day in Butler, Missouri) and published in *Science Fiction Review*, no. 36 (August 1980), Heinlein called the "interstitial notes" of *Expanded Universe* "the closest thing to an autobiography I expect to write." The Truesdale interview is republished in the Virginia Edition, vol. xxxviii, *Nonfiction 2*.

28.   A card from "Shel Dorf" thanking them for the check is dated 09/10/79.

29.   Dr. Zimmerman's self-introducing letter, not on Anderson campaign stationery, dated 09/18/79, has a notation in Heinlein's handwriting on the accompanying envelope: "(He showed up without appt. We did not let him through the gate.)"

30.   Virginia Heinlein, IM with the author, 06/17/02. Mrs. Heinlein was quite definite about Heinlein making a permanent affiliation with the Republican Party specifically because of the Reagan candidacy in 1980. If Heinlein had registered Republican for the Goldwater campaign in 1964, he had since allowed it to lapse, presumably registering as an independent. Possibly Heinlein was disillusioned with the mainstream Republicans he found in Colorado Springs—and somewhat out of touch with local politics after the move to the Santa Cruz area.

31.   In her guest of honor speech at Moscon, given on September 29, 1979, Trestrail revealed what John W. Campbell had told her father: Chester Nimitz had acknowledged to him, long after World War II, that Doc Smith's fictional battlefield information technology devised for his Lensman series had influenced the course of Navy CIC ("Combat Information Center") systems during World War II—which Heinlein already knew: The arrangements Cal Laning was working on for CIC in the South Pacific in the last year of the war had sounded a lot like the Lensman's capital ship *Directrix* . . .

Cal Laning had told Heinlein that his and other writers' science-fiction stories were at the root of Laning's own work organizing an enhancement for Naval CIC in the last years of the war. This material is covered in *Learning Curve*, chapter 24, 333–4. The Campbell letter is cited in an online biography of Smith at http://www.thefullwiki.org/Edward_Elmer_Smith, in the section titled "Influence on Science and the Military," and in http://objectswww.academickids .com/encyclopedia/-index.php/E._E._Smith (both sites accessed 03/04/2014). The letter was in Verna Trestrail's estate, though its current whereabouts are not known. One contributor to the fullwiki talk page tantalizingly said the letter was not from Chester Nimitz. Science historians tend to doubt Campbell's assertions. For an overview of the reasoning, see Edward Wysocki's *The Great Heinlein Mystery: Science Fiction, Innovation and Naval Technology*, 2012. Heinlein included "Larger Than Life" in *Expanded Universe*.

32.   *Apota (A Piece of the Action)* was a publication of the *Star Trek* Welcommittee from its founding in 1973 until 1982 under the editorial direction of KathE Donnelly and Karolyn Popovich, after 1976.

33. *Apota* Guest Editorial, undated but presumably 1979 as the text refers to events that would take place in the summer of 1980.

34. Virginia Heinlein, letter to Michael Cassutt, 10/28/79. In this letter Mrs. Heinlein mentions specifically the good reception among German publishers as well as the domestic United States and English.

35. Virginia Heinlein, letter to Michael Cassutt, 10/28/79.

30. New Beginnings (pages 418–431)

1. Virginia Heinlein, letter to Giles Welch, 05/11/80.

2. Virginia Heinlein, taped interview with Leon Stover, Tape 1, Side B (October 21, 1988).

3. Virginia Heinlein, letter to George Warren, 05/10/80.

4. Virginia Heinlein, letter to George Warren, 05/10/80.

5. McAleer, *Visionary* (2010), 228.

6. Truesdale, David A., "Robert A. Heinlein" Interview, *Science Fiction Review,* no. 36 (August 1980): 49.

7. Truesdale, David A., "Robert A. Heinlein" Interview, *Science Fiction Review,* no. 36 (August 1980): 49. The Truesdale interview actually contains more information about the event than do the local newspaper articles.

   By kind permission of Mr. Truesdale (the practice of *Science Fiction Review* was to reserve copyright to authors), the interview was reprinted in the Virginia Edition, vol. xxxviii, *Nonfiction 2.* One illuminating remark from the interview may be well worth repeating here: In response to a question from Mr. Truesdale as to whether Heinlein thought the new commercial markets for science fiction "spoils a writer into writing only what the audience wants, instead of being creative?" Heinlein replied:

   > You have a hidden premise in your question. You assume that writing what the audience wants is not being creative. You have to be *extremely* creative to write what the audience wants, instead of writing what everybody else is and the audience is tired of. (50)

   Later he went on to say "You have to be a born gambler if you want to be a freelance writer" (50).

8. Uncredited and otherwise unidentified newspaper article found among miscellaneous Heinlein Day newspaper clippings in Virginia Heinlein's files and discussed in Virginia Heinlein, taped interview with the author, Tape 5, Side A (late February 2000).

9. Virginia Heinlein, letter to Wes and Millie Posvar, 05/10/80.

10. Virginia Heinlein, letter to Gay and Halsey Cowan, 05/19/80.

11. Virginia Heinlein, letter to Denis Paradis, 08/17/80.

12. Virginia Heinlein, letter to Denis Paradis, 08/17/80.

13. *New York Times Book Review* VII (08/24/80): 26. "Behind the Best Sellers by Edwin McDowell."

14. Virginia Heinlein, letter to George Warren, 09/03/80.

15. Virginia Heinlein, letter to George Warren, 09/03/80.

16. Heinlein's attitudes changed after the Scribner's rejection of *Starship Troopers,* as is documented in chapter 15, *supra.*

17. Gerald Jonas, "Other Worlds," *New York Times Book Review* VII (09/14/80): 12.

18. Virginia Heinlein, letter to George Warren, 09/03/80.

19. Virginia Heinlein, letter to Jon Crusoe, 04/11/81.

20. Available online through Pournelle.com.

21. U.S. Army Brig. Gen. Stewart Canfield Meyer, Ret. (USMA class of 1943) commanded the Ballistic Missile Defense Systems Command at Huntsville, Alabama, from November 1977 to June 1979, and was in charge of the Homing Overlay project for the Strategic Defense Initiative.

22. Dr. Jerry E. Pournelle, e-mail to the author, 02/13/06.

23. Dr. Jerry E. Pournelle, e-mail to the author, 11/07/03. Dr. Pournelle added:

> It would be unfair to say that any one of those efforts was responsible for SDI, although it is almost certainly the case that without the Council reports the United States would not have engaged in the Strategic Defense Initiative.
>
> The Council wrote a draft of the President's SDI memo. Much of it was incorporated into the President's speech, including several phrases, the authorship of which is not recorded. Heinlein participated in that effort. Reagan himself added several key phrases. He was a better speech writer than any of those he employed, and he and they all knew it. Reagan was the real author of SDI in that he was open to strategic advice from all of us.

However, in another e-mail to the author, 02/13/06, Dr. Pournelle notes: "One sentence by Jim Baen was copied intact into that speech. Jim was pretty proud of that, with reason."

24. Dr. Jerry E. Pournelle, e-mail to the author, 11/07/03.

25. Virginia Heinlein, e-mail to David Silver (AGPlusOne), 07/13/00.

26. This interpretation was first advanced by David Silver in 2003 in an online Heinlein Readers' Group discussion and then published by Silver in two parts, "Blame It All on H. Bruce Franklin: A Sketch of the Motivation Behind the Final 'World As Myth' Novels of Robert A. Heinlein, Part 1—Introduction," *The Heinlein*

Journal, no. 16 (January 2005): 16–20; and "The Lonely Silver Rain: Part II of a Sketch of the Motivations of Robert A. Heinlein's World As Myth," *The Heinlein Journal,* no. 17 (July 2005): 26–36. The rape scene in *Friday* is thus a direct evocation of Cunegonde's rape at the invasion of Westphalia in *Candide.*

27. Heinlein's working notes, Preliminary Notes folder for *Friday,* Op. 185, titled "Heinlein-FRIDAY-chronology."

28. Virginia Heinlein, taped interview with Leon Stover (1988), Tape 3, Side B (p. 38 of Transcript in RAH Archive, UC Santa Cruz). The specific time of the travel is not recorded, but he began writing in November 1980, so the travel was presumably complete by that time. The Heinleins ceased to keep complete paper files of correspondence after becoming proficient on their computers, and the RAH Archive has not attempted to make the Magic Wand disc contents accessible, so the quantity of correspondence after 1981 that is currently accessible declines precipitously.

29. RAH, letter to Donald T. Clark, 04/02/67.

30. Virginia Heinlein, letter to George Warren, 04/03/81.

31. Virginia Heinlein, taped interview with the author, Tape 11, Side A (March 2? 2000); Virginia Heinlein, letter to the author, 08/14/00.

32. *Science Fiction Digest,* vol. 1, no. 4.

33. RAH, letter to Stephen Goldin, 06/13/81, thanking him for the joint dedication of *And Not Make Dreams Your Master.*

34. In September 1984, Milt Stevens, an L.A.-based science-fiction fan and convention organizer, was co-chair of the 42nd World Science Fiction Convention at the Anaheim Convention Center.

35. Art Dula, e-mail to the author, 03/16/06.

36. H. Bruce Franklin, "Genius and Supergenius," *New York Times Magazine* (July 4, 1982): 32.

37. Darrell Schweitzer's review for *Science Fiction Review,* no. 45 (1982), "The Vivisector" Department: "The Old Master's Return: Part 1—Old Heinlein Collaborates with New Heinlein," at 33, was particularly articulate on this point:

> There are *two* Robert Heinleins. Heinlein #1, the Old Heinlein, began his career with "Life-Line" in 1939, and rapidly developed into a brilliant talent, arguably the best science fiction writer since the early Wells. He was head and shoulders over everyone else for decades. He was a natural storyteller, and endlessly coming up with new angles and insights . . .
>
> One is tempted to say that, in the beginning, there was pulp sludge and in the legacy of Gernsback science fiction was void and without form and rather

tedious, and darkness was on the face of the deep; and Heinlein divided the waters from the waters, calling one type of SF "the gadget story" and the other "the human interest story," had [sic] He directed the entire field down the path of the latter. Heinlein #1, the Old Heinlein, was that important.

Heinlein #2, the cancerous growth, became manifest as early as *Starship Troopers* in 1959. He had none of the virtues of Heinlein #1. He lectured endlessly in cute dialogue, often blathering completely stupid things. We saw more of him in *Stranger in a Strange Land,* a novel constructed out of an abandoned draft of something written much earlier than the final version. The corpse came out of the author's trunk covered with fungus or something. It grew.

With *The Moon Is a Harsh Mistress,* the Old Heinlein regained temporary control, but by *I Will Fear No Evil,* the blatherer had taken over completely. It indeed looked like Heinlein #1's career was over.

I think what happened was Heinlein began to take himself entirely too seriously . . . .

38. *Locus* reports, issue 258, vol. 15, no. 7, "Robert A. Heinlein Stars at ABA."
39. Virginia Heinlein, letter to Denis Paradis, 06/21/82.
40. General Daniel O. Graham (1925–95) founded High Frontier, Inc., in 1982 as a lobbying organization (with K Street offices) specifically to promote the kinetic-weapons aspect of the overall strategic defense recommendation of the Citizens Advisory Council that became President Reagan's Strategic Defense Initiative. Because of his constant presence in Washington, D.C., he is sometimes erroneously regarded as the creator of SDI. In an e-mail to the author, 02/13/06, Dr. Jerry Pournelle recalled:

It was this [first] meeting [of the Citizens Advisory Council] or the second (Robert was at all of the early meetings) that we hammered out the Treaty of Tarzana on strategic defense policy, and came to an agreement that included Hunters' Gang of Four, Graham, Lowell Wood, and other rivals; that "treaty" gave us a single policy recommendation that became SDI and I am convinced was a key factor in winning the goddam Cold War . . . .

By 1982 the Treaty of Tarzana had been signed, and Graham was the Washington point man for the strategy the Council had put together. As Reagan used to put it, it's amazing how much you can get done if you don't care who gets the credit.

41. Record of RAH telephone call with Robert Himber, 06/07/82.
42. RAH, letter to *Survive!* magazine (September–October 1982): 57.

43. Tor Books, 1982; substantially revised and reissued in 1983 under the same title.

44. Virginia Heinlein, taped interview with Leon Stover (1988), Tape 1, Side B.

45. The author searched for this letter while going through all of Heinlein's surviving correspondence, but was unable to locate it, although a number of other letters and cards from Asimov were preserved. Perhaps this letter was moved to a "story notes" desk file and lost over the years.

46. RAH, letter to Isaac Asimov, 08/08/84.

47. The counterintuitive basing of morality in esthetics is a trope drawn (almost uniquely) from F. W. Nietzsche. Although Heinlein had a "low opinion" of Nietzsche (RAH, letter to Robert E. Turner, 07/18/73), having read *Also Sprach Zarathustra* in the early 1920s (probably as a result of a Wil Durant lecture in Kansas City and probably in the somewhat unfortunate 1909 Thomas Common translation), he was educated at a time when Nietzschean ideas framed the cutting edge of many intellectual fields—the anthropology of Franz Boaz, for example, and his students Margaret Mead and Ruth Benedict. Nietzsche was arguably the most highly influential philosopher of the twentieth century—and he died in 1900. Much of Heinlein is saturated with Nietzschean ideas. In particular, the pivotal incident of judgment in *Job: A Comedy of Justice* seems drawn from Cabell's *The High Place* (1923), but much of Cabell's philosophical underpinnings come from Nietzsche by way of Vaihinger and the debates on esthetics that were taking place among the American Pragmatists during the 1920s, particularly the rather acrimonious debate between Dewey and Santayana—Pragmatism itself influenced by Nietzsche.

    Heinlein had written a trial-by-esthetic-judgment once before, in the opening month of World War II: "The Unpleasant Profession of Jonathan Hoag."

48. Virginia Heinlein, taped interview with the author, Tape 10, Side A (March 3? 2000).

49. Osamu Tezuka (1928–89), letter to RAH, 08/12/83. Tezuka goes on to add that the exception was the club president, Sakyo Komatsu (1931–2011), who was on location shooting a movie at the time. (Spellings differ slightly in some reference works—e.g., Tesuko for Tezuko—but I have used Tezuka's spellings in his letter to Heinlein.)

    No historical or documentary trace could be found of Tezuka's "Japan Sci-Fi Writer's Club" in any reference source, including a three-part survey of Japanese science fiction in *Science Fiction Studies* (the third installment of Takayuki Tatsumi's "Generations and Controversies: An Overview of Japanese Science Fiction, 1957–1997. *Science Fiction Studies* no. 80 [March 2000] contains a brief summary of the preceding two parts). It is possible that the wording Tezuka used is a variant of the "Science Fiction and Fantasy Writers of Japan" organization formed in 1963 and of which Komatsu was president from 1980–83. Heinlein's visit was in the middle of the "Wintry Age" decline of written-form science fiction in Japan, when public attention was shifting over to anime and manga.

50. Virginia Heinlein, untitled first written trip report. Not dated exactly, but about 11/15/82.

51. Virginia Heinlein, untitled first written trip report, not dated exactly, but about 11/15/82. This trip report was included in the Virginia Edition, vol. xxxviii, *Non-fiction 2,* along with the two other extended trip reports Mrs. Heinlein wrote, for the Northwest Passage and the visit to Antarctica.

52. Virginia Heinlein, untitled first written trip report, not dated exactly, but about 11/15/82.

53. Virginia Heinlein, untitled first trip report, not dated exactly, but about 11/15/82.

54. An outline of the full story of Mark Hubbard's service, capture, and death, is given in volume 1 of this biography, *Learning Curve,* in chapter 25, 347–8.

55. RAH, letter to Poul Anderson, 09/06/61.

56. RAH, letter to L. Ron Hubbard, 12/16/82.

31. Entotic (pages 432–446)

1. "Ships of the World: An Historical Encyclopedia—Lindblad Explorer," web-published at http://college.hmco.com/history/readerscomp/ships/html/sh-055500_lindbladexpl.htm.

2. The incident is detailed in chapter 25 of *Learning Curve,* 341–2.

3. The penguins were definitely the stars of their Antarctic outings. Mrs. Heinlein commented:

> After our association with penguins, we look on them as not being birds, but little people. They manage to endear themselves to anyone who comes into contact with them. Perhaps it is their upright posture, perhaps it's their clumsy locomotion on their feet—or possibly the "academic processions" going to and from the shore. But everyone seemed to love them . . . . Penguins are wonderful!

(Virginia Heinlein, "Entotic," undated but about April 1983, 4.)

4. RAH, letter to Tetsu Yano, 03/19/83.

5. Denis Paradis, letter to Virginia Heinlein, 03/11/83.

6. RAH, letter to Jack Williamson, 04/29/83.

7. RAH, letter to Brad Linaweaver, 03/19/83.

8. Ronald Reagan's memoir and daily diaries ignore entirely the matter of input to this decision.

9. "Dignity committee" is a term of art used in both politics and in the community

of charitable organizations—a committee or board of people who lend their names if not often effort to the organization, i.e., to enhance its dignity.

10. Stan Kent, e-mail to the author, 05/20/06. The Viking Fund actually raised $100,000—one-tenth of the goal from a single effort. However, it became moot when in November 1982 an operator accidentally sent the probe a shut-down command during a software update, and it went permanently off-line.

11. Art Dula, e-mail to the author, 03/14/06.

12. Paul Bohannan (1920–2007) was an anthropologist whose principal work was on the Tiv people of Nigeria but also on the anthropology of divorce. How Dr. Bohannan happened to be invited to this dinner was not recorded.

13. Virginia Heinlein, letter to Denis Paradis, 08/20/83.

14. RAH, letter to Clifford D. Simak, 07/04/83.

15. H. G. Wells, Preface to *Seven Famous Novels by H. G. Wells* (New York: Alfred A. Knopf, Inc., 1934), 2.

16. The earliest known representation of the tail-swallowing Ouroboros comes from the Egyptian Book of the Netherworld found in a Tutankhamen shrine—and therefore dating from approximately 1330 BCE.

17. February 8, 1984.

18. "Custard-head" was one of Heinlein's favorite epithets for the foolish; he specifically applied the term to pacifists in the Forrestal Lecture in 1973 and again in a then-recent letter. He attributed resistance to the High Frontier concept to "the Nervous Nellies and Custard Heads who regard even defensive measures as 'destabilizing' because it would 'provoke the Russians into first strike.' Ah, me!" RAH, letter to Pete and Jane Sencenbaugh, 07/25/73.

19. Information provided by Timothy B. Kyger, e-mail to the author, 03/18/06. In hindsight, the succession of compromises was not good for the L5 Society. The people who were interested in doing practical projects found other ways of accomplishing their purposes, and within ten years the Society folded up its tents and merged with the National Space Society. Essentially, nobody got what they wanted out of this deal.

20. RAH, letter to Andre Norton, 06/03/84. Norton's first published novel, *The Prince Commands,* was issued in 1934. Her second published novel, *Ralestone Luck* (1938) was actually the first written, in about 1930.

21. RAH, letter to Clifford D. Simak, 10/08/78. Heinlein does not seem to have realized that he qualified under his own rule of being a witness to history.

22. Canadians pronounce Newfoundland with the consonants sharpened and the accent on the third syllable—Newf'nLAND (sometimes NewFOUNDl'nd). The locals say it with a rising pitch, but the rest of Canada can't manage the same lilt and pronounce it with descending pitch.

23. Just three days after the *Lindblad Explorer* departed Beechey Island, a scientific expedition sponsored by the recently created Franklin Forensic Project of the University of Alberta dug up three of the bodies, taking samples of the ice at 10 cm. intervals to determine whether the bodies had lain undisturbed all this time (and found they had). Beattie, O. B. and Geiger, J. *Frozen in Time* (Saskatoon, Canada: Western Producer Prairie Books, 1987).

24. Grise Fjord (76.416 N.) is farther north than Resolute (=Qausuittuq at 74.683 N.). In addition, there is the permanent Canadian scientific and military station at Eureka 82.483, *far* north of that, but Eureka is a scientific station like Little America with rotating staff rather than a permanent habitation.

    Barrow, Alaska, is the northernmost settlement in the United States, but hundreds of miles farther south, even though many maps don't represent this fact very well.

25. Mrs. Heinlein pronounced it "Joe Haven," though other pronunciation guides give it as "ee-yoo-ah."

26. Virginia Heinlein, "The Northwest Passage to the Orient" trip report, undated but about October 1984, 6.

27. New discoveries keep pushing the time frame back, to thirty thousand years ago, and possibly as much as fifty thousand years ago. North America was apparently populated in (at least) two different migrations from Asia, the later one skirting the coast because of glaciation. This second migration populated Central and South America, then North America.

28. Although this condemnation was widely remarked upon at the time, a search for the piece was not successful. It is possible that it was a passing remark in an article about something else.

29. In 2000, bookseller Alice Massoglia told Robert James, Ph.D., that Heinlein said that he was going to have to take up writing under a pseudonym again, as he had exhausted the potential market of toes he could step on under his own name.

30. Leon Stover, letter to Virginia Heinlein, 12/03/84.

31. "War and Peace in the Space Age," *Analog Science Fact, Science Fiction* (March 1982).

32. Clarke, Arthur C., *Spring: 1984, A Choice of Futures: Apocalypse May Yet be Cancelled* (New York: Ballantine Books, 1984).

33. Virginia Heinlein, letter to the author, 01/20/00.

34. Virginia Heinlein, letter to the author, 12/20/99.

35. Jerry Pournelle, e-mail to the author, 02/13/06, 12:31 P.M. McAleer's *Visionary* (2010), at 254, has Clarke's remark as "Because I learned all I know about orbital mechanics from you, Max." Max Hunter's rejoinder: "You didn't learn enough, Arthur."

36. Quoted in Neil McAleer, *Visionary* (2010), 255.

37. Jerry Pournelle, e-mail to the author, 02/13/06, 12:31 P.M.

38. McAleer, *Visionary* (2010), 255. The language of this confrontation was changed slightly from the earlier *Arthur C. Clarke: The Authorized Biography* (1992), 327. The words in brackets were in 1992 but not in 2010—possibly because the 2010 revision gives an expanded and somewhat more nuanced treatment of Clarke's position.

   Mr. McAleer kindly sent an expedited copy of the new trade paper edition of *Visionary* (the original was released in limited edition) when the final revisions of this biographer were being made, collegial generocity greatly appreciated.

39. McAleer, *Visionary* (2010), 255.

40. McAleer, *Visionary* (2010) treats this material at 255 as:

> At some point Clarke said he had doubts about it as a moral issue. This outraged Heinlein, who then loudly told Clarke that *he* had no moral right to frame a moral argument about something in which he had no stake. This was a matter of national sovereignty, and Clarke was not a citizen—

and follows with a comment by Gregory Benford:

> Heinlein was always big on freedom and the balance with responsibility . . . I mean that's what *Starship Troopers* is all about. You don't get to vote unless you fight. And similarly, you don't get an opinion unless your skin is personally risked.

41. McAleer, *Visionary* (2010), 256.

42. Arthur C. Clarke, "Robert Heinlein," *Requiem,* Yoji Kondo ed., 264.

   Over the next couple of years Heinlein and Clarke did become reconciled, though they never saw each other again. When Leon Stover was on the dais at a London meeting of the H. G. Wells Society, he recalls that Clarke approached him to help effect the reconciliation. Clarke and Heinlein did correspond—which is to say that Clarke sent letters which Ginny answered cordially. There is nothing particularly unusual or telling about this: Ginny answered almost all Robert's personal correspondence when he was writing or ill, and these two factors accounted for almost all the time he had left. Clarke credits Ginny's help—but it was Clarke's change of attitude, more than any personal intervention, that did the trick.

32. After 1984 (pages 447–460)

1. Heinlein's opus card shows that he recommenced work on *The Year of the Snake* on June 13, 1984, finishing the draft on July 23, 1984.

2. It is not entirely clear at what point in the process of his last five books the World As Myth as an overarching story pattern emerged in Heinlein's mind, though it seems that it exists by the time of *The Cat Who Walks Through Walls,* which contains quite a number of transitional details that would point forward, to the cosmic (and inter-cosmic) war that is made much clearer in *To Sail Beyond the Sunset.*

 Mrs. Heinlein told David Silver in 2003 that before the writing of *Friday* began in 1981, she and Heinlein discussed what he might write, so it is probable that *The Number of the Beast* did not itself suggest the World As Myth story. (David Silver, preliminary material for RAH Reading Group on AIM The "Gulf" (_Starman Jones_?)-_Friday_ Universe. Meeting Dates and Times: Thursday, March 20, 2003, from 8 to 11 P.M., EST.) Sometime after either *Friday* or *Job* it appears that the overarching story concept must have occurred to him. Bringing Jubal Harshaw into the story that connects *The Number of the Beast, The Cat Who Walks Through Walls,* and *To Sail Beyond the Sunset* is a clear marker of the larger structure, which may have evolved out of the unused *Panki-Barsoom Number of the Beast* written in 1977. That suppressed novel was oriented to an interdimensional war in the Cosmic All against the villains of E. E. Smith's Lensman series.

 Curiously, Heinlein's late invention of a master story that incorporates previously written material echoes James Branch Cabell's late (1915) invention of the Biography of the Life of Manuel, which incorporates all the material Cabell had written since 1904.

 Since *The Cat Who Walks Through Walls* clearly incorporates material from "All You Zombies—" and *The Moon Is a Harsh Mistress,* there is some suggestion that Heinlein intended to incorporate other material from his own corpus into the World as Myth—and therefore that both *Friday,* with its incorporation of materials from "Gulf," and *Job,* which incorporates material from "They" (and possibly also from "The Unpleasant Profession of Jonathan Hoag"), might have been intended to become parts of the World As Myth superstory.

3. Virginia Heinlein, letter to Leon Stover, 02/28/85.

4. Virginia Heinlein, taped interview with Leon Stover, Tape 1, Side B (1988).

5. The date of the visit mentioned by Virginia Heinlein in taped interview with the author, Tape 10, Side B, is not recorded, but the transmittal letter of the manuscript which Jayne Sturgeon sent to Heinlein was dated August 21, 1985.

6. Both Jane Gallion, citing Harriet Emerson (www.wussu.com/writings/jane_gallion .html, accessed 09/16/11), and Norman Spinrad (*Science Fiction in the Real World,* Carbondale, IL: Southern Illinois University Press, 1990) independently

mentioned that Sturgeon originally wrote *Godbody* for Brian Kirby at Essex House, a Los Angeles-based publisher of literary pornography, but never finalized the manuscript because the advance offered by Essex House was too low—either $1,000 or $1,500 compared to the then-usual rate of $5,000 for major publishers. Neither Gallion nor Spinrad fixed the date of the writing, though Essex House had failed by 1972 (http://www.wordservices.com/hobbit, accessed 09/16/11). The manuscript for *Godbody* was, therefore, not less than about fifteen years old when Sturgeon died in 1985.

7. In a postscript to a card Jayne Sturgeon sent to Heinlein on 01/30/86 she indicated that her talk with Heinlein about editing the manuscript made her realize she had gone "editorially soft" since Sturgeon's death.

8. The manuscript is in Ms. Box 147 of the RAH Archive, UC Santa Cruz.

9. Jayne Sturgeon, postscript to postcard to RAH, 01/30/86.

10. Remy de Gourmont, *A Night in The Luxembourg*, 1919.

11. Virginia Heinlein, letter to the author, 08/18/00.

12. Robert Silverberg, letter to RAH, 09/04/85.

13. Virginia Heinlein, taped interview with Leon Stover, Tape 2, Side A (1988).

14. Judy-Lynn del Rey died in February 1986.

15. Heinlein voiced this sentiment a number of times over the years, often in passing remarks. Virginia Heinlein explained their position to Margot Fisher (Lurton Blassingame's assistant) on 02/11/81:

> . . . we left Putnam as of Robert's recent book, TNOTB, for various reasons . . . Since Walter [Minton] was no longer at Putnam, we departed. [See Virginia Heinlein to George Warren, 03/15/79.] Our real loyalty was to him, rather than to the publishing house. . . .
>
> There were other reasons, of course. But that was the primary one. MCA was running it for the balance sheet.

16. During the editing of this volume in 2010 and 2011, editor David Hartwell added that the Heinleins' friend Walter Minton had gone to law school since selling his ownership of Putnam's to MCA in 1975 and leaving the presidency of Putnam's in 1977 or 1978 (he took the bar examination in 1982). Minton offered to represent Heinlein, and Hartwell himself testified on their behalf, noting that Signet had been reissuing the paperbacks Hartwell had repackaged for them in the early 1970s for nearly fifteen years by that time.

17. A transcription of Heinlein's "Message to the Berkeley Sales Staff Concerning *The Cat Who Walks Through Walls*" is published in the Virginia Edition, vol. xxxviii, *Nonfiction 2*.

18. Spider Robinson, untitled review in *Analog* dated "mid-December" 1985, 184.

19. David Bradley, "Superlunarian Follies," *New York Times Book Review,* VII, 6. There is no particular significance to the specific placement on p. 6, but over the previous fifteen years or so, reviews of science-fiction books in *The Times* had been migrating from the back toward the front of the magazine.

20. Virginia Heinlein, letter to Denis Paradis, 12/22/85.

21. Hensen's discussions with Heinlein are mentioned in Edward Regis, Jr., *Great Mambo Chicken and the Transhuman Condition: Science Slightly Over the Edge* (Addison-Wesley, 1990).

22. Spider Robinson, "Robert," *Requiem,* Yoji Kondo, ed.

23. Virginia Heinlein, letter to Leon Stover, 04/17/89.

24. Leon Stover, letter to Virginia Heinlein, 04/22/89.

25. Rita Bottoms recalled in personal conversation with the author that Heinlein told her quite early that Stover was to be his designated biographer—before, in fact, he told Stover. Although Mrs. Bottoms was unable to date this communication specifically, it was in 1986 that Heinlein began communicating biographically useful facts to Stover—see especially RAH, letter to Leon Stover, 06/08/86, which is published in the Virginia Edition, vol. xli, *Letters 3* [1960–87]. Heinlein must have discussed the matter explicitly with Stover some time before the end of 1987, as Stover signs himself ". . . I remain your loving friend and loving biographer, Leon" in a letter to Heinlein dated 01/08/88—exactly five months before Heinlein's death.

26. RAH, letter to Leon Stover, 06/08/86.

27. From Alfred, Lord Tennyson (1809–92), "Ulysses" (1842). Quoted as epigraph to *To Sail Beyond the Sunset.*

28. This incident of the hemorrhage from Heinlein's nose, including the detail following, is related in Virginia Heinlein, taped interview with the author, Third Series, Tape A, Side A (March 27, 2001).

29. The incident is described in a circular letter dated 08/09/86; Denis Paradis's copy is preserved in the RAH Archive.

30. Virginia Heinlein, IM with the author, 04/22/00.

31. The copy sent to Denis Paradis is dated August 9, 1986.

32. This information comes from the August 18, 1986, continuation of the circular letter Mrs. Heinlein wrote for friends.

33. August 18, 1986, continuation of Mrs. Heinlein's circular letter about Heinlein's medical state.

34. Virginia Heinlein, letters to Denis Paradis, 08/26/86, 10/14/86, and 11/07/86.

35. Missouri does not actually have a state fruit.

36. Virginia Heinlein, letter to Denis Paradis, 09/26/86.

37. Virginia Heinlein, letter to Denis Paradis, 11/07/86.

38. "Three Men in a Starship," *The Economist* (11/15/86).

39. Probably the purest statement of Heinlein's view of the difference between mass market science fiction and genre-audience science fiction is contained in his 1950 correspondence with Forrest J. Ackerman, 02/19/49, which is quoted in chapter 1 of this volume.

40. Daniel Dickinson, "What Is One to Make of Robert Heinlein?" *Modern Fiction Studies,* XXII: 1 (Spring 1986): 127–32.

41. Leon Stover, letter to Virginia Heinlein, 01/14/87.

42. Virginia Heinlein, letter to Denis Paradis, 01/25/87.

43. Leon Stover, letter to Virginia Heinlein, 02/25/86.

44. Leon Stover, letter to Virginia Heinlein, 03/08/87.

45. Jim Eason, e-mail to "David Silver and the Heinlein Society," 07/17/07.

46. Virginia Heinlein, letter to Denis Paradis, 07/30/87.

47. Notes of phone conversation with Rita Bottoms by the author, 01/18/03.

48. Leon Stover, letter to Virginia Heinlein, 07/21/87.

49. Leon Stover, letter to Robert Heinlein, 07/18/87. "At that time [the June 9, 1984, interview with Heinlein] I got a bigger vision, and wrote back [to Unger] saying, RAH really is a significant American author, not just another genre writer." Stover goes on to say that for this reason the book deal with Unger collapsed: They only wanted a treatment as a science-fiction figure.

50. Gerald Jonas, *New York Times Book Review,* VII: 36:2 (10/18/87).

51. Leon Stover, letter to RAH, 09/22/87. In (unmemorialized) conversation with the author in 1999, Stover indicated that the inscription identified the Uncle Podger character with Heinlein himself and that Heinlein told him that anyone who wanted to understand him needed to understand this book.

52. Virginia Heinlein, taped interview with the author, Tape 7, Side A; Virginia Heinlein, letter to the author, 06/04/99.

53. There was at least one copy of the manuscript not in Heinlein's files, a copy he had given to Cal Laning many years earlier. A copy of a copy of a copy of that manuscript eventually was tracked down by Dr. Robert James in 2003 and was published after Mrs. Heinlein's demise as *For Us, the Living: a Comedy of Customs* (New York: Simon & Schuster, 2004).

54. Virginia Heinlein, letter to the author, 03/12/00.

55. Virginia Heinlein, letter to Leon Stover, 03/29/89.

56. The incident is told in chapter 29 of *Learning Curve,* 421–2.

57. Virginia Heinlein, taped interview with the author, Tape 12, Side A.

33. Last Act (pages 461–468)

1. Virginia Heinlein, taped interview with the author, Series 2, Tape C, Side A.
2. Virginia Heinlein, letter to the author, 11/03/00.
3. Virginia Heinlein, taped interview with the author, Series 3, Tape A, Side A (March 27? 2001).
4. Heinlein's typed notes of this telephone conversation are dated 12/27/87.
5. Information about the operation in this and subsequent paragraphs from Virginia Heinlein, letter to Denis Paradis, 01/20/88.
6. Virginia Heinlein, letter to RAH, 06/05/88.
7. Virginia Heinlein, letter to Leon Stover, 03/29/89.
8. Mrs. Heinlein never found out how Heinlein had managed while she was down, and he never wrote about it or discussed it, so how he managed during this three-day period remains an unresolvable mystery. But he was not an invalid at the time—just tired. He undoubtedly got his own meals and did not attempt to waken her.
9. The Lermers had moved to Pacific Grove in 1979, about seven or eight miles from Carmel.
10. Virginia Heinlein, letter to Denis Paradis, 01/20/88.
11. The number was provided by Leon Stover in a letter to Virginia Heinlein dated 05/08/88.
12. Stover's *Robert Heinlein* would go on to sell more than two thousand copies in the first six months of its first issue, and Twayne asked Stover for a second edition, in which he could correct some of the errors and omissions that had crept in (particularly an error in the time line that had Heinlein going back to Fitzsimmons for a tubercular relapse after 1934).
13. Virginia Heinlein, letter to the author, 11/03/00.
14. Virginia Heinlein, letter to the author, 11/03/00.
15. Virginia Heinlein, letter to the author, 11/03/00.
16. Virginia Heinlein, taped interview with the author, Series 3, Tape A, Side A (March 27, 2001).
17. Virginia Heinlein, letter to the author, 09/20/00; some of the same material is covered in Virginia Heinlein, letter to the author, 04/22/00.
18. Virginia Heinlein, letter to the author, 09/20/00.
19. Virginia Heinlein, circular bulletin 03/13/88, continuation dated 03/15/88.
20. Catherine Crook de Camp, *Requiem*, Yoji Kondo, ed. Mrs. de Camp did not date her recollection, but it must have taken place shortly after March 18, 1988.
21. Virginia Heinlein, letter to RAH, 06/05/88.
22. Denis Paradis, letter to Virginia Heinlein, 03/12/88.
23. Sometime in 1978, the Heinleins' friend Michael Cassutt had suggested that

George A. Warren (1934–89?) send the Heinleins a copy of his first book, *Destiny's Children,* a historical novel about the Mormon migration (a subject of perennial interest to Robert Heinlein, though Cassutt might not have known that at the time). The book had been released without publicity after the sponsoring editor left Simon & Schuster. Both Heinleins were impressed with the book, and a warm epistolary friendship developed over the years.

There is little available biographical material about Warren, but Cassutt recalled that he had met Warren in the spring of 1978,

> at the L.A.-based Nebula weekend. I had been reading his pieces in [Richard E.] Geis' *Alien Critic* before that. We would talk from time to time on the phone, and write more than a few letters. When Cindy and I moved to L.A. in Dec 1978, we wound up seeing George and his wife, Jackie, several times a year until they moved north [to Pacific Grove, near Carmel] . . . [sic] and George vanished.

Cassutt was able to provide some further biographical details:

> I believe he spent most or all of his life in southern California. He was involved with some shady publishers here . . . [sic] porn houses . . . [sic] and also with Leo Margulies and *Mike Shayne* [*Mystery Magazine*] (George wrote a lot of the MS novels for the magazine in the late 1970s, early 1980s). He was primarily a book reviewer for a number of small L.A.-based pubs.

There is some mystery associated with Warren's disappearance and presumed death. Cassutt concludes: "The last I heard of him was that he had disappeared, that a body matching his description had washed up on the shore of Monterey Bay. Very sad. This was probably twenty years ago, but might have been as late as the mid-1990s." Michael Cassutt, e-mail to the author, 09/23/11.

24. George Warren, "On The Arts" Column in the *Los Angeles Herald,* undated on clipping.
25. Spider Robinson, untitled appreciation in *Locus,* June 1988, 82.
26. Virginia Heinlein, letter to the author, 11/03/00.
27. Virginia Heinlein, taped interview with the author, Series 3, Tape A, Side A (March 27, 2001).
28. Virginia Heinlein, letter to the author, 11/03/00.
29. Virginia Heinlein, letter to Denis Paradis, 08/15/88.

Appendix 1: After (pages 469–477)

1. Mrs. Heinlein wrote *two* heartfelt letters to Robert Heinlein after his death, of which this was the second. Both letters deal with the same issues—often in the

same words. It might be that one was a discarded draft, and the other what she intended. It might equally be that both were discarded drafts and Mrs. Heinlein was never able to find the words she wanted to say, as if she were struggling to find some expression of the meaning Robert Heinlein had for her and found the subject too big for words. Virginia Heinlein never had confidence in her writing as anything more than serviceable.

Both letters are a jumble of expressions of grief, newsy items, the kinds of day-to-day events that they would have talked over in person—and an expression of something more universal, something Ginny shared with all of "Heinlein's children"—the sense that he made her want to be a better person, to live up to his vision of her. Some of the more routine matters have been elided from this second letter.

The two letters are so repetitive with each other that I have elected not to include one in text, but the earlier letter is also expressive of those qualities that others found so meaningful about Heinlein. The full text of the earlier letter, with minor, daily household business elided, is as follows:

June 5, 1988

My love, It is just four weeks today since you left me. Most of that time I have spent weeping, wondering whether there was *anything* that might have saved you a while longer. Sometimes it seems as though you had just tired of the burden of your condition—other times it seems as if it hadn't been that I slipped and fell that day down in LA, leaving Doctors Hospital, things might have been better for you.

For the past several days I've been reading over letters from you to me, from me to you, and lots of other letters which you wrote to other people, about lots of things.

I want to tell you that all of it, troubles and love and all the various things which happened to us together were worth while. Even when we quarreled about things—things I can't even remember now. I love you so, and I miss you so!

I even miss that sick old man who had a cheery word and smile for those who came to see him, even me, although I'm sure I disappointed and hurt you many times. But I really tried to live up to your vision of me.

What I will do with this is to write it all out and then burn it up—somehow you might know about it.

Those letters from that heart-broken young woman I was, and your replies. I didn't mean to be thorny, it's just the nature of the beast, probably.

I've felt terrible that for those three weeks when we both lay in bed unable to do anything after that trip down to LA I wasn't able to get you to your doctor. Perhaps, even then, something might have been done to keep you from slipping away, if I'd been able to get you to Dr. Lola before those three weeks had passed.

Although we had insurance, I was scared that it would run out, and that those expenses would make us paupers, and then what would happen? You didn't have any idea about those hospital and doctors bills—that monitor you had so long cost $750 a day in rental! I was prepared to liquidate all our holdings and spend it all on you, if it would have made you feel any better. But you'd always said that you didn't approve of those heart-lung transplants, "one to a customer" was the way you phrased it.

I don't know why they didn't send you home by ambulance that 17th of March—the day you fell in the doorway leading into this office. That nurse who helped get you into the car should have known better, and so should the others . . . [sic] you hadn't walked in a long time, and only very short walks before that. But it wasn't so long before that CPR crew came and got you into bed. The nurse had left, which vexed me . . . [sic] she might have helped.

Oh, dear, regrets, regrets and more of those. How vain they are.

It seems to me that I always did things wrong—but I hope not.

* * *

Absolutely none of those rabid science fiction people ever realized that you'd gone way beyond their little world, and become a world figure. Next to none of the mail which came flooding in was from organized fans—oh, some of those did write, but few. Most of it was from others—those people who never went to conventions, never joined those clubs. And their from-the-heart words touch me most of all, particularly the ones who say that your books moulded their lives. Not that they took all of your ideas in toto, but they tell me how much you influenced their sense of values and guided them into their careers.

They all tell me that your influence will last beyond your human life, here, and that your books will last as long as there is print. Some will, I'm sure.

But I am bereft. People have been very good to me, especially Mary Jean and Andy. Andy has been doing some of those little fixing-up things around here. They come over and help me out.

* * *

The plans for the foundation are under way. And today I will sign the amendment to the trust, which changes the beneficiary of what is left when

I go. Our accountant, Mark Gordon, is helping with putting assets over into the foundation. Copyrights will go to the foundation, along with other assets—don't worry, I will be taken care of, I will have a lifetime interest in the copyrights. But, with careful management, Uncle Sam and California won't tax that money a second time. God knows, we've paid enough in taxes already on it!

I am putting a power of attorney in Ralph's hands. But I'm really stuck about what to do about what happens to me if I should get sick or something like losing my marbles. Probably it will have to be a court-appointed conservator . . . [sic] My plans for disposal of remains are like yours, as you know. And I hope to join you in the not-too-distant future—I don't like living alone. I miss you like hell. It's lonely.

There are other things I need to burn up—our love letters to each other during that period, forty years ago—that unhappy period, when I yearned for you, but you had to pursue your career. *Destination Moon* was worth it. There will be a new showing of it at Kennedy Center on July 24th and 25th. I don't know what else is planned but Yoji Kondo is going to send me a copy of the program. He and Charles Sheffield are in on the planning, I think. You would have liked that. I think you'd have braved the Washington heat to see it!

But I don't want to take any chances, so I won't be going anywhere for a while—I want to get that foundation tied down tight so that it will be as you wished. Betty Noe has been helping from the Butler end. She told me that there's a county library in Butler, but it needs changes etc. So the new lawyer, Bill Brandwein, is going to see what can be done to promote your wishes—he thinks a supporting foundation would be the way to go, and Mark Gordon agrees with him. They will guide me through the legal maze.

But I need some reassurance: Were you happy with me? It bothers me, rereading those letters about how much you missed Leslyn back forty years ago. I hoped that I aged gracefully—I certainly tried to. And become a gracious lady, as you wanted me to be. I regret all the mistakes I made—my judgment wasn't always as sure as yours was. I hope it is now!

My love, my beloved, my dearest one—I miss you and always shall, as long as I live.

Ginny

2. Written versions of these memorial speeches were later published in Kondo's *Requiem: New Collected Works by Robert A. Heinlein and Tributes to the Grand Master* (Tor Books, 1992).

3. The videotape of this reading (a part of the videotape of the entire event), though not of professional quality, was enhanced and processed by James D. Gifford for re-presentation as the concluding moments of the Robert A. Heinlein Centennial Gala on July 7, 2007 (Heinlein's hundredth birthday), combining this video with Heinlein's original audio recording to create a very effective joint reading of "This I Believe." It is hoped that this re-presentation will one day be made publicly available.

4. Stover had collected a large number of documents in addition to photocopies from the RAH Archive—particularly Laning's complete file of correspondence with Heinlein and Robert and Suzie Clifton's file of material relating to Heinlein's involvement in EPIC from 1934–38 and his campaign for the Assembly District 55 seat in 1938, as well as family history documents provided by Heinlein to the Heinlein Family Association and in the possession of his cousin, Oscar Heinlein, Jr. These documents were used to write a stub biography of Heinlein's youth, up to 1939, titled *Before the Writing Began*. In 1999, Stover sent the present author a copy of the first and second chapters, and then allowed him to read the complete manuscript on a visit to Chicago.

    Although he had promised to lodge these documents with the Archive, out of concern for his wife's financial well-being after his death, Stover sold them instead to a private collector, who has not made them available for research.

    After Virginia Heinlein's death in 2003, Stover attempted to have *Before the Writing Began* published but stopped the publication when the Heinlein Prize Trust, successor holders of Heinlein's intellectual property rights, asked to review the text before extending permission to quote. Dr. Stover died on November 25, 2006.

5. The magazine serial publication of *The Puppet Masters* in *Galaxy Science-Fiction,* at 60,000 words, was an entirely different edit/cut/rewrite. Most of H. L. Gold's changes to Heinlein's texts are in the first and second installments; the third installment was restored to Heinlein's original manuscript.

6. *Take Back Your Government!* was partially edited by Jerry Pournelle, who also wrote an introduction for the book. The original manuscript and title were restored for the Virginia Edition publication of the book as its vol. viii, and a new edition in soft covers was issued in 2011 by Arc Press.

7. RAH, letter to Lloyd Biggle, 09/30/76.

8. The "later commentator" was James D. Gifford, in the Introduction to his *Robert A. Heinlein: a Reader's Companion* (Citrus, Calif.: Nitrosyncretic Press, 2000). Gifford's comments in full are quite temperate, but he accurately characterizes many of these "scholarly" papers as "poorly researched and ill-developed."

9. One of the aspects of Mrs. Heinlein's life that has scarcely been remarked upon,

even in her obituaries, is that she was a highly successful manager of one of the very largest literary estates in the world.

10. Quotation taken from the Heinlein Prize Trust website, http://www.heinlein-prize.com/ (accessed 09/29/11).

   In addition to the Heinlein Prize itself, the Prize Trust undertakes other legacy projects, incorporating support for the biography into its legacy mission, as well the Virginia Edition project, forty-six volumes constituting a complete collected works in a library- and archival-quality limited edition. The Heinlein Prize Trust has also undertaken to scan the entirety of the documentary content of the Heinlein Archive and make it available online through www.heinleinarchives.net.

Appendix 2: "The Good Stuff" (pages 478–486)

1. In the case of this biography in particular, Mrs. Heinlein told me early on that, while there were things she would not care to have written about or published while she was alive (since they might cause her social difficulties if known), once she was gone she did not care any longer. She did not merely loose the surly bonds of privacy, she tore them up and cast them from her.

2. Possibly a shortened form of "MacDonald," meaning her mother, Florence Gleason "Skipper" MacDonald. Leslyn's father, Colin MacDonald, had died (of advanced alcoholism) in 1929; her mother lived until some time late in 1944.

3. "Fair white body" is a cliché of turn-of-the-twentieth-century melodrama.

4. The Heinleins had made the Corsons a $1,000 loan; in the divorce settlement, Leslyn got the Corsons' promissory note.

5. That is, Heinlein speculates that Leslyn might not carry through the divorce proceedings if he leaves the area, and he might have to go to Reno, Nevada, where it was notoriously easy to get a divorce in the era before no-fault dissolutions, and institute proceedings himself.

6. Even though this is a nearly contemporaneous account of events, the time sequencing of events is unclear. This reference to "someplace in Arizona" might date the events of this passage to January and early February 1947, as Heinlein mentioned the trip to the desert to take place early in March in a letter to John W. Campbell, Jr., 02/14/47. However, Henry Sang mentioned a prospective trip of the Heinleins to Prescott, Arizona, in his entry for June 17, 1947—by which time the divorce consultations were well under way, and a letter by Heinlein to Lurton Blassingame dated 06/24/47 speaks of the ongoing effort to close up the house. The following day, Henry Sang's journal has Leslyn showing the house to a prospective purchaser.

7. ". . . when we [Henry and Grace Dugan Sang] moved in at the Hicks house . . ." means early June 1947. In May 1947 Leslyn was again confined to bed by doctor's

orders. Ginny Gerstenfeld had been ordered out in April (a fact not mentioned in this recounting, which seems at this stage to be of events not directly witnessed by Mrs. Sang, as she and Henry Sang were still living in Fallbrook near San Diego). The separation took place in mid-June 1947; Heinlein closed their joint checking account on June 16, 1947; the complaint for divorce was filed on June 20, 1947.

8. Virginia Heinlein recalled that Leslyn was being sent $40 a month in the summer of 1947. Virginia Heinlein, taped interview with the author, Series 2, Tape A, Side B (September 6, 2000).

9. From this point, Mrs. Sang is recounting events she personally experienced.

10. Philip Wylie—A favorite writer and moralist of both Robert and Leslyn Heinlein. It was, in fact, Leslyn who wrote Wylie a fan letter, rather than Robert Heinlein.

11. Heinlein had relocated to Ojai on July 7, 1947—his fortieth birthday. These events are covered in chapter 29 of *Learning Curve,* the first volume of this biography.

12. Grace Dugan Sang had recommended Fink to the Heinleins.

WORKS OF ROBERT A. HEINLEIN

A WORD ABOUT THE VIRGINIA EDITION (VE)

The Heinlein Prize Trust assembled the Virginia Edition as a Collected Works edition of the best text available for each work. In addition to all the expected fiction and nonfiction, the Virginia Edition found material that had been published once and never reprinted, and also some manuscripts that had never been published in any form. By adding more than a million words of Heinlein's correspondence (including both sides of the correspondence between Heinlein and John W. Campbell, Jr.), together with all the major print interviews, the Virginia Edition brings substantially all of Heinlein into print together for the first time, and almost any individual work may be found there, whether or not special notice of this fact is made in the listings here.

BOOKS

Assignment in Eternity (1953). Collects: "Gulf," "Elsewhen," "Lost Legacy," and "Jerry Was a Man."

The Best of Robert Heinlein (1973). Ed. Angus Wells. British collection containing: Introduction by Peter R. Weston, "Life-Line," "The Roads Must Roll," "'—And He Built a Crooked House—,'" "The Unpleasant Profession of Jonathan Hoag," "The Green Hills of Earth," "The Long Watch," "The Man Who Sold the Moon," and "'—All You Zombies—.'"

Between Planets (1951). Serial publication as "Planets in Combat" in *Blue Book* (September, October 1951).

Beyond This Horizon (1948). Serial publication as by "Anson MacDonald" in *Astounding Science-Fiction* (April, May 1942).

The Cat Who Walks Through Walls (1985).

Citizen of the Galaxy (1957). Serial publication in *Astounding Science Fiction* (September, October, November, December 1957).

The Day After Tomorrow. See *Sixth Column.*

Destination: Moon. Ed. David G Hartwell. (1979)

The Door into Summer (1957). Serial publication in *The Magazine of Fantasy and Science Fiction* (October, November, December 1956).

Double Star (1956). Serial publication in *Astounding Science Fiction* (February, March, April 1956). Hugo Award Winner.

Expanded Universe: The New Worlds of Robert A. Heinlein (1980). Collection, expanded from *The Worlds of Robert A. Heinlein.* collects: "Life-Line," "Successful Operation," "Blowups Happen," "Solution Unsatisfactory," "The Last Days of the United States," "How to Be a Survivor," "Pie from the Sky," "They Do It With Mirrors," "Free Men," "No Bands Playing, No Flags Flying—," "A Bathroom of Her Own," "On the Slopes of Vesuvius," "Nothing Ever Happens on the Moon," "Pandora's Box," "Where To?," "Cliff and the Calories," "Ray Guns and Rocket Ships," "The Third Millennium Opens," "Who Are the Heirs of Patrick Henry?," " 'Pravda' Means 'Truth,' " "Inside Intourist," "Searchlight," "The Pragmatics of Patriotism," "Paul Dirac, Antimatter, and You," "Larger Than Life," "Spinoff," "The Happy Days Ahead." Short essays by Heinlein before and after each piece.

The Fantasies of Robert A. Heinlein (1999). Combines *The Unpleasant Profession of Jonathan Hoag* and *Waldo and Magic, Inc.*

Farmer in the Sky (1950). Serial publication as "Satellite Scout" in *Boys' Life* (August, September, October, November 1950).

Farnham's Freehold (1964). Serial publication in *Worlds of If* (July, August, October 1964).

For Us, the Living: A Comedy of Customs (2004).

Four Frontiers (2005). Collects *Rocket Ship Galileo, Space Cadet, Red Planet,* and *Farmer in the Sky.*

Friday (1982). Selection published in *Science Fiction Digest,* vol. 1, no. 4 (September-October 1982).

Glory Road (1963). Serial publication in *The Magazine of Fantasy and Science Fiction* (July, August, September 1963).

The Green Hills of Earth (1951). Collects: "Delilah and the Space-Rigger," "Space Jockey," "The Long Watch," "Gentlemen, Be Seated," "The Black Pits of Luna," " 'It's Great to be Back!,' " " '—We Also Walk Dogs,' " "Ordeal in Space," "The Green Hills of Earth," and "Logic of Empire." See also *The Past Through Tomorrow.*

Grumbles from the Grave (1989). Ed. Virginia Heinlein.

Have Space Suit—Will Travel (1958). Serial publication in *The Magazine of Fantasy and Science Fiction* (August, September, October 1958).

A Heinlein Triad (UK, 1966). See *Three by Heinlein*.

A Heinlein Trio (1980). Science Fiction Book Club collection containing *The Door into Summer*, *Double Star*, and *The Puppet Masters*.

I Will Fear No Evil (1970). Serial publication in *Galaxy Science Fiction* (July, August-September, October-November, December 1970). *Infinite Possibilities* (2002). Science Fiction Book Club posthumous collection containing *Tunnel in the Sky*, *Time for the Stars*, and *Citizen of the Galaxy*.

Job: A Comedy of Justice (1984). World As Myth continuation of the Future History.

Lost Legacy (1960). British, collects "Lost Legacy" and "Jerry was a Man." From *Assignment in Eternity*.

The Man Who Sold the Moon (1950). Collects: Introduction by John W. Campbell, Jr., preface by Heinlein ("It Does Not Pay a Prophet to be Too Specific"), "Life-Line," " 'Let There Be Light,' " "The Roads Must Roll," "Blowups Happen," "The Man Who Sold the Moon," and "Requiem." See also *The Past Through Tomorrow*.

The Menace from Earth (1959). Collection containing: "The Year of the Jackpot," "By His Bootstraps," "Columbus Was a Dope," "The Menace from Earth," "Sky Lift," "Goldfish Bowl," "Project Nightmare," and "Water Is for Washing." See also *Off the Main Sequence*.

Methuselah's Children (1958). Serial publication in *Astounding Science-Fiction* (July, August, September 1941). See also *The Past Through Tomorrow* (1967) and *A Robert A. Heinlein Omnibus*.

The Moon Is a Harsh Mistress (1966). Serial publication in *Worlds of If* (December 1965, January, February, March, April 1966).

The Notebooks of Lazarus Long (1978). Extracted from two chapters in *Time Enough for Love* (1973). Published in *Analog Science Fiction/Science Fact* (June 1973) and *Omni* (August 1979).

The Number of the Beast (1980). Serial publication, abridged, in *Omni* (October, November 1979).

Off the Main Sequence: The Other Science Fiction Stories of Robert Heinlein (2005). Ed. Andrew Wheeler. collects: Introductions by Greg Bear and Michael Cassutt, "Successful Operation," " 'Let There Be Light,' " " '—And He Built a Crooked House—,' " "Beyond Doubt," "They," "Solution Unsatisfactory," "Universe," "Elsewhen," "Common Sense," "By His Bootstraps," "Lost Legacy," " 'My Object All Sublime,' " "Goldfish Bowl," "Pied Piper," "Free Men," "On the Slopes of Vesuvius," "Columbus Was a Dope," "Jerry Was a Man," "Water Is for Washing," "Nothing Ever Happens on the Moon," "Gulf," "Destination Moon," "The Year of the Jackpot," "Project Nightmare," "Sky Lift," "Tenderfoot in Space," and " '—All You Zombies—.' "

Orphans of the Sky (1963 UK; 1964 US). Collects "Universe" and "Common Sense."

Outward Bound (2006). Collects *Have Space Suit—Will Travel, Starship Troopers,* and *Podkayne of Mars.*

The Panki-Barsoom Number of the Beast (1977). Suppressed by Heinlein but significant sections cannibalized for *The Number of the Beast.* Manuscript available from online Heinlein archives, www.heinleinarchives.net.

The Past Through Tomorrow (1967). Omnibus. Collects *The Man Who Sold the Moon, The Green Hills of Earth, Revolt in 2100,* and *Methuselah's Children,* with a few additional Future History stories written between 1953 and 1967.

Podkayne of Mars (1963). Serial publication in *Worlds of If* (November 1962, January, March 1963). Heinlein's original provided in *Grumbles from the Grave* and in some paperback editions published after 1990.

The Puppet Masters (1951, 75,000 words). Serial publication in shortened (60,000 words) and heavily edited form in *Galaxy Science Fiction* (September, October, November 1951). A restored 100,000-word version was published in paperback in 1990, and reprinted in VE.

Red Planet (1949).

Requiem: New Collected Works by Robert A. Heinlein and Tributes to the Grand Master (1992). Ed. Yoji Kondo. Collects: Preface by Virginia Heinlein; Editor's Foreword by Yoji Kondo; "Requiem"; "Tenderfoot in Space"; "Destination Moon"; "Shooting 'Destination Moon'"; "The Witch's Daughters"; "The Bulletin Board"; "Poor Daddy"; Guest of Honor Speech at the Third World Science Fiction Convention—Denver, 1941; Guest of Honor Speech at the XIXth World Science Fiction Convention—Seattle, 1961; Guest of Honor Speech—Rio de Janeiro Movie Festival, 1969; Guest of Honor Speech at the XXXIVth World Science Fiction Convention—Kansas City, 1976; NASA Medal for Distinguished Public Service for Robert A. Heinlein; "This I Believe"; Speeches by the Panelists: Tom Clancy, L. Sprague de Camp, Jerry Pournelle, Charles Sheffield, Jon McBride; Speeches by the Special Guests: Catherine Crook de Camp, Tetsu Yano; "RAH: A Memoir" (Poul Anderson); "Jim Baen's RAH Story" (Jim Baen); "Remembering Robert Heinlein (Greg Bear); "Recalling Robert Anson Heinlein" (J. Hartley Bowen, Jr.); "Robert Heinlein" (Arthur C. Clarke); "Robert Heinlein" (Gordon R. Dickson); "Robert A. Heinlein and Us" (Joe Haldeman); "The Return of William Proxmire" (Larry Niven); "Rah Rah R.A.H.!" (Spider Robinson); "Robert" (Spider Robinson); "Heinlein" (Robert Silverberg); "Thank You" (Harry Turtledove); "Who Was Robert Heinlein?" (Jack Williamson); and "Farewell to the Master" (Yoji Kondo and Charles Sheffield).

Revolt in 2100 (1953). Future History collection containing: Introduction by Henry Kuttner ("The Innocent Eye"), " 'If This Goes On—,' " "Misfit," "Coventry," and Afterword by Heinlein ("Concerning Stories Never Written").

Robert A. Heinlein Centennial Souvenir Book (2007).

A Robert Heinlein Omnibus (1966). Collects *The Robert A. Heinlein Omnibus* and *Methuselah's Children*

The Robert Heinlein Omnibus (1958). British collection combining *The Man Who Sold the Moon, The Green Hills of Earth,* and *Beyond This Horizon.* Reprinted as *A Robert Heinlein Omnibus (1966)* with more material.

Rocket Ship Galileo (1947).

The Rolling Stones (1952). Serial publication as "Tramp Space Ship" in *Boys' Life* (September, October, November, December 1952).

6XH (1961). See *The Unpleasant Profession of Jonathan Hoag.*

Sixth Column (1947). Serial publication as by "Anson MacDonald" in *Astounding Science-Fiction* (January, February, March 1941). Slightly expanded for hardcover publication. Published in paperback as *The Day After Tomorrow.*

Space Cadet (1948).

The Star Beast (1954). Serial publication as "Star Lummox" in *The Magazine of Fantasy and Science Fiction* (May, June, July 1954).

Starman Jones (1953).

Starship Troopers (1959). Serial publication as "Starship Soldier" in *The Magazine of Fantasy and Science Fiction* (October, November 1959).

Stranger in a Strange Land (1961).

Take Back Your Government!: A Practical Handbook for the Private Citizen who Wants Democracy to Work (1992). Published as *How to Be a Politician.* Published with Heinlein's title restored in V E.

Three by Heinlein (1965). Collects combines *The Puppet Masters,* "Waldo," and "Magic, Inc." In England as *A Heinlein Triad (1966).*

Time Enough for Love (1973).

Time for the Stars (1956).

To Sail Beyond the Sunset (1987).

To The Stars (2004). Collects *Between Planets, The Rolling Stones, Starman Jones,* and *The Star Beast.*

Tomorrow, the Stars (1952). Anthology, ed. Robert A. Heinlein.

Tramp Royale (1992).

Tunnel in the Sky (1955).

Universe (1951).

The Unpleasant Profession of Jonathan Hoag (1959). Also published in early paperback as *6xH.* Collection containing: "The Unpleasant Profession of Jonathan Hoag," "The Man Who Traveled in Elephants," " '—All You Zombies—,' " "They," "Our Fair City," and " '—And He Built a Crooked House—.' "

Waldo and Magic, Inc. (1950).

The Worlds of Robert A. Heinlein (1966). Collects: "Pandora's Box," "Free Men," "Blowups Happen," "Searchlight," "Life-Line," "Solution Unsatisfactory." Ccontents incorporated in *Expanded Universe* (1980).

SHORT FICTION

" '—All You Zombies—'." *The Magazine of Fantasy and Science Fiction* (March 1959). Collected in *The Unpleasant Profession of Jonathan Hoag* (1959).

" '—And He Built a Crooked House—'." *Astounding Science-Fiction* (February 1941). Collected in *The Unpleasant Profession of Jonathan Hoag* (1959).

"A Bathroom of Her Own." *Expanded Universe* (1980).

"Beyond Doubt." *Astonishing Stories* (April 1941 as by "Lyle Monroe and Elma Wentz"). Collected in *Off the Main Sequence* (2005).

"The Black Pits of Luna." *The Saturday Evening Post* (January 10, 1948). Future History story collected in *The Green Hills of Earth* (1951).

"Blowups Happen." *Astounding Science-Fiction* (September 1940). Future History story revised for collection in *The Man Who Sold the Moon* (1950). Restored 1940 version collected in *Expanded Universe* (1980).

"The Bulletin Board" (a Puddin' story). *Requiem*, ed. Yoji Kondo (1992).

"By His Bootstraps." *Astounding Science-Fiction* (October 1941 as by "Anson MacDonald"). Collected in *The Menace from Earth* (1959).

"Cliff and the Calories" (a Puddin' story). *Senior Prom* (August 1950 as "Mother and the Balanced Diet"). Collected in *Expanded Universe* (1980).

"Columbus Was a Dope." *Startling Stories* (May 1947 as by "Lyle Monroe"). Collected in *The Menace from Earth* (1959).

"Common Sense." *Astounding Science-Fiction* (October 1941). Future History story, collected in *Orphans of the Sky* (1963).

"Complaint." Story in form of a thank-you letter to George Zebrowski and Thomas N. Scortia (11/30/75). Collected in V E.

"Coventry." *Astounding Science-Fiction* (July 1940). Future History story, collected in *Revolt in 2100* (1953).

"Delilah and the Space-Rigger." *Blue Book Magazine* (December 1949). Future History story, collected in *The Green Hills of Earth* (1951).

"Destination Moon." *Short Stories* (September 1950). Novelization of film script. Collected in *Destination Moon*, ed. David G. Hartwell (1979).

"Elsewhen." *Astounding Science-Fiction* (September 1941 as "Elsewhere" by "Caleb Saunders"). Collected in *Assignment in Eternity* (1953).

"Free Men." *The Worlds of Robert A. Heinlein* (1966).

"Gentlemen, Be Seated." *Argosy* (May 1948). Future History story, collected in *The Green Hills of Earth* (1951).

"The Green Hills of Earth." *The Saturday Evening Post* (February 8, 1947). Future History story, collected in *The Green Hills of Earth* (1951).

Opera Libretto (fragment) of *The Green Hills of Earth* (1971). Published in V E.

"Goldfish Bowl." *Astounding Science-Fiction* (March 1942 as by "Anson MacDonald"). Collected in *The Menace from Earth* (1959).

"Gulf." *Astounding Science Fiction* (November, December 1949). Collected in *Assignment in Eternity* (1953).

"'If This Goes On—'." *Astounding Science-Fiction* (February, March 1940). Future History story, collected in *Revolt in 2100* (1953).

"'It's Great to be Back!'" *The Saturday Evening Post* (July 26, 1947). Future History story collected in *The Green Hills of Earth* (1951).

"Jerry Was a Man." *Thrilling Wonder Stories* (October 1947 as "Jerry Is a Man"). Collected in *Assignment in Eternity* (1953).

"'Let There Be Light'." *Super Science Stories* (May 1940 as by "Lyle Monroe"). Future History story, collected in *The Man Who Sold the Moon* (1950) but omitted from most subsequent issues and *The Past Through Tomorrow* (1967). It is re-incorporated into the Future History in VE.

"Life-Line." *Astounding Science-Fiction* (August 1939). Future History story, collected in *The Man Who Sold the Moon* (1950).

"Logic of Empire." *Astounding Science-Fiction* (March 1941). Future History story, collected in *The Green Hills of Earth* (1951).

"The Long Watch." *American Legion Magazine* (December 1949 as "Rebellion on the Moon"). Future History story, collected in *The Green Hills of Earth* (1951).

"Lost Legacy." *Super Science Stories* (November 1941 as "Lost Legion" by "Lyle Monroe"). Collected in *Assignment in Eternity* (1953).

"Magic, Inc." *Unknown* (September 1940 as "The Devil Makes the Law"). Collected in *Waldo and Magic, Inc.* (1950).

"The Man Who Sold the Moon." Future History story, collected in *The Man Who Sold the Moon* (1950).

"The Man Who Traveled in Elephants." *Saturn* (October 1957 as "The Elephant Circuit"). Collected in *The Unpleasant Profession of Jonathan Hoag* (1959).

"The Menace from Earth." *The Magazine of Fantasy and Science Fiction* (August 1957). Future History story collected in *The Menace from Earth* (1959).

"Misfit." *Astounding Science-Fiction* (November 1939). Future History story, collected in *Revolt in 2100* (1953).

"'My Object All Sublime'." *Future Combined with Science Fiction* (February 1942 as by "Lyle Monroe"). Collected in *Off the Main Sequence*, ed. Andrew Wheeler (2005).

"No Bands Playing, No Flags Flying—." *Vertex* (December 1973). Publication title of "Three Brave Men". Collected in *Expanded Universe* (1980).

"Nothing Ever Happens on the Moon." *Boys' Life* (April, May 1949, significantly edited). Collected in *Expanded Universe* (1980). Manuscript version reprinted in hardcover first edition of *Requiem*, ed. Yoji Kondo (1992), (but not paperback editions).

"On the Slopes of Vesuvius." *Expanded Universe* (1980).

"Ordeal in Space." *Town & Country* (May 1948). Future History story, collected in *The Green Hills of Earth* (1951).

"Our Fair City." *Weird Tales* (January 1949). Collected in *The Unpleasant Profession of Jonathan Hoag* (1959).

"Pied Piper." *Astonishing Stories* (March 1942 as by "Lyle Monroe"). Collected in *Off the Main Sequence*, ed. Andrew Wheeler (2005).

"Poor Daddy" (a Puddin' story). *Calling All Girls* (August 1949). Collected in *Requiem*, ed. Yoji Kondo (1992).

"Project Nightmare." *Amazing Stories* (April/May 1953). Collected in *The Menace from Earth* (1959).

"Requiem." *Astounding Science-Fiction* (January 1940). Future History story, collected in *The Man Who Sold the Moon* (1950).

"The Roads Must Roll." *Astounding Science-Fiction* (June 1940). Future History story, collected in *The Man Who Sold the Moon* (1950).

"Searchlight." *Scientific American* (August 1962), *Fortune* (September 1962). Future History story, collected in *The Past Through Tomorrow* (1967).

"Sky Lift." *Imagination* (November 1953). Collected in *The Menace from Earth* (1959).

"Solution Unsatisfactory." *Astounding Science-Fiction* (May 1941 as by "Anson MacDonald"). Collected in *The Worlds of Robert A. Heinlein* (1966).

"Space Jockey." *The Saturday Evening Post* (April 26, 1947). Future History story, collected in *The Green Hills of Earth* (1951).

"Successful Operation." *Futuria Fantasia*, ed. Ray Bradbury (Spring 1940 as "Heil!" by "Lyle Monroe"). Collected in *Expanded Universe* (1980).

"Tenderfoot in Space." *Boys' Life* (May, June, July 1958 in slightly condensed version). A variant of the manuscript version appeared in *Requiem*, ed. Yoji Kondo (1992); paperback issues of *Requiem* have the original manuscript version.

"They." *Unknown* (April 1941). Collected in *The Unpleasant Profession of Jonathan Hoag* (1959).

"They Do It With Mirrors." *Popular Detective* (May 1947 as by "Simon York"). Collected in *Expanded Universe* (1980).

"Universe." *Astounding Science-Fiction* (May 1941). Future History story, published separately as a papaerback in 195? and collected in *Orphans of the Sky* (1963).

"The Unpleasant Profession of Jonathan Hoag." *Unknown Worlds* (October 1942 as by "John Riverside"). Collected in *The Unpleasant Profession of Jonathan Hoag* (1959).

"Waldo." *Astounding Science-Fiction* (August 1942). Collected in *Waldo and Magic, Inc.* (1950).

"Water Is for Washing." *Argosy* (November 1947). Collected in *The Menace from Earth* (1959).

"'—We Also Walk Dogs'." *Astounding Science-Fiction* (July 1941 as by "Anson Mac-Donald"). Collected in *The Green Hills of Earth* (1951). "Weekend Watch" (written ca. 1930). Collected in the *Robert A. Heinlein Centennial Souvenir Book* (2007) and in *VE*.

"The Year of the Jackpot." *Galaxy Science Fiction* (March 1952). Collected in *The Menace from Earth* (1959).

SCREENPLAYS AND TELEPLAYS

"Abbott and Costello Move to the Moon." Film treatment co-written with Ben Babb.

The Adventure of the Double Gambit (written 1963–64). Pilot M.O.W. screenplay for unproduced TV series titled *Century XXII*. Several varying titles for rewrites, including *The Adventure of the "Gambit"* and *The Adventure of the Man Who Wasn't There*.

The Black Pits of Luna (written 1952). Teleplay for *The World Beyond*.

Century XXII. Series bible, letters between Heinlein and his producer and his agent. All published in the Virginia Edition.

"*—And He Built a Crooked House—*" (written 1952). Teleplay for *The World Beyond*.

Delilah and the Space-Rigger (written 1952). Teleplay for *The World Beyond*.

Destination Moon (1950). Four feature film scripts, treatment, and miscellaneous material, including novelization, all of which are published in V E. The novelization, "Shooting 'Destination Moon,'" and publicity materials were gathered into a book for Gregg Press in 1979 (*Destination Moon*, ed. David G. Hartwell).

Home Sweet Home (written 1952). Exists only as a treatment for a teleplay, published in V E.

"*It's Great to be Back!*" (written 1952). Teleplay for *The World Beyond*.

Life-Line (written 1952). Teleplay for *The World Beyond*.

The Long Watch (written 1952). Teleplay for *The World Beyond*.

Misfit (written 1952). Teleplay for *The World Beyond.*

Nothing Ever Happens (1959).Unproduced script for abortive TV series, *Crater Base One* .

Ordeal in Space (written 1952). Teleplay for *The World Beyond.*

"Patterned Opening." Teaser hook for *The World Beyond.*

Project Moonbase (written 1953). Feature film; pilot script for *The World Beyond* as *Ring Around the Moon.*

Project Nightmare (written 1952). Teleplay for *The World Beyond.*

Requiem (written 1952). Teleplay for *The World Beyond.*

Ring Around the Moon (written 1952). Pilot script M.O.W. for *The World Beyond*; see *Project Moonbase.*

Space Jockey (written 1952). Teleplay for *The World Beyond.*

The Tourist (written 1952). Exists only as a treatment for a teleplay, in V E.

"*—We Also Walk Dogs*" (written 1952). Teleplay for *The World Beyond*

INTRODUCTIONS, ARTICLES, MISCELLANY

"Accession Notes" (1967, 1968). Unpublished except in V E.

Review: *Across the Space Frontier*, ed. Cornelius Ryan. *Colorado Springs Free Press* (September 28, 1952). Published as "The Ever-Widening Horizons." Collected in V E.

"Agape and Eros: The Art of Theodore Sturgeon." Introduction to Sturgeon's posthumous final novel, *Godbody* (1985).

"All Aboard the Gemini." *Popular Mechanics* (May 1963). Publication title of "Appointment in Space." Heinlein's original article published in V E.

"America's Maginot Line" (1946). Unpublished except in V E.

"Analysis: Kokjohn book" (1974–75). Lost.

"Analysis: *The Mote in God's Eye*" (1973). Unpublished except collected in V E.

"Analysis: Untitled" (1975). Pat Wilson book, *My Three-Ring Circus & Kangaroo in the Kitchen.* Lost.

"Are You a Rare Blood?" *Compton Yearbook* (1976). Encyclopedia article. Unpublished except collected in V E.

"Atlantis" (written ca. 1920–24). Juvenile poem. Unpublished except in the *Robert A. Heinlein Centennial Souvenir Book* (2007).

"Author! Author!" (1949). Biographical sketch written for a fanzine. Collected in V E.

"Back of the Moon." *The Elks Magazine* (January 1947). Half of Heinlein's manuscript version, "The Man in the Moon." Full manuscript in V E.

Introduction to *The Best From Startling Stories*, ed. Sam Mines (1953).

"Bet on the Future and Win." *Writer's Digest* (March 1950). One of two publication titles, the other being "The Historical Novel of the Future," *Bookshop News* (February 1950).

Foreword to *Beyond Jupiter: The Worlds of the Grand Tour* by Chesley Bonestell and Arthur C. Clarke. Collected in V E.

"The Billion Dollar Eye" with Capt. Caleb B. Laning, USN. Collected in V E (as "System in the Sky").

Books. The Heinleins' 1975 catalog of their personal library. Collected in V E.

Message to the Berkley Sales Staff regarding *The Cat Who Walks Through Walls* (1985). Unpublished except in the Virginia Edition.

"Channel Markers." *Analog Science Fiction/Science Fact* (January 1974). Full version of Heinlein's 1973 Forrestal lecture. A slightly different restoration to Heinlein's original text is published in the Virginia Edition as "Forrestal Lecture."

"Cockpit Canopies—Free Blown Type—Thermal Stability—Examination of" (1945). World War II Engineering Report collected in V E.

"Concerning Stories Never Written." Future History postscript (nonfiction) to *Revolt in 2100* (1953).

Review: *The Conquest of Space* by Chesley Bonestell and Willy Ley. *Saturday Review of Literature* (December 24, 1949 as "Baedeker of the Solar System"), *Thrilling Wonder Stories* (February 1950). Collected in V E.

"Creativity Is Not Divisible" (1969). Guest of honor speech at Rio de Janeiro Movie Festival. Published in *Requiem*, ed. Yoji Kondo (1992).

Current Biography (March 1955). Entry for Robert A. Heinlein presumed written by him.

"Dance Session" (July 1946). Verse. *New Destinies: Volume VI* (1988).

Review: *The Days of Creation* by Willy Ley. *Astounding Science-Fiction* (May 1942). Collected in V E.

"Death Song of a Wood's Colt" (written 1946). Verse. A slightly revised version was incorporated into *Stranger in a Strange Land*. In V E.

"Paul Dirac, Antimatter, and You." *Compton Yearbook* (1975).

"The Discovery of the Future" (1941). Guest of Honor Speech at the Third World Science Fiction Convention (Denvention). Published as a chapbook by Forrest J. Ackerman; collected in *Requiem*, ed. Yoji Kondo (1992).

"Flight into the Future." *Collier's* (August 30, 1947). Co-written with Capt. Caleb B. Laning, USN. Collected in V E.

"Forrestal Lecture" (1973). In the V E. See "Channel Markers."

"A Future History Essay." *SFWA Bulletin*, vol. xiv, no. 3 (Fall 1979).

Future History Chart. There are four versions of this chart extant: (1) Heinlein's handwritten original; (2) the May 1941 *Astounding Science-Fiction* publication; (3) the revised 1950 version used as endpapers on the three Shasta books (*The Man Who Sold the Moon*, *The Green Hills of Earth*, and *Revolt in 2100*); and (4) a 1967 further revision for *The Past Through Tomorrow*. All four are collected together with the introductions of the two volumes of Future History stories in V E.

"The Future Revisited" (1961). Guest of Honor Speech at the XIXth World Science Fiction Convention, Seattle. Collected in *Requiem*, ed. Yoji Kondo (1992).

Introduction to *The Glory That Was* by L. Sprague de Camp (1960). Written 1952.

"The Good News of High Frontier." *Survive* (September-October 1982). A shortened version of this letter was used as a Foreword to *High Frontiers: A New National Strategy* by Daniel O. Graham.

Review: *Green Fire* by John Taine (1928). Collected in V E.

Guest of Honor Speech at the XXXIVth World Science Fiction Convention, MidAmeriCon (1976). Collected in *Requiem*, ed. Yoji Kondo (1992).

"The Happy Days Ahead." *Expanded Universe* (1980).

"The Happy Road to Science Fiction." *McClurg's Book News* (1964). Collected in V E.

"How to Be a Survivor: The Art of Staying Alive in the Atomic Age." *Expanded Universe* (1980). Written 1946.

"How to Write a Story" (1941). In condensed form in *Spaceways* (January 1941), ed. Harry Warner, Jr. The full manuscript version is collected in V E.

"If You Don't See It, Just Ask: A Preview for Playboys" (1963). Collected in the *Robert A. Heinlein Centennial Souvenir Book* (2007) and a different edit in V E.

"Inside Intourist." *Expanded Universe* (1980). Written 1960.

"It Does Not Pay a Prophet to be Too Specific." Preface to *The Man Who Sold the Moon* (1950).

"The Journey of Death" (written 1946). Collected in V E, together with Leslyn Heinlein reportage of the same event.

"Larger Than Life: A Memoir in Tribute to Dr. Edward E. Smith." MosCon I Program Book (1979). Collected in *Expanded Universe* (1980).

"The Last Adventure" (written ca. 1923). Verse. Published in the *Robert A. Heinlein Centennial Souvenir Book* (2007).

"The Last Days of the United States." *Expanded Universe* (1980). Written 1946. .

Letter-Appreciation of Grand Master Clifford D. Simak (1977). Collected in V E.

Letter-Article for Clifford Simak (1965)

Letter to LASFS on Its New Clubhouse (1973).

"A Letter from Robert A. Heinlein." *Harris Children's Library Magazine* (1966). Collected in V E.

Letter-Article for *The Saturday Evening Post* "Keeping Posted" department (1947).

Letter Appeal for Stanford Hospital (1985).

Letter-Appreciation of Jack Williamson (1983).

Letter-Tribute to Grand Master Jack Williamson (1976).

Letter-Article for *Young Wings* (1948).

Liner notes for Avalon Hill Starship Troopers board game (1976).

Liner notes for Caedmon recording of Leonard Nimoy reading "The Green Hills of Earth" and "Gentlemen, Be Seated" (1977).

Untitled Portrait Sketch (1929). Graduating prose-portrait of Sebastian Bach Perreault (and of Heinlein by Perreault).

"A Method for Arranging All Fractions from Zero to One in a Single Sequence" (1954). A reconstruction from Heinlein's notes, published in V E.

Muster Notes (1935, 1949, 1962, 1974, 1979). Short, autobiographical reports for his classmates.

"The Names of the Beast." *Robert A. Heinlein* by Leon Stover (1987). Collected in V E.

Naval Air Materials Center Memorandum (1945).

Octocon Blood Drive Remarks (1977). Published in V E.

"On the Writing of Speculative Fiction." Published in *Of Worlds Beyond,* ed. Arthur Lloyd Eshbach (1947).

"An Open Letter from Robert A. Heinlein." *Destinies* (August-September 1979). Collected as "Open Letter Re L-5 Society" in V E.

"Pandora's Box" / "Where To?" (written 1949). Published as "Where To?" in *Galaxy Science Fiction* (February 1952). Updated and collected as "Pandora's Box" in *The Worlds of Robert A. Heinlein* (1966) and updated again for *Expanded Universe* (1980).

"Pie from the Sky." *Expanded Universe* (1980). Written 1946.

Poetry Center Speech (1974). No transcript exists of this appearance at the Poetry Center of the 92nd Street YM-YWHA in New York City on May 29, 1974. Tom Collins, a fan who was present, reconstructed Heinlein's talk from memory as the first part of "Tonight I Met Heinlein," first published in *Transient* no. 31 (1974), and web-published by Alexei Panshin at http://www.panshin.com/critics/Showdown/tom collins.html. Collins's recollection is incorporated into an endnote in volume 2 of *Robert A. Heinlein: In Dialogue With His Century.*

"The Pragmatics of Patriotism" (written 1973). Last half of the Forrestal Lecture, published in a number of places, including the four U.S. military service academies.

Collected in *Expanded Universe* (1980). Also published by the alternate title of "The Politics of Patriotism."

"'Pravda' Means 'Truth'." *The American Mercury* (October 1960). Collected in *Expanded Universe* (1980).

"Ray Guns and Rocket Ships." *Bulletin of the School Library Association of California* (November 1952). A shorter version was published in *Library Journal* (July 1953) and collected in *Expanded Universe* (1980); the full manuscript and first publication version are published in V E.

Review: *Rockets: A Prelude to Space Travel* by Willy Ley. *Astounding Science-Fiction* (July 1944). Reprinted in the Virginia Edition.

The Saturday Evening Post Fillers (written 1949). For "The Perfect Squelch" department of *The Saturday Evening Post*. Published in V E.

"Science Fiction: Its Nature, Faults and Virtues." Lecture given 1957. Published in *The Science Fiction Novel: Imagination and Social Criticism* (1959).

"Science Fiction: The World of 'What If'." *The Book of Knowledge* (1964, extensively cut). Original uncut version published in V E.

Review: *Shells and Shooting* by Willy Ley. *Astounding Science-Fiction* (November 1942). Not on table of contents. Collected in V E.

"Shooting 'Destination Moon'." *Astounding Science Fiction* (July 1950). Collected in *Destination Moon*, ed. David G. Hartwell (1979).

"Some Applications of Space Technology for the Elderly and the Handicapped." Transcription of Heinlein's Congressional Testimony (July 19, 1979). See "Spinoff."

Review: *Space Medicine: The Human Factor in Flights Beyond the Earth*, ed. John P. Marberger. *The Denver Post* (August 20, 1951), *Galaxy Science Fiction* (December 1951). Collected in V E.

"Spinoff." *Omni* (March 1980). Revised version of Heinlein's Congressional Testimony. Collected in *Expanded Universe* (1980).

"Sworn Statement of Robert A. Heinlein Concerning Robert Cornog." (1949). Published in V E.

"The Third Millennium Opens." *Amazing Stories* (April 1956 as "As I See Tomorrow"). Collected in *Expanded Universe* (1980).

"This I Believe." (1952). Address given on the radio show *This I Believe*. Reprinted in *Requiem*, ed. Yoji Kondo (1992).

"Three Wise Mice." Verse. Published in *VE*.

"Tomorrow the Moon" (1947). Original publication not located; Collected in V E.

Introduction to *Tomorrow, the Stars*, ed. Robert A. Heinlein (1952).

"A U.S. Citizen Thinks About Canada." *Canada and the World* (1975). Collected in V E.

"The Witch's Daughters." (1946) *New Destinies: Volume VI* (1988). Verse. Collected in *Requiem*, ed. Yoji Kondo (1992), and in the Virginia Edition.

"Who Are the Heirs of Patrick Henry?" *Colorado Springs Gazette-Telegraph* (April 12, 13, 18 1958). Reprinted in *Expanded Universe* (1980).

"Why Buy a Stone Ax?" (1946). Published in *VE*.

"Why I selected 'The Green Hills of Earth'." *My Best Science Fiction Story*, ed. Leo Marguiles and Oscar J. Friend (1949). Collected in *VE*.

INDEX